Visit **Hot Wacks Press**

on the Web at

http://www.bootlegs.com
http://log.on.ca/hotwacks
e-mail hotwacks@log.on.ca

buy, sell, trade - advertise for free!

The Rolling Stones

Sticky Fingers

Sticky Fingers is a magazine completely about the Rolling Stones and their great music. We also cover the latest Stones news, tour plans, recording sessions and new releases. Tired of hearing about great bootlegs only after they disappear? Read **Sticky Fingers** and learn about the Hot Rocks while they are still available. With the new bootleg crackdown in Europe and Japan, timely information is more important than ever. Release times are growing shorter and new issues are being pressed in smaller numbers. A subscription to **Sticky Fingers** cost less than one bad bootleg.

Subscriptions (6 Issues):
USA: $20.00 ($36 for 2-Years)
Canada: $25.00   Foreign: 30.00 US

Sample Issue $4.00 US/$5.00 Overseas.

Make Checks or $ International Money Orders payable to:
Sticky Fingers, P.O. Box 3474, Granada Hills, CA 91344

HOT WACKS BOOK

Supplement 5

THE HOT WACKS PRESS

POB 544, Owen Sound, ON, N4K 5R1, CANADA
Fax 519 376 9449 - E-Mail hotwacks@log.on.ca
Web-Pages http://www.bootlegs.com - http://log.on.ca/hotwacks

Dedicated to Doug Regan, a fan of live music, a musician and a gentle man with an intense edge who left us far to soon. I have no doubt he's trading bass licks with Cliff and Phil and jammin' with Jimi. Turn it up Doug and rock on.

Also dedicated to producers of fine recordings the world over and collectors who take the time to write and share information on these recordings.

With thanks to:
Beanie, Pirate and Paddy for patience. Mom for encouragement. Kurt for feeding the monster. Elvis for the attitude. Ed Sullivan for February 9 1964. CGP for support. Simon Pallett for Led ears. And, last but not least, Trainspotters everywhere.

© 1997

HOT WACKS BOOK
Supplement 5

is a copyright protected publication of

ROBERT WALKER AND THE HOT WACKS PRESS

POB 544, Owen Sound, ON, N4K 5R1, CANADA
Fax 519 376 9399 - E-Mail hotwacks@log.on.ca
Web-Pages http://www.bootlegs.com OR http://log.on.ca/hotwacks

PRINTED IN CANADA
ISBN 0-9698080-8-9

PLEASE NOTE:
All opinions expressed in articles written by someone other than the current editor/publisher Robert Walker are those of that writer and do not necessarily reflect the views or thoughts of THE HOT WACKS PRESS.

All rights reserved. No part of this book may be reproduced in any form or by any digital, electronic or mechanical means including information storage and retrieval systems, without permission in writing from the publisher except by a reviewer who may quote brief passages in a review.

Intro: Future Wacks

Hot Wacks Book XV (1992 - see page 230/31) was the last complete bootleg discography. Up until Book XV, each edition contained the information from the previous book plus any new releases. However, the book was becoming too big. Book XIV was 496 pages and, with the explosion of new releases on both vinyl and CD, Book XV was more than 800 pages. This was not only a monster to produce but expensive to ship. On top of that, it became a bit redundant and expensive for those of you who bought every edition of the book to have to buy the old information with the new.

Hot Wacks Book Supplements (see page 230/31) are designed to keep you up-to-date with the ever-expanding world of bootlegs. They contain new releases along with old listings not found in Hot Wacks Book XV.

Plans call for THE ULTIMATE WACKS to now be published in late 1998. This will be a large-format book jam-packed with: interviews with bootleggers, photo discographies, bootleg memorabilia as well as the most complete bootleg listings ever. Hot Wacks also has a Web-site (http://www.bootlegs.com or http://log.on.ca/hotwacks) listing books and a free classifieds page to buy, sell and trade.

As many of you well know, Hot Wacks does not include every bootleg that has ever been released. Not everything that comes out is available here in Canada because of the limited runs of some items and because contacts with some producers or distributors have not been established. While we have access to a great number of items through various collections, there are still some things that get by.

With this in mind, The Hot Wacks Press asks for your help to keep future books up to date. If you have some things in your collection that do not appear in Book XV or Supplements 1 to 5, please write with the information about these items. Please send a picture or photocopy of the cover(s) along with song listings, the source and sound quality of the recording. Feel free to include any comments you want about the recording, performance, or cover.

If you have a collection that you feel is unique and would care to share it with the rest of the world please write or FAX (519-376-9449) or E-mail (hotwacks@log.on.ca) with information about your collection.

If you are a producer of bootlegs, vinyl or CD, please send sample copies or information about your product. We don't need your address or number, just the tracks facts.

A History Of Bootlegs

In 1969 bootleg Rock records made their appearance in the United States and Europe. Previously bootlegs consisted mainly of Jazz and Blues artists. These, however, did not receive the attention that Rock bootlegs did as the artists were not big money-makers. Dean Meador, writing in "Hot Wacks Quarterly" (A History Of Bootleg Recordings, Issue #4), traced bootlegs back to the turn of the `century.

"Mapleson, the librarian of the Metropolitan Opera at that time, received a cylinder recorder from Thomas Edison. He took his gift up into the fly-loft on several occasions during the Met's 1901-03 seasons and recorded bits and pieces of performances. Even though Mapleson had his machine a long way from the stage area and his medium had limitations (his cylinders ran for only a few minutes at a time, making it impossible to capture all of a long aria or duet), he produced an astonishing number of unique recording documents".

"Mapleson and his cylinders provided a taste of actual performances during that period. Mapleson gave collectors a chance to obtain and hear performers, singers, artists and speakers of that era who never appeared on commercial recordings, others in roles they didn't duplicate on authorized discs".

The record that started it all for Rock boots was Bob Dylan's "Great White Wonder". This double album originally came in a plain white jacket without any printed label or title. Since sound recordings did not receive copyright protection in the USA until February 15, 1972, GWW received wider distribution than the bootlegs of today. However, claims that it sold some 350,000 copies are extremely unlikely. It is further interesting to note that when Columbia Records released the same material in authorized form years later as "The Basement Tapes" the official version sold quite well.

A distinction had best be made at this point between bootleg, pirate and counterfeit records. A bootleg consists of unreleased material recorded at concerts, studio outtakes, and radio or TV broadcasts. A pirate album consists of released material without attempting to make the LP look like an original. A counterfeit album is an exact copy of an officially released album.

Record industry spokespeople often include bootlegs with counterfeit and pirate recordings when making statements about the loss of revenue from record piracy. Bootlegs, with their small pressings, should not be included in this figure as the record labels do not lose revenue from a recording which is not in their catalog.

These same spokespeople completely overlook the historical significance of bootlegs as well. While this is obvious when speaking in terms of Opera, Jazz and Blues boots, Rock has not been around for the same amount of time. With Rock's seemingly unending loss of performers due to untimely deaths, this will soon become evident. Albert Goldman, in his bestseller "Elvis", is one of the first biographers to appreciate the historical significance bootlegs have.

"Not just the man but the performer continued to emerge after his death. Though RCA had nothing better to offer than gleanings from its soon-exhausted archives, the record bootleggers, those great friends of the fans, cut the legal knots that had long restrained the release of Elvis's most significant live sessions. The legendary Elvis of the Louisiana Hayride, the Dorsey Brothers shows and the Hawaiian benefits appeared. All the jams from the Singer Special were offered in two beautifully-packaged albums from California that far surpassed both in interest and in appearance any legitimate offerings of RCA Victor. In yet another illicit release came at last the most sought-after tape in the history of rock 'n' roll: the fabled 'Million Dollar Quartet', an impromptu sing in the Sun Studio around Christmas 1956, by the three greatest heroes of rockabilly: Elvis, Jerry Lee Lewis and Carl Perkins (minus the anticipated fourth voice, Johnny Cash). Though in this instance the reality of the recording hardly matched the glamour of its legend, the value of the disc as a document was enormous. At last you were inside the Sun Studio listening attentively as Sam Phillips' greatest singers did what they most enjoyed doing: pickin' and singin' their favorite rock songs and hymns".

Currently the average pressing in the USA of a bootleg is 1,000 copies; in Europe 500 to 1,000 copies; and a few hundred copies in Japan. Australia, which just recently became a steady source of supply, quite likely has runs as small as Japan. Canada deserves mention if only for the fact that an entire run of Bruce Springsteen boxed sets was seized before they could be distributed. With that exception, Canada is not a bootleg-producing country.

All of the early American bootleg labels have ceased operating. This is the case with RUBBER DUBBER, IMMACULATE CONCEPTION RECORDS (ICR), CONTRABAND MUSIC (CBM), DITTOLINO DISCS, KUSTOM RECORDS, TRADE MARK OF QUALITY (TMOQ), PIG'S EYE, HIGHWAY HI FI (HHCER), PHONYGRAF and one outfit that used a different name for each release (Hen, Steel Led, etc.). Their product was a thick, black record in a white jacket. To simplify matters they are referred to in this text as White Cover Folks (WCF).

The second generation of bootleggers, which includes WIZARDO RECORDS (WRMB), IDLE MIND PRODUCTIONS (IMP), HOFFMAN AVENUE RECORDS (HAR), K&S RECORDS and THE AMAZING KORNYFONE RECORD LABEL (TAKRL), is also out of business.

At the present time the vast majority of releases is coming out of Europe. If anything, the Europeans have improved on their sound quality and packaging, both of which they have been leaders in for years. Most of their product matches, and in some cases surpasses, legitimate record releases.

(December 22 1985 Kurt Glemser - Editor of HOT WACKS - Books I thru XI)

Then 'til now

1986 saw the rise and fall of BOX TOP RECORDS. This label re-released many old classics, most on colored vinyl, from original plates. These came in a thin cover with a color snap-shot of the artist on the front and a sticker with the song listings on the back. Titles were rubber-stamped on the front. In the spring of 1987, after two years of production, ROCK SOLID RECORDS/INTERNATIONAL RECORDS (RSR/International) went out of business.

1988 witnessed the short-lived return of the TRADE MARK OF QUALITY (TMOQ or TMQ) and THE AMAZING KORNYPHONE RECORD LABEL (TAKRL) labels working together to provide 'A High Standard Of Standardness'. Records came in one-color covers with the artists' name and the album title on the front and a jacket-sized label logo on the back. There were two separate batches of releases and each had the song listings for all albums in that batch on sheets enclosed in the record jackets. Each release was limited to 500 copies.

1989 brought the introduction of the bootleg CD and the demise of vinyl. In some cases bootleg CDs are a waste of technology since these are taken from the original boots of the same name, not new or better sources. After all, who wants a bad recording containing pops and crackles that'll last forever. In other instances when a good source is available, such as with "Ultra Rare Trax" (The Beatles) or "Dallas '75" volumes 1 and 2 (Led Zeppelin), the results are incredible.

1990 through 1995 can only be described as the time of the bootleg CD. Using loopholes in the copyright laws of some European and Far East countries, bootleggers flooded the market with CD re-issues of old boots as well as a wealth of new, often soundboard, recordings.

1996 - The year of the bust... stores in New York... record fairs across the United States ... record fairs in England... bootleg manufacturers in Italy... who's next?

1997 - THE END? see page 23.

HOT WACKS BOOK SUPPLEMENT 5

Please note, THE HOT WACKS PRESS does not sell the records or CDs listed in this book, this is a discography not a catalog. Most of these items are long out of circulation and not available.

(July 1997 Bob Walker - Editor/Publisher of HOT WACKS Books XII to SUPPLEMENT 5).

Sound Quality

The HOT WACKS rating system is based on the sound quality of bootleg releases, not legitimate albums and CDs. Sound quality has come a long way since the old days of boots in the early 70s. We were very forgiving in those days, simply amazed that we could hear our faves live and ignoring some of the less than perfect recordings. So what if it was an audience recording from the back of a stadium with some drunken lout yelling for "Hard Rain", "Heart Breaker" or "Whipping Post". It was our band LIVE.

The introduction of high quality bootleg CDs has spoiled some of us. No longer will some collectors accept less than perfect recordings. I've talked to some collectors who will not even consider listening to an audience recording. How soon we forget.

Sure, excellent sound quality is desirable but sometimes it's just not available. Do we ignore the Australian Zep shows or Quarrymen rehearsals because of the less than perfect quality? I think not. I hope not. When we start putting the sound quality of recordings ahead of historic importance we are buying bootlegs for the wrong reasons.

Enough soapboxing, let's look at how recordings are graded for this 4th edition of The Hot Hot Wacks Book Supplement. The big thing to keep in mind is the state of live recording at the time of the performance. Remember, DAT portables did not always exist.

Excellent: Everything is nice and clear - instruments and voice(s) are well defined. Very Good: Lacks the edge of an Excellent recording. Good: Still quite listenable but not for everyone. Poor: For the hard-core collector.

Soundboard Recording (Soundboard): Professional recording from the mixing board at a concert, a recording studio source or from a radio or television broadcast. Audience Recording (Audience): Amateur recording on portable audio or video equipment.

An Excellent Soundboard recording more often than not differs from an Excellent Audience recording and this should be kept in mind when looking at the gradings. Soundboard recordings tend to provide an even balanced recording while Audience recordings rely on the quality of the sound system, the recording equipment and the position of the recorder.

From The Trenches

The following articles have been written by people in the trenches... collectors. Some say that we at HOT WACKS are (or should be) the experts. The way I see it, it's you the collectors compiling that seemingly never-ending collection who are the real experts. Sure, we listen and document a lot of the material that goes into HOT WACKS but it's the collectors who write with new information and facts missing from past editions that make the book as complete as it is. Please feel free to send in any data you may have or to contribute an article about your favorite group.

BUILDING A COLLECTION: TIPS, PHILOSOPHIES & OBSERVATIONS FROM A 25-YEAR VETERAN OF THE GAME

By Hugh Jones © 1997 HJR/Proximity Productions

(Hugh Jones is the editor and publisher of the Led Zeppelin Collectors Journal *Proximity* and has been collecting rock & roll music and memorabilia since 1964. He has been known to show up at Led Zeppelin conventions with a bottle of tequila, pontificating about the Seattle '75 boots and "karma.")

One of the questions that frequently seems to come my way is, "how did you start collecting?," and the obvious extension of this, "how do I start a collection?"

Most novice collectors have little to go on but their own enthusiasm, and the prospect of building a good collection can seem daunting, especially in the face of long-time serious collectors who have set standards for the hobby. The thing to remember, however, is that every collector started somewhere in the very same position—with very little or nothing.

When the Beatles came to American in 1964, I got caught up in the fever in a big way, which in turn led to a passion for rock & roll that became all consuming and has endured for 30 years now. From the Beatles & Stones in grade school, and later to Hendrix & Zeppelin, Cheap Trick & Rockpile, Richard Thompson and right on through to bands like Wilco and Blue Mountain today, music, and the constant accumulation of it and everything related to the people who make it, is what makes me get out of bed every morning.

Of course, the day I got "Introducing The Beatles" on Vee Jay (which I still have) or my first Led Zeppelin promo poster (begged from a record store to decorate my room), I never dreamed that 30-plus years later I'd have built up a collection of thousands of like items—records, CDs, boots & live tapes, posters, clippings, magazines and promo items of every variety. I didn't start out thinking, "I'm going to collect this band," I just fell in love with the music and consequently snatched up every single thing I could find, be it music, memorabilia or artifacts.

As it happened, in the mid '70s the world of rock music and memorabilia collecting blossomed into a golden age, fueled by magazines such as *Goldmine* and *Trouser Press*, as well as the easy availability of many then-forgotten '60s rarities often found in junk stores and cutout bins.

For example, original '60s issues of Who, Nazz and Yardbirds albums, which at their peak in the mid-70's could fetch up to $100 on the collectors market, could easily be found in Woolworth and K-Mart cut-out bins as late as 1973 or '74 for a measly $2.99. And while a few savvy folks saw the potential value of things like the Led Zeppelin 1 inflatable Atlantic promo blimp (1997 market value: $500+), the vast majority of people in the record biz were more than happy to give (or throw!) stuff like that away, and many items of this type were procured free or for spare change by fledgling collectors in the early '70s.

Collectors today face a vastly inflated market in original, vintage rock collectibles of the "classic" bands, which certainly makes building a collection an expensive proposition. What one has to remember is that those deluxe all-color *16 Magazine* Beatles specials that fetch over fifty dollars now were once available new for fifty cents—and that there are still new items on bands like the Beatles and Zeppelin being released all the time and sold for regular prices. While items from the '80s and '90s may never have the intrinsic value of items released during a band's lifespan or heyday, they will still unquestionably increase in value over time. And obviously if you're collecting a current band such as U2 or REM, you are in a position to score original current items that will appreciate greatly in years to come.

Of course, good luck can always play a part in scoring those choice items—possibly the best deal I ever got was on a 1971 family vacation in Cambridge, Massachusetts, when I walked into a Budget Tapes & Records store and found an album in the new release bin called "Live Yardbirds Featuring Jimmy Page," priced at the princely sum of $3.99. I only had a passing familiarity with the Yardbirds at that time, but of course as a Zeppelin fan the appeal of any record featuring Jimmy Page was strong—still, I hesitated as I considered carrying it up to the counter.

After putting the record back on the rack, looking around the store some more, picking it up again and hemming and hawing for about half an hour, I finally took the plunge and bought it. Not only did I take it home to find a most amazing 40 minutes of Page guitar and classic Yardbirds tunes which I loved, I later found out that the record was only on the racks for one week—the week I happened to be in Cambridge—before Page and Peter Grant filed an injunction against Epic and had it pulled off the shelves. That record, which I still own, is now impossible to find and goes for upwards of $100.00.

By putting one's self in a position to stumble on deals like this, i.e. haunting record stores, becoming educated and paying attention, anyone with a little patience, some dedication and a healthy constitution can start and build a rock & roll collection of cool items on their favorite band. Oh, and I guess you need at least a small amount of disposable income, too—but perhaps not as much as you might think!

Following are a few basic tenets of collecting that have always worked for me—call it the gospel according to Mr. Prox—which I hope will help some of you achieve success in this most challenging and rewarding of hobbies.

· COLLECT FOR LOVE, NOT MONEY ·

While this is a matter of choice to anyone planning to accumulate goods of value, I personally view this as one of the most important things about collecting anything, especially a band. While it amuses me that items I paid $3 for are now worth hundreds, it doesn't really mean that much to me since I never plan to sell them anyway—the only real gain in knowing the value of an item is when you're using it for trade.

The thing that first excited me about Led Zeppelin—my "main band" in terms of collecting—was their music, and it's still the music that fuels my fire in gathering all the related stuff. I've known collectors over the years who collect only for the value, and in fact don't even care about the music that much. Some of them have done well wheeling and dealing in the collecting world, but they're not much fun to deal with and I am always reluctant to pass something good along to them. It's kind of a matter of principle.

· CHOOSE A POISON, ER. . . PASSION ·

While I have an annoying tendency to collect absolutely anything and everything related to Led Zeppelin (or even not exactly related—my latest obsession is vintage postcards from the '30s and '40s with images of actual Zeppelins on them), it can be more practical to focus attention on one area—7- inch single picture sleeves, for example. While it's advisable to pick up anything of value that's within your price range for trade bait if nothing else, it's easier to pass on that $450 Bath Festival program when you know that you can probably score five or six European picture sleeves for that kind of money if you concentrate your efforts on finding them.

If you decide to collect something fairly common and reasonably priced—American rock magazines with Zeppelin covers or articles, for example—you'll find that as you accumulate more and more of them you'll also end up with duplicates—excellent for trading and possibly helping you step up to a higher level or another facet of collecting, like tour programs. Which brings us to the next directive:

· BUY 2 OF EVERYTHING ·

Any time you come across something that is new, available in quantity, and priced within your budget, buy at least two copies of it! I cannot over-emphasize the benefits this practice has paid me over the years. I've winced a few times at shelling out the extra money, but I've never regretted it even once in the long run. Every time *Circus* Magazine put Jimmy Page or Robert Plant on the cover—which seemed like three or four times a year in the late '70s—I bought two or three copies off the newsstand. When I went to see a band and they had a tour program available, I bought two. When I found a cool poster at Woolworth's for $2.99, I bought three. And over the years, all these multiple purchases have been siphoned off and traded, in most cases for items worth many times the price originally paid for the magazine, program or poster I bought.

And if you think this only applies to vintage items, guess again—copies of the 1994 *Mojo* with Zeppelin on the cover, the '95 Jimmy Page special issue of *Guitar Player*, and any number of other recently produced items are already trading at more than double their original worth on the Zeppelin market. So the next time you see your band on the cover of a magazine, dig deep and buy a few copies! If you're planning to build a collection, it will definitely pay off down the road.

· TRADE, DON'T BUY ·

While it's hard to trade when you're just getting started and don't have anything to offer, it's well worth building up a pool of tradable material, because it's vastly preferable to cut deals with people for the stuff you want than to actually pay cash for it. In a good trade everybody wins. Both parties have paid less than market value for items they're swapping, both can live without the item they're letting go, and both are desirous of the item they're getting. So much more substantial and satisfying than a cash transaction!

Building a collection, and especially a pool of duplicates and 'trade bait,' takes a lot of energy. If all you do is occasionally browse *Goldmine* (where most items sell for full market value) and drop into your local used record store (where the employees scoop all the heaviest stuff), you're never going to do very well. You've got to be willing to spend some time and get your hands dirty. You've got to get into the thrill of the hunt!

Junk shops, swap meets, and especially garage sales are prime places to find great deals. I know of several instances where people scored Beatles "Butcher Covers" for under a buck at garage sales, simply because they knew what to look for and the seller had no idea what they had, and on more than one occasion I have found valuable 7-inch single picture sleeves, 78's and other vinyl rarities in boxes marked "10¢ each" sitting on someone's front lawn! While it may seem obvious to most of us that an old picture sleeve or some other '60s rock artifact has inherent value, there is a huge uneducated public out there who might have picked up some stuff in the '60s or '70s and never thought about it again until it came out of the attic in the Great Garage Sale Purge of '97—and they slapped a "$1.00" price tag on it.

Get out early on Saturdays and drive around to sales. Become a regular and get to know the people running your local junk shop or antique mall, and make sure they know what band you're looking for. While they're not as common as they used to be, great deals on vintage rock collectibles still pop up all the time, usually in the most unexpected of places.

· LEARN THE MARKET ·

Rather than dive in blind and start snapping up every item you see, it's a good idea to learn what the collecting world is all about and in turn get a feel for market value not only on items relating to the band you collect, but on similar collectibles from the same era, be it current or vintage. Probably the most comprehensive and easily available source of information is *Goldmine* magazine, which is pretty much the bible of record and music collectors, and with good reason—it's articles are extremely in-depth and very well researched, and it's advertisements give a fascinating view of the collectors world—what's out there and how much it's worth (or at least how much someone thinks it's worth).

As anyone reading a Hot Wacks book probably already knows, the other place to get a crash course in collecting is at record conventions, and also at band-specific events such as the recent Zeppelin and Kiss conventions and the ubiquitous Beatles gatherings. If you're a newcomer to the world of collecting, going to a record convention is a very good way to find out if this world is for you or not. The level of passion, commitment, fanatacism (and yes, geekiness) at these events is quite staggering, really, and while it's a blast for those who are into it, it can be a reality check for those dabblers who aren't quite sure what they're in for.

If the vibe doesn't scare you away right off the bat, then record conventions can be fun and educational, and of course a good place to find collectibles. While great deals on rarities are unlikely to surface at a convention, occasionally you'll find someone who doesn't know what they have, and of course unlike dealing through the mail out of *Goldmine*, dealing with someone face to face at a convention provides the opportunity to haggle, which one should always be prepared to do. And, you can always bring some of your own items for trade.

· TRADING ·

Actually engineering a trade can be a tricky and sometimes intimidating business. In my mind the best way to play it is to be as honest and forthright as possible. If you're initiating a transaction, take an objective look at what you've got and what you want, and make an offer that's fair. Don't insult someone by trying to pull a scam (see "karma" below), and if you're unsure of the value of something don't be afraid to ask the person's opinion. Think before you make an offer, and make it in good faith. The worst thing that can happen is that the person will say 'no,' and then you can adjust the offer or pass the trade by. Nothing ventured, nothing gained, as they say.

· ATTITUDE ·

Stay cool. If you're at a convention and you just found your heart's desire for mere pennies, don't start doing backflips for the crowd—keep your cards close to your chest and simply purchase the item with a smile. Try not to brag, and never gloat—especially to someone you just scored a deal from unbeknownst to them—if you ever have to deal with that person again, you don't want them thinking they got bilked by you the last time!

· HONESTY & KARMA ·

Call me a crusty old ex-hippie if you like, I don't care: karma is an important thing in this world, and that's especially true in the world of collecting music. If you do nice things for people, treat them fairly, and show respect, it will come back to you in kind. The support I get in publishing my fanzine *Proximity* and the goodies that show up on a regular basis in my P.O. box are living proof of that. And I thank you all! Hopefully some of the thoughts in this article will prove useful to you as you seek that next elusive goodie. Happy hunting. .

PINK FLOYD
COLLECTING HIGHS AND LOWS AND YET ANOTHER FRESH DOSE OF FLOYD MUSINGS
By Keith From Toronto

"The dream is over." (John Lennon "God", 1972)

I've been collecting music since 1969. I'm a completest. I have purchased everything commercially available by virtually all of my favorite artists, led by Floyd, Beatles and Tull.

Remember now, that's everything. Literally!

So, when I innocently stumbled on a Beatles Bootleg (TOP OF THE POPS, Highway High Fi 111) in 1977, I was amazed that there was more material "out there". More Beatles. More Floyd. More Tull. More! More! More! It was a great day indeed.

Now, let's fast track to the late 1980s. All of a sudden, the vinyl bootlegs start to come out on Compact Disc. And they're available in commercial record shops! Great!! I can start the fun all over again!!!

But, alas, we arrive at today. And, as you must know by now, Governments world wide finally agreed music copyright infringements had to stop. The death knell to the small loopholes in copyright law struck at 12:01 a.m. January 1, 1996. Releases of in-concert performances no longer make the cut as "legal" product. As a collector and a fan, the dream appears to be over.

So, maybe it's a good time to contemplate the sum total of all this collecting. The good, the bad and the ugly, so-to-speak. When it comes to Floyd, there's a bit of everything involved.

First, as usual, a bit of business. Unlike previous contributions to HOT WACKS, many of the items mentioned here are not listed in previous volumes or this Supplement (see Keith's other articles in HOT WACKS Supplements 2 to 4 -- we hope to have an adjusted Floyd section for our final coffee table edition--Ed.).

THE GOOD
Let's begin with some good experiences. While I'm saving a definitive Pink Floyd top ten list for the deluxe table top edition of HOT WACKS, I do have some pet "best finds" I'd like to tell you about. Certainly (finally) hearing the debut of DARK SIDE OF THE MOON (Rainbow Theatre Show from February 1972) is right up there.

The RAINBOW show came a year before the commercial album release of DARK SIDE and helps account for why the legitimate album, in fact, did so well. Shows what performances of material live in front of audiences can do. What better way to get the bugs out?

When first performed, DSOTM was actually called ECLIPSE. The group Medicine Head had just released an album using the DARK SIDE OF THE MOON title and Floyd decided to change theirs to avoid confusion (even though Floyd really preferred "the Dark Side..." moniker).

As it worked out, by the time Floyd was ready to actually release their album in 1973, Medicine Head's album had totally faded from view. So, Floyd felt confident enough to use their preferred title after all. And the rest, as they say, was history.

As for the early performance of the work itself? Well, a great deal is missing but the core is there and it is special! Here's what's different from the eventual album release: there's no overture (SPEAK TO ME) featuring effects and voices. ON THE RUN is more or less a group jam and GREAT GIG IN THE SKY is church-service-like in words and organ -- no orgasmic vocal stylings yet. After being so familiar with the released commercial album for so long, hearing the earliest incarnations is, well, just plain fun. It's still a great set and a great set of songs. The pace is just a tad slower.

The RAINBOW show is widely bootlegged under many titles, ironically, none featuring the name of the venue itself. Here are just a few of the Cd titles: FORBIDDEN SAMPLES (Neutral Zone NZ CD 89007, 1989), TIME (Great Dane Records GDR CD SAT 4, 1994), DARK SIDE OF THE SKY (Chapter One 25117, 1992), IN THE SKY (Triangle CD 044 1992), and BEST OF TOUR '72 (The Swingin' Pig TSP CD 049, 1994).

For those really interested in this time period, there is also another worthwhile find in the DARK SIDE REHEARSALS (Triangle Records PYCD 065-2, 1991). This is from a show a month earlier at the start of the 1972 tour (January 20 in Brighton). Listen for the break down altogether of MONEY via equipment failure.

By the way, the song ECLIPSE, was yet to be written at this point. But it was added to the set by the time of the RAINBOW shows.

The whole ECLIPSE-to-DARK SIDE OF THE MOON period presents probably the most important study in the band's development. Through the bootlegs you get to hear Pink Floyd move from a band with a cult following to a cult in and of itself.

As 1972 moved along (you can also find performances of ECLIPSE/DSOTM in Japan, France and the USA) you hear a new Floyd emerging. A new audience response emerges as well. Crowds will never listen quite the same once DARK SIDE is commercially released. Indeed, if Floyd were to opt for an ANTHOLOGY package similar to what the Beatles have done, the RAINBOW Show (or other venue through 1972) would be a must include -- even with inferior sound.

No matter your view on the legality of bootlegs or the artist's right-to-control-their-artistic-output issue, for fans interested in the group, hearing this material is superior to only reading about it in books or fanzines. DAH! This should be obvious to everyone including the artist and record companies. It is history comes alive (with apologies to Peter Frampton).

I feel lucky in having had the pleasure to sample all of the material I've been writing about. But how many other (and newer) fans will be as lucky?

Here's a formal request to all bands to consider releasing the stuff in the vaults. Especially groups who've been with us for a while. Actually, I think it's fair to say the bootleg industry has really prompted many artists and their record companies to do just this. And, please note, in the end, we would rather pay the artist anyway. So legally bootleg yourself folks -- even if only in limited editions for the hard core fans.

But back to more "good stuff". For me, the collecting/research highlight came in locating shows with live performances of the OBSCURED BY CLOUDS album. First find was a show from Toronto (on cassette) followed by another cassette tape of the show at Earl's Court (both 1973). But the capper came via an obscure double Cd release called OBSCURITY (Sugarcane Records SC 52005/6, 1995).

As I said, I'd been searching vigorously for live versions of OBSCURED BY CLOUDS material for years. While HOT WACKS lists a number of releases with live material from this album, I simply could never find anyone who had any of it on Cd (my preferred format).

Actually, it was a collecting buddy who eventually found OBSCURITY for himself. After much salivating I was fortunate to locate a second copy. Phew! War between nations avoided. But why such intensity? Well, this fine Cd features more than WHEN YOU'RE IN and the album's title track, both in excellent live versions. You also get an elongated EMBRYO.

This is the only time, to my knowledge, where the band jams to such an extent. This comes in contrast to what I stated in Supplement 3, referring to Led Zeppelin as the band with long live versions of material and not Floyd. I stand corrected for this one Pink Floyd performance. (By the way, I also did not mean jams were not a part of Floyd's modus operandi during Syd Barrett's reign -- they obviously were.)

This long and live version of EMBRYO (itself never commercially released in an approved studio version by the band), has trace elements of the coming DARK SIDE OF THE MOON material. (I should explain here. The first Cd is actually from a US concert in 1970 and has the EMBRYO material. The second Cd is from a show in 1973 and has the OBSCURED BY CLOUDS stuff.)

Many people might say the thrill of collecting comes in the hunt and not the actual find. I disagree and this surprise Cd ends up on my player regularly.

I suppose I should add finding the COMMITTEE soundtrack and the live performance of ALAN'S PSYCHEDELIC BREAKFAST as significant moments too. (Interestingly, the Cd version called A PSYCHEDELIC NIGHT PART 1 (Triangle Records PYCD 038, 1991) is edited and is not the full performance found on vinyl as ALLEN'S (sic) PSYCHEDELIC BREAKFAST (Circus Sun, 19??)).

The non-music bits of Alan's breakfast finds the band well, er, actually serving up breakfast on stage while the COMMITTEE features early version of CAREFUL WITH THAT AXE EUGENE (more a variation in the same ballpark than an actual version -- comes complete with the dialogue from the movie which is a bit PRISONERish, if you remember that TV series).

THE BAD
Ah, but with the good comes some bad. The RAINBOW show actually has a "bad" story associated to it. For the longest time it was on my list of needed acquisitions. The first Cd I saw stating the right time period was LONDON 1972 (Golden Stars GSCD 1138, 1991). But hey, this is not the right show -- featuring a 1974 BBC version of the completed DARK SIDE OF THE MOON instead.

But inaccuracy is a trait in bootlegdom. Through all of these articles, I've done my best to sort through the untrue or misinformation. It's quite a challenge! The reasons for such frequent mistakes are two fold. Often, it is deliberate. Deliberate as in: "say, the other guys just released a boot so let's copy theirs and change the name and time period altogether." The other reason may not be as blatant in intent but arises from fuzzy information. Perhaps the person who owned the original tape never communicated where it was recorded. More likely the information was ignored, mixed up or just lost in subsequent releases.

The books GREAT WHITE WONDERS by Clinton Heylin (see page 235) and BLACK MARKT BEATLES by Jim Berkenstadt and Belmo (see page 234) -- both available through the HOT WACKS Press -- are interesting reading for tracing bootlegger family trees -- this, in spite of some of the reservations articulated in HOT WACKS (see pages CC to GG, Hot Wacks Supplement 3, for a review of GREAT WHITE WONDERS-- Ed.)

Suffice to say, you can't depend on the sleeves or liner notes. I'm sure all collectors will agree on how frustrating it is to guess your way through the process. I mentioned in HOT WACKS Supplement 2 that the "not-in-it-solely-for-whatever-profit-can-be-made" dealers would give you an opportunity to preview first. It's just unfortunate not all dealers, or even traders, are so inclined.

Certainly with the move to the underground (or is it a return?) anyone left actually selling the illegal product will probably not be inclined to let you preview. But, no matter what I write here, it won't change the credo will it?

THE CREDO
At the end of the HOT WACKS Supplement 2, you will find the bootleg collectors credo: Nunc hic aut numquam. Translated this means: it's now or never! Sad but true. A caveat to this is: here today gone tomorrow and never to be found again! (in Latin I think this translates over to "there is a sucker born every minute").

THE UGLY
Which moves us to the ugly. The capper for me was a Syd Barrett disc: SYD BARRETT LUCY LEAVE AND OTHER RARITIES (DIYE 16, 1995). This is a picture disc listing outtakes of INTERSTELLAR OVERDRIVE, early Floyd demos and also material from Syd's solo period. Looked good alright. But it came sealed and with a gruff, "no-way-I'll-open-it-up-for-you-and-let-you-listen-to-it--buy-it-or-get-out-of-my-face" attitude behind the cash (and it was cash they wanted).

Busted! When I actually listened to the Cd at home, I ended up with Glenn Miller and his Orchestra's GREATEST HITS. No fooling! So much for quality control at the plant.

As for the song called LUCY LEAVE (and another track called KINGBEE -- both songs have also appeared on other boots), there is some speculation that this is not actually early Floyd at all. But, if the bootlegs featuring this material aren't really Pink Floyd and Syd Barrett, then they are great forgeries. (The two songs are found on MAGNESIUM PROVERBS (Golden Standard Night Tripper GD--10, 1994) and A SAUCERFUL OF OUT-TAKES (Chapter One CO 25195, 1994), among others).

I implied in both Supplement's 2 and 3 that these songs are legit early Floyd demos. I stand behind this even though some Floyd books suggest otherwise. (See PINK FLOYD THROUGH THE EYES OF..., edited by Bruno MacDonald, Sedgwick & Jackson 1996, for an example).

Again, for what it's worth, when you hear the songs, it sounds like a young Syd doing vocals. And the attitude is absolutely right ... "Leave but don't you leave me, Lucy."

In the booklet for CRAZY DIAMOND, the commercially released Syd Barrett box set, these songs are discussed as being credible. If the bootlegged material is, in fact, a forgery, then the bootleggers went to great lengths -- complete with scratched record sounds and surface noise. Let's put the questionable factor down as an "ugly" rumour instead. But perhaps Roger Waters or Pink Floyd could finally settle this one for us? Oh yeah, I didn't bother to go back to the store with the Barrett disc (actually it was at a record collector show and the seller was not a local guy anyway). But buyer beware eh!

FLOYD: THE NEXT GENERATION
The transition from vinyl to Cd has allowed exact replicas of material to be reissued and repackaged with no signal loss. But what's interesting here is how many bootleggers did not provide any kind of an audio clean up from their source tapes -- not taking advantage of the newer technologies available. In many cases, it's obvious the bootleggers were taking material directly from a vinyl release -- LUCY LEAVE and KINGBEE aside.

In listening to the same material, cleaned verses uncleaned, it's a shame many bootleggers did not bother to take the extra step of a clean up. The Cd release, PINK FLOYD: STRANGER THAN FICTION (Value For Money Records VFM 430 318, 1995), goes as far as to feature the sounds of the record skipping for 10 seconds or so -- fading down and up again -- midway through a performance of ATOM HEART MOTHER. Yikes!

On the "extra care taken" side of the column, we have OAKLAND COLISEUM (Stonehenge STCD 2016/2017, 1995), WALLPOWER (cd 64-64-32/35, 1995) and the VARIATIONS ON A THEME OF ABSENCE (CD Company DIA 001 through 008, 1995) box set. These three samples in particular represent exceptional sound. (Many second generation Cd releases, in fact, are better quality sound than the first generation.)

While we're talking about this, in HOT WACKS Supplement 3, Ron from Chicago writes about his efforts producing Floyd releases for the Great Dane Record Company in Italy. I agree Great Dane took a great deal of pride in their product and, for the most part, deserve high marks.

But, just to comment on the list provided in his article for a moment. There are better sounding releases of the Top Gear material (BBC). TRANSCENDENTAL MEDICATION (Turtle Records TR-223) and A SAUCERFUL OF OUTTAKES (Chapter One CO 25195, 1994) are examples -- but it is true they do not include everything from the Top Gear appearances.

RANDOM PRECISION (GDR CD) does not, in my opinion, rate with IVOR WYNNE and other shows of the 1975 tours. Meanwhile, IN THE FLESH (Great Dane Records GDR), while good, is now surpassed by the above mentioned OAKLAND COLISEUM.

But I'm quibbling here. Without Great Dane and Ron, we'd be in a lot worse shape. And the TOTAL ECLIPSE 4 Cd box set (GREAT DANE Records GDR CD 9320, 1993) is a real winner and crosses Floyd's career with style. Congratulations for giving fans a shot at hearing some truly rare and historic material and doing so legally!

As to the future? Well, the DIVISION BELL tour was covered rather completely. And, maybe, this is one of the reasons Floyd chose to release such a complete live package of the tour. PULSE certainly did out bootleg the bootlegs in sound and presentation didn't it? And it was cheaper to buy to boot!

NEW MOST WANTED
If, however, Floyd played the song MAROONED at all during the DIVISION BELL tour (as indicated in Andy Mabbett's THE COMPLETE GUIDE TO THE MUSIC OF PINK FLOYD (Omnibus Press, 1995)), it has yet to show up on any bootleg.

So, there's the next item on the top of my wish list for a future find or trade! (Mabbett also states in the re-issued PINK FLOYD THE VISUAL DOCUMENTARY BY MILES & ANDY MABBETT (Omnibus Press, 1994) that, as a treat on Tim Renwick's birthday, August 7, in a concert in Switzerland, Dave Gilmour allowed Tim Renwick to play the solo on LEARNING TO FLY. Sorry Andy, but Tim was playing the solos on this right from the beginning of the MOMENTARY LAPSE OF REASON tour! How did you miss that?)

But I truly doubt we'll see much more new and bootlegged product at all. I would only hope Floyd would consider an arrangement similar to what the Grateful Dead offered -- a taping section for fans. Bottom line, a recording of the show and hearing the performances is what matters to us completest, obsessives most. Are there that many of us around? I suspect a few anyway. But most of us aren't interested in selling or making money from these souvenirs.

Of course, the Internet may offer some possibilities for trades and sound bites. HOT WACKS information is available there already. Maybe you're reading this on a computer screen right now. Greetings from Toronto!

SEE YOU AROUND THE TRENCHES
To paraphrase one of the most bootlegged artists ever, Bob Dylan: the "trenches" they are a changing.

In fact, who knows what technology awaits and what, if any, other forms bootlegs may take. I suspect copyrights will actually be harder to enforce, rather than easier, in spite of the loophole-less laws. This will be especially true as technology gets smaller and recording device chips that fit into the ear (or perhaps another orifice) become the norm. Well, that gives new implications to the search as you go through the concert gate doesn't it?

Whatever! Keep an eye out for me will you? And, if you have any live shows etc., let's talk!

Address any responses to HOT WACKS.

Please note: As this was going to press, Keith let us know that he did find a tape of the show where MAROONED was played. Good things come to those who wait.

THE ROLLING STONES
STICKY FINGERS' ESSENTIAL BOOTLEGS OF 1996
By John Carr
(John Carr is the Editor of 'Sticky Fingers Magazine' which is dedicated to the Rolling Stones and their music. John Carr can be reached at Sticky Fingers, P.O. Box 3474, Granada Hills, CA 91344. Send $4 for sample issue or $20 for a 1-year subscription.)

1996 was an incredible year for Rolling Stones bootlegs. More high quality Rolling Stones releases came out last year than the previous 3 years! [I direct those readers who want more information on earlier Rolling Stones bootleg titles to 'Hot Wacks Book: Supplement #4' for the 'Sticky Fingers' Essential Rolling Stones bootleg list.] Plus, a large number of essential recordings were re-issued in improved sound. One could build a great Rolling Stones alternative music collection, spanning the history of the group, from the releases of the last year and a half alone.

Until 1996 there were only a few official release quality Rolling Stones studio outtake bootlegs on the market. Half a dozen spectacular new releases came out in 1996, many of them with new outtakes and previously available songs in better sound quality than ever before. Enough that 1996 could easily be called the year of the Ultimate Outtakes. And, without a doubt, the most important and significant release of the entire year-no the decade-was the massive 4 CD box set, "Voodoo Brew" released by Vigotone Records.

This was a groundbreaking release, not only because of its superb sound quality and graphics, but because it documented the Stones at work in the studio to a degree never previously heard. While some have argued that its sister release, "Voodoo Stew," has more early takes and unknown songs, "Voodoo Brew" was the first one released and contains an entire CD of a relaxed Keith Richards in the studio singing and playing some of his favorite tunes. Truly, an amazing performance. Already, this box has almost disappeared so go and find one before they're gone-you'll thank me.

Most Rolling Stones fans and collectors divide their lengthy career into three bodies of work: the Brain Jones era, the Mick Taylor era and the Ron Wood era. Each period has its own distinctive sound and wonderful body of work.

THE BRIAN JONES ERA

1. AROUND AND AROUND (Invasion Unlimited/IU-9531-1)
Named after a famous German LP, this single CD contains the best collection of early Rolling Stones outtakes ever compiled on a single CD. A nice thing about "Around And Around" is that it concentrates on the early Blues covers and Blues influenced numbers, not the pop dreck that Andrew Loog Oldham originally wanted them to record as the latest Mersey sensation. [See Invasion Unlimited's second outtakes "Songbook" for most of those amusing, when collected together, but eminently forgettable, pop songs.] "Around And Around" is an essential disc for every Stones music lover. If only "Metamorphosis" had been half this good!

2. BRIAN JONES-STILL I'M GONNA MISS YOU (VGP-073)
There are very few Rolling Stones live radio broadcasts available from the Sixties. Probably the best known are the Europe 1 shows broadcast from Paris, France in 1965, 1966 and 1967. The latter two are the most important since they're from a time when the Stones had put a moratorium on touring. Blue Moon Records' "Raw Power" and Scorpio's "Paris Match" gave us significant upgrades of the Paris, Olympia Theatre April 18th, 1965 radio show; however, at the end of the year, a new release came out that put them all to shame, "Still I'm Gonna Miss You," which was sourced from a recent re-broadcast of the best of the Radio Europe 1 shows called "Musicorama." There are 12 songs from three shows broadcast in 1965, 1966 and 1967. The first 4 are from April 18th 1965 and they've never sounded so good. But the real treat on this disc are the amazing songs from the March 29th 1966 and April 11th 1967 Paris Olympia Theatre shows. While not perfect (after all these were recorded in the infancy of rock radio broadcasting and Mick Jagger's voice is over-miked), they're still amazing sounding documents of a series of shows of great historical importance. The version of 'Get Off My Cloud' with the 'Hang On Sloopy' verse is a hoot. 'Paint It Black' from the 1967 broadcast rolls through the speakers like a run-away locomotive! A knock-off of the Vinyl Gang disc was recently released as "Du Fond du Coeur." (no label), which in addition to the Europe 1, shows contains the May 26th, 1965 'Shindig' show. Actually, if you are looking for a good early Stones soundboard, any of these will do. "Paris Match" includes the entire 1965 Europe 1 show, plus the Honolulu 1966 radio broadcast ("In Action"), as well as two 'Sunday Night At the London Palladium' 1967 TV soundboard shows and one more song (that doesn't appear on "Still I'm Gonna Miss You") from the Paris 1967 broadcast - a Yardbirds-style rave-up of 'Going Home/Satisfaction' which is pure dynamite!

3. BRIAN JONES-GROOVIN' AROUND (Vinyl Gang/VGP-074)
"Groovin' Around" is more a historical document, than an easy listening collection, combining together the only 2 (known) audience tape recordings of the Rolling Stones from the 1967 European Tour - yes, these shows pre-date "Live'r Than You'll Ever Be" by 2 years! The first show, recorded at Stadhalle in Austria, has the best sound. It's really surprisingly good, considering the date. The second show, recorded in Hague, Holland on April 15th 1967 is barely listenable, but, again, historically interesting nonetheless. These rare tapes

of the Rolling Stones 'lost years' (1967-1968) have rarely appeared outside of tape trading circles and we have Vinyl Gang to thank for making them widely available.

4. R.S.V.P. (Cool Blokes)
While there is little evidence of Brian Jones on this new CD, the outtakes presented in this collection give us a completely different take on "Beggars Banquet" - the Back To The Roots album that put the Stones on their most creative course ever. These tracks are sourced right from the master reels and, frankly, some of the early mixes presented on "R.S.V.P." sound better than many of those that made the final album cut! The sound here is much cleaner, and songs like 'Parachute Woman' and 'Jigsaw Puzzle' jump right off this great disc. Here is one outtakes CD you will not want to miss.

THE MICK TAYLOR ERA

5. LIVE'R THAN YOU'LL EVER BE (Master of Sounds)
It's great to hear the Father of All Bootlegs restored to it's original sound, unlike the No-Noised Swingin' Pig title of the same name - which included songs from New York and San Diego. Master of Sounds has given us not only the entire original song list, but all the songs from the Oakland, 2nd show - even the opening 'Jumping Jack Flash' with the drop-outs. I like the rough, tough and in-your-face sound of this disc. It's even better than Vinyl Gang's "The Original Live'r Than You'll Ever Be"-it doesn't have the VGP's vinyl surface noise. Usually, I don't like those cardboard LP replica covers, but this one is sooo cool-it's like holding a piece of history in the palm of your hand! Plus, like the Vinyl Gang version, it has the 'Rolling Stone Magazine' "Live'r" review on the back.

6. COCAINE ON A DENTIST CHAIR (Vinyl Gang/VGP-068 2-CDs)
In tape trading circles, this recording of the 1969 Rolling Stones Tour at the LA Forum didn't show up in decent sound until the early Nineties. It was quickly booted onto CD as "Lost Satanic Tour '69" and "Street Hassle in LA." Several of the performances from the Forum show were superb, especially rarely played gems like 'I'm Free' and 'Under My Thumb.' In 1995/1996 this show appeared on 2 bootlegs from 2 different tape sources in the best sound ever. The first was Vinyl Gang's "Cocaine On A Dentist Chair," which sounds like it was taken straight from the original audience tape, and is head and shoulders above the previous titles. There are some drop-outs in the first few numbers (like on most of these 1969 Ken and Dub recordings), but I've never heard Mick Taylor and Keith's guitars jump out of the speakers like they do on 'Jumping Jack Flash.' Wow! Then a completely new audience tape showed up on a CD from the Sonic Zoom label called "Born In The Crossfire Hurricane." While it's not as clean or clear as the Vinyl Gang title, the mix on "Crossfire Hurricane" is better, with Mick Jagger's vocals up where they belong. You can't go wrong with either one, although the Sonic Zoom title has almost completely disappeared.

7. LIVE IN BALTIMORE & MORE (Moonlight/ML-9637)
Some might think this recording is an odd choice, since there are only 5 new songs on the whole disc. The rest is an upgrade of the 'Gimme Shelter' movie soundtrack. But these 5 tracks include the longest and most dynamic 'Sympathy For The Devil' ever heard - with the 'Hey Jude' refrain. Plus, the audience recording of the 'Love In Vain' that appears on "Get Yer Ya-Ya's Out!." Finally, this is the only live audience tape to show up from the 1969 Tour that is comparable to the great West Coast shows recorded by Ken and Dub.

8. SHAKE YOUR HIPS (Vinyl Gang/VGP-078 2-CDs)
Vinyl Gang has once again upgraded a rare recording that has long been coveted by Stones fans, including yours truly. "Shake Your Hips" features a copy of the Paris, September 22nd 1970 concert soundboard from radio Europe 1. This show was recorded early in the game and in the middle of a riot so it's not really comparable to modern soundboards. In sound quality it is closest to the Bill Graham mixing board tape from

Oakland 1969, released by Vinyl Gang as "Oakland Sixty-Nine." It is, however, the best document we have of the forgotten European tour of 1970, and a significant improvement over Vinyl Gang's earlier version of the Paris soundboard, "Some Like It Hot!." The highlight of this show is a great version of Chuck Berry's 'Roll Over Beethoven' played live only in the early Sixties and on the 1970 Tour. The second CD contains a tolerable audience recording of the 1970 Berlin concert.

9. THE LOST MARQUEE TAPES (Vinyl Gang/VGP-030 2-CDs)
The Marquee Club TV broadcast and rehearsal tapes have been released on a number of CDs, but Vinyl Gang's "The Lost Marquee Tapes" is the best sounding recording of this show I've ever heard. There are some inherent problems with the sound of this show; for one, the guitars are too low in the mix. However, it's nice to finally hear this legendary concert in very good sound quality. This is the only concert where the Stones played 'I Got The Blues.' The second CD consists of an audience recording of the 1971 Chalk Farm Round House show. While the Round House recording is sourced from an LP, the sound is an improvement over earlier Vinyl Gang CDs.

10. IN EXOTIC HONOLULU (Vinyl Gang/VGP-040 2-CDs)
Unfortunately, there are not a lot of great audience (or soundboard for that matter) recordings from the 1972 Exile Tour, which many people believe was the greatest Stones tour of all time. In January of 1973, there was a mini-Exile Tour which started in Los Angeles and ended in the Far East. This Honolulu show is best surviving audience recording of those great Exile tours we have-and never has it sounded as good as it does here on this Vinyl Gang upgrade. The first CD, which includes the complete first show, captures Mick Jagger and the Rolling Stones at the height of their powers. This is an essential concert. The second disc has the 2nd Honolulu January 21st performance in very good sound: it's slightly better than last years "Tropical Windsongs."

11. HEADIN' FOR AN OVERLOAD (Totonka/CD Pro-18 2-CDs)
This fantastic 2 CD live album contains both the King Biscuit Flower Hour 1973 Rolling Stones radio broadcasts (actually aired in 1974) in their entirety in flawless sound. True, many of these KBFH songs had been put out before in great quality (best known as "Brussels Affair 1973"), but now we hear them as they were first aired. These are among the finest Stones performances ever recorded. You can't go wrong with this 2 CD set: don't worry about a few repeats, it is the way they were originally aired and these songs are worth hearing again, and again, and again!

12. ACETATES (Midnight Beat/MB-045)
"Acetates" gives us a wonderful look at the end of the Mick Taylor Era, as the Stones began to display an increased interest in R&B dance music and Soul. This disc contains the cleanest version of 'Drift Away' I've ever heard. I'm sure several of these songs were under consideration for the half studio/half live album Mick Jagger talked about in a Scandinavian interview that was nixed by the Klein/Decca Records settlement - the one which would have featured a live version of 'You Can't Always Get What You Want.' Take your favorite studio outtakes from "Acetates" and put them on one side of a tape, while on the other, take your favorite live songs from "Headin' For An Overload." Viola! You now have a damn good facsimile of a Rolling Stones album that never was. This is one of the top five Stones outtakes albums ever released!

THE RON WOOD ERA

13. L.A. CONNECTION (Vinyl Gang/VGP-085 2-CDs)
After years of neglect by bootleggers, the Stones 1995 Tour Of America has finally gotten some respect! This double disc set is sourced from a video soundboard of the July 11th 1975 Forum show titled, "L.A. Connection." Neither the performance nor the sound are equal to the quality of the Sunday show on "LA Friday '75," but it is far superior to the

Buffalo 1975 soundboard. The sound is surprisingly good (better than the Big Music's "Rockin' At The Forum") until the middle of the show, when Mick's voice dominates the mix. It does pick up again with 'Brown Sugar' through the end of the disc.

14. LA FRIDAY '75 (Vinyl Gang/VGP-082 2-CDs)
While this July 13th LA Forum show from 1975 takes place on Sunday rather than Friday, that's the only miscue in this wonderful 2 CD set. We've seen this show before, most notably on Silver Rarities 2 CD release "I Never Talked To Chuck Berry," which was in excellent sound, but incomplete. This great double CD is not only better sounding - the bass is much more prominent, but includes the entire show in high quality sound. Some authorities on the Net have called this CD the best sounding live Stones CD of all time. I don't know if I'd go that far, but this album should be a part of any serious Stones collection.

15. IT'S ONLY ROCK AND ROLL (Vinyl Gang/VGP-036/037 2-CDs)
'Sticky Fingers' staff member Steve Currin calls this double CD from the same 1975 Tour his all time '75 Tour favorite. Another excellent quality audience recording, this Cow Palace show has all the depth and resonance we expect from a good soundboard recording. You can't go wrong with either "LA Friday '75" or "It's Only Rock And Roll" - both if you can afford them! Idol Mind also has a 4 CD set of both San Francisco shows called "The Cow Palace Tapes;" however, the sound isn't as good as the Vinyl Gang double disc of this show, and the Gang has clearly singled out the best night for "It's Only Rock And Roll."

16. THE BEST OF KNEBWORTH FAIR (Midnight Beat/MB-088)
After Keith's car crash and the subsequent disastrous concert at Earl's Court in 1976, the Rolling Stones decided to show their fans they still cared and could rock with the best of them. This recording is a soundboard from the Knebworth Fair outdoor concert and shows the Stones in fine form, with updated versions of 'Around And Around,' 'Little Red Rooster,' and 'Route 66.' Unfortunately, this soundboard recording is not the complete concert and on some cuts we lose Keith's guitar almost completely! Still, it's a fascinating look at the Stones, in the midst of their Torn and Frayed period, rocked by busts and drugs, trying, and succeeding, in wrestling their Rock crown back.

17. BLIND DATE REVISITED (Swingin' Pig/TSP-202-2 2-CDs)
These Canadian recordings are from Keith's post-drug bust period. This 2 CD Swingin' Pig set is a welcome update of these 1977 court mandated performances. Both CDs were sourced from PA mixing boards and have the same ghost audience sound as "Welcome To New York." These are very low generation recordings and I've never heard either show sound any better. The first CD is of Keith and the New Barbarians and we get an especially nice version of Chuck Berry's 'Sweet Little Rock And Roller.' For fans of the New Barbarians, this is one of the best 'boards available. The second CD showcases the Rolling Stones obligatory Canadian show. This is not an inspired show, but it does have a few nice touches, and - other than the El Mocambo Club - our only record of the band during this trying time.

18. STATIC IN THE ATTIC (Midnight Beat/MB-084)
Another wonderful outtakes album from the folks at Midnight Beat. The sound here is comparable to "Voodoo Brew" and it provides a wonderful look at the late Seventies Stones in the studio. Although many of these songs have been bootlegged before, they've never been heard in this quality. The two versions of 'Claudine' could be right off an official album. Like Swingin' Pig's "Lonely At The Top," this collection works as an album, too. In any other year, this might well have been Best Bootleg of the Year!

19. CHAIN SHOOTING (Show Company/SC-9447-23/24)
This is a new version of the Memphis, Tennessee 1978 show as broadcast on the King Biscuit Flower Hour. "Chain Shooting" is of equal, or better quality, than the classic "Some Girls Are Bigger Than Others," which is almost impossible to find these days. Most of these 1978 KBFH CDs are listed as Memphis, Lexington, Detroit or Houston and really contain a mixture of all 4 shows as originally broadcast. However, there are more actual Memphis tracks on this CD than is usually the case. This disc contains great versions of "Let It Rock," "Honky Tonk Women" and the rip-roaring "Hound Dog" played only in Memphis. Next to the 1973 Brussels KBFH shows, these '78 tracks are the finest live '70s and '80s soundboards available. Far better than the weak official albums of the time, such as "Love You Live" and "Still Life."

20. MADE IN THE SHADE (Invasion Unlimited/IU-9537-1)
"Made In The Shade" is Invasion Unlimited's outtakes collection from the "Some Girls" sessions at the Pathe-Marconi studios in Paris, from October 1977 to March 1978. This is another fine outtakes collection and, while there is some overlap between this and "Static In The Attic," this disc contains the best outtake of "Linda Lu" I've ever heard. It also features the 'early' version of 'So Young," which was resurrected 16 years later, re-recorded and released as the 'B' side to the 'Out Of Tears' American single.

21. SHATTERED IN EUROPE (Swingin' Pig/TSP-185)
We have here not only a great soundboard recording, but a wonderful document of the 1982 European tour that had never been properly showcased. Swingin' Pig's "Shattered In Europe" throws new light on this little known tour and provides a performance as good as, if not better, than the best of the 1981 shows. Plus, for those lucky few, there was a bonus CD of backstage rehearsals and one song with Keith in his hotel room. Bonus CD or not, "Shattered In Europe" is one of the top live albums of this year, or any other year.

22. JUST A SHOT AWAY (Continental Drift/CD003/4 2-CDs)
The complete soundtrack from 'The Rolling Stones Live At The IMAX.' This is a different take on the 1989 Steel Wheels Tour, since in the IMAX production the music became part of the stage show. Thus, we hear some of the intricacies of Ronnie and Keith's guitar sound weave that don't usually survive the sonic blast of a stadium concert. The second CD is padded with some of the great "Flashpoint" 'B' side bonus singles, including the wonderful slow 1989 live version of 'I Just Wanna Make Love To You' and the brilliant reprise of 'Play With Fire.'

23. STEEL WHEELS TOKYO 1990 (Vinyl Gang/VGP-080 2-CDs)
This is the complete February 26, 1990 Rolling Stones Tokyo Dome "Big Egg" show in wonderful soundboard quality. The Tokyo shows were the link between the American Steel Wheels Tour and the European 1990 Urban Jungle Tour. It's great, for the first time, to have this wonderful show complete.

24. VOODOO BREW (Vigotone/147-150 4-CDs)
An absolutely dynamite 4 CD box set that has set a new sound and packaging standard for bootleg Rolling Stones box sets. This will be a hard one to top! Vigotone went beyond anything ever done in Stones history to source dozens of low generation "Voodoo Lounge" demos and outtakes. On these CDs you get to overhear Mick, Keith, Woody and Charlie at work in the studio, which is the next best thing to being there. I can't imagine any legitimate label ever digging this deep into the vaults for an outtakes album, but Vigotone did and we are the richer for it. Also, highly recommended is "Voodoo Brew's" sister box set "Voodoo Stew," which contains many more outstanding "Voodoo Lounge" outtakes, including several songs that were never released. 'Ice Newsletter' had this to stay about "Voodoo Brew:" (this) "package, with its meticulous design and comprehensive liner notes, (is) one of the top five packages ever."

26. THE FOOTTAPPERS AND WHEEL SHUNTERS CLUB GIG (Vinyl Gang/VGP-084 2-CDs)
Vinyl Gang's legendary "Foottappers" Paradiso 'club gig,' became the hardest to find bootleg of the year, when most of the first pressing got dumped into the Sea of Japan over a copyright scare. (Don't be fooled by the imitations on Idol Mind Productions and Real Live: only the VGP discs have both stereo channels.) It's been recently re-issued on gold discs and is again available. Does it live up to the legend? Yes. Is it a soundboard? Who knows. . ? It's either a soundboard or a great audience recording of a soundboard. The incredible live take on Muddy Water's 'Still A Fool' (that's been a bootleg staple for 25 years under the title 'Two Trains Runnin') is played here live for the first time. It displays all the promise, with better sound, that the original outtake promised-it's worth the price of the entire package! "Foottappers" was recorded at the Paradiso Club on the second night of the European Voodoo Lounge Tour, and was officially recorded for a possible 'Unplugged' album, which later metamorphosed into "Stripped."

26. FRENCH MADE '95 (Vinyl Gang/VGP-059 2-CDs)
From the Olympia Theatre comes another superb audience recording of one of the great 'club gigs.' These small club appearances, where the Stones played different songs, were the highlight of the Voodoo Lounge Tours. This recording has most of the depth and range of a good soundboard. This is the second, and best, of 2 audience recordings made at the Olympia Theatre on July 3rd 1995. The first audience tape of this concert appeared under the titles "Back To The Roots" (no label) and "Olympia" on Moonraker, but was marred by the '2 dudes' who talk through and over a number of songs. This is the best audience recording of the 'club gigs' and even surpasses "Having A Laugh In Brixton." The guitars are right there in the mix and really shine on 'Beast Of Burden' and 'Shine A Light.' Highly recommended.

27 CENSORED (Electric/30041 2 CDs)
"Censored" contains the complete European "Stripped" promotional video soundtrack with all the songs, including the 2 that were left off when it played on MTV. Most of the live cuts are different selections (even though many are the same songs) than the ones used on "Stripped," which makes this a very interesting listen. It also includes the great version of 'Gimme Shelter' that was released as the 'B' side bonus track on the Dutch 'Wild Horses' single. This is the video mix, not the audio soundboard, and contains more bass and audience noise than the tracks used on "Stripped.". For those who thought "Stripped" was a little to antiseptic, with "Censored," there's no doubt that these tracks are real live recordings.

With 35 years of studio outtakes and live recordings, the end of new Rolling Stones music is nowhere in sight! We are hoping that the long anticipated official release of "The Rock And Roll Circus" is evidence that we'll see more official releases, as well as bootlegs, of the Stones great back catalog. While Swingin' Pig has sadly announced that it is closing its doors, Vinyl Gang continues to pump out 4 or 5 new titles a month! Midnight Beat has come out of nowhere to become a Rolling Stones bootleg mainstay, and I'm sure there are other outfits in the wings. Already, 1997 has seen some titles that rival the great releases of 1996 - "Handsome Girls," "The Lost Brussels Tapes," "It's No Hangin' Matter," "Rolling Stones Gather No Moss," and "Get Your Leeds Lungs Out - Revisited." Now, with a new Rolling Stones album in the works and a new tour on the horizon, there should be no letup in sight for lovers of Rolling Stones music!

Legal Issues – The End?

BLACK FRIDAY

By John Carr

(John Carr is the Editor of 'Sticky Fingers Magazine' which is dedicated to the Rolling Stones and their music. John Carr can be reached at Sticky Fingers, P.O. Box 3474, Granada Hills, CA 91344. Send $4 for sample issue or $20 for a 1-year subscription.)

In the last week of January, Friday the 31st, the venerable Rolling Stones bootlegger Swingin' Pig (TSP) announced to their dealers that they were closing up shop permanently - this time. Some on the Internet saw this as a clever marketing ploy, since Swingin' Pig had shut down twice before, only to resurrect themselves once again. Others, like myself, saw it as the end of an era.

In the past few years the legal position of the bootleg industry has changed substantially, since the Recording Industry Association of America's copyright noose tightened around the European Economic Union, ending the so-called Protection Gap - a loophole which allowed the creation of an entire bootlegging market in a number of European countries. In 1985 a German court decision (later upheld in 1990) said that, "Under German Copyright Laws, foreign artists cannot claim protection in Germany against the sale of unauthorized recordings, if the performances take place in countries that are not signatories to the Rome Convention." The US, due to pressure from the American Record Industry and their tool the Recording Industry Association of American (RIAA), never signed the Rome accord. And refused to accept it's validity over American music copyrights.

A lawsuit brought by Phil Collins in Germany, regarding the bootleg CD of "Live USA," caused the intervention of a law court outside the national court system to decide whether the Treaty of Rome copyright protection for artists outside Germany should override local copyright laws, primarily protecting German artists. A judgment in late 1993 in favor of Phil Collins, meant that German Copyright law now applied to all European Community artists, regardless of where the recordings took place - thus, the sale of and manufacture of bootleg recordings became illegal in Germany, the home of Swingin' Pig records. Fortunately, Swingin' Pig was actually based in Luxembourg (probably for just this contingency). Italy, one of the most prolific bootlegging countries in the early nineties, followed Germany in 1995, when the government (due to increased pressure from the big labels and RIAA) caused the SIAE (the Italian equivalent of ASCAP, which collects royalties for musicians) to stop collecting from 'live' (read bootleg) CDs.

The Swingin' Pig and a few other intrepid labels moved to Luxembourg, where lax laws and a long history of relaxed copyright and banking laws, has allowed this tiny country to prosper. But the RIAA and it's lackeys have not let up. In early February of 1996, officials in Luxembourg confiscated a number of new titles and even put a few imprints out of business. This increasing harassment, I'm sure, had much to do with Swingin' Pig's recent decision to finally close its doors.

This was verified by the following post on 'Sticky Fingers Journal' Issue 107, Feb. 11, 1997: "A very reliable source from Swingin Pig's home of Luxembourg stated that he did not know for sure why the Pig shut down all operations so suddenly, but is aware that they are currently facing customs problems in Luxembourg. He didn't come out and say it, but I read that to mean one thing: if you can't ship your product out of the country (without having it seized), then your business is pretty much finished."

What are the origins of the Swingin' Pig? According to Clinton Heylin in "Bootleg" (see page 235), Swingin' Pig first appeared in the mid-eighties as one of several labels run by Dieter Schubert. Swingin' Pig, as a reflection of its commitment to quality, revived the old logo of Trade Mark of Quality (TMoQ) label. Many of these now scarce records, released on the Swinging Pig (the g disappeared from Swinging when they began manufacturing CDs) label, were released with colored vinyl and elaborate packaging. According to Heylin, "As a vinyl label, The Swingin' Pig issued a mere fifteen titles. But Mr. Schubert was just gearing up for the next bootleg revolution." It was Swingin' Pigs release of Ultra Rare Trax by the Beatles which jump-started the CD bootleg revolution.

Heylin quotes founder Dieter Schubert: "The basic philosophy of Swingin' Pig is to make available historically important, previously unreleased recordings which would otherwise never see the light of day. . .the tapes ("Ultra Rare Tracks" by the Beatles) are over twenty years old now, some nearly thirty. Twenty more years in the archives would possibly destroy the tapes, like many outtakes from the Fifties, and they'll be lost forever."

Swingin' Pig mostly stuck to that philosophy during the first few years of the CD era, releasing a number of "Ultra Rare Trax" volumes by the Beatles and a number of classic Rolling Stones reissues. Swingin' Pig even re-designed William Stout's famous Smokin' Pig logo, giving him a fedora and hunching him over in a finger-snapping musical (one assumes) frenzy! After the success of "Ultra Rare Trax" Dieter Schubert released a number of famous Rolling Stones 'TMoQ' titles, "Bright Lights, Big City," "Get Your Leeds Lungs Out," "Welcome To New York," and "Live'r Than You'll Ever Be," producing a definitive list of Stones titles that hold up even today. Most of the early CD bootlegs were sourced from vinyl, (and some of them not very good vinyl) which is why Swingin' Pigs first releases had such a profound effect on the bootleg market. Today it's hard for those who were not there to realize the impact of hearing those early Stones classic titles re-mastered from original or low generation tapes for the first time.

Swingin' Pig also put out a number of bootlegs of other Sixties artists, e.g.: Cream, Jimi Hendrix, the Doors, Pink Floyd and Led Zeppelin. At that time, Swingin' Pig was attempting to transform itself into a legitimate label (much like Rhino Records did at about the same time in the US). As a first step, it stopped releasing studio outtakes and began releasing live albums where the legal issues (under the Rome Convention's 'Protection Gap') were much clearer.

Rhino Records Store cleaned up their act, stopped releasing bootleg, separated the label from the Los Angeles store and started releasing vintage albums, many long out of print. For many years they were the most prominent independent reissue label in the US until they were eventually bought up by the Warner/Atlantic mega label. Swingin' Pig was not able to make the transition to legitimate label, probably because Schubert couldn't resist continuing to challenge the limits of European copyright law. To test the limits of the Rome Convention, Swingin' Pig released "Basel '90," which was an average audience recording of a 1990 European Tour concert in Switzerland. At that time, Switzerland had not signed the Convention and this looked to be a good test case. It also led to an injunction by Columbia Records, which was defeated since America herself was not a signatory to the Rome Convention. This paved the way for Swingin' Pigs greatest coup, the 3 CD box set of "Atlantic City '89," mastered directly from the American Steel Wheels Pay-Per-View, which pre-empted both the Stones official release of the tour, "Flashpoint," and their bootleg competitors. This big release led to several lawsuits and forced Swingin' Pig to remaster the first CD and to take out the copy written musical introduction. But Swingin' Pig complied, but Columbia wasn't so lucky with their suit regarding copyright infringement over the cowbell introduction to Honky Tonk Women.

Unlike bootlegs today, many of the early Swingin' Pig titles were sold openly in German record stores, accounting for the eye-popping total of 70,000 copies of "Atlantic City '89" which were sold in Europe less than a year! As Heylin put it: "No Swingin' Pig release would ever again have such an impact. Though Swingin' Pig had broken the dam, Schubert lacked the vision, the source material and the collector mentality to follow-through on his promise of a high-fidelity future in bootleg heaven. It was left to others to realize the potential hinted at when Swingin' Pig first rode the One After 909." Soon a rainbow of different labels were releasing their own quality Stones titles, some new quality labels like Scorpio, Oh Boy! and Vinyl Gang.

By 1992 Swingin' Pig had relinquished the lead as Quality bootleg imprint to Scorpio, Yellow Dog and Great Dane. In part, it was due to their policy of pirating (ironic considering their current difficulties with pirates today) quality releases from other labels, such as Scorpio's "Bowie At the Beeb" and a number of others. Swingin' Pigs' higher wholesale prices and short running times didn't help either. Neither did the No-Noise process which they used to master many of their titles, including "Live'r Than You'll Ever Be" and "Welcome To New York," which lost much of their 'edge' over the vinyl originals. Plus there were few important Swingin' Pig Rolling Stones releases during this period, 1992 to 1994, partly due to the legal battles that the label was embroiled in as the pioneer bootlegging label. One of their biggest losses involved a 2 CD Dire Straits package recorded in Bale, Switzerland, which resulted in an interim judgment against Swingin' Pig. Dire Straits were based in the European Community and as such allowed protection in German courts.

The company's stature as the premier bootleg label was undermined by a major shift in the bootleg market from classic rock to more contemporary music, with an emphasis on Alternative and Progressive Rock. The new music spawned a number of vital younger labels. Soon older companies, like TSP, were left out of the mainstream of a new and growing market. Huge legal bills and the tightening of the RIAA noose, left Swingin' Pig losing its fight for legitimacy and market share. Plus, labels like Oil Well put out a budget series of Rolling Stones titles (Oil Well's Jumping Jack Flash , July 1972 , Madison Square Garden is a copy of TSP's Welcome To New York, etc.) that were mastered 'directly' from the TSP originals.

While it's true that Swingin' Pig lacked the resources to dominate the Stones bootleg market, they did keep up a list of quality titles that head the list of any good Rolling Stones essential bootleg collection-"Philadelphia Special I & II," "Hampton '81," "Live In Toronto," "Bright Lights, Big City (20th Anniversary Edition)" and others. However, it wasn't until 1996 that the Swingin' Pig once again showed its prowess as the Rolling Stones 'Unofficial label' with a barrage of strong Stones titles, including "Shattered In Europe," "Blind Date Revisited," "The Da'Lapa Incident," "Live In Johannesburg," and many more. In retrospect, it almost appears that they were emptying out the shelves in anticipation of the labels death.

Now, what was really behind the sudden closure of this venerable bootleg label? Several theories have been brought up on the Internet and I suspect all of them contain a grain of truth. According to my European friends and contacts, bootlegs have disappeared from much of Europe. Italy, in particular, has been very dry. Meanwhile, with increasing harassment from Luxembourg customs, the bootleg business has been getting more costly, complicated and less profitable. Plus, according to one source, Swingin' Pig has continued to pay royalties (under GEMA-the German office responsible for collecting royalties for recording royalties), whereas few (certainly none of the Far East labels) of the Pigs' competitors bother about this holdover from the "Protection Gap" days. This adds a considerable expense (a dollar or two) to each release, and can grow to considerable amounts on a box set such as "Handsome Girl," with 51 copyright protected songs!

Which brings us to the crux of the matter, "Handsome Girls," Swingin' Pigs new 4 CD release of excellent sounding King Biscuit Flower Hour tapes, which according to one source came right out of DIR. (King Biscuit's parent company) vaults. But more on that later. In some ways "Handsome Girls" may have been the straw that broke the camel's back, since it was a very 'expensive' package - not only due to the quality 12"X12" box and 4 CDs, but because of royalty payments and the cost of the original tape. One correspondent sent me this note (which has been edited to protect the source) about the Swingin' Pig's closure: "I spoke with both (the sales manager) and S. this morning. They are indeed closing down for good, which is a total friggin' bummer for obvious reasons. Back to the bottom line: They told me that they are not making enough money, since volumes are way down due to pirated copies, and especially other new labels that don't pay royalties to the bands like TSP does. Yes, they told me they actually pay royalties to the Stones and other bands for titles like "Get Your Leeds Lungs Out." Big surprise to me, but interesting that my Royal Sound Label of Leeds has a statement written on the back of the jacket that the tracks are licensed from the artists. I guess they aren't kidding. Maybe, this somewhat explains Vinyl Gang's high prices? I would raise prices if I were TSP, so it's odd to me that they haven't taken that route. I didn't ask if they got into trouble by releasing "Handsome Girls," but I'll probably ask next time we speak. The manager may be going back to the UK, since he doesn't want to stay in Luxembourg, since the only thing there is Banking."

Considering the exorbitant prices of Japan's Vinyl Gang releases, there's no doubt that Swingin' Pig could increase the price of their Stones titles. But, unlike Vinyl Gang, Swingin' Pig does not specialize in only one group, nor can TSP afford to since it doesn't have it's own 'captive market' as Vinyl Gang has in Japan. Therefore, when you look at the big picture, hiking prices may mean significantly lower sales when it come to selling, say, Who/Springsteen/Hendrix bootlegs. Plus, it encourages smaller labels to pirate your CDs, which they don't have to pay for, and flood the local European markets - result lower sales. It's doubtful that Swingin' Pig has access to enough new Rolling Stones source material (look at their release of "All Hallows Eve," the inferior monitor mix, of the Oakland Halloween show last year) to exist solely on Stones bootlegs. There are also only so many times you can upgrade the old catalog before the fans cry 'enough is enough' as many are already beginning to do, with the simultaneous release of Swingin' Pig's "San Diego '69 20 Bit Remaster" and Vinyl Gang's San Diego upgrade, "It's No Hangin' Matter."

Then there's the "Handsome Girls" situation. Not only did this wonderful box set cost a fortune to produce, but it has unleashed some unforeseen consequences, as another correspondent reported: "I heard that the source tape used was not simply obtained from someone who traded or sold it to them. It was stolen, copied, and put back. DIR. Broadcasting has a contractual obligation that the recordings will not be released to "anyone". The person who did the actual "borrowing" was paid a lot of money as far as bootleg sales go, but is now embroiled in a lawsuit. DIR., if it wins (and I can't see how they won't) will not be liable since they can show that it slipped out by the unlawful act of an individual and not through negligence on their part."

Now it's possible that this legal action could stretch as far as Luxembourg, which may well have provoked Swingin' Pig into closing its doors for the third time this decade. If they're out of business and the DIR. employee who provided them with the master tapes (which is where the unreleased Ft. Worth, Texas material and the rest of the upgraded 1978 concert material was from) informs on who at Swingin' Pig he sold the tapes to: well, it's a moot point if Swingin' Pig is out of business, isn't it? Will this be the last time for Swingin' Pig? We don't know, and possibly the principals involved in owning and running Swingin' Pig don't know either. However, unlike previous closures, this appears more serious than past shut downs, due mostly to the increased copyright and customs enforcement within Luxembourg itself.

Meanwhile, Rolling Stones fans will hope for the best. At least, with "Handsome Girls," the best live Stones box ever, Swingin' Pig went out with a bang-the same way they came in! I don't know how many lives Pigs have, but I do know cats have nine. Let's hope that this pig has at least one more.

13 ALLEGED MAJOR BOOTLEGGERS INDICTED 800,000 ALLEGED BOOTLEG CDS CONFISCATED IN LARGEST CRIMINAL BOOTLEG INVESTIGATION.

For Immediate Release - March 31, 1997
(The following is a press release from U.S. Department of Justice and the Recording Industry Association of America)

Washington: Charles R. Wilson, United States Attorney for the Middle District of Florida, and Joseph Henderson, Resident Agent in Charge, United States Customs Service, Orlando, Florida, announced today that a federal grand jury sitting in Orlando has returned a 40-count indictment charging 13 individuals with conspiracy and substantive charges involving the manufacturing, importing, and distributing of unauthorized or "bootleg" compact music discs. The Indictment alleges that the defendants, on various dates, manufactured, smuggled, and/or distributed bootleg compact music discs from artists including the Grateful Dead, Stevie Ray Vaughan, the Dave Matthews Band, Tori Amos and Van Halen.

Charged in the Indictment are:

Jorge Garzon, 29, of Orlando, Florida
Hans Heimann, 38, of Wuppertal, Germany
Roger Moenks, 34, of Goch, Germany
Charles Leidelmeyer, 40, of Gravenhaag, the Netherlands
Mark Purseglove, 25, of London, England
Simone Romani, 34, of Milan, Italy
Scott Johnson, 32, of Long Island, New York
Simon Carne, 34, of West Palm Beach, Florida
Alfonso Degaetano, 34, of West Palm Beach, Florida
Ali Moghadam, 30, of Las Vegas, Nevada
Georgio Serra, 32, of the Repulic of San Marino, Italy
Caroline Albanese, 29, of the Republic of San Marino, Italy
Robert Pettersen, 41, of Los Angeles, California

The defendants face the following maximum terms of imprisonment: Garzon, 5 years; Heimann, 15 years; Moenks, 20 years; Leidelmeyer, 15 years; Purseglove, 20 years; Romani, 25 years; Johnson, 25 years; Simon, 10 years; Degaetano, 10 years; Moghadam, 5 years; Serra, 35 years; Albanese, 35 years; and Pettersen, 10 years.

The charges are the result of a year-long undercover operation conducted by agents of the United States Customs Service, with the assistance of the Recording Industry Association of America, of international bootlegging in compact music discs and the smuggling of these items into the United States. A spokesman for the Recording Industry Association of America has indicated that bootlegging of musical recordings accounts for an estimated loss of $300,000,000.00 per year to the music industry. The case will be prosecuted by Assistant United States Attorney A.B. Phillips of the Orlando Division of the United States Attorney's office.

An indictment is merely a formal charge that a defendant has committed a violation of the federal criminal law and every defendant is presumed innocent until, and unless, proven guilty.

Frank Creighton, RIAA Vice President, Associate Director of Anti-Piracy, states, "this operation marks the largest criminal bootleg investigation of its kind - both in terms of the number of individuals indicted and the transnational scope of their operations, as well as the sheer volume of bootlegs seized (80% of 1996's total bootleg confiscations). Without a doubt, the removal of so many major players will substantively and severely disrupt the global bootleg industry. This incredibly successful blow to bootleggers was only possible with the exceptional efforts of Charles Wilson, U.S. Attorney for the Middle District of Florida and Assistant U.S. Attorney A.B. Phillips, and at Customs, Regional Agent in Charge Joseph Henderson and Special Agent T.J. Nelson."

The alleged bootleggers were operating in 12 foreign countries, as well as the United States. Many of the 13 indicted are among the most notorious international bootleg manufacturers and distributors, according to the RIAA. Of those foreign nationals, five were indicted while in the United States allegedly conducting their illicit business affairs. In addition to the indictments, U.S. Customs announced that approximately 800,000 alleged bootleg recordings had been confiscated over the course of the investigation.

ABOUT THE RIAA
The RIAA represents companies that create, manufacture or distribute more than 90% of the legitimate sound recordings sold in the United States. The RIAA's Anti-Piracy Unit investigates the illegal production and distribution of pirated sound recordings, which cost the U.S. music industry hundreds of millions of dollars a year domestically. Consumers and retailers can report suspected music piracy to the RIAA by dialing a toll-free hotline, 1-800-BAD-BEAT or via e-mail to badbeat@riaa.com.

GOING UNDERGROUND

The following has been reprinted with permission from the May 1997 issue of ICE - THE MONTHLY CD NEWSLETTER (PO Box 3043, Santa Monica, CA 90408 USA)

IN THE NINE YEARS since the birth of the bootleg CD business, the marketplace has seen its share of high-profile busts and legal changes which, at the time, appeared to sound the death knell for the industry. Yet, one by one, the resonance of such tolls turned out to be remarkably short-lived. Those events were not ignored by the bootleg industry so much as it had simply grown strong and broad enough to absorb them. For example, when one country's copyright loophole closed, enterprising bootleggers simply moved production to another nation.

Although several U.S. retailers and a few notable distributors have been nabbed in the past two years, U.S. Customs officials and the R.I.A.A. appeared to be fighting the same losing battle with bootlegs as their counterparts in the drug war; when contraband is produced overseas, busting domestic dealers and users does little to hurt foreign manufacturers. The advent of the Internet only made the situation worse by allowing bootleg customers to buy directly from the source.

In mid-March, however, customs officials struck a blow of unprecedented magnitude against the industry in a sting operation that sounds like something out of a gangster movie. Principal figures behind some of the world's biggest and best-known bootleg labels - said to include Midnight Beat, Oxygen, Flashback and Blue Moon - were arrested in Florida after being lured into a trap by a major U.S. distributor.

While the complete details remain to be confirmed, sources say the story dates back to April 1996, when a U.S. Customs official began investigating the importation of bootleg CDs into this country. That investigation eventually led to an association with a large Orlando based wholesaler. At that time, the government agent reportedly offered to assist the wholesaler in importing bootleg CDs into the U.S. Thus began a nine-month period during which the wholesaler is said to have received more than 100,000 bootlegs, all under the watchful eye of the customs official - who monitored and recorded every transaction. Late last year, the wholesaler was finally popped. Following his apprehension, he agreed to cooperate with customs officials and facilitate their investigation of the bootleg labels themselves.

The second phase of the operation involved massive new orders of compact discs from the aforementioned labels (and others) in late 1996 and early '97, reportedly totaling nearly 200,000 CDs. Live! Music Review reported that the wholesaler "approached European manufacturers" on the premise that he could reopen the U.S. market to them "without the costly expense of setting up mail-order facilities in safe countries," and he claimed to have an undetermined number of Customs officials "in his pocket." The Orlando distributor also made arrangements for the manufacture of two specific titles, even acquiring the tapes. Once the wholesaler had run up a huge debt to the labels, the plan apparently called for him to invite the principals to Florida for a summit meeting, where moneys owed would be paid and future arrangements for the U.S. market would be made.

Beyond the European label chiefs, the wholesaler invited others in the domestic bootleg trade, including U.S. distributors. Interestingly, officials from Europe's most famous bootleg label, Kiss the Stone, are rumored to have been invited but did not attend, though they are still involved in the case. The principals from Midnight Beat, Blue Moon, Flashback and Oxygen arrived in Florida, and, according to reports, spent a day sightseeing (including a trip to Disney World) before the meeting on March 14. Two days earlier, the customs official swore out a complaint in the Orlando Division of U.S. District Court against the European label owners in attendance and some of the domestic distributors. With a judge's approval, the customs agent now had the legal authority to arrest the parties involved. The group was said to have been gathered at a restaurant when the raid occurred, and never saw it coming.

Unlike previous actions, such as the closing of Greenwich Village stores last year, the fact that several European bootleggers were actually in custody on American soil put the potential repercussions from the event on a whole new scale. Add to that the fact that at least three of the country's major wholesalers were also captured, and bootleg retailers in the U.S. had plenty of reason to be scared. There have already been stories of stores and dealers dumping their remaining stock at fire-sale prices, though others feel that the value of their remaining titles may have actually increased overnight.

In the days following the bust came word that Hurricane, Totenko and several other labels were tied to persons indicted, as well as a report that the principals of Kiss the Stone were also being charged. While its owner presumably remained free, the label reacted by declaring that KTS would be closing. At press time, a message on the KTS web site read: "Official Notice: The End of An Era. KTS Records are sorry to announce that they will be closing down from the end of April '97. This is the last chance to get the best live CDs in the world at the lowest possible prices."

There are sure to be months of legal proceedings before the events in Florida are completely sorted out, but it seems that this time, KTS's declaration of "The End of An Era" is accurate. The European labels that once defined the bootleg industry are no more. Early players like Great Dane and Swinging Pig closed up shop by their own accord over the past two years, and now the higher-profile labels they helped to spawn have been brought down in one fell swoop. The Florida bust also closes what had been the major point of distribution for bootlegs into this country, and its reverberations have already caused some U.S. dealers to get out of the business.

It does not, however, signal the end of the domestic bootleg CD industry altogether. While we are unlikely to see a bootlegger advertising in Spin magazine again anytime soon, smaller no-name players will continue to ply the trade, and CDs pressed overseas will find their way into this country, though undoubtedly in much smaller quantities. The situation may parallel the state of the American bootleg LP industry in the early '80s, when famous names of the past like TMQ and TAKRL had functionally disappeared and there were few identifiable imprints. With fewer dealers, smaller pressings and a lower industry profile, collectors were forced to be much more diligent in tracking down desirable bootleg albums, especially European imports. History may just be repeating itself.

GOING UNDERGROUND

The following has been reprinted with permission from the June 1997 issue of
ICE - THE MONTHLY CD NEWSLETTER (PO Box 3043, Santa Monica, CA 90408 USA)

Reverberation from the Unprecedented bust in Florida reported here last month continue to resonate with the bootleg community, and the fate of some of those indicted will probably be decided in a major court battle. Word has it that most of U.S. citizens arrested have chosen a plea bargain, while the foreign nationals (who are out of jail, but remain under house arrest and are being monitored with electronic ankle bracelets) are poised to fight the charges. The men behind the Midnight Beat and Oxygen labels have reportedly hired what one source characterized as "two of the best attorneys money can buy," with up-front retainer fees well into the hundreds of thousands of dollars.

Their plight is relevant to bootleg consumers because the litigation will likely bring into question the legal definitions of copyright infringement in the US, particularly the new language put into place by the GATT treaty which outlaws "unauthorized fixation" of "live music performances." The defendants are, of course, fighting for their own freedom, first and foremost, but there's also a belief that existing copyright law might not withstand a true - and perhaps more importantly, well-funded - legal challenge, something it has never faced with regards to bootlegs.

GOING UNDERGROUND

The following has been reprinted with permission from the July 1997 issue of
ICE - THE MONTHLY CD NEWSLETTER (PO Box 3043, Santa Monica, CA 90408 USA)

THE LETTER "R" IN CD-R MAY REFER to "recordable," but in the bootleg world at the moment it could just as easily stand for "revolution." Mere months after the Florida bust appeared to put an end to Europe's big bootleg labels and the importation of most CDs into the country, CD-R bootlegs are booming, turning up like never before. One longtime industry observer calls it "a juggernaut of opportunity and necessity," and the point is well taken; CD recorders and blanks hit a level of affordability and accessibility at precisely the moment when the pipeline to foreign factories closed. Goldtone was the first label to issue a full line of CD-R titles, and the format came of age over the past month when four Beatles-related bootlegs originally issued by Midnight Beat and ostensibly unavailable in America were copied and reissued on CD-Rs by the Repro Man label (Editors note: there are rumors that Repro Man is an offshoot of the Vigotone/Pegboy labels).... One major upside to CD-Rs for collectors is that the format allows hard-to-find titles to be easily copied in accessible quantities, which could make some scarce Japanese pieces a great deal more common.... The CD-R craze has apparently hit in Japan as well, and while we can't confirm this story, we wouldn't doubt it either. The Tokyo bootleg district now includes a handful of vendors who will "cook to order" the bootleg of your choice. Customers pick the title they want from a catalog, pay their money, and return in an hour to pick up their freshly pressed CD-R.

DIGITAL UNDERGROUND
by Don Steinberg

(The following article appeared on the WIRED web site (http://wwww.wired.com/wired) and was re-printed with the permission of the author, Don Steinberg (dons@cynet.net). Mr. Steinberg writes the technology column for GQ and edits the humor zine "Meanwhile" on America Online.)

New technologies that make it possible to send high-quality sound clips over the Net have created a crafty distribution highway for music pirates. And the multi-billion-dollar recording industry is scrambling to catch up.

Early one Tuesday morning in July 1996, Dorothy Sherman was doing what her rock-star clients hire her to do: getting the goods on music bootleggers. Sherman is founder and president of GrayZone, a Brooklyn-based research firm that works with performers, record labels, a tangle of government agencies, and industry groups such as the Recording Industry Association of America (RIAA) to ferret out those digital desperados who electronically distribute unauthorized musical performances. Sherman was going about her business - examining messages on alt.music.bootlegs, ordering illegal CDs from Web pages - when the phone rang. It was a law enforcement agent.

"It's happening today," he said. "In about an hour."

"It?" she asked.

"The big it," the agent replied.

Across the Brooklyn Bridge, federal and state investigators were taking down two Greenwich Village institutions. With badges flashing, plainclothes detectives strode into Second Coming Records on Sullivan Street. The store was widely known to carry bootleg discs (often sneakily labeled as "rare imports"), but nobody made such a fuss before. Now, some seriously armed officers were combing the place, grabbing every Pearl Jam, Hootie, and Hendrix disc that looked suspicious. They told the stunned salesdudes that they were being busted under a newly amended state law that criminalizes distribution of bootlegged music recordings. Moments before, agents grabbed Second Coming's owner near his warehouse in Queens, seizing 70,000 unauthorized CDs that were feeding the store and a thriving mail-order business.

A few blocks away, at Revolver Records on 8th Street, uniformed cops and FBI agents broke down the door. Word had already hit the street about the Second Coming raid, and Revolver's staff, correctly assuming they'd be hit next, had locked the entrance, tried hastily to hide offending inventory in a storage room, and fled out a back door.

In a triumphant postbust press conference, New York Attorney General Dennis Vacco stood at the entrance of Second Coming Records and crowed. The busts netted 17,800 CDs and capped the biggest week of bootleg disc seizures in history. Days earlier, US Customs agents had stormed a Long Island warehouse to confiscate 425,000 imported discs and 2.3 million label inserts (the artwork that slides into CD jewelboxes). Vacco declared lower Manhattan safe from unauthorized concert recordings.

Not entirely. On the day of the bootleg busts, if you'd been planning to swing by Second Coming to pick up, say, Perfect Timing - a CD of an illicitly taped 1995 Alanis Morissette show in Los Angeles - and you'd been put off by the phalanx of patrol cars around the store, you simply could have walked a few extra blocks to one of the Village's cybercafés. Sipping a latte, you could have pointed your browser to the Web page of an online bootleg shop called Magic Com, select Perfect Timing from an elaborate catalog featuring hundreds of artists, place the bootleg into a whimsically illustrated shopping cart, and order it for home delivery for a cool US$21 plus postage. Visa and Mastercard accepted. And no laws would have been broken. Isn't it ironic? Don't you think?

But this is far more than an elaborate legal cat-and-mouse game. Thanks to rapid developments in online audio technology, the efficient digitization and distribution of unauthorized music threatens to radically reorder an infrastructure that major labels have spent decades creating. Bootleggers have demonstrated that it's easy to eradicate the need for a go-between (read: record label) when shuttling a song from performer to fan. Illicit electronic music files are few and far between now, but their very existence portends huge ramifications. Unwittingly, bootleggers are forcing the music industry to tangle with a future that the bigwigs are still unprepared to embrace.

THE INTERNET JUKEBOX

The RIAA says the American recording industry loses approximately $300 million a year in "displaced sales" from unauthorized recordings. First, let's clarify some terminology (which record companies sometimes prefer to blur). A bootleg is a recording of a concert or unreleased studio session - something consumers aren't supposed to be able to buy. Prince's so-called Black Album, for instance, was bootlegged in about 75 different versions in the five years between its still-unexplained liberation from the recording studio and its official release by Atlantic Records.

Counterfeits, by contrast, are whole-hog duplicates of released albums, while pirate recordings are hybrids that combine, say, concert material, B-sides, and studio outtakes with whatever else is lying around.

The dollar damage attributed to bootlegs is high but somewhat misleading. The RIAA multiplies the discs and label-inserts seized by the street price of a bootleg disc ($20 to $40). It adds up fast, but in fact the RIAA's "displaced-sales" figures are actually an extrapolation based primarily on seizures of counterfeit cassettes.

Some argue that bootlegs don't displace the sale of legitimate records, because they're primarily obtained by diehard fans who have already bought all the legal stuff. Further rationalizations defending bootlegs are served up fresh daily on alt.music.bootlegs, including: "Rock stars are so rich, fans deserve to get some of their stuff for free"; "We're only capturing a little magic that would have been lost otherwise"; and "Copyright is a doomed concept anyway, so who cares?"

But many musicians complain that any unauthorized release usurps their artistic control. Bootlegs constitute illegal use of someone else's creative work, and for organizations such as the RIAA and ASCAP that exist to protect usage rights, they glow large on the radar screen.

In the past, curtailing bootlegged CDs and albums was pretty straightforward: bust the manufacturing plants or distribution points (i.e., stores like Second Coming and Revolver). But the many-to-many design of the Internet quickly destroys this traditional method of enforcement. And it offers a clue as to why music copyright holders fear the Net, a place where they see a horrifying collusion of the information-wants-to-be-free attitude with rapidly improving audio transmission technologies.

Until recently, the biggest drawbacks to downloading music from the Internet were time and quality. With a 14.4 modem, for instance, it can take four minutes to download one minute of a tune in FM radio-quality mono. For stereo-CD quality, that same clip could take an hour. Suddenly, the prospect of waiting and waiting and waiting for a scratchy audio clip from an old Nirvana show makes the novelty a good deal less charming than it first seemed.

But those problems are disappearing. Since last summer, breakthroughs in the Net's ability to carry high-quality streaming audio have come fast. Macromedia Internet Products Manager Joseph Ansanelli promised to "turn the Internet into a jukebox" when the company added CD-quality streaming audio to its popular Shockwave plug-in for Web browsers (although you still get only "mono FM quality" at 28.8 Kbps). And Shockwave doesn't require a dedicated server, so anyone can cheaply put high-quality audio on any Web page.

Progressive Networks came out with a stereo upgrade of its RealAudio Player, as well as RealAudio Player Plus, which lets originators of RealAudio 2.0 transmit sound without recording-prevention. This feature is meant to let music owners sell discs online, but it also provides a mechanism for a bootlegger or a pirate to distribute unlicensed material on demand. In October, 40 companies (including Progressive Networks, Macromedia, and Netscape) announced support for Real Time Streaming Protocol, a proposed standard for instantly slinging audio and video over the Internet.

Liquid Audio, a new company formed by music industry veterans, has just delivered software that may provide the highest quality online audio of all. Using Dolby-based compression, Liquid Audio's software delivers near-CD quality streaming music at 28.8 Kbps. It can transfer a full, CD-quality (44-MHz, 16-bit stereo) file of a three-minute song, over a 28.8 connection, in about 12 minutes. With the faster link of a cable modem, the same song file could move "faster than real time" - perhaps in one minute, says Liquid Audio's Robert Flynn.

The next step is to connect your computer to a recordable CD - and voila! - you've got yourself a new disc. And the major labels haven't pocketed a penny. Not coincidentally, Liquid Audio is about to release software called Master ProPlayer, for improving the sound quality of recordable CDs at home.

Clinton Heylin, author of "Bootleg: The Secret History of the Other Recording Industry" (see page 235) says the bootleg community "has always embraced new technologies that the music industry feared," from CDs to digital audio tape - which due to its luxury price has come to be used almost exclusively for material you can't buy on a legitimate CD.

Record company executives rarely see the enormous potential for selling their product by wire. Instead, they panic. Albhy Galuten, VP of interactive programming for MCA Music Entertainment, is one of the few insiders who sees the positive potential but understands the concerns. "Someone could make a file of a complete CD and send it to 25 of their closest friends," Galuten recently told Billboard. "The potential impact on the music industry is very scary."

But only to the timid. Early last year, AudioNet, the largest provider of audio content on the Internet, started a "CD Jukebox," which allowed anyone with an Internet connection, RealAudio Player software, and a soundcard to listen to sound samples from hundreds of albums. AudioNet president Mark Cuban hadn't asked most of the record companies for permission. He figured they'd like the exposure. And since his service wasn't charging people to listen, and the streaming audio didn't let people keep copies of the music they heard, it was exactly like a radio station. Wrong.

Sony Music and the RIAA reminded him of the Digital Performance Right in Sound Recordings Act, which went into effect in February 1996 after intense lobbying by the RIAA. The law established interactive, digital delivery of music as a different beast from analog broadcasts. Owners of sound recordings (i.e., the record labels) now have exclusive say over how their music is used online. That's a right they don't have on, say, radio, where stations can play whatever they please without the label's permission (radio stations do need licenses from songwriters' organizations such as ASCAP and BMI - as do sites that play music online).

The RIAA claims the on-demand inter-activity of online music makes the law a necessity. Cuban says it's unjustified. "Say you're planning your bar mitzvah, and the DJ wants to preview some of the music over the Internet for your grandparents," he says. "One's in Miami and the other's in Chicago. So, what? You go to jail?"

OLD LAWS, NEW TECHNOLOGIES

As in all earthly matters, the first line of defense is law - and belligerent lawyers. Internationally, agreements such as the Berne Convention have forced signatory nations to incorporate universal principles protecting intellectual property into their national laws. In April 1996, for instance, students in the Nettverksgruppa computer society at the Norwegian University of Science and Technology loaded several hundred rock albums onto a university server and made them downloadable for free through the Net. The catalog literally went from ABBA to Zappa. The hammer came down quickly. Since Norway supports international trade agreements, the International Federation of the Phonographic Industry, a global alliance of 1,200 record companies promoting copyright protection, was able to make the kids reconsider their decision.

President Clinton's 1994 signing of the General Agreement on Trade and Tariffs has also helped put the pinch on purveyors of unauthorized music. GATT required its participants to punch up antibootleg laws. So now we have the first federal antibootleg statute to supplement state laws. When, in August 1996, a public area of America Online was promoting bootleg tape trading, horrified record industry officials shut it down by waving a copy of GATT. Tape Traders' Central, a section of ABC's Rock and Road site within AOL, brazenly listed must-have bootlegs, hosted message boards where fans arranged trades and sales, and even offered special downloadable artwork to slip into bootleg cassette cases. The main sponsor of the site was Maxell, the blank cassette manufacturer. "It was unbelievable," says Richard Gusler, attorney for Hootie and the Blowfish. The response from AOL and ABC? Whoops! The site was nuked within hours of the music industry's complaints.

Such tape trading sites are distressingly common. So some of the biggest names in music turn to Sherman, who provides research on bootlegging activity for the likes of Prince, Lou Reed, and Hootie and the Blowfish. She and her small band of "cyberpunk operatives" in London, Paris, New York, and San Francisco are plugged into a "tape traders' network" where fans exchange concert tapes, post critiques and want-lists (i.e., "WANTED: Pumpkins, 2/10/96 at the Moore"), or seek recommendations from kindred souls about microphones, digital audio tape recorders, and illicit soundboard-patching techniques.

But tape traders are small potatoes. The long-term threat remains the instant (and surreptitious) gratification provided by streaming-audio technology. And while the lawyers try to punch up existing laws, the recording industry works on antipiracy technology. Early in 1996, the RIAA formed a New Technology Division and hired David Stebbings to run it. Stebbings is described as "one of the industry's top scientists" who previously worked at Sony on copyright protection for the Digital Versatile Disc (not coincidentally, a technology that's been long delayed by content-owners' piracy issues).

One of Stebbing's top missions is to "develop monitoring systems for finding unauthorized sound recordings on the Internet and formulate high-speed searches." The idea is to take data that's already written into a subchannel of all audio CDs - information about the music, who owns it, where it originated - and embed it in the audio in a way that doesn't audibly interfere with the music (sort of like the subliminal suicide messages in Judas Priest tracks). This "digital watermark" would be inseparable from the music, capable even of "surviving all analog links," Stebbings says.

The RIAA would then set up powerful search engines to continually scan files for the encoded information. This would let the industry "monitor a certain small percentage of what was going on the Net and say 'Ah-ha' every time we came across one of our recordings," Stebbings says.

He admits that this scheme, at best, will track where a portion of copyrighted music is moving, not stop the sale of illegal recordings or the transmission of concert recordings. Says Stebbings, "I don't know of any technical way of actually stopping the stuff from getting on the Web in the first place."

The industry's concerns have pressured some streaming-audio companies to build digital watermarking into their software. But these sometimes seem, well, watered down. While listening to a RealAudio clip of the Beatles in the studio recording "All You Need Is Love" from a fan's well-stocked Web page of rare Beatles recordings, I noticed that RealAudio Player software indeed has a copyright field that appears while the music plays. But for this clip, the fan who digitized it had entered "1967."

Liquid Audio has built an elaborate system for selling music via the Net that encapsulates a recording's copyright data with the audio (plus lyrics, cover art, and liner notes) in a single master file. The software also lets the music's originator be all but certain that the receivers can make only as many copies of the recording as they pay for. Again, there's a hitch: it doesn't prevent a bootlegger in Luxembourg from using the software to sell files of taped concerts, which have no copyright.

If all this watermarking and search-bot stuff sounds over ambitious - and possibly somewhat desperate - maybe it makes sense to turn the recording industry's fervent antipiracy effort on its head. Perhaps it feels as threatened by the completely legal prospect of online music as by the scattershot illegal activity.

"I don't think digital copying is really the major issue here," asserts Larry Rosen, whose N2K Entertainment has created the online music sites Music Boulevard, Rocktropolis, and Jazz Central Station. Rosen implies that the stink over copyright problems may be partly a stalling tactic as established companies contemplate how to deal with the new technology - and the fundamental shift it may bring to the way they do business. "They're trying to protect the status quo," Rosen says.

Already, N2K and Liquid Audio say they have been approached by recording artists who are contemplating skipping the major labels entirely in the future and releasing their music online.

In a sense, music could become the first major packaged product to make the fabled transition from atoms to bits. That's a scary concept to those with a heavy investment in atom-based commerce.

Indeed, one might suspect that recording industry officials took some gratification from the fact that the pair of Greenwich Village busts punished stores that not only sold tons of bootleg recordings but also happened to be two of the city's leading sellers of used CDs and tapes. That's a completely legal practice that robs record companies of sales.
One might similarly suspect that the industry's hand-wringing about putting music online represents a way to, in the absence of being able to outsmart the future, at least delay it.

"But they're also smart enough to know that they can't just stand in the way of this," says Liquid Audio's Flynn. "Because it's gonna happen, with or without them."

HOT WACKS BOOK SUPPLEMENT 5 — page 36

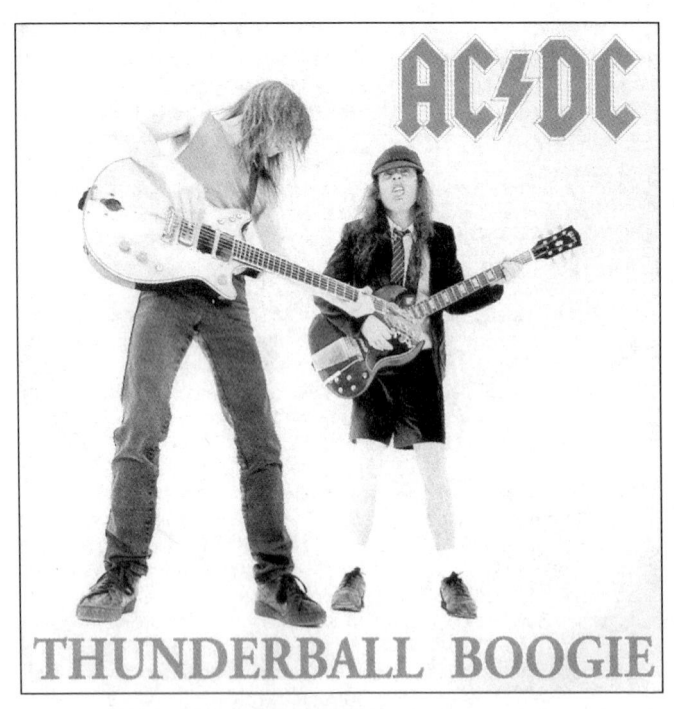

AC/DC — THUNDERBALL BOOGIE

TORI AMOS — WEDDING PERFORMANCE

A

AC/DC

CD - BACK IN RHYTHM
BIR01/02
CD1: Shot Down In Flames (3:52)/ Thunderstruck (5:52)/ Girls Got Rhythm (4:08)/ Hard As A Rock (4:59)/ Shoot To Thrill (6:07)/ Boogie Man (11:03)/ Hail Caesar (5:35)/ Hell's Bells (6:26)/ The Jack (6:57)/ Ballbreaker (5:08)/ Rock 'N Roll Ain't Noise Pollution (5:18)/ Dirty Deeds Done Dirt Cheap (4:26)
CD2: You Shook Me All Night (4:16)/ Whole A Lotta Rosie (5:38)/ TNT (3:32)/ Let There Be Rock (15:55)/ Highway To Hell (5:15)/ For Those About To Rock (6:58)/ Fire Your Guns (3:08)/ Sin City (5:27)/ Heatseeker (3:22)/ Who Made Who (4:52)/ That's The Way I Wanna Rock 'N Roll (3:57)/ Money Talks (3:54)
Recording: Excellent. Audience.
Source: CD1 tracks 1-12 and CD2 tracks 1-6 Superdome, New Orleans August 24 1996. CD2 tracks 7-12 Paris Bercy, March 28 1991.
Comments: European CD. Deluxe color cover. Picture CDs.

CD - THE BALLBREAKER TOUR
SNAKE 004/5
CD1: Intro Beavis & Butthead/ Back In Black/ Shot Down In Flames/ Thunderstruck/ Girls Got Rhythm/ Cover You In Oil/ Caught With Your Pants Down/ Boogie Man/ Hard As A Rock/ Hell's Bell/ Dog Eat Dog
CD2: The Jack/ Ballbreaker/ Rock N' Roll Ain't Noise Pollution/ Dirty Deeds/ You Shook Me All Night Long/ Whole Lotta Rosie/ T.N.T./ Let There Be Rock/ Highway To Hell/ For Those About To Rock
Recording: Very good to excellent. Audience.
Source: Pittsburgh, March 25 1996.
Comments: European CD. Deluxe color cover. Picture CDs.

CD - BREAKING MADRID
RSM RECORDS 187
Back In The Black (4:24)/ Shot Down In Flames (3:44)/ Thunderstruck (5:33)/ Girls Got Rhythm (3:56)/ Hard As A Rock (4:50)/ Shoot To Thrill (5:46)/ Boogie Man (10:26)/ Hail Caesar (5:28)/ Whole Lotta Rosie (5:24)/ T.N.T. (3:59)/ Let There Be Rock (16:26)/ Highway To Hell (4:18)
Recording: Excellent stereo. Soundboard.
Source: Plaza De Tores, Madrid, Spain during The Ballbreaker Tour July 10 1996.
Comments: European CD. Deluxe color cover.

CD - BREAKING THE WALL
DO 08.05.96 1/2
CD1: Intro/ Back In Black/ Shot Down In Flames/ Thunderstruck/ Girls Got Rhythm/ Cover You In Oil/ Shoot To Thrill/ Boogie Man/ Hard As A Rock/ Hells Bells/ Dog Eat Dog/ Down Payment Blues/ The Jack
CD2: Ballbreaker/ Rock 'N' Roll Ain't Noise Pollution/ Dirty Deed Done Dirt Cheap/ You Shook Me All Night Long/ Whole Lotta Rosie/ TNT/ Let There Be Rock/ Highway To Hell/ For Those About Rock (We Salute You)
Recording: Poor to Good. Audience.
Source: Westfalenhalle, Dortmund, May 8 1996.
Comments: European CD. Blue cover. Red/yellow text.

CD - DIRTY WATER
GOLD STANDARD GOLD S.-95004
Live Wire/ Problem Child/ Sin City/ Gone Shooting/ Bad Boy Boogie/ The Jack/ High Voltage/ Rock And Roller/ Dog Eat Dog/ Up To My Neck In You*/ Kicked In The Teeth Again*
Recording: Very good to Excellent.
Source: The Paradise Theatre, Boston, MA August 21 1978. *The Old Waldorf, San Francisco, CA September 2 1977.
Comments: Deluxe color cover. Time 71:01.

CD - FIRE YOUR GUNS
DEEP RECORDS 004
CD1: Thunder Struck/ Shoot To Thrill/ Back In Black/ Fire Your Guns/ Sin City/ Heat Seeker/ Who Made Who/ Jailbreak/ The Jack/ The Razors Edge/ That's The Way - I Wanna R&R
CD2: Money Talks/ Hells Bells/ High Voltage/ You Shook Me/ Dirty Deeds/ Whole Lotta Rosie/ Let There Be Rock/ Angus - Solo/ Highway To Hell/ T.N.T./ For Those About To Rock - We Salute You
Source: Joe Louis Arena, Detroit 1991.

AC/DC

Comments: European CD.

CD - HELL'S BELLS
AC/DC 001/2
CD1: Back In Black/ Shut Down In Flames/ Thunderstruck/ Girls Got Rhythm/ Cover You In Oil/ Shoot To Thrill/ Boogie Man/ Hard As A Rock/ Hell's Bells/ Dog Eat Dog/ The Jack
CD2: Ballbreaker/ Rock N' Roll Ain't Noise Pollution/ Dirty Deeds/ You Shook Me All Night Long/ Whole Lotta Rosie/ TNT/ Let There Be Rock/ Highway To Hell/ For Those About To Rock
Recording: Good. Audience.
Source: Ballbreaker Tour, Paris May 24 1996.
Comments: Japanese CD. Deluxe color cover. Picture CDs. Time CD1 62:35. CD2 56:06.

CD - LIVE FROM THE BULLRING
MOONRAKER 196
Back In Black/ Shot Down In Flames/ Thunderstruck/ Girls Got Rhythm/ Hard As A Rock/ Shoot To Thrill/ The Jack/ You Shook Me All Night Long/ Whole Lotta Rosie/ TNT/ Let There Be Rock/ Highway To Hell/ For Those About To Rock
Recording: Excellent stereo. Soundboard.
Source: The Bullring, Madrid July 10 1996.
Comments: European CD. Deluxe color cover. Picture CD. Time 79:30.

CD - RUFF STUFF
DIRTY DEEDS REC. DDR 001
CD1: Intro/ Back In Black/ Shoot Down In Flames/ Thunderstruck/ Girls Got The Rhythm/ Cover You In Oil/ Shoot To Thrill/ Boogie Man/ Hard As A Rock/ Hells Bells/ Dog Eat Dog
CD2: The Jack/ Ballbreaker/ Rock And Roll Ain't Noise Pollution/ Dirty Deeds Done Dirt Cheap/ You Shook Me All Night Long/ Whole Lotta Rosie/ T.N.T/ Let There Be Rock/ Highway To Hell/ For Those About To Rock (We Salute You)
Recording: Excellent. Audience.
Source: Scandinavium Gothenburg, Sweden April 26 1996.
Comments: European CD. Deluxe color cover. Time CD1 58:43. CD2 62:23.

CD - SHOW YER ASS
SYA961/2
CD1: Hard As A Rock/ Back In Black/ Shot Down In Flames/ Thunderstruck/ Girls Got Rhythm/ Hard As A Rock/ Shoot To Thrill/ Boogie Man/ Cover You In Oil/ Hell's Bells/ Dog Eat Dog/ The Jack/ Ballbreaker
CD2: Dirty Deeds Done Dirt Cheap/ You Shook Me All Night Long/ Whole Lotta Rosie/ TNT/ Let There Be Rock/ Highway To Hell/ For Those About To Rock/ Down Payment Blues/ Rock 'N Roll Ain't Noise Pollution/ Hail Caesar
Recording: Good. Audience.
Source: Barcelona 1996.
Comments: European CD. Deluxe color cover.

CD - THE STUDIO BREAKERS
STUDIO B RECORDS
Announcement/ Interview/ Riff Raff/ Go Down/ You Shook Me All Night Long/ Shoot To Thrill/ Rock'n'Roll Ain't Noise Pollution/ Down Payment Blues/ The Jack/ Whole Lotta Rosie/ Gone Shooting/ Ballbreaker/ Highway To Hell/ Rocker/ Boogie Man/ Boom Boom
Recording: Excellent stereo. Soundboard.
Source: Tracks 1-12 VH-1 Studios, London 1995. Tracks 13-16 Fun Radio Session, Paris September 13 1995.
Comments: European picture CD.

CD - THUNDERBALL BOOGIE
KOBRA KRCR 08/9
CD1: Intro, Back In Black/ Shot Down In Flames/ Thunderstruck/ Girls Got Rhythm/ Cover You In Oil/ Shoot To Thrill/ Boogie Man/ Hard As A Rock/ Hell's Bells/ Down Payment Blues/ The Jack/ Ballbreaker/ Rock'N'Roll Ain't Noise Pollution
CD2: Dirty Deeds Done Dirt Cheap/ You Shook Me All Night Long/ Whole Lotta Rosie/ T.N.T./ Let There Be Rock includes A. Young guitar solo/ Hail Caesar/ Highway To Hell/ For Those About To Rock (We Salute You)/ Fire Your Guns/ Sin City/ Heatseeker/ Who Made Who/ That's The Way I Wanna Rock'N'Roll/ Money Talks
Recording: Excellent.
Source: Arco Arena, Sacramento, CA February 5 1996. CD2 tracks 9-14 Bercy, Paris, France March 28 1991.
Comments: European CD.
Time CD1 73:39. CD2 73:58.

CD - THUNDERSTRUCK
RAVEN RECORDS 001/002
CD1: Thunderstruck/ Shoot To Thrill/ Back

In Black/ Fire Your Guns/ Sin City/ Heatseeker/ Who Made Who/ Jailbreaker/ The Jack
CD2: The Razor Edge/ That's The Way I Wanna Rockn' Roll/ Money Talks/ Hells Bells/ High Voltage/ You Shook Me All Night Long/ Dirty Deeds Done Dirt Cheap/ Whole Lotta Rosie/ Let There Be Rock/ Highway To Hell
Source: Charlotte, USA February 16 1991
Comments: European CD.

CD - UNCUT
SBC 015
Riff Raff/ Go Down/ You Shook Me All Night Long/ Shoot To Thrill/ Rock 'N Roll Ain't Noise Pollution/ Down Payment Blues/ The Jack/ Whole Lotta Rosie
Recording: Excellent stereo. Soundboard.
Source: Tracks 1-12 VH-1 Studios, London 1995.
Comments: European CD. Deluxe color cover. Time 41:43.

CD - WE SALUTE YOU
MAY DAY-001/002
CD1: Intro, Back In Black/ Shot Down In Flames/ Thunderstruck/ Girls Got Rhythm/ Cover You In Oil/ Shoot To Thrill/ Boogie Man/ Hard As A Rock/ Hell's Bells/ Down Payment Blues/ The Jack/ Ballbreaker/ Rock 'N Roll Ain't Noise Pollution
CD2: Dirty Deeds Done Dirt Cheap/ You Shook Me All Night Long/ Whole Lotta Rosie/ T.N.T./ Let There Be Rock/ Hail Caesar/ Highway To Hell/ For Those About To Rock (We Salute You)/ Fire Your Guns*/ Sin City*/ Heatseeker*/ Who Made Who*/ That's The Way I Wanna Rock 'N Roll*/ Money Talks*
Recording: Excellent stereo. Soundboard.
Source: Acro Arena, Sacramento, CA February 5 1996. *Paris Bercy, March 28 1991.
Comments: European CD. Deluxe color cover.

AEROSMITH

CD - GIGS IN THE ATTIC
BANG 010/11
CD1: Intro . Mama Kin/ Write A Letter/ S.O.S.(Too Bad)/ Lick And A Promise/ Big Ten Inch Record/ Sweet Emotion/ Rats In The Cellar/ Dream On/ Lord Of The Thing
CD2: Last Child/ Walk This Way/ Sick As A Dog/ Same Old Song And Dance/ Train Kept A Rollin'(includes drum solo)/ Toys In The Attic
Source: Japan 1977.
Comments: Japanese CD.

ALCATRAZZ

CD - NEVADA DESERT
Too Young To Die, Too Drunk To Live/ Hiroshima Mon Amour/ Desert Song/ Island In The Sun/ Kree Nakoorie/ Yngwie's Solo/ Since You Been Gone/ Lost In Hollywood
Recording: Very good. Audience.
Source: Reno, Nevada March 26 1984.
Comments: Japanese CD. Deluxe color cover. Time 42:00.

CD - NO PAROLE FROM ROCK 'N' ROLL
GRYPHON-007/8
CD1: Opening/ Too Young To Die, Too Drunk To Live/ Jet To Jet/ Night Games/ Island In The Sun/ Desert Song/ Kree Nakoorie
CD2: Guitar Solo/ Since You've Been Gone/ Suffer Me/ Hiroshima Mon Amour/ Lost In Hollywood/ Evil Eyes/ All Night Long
Recording: Good. Audience.
Source: Arizona February 26 1984.
Comments: European CD. Deluxe B&w cover. Yellow type.

ALLMAN BROTHERS BAND, THE

CD - MIDNIGHT RIDING
KISS THE STONE KTS 508/09
CD1: Sailing/ Statesboro Blues/ Blue Sky/ Same thing/ Soul Shine/ Southbound/Seven Turns/ Midnight Rider
CD2: Jessica/ No One To Run With/ Back Where It All Begins/ In Memory Of Elizabeth Reed
Recording: Excellent stereo. Soundboard.
Source: Riverport, St. Louis July 7 1994.
Comments: European CD. Deluxe color cover. Picture CDs. Time CD1 53:38. CD2 57:35.

CD - RETURN TO LUDLOW'S GARAGE
SKYDISC RECORDS SCD24700
Statesboro Blues/ Trouble No More/ In Memory Of Elizabeth Reed/ Mountain Jam
Source: Set 1, Ludlow's Garage, Cleveland, Ohio November 13 1970 .
Recording: Good. Soundboard. Hiss.

AMOS, TORI

CD - BLOOD GIRL
MOONRAKER 195
Intro/ Beauty Queen, Horses/ Blood Roses/ Little Amsterdam/ Cornflake Girl/ China/ Leather/ Caught A Lite Sneeze/ Butterfly/ Tear In Your Hand/ A Case Of You
Recording: Excellent.
Source: The Orpheum Theatre, Vancouver, Canada July 19 1996.
Comments: European CD.

CD - BROKEN STONE
KISS THE STONE KTS 599
Beauty Queen/ Horses/ Leather/ American Pie/ Smells Like Teen Spirit/ Caught A Light Sneeze/ Little Amsterdam/ Cornflake Girl/ Bells For Her/ Precious Thing/ In The Springtime Of His Voodoo/ Father Lucifer, Tubular Bells, Smalltown Boy/ Thank You/ Space Dog/ Sweet/ Putting The Damage On/ Losing My Religion
Recording: Excellent stereo. Soundboard.
Source: Friederich Stadt Palast, Berlin, Germany March 25 1996. Track 15 Ed Sullivan Theatre, New York April 9 1996. Tracks 16-17 Modern Rock Live, New York February 4 1996.
Comments: European. Picture CD. 73:21.

CD - THE PURPLE ROSE
MOONRAKER 084/85
CD1: Beauty Queen, Horses/ Leather/ American Pie, Smells Like Teen Spirit/ Marianne/ Caught A Lite Sneeze/ Little Amsterdam/ Cornflake Girl/ Doughnut Song/ Bells For Her/ Precious Things/ Not The Red Baron/ In The Springtime Of His Voodoo/ Winter
CD2: Father Lucifer/ Me And A Gun/ If 6 Was 9/ Putting The Damage On/ Space Dog/ Hey Jupiter/ American Pie/ Smells Like Teen Spirit/ Crucify/ Jesus My Saviour/ Me And A Gun/ Baker Baker/ Cornflake Girl/ Winter/ Interview
Recording: Excellent stereo. Soundboard.
Source: Friedrichstadtpalast, Berlin March 25 '96. CD2 tracks 7-15 St. Trinitatis Church, Berlin April 9 '94.
Comments: European CD. Purple/black cover. Time CD1 71:02. CD2 73:35.

CD - SAINT AND SINNER
OXYGEN OXY 079
Beauty Queen/ Horses/ Leather/ American Pie/ Smells Like Teen Spirit/ Caught A Lite Sneeze/ Little Amsterdam/ Cornflake Girl/ Bells For Her/ Precious Things/ In The Springtime Of His Voodoo/ Father Lucifer (includes Tubular Bells, Smalltown Boy)/ Thank You/ Space Dog/ Sweet/ Caught A Lite Sneeze
Recording: Excellent stereo. Soundboard.
Source: Tracks 1-14 Friedrichstadtpalast, Berlin, Germany March 25 1996. Track 15 David Letterman Late Show, New York City April 9 1996. Track 16 Jay Leno Tonight Show February 9 1996.
Comments: European. Picture CD. 71:03.

CD - SOME MORE FOR PELE
AMOS 963
Hey Jupiter (Dakota version)/ Professional Widow (Armand's Star Funkin' Mix)/ Tribute To Chas And Dave: London Girls, That's What I Like Mick (The Sandwich Song), Samurai/ Silly Songs: This Old Man, Hungarian Wedding Song, Toodles Mr. Jim, Talula (Tornado Mix)/ Frog On My Toe, Sister Named Desire, Alamo/ Talula (BT's Synthesia Mix)/ Amazing Grace, Til The Chicken, Butterfly (sound track of 'Higher Learning')/ Losing My Religion (sound track of 'Higher Learning')
Recording: Excellent stereo. Soundboard.
Comments: European CD. Deluxe color cover. Picture CD. Time 70:03.

CD - SOMEWHERE OVER THE RAINBOW
WESTWOOD ONE RADIO NETWORKS RARITIES ON CD VOL. 64
Somewhere Over The Rainbow (live)/ Sugar (live)/ Honey (live)/ Samurai (previously unavailable)/ In The Springtime Of His Voodoo (Sugar Dub)/ Frog On My Toe (previously unavailable)/ London Girls (previously unavailable)/ Talula (BT's Synthesia Mix)/ Professional Widow (Armand's Star Trunk Funkin Mix)/ In The Springtime Of His Voodoo (Quiet Mix)/ Professional Widow (MK-Mix)/ Professional Widow (Armand's Instrumental)
Recording: Excellent stereo. Soundboard.
Comments: European CD. Deluxe color cover. Time 69:50.

CD - UNPLUGGED
MOONRAKER 153
Cornflake Girl/ Blood Roses/ Silent All These Years/ Icicle/ Caught A Lite Sneeze/

Somewhere Over The Rainbow/ Hey Jupiter, Purple Rain/ In The Springtime Of His Voodoo/ Losing My Religion/ I'm On Fire/ Sugar/ Somewhere Over The Rainbow/ Hey Jupiter
Recording: Excellent stereo. Soundboard.
Source: Tracks 1-8 MTV Unplugged, Brooklyn Academy Of Music, New York April 11 1996. Tracks 9-12, VH-1 Crossroads1996. Track 13 The Tonight Show With Jay Leno February 8 1996.
Comments: European CD. Deluxe color cover. Time 68:47.

CD - UNPLUGGED
SBC 004
Cornflake Girl/ Blood Roses/ Silent All Those Years/ Icicle/ Caught A Lite Sneeze/ Somewhere Over The Rainbow/ Hey Jupiter/ Voodoo/ Putting The Damage On/ Mr. Zehra/ Sugar/ Honey
Recording: Excellent.
Source: Tracks 1-8 Brooklyn Academy Of Music, New York 1996. Tracks 9-10 Later with Jools Holland 1996. Tracks 11-12 UK Tour 1996.
Comments: European CD. Deluxe color cover. Time 60:03.

CD - WEDDING PERFORMANCE
TA 03
Baltimore (3:30)/ Walking With You (4:31)/ A Happy Day (4:06)/ Circle (5:18)/ Cloud On My Tongue (4:30)/ Baker Baker (3:22)/ Pretty Good Year (7:59)/ Piano Improvisation (1:10)/ Evergreen (3:08)/ If (3:27)/ You Needed Me (2:47)/ You Light Up My Fire (3:49)/ We've Only Just Begun (1:22)/ Attila The Honey (2:51)
Recording: Tracks 1-7 and 14 excellent stereo. Soundboard. Tracks 8-13 fair to good audience.
Source: Tracks 1-3 Baltimore sessions. Tracks 4-7 'Under The Pink' solo piano demos. Tracks 8-13 wedding performance spring 1978 with Tori's father presiding. Track 14 a conversation with God.
Comments: European CD. Deluxe color cover.

ASH

CD - PUNK BOYS
KISS THE STONE KTS 595
Lose Control/ Girl From Mars/ Gold Finger/ Seaton/ Lost In You/ Get Ready, Here I Come/ Oh Yeah/ I'd Give You Anything/ Uncle Pat/ Angel Interceptor/ Jack Names The Planet/ Girls From Mars/ Seaton/ Uncle Pat/ Jack Names The Planet/ Petrol/ Kung Fu/ Coasting/ Punk Boy/ Coasting/ Girl From Mars
Recording: Excellent stereo. Soundboard.
Source: Tracks 1-11 Leeds University, UK April 10 1996. Tracks 12-17 Anson Room, Bristol, UK 1995. Tracks 18-19 Glastonbury Festival, UK 1995. Tracks 20-21 Evening Sessions, UK 1995.
Comments: European CD. Deluxe color cover. Picture CD. Time 70:19.

ASIA

CD - ASIA IN N.Y.
ASTEROID AR-12/13
CD1: Time Again/ One Step Closer/ Without You/ Steve Howe guitar solo (The Ancient, The Clap, Ram)/ Midnight Sun/ Only Time Will Tell/ The Smile Has Left Your Eyes
CD2: Cutting In Fine/ Wildest Dreams/ Here Comes The Feeling/ Sole Survivor/ Heat Of The Moment/ The Smile Has Left Your Eyes
Recording: Very good. Audience.
Source: Palladium, New York 1982.

CD - DREAMS AGAIN
BS 22/23
CD1: Time Again/ Wildest Dreams/ Without You/ Guitar Solo (including Mood For A Day, Ram, The Clap/ Midnight Sun/ Only Time Will Tell/ One Step Closer
CD2: The Smile Has Left Your Eyes/ Cutting It Fire, Keyboard Solo/ Here Comes That Feeling, Drum Solo/ Sole Survivor/ Heat Of The Moment/ Ride Easy/ Daylight/ Lying To Yourself
Recording: Very good. Audience.
Source: Italy 1982. CD2 tracks 6-8 non album tracks.

AYERS, KEVIN -JOHN CALE-ENO-NICO

CD - JUNE 1, 1974 OUTTAKES
CD1: Baby's On Fire/ Buffalo Ballet/ Gun/ Das Lied Der Deutschen/ Didn't Feel Lonely Till I Thought Of You/ Whatever She Brings We Sing/ Everybody's Sometime And Some People's All The Time Blues
CD2: Interview/ See You Later/ It Begins With A Blessing, Once I Awaken/ But It

BABYBIRD

Ends With A Curse, The Doctor Dream Theme/ Two Goes Into Four/ One Night Stand/ Baby's On Fire
Recording: Excellent stereo. Soundboard.
Comments: Japanese CD.

B

BABYBIRD

CD - ELECTRIC BALLROOM
KISS THE STONE KTS 641
Corner Shop/ Too Handsome To Be Homeless/ Goodnight/ Dead Bird Sings/ Cooling Towers/ I Didn't Want To Wake You Up/ You're Gorgeous/ Babybird/ Bad Shave/ C F C/ Bog I A Breeze/ Hate Songs/ Lemonade Baby
Recording: Excellent stereo. Soundboard.
Source: Electric Ballroom, London October 30 1996.
Comments: European CD. Deluxe color cover. Picture CD. Time 52:37.

BAD COMPANY

CD - FANTASY HEY JOE
ELEMENT OF CRIME ELEMENTS-031
Bad Company/ Good Lovin' Gone Bad/ Movin' On/ Gone Gone Gone/ Shooting Star/ Rhythm Machine/ Feel Like Making Love/ Ready For Love/ Simple Man/ Running With The Pack/ Evil Wind/ Rock And Roll Fantasy/ Hey Joe/ Can't Get Enough
Source: Capitol Center, Landover, MD August 31 1979.
Comments: Japanese CD.

CD - LOS ANGELES 1991
RARITIES & FEW 1236
One Night/ Rock 'N' Roll Fantasy/ Shake It Up/ Movin' On/ No Smoke Without Fire/ Ready For Love/ Boys Cry Tough/ If You Needed Somebody/ Feel Like Makin' Love/ Can't Get Enough/ Holy Water/ Bad Company
Source: Los Angeles December 1991.
Comments: European CD.

BAD RELIGION

CD - UNKNOWN INFECTIONS
BR 001
American Jesus/ No Control/ We're Only Gonna Die/ The Handshake/ Recipe For Hate/ Stranger Than Fiction/ Struck A Nerve/ You Are The Government/ Too Much To Ask/ Generator/ Heaven Is Falling/ Leaders And Followers/ Mediocrity/ Incomplete/ Infected/ 20th Century Digital Boy/ Generator/ Atomic Garden/ Heaven Is Falling/ Gertile Cresent/ Waiting For The Fire/ Drastic Actions/ Continuous Tuning/ Tired Of The City/ Silent Night includes My Sharona/ Fuck Christmas/ Struck A Nerve (Christmas version)/ I Saw The Light/ American Jesus (includes Feed The World)
Recording: Excellent stereo. Soundboard.
Source: Tracks 1-11, 22-29 live. Tracks 12-21 studio demos.
Comments: European CD. Red/black/white cover. Time 74:00.

BAND, THE

CD - FORBIDDEN FRUIT
DAYS OF HARVEST DH-003-04
CD1: Don't Do It/ The Shape I'm In/ It Makes No Difference/ The Weight/ King Harvest Has Surely Come/ The Twilight/ Ophelia/ Tears Of Rage/ Forbidden Fruit
CD2: This Wheel's On Fire/ The Night They Drove Old Dixie Down/ The Genetic Method, Chest Fever/ Up On Cripple Creek/ Life Is A Carnival/ Time To Kill The Weight/ This Wheel's On Fire/ Up On Cripple Creek
Recording: Good audience. CD2 tracks 6-9 good soundboard.
Source: Music Inn, Lenox, MA July '76. CD2 tracks 6-9 Syria Mosque Arena, Pittsburg, PA November '70.
Comments: Japanese CD. Deluxe color cover. Time CD1 49:58. CD2 49:59.

CD - OPHELIA
DYNAMITE STUDIO DS94F061/62
CD1: Rag Mama Rag/ Long Black Veil/ Up On Cripple Geek/ The Shape I'm In/ In Make No Difference/ Milk Cow Boogie/ Mystery Train/ King Harvest/ Voo Doo Music/ W.S. Welcott Medicine Show/ You Don't Know Me/ Stage Right/ Caledonia
CD2: Chest Fever/ Java Blues/ I Shall Be Released/ Back To Memphis/ The Weight/

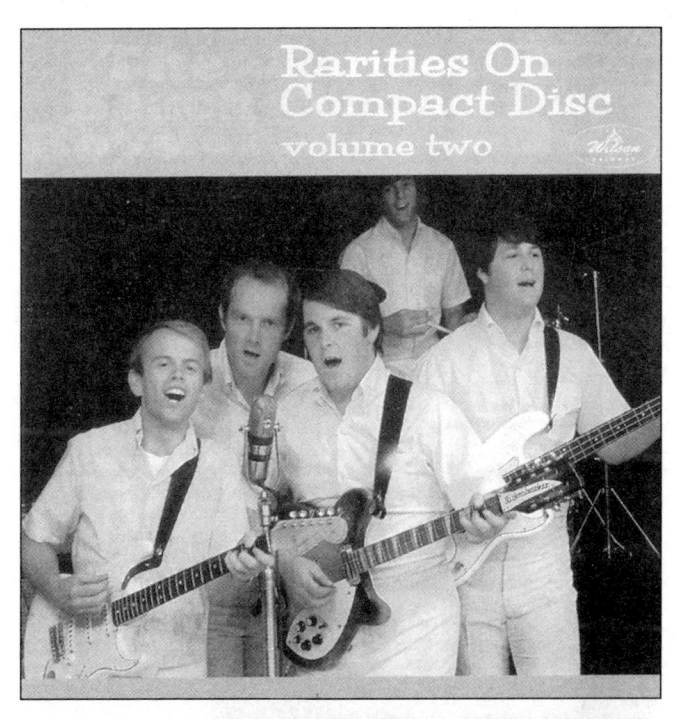

BAND, THE

BAND, THE

Don't Want To Hard Up My Rock'n Roll Show/ Let's Go Out In A Blaze Of Glory/ Willie & The Hard Jive/ Ophelia
Source: Osaka, August 29 1983.
Comments: Japanese CD. Deluxe color cover.

CD - ROYAL ALBERT RAGS
SCORPIO
Time to Kill/ King Harvest/ Strawberry Wine/ Rocking Chair/ Look Out Cleveland/ I Shall Be Released/ Stage Fright/ Up On Cripple Creek/ W.S. Walcott Medicine Show/ We Can Talk/ Loving You (Has Made My Life Sweeter Than Ever)/ The Night They Drove Old Dixie Down, Across The Great Divide/ Unfaithful Servant/ Don't Do It/ The Genetic Method, Chest Fever/ Rag Mama Rag/ Slippin' & Sliding
Recording: Good audience.
Source: The Royal Albert Hall, London June 2 1971.
Comments: Deluxe color cover. Picture on cover reversed. Time 77:59.

BARRETT, SYD

CD - RHAMADAM
9865-4JHG
Love You (fast version - unreleased outtake '69)/ Love You II (slow version - unreleased outtake '69)/ Long Gone (without backing accompaniment - unreleased outtake '69)/ Rhamadam (instrumental - unreleased outtake 6/5/'68)/ Octopus (unreleased outtake '69)/ Clowns And Jugglers (unreleased outtake '69 featuring 'Backwards' guitar)/ Untitled (instrumental segment from Syd Barrett's last ever recording session London '75)/ Dark Globe (unreleased outtake '69)/ Singing A Song In The Morning (rare rejected version of Kevin Ayers song with prominent Syd Barrett guitar and backing vocals - Barrett's only known studio collaboration outside The Pink Floyd '69)/ Mathilda Mother (U.F.O. Club, London, Granada TV Programme 'Underground' 7/2/'67)/ Interstellar Overdrive (U.F.O. Club, London, Granada TV Programme 'Underground' 7/2/'67)/ Interview (unedited 5 minute interview with Roger Waters and Syd Barrett by Hans Keller May '67)/ Sunshine (unreleased backing track from 'Piper At The Gates Of Dawn' sessions, Abbey Road Studios, London June 29 '67)/ Interstellar Overdrive (alternate version with un-broadcast interview July '67)/ Arnold Layne (Advision Studios acetate)/ Candy And A Currant Bun (Advision Studios acetate)/ Interstellar Overdrive (10" one-sided Emidisc acetate)/ Don't Ask Me (Joker's Wild '65)/ Why Do Fools Fall In Love (Joker's Wild '65)/ Interstellar Overdrive (live)
Recording: Very good to Excellent. Some good.
Comments: European CD. Deluxe color cover. Picture CD. Time 63:10.

BE BOP DELUXE

CD - UNFORGETTABLE TUNE
BLAND NEW BEAT BNB-041009
Mill Street Junction/ Unreleased Track/ Third Floor Heaven/ Adventures In A Yorkshire Landscape/ Made In Heaven/ Unreleased Track/ Stage Whispers/ Sister Seagull/ Unreleased Track/ Unreleased Track/ Unreleased Track/ Unreleased Track/ New Precision/ Super Enigmatix (Lethal Appliances For The Home With Everything)/ Possession/ Dangerous Stranger/ Islands Of The Dead/ Lover Are Mortal/ Panic In
Source: 'Sight & Sound', BBC February 1978 plus BBC 7/6/74.
Comments: Japanese CD.

BEACH BOYS, THE

CD - RARITIES ON COMPACT DISC 1
Summer In Paradise (live Wembley, England July 1993)/ Angel Coming Home (Midnight Special April 28 1979)/ Good Timin' (Midnight Special April 28 1979)/ Rockin' Surfer (alternative version)/ Almost Summer (Brian Wilson demo version)/ Almost Summer (playback with Al Jardin)/ Land Ahoy (studio outtake)/ I Get Around (alternative version)/ Honda 55 (outtake)/ Heroes And Villains (outtake segment)/ The Monkey's Uncle (stereo version... just listen to Brian)/ Jingle Bell Rock (Mike Love and Dean Torrence)/ Child Of Winter (rare semi-released single)/ Hot Summer Lovers (Mike Love ...turn both channels off)/ Problem Child (playback version)/ Surf City (Jan and Dean extended version)/ We're Together Again (backing track and vocal outtake)/ We're Together Again (backing track only)/ Sherry She Needs Me (1965 backing track with 1970s vocal overdubbing)/ A Special

Taster For Volume Two
Recording: Good to very good. Some excellent.
Comments: European CD. Deluxe color cover. 'Brother Records' logo. Time 53:39.

CD - RARITIES ON COMPACT DISC 2
SURF 003
Sandy She Needs me (an early version of Sherry She Needs Me)/ Pamela Jean (early demo version)/ Little Saint Nick (single stereo version)/ All I Wanna Do (outtake from Live London album December 1968)/ After The Game (Pamela Jean B-Side)/ Endless Sleep (early 1963 BW production for Ron Wilson)/ The One You Can't Have (demo version produced by BW for The Honey's)/ He's A Doll (same as track 9)/ Malibu Sunset (BW production for Glen Campbell 1963 'One Of Brian's Lost Songs')/ East Meets West (early demo version with basic vocals)/ You Still Believe In Me, Caroline No (live Syracuse University, May 1971)/ Rock N Roll Music, Good Vibrations, Good Vibrations Reprise, Lady Lynda (live on Midnite Special TV show)/ You Are So Beautiful (Dennis 1976)/ If I Could Live My Life Again (unreleased classic from Dennis)/ Baby Blue eyes (original DW version - later recorded for KTSA)/ San Miguel (alternative instrumental version from Dennis)/ Forever (CHR Mix) (John Stamos tribute version from the Australian promo)/ With A Little Help From My Friends (cover of Beatles classic from The Long Lost Rarities Album)
Recording: Very good to excellent. Some good.
Comments: European CD. Deluxe color cover. 'Brother Records' logo. Time 70:30.

BEASTIE BOYS

CD - ULTRA FLY TRACKS
BLUE MOON BMCD45
Ricky's Theme/ Groove Holmes/ Pow!/ Son Of Neckbone/ Bobo On The Corner/ In Threes/ Eugene's Lament/ Futdterman's Rule/ Shambala/ Transitions/ Sabrosa/ Drinkin' Wine/ Vibration Nation/ Something (Ya Know)/ Together (Get It?)/ Sowhatchawant?/ Pass The Skills/ Hot Shot Megamix
Recording: Excellent stereo. Soundboard.
Source: Tracks 1-12 unreleased album '94, 13-18 DJ remixes '92-'94.

Comments: European CD. Deluxe color cover. Time 68:48.

BEATLES, THE
(see pages 232-234)

CD - ABBEY ROAD OUTAKES
NK-001
Maxwell's Silver Hammer (stereo)/ Oh! Darling/ Octopus's Garden/ Something (take 37)/ Because (stereo)/ Part One: The Long One / Huge Melody: You Never Give Me Your Money, Sun King, Mean Mr. Mustard, Her Majesty, Polythene Pam, She Came In Through The Bathroom Window/ Part Two: (quality up): Golden Slumbers, Carry That Weight, The End
Recording: Excellent. Soundboard.
Comments: Deluxe color cover. Time 34:09.

CD - BEATLES FOR SALE
ODEON SMO 83790
Original stereo version of BEATLES FOR SALE plus the following: I'm A Loser (take 2 August 14 1964)/ Leave My Kitten Alone (outtake from Anthology 1)/ Mr. Moonlight (August 14 1964 Anthology 1 Version)/ No Reply (John Lennon studio demo from Anthology 1)/ No Reply (take 2 from Anthology)/ Eight Days A Week (take 5 from Anthology 1)/ She's A Woman (take 1 October 8 1964)/ She's A Woman (take 7)/ I Feel Fine (take 1 - a breakdown October 18 1964)/ I Feel Fine (take 5 October 18 1964)/ Kansas City, Hey-Hey-Hey! (take 2 from Anthology 1)
Recording: Excellent. Soundboard.
Comments: European CD. Deluxe color digi-pack cover - repro of original German cover. Limited edition of 500. Time 63:30.

CD - COME TOGETHER (BEATLES IN THE '90s)
FAB 3
Free As A Bird (full length version with wings intro, clapping outtro and backward message reversed)/ Real Love (Beatles early mix)/ Real Love (Beatles Video mix)/ Strawberry Fields (McCartney Anthology demo)/ I Will (McCartney, Harrison and Starr fragment)/ Derradune (McCartney, Harrison and Starr - unrecorded Harrison composition)/ Free As A Bird (Lennon demo take 1)/ Free As A Bird (Lennon demo take 4)/ Real Love (Lennon demo take 1)/ Real Love (Lennon demo take 4)/ Real Love

(Lennon demo take 5)/ Real Love (Lennon demo take 6)/ Real Love (Lennon demo)/ Real Love (from Imagine)/ It Don't Come Easy (Harrison demo)/ For You Blue (previously unreleased outtake from Let It Be film)/ The Long and Winding Road (previously unreleased outtake from Let It Be film)/ Let It Be (previously unreleased outtake from Let It Be film)/ Come Together (Smokin' Mojo Filters, different mix, Paul on backing vox '95)/ While My Guitar Gently Weeps (Royal Albert Hall 6/4/92, with George, Ringo and Gary Moore)/ Studio Mistakes (collage of outtakes)
Comments: Japanese CD. Deluxe color cover.

CD - COMPLETE HOLLYWOOD BOWL CONCERTS
MIDNIGHT BEAT MB CD 108/109
CD1: Introduction*/ Twist And Shout*/ You Can't Do That*/ All My Loving*/ She Loves You*/ Things We Said Today*/ Roll Over Beethoven*/ Can't Buy Me Love*/ If I Fell*/ I Wanna Hold Your Hand*/ Boys*/ A Hard Days Night*/ Long Tall Sally*/ Introduction**/ Twist And Shout**/ She's A Woman**/ I Feel Fine**/ Dizzy Miss Lizzy**/ Ticket To Ride**/ Everybody's Trying To Be My Baby**/ Can't Buy Me Love**/ Baby's In Black**/ I Wanna Be Your Man**/ A Hard Days Night**/ Help**/ I'm Down**
CD2: Tuning/ Twist And Shout/ She's A Woman/ I Feel Fine/ Dizzy Miss Lizzy/ Ticket To Ride/ Everybody's Trying To Be My Baby/ Can't Buy Me Love/ Baby's In Black/ I Wanna Be Your Man/ A Hard Days Night/ Help/ I'm Down/ Interview with John and Ringo (August 23 1964)/ Press Conference (August 29, 1965)
Recording: Excellent stereo. Line recording.
Source: CD1 *August 23, 1964. **August 30, 1965. CD2 August 29, 1965
Comments: European CD. Box set. Time CD1 73:10. CD2 67:32. Re-released as CDRs on the REPRO MAN label.

CD - DAY TRIPPING - MAGICAL MYSTERY TOUR REMIXED
FAR OUT PRODUCTIONS FOP78
Magical Mystery Tour (Global Insert Mix/Live Overdubs By The Dogs Of Radio) (10:08)/ Fool On The Hill (Day Tripping) (5:45)/ Strawberry Fields Forever (Voices In The Head) (12:19)/ I Am The Walrus (Radio Dogs Live Mash-Up) (9:28)/ Hey Bulldog (Maximum Consternation) (10:20)/ Flying (Lonely Dance Club Mix) (12:58)/ Bonus Tracks: LSD (Wendell Austin) (2:14)/ I'm Only Sleeping (Acetate: Early Mix) (3:01)/ Pink Litmus Shirt (Rare George Harrison Track With Sundry Unidentified Participants, Possibly Including Donovan & Mike Love - Acetate) 3:13)/ The L.S. Bumble Bee (With Peter Cook & Dudley Moore) (2:33)
Recording: Excellent. Soundboard.
Comments: European CD. Deluxe color cover. Time 72:07.

CD - THE ED SULLIVAN SHOWS
YELLOW DOG RECORDS YD 062
Intro, All My Loving (3:44)/ 'Till There Was You (2:11)/ She Loves You (2:54)/ Intro, I Saw Her Standing There (2:52)/ I Want To Hold Your Hand, Outro (3:31)/ She Loves You (2:22)/ This Boy (2:39)/ All My Loving (2:23)/ Intro, I Saw Her Standing There (2:50)/ From Me To You (2:34)/ I Want To Hold Your Hand, Outro (3:19)/ Intro, Twist And Shout (3:04)/ Please Please Me, Speech (2:01)/ I Want To Hold Your Hand (3:02)/ Interview, You Can't Do That (4:40)/ Intro, I Feel Fine (3:22)/ I'm Down (2:25)/ Act Naturally, Speech, Intro (3:01)/ Ticket To Ride (2:46)/ Yesterday (2:26)/ Help, Outro (3:01)/ Ed Sullivan intro without songs (:42)/ She Loves You (2:32)/ This Boy (2:49)/ All My Loving, Intro (3:10)/ I Saw Her Standing There (2:39)/ From Me To You (2:08)/ I Want To Hold Your Hand, Outro (2:34)
Recording: Very good-excellent. Some good. Soundboard.
Source: Ed Sullivan Shows. Tracks 1-5 February 9 '64. Tracks 6-11 rehearsal show Miami February 15 '64. Tracks 12-13 NYC February 23 '64. Tracks 14-15 AHDN outtakes May 24 '64. Tracks 16-21 NYC September 12 '65. Tracks 22 '66. Tracks 23-28 Miami February 16 '64.
Comments: European CD. Deluxe color cover. CD2 of THE ULTIMATE COLLECTION VOL. 1 (YELLOW DOG YDB 101/2/3/4) box set.

CD - FINEST COLLECTORS
THE ONLY ONE PRODUCTION TOO-97 1/2
CD1: Ticket To Ride (no fade out at the end, John's vocals on single track only, February 1965)/ Help (take 5 instrumental

version November 1964)/Paperback Writer (with count in dialogue, no echo April 1966)/ Rain (April 1966)/ Day Tripper (take 3, with count in, no fade November 1965)/ We Can Work It Out (Take 2, no fade out November 1965)/ Norwegian Wood (take 4, extra intros with several false starts)/ I'm Looking Through You (take 1, slower version with hand claps 1965)/ Magical Mystery Tour (different vocal track, spoken interlude by John April 1967)/ I'm The Walrus (long version without strings, bass, chorus and backing vocals 1967)/ Strawberry Fields Forever (Take 4, slow version with false start 1967)/ Penny Lane (rare mono version, count in dialogue with fanfare 1967)/ A Day In The Life (countdown intro January 1967)/ All You Need Is Love (take 1, basic tracks intro May 1967)/ Hey Jude (take 9 July 30 1968)/ Lady Madonna (early version without overdubbed bass and backing vocals February 4 1968)/ Revolution (no organ 1968)/ Ob-La-Di, Ob-La-Da-Christmas Time Is Here Again (early version running into a short reprise of 'Christmas Time Is Here Again' July 68)/ The Continuing Story Of Bungalow Bill (demo with John and George in the background at the beginning 1968)/ Birthday (electric version September 1968)/ A Case For The Blues (not Glass Onion as listed on the cover)
CD2: Back In The USSR/ Dear Prudence/ Ob-La-Di, Ob-La-Da/ Honey Pie/ The Continuing Story Of Bungalow Bill/ While My Guitar Gently Weeps/ I'm So Tired/ Blackbird/ Piggies/ Rocky Raccoon/ Julia/ Yer Blues/ Mother Nature's Son/ Everybody's Got Something To Hide Except For Me And My Monkey/ Sexy Sadie/ Revolution No. 1/ Cry Baby Cry/ Child Of Nature (early version of 'Jealous Guy'/ You Never Give Me Your Money (free jam session at the end, long version 1969)/ Maxwell's Silver Hammer (alternative take 1969)/ Oh! Darling (alternative take, John sings last verse 1969)/ Something (take 37, short version May 1969)
Recording: Very good to excellent. Some surface noise on CD2 tracks 19 - 22.
Source: Versions not on Beatles Anthology Volumes 1-3. CD2 Tracks 1 - 18 are outtakes from the legendary unreleased White UNPLUGGED album. All tracks are recorded in May 1968
Comments: Time CD1 67:21. CD2 71:05.

CD - GONE TOMORROW HERE TODAY
MIDNIGHT BEAT RECORDS MB CD 113
Hey Jude (July 30 1968)/ Dear Prudence (alternate mix, bass up front, longer fade-out, John's vocals heavily echoed, mono)/ Blackbird/ Blackbird, Congratulations/ Blackbird/ Blackbird, Studio Chat/ Studio Chat, Helter Skelter/ Gone Tomorrow Here Today/ Studio Chat/ Blackbird/ Blackbird, Studio Chat/ Mother Nature's Son/ Blackbird (5 takes)/ Organ Play, Drinking Tea/ Blackbird (2 takes)
Recording: Excellent stereo/mono.
Source: Studio outtakes/film. Tony Bramwell film (July 11 1968) used as an Apple promo.
Comments: European CD. Deluxe color cover. Time 51:32. Re-released as a CDR on the REPRO MAN label.

CD - IT'S ALL IN THE MIND Y'KNOW
RED ROBIN BEAT CD 017
A Hard Day's Night (theatrical ad in stereo)/ A Hard Day's Night (long outtro)/ I Should Have Known Better (stereo/harmonica intro now fixed/Lennon's breath between lines in verse more prominent)/ You Can't Do That (slower and bluesier)/ Help (theatrical ad in stereo)/ You've Got To Hide Your Love Away (more spacious mix and guitars mixed out front and cleaner)/ Ticket To Ride (new drums and guitar placement, taken from movie)/ Magical Mystery Tour (different vocals, two drum tracks, basically a different take for some of the early overdubs)/ Fool on the Hill (early mix, plus bass harmonica more prominent; also little or no bass guitar)/ Flying (early mix, snare drum is single tracked, music oddly balanced)/ I Am the Walrus (early mix, closer to finished version, not like any other mix)/ Five Little Dickie Birds (ditty sung and spoken by Lennon)/ There's No Business Like Show Business (sung by Lennon)/ Blue Jay Way (very different mix and noises, especially bass and drums)/ Death Cab For Cutie (sung by Bonzo Dog Band, different version from 'Gorilla' album)/ Your Mother Should Know (medley with 'MMT' and 'Hello Goodbye')/ Yellow Submarine (theatrical trailer)/ Hey Bulldog (unreleased deleted segment from Yellow Submarine)/ Lucy in the Sky With Diamonds (upgraded version)/ It's All Too Much (upgraded version)/ All You Need Is Love (upgraded version with

BEATLES, THE

clipped ending)/ All Together Now (from production master tape)/ Let It Be (theatrical ad in stereo, cool but dated ad for film)/ One After 909 (original mono mix from rare East European pressing from 1971)

CD - JELLY BEANS HAILING IN DREAMLIKE NOISE
WHOOPY CAT WKP-0036
I Want To Hold Your Hand/ Money/ Twist And Shout/ From Me To You (instrumental)/ She Loves You/ You Can't Do That/ Twist And Shout/ Long Tall Sally/ Can't Buy Me Love/ I Saw Her Standing There/ You Can't Do That/ All My Loving/ She Loves You/ Till There Was You/ Roll Over Beethoven/ Can't Buy Me Love/ Twist And Shout/ Long Tall Sally/ She's A Woman/ Ticket To Ride
Recording: Very good mono.
Source: Television. Tracks 1-4 Empire Theatre, Liverpool December 7 1963. Tracks 5-9 Empire Pool, Wembley April 26 1964. Tracks 10-18 Festival Hall, Melbourne, Australia June 15 1964. Tracks 19-20 Empire Pool, Wembley April 11 1965.
Comments: Time 48:59.

CD - LEANING ON A LAMP POST
YELLOW DOG YD 067
Carry That Weight, Castle Of The King Of The Birds, Long Jam (16:19)/ Leaning On A Lamp Post, Long Jam (15:22)/ Two Of Us, Frere Jacques, It Ain't Me Babe, Two Of Us (reprise) (16:23)/ All Things Must Pass (long rehearsal) (16:14)
Recording: Excellent mono.
Source: LET IT BE rehearsals January 6 1969.
Comments: European CD. Deluxe color cover.

CD - SEA OF GREEN
RED ROBIN BEAT CD 018
Help! (original stereo soundtrack, different mix)/ You're Gonna Lose That Girl (with count, original stereo soundtrack, different mix, loud bongos)/ You've Got To Hide Your Love Away (original stereo soundtrack, different mix)/ Ticket To Ride (stereo soundtrack, different mix)/ I Need You (original stereo soundtrack, different mix)/ Another Girl (with count, original stereo soundtrack, different mix)/ Help (with outtro finale, original stereo soundtrack, different mix)/ Yellow Submarine (original stereo soundtrack, different mix)/ Eleanor Rigby (original stereo soundtrack, different mix and intro)/ Submarine Shaped (spoken part with finale climax from 'A Day in the Life' sequence)/ All Together Now (original stereo soundtrack, different mix)/ When I'm 64 (original stereo soundtrack, different mix with spoken intro)/ Only A Northern Song (extra sounds)/ Nowhere Man (spoken outro)/ Foothills Of The Headlands, Lucy in the Sky With Diamonds (different mix with spoken outro)/ Sea of Green (phrase from Yellow Submarine psychedelicized)/ You've Got Time To Rectify (phrase from 'Think For Yourself')/ Tiptoe Through the Tulips (nod to Tiny Tim)/ Sgt. Pepper's Lonely Hearts Club Band (different mix)/ All You Need Is Love (different mix))/ Any Ol' Einstein, Baby You're a Rich Man (replaced 'Hey Bulldog' sequence)/ Beatles To Battle, Dixie Trombone/ It's All Too Much (different mix)/ All Together Now #2 (very different mix)/ It Must Be Baby Glass (spoken ditty)/ 1964 NME Pollwinners Concert, Introductions, She Loves You, You Can't Do That, Twist and Shout, Long Tall Sally, Can't Buy Me Love
Source: Tracks 1-25 are taken from original stereo soundtrack. Tracks 26-32 excellent quality transfer from ABC film broadcast 'Big Beat '64'. The soundtrack contains all five songs without dropouts.

CD - SOME HAVE GONE, SOME REMAIN
BEAT 019
Ain't She Sweet (original stereo version)/ Sweet Georgia Brown (alternate mono mix from acetate)/ She Loves You (German stereo mix)/ And I Love Her (Reel Music stereo mix)/ I'll Cry Instead (US mono mix)/ Any Time At All (US mono mix)/ When I Get Home (US mono mix)/ She's A Woman (US mono mix)/ I Feel Fine (US mono mix)/Help! (Reel Music stereo mix)/ In My Life (rare stereo mix)/ You Won't See Me (UK mono mix)/ What Goes On (UK Mono Mix)/ I'm Looking Through You (UK Mono Mix)/ Paperback Writer (Alternate Mono Mix)/ Taxman (French mono mix)/ And Your Bird Can Sing (UK mono mix)/ Dr. Robert (US mono mix)/ She Said She Said (UK mono mix)/ Good Day Sunshine (UK mono mix)/ Got To Get You Into My Life (UK mono mix)/ Strawberry Fields Forever (US mono mix)/ Baby Your Rich A Man (Us mono mix)/ Hey Jude (edited mix)/ Ballad Of John And Yoko (alternate stereo mix)/

Mean Mr. Mustard Medley (sonic upgrade of Abbey Road sequence), Her Majesty, Polythene Pam, She Came Through The Bathroom Window (outfake - artificially created from the commercial versions)
Recording: Excellent soundboard.
Comments: Japanese CD.

CD - STUDIO 2 SESSIONS AT ABBEY ROAD, VOL. 1
YELLOW DOG RECORDS YD 063
There's A Place (take 1) (2:10)/ There's A Place (take 2) (2:07)/ There's A Place (takes 3, 4) (2:13)/ There's A Place (takes 5, 6) (2:21)/ There's A Place (takes 7, 8) (2:46)/ There's A Place (take 9) (2:06)/ There's A Place (take 10) (2:03)/ I Saw Her Standing There (take 1) (3:05)/ I Saw Her Standing There (take 2) (3:12)/ I Saw Her Standing There (take 3) I Saw Her Standing There (take 4), I Saw Her Standing There (take 5) (2:42)/ I Saw Her Standing There (takes 6-9) (4:57)/ Do You Want To Know A Secret (take 7) (2:40)/ Do You Want To Know A Secret (take 8) (2:06)/ A Taste Of Honey (take 6) (2:12)/ A Taste Of Honey (take 7) (2:13)/ There's A Place (take 11) (2:07)/ There's A Place (take 12) (2:29)/ I Saw Her Standing There (take 10) (3:03)/ I Saw Her Standing There (take 11) (3:41)/ Misery (take 1) (2:02)/ Misery (takes 2-6) (4:51)/ Misery (takes 7, 8) (2:24)
Recording: Excellent. Soundboard.
Source: Recording of 'Please Please Me' LP February 11 1963. Tracks 1-11 morning session. Tracks 12-22 afternoon session.
Comments: European CD. Deluxe color cover. CD2 of THE ULTIMATE COLLECTION VOL. 2 (YELLOW DOG YDB 201/2/3/4) box set.

CD - STUDIO 2 SESSIONS AT ABBEY ROAD VOL. 2
YELLOW DOG RECORDS YD 064
From Me To You (takes 1, 2) (3:32)/ From Me To You (take 3) (1:57)/ From Me To You (take 4) (1:54)/ From Me To You (take 5) (2:18)/ From Me To You (takes 6, 7) (2:19)/ Thank You Girl (take 1) (2:12) Thank You Girl (takes 2-4) (2:37)/ Thank You Girl (take 5) (2:08)/ Thank You Girl (take 6) (2:23)/ Thank You Girl (edit pieces takes 7-13) (4:07)/ From Me To You (take 8) (2:13)/ From Me To You (edit piece takes 9-13) (1:55)/ One After 909 (takes 1, 2) (4:27)/ One After 909 (takes 3-5) (5:41)/ Hold Me Tight (track 2 - take 21) (2:44)/ Hold Me Tight (track 2 - takes 22, 23, 24) (4:04)/ Hold Me Tight (track 2 - takes 25, 26) (3:03)/ Hold Me Tight (track 2 - takes 27, 28) (1:56)/ Hold Me Tight (track 2 - take 29) (2:52)/ Don't Bother Me (remake take 10) (2:52)/ Don't Bother Me (remake takes 11-13) (3:55)
Recording: Excellent. Soundboard.
Source: Tracks 1-14 Abbey Road Studios March 5 1963. Tracks 15-21 Abbey Road Studios September 1219'63.
Comments: European CD. Deluxe color cover. CD3 of THE ULTIMATE COLLECTION VOL. 2 (YELLOW DOG YDB 201/2/3/4) box set.

CD - STUDIO 2 SESSIONS AT ABBEY ROAD, VOL. 3
YELLOW DOG RECORDS YD 065
A Hard Day's Night (take 2) (2:34)/ A Hard Day's Night (take 3) (2:37)/ A Hard Day's Night (take 4) (2:42)/ A Hard Day's Night (takes 6, 7) (4:36)/ A Hard Day's Night (takes 8-9) (2:34)/ I'm A Loser (takes 1, 2) (2:38)/ I'm A Loser (take 3) (2:55)/ I'm A Loser (takes 4-6) (4:43)/ I'm A Loser (takes 7, 8) (1:16)/ She's A Woman (take 2) (3:22)/ She's A Woman (takes 3-5) (3:46)/ She's A Woman (take 7) (6:32)/ I Feel Fine (takes 1, 2) (3:17)/ I Feel Fine (take 5) (2:27)/ I Feel Fine (take 6) (2:49)/ I Feel Fine (take 7) (2:47)
Recording: Excellent. Soundboard.
Source: Studios sessions. Tracks 1-5 March 16 1964. Tracks 6-9 August 14 1964. Tracks 10-12 October 8 1964. Track 13-16 October 18 1964.
Comments: European CD. Deluxe color cover. CD2 of THE ULTIMATE COLLECTION VOL. 3 (YELLOW DOG YDB 301/2/3/4) box set.

CD - WITH THE BEATLES!
ODEON SMO 83568
Original stereo version of WITH THE BEATLES! plus the following: She Loves You (US stereo version)/ I'll Get You (US stereo version)/ It Won't Be Long (early take July 30 1963)/ Please Mr. Postman (early take July 30 1963)/ Don't Bother Me (take 10 September 12 1963)/ This Boy (takes 12 & 13 from 'Free As A Bird' CD)/ Komm, Gib Mir Deine Hand (stereo master)/ Sie Liebt Dich (stereo master)/ I'm In Love (John Lennon - demo summer 1963)

BEATLES, THE

Recording: Excellent. Soundboard.
Comments: European CD. Deluxe color digi-pack cover - reproduction of original German cover. Limited edition of 500. Time 54:13.

CD - WILDCAT!
MADMAN 13-14
CD1: Wild Cat #1 (1:24)/ Wild Cat #2 (2:24)/ I'll Always Be In Love With You (2:19)/ You'll Be Mine (1:42)/ Matchbox (0:53)/ Some Days (1:32)/ Cayenne (2:28)/ One After 909 (1:28)/ Well, Darling (3:19)/ You Must Write Everyday (2:32)/ That's When Your Heartaches Begin (1:14)/ Hello Little Girl (1:51)/ The World Is Waiting For The Sunrise (2:30)/ I Don't Know (improvisation) (5:52)/ I Don't Need No Cigarette, Boy (improvisation) (5:53)/ That's An Important Number (improvisation) (7:49)/ Improvisation (4:56)
CD2: I'll Follow The Sun (1:46)/ Hallelujah I Love Her So (2:12)/ One After 909 (2:25)/ Movin' And Groovin', Ramrod (3:45)/ Improvisation (11:44)/ Improvisation (7:42)/ Improvisation (11:06)/ Improvisation (17:40)
Source: All of the known 1960 rehearsal recordings. Only known recordings of the band with Stu Sutcliff.
Comments: Australian CD. Comes in cardboard slipcase with 32 page booklet of notes and photos. Picture CDs. Time CD1 51:29. CD2 59:36.

CD - YEAH! YEAH! YEAH! & BONUS TRACKS
ODEON SMO 83739
Original stereo version of A HARD DAY'S NIGHT plus the following: Can't Buy Me love (unedited take 2 in stereo)/ You Can't Do That (take 6 from Anthology 1)/ And I Love Her (take 2 from Anthology 1)/ I'll Be Back (take 2 - a breakdown - from Anthology 1)/ I'll Be Back (take 3 from Anthology 1)/ A Hard Day's Night (take 1 from Anthology 1)/ You Know What To Do (George Harrison demo from Anthology 1)/ One And One Is Two (Paul McCartney demo March 1964)/ If I Fell (John Lennon composing demo late 1963)
Recording: Excellent. Soundboard.
Comments: European CD. Deluxe color digi-pack cover - reproduction of original German cover. Limited edition of 500.

BECK

CD - ELECTRIC MUSIC FOR THE KOOL PEOPLE
MOONRAKER 171
Fuckin With My Head (Mountain Dew Rock)/ Devil's Haircut/ Novacane/ Pay No Mind (Snoozer)/ Loser/ Minus/ Truckdrivin' Neighbors Downstairs (Yellow Sweat)/ No Money No Honey/ Puttin' It Down/ Introductions/ Rowboat Where It's At/ Interlude (Fuck Me Up the Ass - East 17 Tribute)/ The New Pollution/ Jack-Ass/ Beercan/ I Wanna Get With You/ High 5 (Rock The Catskills)/ Mutherfuker
Recording: Excellent stereo. Soundboard.
Source: The Paradiso, Amsterdam July 21 1996.
Comments: European CD. Deluxe color cover. Picture CD. Time 79:39.

CD - LOLLIPOP
MOONRAKER 201
Lord Only Knows/ Devil's Haircut/ Novacane/ Sissyneck/ Minus/ Pay No Mind (Snoozer)/ Loser/ Truckdrivin' Neighbors Downstairs (Yellow Sweat)/ Where It's At/ New Pollution/ Jack-Ass/ Beercan/ High Five/ Where It's At/ Where It's At
Recording: Excellent stereo. Soundboard.
Source: Tracks 1-13 Stockholm, Sweden July 26 1996. Track 14 The Late Show With David Letterman, New York September 3 1996. Track 15 the pre-show for the 1996 MTV Video Music Awards, Radio City Music Hall, New York September 5 1996.
Comments: European CD. Deluxe color cover. Time 62:17.

BECK, JEFF

CD - BLUES DELUXE
SCORPIO
You Shook Me (3:12)/ ~Let Me Love You (5:59)/ The Sun Is Shining (9:50)/ Rice Pudding (14:15)/ Shapes Of Things (6:12)/ Jeff's Boogie (7:57)/ Blues Deluxe (7:32)/ I Ain't Superstitious (14:00)/ Bye Bye Baby (Baby Goodbye) (7:31)
Source: Fillmore West, San Francisco December 7 1968.

CD - BOSTON TEA PARTY 1968
SINSEMILLA TOP/JB-68020S
You Shook Me, Let Me Love You/ Jeff's Boogie/ Gambler's Blues/ Rock My

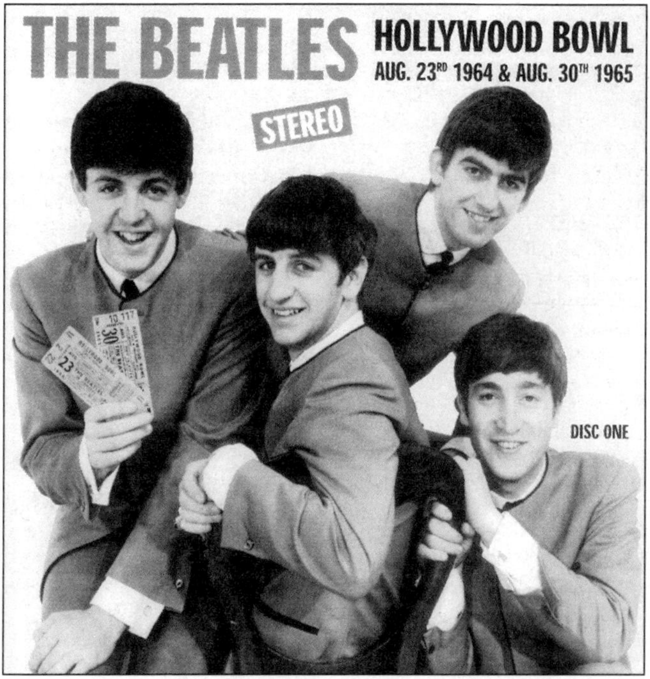
THE BEATLES
HOLLYWOOD BOWL
AUG. 23RD 1964 & AUG. 30TH 1965
STEREO
DISC ONE

björk

BECK, JEFF

Plimsoul/ Shapes Of Things/ Rice Pudding/ Sweet Little Angel/ Rock My Plimsoul/ Hi Ho Silver Lining
Recording: Very good. Audience.
Source: Tracks 1-7 The Tea Party Club, Boston, Massachusetts October 22 1968. Tracks 8-12 Reading Festival August 1967.
Comments: Japanese CD.

CD - ECSTASY HERO
ELEMENTS OF CRIME ELEMENTS 003/4
CD1: Escape/ Get Us All In The End/ Ecstasy/ Ambitious/ Goodbye Pork Pie (Intro) Stop, Look And Listen/ The Pump/ Star Cycle/ Cause We Ended Lovers
CD2: Led Boots/ Love Will/ Miami Vice/ Blue Wind/ People Get Ready/ Freeway Jam/ Wild Thing/ Going Down
Recording: Very good. Audience.
Source: Greek Theater, Los Angels April 1986.
Comments: Japanese CD. Deluxe color cover. Picture CD. Time CD1 49:03. CD2 41:22.

CD - HIGHWAYS
SCARECROW 009
Piano Solo, Going Down (4:17)/ Ice Cream Cakes (7:53)/ Morning Dew (7:30)/ Tonight I'll Be Staying Here With You (4:57)/ I Got To Have A Song (6:46)/ Jody (8:57)/ Jeff's Boogie (4:48)/ Train Train (2:43)/ I Ain't Superstitious (8:57)/ Got The Feeling (12:07)/ Situation (6:04)
Recording: Audience.
Source: Winterland, San Francisco, CA October 30 1971.
Comments: Japanese CD.

CD - JELLYWAY JAM
SCARECROW 026
Rock 'N Roll Jelly/ School Days/ Lopsy Lu/ Rock 'N Roll Jelly (Reha)#1/ Rock 'N Roll Jelly (Reha)#2/ Rock 'N Roll Jelly (Reha)#3/ Rock 'N Roll Jelly (Reha)#4/ Rock 'N Roll Jelly (Reha)#5/ Rock 'N Roll Jelly (Reha)#6/ Rock 'N Roll Jelly (Reha)#7/ Rock 'N Roll Jelly (Basic)#1/ Rock 'N Roll Jelly (Basic)#2/ Rock 'N Roll Jelly (Basic)#3/ Rock 'N Roll Jelly (Basic)#4/ Rock 'N Roll Jelly (Basic)#5
Recording: Soundboard.. Tracks 1-3 very good. Tracks 4-15 good. Some hiss.
Source: Tracks 1-3 Amsterdam June 26 1979. Tracks 4-15 studio session February 1978.
Comments: Japanese CD. Deluxe color cover. Time 70:30.

CD - JONES BEACH 1995
JB-001
Stand On It/ Star Cycle/ Guitar Shop/ Savoy/ You Never Know/ Behind The Veil/ Fee Way Jam/ Where Were You/ Big Block/ Cause We Ended As Lovers/ Sling Shot/ Goodbye Pork Pie Hat/ Blue Wind/ People Get Ready
Recording: Very good. Audience.
Source: Jones Beach, NY August 11 '95.
Comments: Japanese CD. B&W cover. Blue/yellow type. Time 66:44.

CD - THE OLDEST TAPE
SCARECROW 010
Stone Cold Crazy (5:47)/ Talk To Me Baby (3:46)/ Dust My Broom (4:11)/ Let Me Love You (4:48)/ I Ain't Superstitious (5:26)/ Blues Song (6:12)/ Rock My Plimsoul (4:24)/ Jeff's Boogie (4:06)/ Bye Bye Baby (Baby Goodbye) (3:28)/ I'm Losing You (2:18)/ Pretty Woman (2:54)
Recording: Audience.
Source: Marquee Club, London, England 1967.
Comments: Japanese CD.

CD - ORANGE CAKES
SCARECROW 008
Ice Cream Cakes (8:02)/ Morning Dew (6:20)/ Piano Solo, Going Down (4:48)/ Tonight I'll Be Staying With You, Glad All Over (10:15)/ Definitely Maybe (8:20)/ Jeff's Boogie (5:31)/ Situation (5:30)/ New Ways, Plynth, Drum Solo, Train Train (11:23)/ Let Me Love You (7:40)/ Got The Feeling (7:50)
Recording: Audience.
Source: Palace Theater, Waterbury, Connecticut May 17 1972.
Comments: Japanese CD.

CD - PLYNTH
SINSEMILLA TOP/JB-72017S
Going Down/ Ice Cream Cakes/ Over The Hill, Plynth, Shotgun, Drum Solo, Plynth/ Definitely Maybe/ Oleo, Bass Solo, Oleo/ New Ways, Train Train/ Let Me Love You/ Got The Feeling
Recording: Very good. Audience.
Source: Stanley Theatre, Pittsburgh, PA August 1 1972.
Comments: Japanese CD.

CD - RARE RAW ROUGH AND READY
GOLD STANDARD 195-JF-16-04
Going Down/ Goodbye Pork Pie Hat/ Led Boots/ She's A Woman/ New Ways, Train Train/ Got The Feeling/ Definitely Maybe/ Ain't No Sunshine/ Let Me Love You/ Shapes Of Things/ Let Me Love You/ Morning Dew/ You Shook Me/ Rock My Plimsoul/ Beck's Bolero/ I Ain't Superstitious
Recording: Good to very good. Tracks10-16 very good to excellent mono. Some surface noise.
Source: Tracks 1-9 Chicago October '71. Tracks10-16 studio recordings, London '68 from mono 'Truth' LP.
Comments: Deluxe color cover. Time 74:42.

CD - SESSIONS
SCARECROW 011/12
CD1: You Never Know (11:33)/ Stop, Look And Listen (3:59)/ Untitled Jam #1 (1:53)/ Untitled Jam #2 (3:31)/ Untitled Jam #3 (9:15)/ Honky Tonk Women (4:44)/ Sympathy For The Devil (6:24)/ Dead Flowers (4:37)/ Shine A Light (3:33)/ Little Red Rooster (4:31)/ Come On, Don't Stop (3:27)/ Working Demo #1 (3:54)/ Working Demo #2 (3:37)/ Working Demo #3 (1:55)/ People Get Ready (4:49)
Source: Tracks 1-5 Electric Ladyland Studio session 1986. Tracks 6-10 VTR session October 20 1987. Tracks 11-15 Flash out-takes 1985.
Comments: Japanese CD.

BECK, BOGERT & APPICE

CD - ANOTHER SIDE UP
SCARECROW 013/14
CD1: Superstition (4:47)/ Livin' Alone (6:09)/ I'm So Proud (5:42)/ Lady (6:48)/ Morning Dew, Drum Solo (13:20)/ Sweet Sweet Surrender (4:58)/ Lose Myself With You, Bass Solo, Lose Myself With You, Bass Solo (18:19)/ Black Cat Moan Blues De Luxe, You Shook Me, Black Cat Moan (9:41)
CD2: Why Should I Care (7:56)/ Going Down (3:53)/ Jeff's Boogie (4:32)/ Oleo Boogie, The Train Kept A-Rollin (7:42)/ Superstition (4:40)/ Livin' Alone (5:06)/ Tonight I'll Be Staying Here With You (4:42)/ People Get Ready (2:22)/ Lady (6:54)/ Morning Dew, Drum Solo (12:33)
Recording: Audience.
Source: CD1 and CD2 tracks 1-4 Koseinenkin Hall, Osaka, Japan May 18 1973. CD2 tracks 5-10 Nuremburg, Germany June 1973.
Comments: Japanese CD.

CD - COLLECTIVE INDIVIDUALITY
SCARECROW 011/12
CD1: Superstition (5:00)/ Livin' Alone (5:45)/ I'm So Proud (5:08)/ Lady (7:43)/ Morning Dew, Drum Solo (10:34)/ Sweet Sweet Surrender (5:20)/ Lose Myself With You, Bass Solo (11:12)/ Black Cat Moan (8:47)
CD2: Why Should I Care (5:17)/ Plynth, Shotgun, Plynth (7:49)/ People Get Ready (2:57)/ Oleo (5:56)/ Plynth, Shotgun, Bass Solo, Plynth (15:47)/ Let Me Love You (8:29)/ Jeff's Boogie (5:18)/ Why Should I Care (5:30)/ Oleo (6:10)
Recording: Audience.
Source: CD1 and CD2 track 4 Imperial College Of Printing, London, England February 20 1973. CD2 tracks 5-9 Nuremburg, Germany June 1973.
Comments: Japanese CD.

BECK, JEFF WITH THE JAN HAMMER GROUP

CD - PLAY WITH ME
ELEMENTS OF CRIME ELEMENTS 002
Oh Yeah/ Sister/ Darkness (Earth In Search Of The Sun)/ Play With Me/ Freeway Jam/ Scatterbrain/ Earth (Still Out Only Home)/ Diamond Dust/ You Know What I Mean
Recording: Very good. Audience.
Source: Arrowhead Stadium, Kansas City, 1976.
Comments: Japanese CD. Deluxe color cover. Picture CD. Time 57:26.

BJORK

CD - BEAUTY AND THE BEAST
KISS THE STONE KTS 600
Army Of Me/ The Modern Things/ Human Behavior/ Isobel/ Venus As A Boy/ Possibly Maybe/ I Go Humble/ Hyper Ballad/ Enjoy/ I Miss You/ Crying/ Its Oh So Quiet/ Big Time Sensuality/ Aeroplane/ I Miss You
Recording: Excellent stereo. Soundboard.
Source: Warehouse, Toronto, Canada 7/8/95. Track 14 Later Show, London 1995. Track 15 White Room, London, 1995.
Comments: European CD. Time 71:12.

BJORK

CD - LIVE BEHAVIOUR
CRYSTAL CATS RECORDS CC 330
Human Behaviour/ The Harbour/ One Day/ Venus As A Boy/ Come To Me/ The Anchor Song/ Play Dead/ Crying/ Violently Happy/ There's More To Life Than This/ Big Time Sensuality/ If You Complain Once More/ Bonus: Play Dead/ Sperglar (March 1983 with Tappi Tikarrass)/ Ammaeli (1986 Sykurmolarnir-Sugarcubes)/ Kottur (1986 Sykurmolarnir-Sugarcubes)
Recording: Excellent.
Source: The Academy, Manchester, England December 19 1993.
Comments: European CD.

CD - MISS WORLD
OXYGEN OXY 051
Army Of Me (4:01)/ The Modern Things (3:59)/ Human Behaviour (3:27)/ Isobel (5:20)/ Venus As A Boy (2:39)/ Possibly Maybe (5:40)/ I Go Humble (4:02)/ Hyper-Ballad (5:05)/ Enjoy (6:14)/ I Miss You (3:59)/ Crying (5:02)/ It's Oh So Quiet (3:55)/ Big Time Sensuality (4:15)/ Aeroplane (4:36)/ It's Oh So Quiet (3:31)
Recording: Excellent stereo. Soundboard.
Source: Tracks: 1-13 Warehouse, Toronto August 7 1995. Track 14 Later Show, London 1995. Track 15 T.O.T.P., London November 1995.
Comments: European CD.

CD - TIBETAN FREEDOM CONCERT
BLIZZARD RECORDINGS BLZD150
Army Of Me/ Human Behavior/ Venus As A Boy/ Hyper-Ballad/ In Time/ Violently Happy/ Stidgu Mig/ Anchor Song/ I Remember You/ Sidasta Eg/ Gloria (Instrumental)/ Come To Me (Extended Mix)
Recording: Excellent stereo. Soundboard.
Source: Tracks 1-6 Tibetan Freedom Concert, Golden Gate Park, San Francisco, CA June 16 1996. Tracks 7-13 studio outtakes 1994-1996.
Comments: European CD. Deluxe color cover. Time 57:16.

CD - UNPLUGGED PLUS BONUS TRACKS
CARE FOR YOUR EARS CYE 005
Human Behaviour/ One Day/ Come To Me/ Big Time Sensuality/ Aeroplane/ Feeling Like Someone In Love/ Crying/ The Anchor Song/ Violently Happy/ Human Behaviour/ Atlantic/ One Day/ Venus Is A Boy/ Come To Me/ The Anchor Song/ Violently Happy/ Crying
Recording: Excellent stereo. Soundboard.
Source: Tracks 1-8 MTV Unplugged set 1994. Tracks 9-17 London 1994.
Comments: European CD. Time 75:06.

BLACK, FRANK

CD - TUNE IN, TURN ON, BLACK OUT
MOONRAKER 159
The Marsist (4:54)/ Big Red (3:30)/ Brachish Boy (4:22)/ Men In Black (3:04)/ Superabound (3:50)/ Headache (3:19)/ Two Reelers (3:49)/ Freedom Roch (4:11)/ Los Angeles (I (2:13)/ Czar (4:22)/ (I Want to Live On An) Abstract Plain (2:13)/ Calistan (3:43)/ Ten Percenter (4:18)/ Jesus Was Right (2:59)/ White Noise Maker (2:32)/ Los Angeles II (4:17)/ Last Stand Of Shazeb Andleeb (4:54)/ Hiched In The Taco (2:07)/ Headache (3:03)/ You Ain't Me (2:32)/ Jesus Was Right (3:21)
Recording: Excellent.
Source: Tracks 1-16 The Commodore Theatre, Vancouver, Canada April 23 1996. Tracks 17-21 The Loreley Festival, Germany June 22 1996.
Comments: European CD.

BLACK CROWES, THE

CD - LIVE IN NEW YORK
SLEDGEHAMMER RECORDS 30005
No Speak No Slave/ Sting Me/ Twice As Hard/ Thick N' Thin/ Sister Luck/ Black Moon Creeping/ Hotel Illness/ Hard To Handle/ Stare It Cold/ She Talks To Angels/ Remedy/ Jealous Again
Source: Beacon Theatre, New York August 25 1992
Comments: European CD.

CD - OUT OF THE CROWES NEST
BLUE MOON RECORDS BMCD35
Mercenary Man/ Karel The Psychic/ If/ Medicine/ Redneck Blues/ It's Not Fair/ Your Definition/ The Long Day/ Serving Time/ Redneck Blues/ It's Not Fair/ Jealous Again/ She Talks To Angels/ You're Wrong/ She Talks To Angels/ Jealous Again/ She Talks To Angels/ You're Wrong
Recording: Excellent. Soundboard.
Source: Tracks 1-4 garage demos 1986. Tracks 5-7 A&M demos, Chapel Hill, NC

October 1987. Tracks 8-11 studio demos 1988. Tracks 12-13 National Studios, NYC 1990. Tracks 14-16 basement acoustic gig 1990. Tracks 17-18 acoustic rehearsal 1990.
Comments: European CD. Deluxe color cover. Time 75:31.

CD - THE RAVEN
SHINOLA SH 69035
Jealous Guy/ She Talks To Angels/ Hard To Handle/ Sting Me/ My Morning Song/ Thorn In My Pride/ Jealous Again/ Sister Luck/ Struttin' Blues/ No Speak No Slave/ Twice As Hard/ Sometimes Salvation/ Thick And Thin
Recording: Excellent stereo. Soundboard.
Source: Live USA '91 - '93.
Comments: European CD. Time 69:14.

CD - A SOUTHERN FRIED TREAT
RSM 071
Black Moon Creeping (6:21)/ Thick 'N' Thin (2:51)/ A Conspiracy (6:42)/ High Head Blues (6:56)/ Hard To Handle (3:55)/ Waiting Guilty (5:00)/ Cursed Diamond (5:50)/ Jealous Again (5:04)/ No Speak No Slave (5:00)/ She Talks To Angels (6:19)/ Wiser Time (6:42)/ Shake Your Money Maker (3:35)/ Remedy (6:41)/ P. 25 London (4:21)*
Recording: Excellent stereo. Soundboard.
Source: 'Amorica' tour 1995. *US 1994.
Comments: European CD. Deluxe color cover.

CD - SUNFLOWERS
MOONRAKER 106
Ballad In Urgency/ Wiser Time/ Hard To Handle/ Jealous Again/ Stare It Cold/ Remedy/ Champagne & Reefer
Recording: Excellent stereo. Soundboard.
Source: The Music Hall, Cologne, Germany, February 3, '95.
Comments: European CD. Deluxe color cover. Time 41:51.

BLACK FLAG

CD - THE COMPLETE 1982 DEMOS
MANSON REC. 003
What Can You Believe/ Yes, I Know/ Slip It In/ Modern Man/ My War/ Black Coffee/ Beat My Head/ I Can't Decide/ I Love You/ Nothing Left Inside/ I Love You/ My War/ Interview/ Swinging Man
Recording: Excellent. Soundboard. Some hiss.
Source: Tracks 1-10 1982 demos. Tracks 11-14 1984 Radio Tokyo (studio).
Comments: European CD. Time 63:19.

BLACK GRAPE

CD - IN THE NAME OF THE FATHER
KISS THE STONE KTS 571
Tramazi/ In The Name Of The Father/ A Big Day In The North/ New Song/ Shake Well Before Opening/ Reverend Black Grape/ Shake Your Money/ Yeah Yeah Brother/ Kelly's Heroes/ Little Bob/ Fat Neck
Recording: Excellent stereo. Soundboard.
Source: The Brixton Academy, London February 1996.
Comments: European CD.

BLACK SABBATH

CD - ETERNAL SHINING
BONDAGE MUSIC BONO84
Supertzar/ Neon Knights/ Children Of The Sea/ War Pigs/ Born To Lose/ Black Sabbath/ Groly Ride/ Heaven And Hell/ Children Of The Grave/ The Shining/ Paranoid
Recording: Good to very good. Audience.
Source: Bremen, Germany, November 25 1987.
Comments: European CD. Deluxe color cover. Time 73:37.

CD - MIAMI 80
AMSTERDAM AMS 9618-2-1/2
CD1: Supertzar/ War Pigs/ Neon Knights/ Nib/ Children Of The Sea/ Sweet Leaf
CD2: Black Sabbath/ Heaven & Hell/ Iron Man (Tony Iommi solo)/ Die Young/ Paranoid/ Children Of The Grave
Recording: Excellent audience.
Source: Miami Florida September 7 1980.
Comments: Japanese CD. Deluxe color cardboard sleeve cover. Time CD1 45:15. CD2 47:01.

CD - RAY RULES
BS 4
Mob Rules/ Danger Zone/ War Pigs/ Seventh Star/ Die Young/ Black Sabbath/ N.I.B./ Neon Knights/ Paranoid/ Danger Zone/ Tony Iommi Interview Part 1/ Sabbath Bloody Sunday/ Tony Iommi Part 2
Recording: Very good.

BLACK SABBATH

Source: Hammersmith Odeon, London
June 2 1986.
Comments: Japanese CD.

CD - TURN TO GLENN
BS 5
Superzar/ Mob Rules/ Children Of The Sea/ Danger Zone/ War Pigs/ Symptom Of The Universe Stranger To Love
Recording: Very good.
Source: Final live rehearsal, Hollywood March 14 1986.
Comments: Japanese CD.

CD - WELCOME TO THE ELECTRIC FUNERAL
METAL MANIACS MM 001
Sympathy Of The Universe/ War Pigs/ Snow Blind/ Never Say Die/ Black Sabbath/ Dirty Women, Drum Solo/ Rock And Roll Doctor, Guitar Solo/ Electric Funeral/ Children Of The Grave/ Paranoid
Recording: Very good to excellent stereo. Soundboard.
Source: Hammersmith Odeon, London, England 1978.
Comments: European CD. Deluxe color cover. Time 55:24.

CD - WICKED SABBATH
ZA 66
N.I.B./ War Pigs/ Sweet Leaf/ Black Sabbath/ Children Of The Grave/ Wicked World/ Paranoid/ Fairies Wear Boots
Recording: Good to very good. Soundboard.
Source: Toronto, Canada July 18 1971.
Comments: Japanese CD. Time 64:42.

CD - WIZARD OVER STOCKHOLM
FIRE POWER FP-013
Intro/ Neon Knights/ The Shining/ Wizard/ War Pigs/ Headless Cross/ Mercy Angels/ I Ain't Gonna Cry For You No More/ Mob Rules/ Black Sabbath/ Sabbath Bloody Sabbath
Recording: Very good. Audience.
Source: Karl Shamn, Stockholm, Sweden, June 16 1995.
Comments: European CD. Time 54:40.

BLACKMORE, RITCHIE

CD - BY REQUEST
NIGHTLIFE N-053
RAINBOW: Warming Up (June 12 '82)/ DEEP PURPLE: Cosmic Jazz ('84 studio outtake)/ DEEP PURPLE: Smoke On The Water (BBC Studio live)/ DEEP PURPLE: Never Before (BBC Studio live)/ RAINBOW: I Surrender (unreleased '80 instrumental demo version)/ RAINBOW: Make Your Move (extended version)/ RAINBOW: All Night Long (live edited version)/ RAINBOW: Self Portrait (live November 20 '75)/ DEEP PURPLE: Mandrake Root (guitar crush version)/ IAN GILLAN BAND: Rock N Roll Medley
Recording: Very good to excellent. Some good to very good.
Comments: Japanese CD. Deluxe color cover. Time 60:06.

CD - BY REQUEST II
NIGHTLIFE N-054
RAINBOW: Ritchie's Riff (unreleased '80 instrumental demo version)/ RAINBOW: Tarrot Woman (BBC Studio live)/ DEEP PURPLE: Fireball (BBC Studio live)/ DEEP PURPLE: Never Before (Take II) (BBC Studio live)/ RAINBOW: Perfect Strangers (unreleased '80 instrumental demo version)/ RAINBOW: Midnight Tunnel Vision (unreleased '80 instrumental version)/ RAINBOW: Jealous Lover (live December 10 '76)/ RAINBOW: A Light In Black (live December 10 '76)/ DEEP PURPLE: Anyone's Daughter (live June 24, '71)/ JACKIE LYNTON BAND: Blues Shuffle (live March 10 '87)/ IAN GILLAN: Woman From Tokyo (live December 27 '78)/ IAN GILLAN: Lucille (live December 27 '78)
Recording: Good to very good. Some excellent. Soundboard and audience.
Comments: Japanese CD. Deluxe color cover. Time 59:22.

BLUE MURDER

CD - THREE PIRATES... RIOT
LAURA-005/6
CD1: Riot/ Valley Of The Kings/ Out Of Love/ Unreleased Instrumental/ Tony Franklin Solo/ Billy/ Ptolemy
CD2: Jerry Roll/ Carmine Appice Solo/ Hot Legs/ Still Of The Night/ Closer/ Purple Haze/ Blue Murder
Source: Nippon Budokan August 25 1989 not MZA Ariake, Tokyo August 20 1989 as stated on cover.

CD - SCREAMING DALLAS NIGHT
WKD-001
Riot/ Dance/ Cry For Love/ Cold Sweat/ Billy/ She Knows/ Jelly Roll/ We All Fall Down/ Thunder And Lightning/ Blue Murder/ Dancin' In The Moonlight/ Still Of The Night
Recording: Very good. Audience
Source: Dallas, Texas April 8 1994.

BLUETONES

CD - FADE AWAY
KISS THE STONE KTS 567
Don't Stand Me Down/ Vampire/ Bluetonic/ Can't Be Trusted/ Slight Return/ Talking To Clarry/ Putting Out Fires/ Castle Rock/ String Alone/ Are You Blue Or Are You Blind?/ Cut Some Rug/ Time And Again/ Bluetonic/ Slight Return/ Driftwood/ Time And Again
Recording: Excellent stereo. Soundboard.
Source: Bristol, UK February 1996. Leeds April 10 1996. Reading August 26 1995.
Comments: European CD.

BLUES BROTHERS

CD - BLUES FOR YOU
TS RARE RECORDING 012
Intro/ You Go the Blues/ She Caught Katy/ Can't Play The Blues/ The Thrill Is Gone/ Just For You/ Raise Your Hand/ Big Bird/ Knock On Wood, Funky Broadway, Knock On Wood/ Soul Man/ Everybody Needs Somebody To Love/ Outro/ Sweet Home Chicago
Source: Montreux 1992.

BLUES TRAVELER

CD - KING OF NEW YORK
SKYDISC RECORDS SCD2500
But Anyway/ Ivory Tusk/ New Year's Jam/ Optimistic Thought/ Slow Change/ Just Wait/ Come Together/ New York Prophesies/ What's For Breakfast/ Crystal Flame
Recording: Excellent stereo. Soundboard.
Source: The Roseland Ballroom, NYC December 31 1993.
Comments: European CD. Deluxe color cover. Time 73:52.

CD - ROCK ME TONIGHT
BABYFACE BF015
Intro/ Crystal Flame/ Hey Chan/ New York Prophesy/ Mountain Cry/ Rock Me Baby/ Runnin' And Hidin'/ Blues Jam #1/ Blues Jam #2: Conclusion
Recording: Excellent stereo. Soundboard.
Source: Lonestar Roadhouse, New York August 6 '93.
Comments: European CD. Time 71:08.

BLUR

CD - MILE END
KISS THE STONE KTS 483
Tracey Jacks/ Sunday, Sunday/ Chemical World/ End Of A Century/ Globe Alone/ Pop Scene/ Magic America/ Country House/ Jubilee/ To The End/ Advert/ Girls And Boys/ Stereotyper/ Far Out/ Bank Holiday/ For Tomorrow/ Parklife*/ Daisy Bell*/ This Is A Low
Recording: Excellent stereo. Soundboard.
Source: The Mile End Stadium, East London June 17 '95. * With Phil Daniels.
Comments: European CD. Deluxe color cover. Picture CD. Time 70:48.

CD - STOP DREAMING
KOBRA RECORDS KRCD 21
Beetlebum/ Song 11/ Girls And Boys/ Movin' On/ Oily Water/ Stereotypes/ Middle Of The Road/ To The End/ End Of The Century/ Pop Scene/ Chinese Bombs/ Supa Shoppa/ Death Of A Party/ This Is A Low/ On Your Own/ Park Life/ the Universal/ Sing
Recording: Excellent stereo. Soundboard.
Source: London, Astoria Theatre 10/2/97.
Comments: European CD. B&w cover. Blue type. Time 73:16.

CD - YELLOW CLOUDS
MOONRAKER 073
The Great Escape/ Charmless Man/ Popscene/ End Of A Century/ Mr. Robinson's Quango/ Instrumental/ To The End/ Fade Away/ Stereotypes/ Supa Shoppa/ Girls And Boys/ Country House/ He Thought Of Cars/ Parklife/ Globe Alone/ The Universal
Recording: Excellent stereo. Soundboard.
Source: Warehouse, Toronto, Canada October 7 1995.
Comments: European CD. Deluxe color cover. Time 56:38.

BON JOVI

CD - DIAMOND RINGS IN OSAKA!
BYE 95303
Tokyo Road/ Born To Be My Baby/ The Boys Are Back In Town/ Everyday/ Runaway/ Raise Your Hands/ Wild Is The Wind/ Living In Sin/ Cadillac Man/ Livin' On A Prayer/ Diamond Ring/ A Little Help From My Friends
Recording: Good to very good. Audience.
Comments: European CD. Deluxe color cover. Picture CD. Time 70:55.

CD - IN THESE DAYS
KOBRA RECORDS KRCR 11
Keep The Faith/ I Don't Like Mondays/ Save The Last Dance For Me/ Lie To Me/ Something For The Pain/ In These Days/ I'll Sleep When I'm Dead/ Livin' On A Prayer/ Wanted Dead Or Alive/ Someday I'll Be Saturday Night/ In These Days/ Blood Money/ It's Only Rock 'N' Roll/ Blaze Of Glory/ Startin' All Over Again
Recording: Excellent stereo. Soundboard.
Source: Tracks 1-6 TV Show, Paris March 22 1996. Tracks 7-10 acoustic set, Hard Rock Cafe NYC October 28 1995. Track 11 acoustic version, Maidoval Studios March 5 1996. Tracks 12-13 New Jersey December 20 1993. Track 14 New Jersey '92. Track 15 unreleased song.
Comments: European CD. Time 71:50.

CD - LIVE AT WEMBLEY 1995
TD001/2
CD1: Wild In The Streets/ Keep The Faith/ Blood On Blood/ Always/ I'd Die For You/ Blaze Of Glory/ Runaway/ Dry County/ Lay Your Hands No Me/ I'll Sleep When I'm Dead, Jumpin' Jack Flash
CD2: Bad Medicine/ Bed Of Roses/ Hey God/ These Days/ Rockin' All Over The World/ I Don't Like Mondays/ Wanted Dead Or Alive/ Stranger In This Town/ Someday I'll Be Saturday Night/ This Ain't A Love Song
Recording: Excellent stereo. Soundboard.
Source: Wembly, London June 25 '95.
Comments: European CD. Deluxe color cover.

CD - LIVE 20. 12. '93 NEW JERSEY
DEAD DOG RECORDS SE 444
Keep The Faith/ Blaze Of Glory/ In These Arms/ You Give Love A Bad Name/ Born To Be My Baby/ I'll Sleep When I'm Dead/ Blood On Blood/ Bad Medicine/ Shout/ Livin' On A Prayer/ I'll Be There For You/ I'd Die For You/ Wild In The Streets
Recording: Excellent stereo. Soundboard.
Source: New Jersey '93.
Comments: European CD. Deluxe color cover. Time 74:33.

CD - RUNAWAY FROM TOKYO
B-J: ONE/TWO
CD1: Lay Your Hands On Me/ Bad Medicine/ Hey God/ You Give Love A Bad Name/ Runaway/ I'll Be There For You/ Something To Believe In/ Blood On Blood/ Wanted Dead Or Alive/ I'd Die For You/ In These Arms/ Something For The Pain
CD2: Someday I'll Be Saturday Night/ I'll Sleep When I'm Dead (includes Brown Sugar)/ Keep The Faith/ Always/ Blaze Of Glory/ My Guitar Lies Bleeding In My Arms/ Diamond Ring/ Damned/ Livin' On A Prayer
Recording: Excellent stereo. Soundboard.
Source: Yokohama Stadium, Yokohama, Japan May 19 1996.
Comments: Japanese CD. Deluxe color cover. Time CD1 70:37. CD2 68:11.

CD - SEOUL STREET
DR. GIG DGCD 047-2
CD1: Introduction/ You Give Love A Bad Name/ Wild In The Streets/ Keep The Faith/ I'd Die For You/ Diamond Ring/ Bed Of Roses/ Stranger In This Town/ Blaze Of Glory/ Dry County/ Blood On Blood
CD2: Lay Your Hands On Me/ I'll Sleep When I'm Dead, Jumping Jack Flash, Glory Days/ Bad Medicine, Shout/ Always/ Livin' On A Prayer/ Guitar Solo (Acoustic)/ Wanted Dead Or Alive/ Rockin' All Over The World/ Someday I'll Be Saturday Night
Recording: Excellent stereo. Soundboard.
Source: The Olympic Stadium, Seoul, Korea May 10 '95.
Comments: European CD. Deluxe color cover.

CD - THOSE DAYS
SBC 021
Livin On A Prayer/ Just Like A Woman/ Bed Of Roses/ Dead Or Alive/ Sleep When I'm Dead/ Saturday Night/ Mrs. Robinson/ Keep The Faith/ These Days/ On A Prayer/ Hey God
Recording: Excellent stereo. Soundboard.

BLACK FLAG

The Complete 1982 Demos Plus More!

Chuck Dukowski
Chuck Biscuits
Greg Ginn
Dez Cadena
Henry Rollins

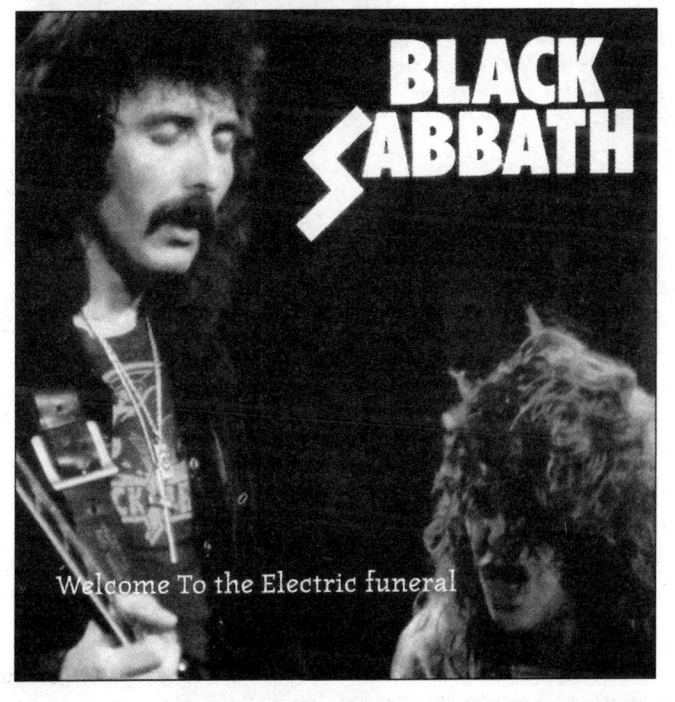

BON JOVI

Source: Tracks 1-4 The Great Music Experience, Japan 1994. Tracks 5-6 Covent Garden, London 1995. Tracks 7-9, TFI 1996. Track 10 Most Wanted, MTV 1995. Track 11 MTV European Music Awards 1995.
Comments: European CD. Deluxe color cover. Time 51:16.

CD - YO-KO-HA-MA
OXYGEN OXY 097.98
CD1: Intro, Lay Your Hands On Me (6:26)/ Bad Medicine (4:58)/ Hey God (6:36)/ You Give Love A Bad Name (3:41)/ Runaway (5:01)/ I'll Be There For You (8:21)/ Something To Believe (6:53)/ Blood On Blood (7:50)/ Wanted Dead Or Alive (4:51)/ I'd Die For You (5:28)/ In These Arms (4:54)/ Something For The Pain (5:33)
CD2: Someday I'll Be Saturday Night (6:26)/ I'll Sleep When I'm Dead, Brown Sugar, I'll Sleep When I'm Dead, (Reprise) (10:48)/ Keep The Faith (6:45)/ Always (7:06)/ Blaze Of Glory (5:43)/ These Days (7:13)/ My Guitar Lies Bleeding In My Arms (6:14)/ Diamond Ring (0:53)/ Damned (5:55)/ Livin On A Prayer (6:52)/ Imagine, Give Peace A Chance (6:06)*
Recording: Excellent stereo. Soundboard.
Source: Yokohama Stadium, Yokohama, Japan May 19 1996. *Jon Bon Jovi and Ritchie Sambora The Rock 'N' Roll Hall Of Fame, Cleveland September 2 1995.
Comments: European CD.

BOSTON

CD - LONG TIME
REAL THING RTCD-025/026
CD1: Star Spangled Banner/ Rock And Roll Band/ Peace Of Mind/ Still In Love/ Cool the Engines/ Surrender To Me/ Holly Ann/ Livin' For You/ Don't Look Back/ The Journey/ unknown/ More Than Feeling/ Guitar & Drum Jam/ A Man/ I'll Never Be
CD2: Amanda/ We're Ready/ The Launch Countdown/ Walkin' At Night/ Walk On/ Get Organized/ Walk On (Some More)/ What's Your Name/ To Be A Man/ I Think I Like It/ Party/ Foreplay, Long Time
Recording: Very good. Audience.
Source: Jones Beach, New York June 6 1995.

CD - MORE THAN THIRD STAGE
CD1: Rock 'N' Roll Band/ Peace Of Mind/ Guitar Solo, Don't Look Back/ The Journey/ More Than A Feeling/ Amanda/ We're Ready/ The Launch/ Cool Engines/ My Destination/ A New World/ To Be A Man/ I Think I Like It/ Can'tcha Say
CD2: Still In Love/ Hollyann/ Foreplay, Long Time/ Feelin' Satisfied/ Used To Bad News/ Let Me Take You Home Tonight
Recording: Very good to excellent stereo. Soundboard.
Source: Oakland, CA July 25 1987.
Comments: Japanese CD. Deluxe color cover. Time CD1 62:32. CD2 40:21.

BOWIE, DAVID

CD - A CAT FROM LONDON
MUSIC HOUSE 003
Hang On To Yourself/ Ziggy Stardust/ Changes/ Moonage Daydream/ John, I'm Only Dancing/ Watch That Man/ Jean Genie/ Time/ Five Years/ Let's Spend The Night Together/ Starman/ Suffragette City/ Rock'N'Roll Suicide/ Round And Round
Source: Japan 1973.
Comments: Japanese CD.

CD - A SEMI-ACOUSTIC LOVE AFFAIR
GOLD STANDARD
Amsterdam/ God Knows I'm Good/ Buzz The Fuzz/ Karma Man/ London Bye Ta-Ta/ An Occasional Dream/ Janine/ Wild Eyed Boy From Freecloud/ Width Of A Circle/ Unwashed And Slightly Dazed/ Fill Your Heart/ Prettiest Star/ Cygnet Committee/ Looking For A Friend/ How Lucky You Are/ Shadow Man/ I've Got Lightning/ Rupert The Riley/ Tired Of My Life/ Don't Sit Down, Andy Warhol/ This Boy
Recording: Tracks very good soundboard. Tracks 14-20 excellent soundboard. Track 21 good.
Source: Tracks 1-13, BBC Radio, recorded at the Paris Cinema Theatre, London February 5 '70. Tracks 14-20 studio out-takes '69-'71. Track 21 live in Bristol, England.
Comments: Japanese CD. Deluxe color cover. Time 74:57.

CD - BOWIE HITS THE ROAD IN JAPAN
THE PORE THE SOUL PRODUCTION PTS 061/2
CD1: The Motel (8:30)/ Look Back In Anger (4:38)/ The Hearts Filthy Lesson (5:16)/ Scary Monsters (And Super Creeps) (5:28)/

Outside (5:10)/ Aladdin Sane (5:06)/ Andy Warhol (3:52)/ The Voyeur Of Utter Destruction (As Beauty) (5:30)/ The Man Who Sold The World (3:31)/ A Small Plot Of Land (7:35)/ Stranger When We Meet (5:00)/ Diamond Dogs (4:470/ Hallo Spaceboy
CD2: Breaking Glass (3:57)/ We Prick On You (4:19)/ Jump They Say (3:32)/ Lust For Life (6:05)/ Under Pressure (3:58)/ Heroes (6:33)/ My Death (10:03)/ White Light, White Heat (4:08)/ Moonage Daydream (6:26)/ All The Young Dudes (4:10)/ I Have Not Been Oxford Town (4:20)/ Baby Universal (3:31)/ Teenage Wildlife (6:46)
Source: Budokan Hall, Tokyo June 5 1996. CD2 tracks 11, 12, 13 Budokan Hall, Tokyo June 4 1996.
Comments: Japanese CD.

CD - DRIVE IN SATURDAY
RAG DOLL MUSIC RDM-942013A/B
CD1: Intro Music/ Hang Onto Yourself/ Ziggy Stardust/ Changes/ Superman/ Life On Mars/ Five Years/ Space Oddity/ Andy Warhol/ Drive In Saturday
CD2: Width Of A Circle/ John, I'm Only Dancing/ Moonage Daydream/ Waiting For The Man/ Jean Genie/ Suffragette City/ Rock & Roll Suicide/ Outro Music
Recording: Good. Audience.
Source: Pirates World, Dania, Florida 1972.
Comments: Japanese CD. Color cover.

CD - EXPOSED LIVE 1996
REAL LIVE DB-9601/2
CD1: Beginning (Sequence)/ Look Back In Anger/ Scary Monsters/ Diamond Dogs/ The Hearts Filthy Lesson/ Outside/ Alladin Sane/ Andy Warhol/ The Voyeur Of Utter Destruction (As Beauty)/ The Man Who Sold The World/ Telling Lies (previously unreleased)/ Baby Universal/ Hallo Spaceboy/ Breaking Grass/ We Prick You/ Jump They Say/ Lust For Life
CD2: Under Pressure/ Heroes/ White Light, White Heat/ Moonage Daydream/ All The Young Dudes/ *Hallo Spaceboy/ ^The Hearts Filthy Lesson/ #Boys Keep Swinging/ +The Man Who Sold The World/ +Strangers When We Meet/ ~The Voyeur Of Utter Destruction (As Beauty)/ ~Hallo Spaceboy/ ~Under Pressure, Warszawa
Recording: Excellent stereo. Soundboard
Source: Lorely Germany Rockpalast Festival 1996 Except *Top Of The Pops-UK ^Late Show-US TV #White Room-UK +Later With Jools Holland Show-UK ~Kanel-Holland TV.
Comments: Japanese CD. Deluxe color cover. Picture CD. Time CD1 74:00. CD2 67:18.

CD - 50TH BIRTHDAY BASH
BPCD 973282-1/2
CD1: Little Wonder/ Heart's Filthy Lesson/ Scary Monsters (with Frank Black)/ Fashion (with Frank Black)/ Telling Lies/ Hallo Spaceboy (with The Foo Fighters)/ Seven Years In Tibet (with Dave Grohl)/ The Man Who Sold The World/ The Last Thing You Should Do (with Robert Smith)/ Quicksand (with Robert Smith)/ Battle For Britain/ The Voyeur Of Utter Destruction (As Beauty)/ I'm Afraid Of Americans
CD2: Looking For Satellites/ Under Pressure/ Heroes/ Queen Bitch (with Lou Reed)/ I'm Waiting For The Man (with Lou Reed)/ Dirty Boulevard (with Lou Reed)/ White Light White Heat (with Lou Reed)/ Moonage Daydream/ Happy Birthday To Bowie/ All The Young Dudes (with Billy Corgan)/ The Jean Genie (with Billy Corgan)/ Space Oddity/ I Can't Read (Dressing Room)/ Repetition (Dressing Room)
Recording: Excellent stereo. Soundboard.
Source: Madison Square Garden, New York January 9 1997.
Comments: European CD. Deluxe color cover. Time CD1 66:27. CD2 62:11.

CD - FUCK YOU ALL NIGHT LONG
MIDNIGHT BEAT MB CD 103
Introduction (1:23)/ Aladdin Sane (4:33)/ The Jean Genie (4:58)/ Can't Stop Loving You (2:35)/ I Can't Read (5:38)/ The Man Who Sold The World (4:35)/ Heroes (6:41)/ Aladdin Sane (5:05)/ The Jean Genie (6:35)/ I Can't Read (5:40)/ The Man Who Sold The World (4:36)/ China Girl (5:05)/ Heroes (6:15)/ White Light, White Heat (4:08)/ Helpless (7:31)
Source: Shoreline Amphitheatre, Mountainview, CA. Tracks 1-8 October 19 1996. Tracks 9-16 October 20 1996.
Comments: European CD.

CD - THE LAST HERO
TUBE TUCD 010
Look Back In Anger (4:39)/ Scary Monsters (And Super Creeps) (5:24)/ Diamond Dogs

BOWIE, DAVID

(4:53)/ The Hearts Filthy Lesson (5:10)/ Outside (5:10)/ Aladdin Sane (4:47)/ Andy Warhol (3:42)/ The Voyeur Of Utter Destruction (As Beauty) (5:27)/ The Man Who Sold The World (3:42)/ Hello Spaceboy (5:18)/ Jump They Say (3:24)/ Under Pressure (4:00)/ Heroes (5:26)/ Moonage Daydream (5:42)/ All The Young Dudes (3:49)
Recording: Excellent.
Source: Loreley Festival, Germany, June 22 1996.

CD - LUST FOR LIFE
KISS THE STONE KTS 601
Heroes (5:00)/ Strangers When We Meet (5:06)/ Lust For Life (6:05)/ All The Young Dudes (3:43)/ White Light White Heat (3:47)/ Moonage Daydream (5:44)/ Look Back In Anger (4:43)/ Man Who Sold The World (3:40)/ Strangers When We Meet (4:31)/ Hallo Space Boy (5:13)/ We Prick You (4:22)/ Teenage Wildlife (6:42)/ Look Back In Anger (4:44)/ New Song (5:20)/ Young Girl (4:43)
Recording: Excellent stereo. Soundboard.
Source: Phoenix Festival, England, July 18 1996. Wembley Arena, England November 18 1996. Lorelei Festival, Germany June 22 1996. Tracks 3-6 - rare live songs.
Comments: European CD. Deluxe color cover. Picture CD.

CD - NITE LIFE
MOONRAKER 087/88
The Motel/ Look Back In Anger/ The Hearts Filthy Lesson/ Scary Monsters/ The Voyeur Of Utter Destruction/ I Have Not Been To Oxford Town/ We Prick You/ White Light, White Heat/ Outside/ Andy Warhol/ The Man Who Sold The World/ A Small Plot Of Land/ Strangers When We Meet/ Diamond Dogs/ Hallo Spaceboy
CD2: Breaking Glass/ Nite Flights/ Introductions/ Teenage Wildlife/ Under Pressure/ Moonage Daydream/ Look Back In Anger/ The Man Who Sold The World/ Strangers When We Meet/ Hallo Spaceboy/ We Prick You/ Teenage Wildlife/ The Man Who Sold The World/ Hallo Spaceboy
Recording: Very good to excellent. Audience. CD2 tracks 7-12 Excellent. Audience. Tracks 13-14 Excellent stereo. Soundboard.
Source: Hamburg January 25 '96. CD2 tracks 7-12 Wembley Arena, London November 14 '95. Tracks 13-14 Swedish TV January 20 '96.
Comments: European CD. Deluxe color cover. Time CD1 74:01. CD2 65:44.

CD - THE PHOENIX
MOONRAKER 172
Heroes/ Strangers When We Meet/ Lust For Life/ All The Young Dudes/ White Light, White Heat/ Moonage Daydream/ The Voyeur Of Utter Destruction/ Under Pressure/ The Man Who Sold The World/ Hallo Spaceboy/ Strangers When We Meet
Recording: Excellent.
Source: Tracks 1-6 The Phoenix Festival, England July 18 1996. Tracks 7-11 Ratatata, French TV, Paris December 10 1996.
Comments: European CD.

CD - TELLING LIES
MOONRAKER 162/3
CD1: Look Back In Anger/ Scary Monsters/ Diamond Dogs/ The Heart's Filthy Lesson/ Outside/ Aladdin Sane/ Andy Warhol/ Voyeur Of Utter Destruction (As Beauty)/ The Man Who Sold The World/ I'm Telling Lies/ Baby Universal/ Hallo Spaceboy
CD2: Breaking Glass/ We Prick You/ Jump They Say/ Lust For Life/ Under Pressure/ Heroes/ Introductions/ White Light, White Heat/ Moonage Daydream/ All The Young Dudes
Recording: Excellent.
Source: The Loreley Festival, Germany, June 22 1996.
Comments: European CD.

CD - WHERE IS BLOODY HERMANN
TABORSKY RECORDS TAB002
Look Back In Anger/ Hearts Filthy Lesson/ Scary Monsters/ Outside/ Andy Warhol/ The Man Who Sold The World/ A Small Plot Of Land/ Strangers When We Meet/ Hallo Spaceboy/ Breaking Glass/ We Prick You/ Teenage Wildlife/ Under Pressure/ Moonage Daydream
Recording: Good to very good. Audience.
Source: Wien Stadhalle, Vienna 4/2/96.
Comments: European CD. Deluxe color cover. Picture CD. Time 69:47.

CD - WITH LOU REED
DB72-5-4 / DB72-7-8
CD1: Hang On To Yourself/ Ziggy Stardust/ Superman/ Queen Bitch/ Song For Bob

Dylan/ Changes/ Starman/ Five Years/ Space Oddity/ Andy Warhol/ Amsterdam/ I Feel Free/ Moonage Daydream/ White Light, White Heat/ Got To Get Job/ Suffragette City/ Rock 'N Roll Suicide/ Waiting For My Man
CD2: Introduction/ Hung On To Yourself/ Ziggy Stardust/ Life On Mars/ Superman/ Starman/ Changes/ Five Years/ Space Oddity/ Andy Warhol/ Amsterdam/ I Feel Free/ Moonage Daydream/ White Light, White Heat*/ Waiting For My Man*/ Sweet Jane*/ Suffragette City
Recording: Good audience. CD2 fair to good audience.
Source: CD1 Kingston Poly, London May 6 1972. CD2 Royal Festival Hall, London July 8 1972. *With Lou Reed.
Comments: Japanese CD. Deluxe color cover. Time CD1 74:39. CD2 71:52.

CD - ZIGGY WITH SOUL
DANCING HORSE DH-001
My Death (previously unreleased live recording from The Music Hall, Boston October10 1972)/ Sorrow*/ Time*/ Everything Alright*/ Space Oddity*/ I Can't Explain*/ The Jean Genie*/ 1984, Dodo*/ I Got You Babe (duet with Marienne Faithful 1973)/ Rebel Rebel (special dry mix made for BBC's 'Top Of The Pops' broadcast in 1974)/ Dodo (duet with Lulu, original full length version recorded late 1973)/ Can You Hear Me**/ Right**/ Somebody Up There Likes Me**/ Golden Years (dry mix made for BBC's 'Top Of The Pops' broadcast in 1975)
Recording: Excellent. Soundboard.
Source: *Alternative recordings of 'The 1980 Floor Show', Marquee Club, London October 18-20 1973. **'Young Americans' sessions alternative versions recorded at Sigma Sound Studios 1975.
Comments: Japanese CD. Deluxe color cover. Time 69:26.

BROUGHTON, EDGAR BAND

CD - LIVE ON BBC-72
ALMO REC.
Intro/ Side By side/ Call Me A Liar/ Poppy/ The Rake/ Gone Blue/ Chilly Morning Mama/ Band Intro/ I Got Mad/ Its Not You
Source: Live on BBC 1972.
Comments: Time 54:58.

BROWN, JAMES

CD - A FUNKY GOOD TIME
MOONRAKER 151
Intro/ Brother Rapp/ Ain't It Funky/ Georgia On My Mind/ Bewildered/ Get Up (I Feel Like Being A) Sex Machine/ Try Me (I Need You)/ Papa's Got A Brand New Bag, I Got The Feelin'/ Give It Up Or Turnit A Loose/ It's A Man's Man's Man's World/ Please Please Please/ Get Up (I Feel Like Being A) Sex Machine (Return)Super Bad/ Get Up, Get Into It And Get Involved/ Soul Power, Outro
Recording: Excellent.
Source: The Olympia, Paris March 8 1971.
Comments: European CD.

BROWNE, JACKSON

CD - ALIVE AND KICKING
HOME RECORDS HR 5988-3
I'm Alive (6:07)/ World In Motion (5:14)/ Everywhere I Go (5:42)/ My Problem Is You (5:36)/ In The Shape Of A Heart (6:14)/ Late For The Sky (5:56)/ Your Bright Baby Blues (6:08)/ Our Lady Of The Well (8:14)/ Too Many Angels (6:51)/ For Every Man (3:35)/ Sky Blue And Black (6:13)/ The Pretender (6:34)/ I Am A Patriot (4:26)
Recording: Excellent. Audience.
Source: The Universal Amphitheatre, Los Angeles August 31 1994.
Comments: European CD. Deluxe color cover. Picture CD.

CD - AMSTERDAM 1976
DAYS OF HARVEST DH-002
The Fuse/ Farther On/ For Everyman/ The Only Child/ Late For The Sky/ Fountain Of Sorrow/ Something Fine/ For A Dancer/ Rock Me On The Water/ The Load And The Sky/ Before The Deluge/ Our Lady Of The Well
Recording: Very good. Soundboard. Hiss.
Source: Amsterdam, Netherlands March 12 '76.
Comments: Japanese CD. Deluxe color cover. Time 73:14.

CD - DREAMING OF BABYRON
DAYS OF HARVEST DH-001
A Child In These Hills/ Rock Me On The Water/ Take It Easy/ Our Lady Of The Well/ For A Dancer/ Ready Or Not/ Fountain Of Sorrow/ For Everyman/ Walking Slow/

Doctor My Eyes/ These Days/ The Load And The Sky
Recording: Excellent. Soundboard.
Source: Tulane University, New Orleans, LA March 2 1975.
Comments: Japanese CD. Deluxe color cover. Time 69:48.

BRUFORD, BILL

CD - THE BRUFORD TAPES II
DYNAMITE STUDIO 94M066
Hell's Bells/ Sample And Hold/ Fainting In Coils/ Forever Until Sunday/ Travels With Myself - And Someone else/ The Sahara Of Snow part 1/ The Sahara Of Snow part 2/ Beelzebub
Source: Ol' Man Rivers 1979
Comments: Japanese CD.

CD - FAINTING IN COILS
OFF BEAT RECORDS XXCD 17
Hell's Bells/ Sample and Hold/ Fainting In Coils . Back To The Begging/ Fainting In Coils/ Forever Until Sunday/ Joe Frazier/ Travels With Myself/ And Someone Else/ Breelzebub/ Seems Like A Lifetime Ago/ Five G/ Feels Good To Me/ Back To The Beginning
Source: Roxy Theater, LA 1979. Tracks 10-11 BBC 1978.
Comments: Japanese CD.

CD - THE STONE CLUB TORNADO
HIGHLAND HL 021#B1
Hell's Bells/ Joe Frazier/ Land's End/ The Sliding Floor/ The Sahara Of Snow (Part 1)/ Gothic 17/ Fainting In Coils/ Age Of Information
Source: The Stone Club, San Francisco CA 1980.
Comments: Japanese CD.

BUFFALO TOM

SPRING FLOOR
KISS THE STONE KTS 527
Velvet Roof (4:13)/ Clobbered (3:36)/ Kitchen Door (3:16)/ Sparklers (4:50)/ Summer (4:07)/ Tangerine (2:34)/ When You Discover (2:18)/ Late At Night (4:11)/ Your Stripes (3:24)/ Latest Monkey (2:46)/ Mineral (4:57)/ Treehouse (4:21)/ I'm Allowed (4:34)/ Impossible (3:02)/ Crutch (5:31)
Recording: Excellent stereo. Soundboard.

Source: The Commodore Ballroom, Vancouver, Canada October 15 '95.
Comments: European CD. Deluxe color cover. Picture CD.

BUFFETT, JIMMY

CD - COCKTAILS AT SUNRISE
FLOOD RECORDINGS FLD 1006/7
CD1: The Wino And I Know/ Pencil Thin Moustache/ They Don't Dance Like Carmen No More/ Tryin' To Reason With Hurricane Season/ Fuji Wuji Song/ My Whole World Lies Waiting (Behind Door #3)/ Livingston's Gone To Texas/ Railroad Lady/ Dallas/ A Pirate Looks At Forty/ Cousin In Miami/ Come Monday/ Land Fog/ Volcano
CD2: Cheeseburger In Paradise/ Sunny Afternoon, Summertime/ In The Shelter/ Why Don't We Get Drunk/ Instrumental (Coral Reefer Band)/ Grapefruit, Juicy Fruit/ Island/ Son Of A Son Of A Sailor/ Changes In Latitude, Changes In Attitude/ The Pascagoula Run/ Livingston's Saturday Night/ Fins/ Margaritaville/ Cheeseburger In Paradise/ Brown-Eyed Girl/ Defying Gravity
Source: Tracks 1-10 San Francisco 1973. Tracks 11-14 New York 1994. CD2 New York 1994.
Comments: European CD. Deluxe color cover.

BURDON, ERIC AND THE ANIMALS

CD - LIVE IN POUGHKEEPSIE
THE SWINGIN' PIG TSP-CD-219-2
CD1: It's Too Late/ Melt Down/ Don't Let Me Be Misunderstood/ The Night/ My Favorite Enemy/ Trying To Get You/ Loose Change/ Just Can't Get Enough/ I'm Crying/ No John No/ Bring It On Home To Me/ Prisoner Of The Light
CD2: Love Is For All Time/ Heart Attack/ House Of The Rising Sun/ Hard Times/ Being There/ It's My Life/ Don't Bring Me Down/ Young Girls/ Boom Boom/ We've Gotta Get Out Of This Place
Recording: Excellent. Soundboard.
Source: Puoghkeepsie, NY '83.
Comments: European CD.
Time CD1 53:26. CD2 48:50.

BUSH

CD - A GREEDY FLY IN TOWN
LHJ 86348
A Tendency To Start Fires/ Personal Holloway/ Machine Head/ Insect Kin/ Greddy Fly/ Comedown/ History/ X-Girlfriend/ All Its About/ Cold Contagious/ Bonedriven/ Glycerine/ Bomb/ Everything Zen/ Swallowed/ Broken TV
Recording: Excellent stereo. Soundboard.
Source: Mortinhal, Groningen February 25 1997.
Comments: European CD. Deluxe color cover. Time 71:53.

CD - BROTHER ZEN'S DINER
BLIZZARD RECORDINGS BLZD125
Alien/ Monkey/ Machine Head/ Everything Zen/ Give It All Away/ X-Girlfriend/ Come Down/ Little Things/ Machine Head/ Everything Zen/ Come Down/ Bomb/ Glycerine
Recording: Excellent stereo. Soundboard.
Source: Tracks: 1-8 Shoreline Amphitheatre, Mountain View, CA June 4 1995. Tracks 9-13 KROQ acoustic X-Mas, Los Angeles, CA December 17 1995.
Comments: European CD. Deluxe color cover. Time 75:04.

CD - THE CROSS
MOONRAKER 177
Monkey/ Machinehead/ Comedown/ Broken TV/ Comedown/ Ex-Girlfriend/ Bubbles/ Swim/ Little Things/ Glycerine/ The Cross/ Everything Zen/ Bonus tracks: Machinehead/ Interview
Recording: Excellent. Soundboard.
Source: Tacoma Dome, Tacoma, Washington April 26 1996. Track 12 MTV Video Music Awards, Radio City Music Hall, New York September 5 1996.
Comments: European CD.

CD - OVERHEAT
OXYGEN OXY 052
Monkey (5:33)/ Old (3:11)/ Testosterone (4:32)/ Bomb (5:27)/ Little Things (6:12)/ Swim (7:09)/ Comedown (5:43)/ Machinehead (4:54)/ Bubbles (3:39)/ Everything Zen (7:15)/ Glycerine (4:26)/ Everything Zen (5:24)/ Swim (5:03)
Recording: Excellent stereo. Soundboard.
Source: Tracks 1-11 The Warehouse In Toronto, Canada August 15 '95. Tracks 12-13 The Splash Club, London, UK March '95.
Comments: European CD. Picture CD.

CD - TESTOSTERONE
TORNADO TOR024
Body/ Monkey/ It's Always Going To Be This Way/ Everything Zen/ Janie Jones/ X-Girlfriend/ Testosterone/ Swim/ Come Down/ Give It Up/ Little Things/ Believe In You/ Machinehead
Recording: Good to very good. Audience.
Source: Rendon Inn, New Orleans March 15 '95.
Comments: European CD. Deluxe color cover. Time 68:41.

CD - WORLD DOMINATION
MOONRAKER 207
Machinehead/ Greedy Fly/ Little Things/ Personal Halloway/ Comedown/ Insect Kin/ Swallowed/ A Tendancy To Start Fires/ Glycerine/ Everything Zen/ Interview
Recording: Excellent stereo. Soundboard.
Source: The Much Music TV Studios, Toronto, Canada November19 1996.
Comments: European CD. Deluxe color cover. Time 62:11.

BYRDS, THE

CD - DOIN' ALRIGHT FOR OLD PEOPLE
THE SWINGING PIG RECORDS TSP-CD-217
Don't You Write Her Off/ Crazy Ladies/ Train Leaves Here This Morning/ Back For Money/ Release Me Girl/ Fair And Tender Ladies/ Chestnut Mare/ Mr. Tambourine Man/ Feelin' Higher/ Turn Turn Turn/ You Ain't Goin' Nowhere/ Knockin' On Heaven's Door/ So You Want To Be A Rock 'N' Roll Star/ Eight Miles High/ Bye Bye, Baby/ 5D (Fifth Dimension)
Recording: Excellent. Soundboard.
Source: Bottom Line Club, New York City October 1977.
Comments: European CD. Time 64:09.

BYRNE, DAVID

CD - NO TITLES PLEASE
CRYSTAL CAT RECORDS CC 349/50
CD1: Intro Drums/ A Long Time Ago/ God's Child/ My Love Is You/ Girls On My Mind/ And She Was/ Road To Nowhere/ A Walk In The Dark/ (Nothing But) Flowers/ This Must

Be The Place (Naive Melody)/ Don't Worry About The Government/ Lilies Of The Valley/ Stay Up Late/ Sad Song/ I Zimbra/ Strange Ritual/ Empire/ Back In The Box CD2: Once In A Life Time/ Angels/ You & Eye/ Buck Naked/ Psycho Killer/ Love - Building On Fire/ Burning Down The House/ She's Mad/ Burning Down The House/ Sympathy For The Devil/ Heaven/ (Nothing But) Flowers/ Take Me To The River/ Blind/ Psycho Killer
Recording: Excellent.
Source: Stockholm, Sweden, October 2 1994.
Comments: European CD.
Time CD1 75:54. CD2 74:28.

C

CARDIGANS

CD - TRAVELLING WITH CHARLEY
ZA 63
Introduction/ Travelling With Charley/ Hey! Get Out Of My Way/ Daddy's Car/ Gordon's Gardenparty/ Sick & Tired/ Plain Parade/ Tomorrow/ In The Afternoon, The Boys Are Back In Town, In The Afternoon/ Over The Water/ Step On Me/ After All.../ Carnival/ Fine/ Celia Inside (Encore 1)/ Rise And Shine*/ Sabbath Bloody Sabbath**
Recording: Very good. Audience.
Source: Air West, Shibuya July 13 1995. *Air West, Shibuya July 12 1995. **Club Quattro, Shibuya July 9 1995.
Comments: Japanese CD.

CAREY, MARIAH

CD - OUT IN JAPAN
OXYGEN OXY 083
Emotions/ Open Arms/ Forever/ I Don't Wanna Cry/ Fantasy/ Always Be My Baby/ Underneath The Stars/ Without You/ Make It Happen/ Just Be Good To Me/ Dreamlover/ Vision Of Love/ Hero/ Anytime You Need A Friend/ All I Want For Christmas Is You
Recording: Excellent stereo. Soundboard.
Source: Tokyo Dome, Japan March 7 '96.
Comments: European CD. Picture CD.
Time 74:01

CASH, JOHNNY

CD - AMERICAN OUTTAKES
EMPIRE RECORDS EMO7
What On Earth (2:13)/ The Drifter (2:52)/ I Witnessed A Crime (2:36)/ Banks Of The Ohio (4:44)/ The Next Time I'm In Town (2:28)/ Breaking Bread (3:27)/ To Beat The Devil (4:26)/ Friends In California (1:57)/ The Caretaker (1:55)/ The Wonder Of You (2:45)/ East Virginia Blues (2:36)/ Bury Me Not (take 2) (3:51)/ Old Chunk Of Coal (1:59)/ Go On Blue (2:21)/ Flesh And Blood (2:55)
Recording: Excellent.
Source: Rick Rubin's living room, Los Angeles, CA May 17-20 1993.

CAST

CD - LET IT IN
KISS THE STONE KTS 576
Back Of My Mind/ Sandstorm/ Mankind/ Walkaway/ Finetime/ Mirror Me/ Alright/ History/ Follow Me Down/ Back Of My Mind/ Sandstorm/ Mankind/ Finetime Reflections/ Alright/ Tell It Like It Is/ History/ Back Of My Mind/ Sandstorm/ Finetime
Recording: Excellent stereo. Soundboard.
Source: Leeds, UK April 4 1996 and London October 30 1995.
Comments: European CD.

CAVE, NICK AND THE BAD SEEDS

CD - DEAD IS NOT THE END
NC-001
Brother, My Cup Is Empty/ Loverman/ Mercy/ Your Funeral, My Trial/ Where The Wild Roses Grow/ The Weeping Song/ The Mercy Seat/ Nobody's Baby Now/ Knocking On Joe Part 1/2/ City Of Refuge/ From Here To Eternity/ Well Of Misery/ Sad Dark Eyes/ Blind Lemon/ Wanted Man
Source: Koln August 17 1996 and USA 1992.
Comments: European CD. Time 73:31.

CD - RING OF WILD ROSES
KISS THE STONE KTS 622
Brother My Cup Is Empty/ Loverman/ Mercy/ Your Funeral Trail/ Where The Wild Roses Grow/ The Weeping Song/ The Mercy Seat/ Nobody's Baby Now/ Jack The Ripper/ Stagger Lee/ Henry Lee/ Do You Love Me/ Into My Arms/ Where The Wild

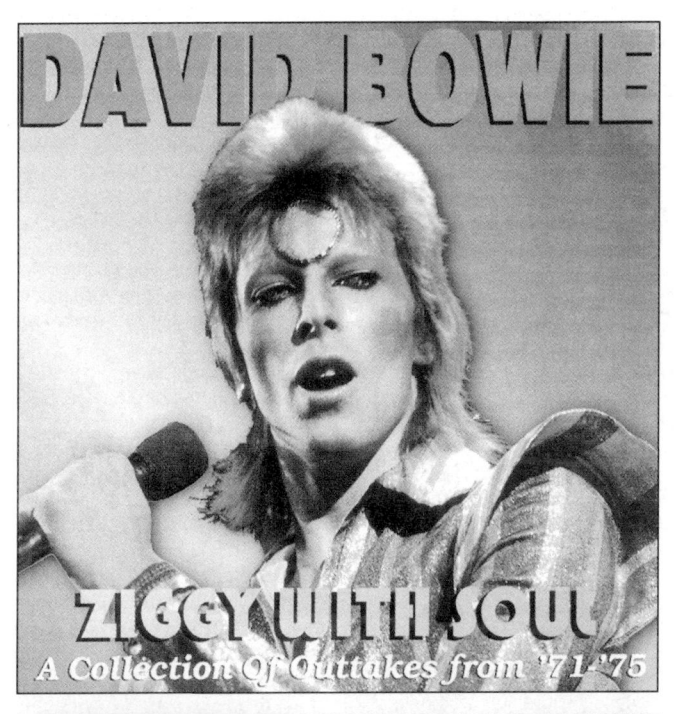

CAVE, NICK AND THE BAD SEEDS

CHICAGO

Roses Grow
Recording: Excellent stereo. Soundboard.
Source: Tracks 1-9 Bizzarre Festival, Germany August 17 1996. Tracks 10-11 White Room, London January 1996. Tracks 12-14 Brixton Academy, London August 14 1996.
Comments: European CD. Picture CD. Time 58:56.

CHICAGO

CD - 4673
Magical Mystery Tour/ State Of The Union/ Just You'An Me/ Aire/ Beginnings/ Re Discovery/ Now That You're Gone/ Saturday In The Park/ Dialogue/ 25 Or 6 To 4/ Make Me Smile
Recording: Very good. Audience.
Source: Tokyo Sapporo, Japan, April 6, '73.
Comments: Japanese CD. Deluxe color cover.

CLAPTON, ERIC

CD - COMPLETE MIAMI REHEARSAL '75
ELEMENT OF CRIME 011/012/013/014
CD1: Motherless Children#1/ Motherless Children#2/ Motherless Children#3/ 1st Unknown#1/ 1st Unknown#2/ 1st Unknown#3/ 1st Unknown#4/ Why Does Love Got Be So Sad#1/ Bell Bottom Blues#1/ Keep On Growing#1/ Knockin' On Heaven's Door#1/ Knockin' On Heaven's Door#2/ Knockin' On Heaven's Door#3/
CD2: Knockin' On Heaven's Door#4/ Eye Sight To The Blind#1/ Eye Sight To The Blind#2/ Eye Sight To The Blind#3/ 1st Unknown#5/ Motherless Child#4/ Teach Me To Be Your Woman#1/ Teach Me To Be Your Woman#2/ Knockin' On Heaven's Door#5/ Knockin' On Heaven's Door#6/ Layla/ Mainline Florida
CD3: Easy Now/ Twist & Shout/ After Midnight/ Jammin#1/ Eye Sight To The Blind#4/ Knockin' On Heaven's Door#7/ It's Too Late/ Well All Right/ Keep On Growing#3/ Bell Bottom Blues#2/ Why Does Love Got Be So Sad#2/ Knockin' On Heaven's Door#8/ Knockin' On Heaven's Door#9
CD4: 2nd Unknown#2/ 2nd Unknown#3/ Jamming#2/ Bell Bottom Blues#3/ Keep On Growing#3/ Jamming#3/ Eye Sight To The Blind#5/ Keep On Growing#4/ Why Does Love Got Be So Sad#3/ Bell Bottom Blues#4/ Knockin' On Heaven's Door#10/ Knockin' On Heaven's Door#11
Recording: Excellent. Soundboard.
Source: Criteria Recording Studios, Miami June 11 1975.
Comments: Japanese CD. Deluxe B&W cover.

CD - CROSSROADS IN LA
BLACKIE 06
Bad Love/ Before You Accuse Me/ Old Love/ Tearing Us Apart/ Cocaine/ A Remark You Made/ Layla/ Instrumental Jam/ Crossroads
Recording: Good to very good. Audience.
Source: Forum, Los Angeles, CA May 1 1990.
Comments: European CD. Deluxe color cover. Time 67:33.

CD - GLASGOW APOLLO
ZEALOT 02
CD1: Layla (7:39)/ Worried Life Blues (6:14)/ Tulsa Time (4:52)/ Early In The Morning (8:10)/ Badge (10:25)/ Wonderful Tonight (8:10)/ Kind-Hearted Woman Blues (5:55)
CD2: Key To The Highway (9:25)/ Further Up The Road (7:06)/ Cocaine (8:08)/ Double Trouble (14:54)/ Crossroads (6:29)
Source: Apollo Theatre, Glasgow, UK November 24 1978.
Comments: Japanese CD.

CD - GUNFIGHT AT THE APOLLO
QR3
Rock Me Baby/ Sweet Little Angel, I'm Tore Down/ Let The Good Times Roll/ Let The Good Times Roll Reprise/ Why Does Love Got To Be So Sad/ Willpower/ Instrumental Jam #1/ Instrumental Jam #2
Recording: Excellent stereo. Soundboard.
Source: Tracks 1-4 Apollo, New York City June 15 1993 with BB King, Albert Collins and Buddy Guy. Track 5 August 1988 with Buckwheat Zydeco. Track 6 February 15/16 1987 with Jack Bruce. Tracks 7-8 Derek And The Dominos Rehearsals, Criteria Studios, Miami, FL August 1970.
Comments: European CD. Deluxe color cover. Time 71:28.

CD - THE LAST REHEARSAL
THE SWINGIN' PIG TSP-CD-183
Hoochie Coochie Man/ I'm Tore Down/ Sinner's Prayer/ Motherless Child/ Malted

Milk/ Born Under A Bad Sign/ Someday After A While/ It Hurts Me Too/ 44/ Five Long Years/ Crossroads/ Ain't Nobody's Business
Recording: Excellent stereo. Soundboard.
Source: 'From The Cradle' tour rehearsals, Manhattan Center Studios, NYC September 28 1994.
Comments: European CD. Time 50:15.

CD - ROYAL ALBERTA
ECRA001/2
CD1: Badge/ Bell Bottom Blues/ Knockin' On Heaven's Door/ Lay Down Sally/ Wonderful Tonight/ I Shot The Sheriff/ Old Love/ Behind The Mask/ White Room/ Sunshine Of Your Love/ The Circus Left Town/ Tears In Heaven
CD2: My Father's Eyes/ Alberta/ Layla/ Reconsider Baby/ Third Degree/ Tearing Us Apart/ Hoochie Coochie Man/ Tore Down/ Have You Ever Loved A Woman/ It Hurts Me Too/ Five Long Years/ Every Day I Have The Blues
Recording: Very good. Audience.
Source: Royal Albert Hall, London February 18 1996.
Comments: European CD.

CD - STANDING AROUND CRYING
ER-9401-2
CD1: Motherless Child/ Malted Milk/ How Long/ Kidman Blues/ Country Jail/ "44"/ Blues Leave Me Alone/ Standing Around Crying/ Hoochie Coochie Man/ It Hurts Me Too/ Blues Before Sunrise/ Third Degree/ Reconsider Baby
CD2: Sinner's Prayer/ I Can't Judge Nobody/ Someday After A While/ I'm Tore Down/ Have You Ever Loved A Woman/ Crosscut Saw/ Five Long Years/ Crossroads/ Groaning The Blues/ Ain't Nobody's Business
Recording: Excellent. Soundboard.
Source: San Francisco, USA, '94.
Comments: Japanese CD. Deluxe b&w cover.

CD - UNSTEADY ROLLIN' MAN
VINTAGE RARE MASTERS VRM-010-11
CD1: Badge/ Milk Cow Blues/ Steady Rollin' Man/ Let It Rain/ Nobody Knows/ I Shot The Sheriff
CD2: Tell The Truth/ I Shot The Sheriff/ Steady Rollin' Man/ Key To The Highway/ Can't Find My Way Home/ Blues Power/ Driftin' Blues/ Layla
Recording: Excellent stereo. Soundboard.
Source: CD1 Festival Hall, Brisbane, Australia April 14 '75. CD2 Opera House, Sydney, Australia April 20 '75.
Comments: Japanese CD. Deluxe color cover.

CLASH

CD - CLASH OVER
SONIC ZOOM SZ 2015/2016
London Calling/ Safe European Home/ Train In Vain/ Washington Bullets/ The Leader/ Spanish Bomb/ The Magnificent Seven/ Guns Of Brixton/ White Man In Hammersmith Palais/ Charlie Don't Surf/ Ivan Meets G. I. Joe/ Brand New Cadillac/ Janie Jones/ Koka Koka/ I Fought The Law/ Somebody Got Murdered/ Clamp Down/ Armagideon Time/ Stay Free/ Clash City Rockers/ Garage Land/ Tommy Gun/ Complete Control/ White Riot
Source: Osaka February 2 1982.
Comments: Japanese CD.

COCTEAU TWINS

CD - PEARLY, PINK & WHITE
TORNADO TOR025
Pure/ Pitch The Baby/ Heaven Or Las Vegas/ For Phoebe Still A Baby/ Know Who You Are/ Road River/ Evangeline/ Whale Tales/ Carolyn's Fingers/ Bluebeard/ Summerhead/ Ice Blink Luck/ Blue Bell Knoll/ Cico Buff/ A Kiss/ Ellamegablast/ Pink
Recording: Good. Audience.
Source: New Orleans February 28 1994.
Comments: European CD. Deluxe color cover. Time 74:38.

CONCRETE BLONDE

CD - ACOUSTIC HUMILIATION
TORNADO TOR-023
Tomorrow, Wendy/ Little Conversations/ You're The Only One/ Carry Me Away/ I Don't Need A Hero/ Skyway/ The Ship Song/ Darkening Of The Light/ Joey/ And I Fell Back Alone/ Nevermore/ Ain't The Kind Of Man I Need/ I'm Going Home/ Debbie Don't Do Dicks/ Whiskey On Your Willy/ Christmas Advice Song/ Mercedes Benz/ Roses Grow
Recording: Very good. Audience.

COOPER, ALICE

Source: Backstage, Seattle, WA December 12 1991.
Comments: European CD. Time 67:30.

COOPER, ALICE

CD - GOES TO CHILE
KISS THE STONE KTS 512
Under My Wheels/ Hey Stupid/ 18/ No More Mr. Nice Guy/ Killer/ Billion Dollar Babies/ I's Me/ Lost In America/ Burn It Down/ Go To Hell, Gutter Cat VS The Jets/ Street Fight, Feed My Frankenstein/ Only Women Bleed/ Welcome To My Nightmare/ Ballad Of Dwight Fry/ Schools Out/ Elected
Recording: Excellent stereo. Soundboard.
Source: Santiago, Chile 7-9-95.
Comments: European CD. Deluxe color cover. Picture CD. Time 73:40.

COODER, RY

CD - DO RE MI
TNT STUDIO 930134
CD1: Low Commotion/ Little Sister/ Go Home Girl/ Let's Have A Ball/ He'll Have To Do/ Jesus On The Maine/ How Can A Poor Man Stand Such Time And Live?/ 13 Question Method/ Dark Is the Night/ Down In Mississippi/ Just A Little Bit
CD2: Do Re Mi/ Across The Borderline/ Down In The Boondocks/ The Very Thing That Makes You Rich/ All Shook Up/ Get Rhythm/ Going Back To Okinawa/ China Gang/ Goodnight Irene
Source: Nakano-Sunplaza, Tokyo, Japan Jun. 29 1988
Comments: Japanese CD.

COSTELLO, ELVIS

CD - BACK WITH A VENGEANCE (VOLUME ONE)
DOBERMAN 043/44
CD1: Opportunity/ New Lace Sleeves/ 13 Steps Lead Down/ Why Can't A Man Stand Alone/ Little Atoms/ Still So Far From The Prize/ Motel Matches/ Veronica/ A Passionate Fight/ Almost Blue/ My Funny Valentine/ Oliver's Army/ Brilliant Mistake/ All This Useless Beauty/ Man Out Of Time/ Distorted Angel/ (I Don't Want To Go To) Chelsea/ Pump It Up
CD2: This Years Girl/ You Belong To Me/ Riot Act/ Accidents Will Happen/ Complicated Shadows/ Indoor Fireworks/ The Other End Of The Telescope/ Human Hands/ Watching The Detectives/ You Bowed Down/ (The Angels Wanna Wear My) Red Shoes/ No Action/ Shipbuilding/ I Want To Vanish/ Shallow Grave/ Allison/ Rocking Horse Road/ (What's So Funny 'Bout) Peace, Love And Understanding
Recording: Very good-excellent. Audience.
Source: Shepherds Bush Empire, London July 26 1996.
Comments: UK CDR.

CD - BACK WITH A VENGEANCE (VOLUME TWO)
DOBERMAN 045/046
CD1: Clown Strike/ Pills And Soap/ The Long Honeymoon/ Poor Fractured Atlas/ Sulky Girls/ Allison Medley-Includes-You Win Again, He'll Have To Go, Tracks Of My Tears, Clowntime Is Over/ Honey Are You Straight Or Are You Blind?/ Just About Glad/ I Don't Know What To Do With Myself/ Beyond Belief/ Clubland/ It's Time/ Possession/ Just A Memory/ King Horse/ Miracle Man
CD2: Unwanted Number/ I Can't Stand Up For Falling Down/ Deep Dark Truthful Mirror/ You'll Never Be A Man/ Black Sails In The Sunset/ Roundhouse Theme/ Pump It Up, Slow Down/ Lipstick Vogue/ I Want You/ London Brilliant Parade/ All The Rage/ Mystery Dance/ God's Comic/ God Give Me Strength/ Almost Ideal Eyes/ Speak Darkly My Angel
Recording: Very good-excellent. Audience.
Source: CD1 tracks 1-6 Shepherds Bush July 5 1996. Tracks 7-12 Roundhouse, London July 6 1996. Tracks 13-16 Shepherds Bush July 12 1996. CD2 tracks 1-2 Shepherds Bush July 12 1996. Tracks 3-13 Roundhouse July 27 1996. Tracks 14-15 Beacon Theatre August 5 1996. Track 16 Beacon Theatre, August 4 1996.
Comments: UK CDR.

CD - MAIN ATTRACTION
KISS THE STONE KTS 598
Accidents Will Happen/ Little Atoms/ Pump It Up/ Why Can't A Man Stand Alone/ Wide Eyed/ Veronica/ Indoor Fireworks/ Pills And Soap/ Banish/ Tongue Is Tied/ All This Useless Beauty/ You Bow Down/ Complicated Shadows/ Watching Detectives/ I Want To Vanish
Recording: Excellent stereo. Soundboard.
Source: Later Show, London 7/6/96. Tracks

8-11 with The Brodsky Quartet.
Comments: European CD. Deluxe color cover. Picture CD.

CD - THE RISE & RISE OF DECLAN MACMANUS
TONE-2 CD004
Mystery Dance/ Waiting For The End Of The World/ Lip Service/ Two Little Hitlers/ The Beat/ Night Rally/ This Years Girl/ No Action/ (I Don't Want To Go To) Chelsea/ Lipstick Vogue/ Watching The Detectives/ Pump It Up/ You Belong To Me/ Paul McCartney Introduces Elvis Costello/ I Almost Had A Weakness*/ The Birds Will Still Be Singing*/ Elvis Costello Introduces Paul McCartney/ One After 909**/ Mistress & Maid**
Recording: Excellent stereo. Soundboard.
Source: Tracks 1-13 WDR Studio Complex, Bremen, Germany June 15 1978. Tracks 14-18 Royal College Of Music March 23 1995.
Comments: European CD. Deluxe color cover. Picture CD. *With The Brodsky Quartet. **With McCartney. Time 62:52.

COUNTING CROWS

CD - FLYING DEMOS
KISS THE STONE KTS 609
Rain King/ Omaha/ Einstein On The Beach (For An Eggman)/ Shallow Days/ Love And Addiction/ Mr. Jones/ Round Here/ 40 Years/ Margery Dreams Of Horses (And So Do I)/ Bulldog/ Lightning/ We're Only Love
Recording: Excellent stereo. Soundboard.
Source: Demos From '91.
Comments: European CD. Picture CD. Time 52:44.

CRAMPS

CD - TEENAGE WEREWOLF
CENTERFOLD 321
Twist And Shout/ All Tore Up/ Mystery Plane/ T.V. Set/ Rockin' Bones/ What's Behind The Mask/ Uranium Rock/ Under The Wires/ Teenage Werewolf/ Sunglasses After Dark/ Jungle Hop/ Mad Daddy/ Hurricane Fighter Plane/ I'm Cramped/ Drug Train/ Under The Wires/ Garbage Man/ Louie, Louie/ Mule Skinner Blues/ Journey To The Center Of A Girl/ All Women Are Bad/ Drug Train
Recording: Tracks 1-12 and 19-22 Excellent. Soundboard. Tracks 13-18 very good audience.
Source: Tracks 1-12 studio outtakes 1979. Tracks 13-14 Max's Kansas City, NYC January 1977. Tracks 15-18 Italy, Venue 1980. Tracks 19-22 Brixton Academy, London February 28 1990.
Comments: European CD. Deluxe color cover. Time 66:06.

CRANBERRIES

CD - ABSOLUTELY ACOUSTIC
BLUE MOON RECORDS BMCD43
Dreaming My Dreams/ Ode To My Family/ Linger/ Free To Decide/ I'm Still Remembering/ Empty/ Zombie/ Yesterday's Gone/ No Need To Argue/ Put Me Down/ Ode To My Family/ Wanted/ Sunday/ Empty/ Linger/ I Can't Be With You/ How
Recording: Excellent stereo. Soundboard.
Source: Tracks 1-9 MTV Unplugged, Brooklyn Academy Of Music, New York February 13 '95. Tracks 10-17 acoustic performance, Fleadh Festival June 11 '94.
Comments: European CD. Deluxe color cover. Time 71:35.

CD - FOREVER LIVE
MOONRAKER 213
Forever Yellow Skies/ Free To Decide/ Sunday/ Linger/ Wanted/ Still Can't.../ Waltzing Back/ I Can't Be With You/ I Just Shot John Lennon/ Ridiculous Thoughts/ Salvation/ Zombie/ Will You Remember?/ Hollywood/ Dreams/ Salvation*
Recording: Excellent stereo. Soundboard.
Source: Molson Amphitheatre, Toronto August 29 1996. *1996 MTV Video Music Awards, Radio City Music Hall, New York September 5 1996.
Comments: European CD. Grey/white cover. Black text. Time 59:28.

CD - SCREAM
KISS THE STONE KTS 557
Sunday/ Zombie/ Wanted/ Linger/ Dreaming My Dreams/ Dreaming My Dreams/ Linger/ I Can't Be With You/ The Icicle Melts/ Dreams/ Zombie/ Ode To My Family/ Linger (with Simon Le Bon)/ Ave Maria (with Pavarotti)/ Free To Decide/ John Lennon Died
Recording: Excellent stereo. Soundboard.
Source: Tracks 1-5 acoustic set WNNX Studios, Atlanta, GA August 19 1994.

CREAM

Tracks 6-12 The Mayflower, Newcastle, UK October 12 1994. Tracks 13-14 The Parco Novi Sad, Modena, Italy September 12 1995. Tracks 15-16 Utrecht, Holland, February 8 1995. Track 13 Dolores with Simon Le Bon. Track 14 Dolores with Luciano Pavarotti.
Comments: European CD. Deluxe color cover. Picture CD. Time 69:43.

CREAM

CD - BLIND SPOT
DR. GIG DGCD 058
Sunshine Of Your Love/ Born Under A Bad Sigh/ Tales Of Brave Ulysses/ Sunshine Of Your Love/ N.S.U./ Sitting On Top Of The World/ Traintime
Recording: Tracks 1-3 Very good to excellent. Tracks 4-8 Poor-Good.
Source: Tracks 1-3 Rock And Roll Hall Of Fame '93. Tracks 4-8 Brandeis University, Waltham, UK September 9 1967.
Comments: European CD. Time 66:14.

CD - CREAMSET
SCORPIO
CD1: Tales Of Brave Ulysses/ N.S.U./ Sitting On Top Of The World/ Sweet Wine/ Rolling & Tumbling/ Spoonful
CD2: Stepping Out/ Train Time/ Toad/ I'm So Glad/ Sunshine Of Your Love/ Spoonfull
Recording: Very good. Soundboard.
Comments: Deluxe color cardboard gatefold cover. Time CD1 67:37. CD2 73:09.

CD - FRESH AS CREAM
SLOW HAND SH-01
Tales Of Brave Ulysses/ Sunshine Of Your Love/ NSU/ Sitting On Top Of The World/ Traintime
Recording: Poor to good. Audience.
Source: Brandeis University, Waltham, UK September 9 1967.
Comments: Japanese CD. Deluxe color cover. Time 52:11.

CD - SAN JOSE
H-BOMB MUSIC HBM9504
I'm So Glad/ Sitting On Top Of The World/ Steppin' Out/ Train Time/ Toad/ Tales Of Brave Ulysses/ Sunshine Of Your Love
Recording: Good. Audience.
Source: San Jose May 25 1968.
Comments: Japanese CD. Deluxe color cover. Time 59:46.

CREEDENCE CLEARWATER REVIVAL

CD - ROCK ON THE ROAD
MUM MUCD 016
Born On The Bayou/ Green River/ Tombstone Shadow/ It Came Out Of The Sky/ Travelin' Band/ Who'll Stop The Rain/ Bad Moon Rising/ Proud Mary/ Fortunate Son/ Commotion/ Midnight Special/ The Night Time Is The Right Time/ Down On The Corner/ Keep On Chooglin/ Ninety Nine And A Half (Won't Go)/ Bootleg/ I Put A Spell On You/ Suzie Q
Recording: Excellent. Soundboard.
Source: Tracks 1-14 Oakland Coliseum, CA January 31 1970. Tracks 15-18 Woodstock August 16 1969.
Comments: European CD. Time 68:56.

CROSBY, STILLS, NASH & YOUNG

CD - BALBOA PARK
COLOSSEUM RECORDS 97-C-011
Suite: Judy Blue Eyes/ Blackbird/ On The Way Home/ Helplessly Hoping/ Helpless/ Black Queen/ 49 Bye-Bye includes For What it's Worth/ America's Children/ Pre-Road Downs/ So Begins The Task/ Long Time Gone/ Wooden Ships/ Down By The River/ Star Of Bethlehem
Recording: Good to very good. Audience.
Source: Balboa Stadium, San Diego December 21 1969. Track 13 Wembley Stadium, London September 14 1974 (not listed on cover).
Comments: Japanese CD. Deluxe color cover. Made up names for songs on CD. Time 76:07.

CD - ROOSEVELT RACEWAY
GOLD STANDARD
CD1: Love The One You're With/ Wooden Ships/ Immigration Man/ Helpless/ Military Madness/ Johnny's Garden/ Walk On/ Almost Cut My Hair/ Teach Your Children/ Only Love Can Break Your Heart/ The Lee Shore/ Time After Time/ Southbound Train
CD2: Another Sleep Song/ Our House/ Hawaiian Sunrise/ Long May You Run/ Ambulance Blues/ Old Man/ Change Partners/ Myth Of Sisyphus/ You Can't Catch Me, Word Game/ Suite: Judy Blue Eyes/ Deha Vu/ First Things First
CD3: Don't Be Denied/ Black Queen/ Revolution Blues/ Pushed It Over The End/ Pre-Road Downs/ Carry On/ Sugar

Mountain/ Ohio
Recording: Excellent. Soundboard.
Source: Roosevelt Raceway Westbury Long Island September 8 1974.
Comments: Deluxe color cardboard tri-fold cover. CDs in color picture sleeves.

CROW, SHERYL

CD - SUNDAY NIGHT AT THE PARADISO
MIDNIGHT BEAT MB CD 090/91
CD1: Hard To Make A Stand (5:35)/ Every Day Is A Winding Road (5:44)/ A Change (4:26)/ Leaving Las Vegas (6:49)/ If It Makes You Happy (5:40)/ Run, Baby, Run (7:08)/ Sweet Rosalyn (5:33)/ On The Outside (7:35)/ Redemption Day (5:33)
CD2: Strong Enough (4:26)/ Maybe Angels (4:11)/ Solidify (6:06)/ All I Wanna Do (5:17)/ Introduction, Superstar (10:27)/ Sway (3:43)/ The Na, Na, Song (7:11)/ Ordinary Morning (5:01)/ Interview (2:45)/ If It Makes You Happy (4:17)
Recording: Excellent stereo. Soundboard.
Source: Paradiso, Amsterdam, Holland, November 3 1996. CD2 Track 10 The Late Show With David Letterman October 22 1996.
Comments: European CD. Deluxe color cover. Picture CD.

CROWDED HOUSE

CD - DON'T SCREAM, IT'S OVER
KISS THE STONE KTS 363/37
CD1: Intro, Mean To Me/ World Where You Live/ When You Come/ Private Universe/ Four Seasons In One Day/ Fall At Your Feet/ Whispers And Moans/ Better Be Home Soon/ Distant Sun/ Into Temptation/ Everything Is Good For You/ Been Locked Out/ Something So Strong
CD2: Sister Madly/ Weather With You/ It's Only Natural/ Fingers Of Love/ In My Command/ Don't Dream It's Over/ Been Locked Out/ Private Universe/ In My Command/ Nails In My Feet/ Chocolate Cake/ Throw Your Arms Around Me
Recording: Excellent stereo. Soundboard.
Source: CD1 plus CD2 tracks 1-6 steps of the Sydney Opera House August 23 1996. Tracks 7-10 acoustic sessions, London 1993. Tracks 11-12 London Studios (acoustic) 1991. CD2 tracks 2 and 3 with Tim Finn.
Comments: European CD. Deluxe color cover. Picture CD. Total time 01:51:20.

CD - THE FINAL SESSIONS
KISS THE STONE KTS 592
Distant Sun/ Weather With You/ Into Temptation/ Instinct/ In My Command/ The Fingers Of Love/ Four Seasons In One Day/ Private Universe/ Pineapple Head/ Fall At Your Feet/ Locked Out/ Better Be Home Soon/ Weather With You/ Private Universe/ Don't Dream It's Over/ Fall At Your Feet/ You're Not The Girl You Think You Are
Recording: Excellent stereo. Soundboard.
Source: Tracks 1-12 GLR Basement Studio, London, England June 21 1996. Tracks 13-17 London, England June 16 1996 (acoustic). Track 18 Virgin Music Cafe, London, England June 13 1996 (acoustic).
Comments: European CD. Deluxe color cover. Picture CD. Time 70:14.

CD - REVOLVER
MONTANA MO10023
Don't Dream It's Over (4:30)/ It's Only Natural (4:03)/ Weather With You (6:23)/ Fall At Your Feet (4:05)/ Better Be Home Soon (3:30)/ Distant Sun (4:25)/ Locked Out (3:29)/ Into Temptation (4:49)/ Kari Kan (3:25)/ Fingers Of Love (5:02)/ Four Seasons In One Day (2:56)/ World Where You Live (3:21)/ Born On The Bayou (2:19)/ In My Command (4:08)
Recording: Excellent stereo. Soundboard.
Source: New York 1993.
Comments: European CD.

CURE, THE

CD - COLD
THE SWINGIN' PIG TSP-CD-223-2
CD1: Shake Dog Shake/ Piggy In The Mirror/ Wailing Wall/ M/ Primary/ Cold/ The Hanging Garden/ Charlotte Sometimes/ Secrets/ The Wall/ Let's Go To Bed
CD2: One Hundred Years/ Give Me It/ A Forest/ Happy The Man/ The Caterpillar/ Three Imaginary Boys/ Boys Don't Cry/ 10:15 Saturday Night/ Killing An Arab/ Five
Recording: Excellent stereo. Soundboard.
Source: Washington, DC November 15 1984.
Comments: European CD.
Time CD1 45:19. CD2 42:51.

CURE, THE

CD - FACEPAINT
HURRICANE HUR007/8
CD1: Lullaby/ Just Like Heaven/ Trust/ Jupiter Crash/ High/ The Walk/ Let's Go To Bed/ Dressing Up/ Strange Day/ Push/ Mint Car/ Friday I'm In Love/ Inbetween Days / The Edge Of The Deep Green/ Shiver And Shake
CD2: Disentepration/ End/ Want/ Pictures Of You/ Fascination Street/ A Night Like This/ Apart/ Friday I'm In Love/ Close To Me/ Boy's Don't Cry/ A Forest
Recording: Very good. CD 2 tracks 4-11 G- Very good. Audience.
Source: Glastonbury Festival, England June 25 '95. CD 2 tracks 4-11 Frank T. Ervin Center, Austin, TX June 11 '92.
Comments: European CD. Deluxe color cover. Time CD1 66:53. CD2 73:57.

CD - MESSAGE FROM JUPITER
MOONRAKER 202
Want/ Club America/ Lullaby/ Round & Round & Round/ Just Like Heaven/ Strange Attraction/ Return/ Trap/ Prayers For Rain/ Inbetween Days/ From The Edge Of The Deep Green Sea/ Disintegration
Recording: Excellent stereo. Soundboard.
Source: Live At The Queen Elizabeth Theatre, Vancouver, Canada, August 1 1996.
Comments: European CD. Deluxe color cover. Time 58:48.

CD - OBSCURTIES
Burn (from The Crows soundtrack)/ Want, This Is A Lie, Club America, Jupiter Crash, The Two Chord Cool, Mint Car ('First Pass' Mixes From Promo-Only Tape)/ Dredd Song (full length version from 'Judge Dredd' soundtrack)/ The Love Cats (extended remix)/ In Between Days (extended version from US 12")/ Purple Haze (full length version from 'Stone Free - A Tribute To Jimi Hendrix' compilation)/ Friday I'm In Love (edited version of the 'Strangelove' mix)/ Just Like Heaven (special remix by Bob Clearmountain)/ High (different vocal version from limited 12")/ Snow In The Summer, Sugar Girl (from 'Kiss Me, Kiss Me, Kiss Me' bonus 12")/ Killing The Arab (1982 live version from 'Hanging Garden' 10")/ Cats Like Cheese (early demo of 'Give Me It' with different lyrics)/ Boys Don't Cry (Chestnut Studios May 26 1978)/ Hello I Love You (Slight Return) (from the Elektra Anniversary compilation 'Rubaiyat')
Recording: Excellent stereo. Soundboard.
Comments: European CD. Deluxe color cover. Time 70:71.

CD - STRAWBERRY KISSES
KISS THE STONE KTS 548
Want (5:26)/ Club America (5:03)/ This Is A Lie (4:59)/ Mint Car (3:50)/ Jupiter Crash (4:22)/ Round & Round And Round (2:53)/ Return (3:38)/ Trap (3:42)/ Treasure (4:06)/ Bare (7:07)/ Friday I'm In Love (3:25)/ Mint Car (3:34)/ Just Like Heaven (3:36)/ Club America (4:58)/ This Is A Lie (4:37)/ Gone! (4:33)
Recording: Excellent.
Source: Tracks 1-10 The Adrenaline, London May 7 '96. Tracks 11-13 London December '95. Tracks 14-16 London May 11 '96.
Comments: European CD. Deluxe color cover. Picture CD.

CD - SWINGING CROWDS
KOBRA RECORDS KRCD 12/2
CD1: Plainsong/ Want/ Club America/ Fascination Street/ Lullaby/ Picture Of You/ Jupiter Crash/ Round And Round/ Just Like Heaven/ Cold/ Friday I'm In Love/ Catch/ Mint Car/ Strange Attraction/ Love Song/ Return/ Trap/ Treasure
CD2: Prayer For The Rain/ In Between Days/ From The Edge Of The Deep Green Sea/ Bare/ Disintegration/ Dressin' Up/ Let's Go To Bed/ Close To Me/ Why Can't I Be You?/ The Lovecats/ Play For Today/ Boys Don't Cry/ Forest/ Faith
Source: Milan October 23 1996.
Comments: European CD.

CD - TEARDROPS AND TEMPTATIONS
KISS THE STONE KTS 554
Want/ Club America/ This Is a Lie/ Mint Car/ Jupiter Crash/ Round & Round & Round/ Return/ Trap/ Treasure/ Bare/ Let's Go To Bed/ Just Like Heaven/ The Caterpillar/ The Blood/ Boys Don't Cry/ The Walk (Instrumental)
Recording: Excellent stereo. Soundboard.
Source: Tracks 1-10 electric set, New York City May 22 1996. Tracks 11-16 acoustic set, Limehouse, London March 3 1991.
Comments: European CD. Deluxe color cover. Picture CD. Time 64:53.

CURE, THE

D

DAVIES, RAY

CD - SANTA ANA 1995
PHENOMENAL CAT CS-9701
Dedicated Follower Of Fashion/ Autumn Almanac/ Dead End Street/ Sunny Afternoon/ Victoria/ 20th Century Man/ London/ Witchcraft/ That Old Black Magic/ Tired Of Waiting For You/ Set Me Free/ X Ray/ See My Friends/ Money Go Round/ Dead End Street/ Julie/ Lola/ To The Bone/ Village Green/ Days/ Waterloo Sunset
Recording: Very good. Audience.
Source: Santa Ana, California May 1995.
Comments: Japanese CD. Deluxe color cover. Time 76:53.

DAVIS, MILES

CD - NIGHTCRAWLER
TEDDY BEAR RECORDS TB 16
Full Nelson (3:51)/ Tutu (14:53)/ Come And Act it (8:28)/ Human Nature (15:58)/ Time 12 Slowfunk (6:42)/ Jilly (5:44)
Source: Columbus, Ohio January 12 1990.
Comments: European CD. Deluxe color cover. Picture CD.

DEEP PURPLE

CD - A WHITER SHADE OF PURPLE
NIGHTLIFE -040/41
CD1: Intro/ Burn/ Black Night, Child In Time/ Truth Hurts/ Cut Runs Deep, Hush/ Perfect Strangers/ Fire In The Basement/ King Of Dreams/ Love Conquers All
CD2: Ritchie's Blues/ Difficult To Cure, Organ Solo/ Knocking At Your Back Door/ Lazy/ Highway Star/ Smoke On The Water, Drum Solo, Woman From Tokyo/ A Whiter Shade Of Pale*/ King Of Dreams*/ Jon Speaks To The Crowd*/ Love Conquers All*
Recording: Very good to excellent. Audience. *Very good. Audience.
Source: Copenhagen Forum, Denmark March 6 '91. *Hammersmith Odeon, London March 16 '91.
Comments: Japanese CD. Deluxe color cover. Time 65:37. CD2 65:18.

CD - IN YOUR TROUSERS
CRYSTAL CAT RECORDS CC 336/37
CD1: Intro/ Highway Star/ Black Night/ Talk About Love/ A Twist In The Tale/ Perfect Strangers/ Difficult To Cure/ Keyboard Improvisation/ Knockin' At Your Backdoor/ Anyones Daughter/ Child In Time
CD2: Guitar Improvisation/ Anya/ The Battle Rages On/ Lazy/ Drums Improvisation/ Space Truckin'/ Woman From Tokyo/ Paint It Black/ Hush/ Smoke On The Water/ Speed King/ Intro Guitar/ Smoke On The Water
Recording: Excellent. Audience.
Source: Stockholm November 13 1993. CD2 Tracks 11-13 Copenhagen 1993.
Comments: European CD.
Time CD1 64:05. CD2 67:14.

CD - LIVE IN SEOUL
NIGHTLIFE N-026/027
CD1: Fireball, Into The Fire (Intro)/ Black Night/ The Battle Rages On/ Ken The Mechanic/ Woman From Tokyo/ The Perpendicular Waltz/ When A Blindman Cries/ Perfect Strangers/ Pictures Of Home/ Jon Lord Solo, Soldier Of Fortune, Ariran/ Knocking At Your Back Door
CD2: Anyones Daughter/ Child In Time/ Anya/ Steve Morse Solo, Lazy, Ian Paice Solo/ Maybe i'm A Leo/ Speed King/ Highway Star/ Smoke On The Water
Recording: Good to very good. Audience.
Source: Seoul, Korea March 18-19 1995.
Comments: Japanese CD. Silver hinged metal box with color label. Color sticker (same as cover) inside. Time CD1 74:09. CD2 68:23.

CD - LIVE IN TELAVIV
DP-23-4
CD1: Black Night, Long Live Rock 'N' Roll, Child In Time/ Truth Hurts/ Cut Runs Deep, Hush/ Perfect Strangers/ Fire In The Basement/ Hey Joe/ Love Conquers All
CD2: Ritchie's Blues, Difficult To Cure, Organ Solo/ Knocking At Your Back Door/ Lazy, Space Truckin'/ Highway Star/ Smoke On The Water
Recording: Excellent stereo. Soundboard.
Source: Telaviv, Israel 1991.
Comments: Japanese CD. Purple/black cover. Red Type. Radio announcer talks over songs.

CD - WE FOUND THE GUITAR
DDR 004
CD1: Fireball/ Ted The Mechanic/ Pictures Of Home/ Black Night/ Cascades, I'm Not Your Lover/ Sometimes I Feel Like Screaming/ Woman From Tokyo/ No One Came/ Smoke On The Water
CD2: When A Blind Man Cries/ Speed King/ Perfect Strangers/ Highway Star/ Speed King (Halmstad July 5 1996)/ Hey Cisco (Halmstad July 5 1996)/ Strange Kind Of Woman (Oslo August 22 1987)/ Blues, A Gypsy's Kiss (Stockholm June 15 1985)
Recording: Good to very good audience.
Source: Kungshamnsvallen, Smogen July 4 1996.
Comments: European CD. Deluxe color cover.

CD - WHEN A BLIND MAN CRIES
DP96/1/2
CD1: Fireball (No, No, No)/ Maybe I'm A Leo/ Ted The Mechanic/ Pictures Of Home/ Black Night/ I'm Tokyo/ Bloodsucker/ Perpendicular Walls/ No One Came
CD2: Rosas Cantina/ Smoke On The Water/ John Lord Solo/ When A Blind Man Cries/ Somebody Stole My Guitar/ Speed King/ plus bonus tracks
Recording: Good to very good audience.
Source: Munchen, March 27 1996.
Comments: European CD. Deluxe color cover.

CD - WHEN HARRY MET SALLY
EPPEL 1/2
CD1: Fireball (4:17)/ Vavoom, Ted The Mechanic (4:53)/ Pictures Of Home (6:06)/ Black Night (6:57)/ Cascades, I'm Not Your Lover (11:49)/ Sometimes I Feel Like Screaming (8:08)/ Woman From Tokyo (6:19)/ The Aviator (6:23)/ Rosa's Cantina (6:08)/ No One Came (5:52)
CD2: Smoke On The Water (11:50)/ When A Blind Man Cries (7:33)/ Speed King, Peggy Sue, Not Fade Away, Speed King (13:01)/ Perfect Stranger (7:20)/ Hey Cisco (6:59)/ Highway Star (7:22)/ Smoke On The Water (5:15)*
Recording: Good to very good audience.
*Excellent soundboard.
Source: Rhein-Neckar Halle, Heidelberg, Germany, September 27 1996. *The Harald Schmidt Show, Cologne, Germany, September 16 1996.
Comments: European CD. Deluxe color cover. Picture CDs.

CD - WOMAN FROM OSAKA
NIGHTLIFE N-034/035/036/037
CD1: Highway Star/ Nobody's Home/ Strange Kind Of Woman/ Blues, A Gypsy's Kiss/ Perfect Strangers/ Under The Gun/ Lazy, Ian Paice Solo/ Child In Time
CD2: Knocking At Your Backdoor/ Difficult To Cure, Jon Lord Solo/ Space Truckin'/ Smoke On The Water/ Woman From Tokyo*/ Black Night*
CD3: Highway Star/ Nobody's Home/ Strange Kind Of Woman/ Blues, A Gypsy's Kiss/ Perfect Strangers/ Under The Gun/ Lazy, Ian Paice Solo
CD4: Child In Time/ Knocking At Your Backdoor/ Difficult To Cure, Jon Lord Solo/ Space Truckin'/ Woman From Tokyo/ Black Night/ Smoke On The Water
Recording: Good audience.
Source: CD1-2 Jyo Hall, Osaka, Japan May 8 1985. CD3-4 May 9 1985. *Nagoya, Japan May 11 1985.
Comments: Japanese CD. Silver hinged metal box with color label. Time CD1 74:09. CD2 68:23.

CD - WORTH THE WAIT VOL. 1
KIWI RECORDS KR-007
Highway Star/ Nobody's Home/ Strange Kind Of Woman/ A Gypsy's Kiss/ Perfect Strangers/ Under The Gun/ Lazy
Recording: Good-very good. Audience.
Source: Providence, RI March 5 1985.
Comments: Australian CD. Time 44:44.

CD - WORTH THE WAIT VOL. 2
KIWI RECORDS KR-008
Child In Time Knocking At Your Backdoor/ Difficult To Cure/ Space Truckin'/ Woman From Tokyo/ Speed King/ Smoke On The Water
Recording: Good-very good. Audience.
Source: Providence, RI March 5 1985.
Comments: Australian CD. Time 64:49.

DEF LEPPARD

CD - THE EARLY YEARS
BLUDGEON RECORDS
Satellite/ When The Walls Came Tumbling Down/ Medicine Man/ The Overture/ Lady Strange/ Getcha Rocks Off/ The Overture/ Wasted/ Hello America/ Good Morning Freedom/ Me And My Wine

DEF LEPPARD

Recording: Excellent stereo. Soundboard.
Source: Tracks 1-6 Reading Festival, England August 24 1980. Tracks 7-9 original versions from 'Def Leppard EP.' Tracks 10 and 11 original versions from 'Wasted'. Track 12 non-album track from B-Side of 'Hello America.' Track 13 original version from B-Side of 'Bringin' On The Heartbreak.'
Comments: Japanese CD. Deluxe color cover. Time 55:02.

CD - FIRST STRIKE
843 007
Heat Street (2:51)/ Answer To The Master (3:22)/ See The Lights (3:34)/ When The Walls Come Tumbling Down (3:47)/ Wasted (3:28)/ Sorrow Is A Woman (3:49)/ Glad I'm Alive (4:09)
Recording: Excellent stereo. Soundboard.
Source: Studio tracks '79.
Comments: Japanese CD. Deluxe color cover.

CD - WARCHILD
NIGHTLIFE N-049
Glad I'm Alive/ Hello America/ When The Walls Came Tumbling Down/ Overture/ Getcha Rocks Off Wasted/ Getcha Rocks Off/ Tomorrow Seems Like Yesterday/ Warchild/ Got To See The Lights/ Overture/ Beyond The Temple/ Wasted
Recording: Excellent stereo. Soundboard.
Source: Tracks 1-5 BBC 1980. Tracks 6-12 demo tape 1978.
Comments: Japanese CD. Deluxe color cover. Time 65:05.

DEPECHE MODE

CD - THE HEDONIST MIXES
POLITICAL CORRECTNESS PC 20019401
Never Let Me Down Again (Groovy Wax Mix)/ Enjoy The Silence (Violation Mix)/ The Strange People (Mix Medley)/ I Feel You (More Fun Mix)/ Strange Love (Fresh Ground Mix)/ Policy Zoom Megamix/ Mix Of Faith And Devoton/ Master & Servant (Power Mix)
Recording: Excellent stereo. Soundboard.
Comments: European CD. Deluxe color cover. Picture CD. Time 78:10.

DENNY, SANDY

CD - AT THE BBC
NIGHTLIFE N-071
Autopsy/ Fothringay/ Cajun Woman/ 'Sandy Denny' Interview/ Si Tu Dois Partir/ The Way I Feel/ Interview/ Followed By The Sea/ Now Be Thankful/ 'Simon Nicol' Interview/ The Journey Man's Grace/ Eppy Moray/ The Low Low Land Of Holland/ Interview, Gypsy Davy/ Will You Go/ John The Gun/ Jack Donaghue/ Dark Of The Night/ Whispering Grass/ Solo
Recording: Excellent. Soundboard.
Source: Tracks 1-5, 9-11 Fairport Convention. Tracks 6-8, 12-17 Fothringay. Tracks 18-20 Sandy Denny.
Comments: Japanese CD. Deluxe color cover. Time 73:36.

DEPECHE MODE

CD - DARKEST FEELINGS
TORNADO TOR 009/010
CD1: Rush/ Halo/ Behind The Wheel/ Everything Counts/ World In My Eyes/ Walking In My Shoes/ Stripped/ Condemnation/ I Want You Now/ In Your Room/ Never Let Me Down Again/ I Feel You
CD2: Personal Jesus/ Somebody/ Enjoy The Silence/ A Question Of Time/ I Want You Now/ World Full Of Nothing/ Little 15/ Blue Dress/ Here Is The House/ Sweetest Perfection
Recording: Good to very good. Audience.
Source: Gulf Coast Coliseum, Biloxi, Mississippi June 5 '94. CD2 tracks 5-10 acoustic tracks.
Comments: European CD. Deluxe color cover. Picture CD.

DEREK AND THE DOMINOS

CD - DEREK IS ERIC
HIWATT
Why Does Love Got To Be So Sad (4:52)/ Bell Bottom Blues (Instrumental) (5:19)/ I Looked Away (3:10)/ Have You Ever Loved A Woman (7:10)/ Nobody Knows You (When You're Down And Out) (Instrumental) (4:46)/ Why Does Love Got To Be So Sad (False Start) (5:41)/ Keep On Growing (Instrumental) (6:21)/ I Looked Away (3:24)/ Anyday (5:50)/ Tender Love (Instrumental) (2:32)/ Tell The Truth (5:07)/

Instrumental Jam #7 (12:42)/ Evil (4:25)
Source: Layla session at Criteria Studio, Miami late August to mid September 1970. Track 14 2nd album session Olympic Studio, London, UK April 14 1971.

DIO

CD - EVIL EYES '83
GRYPHON-013/14
CD1: Introduction/ Stand Up And Shout/ Straight Through The Heart/ Children Of The Sea/ Rainbow In The Dark/ Holy Diver/ Drum Solo/ Stargazer, Guitar Solo/ Heaven And Hell/ Man On Silver Mountain (includes Star Struck)/ Evil Eyes
CD2: Introduction/ Stand Up And Shout/ Straight Through The Heart/ Shame On The Night/ Children Of The Sea/ Holy Diver/ Drum Solo/ Stargazer/ Heaven And Hell, Guitar Solo/ Rainbow In The Dark/ Man On Silver Mountain (includes Star Struck)/ Evil Eyes
Source: CD1 Monsters Of Rock Festival, Donnington August 20 1983. CD2 Sheffield November 9 1983.
Comments: Japanese CD.

DOORS, THE

CD - ALL HAIL THE AMERICAN NIGHT!
TUFF BITES T.B. 95.1025
CD1: Alabama Song, Back Door Man (5:15)/ The Wasp (Texas Radio And The Big Beat) (1:55)/ Love Me Two Times (3:30)/ When The Music's Over (12:28)/ Unknown Soldier (4:10)/ Tell All The People (5:34)/ Alabama Song, Back Door Man (6:08)/ Wishful Sinful (3:15)/ Build Me A Woman (4:26)/ The Soft Parade (10:00)/ Doors Interview By Richard Goldstein (11:41)
CD2: Love Her Madly (10:24)/ Back Door Man (4:05)/ Ship Of Fools (8:20)/ The Changeling (4:55)/ L.A. Woman (15:40)/ When The Music's Over (13:30)/ The End (15:16)
Recording: Very good to excellent.
Source: CD1 Tracks 1-5 Copenhagen TV-Studio September 17 '68. Tracks 6-11 The Critique Show, PBS TV Studios, New York May 23 '69. CD2 Tracks 1-6 State Fair Music Hall, Dallas December 11 '70 (last recorded show with Morrison on vocals). Track 7 Toronto Pop Festival, Varsity Stadium, Toronto, Canada September 13 '69.
Comments: European CD. Digi-pak fold-open cardboard case.

CD - HIGHSCHOOL CONFIDENTIAL
BUSY BASTARDS BBM08-15
Moonlight Drive/ Money/ Break Through/ Back Door Man/ People Are Strange/ The Crystal Ship/ Wake Up/ Light My Fire/ The End
Recording: Very good. Audience. Hiss.
Source: Danbury Highschool October 17 1967.

CD - LIQUID NIGHT
SCREAMING BUTTERFLY SBR 3169
Medley: Back Door Man, Five To One (15:10)/ Fun Rap (Poem) (0:45)/ Touch Me (Attempt) (1:25)/ Love Me Two Times (3:20)/ When The Music's Over (22:15)/ Wake Up! (1:20)/ Light My Fire (11:50)/ Who Scared You (4:17)/ Spanish Caravan (4:07)/ Wild Child (4:58)/ Touch Me (3:38)/ The Unknown Soldier (4:28)
Recording: Very good. Audience. Tracks 8-12 poor.
Source: Tracks 1-7 Dinner Key Auditorium, Miami, FL March 1 1969. Tracks 8-12 LA Forum, Inglewood, CA December 14 1968.
Comments: European CD. Deluxe cover.

DREAM THEATER

CD - GUITAR TALKIN'
KOBRA RECORDS KRCD 16
Lifting Shadows Off A Dream/ Wait For Sleep/ Tears/ The Silent Man (Radio Veronica session February 14 1995)/ Another Day (US Radio Power Thirty - June 1993)/ Lost Without You/ Untitled (Petrucci demo)/ Final Jamming/ Raise The Knife (John Petrucci and Mike Portnoy Clinic in Milano Auditorium March 3 1996)/ Learning To Live/ Take The Time/ To Live Forever (James La Brie Auditorium demo March 1991)
Recording: Excellent.
Comments: European CD. Time 79:05.

DURAN DURAN

CD - PERFECT DAY: NOW AND THEN
TORNADO TOR033
Anyone Out There?/ Planet Earth/ To The Shore/ Late Bar/ Khanada/ Nightboat/ Last Chance To The Stairway/ Faster Than

DYLAN, BOB

Light/ My Own Way/ Careless Memories/ Girls On Film/ Fame/ Anyone Out There?/ Seven And The Ragged Tiger/ Friends Of Mine
Recording: Very good. Soundboard. Surface noise. Tracks 13-15 Excellent stereo. Soundboard.
Source: Tracks 1-12 USA '81. Tracks 13-15 Detroit, MI July '82.
Comments: European CD. Deluxe color cover. Time 69:54.

DYLAN, BOB

CD - A NIGHT TO REMEMBER
AMSTERDAM AMS 9617-2-1/2
CD1: A Hard Rain's A Gonna Fall (Instrumental)/ Love Her With A Feeling/ One More Cup Of Coffee/ Mr. Tambourine Man/ I Threw It All Away/ I Don't Believe You/ Girl From The North Country/ I'll Be Your Baby Tonight/ Shelter From The Storm/ Ballad Of A Thin Man/ Maggie's Farm/ To Ramona/ Like A Rolling Stone/ I Shall Be Released/ Going Going Gone
CD2: One Of Us Must Know/ Blowin' In The Wind/ Just Like A Woman/ Oh Sister/ You're A Big Girl Now/ All Along The Watchtower/ I Want You/ All I Really Want To Do/ The Man In Me/ Knockin' On Heaven's Door/ It's Alright, Ma/ Forever Young/ The Times They Are A-Changin'
Source: February 26 1978.
Comments: Japanese CD.

CD - ALL ALONG THE ROSELAND
YING YANG RECORDS YY9504/5
CD1: Jokerman/ All Along The Watchtower/ Simple Twist Of Fate/ Tangled Up In Blue/ Positively 4th Street/ Mama You Been On My Mind/ The Lonesome Death Of Hattie Caroll/ Boots Of Spanish Leather/ God Knows
CD2: Joey/ Maggie's Farm/ Most Likely You Go Your Way (And I'll Go Mine)/ My Back Pages/ Rainy Day Woman #12 & 35/ Highway 61 Revisited/ Tears Of Rage/ Leopardskin Pill-Box Hat/ Senor (Tales Of Yankee Power)
Recording: Very good. Audience recording
Source: The Roseland Ballroom, New York October 14 1994. CD2 tracks 7 and 9 US tour 1994. Track 8 Mountainview 1993.

CD - ALL HALLOWS' EVE & MORE
MIDNIGHT BEAT MB CD 079/80
CD1: Intro (0:45)/ The Times They Are A-Changin' (3:14)/ Spanish Harlem Incident (2:58)/ Talking John Birch Paranoid Blues (4:28)/ To Ramona (5:13)/ Who Killed Davey Moore? (5:41)/ Gates Of Eden (7:47)/ If You Got To Go, Go Now (4:52)/ It's Alright, Ma (I'm Only Bleeding) (8:51)/ I Don't Believe You (She Acts Like We Never Have Met) (5:40)/ Mr. Tambourine Man (6:26)/ A Hard Rain's A-Gonna Fall (7:39)
CD2: Talking World War III Blues (5:53)/ Don't Think Twice It's All Right (4:07)/ The Lonesome Death Of Hattie Carroll (7:35)/ Mama, You Been On My Mind (3:10)/ With God On Our Side (6:29)/ It Ain't Me Babe (5:20)/ All I Really Want To Do (4:06)/ Interview (2:37)/ Ballad Of Donald White (4:30)/ Interview (1:11)/ The Death Of Emmett Till (4:39)/ Interview (0:52)/ Blowin' In The Wind
Recording: Excellent. Soundboard.
Source: Philharmonic Hall, New York City October 31 1964 and Broadside Show, WBAI-FM Radio, New York City May 1962.
Comments: European CD. Deluxe color cover. Picture CDs.

CD - BLOWN OUT ON THE TRAIL
MOONTUNES MOON 019/20
CD1: Subterranean Homesick Blues/ Just Like Tom Thumb's Blues/ You're A Big Girl Now/ Tangled Up In Blue/ Master's Of War/ I Shall Be Released/ Stuck Inside Mobile With The Memphis Blues Again/ The Lakes Of Ponchatrain/ A Hard Rain's A-Gonna Fall/ Eileen Arroon/ Boots Of Spanish Leather/ Silvio/ Gates Of Eden/ Like A Rolling Stone
CD2: The Times They Are A-Changin'/ All Along The Watchtower/ Maggie's Farm/ San Francisco Bay Blues/ Pretty Boy Floyd/ With God On Our Side/ Girl From The North Country/ Gates Of Eden/ Forever Young/ I'll Remember You/ Every Grain Of Sand/ Don't Think Twice, It's Alright/ One Too Many Mornings/ Barbara Allen
Source: CD1 and CD2 tracks 1-4 Jones Beach Theatre, Wantaugh, NY June 30 1988. CD2: Tracks 5-9 Shoreline Amphitheatre, Mountainview, CA December 4 1988. CD2 Tracks 10-14 New York State Fair Ground, Syracuse, NY August 31 1988.

CD - DARKNESS AT THE BREAK OF NOON
RAZOR'S EDGE RAZ-021
I'll Be Your Baby Tonight/ The Times They Are A-Changin'/ If You See Her Say Hello/ The Man In Me/ I Don't Believe You/ Tomorrow Is A Long Time/ You're A Big Girl Now/ Knockin' On Heaven's Door/ It's Alright Ma/ Forever Young/ Repossession Blues/ One Of Us Must Know/ Girl From The North Country/ We Better Talk This Over Coming From The Heart/ Simple Twist Of Fate/ If You See Her Say Hello/ I Don't Believe You
Recording: Excellent. Soundboard.
Source: Tour rehearsals, Rundown Studios, Santa Monica 1978. Tracks 1-10 January 30. Tracks 11-13 February 1. Tracks 14-17 April.

CD - DOWN TO THE EARTH
MUM MUCD 015
Like A Rolling Stone (Complete long version, rough mix. No fade. Columbia Studio, NYC June 15 1965 - 6:34)/ Tombstone Blues (Rough mono mix. Long version. Columbia Studio, NYC July 29 1965 - 6:19)/ It Take A Lot To Laugh It Takes A Train To Cry (Long version. Columbia Studio NYC July 29 1965 - 4:18)/ Ballad Of A Thin Man (Long version. Rough mono mix. Frank Owens on piano. Columbia Studio NYC August 2 1965 - 6:08)/ Queen Jane Approximately (Long version. Rough mono mix. Frank Owens on piano. Columbia Studio NYC August 2 1965 - 5:33)/ Highway 61 Revisited (Long version. Rough mono mix. Russ Savakus on bass, Frank Owens on piano, Charlie Mccoy on guitar. Columbia Studio NYC August 2 1965 - 3:42)/ Just Like Tom Thumb's Blues (Extended version. Rough mono mix. Russ Savakus on sass. Columbia Studio NYC August 4 1965 - 5:40)/ Desolation Row (Unreleased version. Rare early slow mix. Russ Savakus on bass, Charlie McCoy on guitar. Columbia Studio NYC July 30 1965 - 12:01)/ Positively 4th Street (Long version. Rough mix. Columbia Studio NYC July 29 1965 - 4:21)/ Can You Please Crawl Out Your Window? (Stereo version. Backing by The Band. Columbia Studio NYC October 20 1965 - 3:37)/ Vision Of Johanna (Rare different take. Columbia Studio, Nashville February 1966 - 7:45)/ Like A Rolling Stone* (The A.B.C. Theatre, Edinburgh, Scotland May 20 1966)
Recording: Excellent. Soundboard. *Good.
Comments: European CD. Time 72:58.

CD - THE EMPIRE STRIKES BACK
LAUGHING CAMEL RECORDS HUMP 001/002
CD1: Leopard-Skin Pillbox Hat/ Tonight I'll Be Staying Here With You/ All Along The Watchtower/ Under The Red Sky/ Just Like Tom Thumb's Blues/ Silvio/ Mr. Tambourine Man/ John Brown/ To Ramona/ Ballad Of A Thin Man
CD2: When I Paint My Masterpieces/ 7 Days/ Alabama Getaway/ It Ain't Me Babe/ Rainy Day Women No. 12 & 35/ Drifters Escape/ The Man In The Long Black Coat/ Positively 4th Street/ Watching The River Flow
Recording: Excellent. Audience.
Source: Liverpool Empire June 27 1996. CD2 Tracks 6-9 Liverpool Empire June 26 1996.
Comments: European CD. Deluxe color cover. Time CD1 71:46. CD2 74:02.

CD - EXCLUSIVE SERIES '94
ES 002
Disease Of Conceit (6:07)/ Man In The Long Black Coat (7:49)/ Every Gain Of Sand (7:41)/ Mr. Tambourine Man (5:32)/ Blowin' In The Wind (5:12)/ Jokerman (7:38)/ Just Like A Woman (6:30)/ Love Minus Zero, No Limit (6:28)/ I Shall Be Released (6:52)/ Knockin' On Heaven's Door (9:58)/ One Too Many Mornings (6:38)
Recording: Excellent. Audience.
Comments: European CD. Deluxe color cover. Picture CD.

CD - GERMANY SUMMER TOUR 1995 VOL. 1
IPPY 012/013
CD1: Down In The Flood/ Man In The Long Black Coat/ All Along The Watchtower/ I Believe In You/ Most Likely You Go Your Way/ Silvio/ Mr. Tambourine Man/ Boots Of Spanish Leather/ To Ramona/ Everything Is Broken
CD2: Every Grain Of Sand/ Highway 61 Revisited/ Like A Rolling Stone/ It Ain't Me Babe/ Rainy Day Woman/ Drifter's Escape/ The Man In Me/ All Along The Watchtower
Recording: Excellent. Audience.
Source: CD1, CD2 tracks 1-5 Terminal 1 Airport Riem, Munchen June 8 '95, tracks

DYLAN, BOB

6-8 Congress Centrum, Stuttgart June 10 '95.
Comments: European CD. Deluxe color cover. Time CD1 75:01. CD2 66:08.

CD - GERMANY SUMMER TOUR 1995 VOL. 2
IPPY 014/015
CD1: All Along The Watchtower/ Shooting Star/ It Takes Alot To Laugh/ Silvio/ Tangled Up In Blue/ Boots Of Spanish Leather/ It's All Over Now Baby Blue/ Stuck Inside Of Mobile
CD2: I Believe In You/ Cat's In The Well/ Knockin' On Heaven's Door/ My Back Pages/ Rainy Day Women #12 & 35/ Born In Time/ Shelter From THe Storm/ Silvio/ Mama You Been On My Mind
Recording: Excellent. Audience.
Source: CD1, CD2 tracks 1-5 Westfalenhalle, Dortmund June 12 '95. CD2 Tracks 6-9 Congress Centrum, Stuttgart June 10 '95.
Comments: European CD. Deluxe color cover. Time CD1 67:45. CD2 75:01.

CD - GUIDED BY THE ETERNAL LIGHT
TUFF BITES T.B. 95. 1026
CD1: Crash On The Levee/ Takes A Lot To Laugh/ All Along the Watchtower/ Simple Twist Of Fate/ Silvo/ The Tombstone Blues/ Mr. Tambourine Man/ Masters Of War/ To Ramona/ Band Introduction
CD2: Stuck Inside Mobile/ Knockin' On Heaven's Door/ I Want You/ Just Like A Woman/ Shooting Star/ Obviously Five Believers/ Shelter From The Storm/ Love Minus Zero, No Limit/ If Not For You
Recording: Very good. Soundboard. CD2 tracks 3-12 very good. Audience.
Source: Laguna Seca Daze, Monterey May 27 1995. CD2 tracks 3-12 various May-June 1995.
Comments: European CD. Deluxe color cover.

CD - GUITARS KISSING AND THE CONTEMPORARY FIX
SCORPIO 51766A/51766E
CD1: She Belongs To Me/ Fourth Time Around/ Visions Of Johanna/ Its All Over Now, Baby Blue/ Desolation Row/ Just Like A Woman/ Mr. Tambourine Man
CD2: Tell Me Mama/ I Don't Believe You (She Acts Like We Never Have Met)/ Baby, Let Me Follow You Down/ Just Like Tom Thumb's Blues/ Leopard Skin Pill-Box Hat/ One Too Many Mornings/ Ballad Of A Thin Man/ Like A Rolling Stone
Recording: Excellent. Soundboard.
Source: Bob Dylan with The Hawks, Manchester Free Trade Hall May 17 '66.
Comments: The first version came in a gatefold cardboard cover with a black and white picture and red type. Each picture CD is in a cardboard sleeve with black and white pictures. Due to the demand for this item, it was re-released by Scorpio with a different cover. Time CD1 49:06. CD2 44:48.

CD - HARD TIMES IN ALABAMA
REAL LIVE RL CD 36 1/2
CD1: Hard Times (5:21)/ Stuck Inside Of Mobile With The Memphis Blues Again (8:35)/ All Along The Watchtower (5:22)/ You're A Big Girl Now (6:00)/ Tangled Up In Blue (10:34)/ Born In Time (6:16)/ Watching The River Flow (5:47)/ Jim Jones (Traditional) (6:04)/ Tomorrow Night (5:38)/ Gates Of Eden (6:49)/ Don't think Twice, It's Allright (8:14)
CD2: Cat's In The Well (5:05)/ I And I (7:43)/ Shelter From The Storm (7:37)/ Everything Is Broken (5:20)/ What Good Am I? (6:47)/ Maggie's Farm (6:13)/ It Ain't Me, Babe (9:01)/ Black Jack Davey (6:03)/ God Knows (5:37)/ Series Of Dreams (5:51)/ Pancho & Lefty (4:32)/ Hard Times (4:15)
Recording: Excellent audience.
Source: CD1 tracks 1-11 and CD2 tracks 1-7 Von Braun Concert Hall, Huntsville April 19 1993. CD2 tracks 8-10 Wolf Trap Farm, Vienna September 8 1993. CD2 tracks 11-12 Austin, TX May 5 1993.
Comments: Euro CD. Deluxe color cover.

CD - HIGHWAY 49 REVISITED
TOP CAT 760501
Mr. Tambourine Man/ Simple Twist Of Fate/ Vincent Van Gogh/ I'll Be Your Baby Tonight/ Maggie's Farm/ One Too Many Mornings/ Isis/ Blowing In The Wind/ I Pity The Poor Immigrant/ Shelter From The Storm/ I Threw It All Away/ Stuck Inside Of Mobile With The Memphis Blues Again/ You're A Big Girl Now/ You're Gonna Make Me Lonesome When You Go/ Mozambique/ Idiot Wind
Recording: Very good audience.
Source:Live At Reid Green Coliseum

DYLAN, BOB

DYLAN, BOB

Hattiesburg May 1 1976.
Comments: Time 75:39.

CD - HOLLIS BROWN AT IVY
CD1: Crash On the Levee (Down In The Flood)/ If You See Her, Say Hello/ All Along The Watchtower/ Just Like A Woman/ It Takes A Lot To Laugh, It Takes A Train To Cry/ Silvio/ Oh Babe, It Ain't No Lie/ Mr. Tambourine Man/ Ballad Of Hollis Brown/ Don't Think Twice It's Alright
CD2: I'll Remember You/ Maggie's Farm/ Like A Rolling Stone/ It Ain't Me Babe/ Rainy Day Woman/ Just Like Tom Thumb's Blues/ The Man In Me/ When I Paint My Masterpiece/ Absolutely Sweet Marie/ Viola Les Blues
Recording: Very good. Audience.
Source: CD1 and CD2 tracks 1-5 Kurashiki Shiminkaikan Okayama February13 1997. CD2 track 6 International Forum Tokyo February 10 1997. CD2 track 7 San Plaza Sendai February 20 1997. CD track 8 Kenminkaikan Akita February 22 1997. CD2 tracks 9-10 Kouseinenkin Kaikan Sapporo February 24 1997.
Comments: Japanese CD. Deluxe color cover. Time CD1 65:05. CD2 75:51.

CD - I'VE GOT A SONG TO SING
BD 96
Sake Sugaree (Berlin, Germany June 17 1996) (5:57)/ This Wheel's On Fire (Madison, WI April 13 1996) (7:06)/ Friend Of The Devil (Lewisburg May 3 1996) (6:36)/ Seven Days (Frankfurt, Germany June 19 1996) (5:19)/ Visions Of Johanna (Differdange, Luxemburg June 24 1996) (7:59)/ Disease Of Conceit (Buffalo, NY May 11 1996) (6:42)/ Hattie Carroll (Orono, FL April 23 1996) (7:37)/ New Minglewood Blues (Differdange, Luxemburg June 24 1996) (5:39)/ Pretty Peggy-O (Mannheim, Germany July 2 1996) (5:56)/ Blowin' In The Wind (Cottbus, Germany July 14 1996) (8:29)/ Like A Rolling Stone (Montpellier, France, July 27 1996) (8:29)
Recording: Excellent.
Source: Compilation of rare performances in 1996.
Comments: European CD. Deluxe color cover. Gold disc.

CD - IN CHRISTIANIA
CRYSTAL CAT RECORDS 407-10
CD1: Intro/ To Be Alone With You/ If You See Her, Say Hello/ All Along The Watchtower/ Tears Of Rage/ I Don't Believe You (She Acts Like We Never Met)/ Silvio/ Boots Of Spanish Leather/ Masters Of War/ Friend Of The Devil/ Tombstone Blues
CD2: She Belongs To Me/ Everything Is Broken/ It Ain't Me, Babe/ Rainy Day Women #12 & 35/ Bonus Tracks: Pretty Peggy-O/ To Ramona/ What Good Am I?/ Alabama Getaway/ Ring Them Bells/ Shelter From The Storm
CD3: Intro/ To Be Alone With You/ I Want You/ All Along The Watchtower/ You're A Big Girl Now/ I'll Be Your Baby Tonight/ Silvio/ Love Minus Zero, No Limit/ Tangle Up In Blue/ The Lonesome Death Of Hattie Carroll/ Maggies Farm
CD4: Lennie Bruce/ Cat's In The Well/ My Back Pages/ Highway 61 Revisited/ Girl From The North Country/ Bonus Tracks: Simple Twist Of Fate/ John Brown/ Mama, You Been On My Mind
Recording: Excellent audience.
Source: Den Gra Hal., Fristaden Christiania, Copenhagen, Denmark CD1-2 July 23 1996. CD3-4 July 24 1996.
Comments: European box set. Fold-out cardboard card with info ans pictures. Picture CDs. Time: CD1 72:53. CD2 75:03. CD3 76:25. CD4 76:13.

CD - LAGUNA BEACH
MIDNIGHT BEAT MB CD 067/68
CD1: Down In The Flood (5:23)/ It Takes A Lot To Laugh, It Takes A Train To Cry (6:37)/ All Along The Watchtower (6:38)/ Simple Twist Of Fate (3:34)/ Silvio (6:50)/ Tombstone Blues (7:48)/ Mr. Tambourine Man (7:22)/ Masters Of War (5:34)/ To Ramona (7:20)/ Seeing The Real You At Last (5:45)
CD2: Every Grain Of Sand (8:55)/ Stuck Inside Of Mobile With The Memphis Blues Again (10:31)/ Knockin' On Heavens Door (7:37)/ All Along the Watchtower (5:53)/ Just Like A Woman (5:16)/ Seeing The Real You At Last (5:14)/ Highway 61 Revisited (5:19)/ Forever Young (5:43)/ I Shall Be Released (6:22)
Recording: Excellent. Soundboard.
Source: Laguna Seca Recreation Area, Monterey, CA May 27 1995. CD2 tracks 4-8 Rock 'N Roll Hall Of Fame, Municipal Stadium, Cleveland, Ohio September 2 1995. CD2 track 9 with Elvis Costello, Brixton Academy, London March 30 1995.

Comments: European CD. Deluxe color cover. Picture CD.

CD - MAESTRO
QR- 1/2
CD1: Senor/ All Along The Watchtower/ Shooting Star/ Most Likely To Go Your Way/ Silvo/ Tangled Up In Blue/ A Hard Rains Gonna Fall
CD2: I Shall Be Released/ Seeing The Real You At Last/ Like A Rolling Stone/ The Times They Are A-Changin'/ Rainy Day Woman/ Like A Rolling Stone/ Drifter's Escape/ It Takes A Lot To Laugh, It Takes A Train To Cry/ All Along The Watchtower/ What Good Am I/ I Want You
Recording: Poor audience recording.
Source: Barcelona, Spain July 24 1995. CD2 tracks 6-9 Montpellier, France July 27 1995. CD2 track 10 Aston Villa April 2 1995. CD2 track 11 Brighton Mar. 26 1995.

CD - MORE SUNRISES
RED SKY RECORDS CD 1015
I'll Remember You/ Simple Twist Of Fate/ Desolation Row/ Boots Of Spanish Leather/ What Was It You Wanted/ A Hard Rain's A-Gonna Fall/ You're A Big Girl Now/ What Good Am I?/ Girl From The North Country/ Ballad Of Hollis Brown/ Man In The Long Black Coat/ Positively 4th Street/ Queen Jane Approximately/ Just Like A Woman/ It's Alright, Ma (I'm Only Bleeding)
Recording: Very good audience recording.
Source: USA '90.

CD - NORTH WIND BLOWING
KISS THE STONE KTS 578/79
CD1: Leopard Skin Pill Box Hat/ Man In The Long Black Coat/ All Along The Watchtower/ Positively 4th Street/ Most Likely Go Your Way (And I'll Go Mine)/ Silvo/ Tangled Up In Blue (acoustic)/ Lonesome Death Of Hattie Carroll (acoustic)
CD2: Ballad Of Hollis Brown (acoustic)/ Absolutely Sweet Marie/ Ballad Of A Thin Man/ Highway 61 Revisited/ Girl Of The North Country (acoustic)/ Rainy Day Woman #12 & 35/ My Back Pages (acoustic)
Recording: Excellent.
Source: The Spektrum, Oslo, Norway July 18 1996.
Comments: European CD.

CD - PARADISE HAWAIIAN STYLE
Q RECORDS QR 11/12
CD1: Rainy Day Women Nos 12 & 35/ Most Of The Time/ Union Sundown/ Just Like A Woman/ Stuck Inside Of Mobile With The Memphis Blues Again/ I'll Be Your Baby Tonight/ She Belongs To Me/ Love Minus Zero, No Limit/ Little Moses/ Golden Vanity/ Mr. Tambourine/ Cat's In The Well/ Idiot Wind
CD2: The Times They're A-Changin'/ Highway 61 Revisited/ Absolutely Sweet Marie/ All Along The Watchtower/ Blowin' In The Wind/ 2x2/ Most Likely You Go Your Way I'll Go Mine/ Simple Twist Of Fate/ Desolation Row/ One Too Many Mornings/ John Brown/ Don't Think Twice It's Alright/ Knockin' On Heaven's Door
Recording: Excellent stereo. Soundboard. CD2 tracks 6-13 good audience.
Source: CD1 and CD2 tracks 1-5 Waikiki Shell, Waikiki, Hawaii April 24 1992. CD 2 track 6 Toronto August 18 1992. CD2 tracks 7-13 Hawkeye Arena, Iowa November 8 1990.
Comments: European CD. Deluxe color cover. Time CD1 63:42. CD2 68:21.

CD - THE PEDLAR NOW SPEAKS
RAZOR'S EDGE RAZ019/20
CD1: Down In The Flood/ If Not For You/ All Along The Watchtower/ License To Kill/ Most Likely You Go Your Way/ Silvo/ Mr. Tambourine Man/ Visions Of Johanna/ Girl From The North Country/ God Knows
CD2: Unbelievable/ Knockin' On Heaven's Door/ Tangled Up In Blue/ Rainy Day Woman #12&35/ Shelter From The Storm/ Masters Of War/ What Good Am I?/ Cat's In A Well/ My Back Pages/ Like A Rolling Stone
Recording: Very good audience recording.
Source: Theatre Of Living Arts, Philadelphia June 21 1995. CD2 tracks 5-10 June 22 1995.

CD - PROTEST AND FOLK SONGS - THE BOOTLEG SERIES TAKE 2
SCORPIO
CD1: The Two Sisters (Karen Wallace's Apartment, St. Paul, Minnesota May '60)/ Lang A-Growing (Carnegie Hall, New York, April 11 '61)/ Corrina, Corrina (Columbia Studios, New York April 24-25 '62)/ That's Alright Mama (Columbia Studio, New York November 14 '62)/ Hero Blues (Columbia

Studios December 6 '62)/ Long Time Gone (recorded for Witmark Music as a publishers demo, New York)/ Lay Down Your Weary Tune (Carnegie Hall, New York October 20 '63)/ Guess I'm Doing Fine (recorded for Witmark Music as a publishers demo, New York)/ Mr, Tambourine Man I (Columbia Studios, New York June 9 '64)/ Mr. Tambourine Man II (Newport Folk Festival, Rhode Island July 26 '64)/ It's All Over Now Baby Blue (Columbia Studios January 13 '65)/ Lunatic Princess Revisited (Columbia Studios, New York June 16 '65)/ I Don't Wanna Be Your Partner (Columbia Studios, New York October 20 '65)/ Freeze Out (Columbia Studios, New York November 20 '65)/ Does She Need Me I & II (Glasgow Hotel Room (May 19 '66)/ Like A Rolling Stone (Royal Albert Hall May 27 '66

CD2: I'm Not There (recorded for The Basement Tapes, Saugerties, New York summer '67)/ Lang A-Growing (recorded for The Basement Tapes, Saugerties, New York summer '67)/ Banks Of The Royal Canal (recorded for The Basement Tapes, Saugerties, New York summer '67)/ Silent Weekend (recorded for The Basement Tapes, Saugerties, New York summer '67)/ Wild Mountain Thyme (Isle Of Wight, U.K. August 31, '67)/ Tomorrow Is A Long Time (Columbia Studios New York June '70)/ Spanish Is The Loving Tongue (Columbia Studios, New York June '70)/ George Jackson (Blue Rock Studios, New York November 4 '71)/ Goodbye Holly (recorded for the soundtrack to 'Pat Garrett And Billy The Kid' at CBS Mexico City Disco Studios, Los Angeles January 20 '73)/ House Of The Rising Sun (Village Recorder Studios, Los Angeles November 2 '73)/ Nobody 'Cept You (Village Recorder Studios, Los Angeles November 2 '73)/ Tangled Up In Blue (A & R Studios, New York September 16 '74)/ Abandoned Love (Other End Club, New York July 3 '75)/ People Get Ready (S.I.R. Rehearsals, New York October '75)/ The Water Is Wide (Shangri-La Studios, Malibu March 30 '76)/ Repossession Blues (Rundown Studios, Santa Monica February 1 '78)/ If You See Her Say Hello (Rundown Studios, Santa Monica January 30 '78)/ Stop Now II (Rundown Studios, Santa Monica May 2 '78)/ Coming From The Heart (Rundown Studios, Santa Monica May 2 '78)

CD3: Ain't Gonna Go To Hell (Massey Hall, Toronto April 20 '78)/ Coverdown Breakthrough (Massey Hall, Toronto April 19 '78)/The Groom's Still Waiting At The Altar (Warfield, San Francisco November 15 '80)/ Magic (Clover Recorder Studios, Los Angeles April '81)/ Heart Of Mine (Clover Recorder Studios, Los Angeles April '81)/Nadine (Lone Star Cafe, New York February 16 '83)/ We Three (Malibu March '84)/ The Dawn Is Gonna Shine (Almost Done I) (Beverly Theatre, Los Angeles May 23 '84)/ Almost Done II (Arena Di Verona, Italy May 27 '84)/ Freedom For The Stallion (Oceanway, Los Angeles November '84)/ Something's Burning Baby (Cherokee Studios, Los Angeles November '84)/ To Fall In Love With You (Townhouse Studios, London, August 27-28 '86)/ Got Love If You Want It (Sunset Sound, Los Angeles April '87)/ Don't Keep Me Waiting Too Long (Club Front, San Rafeal, California May '87)/ Broken Days (Studio On The Move, New Orleans March 89)/ Born In Time (Studio On The Move, New Orleans March 89)/ Most Of The Time (Culver City Studios, California March 2 '90)/ Series Of Dreams (Wolf Trap, Virginia September 8 '93)
Recording: Excellent.
Comments: Tri-fold deluxe color cardboard cover. Another excellent Scorpio product.

CD - PLYMOUTH ROCK
COLOSSEUM 97-C-015
I Don't Believe You/ Hurricane/ Oh Sister/ One More Cup Of Coffee/ Sara/ Just Like A Woman/ This Land Is Your Land/ A Hard Rains A' Gonna Fall/ Romance In Durango/ Isis/ Blowin' In The Wind/ The Water Is Wide/ I Dreamed I Saw St. Augustine/ Never Let Me Go/ I Shall Be Released/ Knockin' On Heaven's Door
Recording: Excellent stereo. Soundboard.
Source: Tracks 1-7 War Memorial Auditorium Plymouth MA October 31 1975. Tracks 8-16 Palace Theatre Waterbury CT November 11 1975.
Comments: Japanese CD. Deluxe color cover. Time 74:55.

CD - RICH FOR POOR
RAMBLING COWBOY MUSIC
CD1: So Long, Good Luck And Good Bye/ Positively 4th Street/ Clean-Cut Kid/ Emotionally Yours/ Trust Yourself/ We Had

It All/ Masters Of War/ Straight Into Darkness/ One Of These Days/ The Waiting/ Breakdown
CD2: To Ramona/ One Too Many Mornings/ A Hard Rains A-Gonna Fall/ I Forgot More Than You'll Ever Know/ Band Of The Hand/ When Night Comes Falling From The Sky/ Lonesome Town/ Ballad Of A Thin Man/ Johnny B. Goode/ The Losing/ Spike/ Refugee
Recording: Very good.
Source: Buffalo, New York July 4 1986. CD2 tracks 13-16 TV charity show September 14 1986.
Comments: With Tom Petty And The Heartbreakers.

CD - RING THEM BELLS
MOONLIGHT ML 9635
Ring Them Bells/ Shooting Star/ God Knows 1/ God Knows 2/ What Good Am I/ Most Of The Time/ Everything Is Broken/ Political World 1/ Political World 2/ Born In Time/ Dignity/ Shooting Star/ Disease Of Conceit/ Ring Them Bells/ Most Of The Time/ Ring Them Bells
Recording: Excellent. Soundboard.
Source: 'Oh Mercy' outtakes, New Orleans, Louisiana March 1989.
Comments: European CD. Deluxe color cover. Time 61:19.

E

EAGLES

CD - VANISHING AWAY
DR. GIG DGCD 057
Peaceful Easy Feeling/ Already Gone/ Good Day In Hell/ Silver Threads And Golden Needles/ Desperado/ It Doesn't Matter Anymore/ Midnight Flyer/ Twenty One/ O'l 55/ Your Bright Baby Blues/ Looking Into You/ James Dean/ Doolin-Dalton, Desperado/ Take It Easy/ Hotel California
Recording: Excellent. Soundboard.
Source: Tracks 1-14 Don Kirshner Rock Concert, TV program USA 1974. Tracks 4-6 with Linda Ronstadt. Tracks10-11 with Jackson Browne. Track 15 reunion concert USA 1994.
Comments: European CD. Time 72:18.

ECHOBELLY

CD - PANTYHOSE & ROSES
KISS THE STONE KTS 540
Car Fiction (3:04)/ Give Her A Gun (3:45)/ Great Things (3:51)/ Pantyhose And Roses (3:12)/ Can't Imagine (3:45)/ Natural Animal (3:49)/ Call Me Names (4:44)/ King Of The Kerb (5:03)/ Go Away (3:10)/ Today, Tomorrow (3:14)/ Father, Ruler King, Computer (2:58)/ Insomniac (4:32)/ Dark Therapy (7:58)
Recording: Excellent stereo. Soundboard.
Source: The Phoenix, Toronto, Canada, November 21 '95.
Comments: European CD. Deluxe color cover. Picture CD.

EMERSON, LAKE AND PALMER

CD - DEBUT
IOW-70CD
The Barbarian (5:22)/ Take A Pebble (11:51)/ Pictures At An Exhibition Promenade (1:26)/ The Gnome (3:46)/ Promenade, The Sage (4:29)/ The Sage (1:02)/ The Old Castle, Blues Variation (7:08)/ Blues Variation, Promenade (2:54)/ The Hut Of Baba Yaga, The Curse Of Baba Yaga, The Hut Of Baba Yaga, The Great Gates Of Kiev (15:06)/ Rondo (4:20)/ Nutrocker (4:48)
Source: Wight Festival, England August 29 1970.
Comments: Japanese CD.

CD - THE 1972 AMERICAN TOUR
BS-12/13
CD1: Tarkus/ The Endless Enigma (Part One)/ Fugue/ The Endless Enigma (Part Two)/ The Sheriff/ Take A Pebble/ Lucky Man
CD2: Take A Pebble (Reprise)/ Pictures At An Exhibition/ Hoedown/ Grand Finale (Rondo)
Recording: Very good.
Source: The Long Beach Arena July 28 1972.

CD - CUT THE ORGAN
ULTRAVIOLET SOUNDS CORP.
CD1: Hoedown/ Tarkus/ The Endless Enigma/ Alan Freeman Theme/ The Sheriff/ Take A Pebble/ Lucky Man
CD2: Piano Improvisation/ Take A Pebble/ Pictures At An Exhibition/ Nutrocker/ Rondo

ENO

Recording: Good to very good.
Source: Hammersmith Odeon '72.

ENO

CD - UNRELEASED TRACKS
Unknown/ Unknown/ Unknown/ Fun Time/ Fear/ Worlds And Music/ Strong Flashes Of Light/ More Volts/ Mist, Rhythm/ Evening Star/ Mel Ancho Ly Wal Tz/ The Secret/ Don't Look Back
Source: Tracks 1-3 outtakes from David Bowie's albums 'Low' And 'Lodger'. Track 4 studio outtake with Iggy Pop and David Bowie. Track 5 studio outtakes with John Cale. Track 6 promotional release only track 1989.
Comments: Japanese CD.

ETHERIDGE, MELISSA

CD - CIRKUS
MOONRAKER 114
An Unusual Kiss/ Come To My Window/ I Want To Come Over/ If I Wanted To/ Shriner's Park/ You Can Sleep While I Drive/ All The Way To Heaven/ Like The Way/ This War Is Over
Recording: Excellent.
Source: Circus, Stockholm February 11 1996.
Comments: European CD.

CD - NO MORE SECRETS
ME 0296-A/B
CD1: An Unusual Kiss (6:19)/ Come To My Window (4:38)/ I Want To Come Over (5:48)/ If I Wanted To (4:25)/ Nowhere To Go (6:30)/ Similar Features (4:47)/ Shriner's Park (8:35)/ Change (6:06)/ Silent Legacy (9:35)/ I Could Have Been You (7:42)/ You Can Sleep While I Drive (4:20)/ Occasionally (3:10)
CD2: All The Way To Heaven (5:30)/ Chrome Plated Heart (7:07)/ Must Be Crazy For Me (7:38)/ I Really Like You (5:02)/ Bring Me Some Water (7:25)/ I'm The Only One (10:00)/ Your Little Secret (4:29)/ Like The Way I Do (16:04)/ This War Is Over (9:51)
Recording: Excellent stereo. Audience.
Source: Sporthalle, Cologne, Germany February 5 1996.

CD - RUN BABY RUN
OXYGEN OXY 081
An Unusual Kiss/ Come To My Window/ I Want To Come Over/ If I Wanted To/ Shriner's Park/ You Can Sleep While I Drive/ All The Way To Heaven/ Like The Way I Do/ Ain't It Heavy (acoustic version)/ Yes I Am/ Let Me Go/ Must Be Crazy For Me/ Heaven Help Us On (with Stevie Wonder, Rev. Al Green And Bonnie Raitt)/ Honkey Tonk Woman (with Sammy Hagar)
Recording: Excellent stereo. Soundboard.
Source: Tracks 1-8 Cirkus, Stockholm, Sweden February 11 '96. Tracks 9-12 Ahoy, Rotterdam, Holland February 2 '96. Tracks 13-14 Shrine Auditorium, Los Angeles, CA June 26 '94.
Comments: European CD. Picture CD. Time 73:52

CD - VALENTINE'S DAY
MOONRAKER 059/60
CD1: An Unusual Kiss/ Come To My Window/ I Want To Come Over/ If I Wanted To/ Nowhere To Go/ Similar Features/ Shriner's Park/ Change/ Silent Legacy/ I Could Have Been You/ You Can Sleep While I Drive*/ Watching You/ Occasionally
CD2: All The Way To Heaven/ Chrome Plated Heart/ Must Be Crazy/ I Really Like You/ Bring Me Some Water/ I'm The Only One/ Your Little Secret/ Like The Way/ This War Is Over
Recording: Excellent stereo. Soundboard.
Source: Huxley's New World, Berlin, Germany February 14 '96. *Cirkus Stockholm February 11 '96.
Comments: European CD.

EVERCLEAR

CD - CONFUSION
KISS THE STONE KTS 558
Electra Made Me Blind/ Like A Whore/ Nervous And Weird/ Summerland/ Heartspark Dollar Sign/ Heroin Girl/ Santa Monica/ Got No Place To Go/ Sin City/ Chemical Smile/ Electra Made Me Blind/ Heartspark Dollar Sign/ Santa Monica/ Heroin Girl/ Santa Monica/ Heartspark Dollar Sign
Recording: Excellent.
Source: Tracks 1-10 The Paradiso, Amsterdam January '96. Tracks 11-14 London, May 20 '96. Tracks 15-16 The 'Later Show' May 25 '96.

Comments: European CD. Deluxe color cover. Picture CD. Time 53:19

CD - HIGHLY ABRASIVE
OXYGEN OXY 075
Strawberry (2:48)/ Electra Made Me Blind (3:03)/ You Make Me Feel Like A Whore (3:31)/ Your Genius Hands (2:31)/ Nervous And Weird (3:05)/ Heartspark Dollarsign (2:55)/ The Twist inside (4:22)/ Her Brand New Skin (1:52)/ Chemical Smile (2:05)/ Loser Makes Good (2:44)/ Summerland (3:49)/ Heroin Girl (2:48)/ Sparkle (2:23)/ Santa Monica (3:16)/ My Sexual Life (4:03)/ Nehalem (1:36)/ American Girl (3:59)/ Electra Made Me Blind (4:01)/ Fire Maple Song (4:13)/ Heartspark Dollarsign (2:59)/ Santa Monica (3:04)/ Sin City (4:42)/ Chemical Smile (1:53)
Recording: Excellent stereo. Soundboard.
Source: Tracks1-17 The Opera House, Toronto, Canada February 14 1996. Tracks18-23 The Paradiso, Amsterdam, Holland March 5 1996.
Comments: European CD. Picture CD.

CD - STRAWBERRY VALENTINE
MOONRAKER 117
Strawberry/ Electric Made Me Blind/ You Make Me Feel Like A Whore/ Your Genius Hands/ Nervous And Weird/ Heartspark Dollarsign/ The Twist Inside/ Her Brand New Skin/ Chemical Smile/ Loser Makes Good/ Summerland/ Heroin Girl/ Sparkle/ Santa Monica/ My Sexual Life/ Nehalem/ American Girl
Recording: Excellent stereo. Soundboard.
Source: The Opera House, Toronto, Canada February 14 1996.
Comments: European CD.

F

FACES, THE

CD - LIVE AT RANDWICK RACECOURSE
WEEPING GOAT WG-043
It's All Over Now/ I'm Losing You/ Angel/ True Blue/ Stay With Me/ I'd Rather Go Blind/ Memphis Tennessee/ My Fault/ Too Bad, Every Picture Tells A Story/ You Wear It Well/ Maggie Mae/ I Wish It Would Rain/ Borstal Boys/ Around The Plynth, Gasoline Alley, Amazing Grace, Borstal Boys/ Twistin' The Night Away
Recording: Good to very good. Muffled.
Source: Randwick Racecourse, Sydney, Australia February 1 '74.
Comments: Japanese CD. Deluxe b&w cover. Red type. Time 73:59

FAITH NO MORE

CD - FOOL'S SMALL VICTORY
EKD 9095
A Small Victory (radio edit)/ The Perfect Crime/ Let's Lynch The Landlord (R-evolution 23 Full Moon Mix)/ I'm Easy/ Das Schutzenfest/ A Small Victory (Sundown Mix)/ Absolute Zero/ I Started A Joke/ Greenfields/ A Small Victory (Sundown Instrumental Mix)/ RV (live)/ Mark Bowen (live)/ Surprise You're Dead (live)/ Chinese Arithmetic (live)/ Midlife Crisis (live)/ Epic (live)/ We Care A Lot (live)
Recording: Excellent. Soundboard.
Source: B-Sides and rarities 1990-1995.
Comments: European CD. Deluxe color cover. Picture CD. Time 79:42.

CD - GOD IS DEAD!
ANTICHRIST RECORDS ACREC 236 765 1
Caffeine/ Be Aggressive/ As The Worm Turns/ The Crab Song/ Midlife Crisis/ RV/ Land Of Sunshine/ We Care A Lot/ Chinese Arithmetic/ Crack Hitler/ Edge Of The World/ Falling To Pieces/ Death March/ Surprise! Your Dead/ Woodpecker From Mars/ Jizzlobber/ Introduce Yourself/ A Small Victory/ I'm Easy/ Possible Bonus Track: Epic
Recording: Fair to good. Audience.
Source: Grosmarkt, Hamburg 5/6/93.
Comments: European CD. Deluxe color cover. Time 78:29.

FIRM, THE

CD - RADIOACTIVE
TAILFIN MUSIC CO. WEM85522
CD1: Closer/ City Sirens/ Make Or Break/ Morning After The Night Before/ Together/ Cadillac/ Prelude/ Money Can't Buy/ Satisfaction Guaranteed/ Radioactive/ Live In Peace/ Midnight Moonlight
CD2: You've Lost That Loving Feeling/ The Chase/ I Just Want to Make Love To You/ Someone To Love/ A Girl Possessed,

FIRM, THE

Boogie Mama/ Everybody Needs Someone To Love
Recording: Very good. Soundboard.
Source: Wembley Arena May 22 1985.
Comments: European CD.

CD - YOU NEVER CLOSE YOUR EYES
MIDAS TOUCH MD95521/22
CD1: Intro, Closer/ City Sirens/ Make Or Break Up/ The Night Before/ Together/ Cadillac/ Prelude/ Money Can't Buy/ Radioactive/ Live In Peace/ Midnight Moonlight
CD2: You've Lost That Lovin' Feeling/ The Chase/ I Just Wanna Make Love To You/ Full Circle/ Someone To Love/ Cut Loose/ A Girl Possessed Boogie, Boogie Mama/ Everybody Needs Somebody To Love
Recording: Excellent. Soundboard.
Source: Pacific Amphitheatre, Cosa Mesa March 16 1985.
Comments: Japanese CD.

FISH

CD - ARE YOU FREAKS OR WHAT?
FREAK RECORDS FR 9702
Vigil In The Wilderness Of Mirrors/ Credo- State Of Mind/ Tongues/ Just Good Friends/ Family Business/ Incubus/ Shadowplay/ Dear Friend/ Kayleigh/ Lucky/ Big Wedge
Recording: Very Good. Audience.
Source: Tivoli, Utrecht October 26 1991.
Comments: European CD.

CD - BACK ON STAGE
FREAK RECORDS FR 9701
Faith Healer/ The Voyeur/ Punch And Judy/ State Of Mind/ The Company/ Script For A Jester's Tears/ Family Business/ Warm Wet Circles/ Slainte Mhath/ Vigil In A Wilderness Of Mirrors/ Big Wedge/ Fugazi/ Kayleigh/ Lavender/ Heart Of Lothian/ Internal Exile/ View From The FER
Recording: Excellent. Audience.
Source: Queenshall, Edinburgh October 23 1989.
Comments: European 2 CD set.

FLEETWOOD MAC

CD - TIGER BEAT
BLUES 'N' GREENS 196869
Merry Go Round/ One Sided Love/ Dust My Broom/ Got To Move/ Sugar Mama/ I Can't Hold Out/ Please Stop Messing Around/ Unknown Blues/ Albatross/ Rattlesnake Shake/ Underway/ Tiger/ The Green Manalishi
Recording: Good. Audience.
Source: Tracks 1-9 Amsterdam 1969. Tracks 10-13 Santa Monica 1968.
Comments: Deluxe color cover. Cover only lists 13 songs but there are 15 on the CD. Time 74:21.

FOCUS

CD - SYLVIA
DYNAMITE STUDIO 94F065
Focus II/ Sylvia/ Harem Scarem/ Untitled/ Tommy (Eruption)/ Birth/ Hamburger Concerto/ Hocus Pocus
Source: Japan June 1975.
Comments: Japanese CD.

FOO FIGHTERS

CD - BRIXTON
KISS THE STONE KTS 518
Enough Space/ This Is A Call/ Winnebago, Wattershed/ For All The Cows/ Weenie Beenie/ Big Me/ I'll Stick Around/ Alone And Easy Target/ Up In Arms/ Gas Chamber/ Exhausted/ My Hero/ Ho, George/ This Is A Call/ Winnebago, Wattershed
Recording: Excellent stereo. Soundboard.
Source: Tracks 1-11 The Brixton Academy, London, England November 11 '95. Tracks 12-13 The Lowlands Festival, Holland June 27 '95. Track 14, New York July '95. Track 15 London, England November 16 '95.
Comments: European CD. Deluxe color cover. Picture CD. Time 56:35.

CD - DAVE GROHL DEMOS
BABYFACE RECORDS BF028
Pokey Little Puppy/ Petrol C.3./ Friend Of A Friend/ Throwing Needles/ Just Another Story About Skeeter Thompson/ Color Pictures Of A Marigold/ Hell's Garden/ Winnebago/ Bruce/ Milk/ X-static/ My Hero/ Down In The Park/ This Is A Call/ Gas Chamber/ Exhausted
Recording: Very good to excellent. Soundboard. Tracks 11-16 Good to Excellent.
Source: Tracks 1-10 Dave Grohl solo demos, Arlington, VA '90. Tracks 11-16 various live recordings '95.
Comments: European CD. Deluxe color

FOO FIGHTERS

Melissa Etheridge
run baby run

the fugees
refugees

FOO FIGHTERS

cover. Picture CD. Time 58:19.

CD - FOO RADIO
MOONRAKER 122
This Is A Call/ Winnebago/ Wattershed/ For All The Cows/ Weenie Beenie/ Butterflies/ Big Me/ Good Grief/ Coot/ How I Miss You/ Alone/ Easy Target/ I'll Stick Around/ Gas Chamber*/ This Is A Call*/ I'll Stick Around*/ Flortie*
Recording: Excellent.
Source: The Concert Hall, Toronto, Canada April 3 1996. *Universal Amphitheatre, Los Angeles, December 17 1995.
Comments: European CD.

CD - HOWLING WIND
TORNADO TOR055
Random Mumblings/ I'll Stick Around/ Not A Fool/ Wattershed/ Big Me/ This Is A Call/ Weenie Beenie/ For All The Cows/ My Hero/ I Will Listen/ Alone And Easy Target/ Exhausted/ Down In The Park/ Random Mumblings/ This Is A Call/ Not A Fool/ I'll Stick Around/ Wattershed
Recording: Very good. Audience.
Source: San Diego, CA July '95. Tracks 14-18 Hollywood, CA May '95.
Comments: European CD. Time 67:54.

CD - UP AGAINST!
OXYGEN OXY 088
This Is A Call (4:54)/ Winnebago (3:06)/ Wattershed (2:16)/ For All The Cows (3:31)/ Weenie Beenie (3:24)/ Butterflies (3:38)/ Big Me (2:28)/ Good Grief (3:39)/ Podunk (2:58)/ How I Miss You (7:56)/ Alone + Easy Target (4:29)/ I'll Stick Around (4:12)/ Pokey Little Puppy (Instrumental) (4:16)/ Petrol (4:41)/ Friend Of A Friend (3:06)/ Throwing Needles (3:20)/ Just Another Story (2:05)/ Hell's Garden (3:18)/ Bruce (Instrumental) (3:51)/ Milk (2:33)
Recording: Excellent.
Source: Tracks 1-12 The Concert Hall, Toronto, Canada April 3 1996. Tracks 13-20 Dave Grohl solo demo, Arlington, VA 1990.
Comments: European CD.

FUGEES

CD - REFUGEES
MOONRAKER 145
Intro/ No Woman, No Cry/ White Lines/ Vocab/ Interlude/ Manifest I/ How Many Mic's/ Introduction/ Interlude/ Fu-Gee-La/ Boof Baf/ Nappy Heads/ Interlude/ Killing Me Softly/ Medley/ Manifest II/ Ready Or Not/ Interlude/ ZeaLots/ Keep On Moving/ Redemption Song/ Bonus: Killing Me Softly (The '96 MTV Movie Awards, Los Angeles, June 13, '96)
Recording: Excellent stereo. Soundboard.
Source: Club Gino, Stockholm, Sweden May 22 1996.
Comments: European CD.

G

GABRIEL, PETER

CD - STONEYBROOK
MOONLIGHT ML9621
Keyboard Intro/ On The Air/ Moriband The Burgermeister/ Perspective/ Humdrum/ no title/ White Shadow/ D.I.Y./ Waiting For The Big One/ Flotsam & Jetsam/ Exposure/ Slowburn/ I Don't Remember/ Solsbury Hill/ Modern Love
Recording: Very good. Audience.
Source: October 24 1978.

GALLAGHER, RORY

CD - LAST OF THE INDEPENDENTS
SBC 026/027
CD1: The Continental OP/ Moonchild/ I Wonder Who/ Don't Start Me Talkin'/ I Could've Had Religion/ Ghost Blues/ Out On A Western Plain/ Walkin' Blues/ Tattoo'd Lady
CD2: Shadowplay/ A Million Miles Away/ Shinkicker/ Last Of The Independents/ Keychain/ Bought & Sold/ Follow Me/ Fly Off The Handle/ Walk On Hot Coals
Recording: Excellent.
Source: CD1 Tracks 1-9 and CD2 Tracks 1-2 Enschede, Holland January 6 1995. CD2 Tracks 3-9 Bottom Line, New York September 6 1979.
Comments: European CD. Deluxe color cover. Time CD1 67:48. CD2 53:45.

GARBAGE

CD - A NIGHT AT THE OPERA
MOONRAKER 054
Intro/ Supervixen/ Stupid Girl/ My Lover's Box/ As Heaven Is Wide/ Fix Me Now/

GARBAGE

Subhuman/ A Stroke Of Luck/ On Fire/ Queer/ Only Happy When It Rains/ Not My Idea/ Vow/ Milk/ Girls Don't Lie
Recording: Excellent stereo. Soundboard.
Source: The Opera House, Toronto, Canada November 10 '95.
Comments: European CD. Deluxe color cover. Time 66:06.

CD - COMPLETE GARBAGE
GB 960902
Driving Lesson/ Dog New Tricks (The Pal Mix)/ Stupid Girl (Red Snapper Mix)/ Alien Sex Fiend/ Stupid Girl (Dreadzone Dub Mix)/ Girl Don't Come/ Sleep/ Butterfly Collector/ Queer/ (F.T.F.O.1. Mix) Queer/ (Danny Sober Mix) Queer/ (The Most Beautiful Woman In Town Mix) Subhuman/ No. 1 Crush/ Vow (Torn Apart)
Recording: Excellent stereo. Soundboard.
Source: B-Sides and remixes.

CD - IN THE CAN
KISS THE STONE KTS 513
Intro-Supervixen/ Stupid Girl/ Sub Human/ Queer/ Trip My Wire/ Fix Me Now/ Only Happy When It Rains/ Not My Idea/ Vow/ Sub Human/ A Stroke Of Luck/ Milk/ Girls Don't Count/ Queer/ Only Happy When It Rains
Recording: Excellent.
Source: Tracks 1-9 The Sting, New Britain CT December 6 1995. Tracks 10-13 Amsterdam, Holland, November 11 1995. Tracks 14-15 Camden, London, England November 11 1995.
Comments: European CD.

CD - LIVE TRASH
KISS THE STONE KTS 541
Intro-Queer (6:46)/ Fix Me Now (4:58)/ Not My Idea (3:52)/ Dog New Tricks (4:15)/ My Lover's Box (3:48)/ Milk (4:21)/ Supervixen (3:52)/ Stupid Girl (4:25)/ Trip My Wire (4:49)/ Only Happy When It Rains (4:21)/ Vow (5:52)/ Supervixen (4:02)/ Fix Me Now (4:36)/ Milk (4:07)
Recording: Excellent stereo. Soundboard. Tracks 12-14 Excellent audience.
Source: Tracks 1-11 Dusseldorf Easter Festival, Germany 07/04/96. Tracks 12-14 Leeds, England 9/04/96.
Comments: European CD. Deluxe color cover. Picture CD.

CD - MUTANTE
ELECTRIC 40022
Queer/ Fix Me Now/ Not My Idea/ Dog New Tricks/ My Lover's Box/ Milk/ Supervixen/ Stupid Girl/ Trip/ I'm Only Happy When It Rains/ Vow/ I'm Only Happy When It Rains/ Stupid Girl
Recording: Excellent stereo. Soundboard.
Source: Tracks 1-11 Germany July 4 1996. Tracks 12-13 UK 1996.
Comments: European CD. Deluxe color cover. Time 58:47.

CD - PINK RADIO
MOONRAKER 156
Queer (4:54)/ Only Happy When It Rains (4:07)/ Vow (5:33)/ Queer (6:41)/ Fix Me Now (4:50)/ Not My Idea (3:44)/ Milk (4:11)/ Supervixen (4:02)/ Stupid Girl (4:32)/ Only Happy When It Rains (4:11)/ Vow (5:13)/ Stupid Girl (4:25)/ Kick My Ass (2:28)/ Only Happy When It Rains (4:05)/ Milk (4:04)/ Only Happy When It Rains (3:47)/ Stupid Girl (4:07)/ Only Happy When It Rains
Recording: Excellent.
Source: Tracks 1-3 The Universal Amphitheatre, Los Angeles December 17 1995. Tracks 4-11 London March 24 1996. Tracks 12-15 Modern Rock Live, Los Angeles April 14 1996. Track 18 MTV Movie Awards, Los Angeles June 13 1996.
Comments: European CD.

CD - THE TRIP
MOONRAKER 103
Queer/ Fix Me Now/ Not My Idea/ Dog New Tricks/ My Lover's Box/ Milk/ Supervixen/ Stupid Girl/ Trip My Wire/ Only Happy When It Rains/ Vow
Recording: Excellent stereo. Soundboard.
Source: The Philipshalle, Dortmund, Germany April 7 1996.
Comments: European CD.

CD - VANILLA GIRL
KOBRA RECORDS KRCD 18
Intro, Queer/ Fix Me Now/ Not My Idea/ Dog New Tricks/ My Lover's Box/ Milk/ Supervixen/ Stupid Girl/ Trip My Wire/ Only Happy When It Rains/ Vow/ #1 Crush/ As Heaven Is Wide/ A Stroke Of Luck/ Girl Don't Come
Recording: Excellent stereo. Soundboard.
Source: Tracks 1-11 Dusseldorf, Philipshalle 7/4/96. Track 12 unreleased song from the 1st single. Tracks 13-15

GARBAGE

Toronto 10/11/95.
Comments: European CD.

CD - VIBECRUSHER
ELECTRIC EL 40087
Supervixen/ Stupid Girl/ My Lover's Box/ As Heaven Is Wide/ Fix Me Now/ A Stroke Of Luck/ Trip My Wire/ Queer/ Only Happy When It Rains/ Not My Idea/ Vow/ Girl Don't Come/ Stupid Girl/ Queer/ Only Happy When It Rains/ Not My Idea
Recording: Excellent stereo. Soundboard.
Source: Tracks 1-12, Opera House, Toronto, Canada November 10 1995. Tracks 13-16 Berkeley Theatre, Berkeley, California December 15 1995.

GARCIA, JERRY

CD - LONESOME PRISON BLUES
DEAD MAN DM014
Deep Elum Blues/ Friend Of The Devil/ Jackaroe/ Oh Babe It Ain't No Lie/ It Takes A Lot To Laugh, A Train To Cry/ Run For The Roses/ Ripple/ I've Been All Around This World/ Valerie/ Dire Wolf/ Ruben And Cherise
Recording: Excellent stereo. Soundboard.
Source: Acoustic set, Oregon State Prison, Salem, OR May 5 '82.
Comments: European CD. Deluxe color cover. Time 53:09.

GASKIN

CD - END OF THE WORLD
RONDELET MUSIC & RECORDS
Sweet Dreamer Maker/ Victim Of The City/ Despier/ Burning Alive/ The Day Thou/ End Of The Day/ On My Way/ Lonely Man/ I'm No Fool/ Handful Of Reasons/ I'm No Fool (Remix)/ Sweet Dream Maker (Remix)
Recording: Excellent stereo. Soundboard.
Source: Studio.
Comments: Japanese CD. Deluxe color cover. Time 52:10.

GENESIS

CD - FANTASIA
EXPOSURE EX-002-1GE
Watcher Of The Skies/ Dancing With The Moonlit Knight/ The Cinema Show/ I Know What I Like/ Firth Of Fifth/ The Musical Box/ Horizons/ Supper's Ready
Recording: Good.

Source: The Roxy, Los Angels December 18 1973.

CD - IMPERIAL COLLEGE '72
NIGHT SUN-001
Watcher Of The Skies/ The Musical Box/ Get' Em Out By Friday/ Supper's Ready/ The Return Of The Giant Hogweed/ The Knife
Recording: Good. Audience
Source: Imperial College, UK November 18 1972.

CD - THE LAMB DESCENDS ON WATERBURY
OXYGEN OXY 089-090
CD1: The Lamb Lies Down On Broadway (4:33)/ Fly On A Windshield (4:06)/ Broadway Melody Of 1974 (0:28)/ Cuckoo Cocoon (2:06)/ In The Cage (7:40)/ The Grand Parade Of Lifeless Packaging (4:00)/ Back In NYC (5:38)/ Hairless Heart (2:22)/ Counting Out Time (3:32)/ The Carpet Crawlers (5:21)/ The Chambers Of 32 Doors (6:14)/ Lilywhite Lilith (2:55)/ The Waiting Room (5:40)/ Anyway (3:26)/ Here Comes The Supernatural Anaesthetist (3:51)/ The Lamia (6:57)/ Silent Sorrow In Empty Boats (3:02)
CD2: The Colony Of Slippermen (8:10)/ Ravine (1:29)/ The Light Dies Down On Broadway (3:31)/ Riding The Scree (4:20)/ In The Rapids (2:18)/ It (5:01)/ The Music Box (10:17) Here Comes The Supernatural Anaesthetist (1:25)/ Instrumental (1:29)/ In The Rapids (5:52)/ It (4:56)/ The Light Dies Down On Broadway (1:27)/ Here Comes The Supernatural Anaesthetist (#1) (4:23)/ Here Comes The Supernatural Anaesthetist (#2) (2:04)/ In The Cage (3:17)/ The Colony Of Slippermen (#1) (2:10)/ The Colony Of Slippermen (#2) (2:28)/ The Colony Of Slippermen (#3) (0:30)/ Fly On A Windshield (#1) (11:58)/ Fly On A Windshield #2) (2:16)
Recording: Excellent. Soundboard.
Source: Waterbury, CT December 1974. CD2 tracks 8-20 'Lamb Compositions' 4CD set, Hedley Grange, UK spring '74.
Comments: European CD

CD - MORE FOOL ME
HIGHLAND HL 029/30#G3
CD1: Watcher Of The Skies (7:44)/ Dancing With The Moonlit Knight (13:47)/ The

Cinema Show (11:38)/ I Know What I Like (9:23)
CD2: Firth Of Fifth (9:05)/ The Musical Box (12:04)/ More Fool Me (3:49)/ Supper's Ready (22:55)
Recording: Good to very good. Audience. Some hiss.
Source: Orpheus Theatre Boston April 24 1974.
Comments: Japanese CD. Deluxe color cover.

CD - SELLING ENGLAND BY THE SESSION
HIGHLAND HL 032/33#G4
CD1: Studio Improvisation #1 (5:57)/ Studio Improvisation #2 (0:20)/ The Battle Of Epping Forest (instrumental take #1) (2:36)/ The Battle Of Epping Forest (instrumental take #2) (2:51) The Battle Of Epping Forest (session take #1) (5:28)/ The Battle Of Epping Forest (session take #2) (6:15)/ The Battle Of Epping Forest (session take #3) (3:04)/ The Cinema Show (fast instrumental take) (0:31)/ The Cinema Show (session take #1) (5:12)/ Dancing With The Moonlit Knight (session take #1) (1:46)/ The Battle Of Epping Forest (session take #1) (4:09)/ The Last Time (1:00)/ You Really Got To Me (0:45)/ The Battle Of Epping Forest (instrumental take #3) (0:55)/ The Battle Of Epping Forest (instrumental take #4) (1:50)/ The Battle Of Epping Forest (session take #5) (12:28)/ I Know What I Like #1 (3:14)/ I Know What I Like #2 (4:12)/ The Cinema Show #1 (3:11)/ Phil's Solo (7:59)
CD2: Firth Of Fifth (instrumental take #1) (4:57)/ Firth Of Fifth (instrumental take #2) (5:07)/ The Cinema Show #2 (0:55)/ After The Ordeal (instrumental take #1) (4:30)/ Dancing With The Moonlit Knight (session take #2) (7:36)/ Dancing With The Moonlit Knight (session take #3) (4:18)/ The Battle Of Epping Forest (instrumental take #5) (7:13)/ The Battle Of Epping Forest (session take #6) (21:30)/ The Cinema show #3 (1:09)/ Dancing With The Moonlit Knight (ending different mix #1) (1:40)/ Dancing With The Moonlit Knight (ending different mix #2) (2:11)/ More Fool Me (studio demo) (3:11)/ After The Ordeal (different mix #1) (2:12)/ After The Ordeal (different mix #2) (2:15)/ I Know What I Like (alternate version) (4:07)
Recording: Good to very good. Soundboard. Some hiss.

Comments: Japanese CD.

CD - TALES OF ORDINARY MADNESS
DREAM WEAVER RECORDS DWR 396078-2
The Lamb Lies Down On Broadway/ Fly On A Windshield, Broadway Melody Of 1974/ Cuckoo Cocoon/ In The Cage/ The Grand Parade Of Lifeless Packaging/ Back In N.Y.C./ Hairless Heart/ Counting Out Time/ The Carpet Crawlers/ The Chamber Of 32 Doors/ Lilywhite Lilith/ The Waiting Room/ Anyway/ The Supernatural Anaestetist/ The Lamia/ The Light Dies Down On Broadway/ Riding The Scree
Recording: Excellent. Audience.
Source: Hippodrome, Birmingham 2/5/75.
Comments: European CD. Deluxe color cover. Time 77:07.

CD - THIS PLANET'S SOIL
NEWOX 73
Watcher Of The Skies/ Dancing With The Moonlit Knight/ Musical Box/ I Know What I Like/ Supper's Ready
Recording: Poor.
Source: New Oxford Theatre '73.

CD - WE
ALIEN SOUND MUSIC ALIEN 003
Fading Lights/ In the Cage/ Medley: Dance On A Volcano, The Lamb Lies Down On Broadway, Musical Box, Firth Of Fifth, I Know What I Like, That's All, Follow You Follow Me, I Know What I Like/ Carpet Crawl/ Domino Parts 1+2/ Throwing It All Away/ Abacab
Recording: Excellent stereo. Soundboard.
Source: Texas 1992. Tracks 2 and 4 USA 1974. Tracks 7 Spectrum, Philadelphia 1984.
Comments: European CD. Time 71:46.

GILLAN

CD - GLORIOUS BIRTHDAY
N-009
Second Sight/ Unchain Your Brain/ Are You Sure?/ Mr. Universe/ If You Believe Me/ Trouble/ No Easy Way/ Nervous/ Vengeance/ Sleeping On The Job/ Happy Birthday Ian/ Smoke On The Water
Recording: Good. Audience.
Source: Friars, Aylesbury, England August 21 1980.
Comments: Japanese CD. Deluxe color

GIN BLOSSOMS

GIN BLOSSOMS

CD - A BEAUTIFUL NIGHT
MOONRAKER 147
Highwire/ Day Job/ Til I Hear From You/ My Car/ Virginia/ Whitewash/ Not Only Numb/ Found Out About You/ I Can't Figure You Out/ Memphis Time/ Perfectly Still/ Hold Me Down/ Mrs Rita/ As Long As It Matters/ Hands Are Tied/ Hey Jealousy/ Follow You Down/ Competition Smile/ I Need To Know/ Allison Road
Recording: Excellent stereo. Soundboard.
Source: Duquesne University, Pittsburgh April 18 1996.
Comments: European CD.

CD - HARD ON IT
KISS THE STONE KTS 559/60
CD1: Highwire/ Day Job/ Til I Hear From You/ My Car/ Virginia/ Whitewash/ Not Only Numb/ Found Out About You/ I Can't Figure You Out/ Memphis Time/ Perfectly Still/ Hold Me Down
CD2: Mrs. Rita/ As Long As It Matters/ Hands Are Tied/ Hey Jealousy/ Follow You Down/ Flaming Moe's/ Competition Smile/ I Need To Know/ Allison Road/ Til I Hear From You*/ As Long As It Matters*/ Competition Smile*
Recording: Excellent stereo. Soundboard.
Source: Duquesne University, Pittsburgh April 18 1996. *New York February 9 1996 (Acoustic Session).
Comments: European CD. Deluxe color cover. Picture CD.

GRATEFUL DEAD, THE

CD - AT KAISER'S PLACE
KISS THE STONE KTS 552/53
CD1: Feel Like a Stranger (9:03)/ Cold Rain & Snow (6:43)/ Mama Tried (2:39)/ Big River (5:32)/ West L.A. Fadeaway (7:20)/ Looks Like Rain (8:21)/ Brown-Eyed Woman (5:14)/ Let It Grow (11:14)/ Keep On Growing (4:52)
CD2: Lost Sailor (13:30/ Saint Of Circumstances (5:49)/ Terrapin Station (6:15)/ Drum Solo Space (12:24)/ Wharf Rat (10:25)/ Throwing Stones (8:46)/ Turn On Your Love Light (5:34)/ Brokedown Palace (5:24)
Recording: Excellent stereo. Soundboard.
cover. Time 75:30.
Source: The Convention Center, Oakland, CA February 14 1986.
Comments: European CD. Picture CD.

CD - BIG BUST
CD1: Here Comes Sunshine/ Walkin' Blues/ Dire Wolf/ It's All Over Now/ Broken Arrow/ Desolation Row/ Tennessee Jed/ Let It Grow/ Scarlet Begonias
CD2: Fire On The Mountain/ Victim Or The Crime/ It's All Too Much/ New Speedway Boogie/ Drums, Space/ Attics Of My Life/ Sugar Magnolia/ Quinn The Eskimo
Recording: Good to very good. Audience.
Source: Deer Creek, Noblesville, IN July 2 1995.
Comments: European CD. Deluxe color cover. Picture CD.

CD - CAUTION
GDD2001/2002/2003
Playing In The Band/ Sugaree/ Mr. Charlie/ Black Throated Wind/ Deal/ Chinatown Shuffle/ Mexicali Blues/ China Cat Sunflower/ I Know You Rider/ It Hurts Me Too/ Beat It On Down The Line/ Brown Eyed Woman/ Jack Straw/ Big Railroad
CD2: Good Lovin'/ Casey Jones/ Morning Dew/ Me And My Uncle/ Two Souls/ El Paso/ Tennessee Ted/ Lied, Cheated/ Dark...
CD3: ...Star/ Sugar Magnolia/ Caution/ Who Do You Love/ Caution/ Truckin'/ Uncle John's Band
Recording: Very good to excellent.
Source: The Netherlands, May 11 1972.
Comments: European CD. Deluxe color cover.

CD - DEAD IN THE GARDEN
KISS THE STONE KTS 620/21
CD1: Hell In A Bucket/ Sugaree/ Walkin' Blues/ Candyman/ Masterpiece/ Bird Song/ Shakedown Tree/ Man Smart-Woman Smarter
CD2: Terrapin Station/ Drums, Space/ Goin' Down The Road Feelin' Bad/ All Along The Watchtower/ Morning Dew/ Good Lovin', La Bamba, Good Lovin'/ Knockin' On Heaven's Door
Recording: Excellent stereo. Soundboard.
Source: Madison Square Garden, New York September 18 1987.
Comments: European CD. Picture CD.
Total time 02:09:57.

GRATEFUL DEAD, THE

CD - DEAD ON TIME
KISS THE STONE KTS 573/74
CD1: Alabama Getaway/ Greatest Story Ever Told/ Candyman/ Good Morning Little Schoolgirl/ Ramblin' Rose/ El Paso/ Bird Song/ Promised Land/ New Speedway Boogie/ That Would Be Something
CD2: Way To Go Home/ Saint Of Circumstance/ He's Gone/ Drums/ Chanting By The Gyoto Monks/ Space/ Easy Answers/ Standing On The Moon/ Round 'N' Round/ Lucy In The Sky With Diamonds
Recording: Excellent stereo. Soundboard.
Source: The Shoreline Amphitheater, Mountain View, California June 2 1995.
Comments: European CD.

CD - FINAL RETURN TO SAM BOYD
CD1: Mississippi Half-Step/ Uptown Toodeloo/ Mississippi Half-Step Uptown Toodeloo/ The Race Is On/ Lazy River Road/ When I Paint My Masterpiece/ Samba In The Rain/ Men Smart, Women Smarter/ Truckin'/ Drums/ Space
CD2: The Last Time/ That Would Be Something/ Walk Me Out In The Morning Dew/ Althea/ Standing On The Moon/ Unbroken Chain/ Tennessee Jed/ China Cat Sunflower/ Lucy In The Sky With Diamonds
Recording: Excellent stereo. Soundboard.
Source: Sam Boyd Silverbowl, Las Vegas May 20 '95.
Comments: European CD. Deluxe color cover. Time CD1 74:01. CD2 64:48.

CD - FIRE IN KNICKERBOCKER ARENA
CD1: Hell In A Bucket/ Loser/ Take Me To The River/ Row Jimmy/ Broken Arrow/ Promised Land/ Down On The Boardwalk/ Scarlet Begonia's/ Fire On The Mountain (Part I)
CD2: Fire On The Mountain (Part II)/ Women Are Smarter/ It's All Too Much/ Playin' In The Band/ Supplication Jam/ Easy Answers/ Morning Dew/ U.S. Blues
Recording: Excellent stereo. Soundboard.
Source: Albany NY June 21 '95.
Comments: European CD. Deluxe color cover. Time CD1 73:36. CD2 60:13.

CD - INSIDE THE PYRAMID
BABY FACE BFBX 006/7/8/9
CD1: Hell In A Bucket/ Candyman/ Take Me To The River/ Lazy River Road/ Masterpiece/ Childhoods End/ Deal/ Foolish Heart
CD2: Long Way Home/ Saint Of Circumstance/ Mexicali/ Wheel/ All Along The Watchtower/ Standing On The Moon/ One More Saturday Night
CD3: Shakedown Street/ Same Thing/ Althea/ Stuck Inside Mobile/ Tennessee Jed/ Promised Land/ Here Comes The Sunshine/ Eternity
CD4: Crazy Fingers/ Last Time/ Wharf Rat/ Not Fade Away/ Unbroken Chain
Source: The Pyramid, Memphis, Tennessee. CD1-2 April 1 1995. CD3-4 April 2 1995.
Comments: European CD. Box set with poster. Time CD1 63:53. CD2 56:14. CD3 71:47. CD4 59:18.

CD - LIVE AT THE NASSAU COLISEUM
OXYGEN OXY 049
Shakedown (14:29)/ Little Red Rooster (11:58)/ Row Jimmy (11:16)/ Elpaso (5:30)/ Might As Well (4:30)/ Promised Land (5:09)
Recording: Excellent stereo. Soundboard.
Source: Nassau Coliseum, New York City March 23 1994.
Comments: European CD. Deluxe color cover. Picture CD.

CD - MEMPHIS BELLE-APRIL FOOL'S DAY 1995
KISS THE STONE KTS 538/39
CD1: Hell In A Bucket/ Candyman/ Take Me To The River/ Lazy River Road/ When I Paint My Masterpiece/ Childhood's End/ Deal/ Foolish Heart/ Way To Go Home
CD2: Saint Of Circumstance/ Eyes Of The World/ Drums-Space/ The Wheel/ All Along The Watchtower/ Standing On The Moon/ One More Saturday Night
Source: The Pyramid Arena, Memphis, TN April 1 1995
Comments: European CD. Deluxe color cover. Picture CDs. Total time 120:39.

CD - MIDNIGHT HOUR
DINOSAUR DNR95003
Cold Rain And Snow/ C.C. Rider/ Cumberland/ Far From Me/ Cassidy/ Ramble On Rose/ Looks Like Rain/ Turn On Your Love Light/ Tell Mama/ Baby What You Want/ Hard to Handle/ Midnight Hour
Recording: Very good. Soundboard.
Source: Auditorium Arena, Oakland December 31 1982.

GRATEFUL DEAD, THE

CD - PSOUND PSYCHILE
HAIGHT STREET RECORDS 215-15-27
CD1: New Potato Caboose/ Viola Lee Blues/ (Turn One Pour) Lovelight/ (A Little Thing Called) Alligator/ In The Midnight Hour (Rio Nido, CA September 3 1967)
CD2: Dark Star/ St. Steven/, The Eleven/ Death Don't Have No Mercy/ Lovelight/ Alligator/ Caution/ Feedback/ And We Bid You Goodnight
Recording: Good-very good. Soundboard.
Source: CD1 O'Keefe Center, Toronto, Canada August 4 '67. CD2 Fillmore West, August 22 1968.
Comments: Deluxe color cover.
Time CD1 76:14. CD2 71:57.

CD - SOUTHERN COMFORT
KISS THE STONE KTS 504/05
CD1: Shakedown Street (11:59)/ The Same Thing (7:05)/ Althea (8:49)/ Stuck Inside Of Mobile With The Memphis Blues Again (7:47)/ Tennessee Jed (7:47)/ Promised Land (5:02)/ Here Comes The Sunshine (6:20)/ Eternity (9:43)/ Crazy Fingers (9:18)
CD2: Estimred Prophet (14:16)/ Drums, Space (25:58)/ The Last Time (6:25)/ Wharf Rat (11:49)/ Not Fade Away (8:20)/ Unbroken Chain (6:22)
Recording: Excellent stereo. Soundboard.
Source: The Pyramid Arena, Memphis, TN April 2 '95.
Comments: European CD. Deluxe color cover. Picture CD.

CD - VIVE LA FRANCE!!
DINOSAUR DNR95004
China Cat Sunflower/ I Know You Rider/ St. Of Circumstance/ Crazy Fingers/ Playing In The Band 2/ Stella Blue/ Throwing Stones/ Not Fade Away/ One More Saturday Night
Recording: Excellent soundboard.
Source: Second set, The Zenith, Paris, France November 27 1990.

GREEN DAY

CD - ALL BY MYSELF
PARTY LINE PLCD-012
Welcome to Paradise/ What Are Lies/ Chump/ Long View/ Burn Out/ Only Of You/ Christy Road/ 2,000 Light Years Away/ Knowledge/ Going To Pasalaqua/ F.O.D./ Paper Lantern (includes Eye Of The Tiger)/ All By Myself/ Dominated Love Slave/ The One I Want
Recording: Good. Audience. Tracking noise.
Source: Trenton, New Jersey March 18 1994.

H

HARRISON, GEORGE

CD - FORTWORTH EXPRESS
HINDUSTANI MUSIC RAGA 001-A/B
CD1: Hari's On Tour (Express)/ While My Guitar Weeps/ Something/ ..Will It Go Round In Circles/ Sue Me Sue You Blues/ Indian Music By Ravi Shankar # 1/ Indian Music By Ravi Shankar # 2/ Indian Music By Ravi Shankar # 3/ Indian Music By Ravi Shankar # 4/ Indian Music By Ravi Shankar # 5/ Indian Music By Ravi Shankar # 6
CD2: For You Blue/ Give Me Love (Give Me Peace On Earth)/ Sound Stage Of Mind/ In My Life/ Tomcat/ Maya Love/ Dark Horse/ Nothing From Nothing/ Outta Space/ What Is Life/ My Sweet Lord
Source: Texas Convention Center, Fort Worth November 22 1974.

CD - LIVE IN SEATTLE 1974
THE GOLD STANDARD GS-96009/10
CD1: Hari's On Tour (Express)/ Something/ While My Guitar Gently Weeps/ Will It Go 'Round The Circles/ Sue Me Sue You Blues/ Indian Interludes #1/ Indian Interludes #2/ Indian Interludes #3/ Indian Interludes #4/ Indian Interludes #5/ Indian Interludes #6
CD2: Krishna, Where Are You?/ For You Blue/ Give Me Love (Give Me Peace On Earth)/ Sound Stage Of Mind/ In My Life/ Tomcat/ Maya Love/ Nothing From Nothing/ Dark Horse/ Outta Space/ What Is Life/ My Sweet Lord
Source: Madison Square Garden, New York December 19 or 20 1974.

CD - MAKING OF ALL THINGS MUST PASS
MIDNIGHT BEAT MBCD 110-112
CD1: What Is Life (5:11)/ What Is Life (5:10)/ Beware Of Darkness (3:55)/ Beware Of Darkness (3:59)/ Beware Of Darkness (3:58)/ Let It Down (6:43)/ Let It Down

Live
Trash
garbage

DEAD inthe garden
GRATEFUL DEAD
http://www.kts.it -- email:mailme@kts.it

HARRISON, GEORGE

(6:43)/ Let It Down (6:50)/ Apple Scruffs (3:20)/ Apple Scruffs (2:55)/ Apple Scruffs (5:23)
CD2: Hear Me Lord (7:34)/ Awaiting On You All (2:58)/ Awaiting On You All (2:53)/ Run Of The Mill (3:01)/ Run Of The Mill (3:01)/ Art Of Dying (3:53)/ Art Of Dying (3:50)/ Apple Scruffs (7:12)/ Apple Scruffs (9:12)/ Momma You Been On My Mind (4:04)/ Apple Scruffs (5:45)
CD3: What Is Life (5:12)/ Beware Of Darkness (4:00)/ Hear Me Lord (7:38)/ Let It Down (6:57)/ Awaiting On You All (2:59)/ Run Of The Mill (3:02)/ Art Of Dying (3:55)/ You (4:48)/ Apple Scruffs (5:34)/ Apple Scruffs (2:35)/ Apple Scruffs (2:35)/ Apple Scruffs (2:35)
Recording: Excellent stereo. Soundboard.
Source: Studio outtakes.
Comments: Picture CDs. 12-page booklet with photos of George from the 'Bangladesh' concert and the ATMP recording sessions. Limited of 3000 copies. Also available on The Repro Man label on CDR. The Repro Man versions included three songs from the Ringo bootleg, IT DON'T COME EASY.

CD - 12 ARNOLD GROVE - PIRATE SONGS PART 2
PEGBOY PEGBOY 1007
Shanghai Surprise (5:05)/ Someplace Else (3:34)/ Breath Away From Heaven (3:22)/ Zig Zag (2:43) I Don't Wanna Do It (2:50)/ It Don't Come Easy (3:25)/ Got My Mind Set On You (5:17)/ Save The World (4:35)/ Rockline Medley: Drive My Car (riff), That's All Right (Mama), Let It Be Me, Something, Every Grain Of Sand (9:02)/ I Don't Wanna Do It (2:51)/ While My Guitar Gently Weeps (5:09)/ Here Comes The Sun (3:36)/ If Not For You (3:57)/ Absolutely Sweet Marie (4:27)/ Abandoned Love (demos) (4:10)/ I Don't Wanna Do It (demos) (2:20)/ Dream Away (5:51)
Comments: Cardboard slipcase. 28 page booklet.

HARVEY, P.J.

CD - LIVE GOES THE NIGHT
KISS THE STONE KTS 486
Long Goes The Night/ Down To The Water/ Come On Billy/ Hook/ Deep Salt Water/ Me Jane/ 50ft Queenie Goodnight Irene/ Send His Love To Me/ Naked Cousin

Recording: Excellent stereo. Soundboard.
Source: Glanstonbury Festival June 24 '95.
Comments: European CD. Deluxe color cover. Picture CD. Time 43:42.

CD - MAYAN MONSTAS
TORNADO TOR034
C'mon And Step Inside/ Send His Love To Me/ Meet Ze Monsta/ Don't Ever Leave Me/ Working For The Man/ It's So Hard/ Teclo/ My Lord/ Down By The Water/ C'mon Billy/ Hook/ Don't Pour It On Me/ Driving/ 50ft Queenie/ Oh My Lover/ I Think I'm A Mother/ Long Snake Moan
Recording: Good. Audience.
Source: Mayan Theatre, Los Angeles, CA May 18 '95.
Comments: European CD. Deluxe color cover. Picture CD. Time 71:38.

CD - PRETTY IN PINK
HUNA 002
Meet Ze Monsta/ Working For The Man/ Naked Cousin/ Water/ Send His Love To Me/ Teclo/ Down By The Water/ C'mon Billy/ Hook/ Long Snake Moan/ Me Jane/ 10 Foot Queenie/ Goodnight/ Working For The Man/ Goodnight/ Meet Ze Monsta/ The Dancer
Recording: Excellent stereo. Soundboard.
Source: Tracks 1-13 Glastonbury June 24 1995. Tracks 14-15 White Room April 15 1995. Track 16 Britpop Now August 16 1995. Track 17 Mercury Music Awards September 23 1995.
Comments: European CD. Deluxe color cover. Time 75:49.

HELLOWEEN

CD - PERFECT PUMPKIN
CD1: Irritation, Soul Survivor/ Ride The Sky/ The Chance/ Mankind/ The Game Is On/ Why?/ Dr. Stein/ Grapowski's Malmsuite 1001/ Eagle Fly Free
CD2: Mr. Ego (Take Me Down)/ Where The Rain Grows/ Perfect Gentleman/ Future World/ Where The Eagle Learn To Fly/ How Many Tears
Recording: Excellent stereo. Soundboard.
Source: January 17 1995.

HENDRIX, JIMI

CD - BACK TO BERLIN!
MIDNIGHT BEAT MB CD 049
Straight Ahead/ Spanish Castle Magic/ Sunshine Of Your Love/ Hey Baby, Land Of The New Rising Sun/ Message To Love/ Machine Gun, The Breeze And I/ Purple Haze/ Red House/ Foxy Lady/ Ezy Rider/ Hey Joe
Recording: Excellent. Audience.
Source: The Deutschland Halle, Berlin, Germany September 4 1970.
Comments: Sepia-tone cover. Time 56:41.

CD - HEAR MY FREEDOM
KOBRA RECORDS KRCR 10
Hear My Freedom (1968)/ Izabella (instrumental with piano, Electric Lady Studios June 15 1970)/ Instrumental Jam (Record Plant May 15 1969)/ Sending My Love To Linda, Live And Let Live (takes 3-5, unknown percussion, Record Plant May 16 1969)/ Ezy Rider Jam (extended stereo version, Record Plant October 23 1970)/ Rainy Day Dream Away Still Raining Still Dreaming (alternate versions, Record Plant June 10 1968)/ Voodoo Child (Slight Return) (Record Plant May 3 1968)
Recording: Excellent. Soundboard.
Comments: European CD. Time

CD - HISTORIC CONCERT VOL. 2 - HIGH TIMES AT SAN JOSE POP
MIDNIGHT BEAT MB CD 050
Intro, Hear My Train A-Comin'/ Fire, Drum Solo/ Spanish Castle Magic/ Red House/ I Don't Live Today/ Foxy Lady/ Purple Haze/ Voodoo Chile (Slight Return)/ Villanova Junction Blues/ Message To Love/ Room full Of Mirrors/ Sunshine Of Your Love
Recording: Very good. Soundboard.
Source: San Jose Pop Festival, Santa Clara, Country Fairground, San Jose, CA May 25 '69.
Comments: Deluxe color cover. Jimi's voice buried. Time 68:53.

CD - LIVE IN COPENHAGEN 1968/70
THE SWINGIN' PIG TSP-CD-220-2
CD1: Catfish Blues/ Tax Free/ Fire/ Voodoo Chile (Slight Return)/ Foxy Lady/ Spanish Castle Magic
CD2: Freedom/ Red House/ In From The Storm/ Purple Haze/ Voodoo Chile (Slight Return)
Recording: Excellent. Soundboard.
Source: CD1 Tivolis Koncertsal, Copenhagen January 7 1968. CD2 K.B. Hallen, Copenhagen September 3 1970.
Comments: European CD.
Time CD1 46:38. CD2 36:17.

CD - MOON AND RAINBOWS
INSECT IST 48
Crash Landing/ Midnight Lightning/ Machine Gun/ Farther Up The Road/ Astro Man/ Country Blues/ Message To Love/ Stone Free/ Instrumental Jam/ Izabella
Recording: Excellent. Soundboard.
Source: Alternate studio versions 1968.
Comments: European CD. Japanese text on cover. Time 55:00.

CD - THE ROMAN COLISEUM
STARQUAKE SQ-11
Lover Man/ Come On (Part 1)/ Red House/ Fire/ Spanish Castle Magic/ Here My Train A Comin'/ I Don't Love Today/ Voodoo Chile (Slight Return)/ Purple Haze
Recording: Poor. Audience.
Source: Madison Square Garden May 18 1969.
Comments: Japanese CD. Deluxe color cover. Time 69:21.

CD - WOODSTOCK MONDAY
JMH 008/2
CD1: Introduction (2:10)/ Message To Love (4:00)/ Hear My Train A Comin' (9:15)/ Red House (5:40)/ Call Me Mastermind (3:27)/ Lover Man (5:37)/ Foxy Lady (4:17)/ Jam Back At The House (8:24)/ Izabella (5:10)/ Gipsy Woman (5:26)/ Fire (3:53)
CD2: Voodoo Chile - Stepping Stone (12:19)/ Star Spangled Banner (3:41)/ Purple Haze (3:25)/ Guitar Improvisation (4:58)/ Villanova Junction Blues (3:04)/ Hey Joe (4:50)/ Woodstock Interview (1:51)/ Lover Man (5:10)*/ Lover Man (5:27)*/ Hear My Train A Comin' (8:28)*/ Spanish Castle Magic (4:52)*/ Hear My Train A Comin' (2:33)**/ Machine Gun** (2:35)/ Izabella (3:24)**
Recording: Excellent stereo. Soundboard. CD2 tracks 8-11 Good-very good.Soundboard. Tracks 12-14 Very good-excellent. Soundboard.
Source:At 'Woodstock Music And Art Fair Festival' Bethel, New York August 18 1969 - 8:00 AM. *Liberty House, Shokan, New York August 14 1969 - Gipsy Sun And

Rainbows Session. **'Dick Cavett Show', ABC Studios, NYC September 9 1969.
Comments: European CD. Deluxe color cover. Picture CDs.

HOLE

CD - VENGEANCE IS MINE
KISS THE STONE KTS 489
Plump/ Miss World/ Sugar Coma/ Credit In The Straight World/ Whose Porno You Burn/ Doll Parts/ Violets/ Time To Kill/ He Hit Me (And It Felt Like A Kiss)/ Doll Parts/ Violet/ Plump/ Beautiful Son/ Drown Soda/ Gutless/ Best Sunday Dress/ Credit In The Straight World/ Doll Parts/ Violet
Recording: Excellent stereo. Soundboard.
Source: Tracks 1-8 Reading Festival, UK August 25 '95. Tracks 9-11 Later Studios, London May 13 '95. Tracks 12-19 Brixton Academy, London May 4 '95.
Comments: European CD. Deluxe color cover. Picture CD. Time 69:27.

HOLLY, BUDDY

CD - APARTMENT DEMOS
DYNAMITE STUDIO 92J022
I Know I'll Have The Blues Again/ Wait Till The Sunshines Nellie/ Peggy Sue Got Married/ That Makes it Tough/ Crying, Wanting, Hoping/ Learning The Game/ Slippin' And Slidin' #1/ Smokey Joe's Cafe #1/ Love Is Strange/ Dearest (Um Yeah)/ That's What They Say/ I Know I'll Have The Blues Again #2/ Smokey Joe's Cafe #2/ Slippin' And Slidin' #4/ You And I Are Through/ Down The Line/ Baby Won't You Come Out/ Don't Come Back Knockin'/ I Was Just A Fool/ Nigger Hatin' Me/ Rip It Up Lubbock/ Blue Suede Shoes
Source: Tracks 1-12 apartment tapes Tracks 13-16 lost apartment tapes. Tracks 17-22 Holley's family acetates. Tracks 23-24 original undubbed versions.
Comments: Japanese CD.

HOLOCAUST

CD - THE NIGHT COMERS
CD-011
Smokin Values/ Death Or Glory/ Come On Back/ Mavrock/ It Don't Matter/ Cryin Shame/ H.M. Mania (Re Mix)/ Push It Around/ The Night Comers/ H.M. Mania/ Loves Power/ Only As Young/ Friend Or Foe/ Out Of My Book/ Comin Through/ Don't Wanna Lose/ Good Thing
Recording: Excellent. Soundboard.
Source: Tracks 1-9 from 'The Night Comers' LP. Tracks 10-12 from 'H.M. Mania' 12". Tracks 13-14 from 'Smoking Values' 12". Tracks 15-17 from 'Comin Through' 12".
Comments: Japanese CD. Time 67:06.

HONEY DRIPPERS, THE

CD - BLUE NOTE CLUB
MIDAS TOUCH MD95421/22
CD1: Little Sister/ Hey Mae/ Lotta Lovin'/ You True Love/ Deep In The Heat Of Texas/ Honky Tonk/ How Many More Years/ Cross Cut Saw/ Bring It On Home/ I Can't Be Satisfied
CD2: Unknown/ Born Under A Bad Sign/ Keep On Loving Me Babe/ What Can I Do/ Tell Me How/ Queen Of The Hop/ She She Little Sheila/ Got My Mojo Working
Recording: Very good. Audience.
Source: Blue Note Club, Derby April 13 1981.

HOOTIE AND THE BLOWFISH

CD - ACOUSTIC
KISS THE STONE KTS 549
Time/ Sad Caper/ Running From An Angel/ She Crawls Away/ The Earth Stayed Cold At Dawn/ Gravity Of The Situation/ I Hope That I Don't Fall In Love With You/ Let Her Cry/ So Strange/ Hold My Hand/ Sad Caper/ The Earth Stayed Cold At Dawn/ Old Man & Me (When I Get To Heaven)
Recording: Excellent stereo. Soundboard.
Source: The Horseshoe, University Of Southern Carolina. Tracks 11-12 GLR Studios, London May 1 '96 (acoustic sessions). Track 13 The Ed Sullivan Theater, NYC May 23 '96.
Comments: European CD. Deluxe color cover. Picture CD. Time 54:50.

HUGHES, GLENN

CD - BIEBOB VOSSELAAR
NIGHTLIFE N-015
Burn/ The Liar/ Muscle & Blood/ Lay My Body Down/ Into The Void/ Coast To Coast/ Getting Tighter/ You Keep On Moving/ Lady Double Dealer/ I Got Your Number/ Stormbringer

Recording: Very good. Audience.
Source: Biebob Vosselaar October 22 ?
Comments: Japanese CD. Deluxe color cover. Time 73:27.

CD - MADE IN SWEDEN
NIGHTLIFE N-025
Smoke On The Water*/ The Liar**/ House Of The Rising Sun**/ Lay My Body Down**/ Coast To Coast**, This Time Around**/ Lay Down, Stay Down (Intro)**, Getting Tighter**/ You Keep On Moving**/ I Got Your Number**/ Georgia On My Mind**/ From Now On (Unplugged)^, Interview^/ Lay My Body Down (Unplugged)^/ So Much Love To Give^^
Recording: Ex. Audience.
Source: *Borlange, January 1 1993.
**Gothenburg September 10 1993.
^Hilversum, August 20 1994. ^^Stockholm July 28 1993.
Comments: Japanese CD.

IRON MAIDEN

CD - BRAZIL 1996
KISS THE STONE KTS 612
Falling Down/ Wrathchild/ Heaven Can Wait/ Lord Of The Flies/ Fortunes Of War/ Bass Intro, Out Of Control/ The Evil That Men Do/ The Aftermath/ The Name Of The Rose/ Two Minutes To Midnight/ Fear Of The Dark/ The Clairvoyant/ Iron Maiden
Recording: Excellent stereo. Soundboard.
Source: Pacaebu Stadium, San Paolo, Brazil August 24 1996.
Comments: European CD. Deluxe color cover. Picture CD. Time 71:04.

CD - MAIDEN AMERICA
BONDAGE MUSIC BON 065
The Ides Of March/ Sanctuary/ Purgatory/ Wrathchild/ Remember Tomorrow/ Another Life/ Genghis Khan/ Killers/ Innocent Exile/ Twilight Zone/ Murders In The Rue Morgue/ Phantom Of The Opera/ Iron Maiden/ Running Free/ Transylvania/ Drifter
Recording: Excellent stereo. Soundboard.
Source: Metal Summerfest, Milwaukee June 26 1981.
Comments: Japanese CD.

CD - PARIS
OLYMPUS OR 004/5
CD1: Man On The Edge/ Wrathchild/ Heaven Can Wait/ Lord Of The Flies/ Fortunes Of War/ Blood On The World's Hands/ Afraid To Shoot Strangers/ The Evil That Men Do/ The Aftermath/ Sign Of The Cross/ Two Minutes To Midnight/ The Edge Of Darkness
CD2: Fear Of The Dark/ The Clairvoyant/ Iron Maiden/ Number Of The Beast/ Hallowed Be Thy Name/ Running Free/ Sanctuary/ The Trooper/ Revelations/ Flight Of The Icarus/ 22 Acacia Avenue/ Twilight Zone/ Wrathchild/ Killers
Recording: Very good audience. CD2 tracks 12-14 excellent soundboard.
Source: Le Zenith, Paris November 16 1995. CD2 tracks 7-11 Westfalenhalle, Dortmund, Germany, December 18 1983. CD2 tracks 12-14 Bruce's audition tapes, London October 1981.
Comments: Time CD1 73:54. CD2 70:01.

CD - PRISONERS LIVE AT READING FESTIVAL 1982
AMSTERDAM AMS720
CD1: Intro, Murder The Rue Morgue/ Wrath Child/ Run To The Hills/ Children Of The Damned/ Number Of The Beast/ 22 Acasia Avenue, Clive Burn Drums Solo/ Transylvania/ The Prisoner/ Hallowed Be Thy Name
CD2: Phantom Of The Opera/ Iron Maiden/ Running Free/ Drifter/ Tush (Special Guest- Black Foot)
Source: Reading Festival, August 28 1982.
Comments: Japanese CD.

CD - WAR MACHINE
KOBRA RECORDS KRHM 12
Intro, Tailgunner/ Public Enemy Number One/ Wrathchild/ Die With Your Boots On/ Hallowed Be Thy Name/ Holy Smoke/ No Prayer For The Dying/ The Clairvoyant/ Two Minutes To Midnight/ The Trooper/ Iron Maiden/ The Number Of The Beast/ Run To The Hill/ Nicko Mc Brain Solo Project: Rhythm Of The Beast
Recording: Excellent stereo. Soundboard.
Source: Wembley Arena, London December 18 1990. Track 14 from a rare 12" picture disc.
Comments: European CD. Deluxe color cover. Time 71:00.

JACKSONS, THE

CD - BLAME IT ON THE BOOGIE
MIDNIGHT BEAT MBCD035
Dancing Machine/ Things I Do For You/ Ben/ I Am Love/ Keep On Dancing/ Medley: I Want You Back, ABC/ The Love Save/ I'll Be There/ Band Introduction/ Enjoy Yourself/ Destiny/ Show You The Way To Go/ All Night Dancing/ Blame It On The Boogie
Recording: Excellent stereo. Soundboard.
Source: The Carre Theater, Amsterdam, Holland February 26 1979.
Comments: European CD.

JAM, THE

CD - FACE ACTION AT FIVE THIRTY
SIDEVENTS LAB SV-001
Girl On The Phone/ Away From The Numbers/ Smithers Jones/ Mr. Clean/ Butterfly Collector/ Thick As Thieves/ When You're Young/ Strange Town/ Eton Rifles/ Down In The Tube Station At Midnight/ Saturdays Kids/ All Mod Cons/ David Watts/ Ghosts/ In The Cloud/ Town Called Malice/ The Modern World/ Move On Up/ Beat Surrender
Recording: Very good to excellent. Soundboard.
Source: Tracks 1-13 Finsbury Park, London, UK December 6 '79. Tracks 14-19 Tube, London TV '82.
Comments: Japanese CD. Picture CD. Time 60:04.

CD - READY, STEADY... GONE
WA21282
Start/ It's Too Bad/ Beat Surrender/ Away From The Numbers/ Ghosts/ In The Crowd/ Boy About Town/ Get Yourself Together/ All Mod Cons/ To Be Someone/ Smithers-Jones/ The Great Depression/ Precious/ Move On Up/ When You're Young/ David Watts/ Private Hell/ Down In The Tube Station At Midnight/ Mr. Clean/ Transglobal Express/ Going Underground
Recording: Very good.
Source: Wembley Arena, London December 2 '82.

JANES ADDICTION

CD - FORGET THE RUMORS WE'RE STILL ALIVE
ALLEY KAT AK 062
Chip Away/ Had A Dad/ Pigs In Zen/ Ain't No Right/ Then She Did/ Been Caught Stealing/ Idiots Rules/ Whores/ Of Course/ Up The Beach/ Oceansize/ Mountain Song/ Stop!
Recording: Excellent stereo. Soundboard.
Source: Mt. Baldy Amphitheater, Mt. Baldy, CA July 7 '90.
Comments: European CD. Deluxe color cover. Picture CD. Time 68:04.

CD - LAST FIXX
KISS THE STONE KTS 569
Up the Beach/ Whores/ Standing In The Shower/ Ain't No Right/ Thank You Boys/ Three Days/ Been Caught Stealing/ L.A. Medley: L. A. Woman, Nausea/ Classic Girl/ Mountain Song/ Top/ Ocean Size/ Trip Away
Recording: Excellent stereo. Soundboard.
Source: Honolulu, Hawaii September 9 1991.
Comments: European CD. Deluxe color cover. Picture CD. Time 63:50.

CD - L.A. WOMAN
TOTONKA CD PRO 15
L.A. Woman Medley/ Ain't No Right/ No One's Leaving/ Whores/ Had A Dad/ Standin In The Shower Thinkin/ Ain't No Right/ No One's Leaving/ Trip Away/ Oceansize/ Stop/ Like A Rolling Stone, Pigs In Zen/ Ted Just Admit It (Nothing's Shocking)
Recording: Excellent stereo. Soundboard.
Source: Northridge, Cal State May 2 1987.
Comments: European CD. B&W cover with red type. Time 59:37.

CD - WHOLE LOTTA LOVE
BABYFACE BF020
Kettle Whistle/ My Time/ Chip Away/ Whores/ Thank You Boys/ 1%/ Ocean Size/ Ain't No Right/ Up The Beach/ Trip Away/ Slow Driver (early version '86)/ Whole Lotta Love ('86)/ Feel Alright ('87)/ Don't Call Me Nigger ('91)/ 100 Ways (Porno For Pyros '93)/ My Time (Porno Do Jane's '93)
Recording: Good. Audience.
Source: USC, Los Angeles 1987.
Comments: European CD. Picture CD.

Time 64:37.

CD - WHORES IN THE SHADOW
TORNADO TOR035
Intro Jam/ Whores/ Caught In The Act/ Idiots/ Funkajamalama/ Nothing Shocking/ Standing In The Shadow/ Thank You Boys/ Pigs In Zen/ Summertime Blues/ N Harm Done/ Mountain Song/ Trip Away/ Jane Says/ End
Recording: Very good. Audience.
Source: L'Armour, Brooklyn, NY.
Comments: European CD. Deluxe color cover. Time 65:29.

JAYHAWKS

CD - POISED FOR STARDOM
KISS THE STONE KTS 443
Blue (3:43)/ I'd Run Away (4:10)/ Two Hearts (3:37)/ Miss William's Guitar (3:34)/ Red's Song (4:25)/ Over My Shoulder (4:25)/ Ten Little Kids (4:36)/ Clouds (6:16)/ Settle Down Like Rain (2:52)/ Martin's Song (3:09)/ Take Me With You (When You Go) (4:44)/ Leave No Gold (4:51)/ Reason To Believe (4:00)/ Two Angels (3:56)/ Waiting For The Sun (4:30)/ Wichita (7:08)
Recording: Excellent stereo. Soundboard.
Source: Tracks 1-7 New York 1995. Tracks 8-16 Chicago July 4 1993.
Comments: European CD. Deluxe color cover. Picture CD.

JETHRO TULL

CD - BACK TO BIRMINGHAM
SBC 010
Roots To Branches/ Rare & Precious Chain/ In The Grip Of Stronger Stuff/ In Your Face/ Beside Myself/ We Used To Know/ Treacherous/ Locomotive Breath
Recording: Excellent stereo. Soundboard.
Source: Festival Hall, Birmingham 1995.
Comments: European CD. Deluxe color cover. Time 53:50.

CD - CURIOUS RIFF
CRYSTAL CAT RECORDS CC 375/76
CD1: Intro/ And Further On, Fylingdale Flyer, Protect And Survive/ Roots To Branches/ Rare And Precious Chain/ Out Of The Noise/ Valley/ In The Grip Of Stronger Stuff/ At Last, Forever/ Dangerous Veils/ Beside Myself/ Intro/ Aqualung/ Instrumental
CD2: Nothing Is Easy/ We Used To Know/ In The Moneylender's Temple/ My God/ Misery/ Fat Man/ Budapest/ Wounded, Old And Treacherous/ Intro/ Locomotive Breath/ Jump Start/ Dambusters March, Brick
Recording: Excellent.
Source: Stockholm, Sweden October 3 1995.
Comments: European CD. Deluxe color cover. Time CD1 68:27. CD2: 73:42.

CD - EAST DREAMS
TURN YOUR PLAYER ON TYPO 01
Locomotive Breath, Hunting Girl/ Living In The Past, Serenade To A Cookoo/ Fly By Night/ Watching Him, Watching Me/ Keyboard/ Drums/ Fat Man/ Thick As A Brick/ Black Sunday/ Unknown Dreams/ Aqualung
Recording: Excellent stereo. Soundboard.
Source: Old Gymnasium, Budapest, Hungry July 2 1986.
Comments: European CD. Deluxe B&w with pink cover. Time 70:13.

CD - VELVET FLUTE
KISS THE STONE KTS 491
Roots To Branches (6:07)/ Rare And Precious Chain (6:59)/ In The Grip Of Stronger Stuff (3:57)/ At Last, Forever (8:13)/ Beside Myself (7:06)/ We Used To Know (6:10)/ Wounded, Old And Treacherous (7:48)/ Locomotive Breath (7:34)
Recording: Excellent.
Source: On tour 1995.
Comments: European CD. Picture CD. Time 53:57.

JEWEL

CD - SALVATION
SNOW 016
Singing At A Gay Bar/ Pieces Of You/ Jewel/ Little Sister/ Drug Bust In Mexico/ You Were Meant For Me/ Catch A Cold With Me/ Race Car Driver/ I'm Sorry/ Growing Up In Alaska/ Fragile Flame/ Near You Always/ Angel Standing By/ Live By Your Passion/ Who Will Save Your Soul/ Dad's Eyebrows/ China Bells Ringing/ Absence Of Fear/ Sunshine Superman
Recording: Excellent.
Source: Tracks 1-17 Tower Records

Hollywood March 28 1996. Track 18 MTV Studios 1996. Track 19 unreleased studio track.
Comments: European CD.

JOEL, BILLY

CD - SONGS FROM THE BACK YARD
WHATEVER WER-09/10
CD1: You May Be Right/ Don't Ask Me Why/ Sleeping With The Television On/ Summer Highland Falls/ You're My Home/ Only The Good Die Young/ Stranger/ Just The Way You Are/ It's Still Rock & Roll To Me/ I'll Cry Instead/ Everybody Loves You Now/ Miami 2017/ Streetlife Serenade
CD2: Sometimes A Fantasy/ Stiletto/ Big Shot/ Movin' Out/ Angry Young Man/ Piano Man/ Zanzibar/ The Ballad Of Billy The Kid/ New York State Of Mind
Recording: Good. Hiss.
Source: Live during the 1980 and 1981 US tours.

JOHN, ELTON

CD - BBC 1973
ELEMENTS OF CRIME ELEMENTS-028
Funeral For A Friend/ Love Lies Breeding/ Candle In The Wind/ Hercules/ Rocket Man/ Bennie And The Jets/ Daniel/ Honky Cat/ Goodbye Yellow Brick Road/ Your Song/ All The Young Girls Love Alice/ Saturday Nights Alright For Fighting
Recording: Excellent stereo. Soundboard.
Source: Hammersmith December 22 1973.
Comments: Japanese CD. Time 72:54.

CD - THE GREATEST DISCOVERY
HIWATT ZA56
Your Song/ Border Song/ Sixty Years On/ Take Me To The Pilot/ The Greatest Discovery/ I Need You To Turn To/ Burn Down The Mission/ Tiny Dancer/ Rotten Peaches/ Razor Face/ Holiday Inn/ Indian Sunset/ Levon/ Madman Across The Water
Recording: Excellent. Soundboard.
Source: Tracks 1-7 BBC television show 'In Concert' May 22 '70. Tracks 8-14 BBC television show 'In Concert' summer '70.
Comments: Deluxe color cover. Time 72:26.

CD - MY SONGS
MUM MUCD 014
Your Song/ Border Song/ Sixty Years On/ Take Me To The Pilot/ The Greatest Discovery/ I Need You To Turn Me On/ Burn Down The Mission/When The First Tear Shows/ Turn To Me/ The Tide Will Turn For Rebecca/ Sitting Doing Nothing/ Thank You For All Your Loving/ Tartan Colored Lady/ Regimental Sgt. Zippo/ Come Down In Town/ Tiny Dancer/ Madman Across The Water
Recording: Excellent. Soundboard.
Source: Tracks 1-7 BBC Broadcast, May 22 1970. Tracks 8-15 Dick James demos '68. Tracks 16-17 BBC Broadcast summer 1970.
Comments: European CD. Time 73:24.

JOPLIN, JANIS

CD - LIGHT IS FASTER THAN SOUND
MIDNIGHT BEAT MB CD 089
Call On Me (4:09)/ Combination Of The Two (6:36)/ Blow My Mind (5:50)/ Down On Me (3:01)/ All Is Loneliness, Drum Solo (12:32)/ Road Block (8:05)/ Light Is Faster Than Sound (6:38)/ Bye Bye Baby (6:13)/ Goin' To Brownsville (9:12)/ Ball And Chain (8:34)/ I Know You Rider (Traditional) (2:56)
Recording: Excellent. Soundboard.
Source: California Hall, San Francisco July 28 1966.
Comments: European CD. Deluxe color cover. Picture CD.

CD - SUMMERTIME
MOONRAKER 101
Instrumental/ Maybe/ Summertime/ Try (Just A Little Bit Harder)/ Can't Turn You Loose/ Combination Of The Two/ Ball And Chain/ Piece Of My Heart
Recording: Excellent. Soundboard.
Source: Amsterdam April 1 1969.
Comments: European CD.

JOURNEY

CD - VISITED TO JAPAN
MY PHENIX BS 1
City Of Angels/ Too Late/ Lovin' You Is Easy/ Of A Lifetime/ Lights/ On A Saturday Night/ Patiently
Recording: Very good to excellent. Soundboard.
Source: Tokyo, Japan April 1979.
Comments: Japanese CD. Deluxe color cover. Time 41:21.

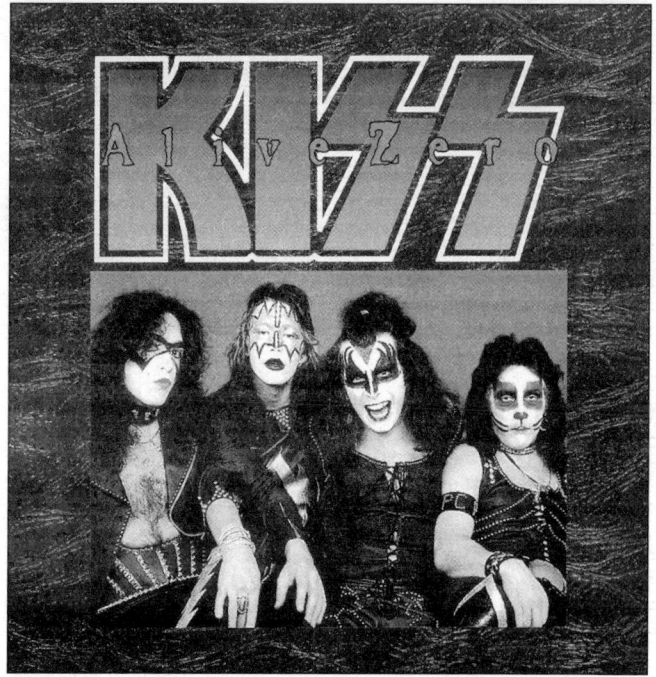

JOURNEY

JUDAS PRIEST

CD - BRITISH STEELER
BONDAGE MUSIC BON073
Hell Bent For Leather/ The Ripper/ Running Wild/ Living After Midnight/ Sinner/ Beyond The Realms Of Death/ You Don't Have To Be Old Be Wise/ Grinder/ Victim Of Changes/ Steeler/ Genocide/ Tyrant/ Green Manalishi
Recording: Very good to excellent. Soundboard.
Source: Calderone Hall, NY 7/5/80.
Comments: Japanese CD. Deluxe color cover. Picture CD. Time 57:26.

K

KING CRIMSON

CD - ASAKUSA
KC-1281 A/B
CD1: Discipline/ Thela Hun Ginjeet/ Red/ Matte Kudasai/ The Sheltering Sky/ Frame By Frame
CD2: Neurotica/ Bill Bruford Percussion Solo/ Indiscipline/ Neal And Jack And Me/ Elephant Talk/ Lark's Tongues In Aspic, Part Two
Recording: Good. Audience.
Source: December 1981.
Comments: Japanese CD.

CD - THE DOUBLE TRIO
OXYGEN OXY 05
Instrumental Intro (2:08)/ Vroom Vroom (4:51)/ Frame By Frame (5:13)/ Dinosaur (6:57)/ One Time (5:45)/ Red (6:12)/ Drum Solo (1:53)/ Vroom (6:47)/ Sex, Sleep, Eat, Drink, Dream (4:43)/ Elephant Talk (6:21)/ Indiscipline (6:44)/ The Talking Drums (3:14)/ Lark's Tongues In As Picture Part Two (6:32)/ Walking On Air (5:57)/
Recording: Excellent stereo. Soundboard.
Source: The Nakano Sun Plaza, Tokyo, Japan October 5 1995.
Comments: European CD. Picture CD.

CD - FRISCO SPACE
KC-013
Pictures Of A City/ Formentera Lady, The Sailors Tale/ Cirkus/ Ladies Of The Road/ Groon/ 21st Century Schizoid Man
Recording: Good. Audience.
Source: Winterland Ballroom, San Francisco March 21 1972.
Comments: Japanese CD.

CD - SCHIZOIDS
K-71-C1/2
CD1: Cirkus/ Pictures Of A City/ Formentera Lady/ Sailors Tale/ The Letters/ Islands
CD2: Ladies Of The Road/ Groon/ 21st Century Schizoid Man/ Devil's Triangle
Recording: Good. Audience. Background noise.
Source: Brighton Dome October 16 1971.
Comments: Japanese CD.

CD - SCREETCH!
KINKY SOUNDS KS280466
CD1: Intro (3:00)/ Vrooom (4:44)/ Frame By Frame (5:04)/ Dinosaur (6:55)/ One Time (5:34)/ Red (6:02)/ B'Boom (6:08)/ Thrak (6:58)/ Matte Kudasei (3:19)/ Vrooom Vrooom (6:58)/ Sex Sleep Eat Drink Dream (4:45)/ People (5:49)/ Improvisation - Two Sticks (2:43)/ Elephant Talk (4:16)
CD2: Indiscipline (6:35)/ Leading Into... (5:35)/ Lark's Tongue In Aspic Part 2 (6:20)/ Walking On Air (4:55)/ Underwater Cage Improvisation (9:39)/ Antartic Improvisation (3:00)/ Sun Storm Improvisation (7:00)/ Dragon Flight Improvisation (11:49)/ Termites Journey Improvisation (4:40)/ Mystic Nippon Improvisation (14:05)
Recording: Good to Very Good. Audience. CD2 Tracks 5-10 Excellent.
Source: San Diego, CA June 28 1995. CD2 Tracks 5-10 Robert Fripp solo performance, San Diego, CA January 27 1995.
Comments: European CD. Deluxe color cover.

CD - SLIDING MYSTIFIED
KC-012
Pictures Of A City/ Cirkus/ 21st Century Schizoid Man/ Earthbound/ Cadence And Cascade/ Improvisation
Recording: Good. Audience.
Source: Municipal Auditorium, New Orleans, Louisiana, March 31, '72,
Comments: Japanese CD.

CD - STUDIO REHEARSAL
HIGHLAND HL 027/28#KC2
CD1: Untitled Tracks (4:27)/ Sleepless (Instrumental #1, 2) (6:10)/ Three Of A

Perfect Pair #1 (3:31)/ Three Of A Perfect Pair #2 (4:59)/ Man With An Open Heart #1 (3:52)/ Man With An Open Heart #2 (2:59)/ Industry #1 (5:55)/ Nuages #1 (6:06)/ Nuages #2 (2:46)/ Model Man (4:22)/ Untitled Tracks with Tony Levin (7:52)/ Untitled Guitar Tracks (3:17)
CD2: Industry #2 (7:24)/ Drum Tracks with Bill Bruford #1,2 (5:51)/ Untitled Tracks (2:23)/ Sleepless (Instrumental #3, 4, 5) (18:20)/ Lark's Tongues In Aspic Part III (5:57)/ Man With An Open Heart (3:27)/ Dig Me (3:29)/ Three Of A Perfect Pair (2:23)/ Model Man (3:29)
Recording: Good to very good. Soundboard. Hiss.
Source: CD1 and CD2 tracks 1-4 studio rehearsals, Bearsville Studio, New York 1983. CD2 tracks 5-9 'Three Of A Perfect Pair' demos.
Comments: Japanese CD.

CD - THE VIRGIN MARY
KC-014-A/B
CD1: The Great Deceiver/ Lament/ Exiles/ Fracture/ Improvisation/ The Night Watch
CD2: Doctor Diamond/ Starless/ Improvisation/ The Talking Drum/ Larks' Tongues In Aspic (Part Two)/ 21st Century Schizoid Man
Recording: Very good.
Source: McMaster University, Hamilton, Ontario May 4 '74.
Comments: Japanese CD.

KINKS

CD - U.S. JIVE
MOD 003
Low Budget/ Apeman/ Sleepwalker/ Come Dancing/ Lost And Found/ Think Visual/ Too Much On My Mind/ Living On A Thin Line/ A Well Respected Man/ All Day And All Of The Night/ The Road/ You Really Got Me/ *Art Lover/ *Welcome To Sleazy Town/ *Guilty/ *Celluloid Heroes
Recording: Excellent stereo. Soundboard.
Source: Riverside Theater, Milwaukee, Wisconsin April 8 1988. *Fox Theater, St. Louis, Missouri April 14 1988.
Comments: Japanese CD. Deluxe color cover. Time 65:29.

KISS
(see page 239)

CD - ALIVE ZERO
YU 52
Deuce/ Nothin' To Lose/ She/ Firehouse/ Strutter/ 100,000 Years/ Black Diamond/ Rock And Roll All Nite/ Deuce/ Cold Gin/ Strutter
Recording: Fair to good. Soundboard.
Source: Tracks 1-7 Academy Of Music, New York Dec. 31 1973. Tracks 9-11 Electric Ladyland Studios, New York June 1973.
Comments: Japanese CD. Deluxe color cover. Time 51:50.

CD - ASYLUM WORLD TOUR 1986
CD 005
Detroit Rock City/ Fits Like A Glove/ Uh! All Night/ Strutter/ Cold Gin/ Guitar Solo/ Bass Solo/ I Love It Loud/ Drum Solo/ War Machine/ Guitar Solo/ Heaven's On Fire/ I Still Love You/ Love Gun/ Rock And Roll All Nite/ Tears Are Falling
Recording: Fair to good. Audience.
Source: Asylum World Tour 1986.
Comments: Japanese CD. B&w cover. Time 74:03.

CD - THE BEST OF...
CD006
New York Groove/ Living In Sin/ See You Tonite/ Rip It Out/ Fractured Mirror/ Don't Let Me Down/ Radioactive/ Tonight You Belong To Me/ Take Me Away (Together As One)/ Rock Me, Baby/ I Can't Stop The Rain/ Hold Me, Touch Me
Recording: Excellent. Soundboard.
Source: Studio tracks.
Comments: European CD. Deluxe color cover. Time 47:25.

CD - CARNIVAL OF SOULS
COSO196
Hate/ Tell Me/ I Will Be There/ Seduction Of The Innocent/ Rain/ Childhood's End/ The Jungle/ It Never Ends/ In My Head
Recording: Excellent. Soundboard.
Source: Studio.
Comments: European CD. Deluxe color cover. Time 44:13.

CD - DESTROY THE U.K.
PGAP0896
Deuce/ King Of Nighttime World/ Do Ya

KISS

Love Me/ Calling Dr. Love/ Cold Gin/ Let Me Go Rock & Roll/ Shout It Out Loud/ Watchin' You/ Fire House/ Shock Me/ Strutter/ God Of Thunder/ Love Gun
Recording: Good to Very Good. Audience.
Source: Donnington August 17 1996.
Comments: European CD. Deluxe color cover. Picture CD. Time 74:02.

CD - GOLDEN TRASHES
KOBRA RECORDS KBHM 13
Sweet Ophelia/ Keep Me Waiting/ Ladies In Waiting/ She/ Too Many Mondays/ In The Darkness/ When The Bells Rings/ Some Other Guy/ We Want To/ Shout It Out Loud/ I Stole Your Love (demo '77)/ Partners I Crime (demo '82)/ Reason To Live (demo '87)/ Bang, Bang You (demo '87)/ My Way (demo '87)/ When Two Hearts Collide/ Don't Let Go/ Hide Your Heart/ Best Man For You/ Time Traveller/ Give It To You Easy
Recording: Excellent. Soundboard.
Source: Tracks 1-10 Wicked Lester demos. Tracks 16-20 Paul Stanley's demos 1990. Track 21 unreleased song.
Comments: European CD. Deluxe color cover. Time 73:55.

CD - H.I.T.S. AT THE PONY
EPGB0490
I Stole Your Love/ Deuce/ Heaven's On Fire/ Fits Like A Glove/ Rise To It/ Betrayed/ C'Mon And Love Me/ Calling Dr. Love/ Hide Your Heart/ Love Gun/ Detroit Rock City/ I Love It Loud/ Black Diamond/ Little Caesar
Recording: Good to Very Good. Audience.
Source: Live At The Stone Pony April 1990.
Comments: European CD. Deluxe color cover. Picture CD. Time 59:55.

CD - KISSING IN THE PINK
CD 004
Detroit City Rock/ Cold Gin/ Creatures Of The Night/ Fits Like A Glove/ I've Had Enough/ Heaven's On Fire/ Burn Bitch Burn/ War Machine/ Drum Solo/ Young And Wasted/ Bass Solo/ I Love It Loud/ I Still Love You/ Love Gun/ Black Diamond/ Untitled/ Lick It Up
Recording: Poor. Audience.
Comments: Japanese CD. B&w cover. Pink text. Time 73:59.

CD - MASKED AGAIN
KOBRA RECORDS KRHM 08
Intro, Deuce/ Love Gun/ Cold Gin/ Calling Dr. Love/ Firehouse/ Shock Me (Including Guitar Solo)/ Bass Solo, 100,000 Years/ Detroit Rock City/ Black Diamond/ Rock'N'Roll All Night/ Cold Gin/ Strutter/ Watchin' You/ Black Diamond
Recording: Good. Audience. Tracks 11-14 Excellent. Soundboard.
Source: Tracks 1-10 first show, Irvine Meadows Amphitheatre, Irvine, CA June 15 1996. Tracks 11-14 original demo 1973.
Comments: European CD. Deluxe color cover. Time 73:02.

CD - RETURN TO CASABLANCA III
INDUSTRIA ARGENTINA 6399 059
Comin' Home/ Plaster Caster/ Goin' Blind/ Do You Love Me/ Domino/ Nothin' To Lose/ Sure Know Something/ Take Me/ A World Without Heroes/ Everytime I Look At You/ Rock Bottom/ C'mon And Love Me/ God Of Thunder/ Shandi/ She/ Strutter/ Hide Your Heart/ Let Me Know/ Christine Sixteen/ Calling Dr. Love
Recording: Excellent. Audience.
Source: Boston July 29 1995.
Comments: Time 73:52.

CD - ROCK DIAMONDS
KOBRA RECORDS KRHM 07
Hate Is What I Am/ Rain Down On Me/ Childhood's End/ I Will Be There/ In The Jungle/ Seduction Of The Innocent/ It Never Ends/ In My Head/ The Street Giveth (demo '90)/ Bad Bad Lovin' (demo '78)/ Reputation (demo '78)/ There's Nothing Better (demo '79-'80)/ Rumble (demo '79-'80)/ Dirty Livin' (demo '79-'80)/ Out Of Control (demo '79-'80)/ Beck (first version of 'Beth')/ Beth (acoustic version '77)
Recording: Very good to excellent. Soundboard.
Source: Tracks 1-9 'Carnival Of Soul' - unreleased album. Tracks 10-18 various demos.
Comments: European CD. Deluxe color cover. Time 76:13.

CD - ROCK 'N ROLL IN GLOBE ARENA
MIXING RECORDS 7005
CD1: Intro (1:11)/ Deuce (3:35)/ King Of The Night Time World (3:31)/ Do You Love Me (3:46)/ Calling Dr. Love (2:59)/ Cold Gin (5:57)/ Watching You (4:27)/ Firehouse

(4:10)/ I Stole Your Love (3:26)/ Shock Me (4:29)/ Ace Guitar Preludium (7:57)/ Let Me Go, Rock 'N Roll (5:08)/ Shout It Out Loud (2:48)
CD2: I Was Made For Loving You (4:16)/ C'Mon And Love Me (2:53)/ God Of Thunder (3:08)/ Drum Solo (5:00)/ God Of Thunder continued (1:06)/ New York Groove (3:21)/ Love Gun (4:06)/ 100,000 Years (5:25)/ Paul Stanley Intro Guitar (3:16)/ Black Diamond (4:42)/ Detroit Rock City (4:25)/ Beth (2:17)/ Rock 'N Roll All Nite (6:11)
Recording: Good to very good. Audience.
Source: Globe Arena, Stockholm, Sweden December 6 1996.
Comments: European CD. Deluxe color cover. Picture CD.

CD - SECRET KISSES I
PGAEP 7395
Love Gun (Detroit '92)/ Deuce (San Francisco '75)/ Nothin' To Lose (San Francisco '75)/ Parasite (San Francisco '75)/ 100 000 Years (Detroit '76)/ Strutter (Detroit '76)/ C'Mon And Love Me (Detroit '76)/ She (Detroit '76)/ Black Diamond (Detroit '76)/ Do You Love Me (New York '77)/ Shock Me (Houston '77)/ Hooligan (Houston '77)/ Radioactive (Largo '79)/ Move On (Largo '79)/ New York Groove (Largo '79)/ Beth (Kiss movie '78)/ Rip And Destroy (Kiss movie '78)
Recording: Very good to excellent. Some good to very good.
Comments: European CD. Deluxe color cover. Picture CD. Time 69:54.

CD - SECRET KISSES II
PGAEP 7395-2
Detroit Rock City (Glasgow '84)/ Strutter (Glasgow '84)/ Fits Like A Glove (Glasgow '84)/ Heaven's On Fire (Glasgow '84)/ War Machine (Glasgow '84)/ I've Had Enough (Glasgow '84)/ Young And Wasted (Glasgow '84)/ I Still Love You (Glasgow '84)/ Lick It Up (Glasgow '84)/ Rock 'N' Roll All Nite (Glasgow '84)/ Car Crash (Houston '85)/ Get All You Can Take (Brighton '84)/ Rock 'N' Roll Hell (Rockford '82)/ Tossin' And Turnin' (Largo '79)/ Intro (London '92)/ I Stole Your Love (London '92)/ Deuce (London '92)
Recording: Very good to excellent. Some good to very good.
Comments: European CD. Deluxe color cover. Picture CD. Time 71:31.

CD - SECRET KISSES III
PGAEP 7395-3
See You Tonight (Los Angeles '95)/ Good-Bye (Los Angeles '95)/ Hard Luck Woman (Los Angeles '95)/ Nothing To Lose (Los Angeles '95)/ Deuce (Bochum '88)/ Black Diamond (Bochum '88)/ Lick It Up (Bochum '88)/ Detroit Rock City (Bochum '88)/ Rock 'N' Roll All Nite (Bochum '88)/ Won't Get Fooled Again (Chicago '86)/ Hard Luck Woman (with Garth Brooks '94)/ Christine Sixteen (with Gin Blossoms '94)/ When Two Hearts Collide (Paul Stanley demos '89)/ Don't Let Go (Paul Stanley demos '89)/ Best Man For You (Paul Stanley demos '89)/ Time Traveller (Paul Stanley demos '89)
Recording: Very good to excellent. Some good to very good.
Comments: European CD. Deluxe color cover. Picture CD. Time 73:11.

CD - WELCOME HOME PETE!
BABYFACE BF023/24
CD1: Coming Home/ Plaster Caster/ Take Me/ A World Without Heroes/ C'mon And Love Me/ Do You Love Me?/ I Will See You Tonight/ Got To Choose/ Domino/ Hard Luck Woman/ Sure Know Something/ Going Blind/ Rock Bottom
CD2: God Gave Rock N Roll To You/ Heavens On Fire/ All The Way/ Goodbye/ Nothing To Lose/ Black Diamond/ Room Service/ Forever/ Hard Luck Woman/ Nothing To Lose/ Calling Dr. Love/ Shandi/ Going Blind
Recording: Excellent. Audience.
Source: CD1-CD2 tracks 9-13 Unplugged Fan Club show, Los Angeles June 17 '95. CD2 tracks 1-8 Fan Club Show, San Francisco June 18 '95.
Comments: European CD. Deluxe color cover. Picture CDs.

KNOPFLER, MARK

CD - BREAK OF DAY
KISS THE STONE KTS 551
Darling Pretty/ Walk Of Life/ Instrumental, Golden Heart/ Rudiger/ Instrumental, Cannibals/ Romeo & Juliet/ Done With Bonaparte/ Money For Nothing/ Brothers In Arms/ Gravy Train
Recording: Excellent stereo. Soundboard.

KNOPFLER, MARK

Source: The Sheppard's Bush Empire, London May 6 1996.
Comments: European CD. Deluxe color cover. Time 68:02.

CD - THE GOLDEN GLOBE
MOONRAKER 179
Darling Pretty (4:00)/ Imelda (6:57)/ Sultans Of Swing (15:58)/ Done With Bonaparte (5:17)/ Golden Heart (5:55)/ Brothers In Arms (9:36)/ Money For Nothing (6:23)
Recording: Excellent.
Source: The Globe Arena, Stockholm June 12 1996.
Comments: European CD.

CD - GOLDEN TEARS
KISS THE STONE KTS 586
Walk Of Life/ Intro, Rudiger/ I'm The Fool/ Intro, Romeo And Juliet/ Done With Bonaparte/ A Night In Summer Long Time Ago/ Intro, Golden Heart/ Cannibals/ Theme From 'Going Home'
Recording: Excellent stereo. Soundboard.
Source: Bristol, England 1996.
Comments: European CD.

KORN

CD - LIVE, DEMO'S & BLIND
BLIZZARD BLZD 105
Blind/ Ball Tongue/ Need To/ Shoots & Ladders/ Lies/ Faggott/ Predictable/ Blind/ Daddy/ Alive/ X-Mas Song/ X-Mas Song/ This Town
Recording: Tracks 1-6 Ex. Audience. Tracks 7-13 Excellent stereo. Soundboard.
Source: Tracks 1-6 The Palace, Los Angeles 1995. Tracks 7-10 four song demo 1994. Track 11 Jonathon with Human Waste Project 1995. Track 12 Squeak by the FCC version. Track 13 Fuck the FCC version.
Comments: European CD. Deluxe color cover. Time 52:50.

KRAVITZ, LENNY

CD - DREAM ON
KISS THE STONE KTS 556
Tunnel Vision/ Stop Draggin' Around/ Circus/ Beyond The 7th Sky/ Can't Get You Off My Mind/ Fields Of Joy/ What The Fuck Are We Sayin/ Mr. Cabdriver/ Let Love Rule/ It Ain't Over Till It's Over/ Are You Gonna Go My Way/ Rock And Roll Is Dead
Recording: Excellent stereo. Soundboard.
Source: E-Werk, Cologne, Germany, October 7 1995
Comments: European CD.

CD - ETERNAL SPIRIT
OXYGEN OXY 045
Tunnel Vision/ Stop Draggin' Around/ Always On The Run/ Rock And Roll Is Dead/ Believe (acoustic version)/ Can't Get You Off My Mind (acoustic version)/ Mr, Cab Driver/ Are You Gonna Go My Way?/ Rock And Roll Is Dead/ Circus/ Let Love Rule/ Are You Gonna Go My Way/ Heaven Help (acoustic)/ Always On The Run
Recording: Excellent stereo. Soundboard.
Source: Tracks 1-8 Much Music Studios, Toronto, Canada February 7 '96. Tracks 9-11 New York City October '95. Tracks 12-14 The 'Later Show', London, UK '94.
Comments: European CD. Picture CD. Time 72:50.

CD - HAPPY BIRTHDAY CINDY
BS - 16/17
CD1: Tunnel Vision/ Stop Draggin' Around/ Freedom Train/ Always On The Run/ Beyond The 7th Sky// Come On And Love Me/ Circus/ Can't Get You Off My Mind/ Fields Of Joy/ What Goes Around Comes Around
CD2: Mr. Cab Driver/ Let Love Rule/ It Ain't Over 'Till It's Over/ Are You Gonna Go My Way/ Rock And Roll Is Dead/ Believe/ Always On The Run/ Be/ Birthday Song/ Let Love Rule/ Believe
Recording: Good to very good. Audience.
Source: Budokan, Tokyo November 9 1995. CD2 tracks 7-11 NK Hall, Urayasu November 18 1995.

KULA SHAKER

CD - BLENDER, BLENDER
KISS THE STONE KTS 643
Baby/ Knight On The Town/ 303/ Grateful When You're Dead/ Jerry Was There/ Ragi One (Waiting For Tomorrow)/ For This Is Love/ Drop In The Sea/ Tattva/ Smart Dogs/ Start All Over/ Hey Dude/ Hush/ Hollow Man (Parts 1 & 2)/ Into The Deep/ Govinda
Recording: Excellent stereo. Soundboard.
Source: Aston Villa Leisure Centre, Birmingham, UK January 27 1997.
Comments: European CD. Deluxe color cover. Picture CD. Time 64:14.

L

LAKE, GREG

CD - MOORE ATTACK '81
NIGHTLIFE N-044
Introduction/ Fanfare For The Common Man/ Welcome Back My Friends/ Nuclear Attack/ The Lie/ Retribution Drive/ Lucky Man/ I Love You Too Much/ 21St. Century Schizoid Man/ In The Court Of The Crimson King
Recording: Excellent stereo. Soundboard.
Source: Hammersmith Odeon, London December 12 1981.
Comments: Japanese CD. Deluxe color cover. Time 49:08.

LED ZEPPELIN
(see pages 236 to 238)

CD - AMERICAN BEAUTY
TARANTURA SFSB-1,2
CD1: The Train Kept A-Rollin' (3:00)/ I Can't Quit You Baby (6:15)/ As Long As I Have You, Flesh Garbage, Shake, Cat's Squirrel, I'm A Man, Cadillac No Money Down (20:01)/ You Shook Me (9:50)/ How Many More Times, The Hunter, Mulberry Bush (19:44)/ The Lemon Song includes Sweet Jelly Baby (7:35)
CD2: Babe I'm Gonna Leave You (7:11)/ Sitting And Thinking (7:48)/ Dazed And Confused (13:13)/ Communication Breakdown (5:22)
Recording: Excellent. Soundboard.
Source: Fillmore West, San Francisco April 27 1969.
Comments: Japanese CDs.

CD - AMERICAN WOMAN
THE DIAGRAMS OF LED ZEPPELIN
TDOLZ 0018/19
CD1: Immigrant Song/ Heartbreaker/ Dazed And Confused/ Bring It On Home/ That's The Way/ Bron-Yr-Aur/ Since I've Been Loving You/ Thank You/ What Is And What Should Never Be
CD2: Moby Dick/ Whole Lotta Love/ Communication Breakdown (Includes American Woman)
Recording: Good to very good audience.
Source: Madison Square Garden, New York September 19 1970.
Comments: Japanese CDs.

CD - ARABESQUE & BAROQUE - THE FOURTH NIGHT
ANTRABATA REFERENCE MASTER ARM
CD1: Rock & Roll/ Sick Again/ Over The Hills And Far Away/ In My Time Of Dying/ The Song Remains The Same/ The Rain Song/ Kashmir
CD2: No Quarter/ Tangerine/ Going To California/ That's The Way/ Bron-Y-Aur Stomp/ Trampled Underfoot
CD3: Moby Dick
CD4: Dazed & Confused/ Stairway to Heaven/ Whole Lotta Love, The Crunge/ Black Dog
Recording: Very good to excellent. Audience and soundboard. Combination of audience and video source tapes.
Source: London May 24 1975.
Comments: Japanese CD. Full color cardboard slipcover. Limited edition of 325 numbered copies.

CD - ARABESQUE & BAROQUE - THE SECOND NIGHT
ANTRABATA REFERENCE MASTER ARM
CD1: Rock & Roll/ Sick Again/ Over The Hills And Far Away/ In My Time Of Dying/ The Song Remains The Same/ The Rain Song/ Kashmir
CD2: No Quarter
CD3: Tangerine/ Going To California/ That's The Way/ Bron-Y-Aur Stomp/ Trampled Underfoot/ Moby Dick
CD4: Dazed & Confused/ Stairway To Heaven/ Whole Lotta Love, The Crunge/ Black Dog
Recording: Very good. Audience.
Source: London May 18 1975.
Comments: Japanese CD. Full color cardboard slipcover. Limited edition of 325 numbered copies.

CD - ARABESQUE & BAROQUE THE - THIRD NIGHT
ANTRABATA REFERENCE MASTER ARM
CD1: Rock & Roll/ Sick Again/ Over The Hills And Far Away/ In My Time Of Dying/ The Song Remains The Same/ The Rain Song/ Kashmir
CD2: No Quarter/ Tangerine/ Going to California/ That's The Way, Bron-Y-Aur Stomp/ Trampled Underfoot
CD3: Moby Dick

LED ZEPPELIN

CD4: Dazed & Confused/ Stairway To Heaven/ Whole Lotta Love, The Crunge/ Black Dog
Recording: Very good to excellent. Audience. Combination of two source tapes.
Source: London May 23 1975.
Comments: Japanese CD. Full color cardboard slipcover. Limited edition of 325 numbered copies.

CD - ARGENTEUM ASTRUM
TARANTURA
CD1: Rock And Roll/ Sick Again/ Over The Hills And Far Away/ In My Time Of Dying/ The Song Remains The Same/ The Rain Song, Kashmir
CD2: No Quarter/ Tangerine/ Going To California/ That's The Way/ Bron-Y-Aur Stomp/ Trampled Underfoot
CD3: Moby Dick/ Dazed And Confused/ Stairway To Heaven
CD4: Whole Lotta Love, The Crunge/ Black Dog
Recording: Very good to excellent. Audience.
Source: London, May 18 1975.
Comments: Japanese CD. Deluxe cardboard slipcover.

CD - BACK TO THE GARDEN
THE DIAGRAMS OF LED ZEPPELIN
TDOLZ 0025/26/27
CD1: The Song Remains The Same/ The Rover, Sick Again/ Nobody's Fault But Mine/ In My Time Of Dying, You Shook Me/ Since I've Been Loving You/ No Quarter
CD2: Ten Years Gone/ The Battle Of Evermore/ Going To California/ Raw Hide/ Black Country Woman/ Bron-Y-Aur Stomp/ White Summer/ Black Mountain Side/ Kashmir
CD3: Out On The Tiles, Moby Dick/ Guitar Solo/ Achilles Last Stand/ Stairway To Heaven/ Whole Lotta Love/ Rock And Roll
Recording: Good to very good audience.
Source: Madison Square Garden, New York June 7 1977.
Comments: Japanese CDs.

CD - BEAST OF TORONTO
IMMIGRANT IM-045
Good Times Bad Times, Communication Breakdown/ I Can't Quit You/ Heartbreaker/ Dazed And Confused/ White Summer,

Leave You/ Moby Dick
Recording: Good to very good. Audience.
Source: O'Keefe Centre, Toronto, Canada November 2 '69.
Comments: Japanese CD. Dbw. Time 68:14.

CD - BERDU
COBRA
CD1: Immigrant Song/ Heartbreaker/ Since I've Been Loving You/ Stairway To Heaven/ Going To California
CD2: That's The Way/ Tangerine/ Bron-Y-Aur Stomp/ Dazed & Confused/ What Is And What Should Never Be/ Moby Dick/ Whole Lotta Love Medley/ Rock & Roll
Recording: Good to very good. Audience.
Source: San Bernardino June 22 1972.
Comments: Japanese CD. Deluxe cardboard slipcover.

CD - BOX OF TRICKS
RED HOT RH-023
Immigrant Song/ Dazed And Confused/ Heartbreaker/ Since I've Been Loving You/ What Is And What Should Never Be/ Moby Dick/ Whole Lotta Love/ Communication Breakdown
Recording: Very good. Audience.
Source: Honolulu, Hawaii, September 6 1970.
Comments: Japanese CD. B&w cardboard sleeve in gold foil bag.

CD - BRADFORD UK 1973
THE DIAGRAMS OF LED ZEPPELIN
TDOLZ 209701/2 VOL.020
CD1: Rock And Roll/ Over The Hills And Far Away/ Black Dog/ Misty Mountain Hop/ Since I've Been Loving You/ Dancing Days/ Bron-Y-Aur Stomp/ The Song Remains The Same/ The Rain Song/ Dazed And Confused
CD2: Stairway To Heaven/ Whole Lotta Love/ Heartbreaker
Recording: Poor to fair. Audience.
Source: Bradford, England January 18 1973.
Comments: Japanese CD. Deluxe cardboard sleeve.

CD - BROKEN FINGERS
IMAGE QUALITY IQ-001/2
CD1: Rock And Roll (4:13)/ Over The Hills And Far Away (5:57)/ Black Dog (6:20)/

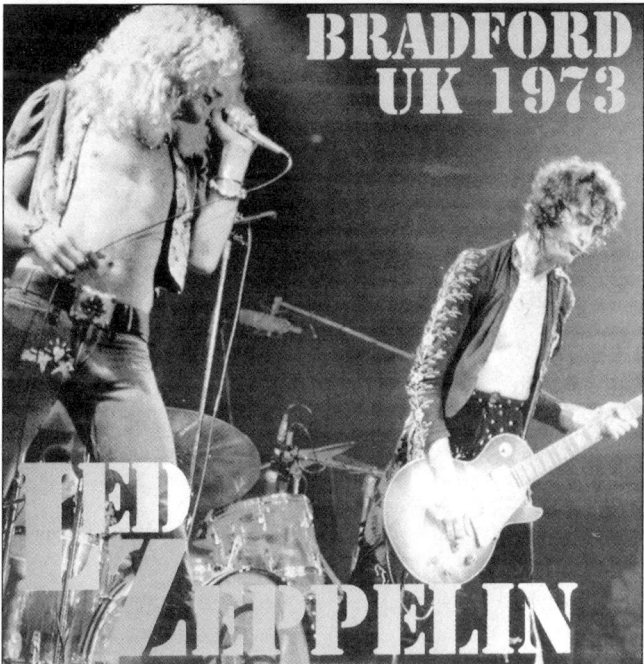

LED ZEPPELIN

BEAST OF TORONTO

BRADFORD UK 1973

LED ZEPPELIN

LED ZEPPELIN page 116

Loving You (8:16)/ Dancing Days (4:32)/ Bron-Yr-Aur Stomp (6:28)/ The Song Remains The Same (5:06)/ Rain Song (7:15)
CD2: Dazed And Confused (includes The Crunge, San Francisco) (29:49)/ Stairway To Heaven (9:47)/ Whole Lotta Love (includes Voodoo Chile, Everybody Needs Somebody To Love, Boogie Woogie, Baby I Don't Care, Let's Have A Party)
Recording: Very good. Soundboard.
Source: Trentham Gardens, Stoke, UK January 15 1973.
Comments: Japanese CD.

CD - CANADIAN GRAFITTI
BLACK ROSE BR-001-2
CD1: Rock And Roll/ Sick Again/ Over The Hills And Far Away/ In My Time Of Dying/ The Song Remains The Same/ The Rain Song
CD2: Dazed And Confused/ Stairway To Heaven/ Whole Lotta Love/ Black Dog/ Heartbreaker
Recording: Poor to good. Audience. Some surface noise.
Source: Montreal, Canada February 6 '75.
Comments: Japanese CD. Deluxe color cover. Time CD1 40:51. CD2 49:52.

CD - CAN'T TAKE YOUR EVIL WAYS
THE DIAGRAMS OF LED ZEPPELIN TDOLZ 019
CD1: Rock And Roll/ Sick Again/ Over The Hills And Far Away/ In My Time Of Dying/ The Song Remains The Same/ The Rain Song/ Kashmir
CD2: No Quarter/ Trampled Underfoot/ Moby Dick
CD3: Dazed And Confused/ Stairway To Heaven/ Whole Lotta Love/ Black Dog/ Heartbreaker
Recording: Excellent audience.
Source: Madison Square Garden, New York February 12 1975.
Comments: Japanese CD. Deluxe gatefold cardboard sleeve.

CD - CHECKPOINT CHARLIE
IMMIGRANT IM-050-51
CD1: Immigrant Song/ Heartbreaker/ Dazed And Confused/ Bring It On Home/ Since I've Been Loving You
CD2: Thank You/ What Is And What Should Never Be/ Whole Lotta Love Medley/ Moby Dick

Recording: Good. Audience.
Source: Deutshlandhalle, Berlin July 12 1970.
Comments: Japanese CD. Deluxe color cover. Picture CD. Time CD1 41:03. CD2 42:59.

CD - CLEVELAND 1969
THE DIAGRAMS OF LED ZEPPELIN TDOLZ 0029
The Train Kept A-Rollin' (3:01)/ I Can't Quite You Baby (7:32)/ Dazed And Confused (14:28)/ White Summer, Black Mountain Side (7:15)/ You Shook Me (11:58)/ How Many More Times, The Hunter, The Lemon Song (17:21)
Recording: Fair audience.
Source: Cleveland, Ohio, July 16, '69.
Comments: Japanese CD. Deluxe color cover.

COME BACK TO BOSTON
HOLY SH 001-A
CD1: Introduction (3:11)/ Immigrant Song (5:41)/ Heartbreaker (6:29)/ Dazed And Confused (16:42)/ Bring It On Home (9:20)/ That's The Way (7:14)/ Bron-Yr-Aur (5:03)/ Since I've Been Loving You (12:15)
CD2: Organ Solo, Thank You (11:03)/ What Is And What Should Never Be (4:48)/ Moby Dick (12:40)/ Whole Lotta Love, Let That Boy Boogie Woogie, Messin' Around, Ramble On, For What It's Worth, Some Other Guy, Honey Be, The Lemon Song (18:27)/ Communication Breakdown (5:44)
Recording: Fair to good audience.
Source: Boston Gardens, Boston September 9 1970.
Comments: Japanese CD.

CD - COMPLETE DANCING DAYS
CD1: Intro/ Rock And Roll/ Over The Hills And Far Away/ Black Dog/ Misty Mountain/ Since I've Been Loving You/ Dancing Days/ Born-Y-Aur-Stomp/ The Song Remains The Same/ The Rain Song/ Dazed And Confused
CD2: Stairway To Heaven/ Whole Lotta Love, Let That Boy Boogie Woogie, My Baby Left Me, The Lemon Song, I Can't Quit You Baby, Unknown Blues/ Heartbreaker/ Immigrant Song/ Communication Breakdown/ How Many More Times*, Let That Boy Boogie Woogie*, Some Other Guy*, Killing Floor*
Source: Budokan Hall, Tokyo, Japan

October 2 1972. *West Germany March 1970.
Comments: Japanese CD.

CD - COPENHAGEN WARM-UPS
LAST STAND DISC LSD-01/02/03/04
CD1: Introduction (2:14)/ The Song Remains The Same (5:36)/ Celebration Day (3:17)/ Out On The Tiles Into, Black Dog (6:00)/ Nobody's Fault But Mine (6:44)/ Over The Hills And Far Away (6:18)/ Misty Mountain Hop (4:40)/ Since I've Been Loving You (9:06)/ No Quarter (14:29)/ Hot Dog (4:33) The Rain Song (8:46)
CD2: White Summer, Black Mountain Side (5:04)/ Kashmir (9:47)/ Trampled Underfoot (6:04)/ Achilles Last Stand (10:19)/ Guitar Solo, Drum Solo (5:33)/ In The Evening (6:36)/ Stairway To Heaven (9:35)/ Rock And Roll (4:43)
CD3: The Song Remains The Same (6:21)/ Celebration Day (3:17)/ Out On The Tiles Intro, Black Dog (6:12)/ Nobody's Fault But Mine (5:49)/ Over The Hills And Far Away (6:00)/ Misty Mountain Side (4:39)/ Since I've Been Loving You (9:44)/ No Quarter (11:08)/ Ten Years Gone (4:43)
CD4: The Rain Song (8:12)/ White Summer, Black Mountain Side (5:01)/ Kashmir (9:05)/ Trampled Underfoot (6:21)/ Sick Again (5:40)/ Achilles Last Stand (9:35)/ Guitar Solo, Drum Solo (5:04)/ In The Evening (7:03)/ Stairway To Heaven (9:57)/ Whole Lotta Love (8:20)
Recording: Excellent. Audience.
Source: CD1, CD2 Falkoner Theater, Copenhagen, Denmark July 23 1979. CD3, CD4 Falkoner Theater, Copenhagen, Denmark July 24 1979.
Comments: Japanese CD.

CD - CONDITION BREAKDOWN
HOLY SH 006-A
CD1: Rock And Roll (4:09)/ Sick Again (5:59)/ Over The Hills And Far Away (7:11)/ The Song Remains The Same (3:56)/ The Rain Song (7:03)/ Kashmir (8:33)/ The Wanton Song (5:15)/ No Quarter (13:54)
CD2: Trampled Underfoot (8:12)/ Moby Dick (4:16)/ How Many More Times (5:41)/ Stairway To Heaven (11:20)/ Whole Lotta Love, Out On The Tiles Intro, Black Dog (9:11)
Recording: Fair audience.
Source: Market Square Arena, Indianapolis, Indiana. January 25, '75.

Comments: Japanese CD.

CD - CONFUSION
LZ-72377A/B
CD1: The Song Remains The Same/ The Rover (Intro)/ Sick Again/ Nobody's Fault But Mine/ Over The Hills And Far Away/ Since I've Been Loving You/ No Quarter/ Ten Years Gone/ The Battle Of Evermore/ Going To California
CD2: Black Country Woman, Bron-Y-Aur Stomp/ Trampled Underfoot/ White Summer, Black Mountain Side/ Kashmir/ Achilles Last Stand/ Stairway To Heaven/ Whole Lotta Love, Rock And Roll/ Black Dog
Recording: Very good to excellent.
Audience.
Source: Oakland Coliseum Stadium, Oakland, CA July 23 1977.
Comments: Japanese CD.

CD - CRAZED ATTACK
CRA-7103CD-1/2
CD1: Immigrant Song (4:54)/ Heartbreaker (6:57)/ Since I've Been Loving You (10:00)/ Out On The Tiles Intro, Black Dog (6:29)/ Stairway To Heaven (9:49)/ Dazed And Confused (18:26)
CD2: Going To California (2:00)/ What Is And What Should Never Be (1:22)/ Moby Dick (14:31)/ Whole Lotta Love, Let That Boy Boogie, Suzie Q, Some Other Guy, Hey Baby Don't Go That Way, Honey Bee, Needle Blues, The Lemon Song/ That's Alright (25:57)/ Communication Breakdown (6:57)/ Rock And Roll (2:28)
Source: National Stadium, Dublin, Ireland March 6 1971.
Comments: Japanese CD.

CD - DANCING BEARS
TARANTURA BEAR-001/2
CD1: Immigrant Song/ Heartbreaker/ Black Dog/ Since I've Been Loving You/ Celebration Day/ Stairway To Heaven/ Bron-Y-Aur Stomp/ Dazed And Confused
CD2: What Is And What Should Never Be/ Moby Dick/ Whole Lotta Love Medley/ Rock And Roll/ Communication Breakdown
Recording: Very good. Audience
Source: Amsterdam May 27 1972.
Comments: Japanese CD.

CD - DESTROYER FINAL EDITION
COBLA STANDARDS
CD1: The Song Remains The Same/ Sick Again/ Nobody's Fault But Mine/ In My Time Of Dying/ Since I've Been Loving You/ No Quarter
CD2: Ten Years Gone/ The Battle Of Evermore/ Going To California/ Black Mountain Side/ Bron-Y-Aur Stomp/ White Summer, Black Mountain Side/ Kashmir
CD3: Moby Dick/ Guitar Solo/ Achilles Last Stand/ Stairway To Heaven/ Rock & Roll/ Trampled Underfoot
Recording: Excellent. Soundboard.
Source: Cleveland April 27 1977.
Comments: Japanese CD. Deluxe cardboard sleeve.

CD - THE DESTROYER 1969
TARANTURA
Train Kept A Rolling/ I Can't Quit You/ Dazed & Confused/ White Summer, Black Mountain Side/ You Shook Me/ How Many More Times
Recording: Good to very good. Audience.
Source: Cleveland July 16 1969.
Comments: Japanese CD. Deluxe cardboard sleeve.

CD - THE DESTROYER STORONGEST EDITION
THE DIAGRAMS OF LED-ZEPPELIN TODOLZ 0015/16/17
CD1: The Song Remains The Same/ The Rover, Sick Again/ Nobody's Fault But Mine/ In My Time Of Dying/ Surrender/ Since I've Been Loving You/ No Quarter
CD2: Ten Years Gone/ The Battle Of Evermore/ Going To California/ Black Country Woman/ Bron-Y-Aur Stomp/ White Summer, Black Mountain Side/ Kashmir
CD3: Out On The Tiles, Moby Dick/ Guitar Solo, Achilles Last Stand/ Stairway To Heaven/ Rock And Roll/ Trampled Underfoot
Recording: Very good to excellent. Audience.
Source: Cleveland April 28 1977.
Comments: Japanese CD. Deluxe cardboard gatefold sleeve.

CD - THE FABULOUS FOUR
TARANTURA FF-1/2
CD1: Over The Hills And Far Away (5:28)/ Out On The Tiles Intro, Black Dog (5:52)/ Misty Mountain Hop (5:00)/ Since I've Been Loving You (7:36)/ Dancing Days (4:24)/ Bron-Y-Aur Stomp (6:02)/ The Song Remains The Same (5:49)/ The Rain Song (5:38)/ Dazed And Confused includes San Francisco (22:50)
CD2: Stairway To Heaven (10:51)/ Whole Lotta Love, Everybody Needs Somebody To Love, Let That Boy Boogie, Baby (You're So Square) I Don't Care, Let's Have A Party, I Can't Quit You Baby, Shape I'm In (23:20)/ Heartbreaker (7:02)/ The Ocean (4:29)
Recording: Very good to excellent. Soundboard.
Source: The Empire, Liverpool, UK January 14 1973.
Comments: Japanese CD.

CD - FEEL ALL RIGHT
COBLA STANDARD SERIES 003
CD1: We're Gonna Groove/ I Can't Quit You, Baby/ White Summer, Black Mountain Side/ Dazed And Confused/ Heartbreaker
CD2: Since I've Been Loving You/ Organ Solo/ Thank You/ What Is And What Should Never Be/ Moby Dick/ How Many More Times (Cut Off)
Recording: Very good. Audience.
Source: Montreaux Jazz Festival Montreaux Switzerland March 14 1970.
Comments: Japanese CD. Deluxe cardboard sleeve.

CD - FILLMORE WEST
LAST STAND DISC LSD-09/10/11
CD1: As Long As I Have You, Flesh Garbage, Shake, Hush Little Baby, Suzie Q (19:34)/ The Lemon Song (7:35)/ White Summer, Black Mountain Side (11:47)/ Babe I'm Gonna Leave You (7:05)/ Pat's Delight (12:37)
CD2: The Train Kept A-Rollin' (3:02)/ I Can't Quit You Baby (6:10)/ As Long As I Have You, Fresh Garbage, Shake, I'm A Man, Cadillac-No Money Down (19:56)/ You Shook Me (9:46)/ How Many More Times, The Hunter, Mulberry Bush (19:37)
CD3: The Lemon Song includes Sweet Jelly Baby (7:34)/ Babe I'm Gonna Leave You (7:06)/ Sitting And Thinking (7:38)/ Pat's Delight (13:39)/ Dazed And Confused (12:57)/ Communication Breakdown (5:22)
Source: CD1 Fillmore West, San Francisco April 24 1969. CD2, CD3 Fillmore West, San Francisco April27 1969.
Comments: Japanese CD

LED ZEPPELIN

CD - THE FINAL TOUR EUROPEAN DAZE 1980
PATRIOT 3-1/2
CD1: Trains Kept A Rollin'/ Nobody's Fault But Mine/ Black Dog/ In The Evening/ The Rain Song/ Hot Dog/ All My Love/ Trampled Underfoot/ Since I've Been Loving You/ Achilles Last Stand
CD2: Stairway To Heaven/ Rock And Roll/ Heartbreaker/ *Stairway To Heaven/ *Rock And Roll/ *Whole Lotta Love
Recording: Excellent stereo. Soundboard.
Source: All Tracks Live In Zurich June 29 1980 *Live In Berlin July 7 1980.
Comments: Japanese CD.

CD - FIRE CRACKER'S SHOW
THE DIAGRAMS OF LED ZEPPELIN TDOLZ 0003/4/5
CD1: Rock And Roll (5:15)/ Sick Again (6:25)/ Over The Hills And Far Away (7:28)/ On My Time Of Dying (12:23)/ The Song Remains The Same (5:14)/ The Rain Song (8:31)/ Kashmir (8:35)
CD2: No Quarter includes Aanjuez Concert (27:11)/ Trampled Underfoot (9:20)/ Moby Dick (22:34)
CD3: Dazed And Confused includes Woodstock (35:03)/ Stairway To Heaven (13:20)/ Whole Lotta Love includes The Crunge (8:46)/ Out On The Tiles Intro, Black Dog (6:33)/ Heartbreaker (8:38)
Recording: Very good to excellent. Audience.
Source: The Forum, Inglewood, CA March 24 1975.
Comments: Japanese CD.

CD - FLAWLESS PERFORMANCE
IMAGE QUALITY IQ-013/14/15
CD1: Introduction (0:42)/ Rock And Roll (3:43)/ Over The Hills And Far Away (6:10)/ Black Dog (5:33)/ Misty Mountain Hop (5:03)/ Since I've Been Loving You (8:00)/ Dancing Days (4:37)/ Bron-Yr-Aur Stomp (5:34)/ The Song Remains The Same (5:25)/ The Rain Song (8:45)
CD2: Dazed & Confused (includes San Francisco) (29:37)/ Stairway To Heaven (10:59)
CD3: Whole Lotta Love (includes Everybody Needs Somebody To Love, Boogie Woogie, Let's Have A Party, Heartbreak Hotel, I Can't Quite You) (27:03)/ Immigrant Song (3:54)/ Heartbreaker (6:59)/ Mellotron Solo, Thank You (10:58)
Recording: Good. Audience.
Source: Alexandra Palace, London UK Dec. 22 1972.
Comments: Japanese CD. Deluxe color cover.

CD - FOR TRAINSPOTTERS ONLY
ANARAC RECORDING COMPANY ARC 01/02/03
CD1: Introduction, Rock And Roll (5:39)/ Sick Again (6:47)/ Over The Hills And Far Away (7:29)/ In My Time Of Dying (11:21)/ The Song Remains The Same (5:43)/ The Rain Song (9:03)/ Kashmir (9:30)
CD2: No Quarter (23:44)/ Tangerine (4:24)/ Going To California (8:06)/ That's The Way (7:17)/ Bron-Y-Aur Stomp (7:22)/ Trampled Underfoot (9:09)
CD3: Moby Dick (20:31)/ Dazed And Confused (27:44)/ Stairway To Heaven (12:41)/ Whole Lotta Love (Inc. The Crunge) (6:51)/ Black Dog (6:10
Recording: Very good to excellent mono. Audience.
Source: Earls Court May 17 1975.
Comments: Deluxe color cover. Picture CD. CDR. Limited edition of 10.

CD - GOIN' MOBILE
MIDAS TOUCH 61921/2
CD1: Rock And Roll (4:19)/ Celebration Day (3:36)/ Bring It On Home Intro, Black Dog (6:17)/ Over The Hills And Far Away (6:47)/ Misty Mountain Hop (4:40)/ Since I've Been Loving You (8:58)/ No Quarter (11:34)/ The Song Remains The Same (5:34)/ The Rain Song (8:37)
CD2: Dazed And Confused includes San Francisco (28:35)/ Stairway To Heaven (11:09)/ Moby Dick (15:54)
Recording: Excellent. Soundboard.
Source: The Auditorium, Mobile, Alabama May 13 1973.
Comments: Japanese CD.

CD - GRACIAS
ANTRABATA REFERENCE MASTER ARM 240680
CD1: The Train Kept A Rollin/ Nobody's Fault But Mine/ Black Dog/ In The Evening/ The Rain Song/ Hot Dog/ All My Love/ Trampled Underfoot (contains 2 small cuts during the guitar solo)
CD2: Since I've Been Loving You/ Achilles Last Stand/ White Summer, Black Mountain

LED ZEPPELIN

Side/ Kashmir/ Stairway To Heaven/ Rock And Roll/ Communication Breakdown
CD3: The Train Kept A Rollin/ Nobody's Fault But Mine/ Black Dog/ In The Evening/ The Rain Song/ Hot Dog/ All My Love/ Trampled Underfoot
CD 4: Since I've Been Loving You/ Achilles Last Stand/ White Summer, Black Mountain Side/ Kashmir (ending cut)/ Stairway to Heaven/ Rock And Roll/ Heartbreaker
Recording: Excellent stereo. Soundboard.
Source: CD1-2 Messehalle, Hannover, Germany June 24 1980. CD3-4 Hallenstadion, Zurich, Switzerland June 29 1980.
Comments: Japanese CD. Full color cardboard slipcover. Limited edition of 325 numbered copies. Time CD1 49:13. CD2 56:13. CD3 52:53. CD4 65:30.

CD - GRAF-ZEPPELIN-MARSCH
TARANTURA
CD1: Rock & Roll/ Sick Again/ Over The Hills And Far Away/ In My Time Of Dying/ The Song Remains The Same/ The Rain Song
CD2: No Quarter/ Tangerine/ Going To California/ That's The Way/ Bron-Y-Aur Stomp/ Trampled Underfoot
CD3: Dazed & Confused/ Stairway To Heaven/ Whole Lotta Love/ Black Dog
Recording: Very good to excellent. Soundboard.
Source: London May 24 1975.
Comments: Japanese CD. Deluxe cardboard slipcover.

CD - HAMPTON '71
THERAMIN MUSIC 020971
CD1: Immigrant Song/ Heartbreaker/ Since I've Been Loving You/ Black Dog/ Dazed And Confused
CD2: Stairway To Heaven/ Celebration Day/ That's The Way/ Going To California/ What Is And What Should Never Be/ Moby Dick
Recording: Excellent. Soundboard.
Source: Hampton Roads Coliseum, Hampton, Virginia September 2 1971.
Comments: Japanese CD. Deluxe color cardboard sleeve.

CD - HEARTBEAT
H-BOMB MUSIC HB-9616
Immigrant Song/ Heartbreaker/ Black Dog/ Bron-Y-Aur Stomp/ Dazed And Confused/ What Is And What Should Never Be/ Rock And Roll/ Whole Lotta Love, Just A Little Hideaway, Trucking Little Mama, Boogie Woogie/ Heartbeat, Hello Mary Lou, Lawdy Miss Clawdy, I Can't Quite You
Recording: Poor to fair audience.
Source: Royal Ballroom, UK December 2 1971.
Comments: Japanese CD.

CD - HEARTBREAK HOTEL
MISSING LINK ML-011/012/013
CD1: Immigrant Song/ Heartbreaker/ Over The Hills And Far Away/ Black Dog/ Since I've Been Loving You/ Stairway To Heaven/ Going To California/ That's The Way/ Tangerine/ Bron-Yr-Aur-Stomp
CD2: Dazed And Confused (includes The Crunge)/ What Is And What Should Never Be/ Dancing Days/ Moby Dick
CD3: Whole Lotta Love/ Boogie Woogie, Let's Have A Party, Mary Lou, Heartbreak Hotel, Going Down/ Rock And Roll/ The Ocean/ Louie Louie/ Thank You/ Communication Breakdown/ Bring It On Home
Recording: Very good. Audience.
Source: The Forum, Inglewood, CA June 25 1972.
Comments: Japanese CD.

CD - HOLIDAY IN WAIKIKI
SCORPIO - GOLD STANDARD
Introduction/ Immigrant Song/ Dazed And Confused/ Heartbreaker/ Since I've Been Loving You/ What Is And Should Never Be/ Moby Dick/ Whole Lotta Love/ Communication Breakdown
Recording: Very good. Audience.
Source: The Honolulu International Center, Honolulu, Hawaii September 6 1970.
Comments: Gold CD.

CD - HOT AUGUST NIGHT
THE DIAGRAMS OF LED ZEPPELIN
TDOLZ 429701/2
CD1: Dazed And Confused (18:40) Stairway To Heaven (10:05) Celebration Day (4:13) That's The Way (7:26) What Is And What Should Never Be (4:50) Moby Dick (14:57)
CD2: Whole Lotta Love (24:34) (includes Truckin' Little Mama), Mess O' Blues, You Shook Me/ Communication Breakdown (0:57)
Recording: Very good. Soundboard.

Source: Fort Worth August 23 1971.
Comments: Japanese CD. Cardboard sleeve with raised lettering. CD1 60:13. CD2 25:32.

CD - HOT RODS IN PONTIAC
THE DIAGRAMS OF LED ZEPPELIN
TDOLZ 0030/31/32 VOL. 013
CD1: The Song Remains The Same/The Rover, Sick Again/ Nobody's Fault But Mine/ In My Time Of Dying/ Since I've Been Loving You/ No Quarter
CD2: Ten Years Gone/ The Battle Of Evermore/ Going To California/ Black Country Woman/ Bron-Y-Aur Stomp/ White Summer, Black Mountain Side/ Kashmir
CD3: Out On The Tiles, Moby Dick/ Guitar Solo (Includes Star Spangled Banner)/ Achilles Last Stand/ Stairway To Heaven/ Rock And Roll/ Trampled Underfoot
Recording: Very good. Audience.
Source: Pontiac Silverdome Pontiac Michigan April 30 1977.
Comments: Japanese CD. Deluxe cardboard sleeve.

CD - IN CONCERT & BEYOND
THE DIAGRAMS OF LED ZEPPELIN
TDOLZ 0001/2
CD1: Rock And Roll (4:56)/ Celebration Day (3:27)/ Bring It On Home Intro, Black Dog (6:34)/ Over The Hills And Far Away (7:04)/ Misty Mountain Hop (4:45)/ Since I've Been Loving You (9:06)/ No Quarter (13:21)/ The Song Remains The Same (5:24)/ The Rain Song (8:19)
CD2: Dazed And Confused includes San Francisco (32:11)/ Stairway To Heaven (10:54)
Recording: Excellent. Soundboard.
Source: Buffalo Auditorium, Buffalo, New York July 15 1973.
Comments: Japanese CD.

CD - INSPIRED
ANTRABATA REFERENCE MASTER ARM 020971
CD1: Immigrant Song (first 30 seconds cut)/ Heartbreaker/ Since I've Been Loving You/ Black Dog/ Dazed And Confused (cut during the guitar solo, last vocal section cut)
CD 2: Stairway to Heaven/ Celebration Day/ That's The Way/ Going To California/ What Is And What Should Never Be/ Moby Dick (last 30 seconds cut)

Recording: Excellent mono. Soundboard.
Source: Hampton Roads Coliseum, Hampton, Virginia September 2 1971.
Comments: Japanese CD. Full color cardboard slipcover. Limited edition of 325 numbered copies. Time CD1 49:28. CD2 46:50.

CD - IT'S BEEN GREAT
IMAGE QUALITY IQ-0010/11/12
CD1: The Song Remains The Same (6:18)/ The Rover, Sick Again (6:51)/ Nobody's Fault But Mine (7:28)/ Over The Hills And Far Away (8:36)/ Since I've Been Loving You (9:40)/ No Quarter (22:47)
CD2: Ten Years Gone (11:34)/ The Battle Of Evermore (7:13)/ Going To California (6:04)/ Black Country Woman (2:32)/ Bron-Yr-Aur Stomp (7:06)/ Trampled Underfoot (8:01)/ White Summer, Black Mountain (9:16) Kashmir (9:36)
CD3: Guitar Solo (10:17)/ Achilles Last Stand (9:57)/ Stairway To Heaven (12:12)/ Whole Lotta Love (3:13)/ Rock And Roll (4:15)/ Black Dog (5:59)
Recording: Very good. Audience.
Source: Alameda County Coliseum Oakland California July 23 1977.
Comments: Japanese CD. Deluxe B&W cover. Blue type.

CD - JAZZ
NPJF 1001
Train Kept A Rollin'/ I Can't Quit You/ Dazed And Confused/ You Shook Me/ How Many More Times (Including, The Hunter, The Lemon Song)/ Communication Breakdown/ Long Tall Sally
Recording: Good to very good. Audience.
Source: Newport Festival, Newport, Rhode Island July 6 1969.
Comments: Japanese CD.

CD - JIM'S PICKS
TARANTURA HAMP-1/2
CD1: Immigrant Song (3:55)/ Heartbreaker (7:41)/ Since I've Been Loving You (8:24)/ Out On The Tiles Intro, Black Dog (7:06)/ Dazed And Confused (22:17)
CD2: Stairway To Heaven (10:49)/ Celebration Day (5:43)/ That's The Way (7:33)/ Going To California (5:30)/ What Is And What Should Never Be (5:26)/ Moby Dick (11:44)
Recording: Excellent. Soundboard.
Source: Hampton Roads Coliseum, Hampton, Virginia September 2 1971.

LED ZEPPELIN

Comments: Japanese CD.

CD - JOHNNY PISTON AND THE DOGS
TM 005/006
CD1: Heartbreaker/ Whole Lotta Love/ Communication Breakdown/ Rock And Roll (first 2 minutes cut)/ Celebration Day/ Bring It On Home introduction/ Black Dog/ Over The Hills And Far Away/ Misty Mountain Hop/ Since I've Been Loving You/ No Quarter
CD2: The Song Remains The Same/ The Rain Song (small cut near the end)/ Dazed And Confused/ Stairway To Heaven/ Moby Dick (contains a small cut near the end of the solo)
Recording: Excellent stereo. Soundboard.
Source: Municipal Auditorium, New Orleans, Louisiana May 14 1973.
Comments: European CD. Deluxe color cover. Original song order altered to allow the concert to be placed on two discs. Time CD1 73:01. CD2 76:11.

CD - KICKS
TARANTURA K&S 974
I Can't Quit You Baby (5:34)/ I Gotta Move (3:31)/ Dazed And Confused (10:08)/ How Many Times More (2:14)
Recording: Excellent stereo from FM broadcast.
Source: Tivoli Gardens, Stockholm, Sweden March 14 1969.
Comments: Japanese CD.

CD - KNEES UP MOTHER BROWN
IMAGE QUALITY IQ-024/25
CD1: Immigrant Song (3:40)/ Heartbreaker (6:43)/ Celebration Day (4:05)/ Black Dog (6:06)/ Since I've Been Loving You (8:12)/ Stairway To Heaven (9:59)/ Going To California (5:33)/ That's The Way (6:54)/ Tangerine (3:49)/ Bron-Yr-Aur Stomp (6:08)
CD2: Dazed And Confused (25:07)/ What Should Never Be (5:08)/ Moby Dick (18:55)/ Whole Lotta Love (7:29)/ Rock And Roll (4:21)/ Communication Breakdown (5:13)
Recording: Very good. Audience.
Source: Coliseum Charlotte North Carolina June 9 1972.
Comments: Japanese CD. Deluxe B&W cover. Purple type.

CD - LEAD POISONING
COBRA STANDARD SERIES 008
CD1: Rock And Roll/ Over The Hills And Far Away/ Black Dog/ Misty Mountain Hop/ Since I've Been Loving You/ Dancing Days/ Bron-Y-Aur Stomp/ The Song Remains The Same/ The Rain Song
CD2: Dazed And Confused/ Stairway To Heaven/ Whole Lotta Love (Inc. Boogie Mama, Let's Have A Party, I Can't Quit You Baby, The Lemon Song/ Heartbreaker
Recording: Good to very good. Audience. Sound deteriorates on CD2.
Source: Vienna March 16 1973.
Comments: Japanese CD.

CD - THE LEGENDARY FILLMORE TAPES VOL. 1
SAVAGE BEAST MUSIC SB-949629
White Summer, Black Mountain Side/ Train Kept A Rollin'/ I Can't Quit You Babe/ Pat's Delight/ How Many More Times/ Communication Breakdown
Recording: Poor. Audience.
Source: Fillmore East, NYC February 1 1969.
Comments: Japanese CD. Deluxe B&W cover. Red and yellow type. Time 46:27.

CD - THE LEGENDARY FILLMORE TAPES VOL. 2
SAVAGE BEAST MUSIC SB-949630
Train Kept A Rollin'/ I Can't Quit You Babe/ Dazed And Confused/ You Shook Me/ White Summer, Black Mountain Side/ How Many More Times/ Communication Breakdown
Recording: Poor. Audience.
Source: Fillmore East, NYC May 30 1969.
Comments: Japanese CD. Deluxe B&W cover. Red and yellow type. Time 60:17.

CD - LIGHT AND SHADE
THE DIAGRAMS OF LED ZEPPELIN
TDOLZ 027
CD1: Immigrant Song/ Heartbreaker/ Since I've Been Loving You/ Black Dog/ Dazed And Confused
CD2: Stairway To Heaven/ Celebration Day/ That's The Way/ Going To California/ Tangerine/ What Is And What Should Never Be/ Moby Dick
CD3: Whole Lotta Love Medley/ Organ Solo, Thank You/ Communication Breakdown
Recording: Very good. Audience.
Source: Tokyo September 24 1971.
Comments: Japanese CD. Deluxe gatefold cardboard sleeve.

ROOM 2/3

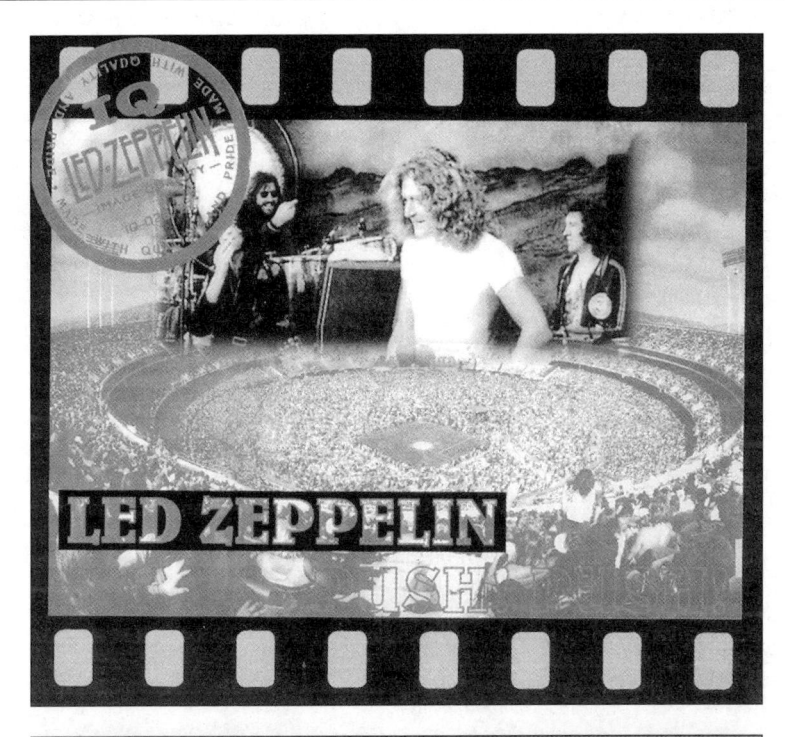

LED ZEPPELIN

CD - LISTEN TO ME, BOSTON
TARANTURA BOS-1/2
CD1: Immigrant Song (4:44)/ Heartbreaker (7:43)/ Since I've Been Loving You (8:32)/ Out On The Tiles Intro, Black Dog (6:34)/ Dazed And Confused (22:31)
CD2: Stairway To Heaven (8:06)/ The Lemon Song, Whole Lotta Love (7:44)/ Communication Breakdown (8:14)/ Organ Solo, Thank You (12:36)/ Rock And Roll (4:04)
Recording: Very good. Audience.
Source: Boston Gardens, Boston September 7 1971.
Comments: Japanese CD.

CD - LIVE FROM THE MIDNIGHT SUN
THE DIAGRAMS OF LED ZEPPELIN TDOLZ 1899701/02
CD1: Immigrant Song (3:43)/ Heartbreaker (7:09)/ Since I've Been Loving You (7:04)/ Out On The Tiles Intro, Black Dog (5:16)/ Dazed And Confused (20:19)/ Stairway To Heaven (9:05)/ Celebration Day (4:23)/ That's The Way (6:29)/ Going To California (4:18)
CD2: What Is And What Should Never Be (4:20)/ Moby Dick (14:09)/ Good Times Bad Times Intro, Whole Lotta Love, Just A Little Bit, Let That Boy Boogie, My Baby Left Me, Mess O'Blues, You Shook Me (20:12)/ Communication Breakdown (7:32)/ Thank You (7:53)
Recording: Very good. Audience.
Source: Maple Leaf Gardens, Toronto, Canada September 4 1971.
Comments: Japanese CD.

CD - LIVE IN COPENHAGEN
COBRA STANDARD SERIES 012
CD1: Immigrant Song/ Heartbreaker/ Since I've Been Loving You/ Dazed And Confused/ Black Dog/ Stairway To Heaven/ Going To California/ That's The Way/ What Is And What Should Never Be
CD2: Four Sticks/ Gallows Pole/ Whole Lotta Love Medley (includes Let That Boy Boogie Woogie, Trucking Little Mama, That's Alright, Mess Of Blues, Lemon Song)/ Communication Breakdown (includes bass solo and Celebration Day) Misty Mountain Hop/ Rock And Roll/ Dazed And Confused (Supershow March 25 1969 listed on cover but doesn't appear on disc)
Recording: Good. Audience.

Source: Copenhagen May 3 1974.
Comments: Japanese CD. Time CD1 72:28. CD2 51:27.

CD - LIVE IN LIVERPOOL '73
THE DIAGRAMS OF LED ZEPPELIN TDOLZ 0008/9
CD1: Over the Hills And Far Away/ Black Dog/ Misty Mountain Hop/ Since I've Been Loving You/ Dancing Days/ Bron-Yr-Aur Stomp/ The Song Remains The Same/ The Rain Song (last 4 minutes cut)/ The Rain Song (last 5 minutes cut)/ Dazed And Confused (first 5 minutes cut)
CD2: Stairway to Heaven/ Whole Lotta Love (includes Everybody Needs Somebody To Love, Boogie Woogie, Baby I Don't Care (cut), Let's Have A Party, I Can't Quit You, Going Down Slow)/ Heartbreaker/ The Ocean
Recording: Good to very good stereo. Soundboard.
Source: The Empire, Liverpool January 15 1973.
Comments: Japanese CD.
Time CD1 74:27. CD2 50:16.

CD - LIVE IN TOKYO
AMSTERDAM AMS 9609-3-1/2/3
CD1: Rock And Roll/ Black Dog/ Over The Hills And Far Away/ Misty Mountain Hop/ Since I've Been Loving You/ Dancing Days/ Bron-Yr-Aur Stomp
CD2: The Song Remains The Same/ The Rain Song/ Dazed And Confused
CD3: Stairway To Heaven/ Whole Lotta Love/ Immigrant Song/ The Ocean
Recording: Very good. Audience.
Source: Budokan Tokyo October 3 1973.
Comments: Japanese CD.

CD - LONG BEACH ARENA FRAGMENT
HOLY SH 002
Stairway To Heaven, Happy Birthday (9:09)/ Whole Lotta Love, The Crunge, Sex Machine (7:54)/ Out On The Tiles Intro, Black Dog (5:49)/ Heartbreaker (includes I'm A Man) (11:09)
Recording: Excellent. Audience.
Source: Civic Arena, Long Beach, CA March 12 1975.
Comments: Japanese CD.

CD - LZ RHODER
TM 007/LZ 008
CD1: Rock 'N Roll/ Celebration Day/ Black Dog/ Over The Hills And Far Away/ Misty Mountain Hop/ Since I've Been Loving You/ No Quarter/ The Song Remains The Same/ The Rain Song
CD2: Dazed And Confused/ Stairway To Heaven/ Moby Dick/ Heartbreaker/ Whole Lotta Love/ The Ocean
Recording: Excellent. Audience.
Source: Rhode Island July 21 '73.
Comments: European CD. Copy of 'LZ Rider' (Tarantura).

CD - MADE IN ENGLAND
TARANTURA 0X73-1/2
CD1: Rock And Roll (3:33)/ Over The Hills And Far Away (5:12)/ Out On The Tiles Intro, Black Dog (5:32)/ Misty Mountain Hop (5:04)/ Since I've Been Loving You (7:44)/ Dancing Days (4:25)/ Bron-Y-Aur Stomp (6:12)/ The Song Remains The Same (5:47)/ The Rain Song (6:41)
CD2: Dazed And Confused includes San Francisco, Walter's Walk (27:59)/ Stairway To Heaven (10:39)/ Whole Lotta Love (4:30)
Recording: Very good to excellent stereo. Soundboard.
Source: New Theatre, Oxford, London, UK January 7 1973.
Comments: Japanese CD. Limited edition of 500 copies.

CD - MARYLAND DE LUXE
DIAGRAMS OF LED ZEPPELIN TDOLZ
Recording: Good. Audience.
Comments: Japanese CD. 12-CD set in a deluxe cardboard box consisting of the following 4 titles: RUNNING ON PURE HEART AND SOUL, THUNDEROUS BREAK, TIGHTEST AND LOOSEST and CD - TIGHTEST AND LOOSEST and YOUR TEENAGE DREAM.

CD - MASTERS OF EXCESS
THE SYMBOLS
CD1: As Long As I Have You, Flesh Garbage, Shake, Hush Little Baby/ I Can't Quit You/ Dazed And Confused/ You Shock Me
CD2: Pat's Delight/ Babe I'm Gonna Leave You/ How Many More Times, For Your Love, The Hunter/ Improvisation, Communication Breakdown

Recording: Poor. Audience.
Source: Boston Tea Party, Boston, Massachusetts May 19 1969.
Comments: Japanese CD. Excessive noise reduction used.

CD - MERRY CHRISTMAS MR. JIMMY
LEMON SONG LS-7208/09
CD1: Rock And Roll/ Over The Hills And Far Away/ Black Dog/ Misty Mountain Hop/ Since I've Been Loving You/ Dancing Days/ Bron-Y-Aur Stomp/ The Song Remains The Same/ The Rain Song/ Stairway To Heaven
CD2: Dazed And Confused/ Whole Lotta Love, The Crunge, Everybody Needs Someone To Love, Boogie Mama, Let's Have A Party, Heartbreak Hotel, I Can't Quit You/ Heartbreaker
Recording: Good to very good. Audience.
Source: Alexandra Palace, London December 23 1972.
Comments: Japanese CD.

CD - MESSAGE OF LOVE
LEMON SONG
CD1: Immigrant Song/ Heartbreaker/ Since I've Been Loving You/ Black Dog/ Dazed And Confused/ Stairway To Heaven/ Celebration Day
CD2: That's The Way/ Going To California/ Tangerine/ What Is And What Should Never Be/ Moby Dick/ Whole Lotta Love/ Communication Breakdown
Recording: Good to very good. Audience.
Source: Hiroshima, September 27 1971.
Comments: Japanese CD.

CD - MIDNIGHT REHEARSALS
0001
Royal Orleans (instrumental) (0.20), Tea For One (Hootchie Kootchie version) (1.55)/ Don't Start Me Talking, All My Loving (4.35)/ Fire (aka Say You Gonna Leave Me) (2.59)/ Carouselambra #1 (3.01)/ Carouselambra #2 (3.46)/ Carouselambra #3 (3.56)/ In the Evening intro (0.56)/ The Battle of Evermore (5.44)/ Swansong demo (aka Midnight Moonlight) (17.59)/ Ten Years Gone demo (7.58)/ Night Flight (alt. mix) (3.43)/ Lucifer Rising (4.03)/ acoustic guitar demo #1 (2.36)/ acoustic guitar demo #2 (0.31)
Recording: Very good to excellent. Soundboard.
Source: Tracks 1 - 2 Malibu, CA October-November 1975. Tracks 3-7 Clearwell

LED ZEPPELIN

Castle, Forest of Dean, Wales, UK May 1978. Track 8 Headley Grange, Hampshire, England January 1971. Tracks 9-10 Headley Grange Studios, Hampshire, UK November 1973 - May 1974. Track 12 Boleskine House, Near Loch Ness, Scotland November 1973. Tracks 13-14 Bron-Yr-Aur Cottage, Wales, UK May 1970.

CD - MYSTERY EUROPEAN GIG
THE SYMBOLS
CD1: We're Gonna Groove/ I Can't Quite You Baby/ Dazed And Confused/ Heartbreaker/ White Summer, Black Mountain Side/ Since I've Been Loving You/ Organ Improvisation, Thank You
CD2: What Is And What Should Never Be/ Moby Dick/ How Many More Times, The Hunter, Boogie Woogie, Truckin' Little Mama, Ramblin, Down By The Riverside, Travelling Riverside Blues, Long Distance Call Blues, Lemon Song/ Whole Lotta Love
Recording: Poor. Audience.
Source: Hamburg, Germany March 11 1970 not Frankfurt March 10 as stated on cover.
Comments: Japanese CD.

CD - NEWCASTLE SYMPHONY
IMAGE QUALITY IQ-022/23
CD1: Rock And Roll (3:50)/ Over The Hills And Far Away (5:59)/ Black Dog (5:46)/ Misty Mountain Hop (5:34)/ Since I've Been Loving You (7:43)/ Dancing Days (5:28)/ Bron-Yr-Aur Stomp (5:20)/ The Song Remains The Same (5:26)/ The Rain Song (8:17)
CD2: Dazed And Confused (includes The Crunge Instrumental) (23:16)/ Stairway To Heaven (10:05)/ Whole Lotta Love (Incls. Everybody Needs Somebody To Love, Boogie Woogie, Let's Have A Party, Going Down Slow) (20:23)/ Immigrant Song (4:12)/ Heartbreaker (5:54)/ Mellotron Solo, Thank You (8:42)
Recording: Fair to good. Audience.
Source: City Hall, Newcastle, UK Nov. 30 1972.
Comments: Japanese CD. Deluxe B&W cover. Blue type.

CD - NICE STARTER!
THE SYMBOLS
CD1: Rock And Roll/ Over The Hills And Far Away/ Black Dog/ Misty Mountain Hop/ Since I've Been Loving You/ Dancing Days/ Bron-Y-Aur Stomp/ The Song Remains The Same/ The Rain Song
CD2: Dazed And Confused (including The Crunge)/ Stairway To Heaven/ Whole Lotta Love, Everybody Needs Somebody To Love, Let That Boy Boogie Woogie, Let's Have A Party, Going Down Slow/ Immigrant Song/ Heartbreaker/ Mellotron Solo/ Thank You
Recording: Poor. Audience.
Source: City Hall, Newcastle, England November 30 1972
Comments: Japanese CD.

CD - 929
H-BOMB MUSIC HBM 9510/9511/9512
Immigrant Song/ Heartbreaker/ Since I've Been Loving You/ Black Dog/ Dazed And Confused
CD2: Stairway To Heaven/ Celebration Day/ That's The Way/ Going To California/ Tangerine/ Friends/ Smoke Gets In Your Eyes/ What Is And What Should Never Be/ Moby Dick
CD3: Whole Lotta Love, Boogie Woogie, Tossin' And Turnin', Twist And Shout/ Fortune Teller, Good Times Bad Times, You Shook Me/ Communication Breakdown/ Organ Solo, Thank You/ Rock And Roll
Recording: Fair to good. Audience.
Source: Festival Hall, Osaka, Japan September 29 1971.
Comments: Japanese CD. Cardboard sleeve. Time CD1 58:36. CD2 64:16. CD3 55:17.

CD - NOT GUARANTEED TO WAKE YOU
THE DIAGRAMS OF LED ZEPPELIN
TDOLZ 0010/11
CD1: The Train Kept A Rollin'/ Nobody's Fault But Mine/ Black Dog/ In The Evening/ The Rain Song/ Hot Dog/ All My Love/ Trampled Underfoot (first 4 minutes cut)/ Since I've Been Loving You/ Achilles Last Stand
CD2: White Summer, Black Mountain Side (middle 3 minutes cut)/ Kashmir/ Stairway To Heaven/ Rock And Roll/ Heartbreaker
Recording: Very good. Audience.
Source: Ahoyhallen, Rotterdam June 21 1980
Comments: Japanese CD.
Time CD1 65:01. CD2 42:16.

CD - ONE DAY AFTER EDDIE
IMMIGRANT IM-054-56
CD1: The Song Remains The Same/ Sick

Again/ Nobody's Fault But Mine/ In My Time Of Dying/ Since I've Been Loving You/ No Quarter
CD2: Ten Years Gone (runs a little fast)/ The Battle Of Evermore/ Going To California/ Black Country Woman, Bron-Y-Aur Stomp/ White Summer/ Kashmir
CD3: Moby Dick/ Over The Hills And Far Away/ Bowed Guitar Solo/ Achilles Last Stand/ Stairway To Heaven/ Whole Lotta Love/ Rock And Roll
Recording: Good to very good. Audience. High pitch squeal during first five songs.
Source: The Forum, Inglewood June 22 1977. CD2 track 1 June 25 1977.
Comments: Japanese CD. Deluxe color cover. Time CD1 77:20. CD2 51:01. CD3 70:15.

CD - ONE FOR THE M6
CRAZY DREAM CDZ-73001/002
CD1: Over The Hills And Far Away/ Black Dog/ Misty Mountain Hop/ Since I've Been Loving You/ Dancing Days/ Bron-Y-Aur Stomp/ The Song Remains The Same/ The Rain Song/ Dazed And Confused
CD2: Stairway To Heaven/ Whole Lotta Love Medley/ Heartbreaker/ The Ocean
Recording: Very good. Soundboard.
Source: The Empire, Liverpool, England January 14 1973.
Comments: Japanese CD. Deluxe color cover.

CD - OOOH MY EARS, MAN
THE THE DIAGRAMS OF LED ZEPPELIN TDOLZ 034
CD1: Immigrant Song/ Heartbreaker/ Black Dog/ Since I've Been Loving You/ Stairway To Heaven/ Going To California/ That's The Way/ Tangerine/ Bron-Y-Aur Stomp
CD2: Dazed And Confused/ Moby Dick/ Whole Lotta Love
Recording: Very good to excellent audience.
Source: Adelaide, Australia February 19 1972.
Comments: Japanese CD. Deluxe gatefold cardboard sleeve.

CD - THE OUT OF SONG REMAINS
HOLY SH 003
CD1: The Rain Song (7:47)/ Dazed And Confused includes San Francisco (30:42)/ Stairway to Heaven (11:18)
CD2: Moby Dick (19:40)/ Heartbreaker (7:03)/ Whole Lotta Love, Let That Boy Boogie (15:42)/ The Ocean (5:16)
Recording: Fair to good. Audience.
Source: Madison Square Garden, New York City June 27 1973.
Comments: Japanese CD.

CD - OUT OF THE WAY
THE DIAGRAMS OF LED ZEPPELIN TDOLZ 0036/37/38
CD1: The Song Remains The Same (6:17)/ The Rover Intro, Sick Again (6:42)/ Nobody's Fault But Mine (7:30)/ In My Time Of Dying (12:09)/ Since I've Been Loving You (9:23)/ No Quarter (21:06)
CD2: Ten Years Gone (13:41)/ The Battle Of Evermore (6:18)/ Going To California (4:54)/ Black Country Woman (1:48)/ Bron-Y-Aur Stomp (6:11)/ White Summer, Midnight Moonlight, Black Mountainside (6:03)/ Kashmir (9:49)/ Out On The Tiles, Moby Dick (20:26)
CD3: Guitar Solo includes Star Spangled Banner (9:45)/ Achilles Last Stand (10:27)/ Stairway To Heaven (11:27)/ Rock And Roll (4:44)
Recording: Good. Audience.
Source: Jefferson Coliseum, Birmingham, Alabama May 18 1977.
Comments: Japanese CD.

CD - OUTTAKES
ANTRABATA REFERENCE MASTER ARM
CD1: Babe I'm Gonna Leave You (7:01)/ Babe I'm Gonna Leave You (6:16)/ You Shook Me (7:56)/ Baby Come On Home (8:53)/ Guitar, Organ Instrumentals (15:53)/ Guitar, Organ Instrumentals (21:37)/ Sugar Mama (2:58)
Source: CD1 tracks 1-4, Olympic Studios, London September 20 to October 10 1968. Tracks 5-6 Olympic Studios, London October '68? Track 7 Morgan Studios, London June 1969.
CD2: Jennings Farm Blues (24:53)/ No Quarter (25:08)/ That's The Way (5:37)/ Feel So Bad, Fixin' To Die, That's Alright (7:06)/ Since I've Been Loving You (7:34)
Source: CD2 track 1 Olympic Studios, London November 1969. Track 2 Electric Ladyland Studios, New York June 1972. Track 3-5 Headley Grange Studios, Hampshire, UK May-June 1970.
CD3: Since I've Been Loving You (vocal track) (3:06)/ Moby Dick (1:41)/ Drum Set (7:01)/ I Wanna Be Her Man (1:46)/ Guitar

LED ZEPPELIN

Instrumentals including Down By The Seaside, Stairway To Heaven (Instrumental Take), Blues Guitar Instrumentals (54:41)/ Blues Guitar Instrumentals (0:28)
Source: CD3 track 1 Headley Grange Studios, Hampshire, UK May-June '70. Track:2-3 Mirror Sound Studios, Los Angeles May '69. Track 4-5, Bron-Yr-Aur Cottage, Wales, UK May '70. Tracks 5-6 Headley Grange Studios, Hampshire, UK December 1970 and January 1971.
CD4: Guitar Instrumentals includes Piano Instrumentals (42:59)/ Poor Tom (3:21)/ Walter's Walk (4:39)/ Guitar Instrumentals (0:09)
Source: CD4 track 1 unknown. Track 2 Olympic Studios, London June 5 1970. Track 3 Rolling Stones, Mobile Studio, Stargroves, UK May 1972. Track 4 unknown.
CD5: Friends (3:28)/ Immigrant Song (2:42)/ Out On The Tiles (3:35)/ Bron-Yr-Aur (1:40)/ Poor Tom (3:22)/ Hey Hey What Can I Do (1:49)/ Guitar Instrumentals (2:08)/ Guitar Instrumentals (1:33)/ That's The Way (9:10)/ Friends (1:22)/ Bron-Yr-Aur, Guitar Instrumentals (8:31)/ Guitar Instrumentals (2:00)
Source: CD5 tracks 1,7-15, Bron-Yr-Aur Cottage, Wales May 1970. Tracks 2-6, Headley Grange Studios, Hampshire, UK May-June 1970.
CD6: Black Dog (6:59)/ No Quarter (4:07)/ Stairway To Heaven (Instrumental Take) (7:04)/ Guitar Instrumentals (1:03)/ Stairway To Heaven (6:10)/ Stairway To Heaven (8:20)/ The Battle Of Evermore (5:47)/ Guitar Instrumentals (4:21)/ Ten Years Gone (7:12)
Source: CD6 tracks 1-6 Headley Grange Studios, Hampshire, UK December 1970 and January 1971. Track 7 Headley Grange, Hampshire, UK January 1971. Track 8 Jimmy Page's home studio, UK January 1972? Track 9 unknown.
CD7: Friends (31:42)/ Four Sticks (5:18)/ Friends (4:52)/ Friends (4:40)/ Four Sticks (2:17)
Source: CD7: Bombay, India April 1972.
CD8: Drums, Mellotron Tuning, Love Me, Frankfurt Special (Station Blues) (5:52)/ Sugar Baby (5:07)/ The Wanton Song (2:39)/ The Rover (8:22)/ Night Flight (11:04)/ School Days (3:10)/ Nadine (1:03)/ Round And Round (3:25)/ Move On Down The Line (2:54)/ Love Me Like A Hurricane (2:43)/ C'mon Pretty Baby (3:03)/ Shakin' All Over (2:51)/ Hungry For Love (2:27)/ I'll Never Get Over You (2:13)/ Reelin' And Rockin' (1:46)/ Surrender (3:38)
Source: CD8 track 1 Southampton University, Southampton January 20 1973. Tracks 2-16 Chicago Auditorium, Chicago July 6 1973?
CD9: The Wanton Song (5:35)/ Take Me Home (4:45)/ In The Morning (6:13)/ Sick Again (3:49)/ The Rover (1:21)/ Rhythm Exercise (3:16)/ In My Time Of Dying (12:59)/ The Wanton Song (3:56)
Source: CD9 tracks 1-9 Headley Grange Studios, Hampshire, UK November 1973 to May 1974. Track 10 WLIR 92.7 Radio Broadcast, Westbury, New York spring '75.
CD10: Carouselambra (11:30)/ Untitled, Wearing And Tearing (6:00)/ Fool In the Rain (6:27)/ Hot Dog (3:31)/ In The Evening (6:39)/ South Bound Suarez (4:20)/ Darlene (5:21)/ Fool In The Rain (6:21)/ Carouselambra (8:48)/ All My Love (7:55)
Source: CD10 Polar Studios, Stockholm, Sweden November to December 1978.
CD11: White Summer (2:26)/ White Summer, Black Mountain Side (6:19)/ Kashmir (8:35)/ Achilles Last Stand (10:15)/ Stairway To Heaven (10:11)/ Say You're Gonna Leave Me (4:46)/ Carouselambra (12:38)/ Lucifer Rising (5:14)/ Royal Orleans (0:21)/ Tea For One (Hootchie Kootchie Version) (2:46)/ Don't Start Me Talkin', Blues Medley, All My Lovin' (4:55)
Source: CD11 tracks 1-5 Victoria Theatre, London May 1980. Tracks 6-7 Clearwell Castle, Forest Of Dean, Wales May 1978. Track 8 Boleskin House, Near Loch Ness, Scotland, UK November 1973. Tracks 9-11 Malibu, CA October to November 1975.
Comments: Limited edition of 325 numbered copies. The first 20 came in a metallic silver box. The rest were in a gunmetal grey box.

CD - PERSISTENCE KEZAR
HOLY SH 004-A
CD1: Introduction (2:36)/ Rock And Roll (3:50)/ Celebration Day (2:39)/ Bring It On Home Intro, Black Dog (6:09)/ Over The Hills And Far Away (7:00)/ Misty Mountain Hop (5:10)/ Since I've Been Loving You (8:20)/ No Quarter (10:08)/ The Song Remains The Same (6:23)/ The Rain Song (8:17)
CD2: Dazed And Confused includes San

Francisco0 (30:31)/ Stairway To Heaven (10:54)/ Moby Dick (4:28)
CD3: Heartbreaker (8:02)/ Whole Lotta Love, Let That Boy Boogie (12:25)/ Communication Breakdown (4:09)/ The Ocean (5:31)/ Heartbreaker (7:52)/ Whole Lotta Love, Let That Boy Boogie (12:27)
Recording: Good. Audience.
Source: Kezar Stadium, San Francisco, CA June 2 1973.
Comments: Japanese CD. The last three tracks are from vinyl.

CD - PHILADELPHIA SPECIAL
LZ 001/002
CD1: Rock And Roll (beginning cut)/ Sick Again (garbled in one spot)/ Over The Hills And
Far Away (beginning slightly cut)/ In My Time of Dying/ The Song Remains The Same/ The Rain Song, Kashmir/ No Quarter (garbled and cut in 2 separate spots)/ Trampled Underfoot
CD2: Moby Dick (cut in 2 separate sections)/ Dazed And Confused (includes San Francisco)/ Stairway To Heaven (small cut right before guitar solo)/ Whole Lotta Love/ Out On The Tiles introduction/ Black Dog/ Heartbreaker
Recording: Good to very good. Audience.
Source: The Spectrum, Philadelphia February 8 1975.
Comments: Japanese CD.
Time CD1 75:45. CD2 75:37.

CD - PSYCHEDELIC EXPLOSION
THE DIAGRAMS OF LED ZEPPELIN
TDOLZ 0006/7
CD1: Communication Breakdown (4:18)/ I Can't Quit You Baby (7:01)/ Dazed And Confused (16:17)/ You Shook Me (11:07)/ How Many More Times, Smoke Stack Lightning, The Hunter, Girl Of The North Country (19:35)/
CD2: White Summer, Black Mountain Side (11:50)/ The Lemon Song includes That's Alright (9:15)/ Babe I'm Gonna Leave You (7:16)/ Pat's Delight (6:40)/ As Long As I Have You, Fresh Garbage, Shake, Hush Little Baby (18:20)/ Whole Lotta Love (8:55)
Recording: Very good to excellent. Audience.
Source: Winterland Ballroom, San Francisco, CA., April 26, '69.
Comments: Japanese CD.

CD - PUSH! PUSH!
IMAGE QUALITY IQ-026/27
CD1: The Song Remains The Same (5:30)/ The Rover, Sick Again (7:17)/ Nobody's Fault But Mine (6:23)/ Over The Hills And Far Away (5:32)/ Since I've Been Loving You (9:05)/ No Quarter (23:13)/ Ten Years Gone (9:49)/ The Battle Of Evermore (5:34)
CD2: Going To California (6:19)/ Mystery Train (0:54)/ Black Country Woman (1:52)/ Bron-Yr-Aur Stomp (6:24)/ Trampled Underfoot (7:40)/ White Summer, Black Mountain Side (7:37)/ Kashmir (10:39)/ Guitar Solo (includes Star Spangled Banner) (7:11)/ Achilles Last Stand (9:26)/ Stairway To Heaven (10:56)/ Whole Lotta Love (1:11)/ Rock And Roll (4:18)
Recording: Very good. Audience.
Source: Oakland Alameda County Coliseum, Oakland, California July 24 1977.
Comments: Japanese CD. Deluxe B&W cover. Purple type.

CD - RARE SHORT PARTY
IMAGE QUALITY IQ-003/4
CD1: Immigrant Song (3:45)/ Heartbreaker (6:18)/ Dazed And Confused (17:25)/ Bring It On HOme (9:43)/ Since I've Been Loving You (6:52)
CD2: What Is And What Should Never Be (4:16)/ Moby Dick (15:34)/ Whole Lotta Love (includes Boogie Mama, Shake, Move On Down The Line, Honey Bee, The Lemon Song) (12:58)/ Communication Breakdown (includes Good Times Bad Time) (8:49)
Recording: Good audience.
Source: Yale Bowl, New Haven, Connecticut August 15 1970.
Comments: Japanese CD.

CD - RAVE ON
THE THE DIAGRAMS OF LED ZEPPELIN
TDOLZ VOL.029
CD1: Immigrant Song/ Heartbreaker/ Black Dog/ Since I've Been Loving You/ Celebration Day/ Stairway To Heaven/ Going To California/ That's The Way/ Tangerine/ Bron-Y-Aur Stomp
CD2: Dazed And Confused/ What Is And What Should Never Be/ Rock And Roll/ Whole Lotta Love/ Thank You
Recording: Good audience.
Source: Freedom Hall, Manchester, UK November 24 1971.

LED ZEPPELIN

Comments: Japanese CD. Deluxe gatefold cardboard sleeve.

CD - REFLECTIONS FROM A DREAM
THE DIAGRAMS OF LED ZEPPELIN
TDOLZ 026
CD1: Immigrant Song/ Heartbreaker/ Since/ Black Dog/ Dazed And Confused/ Stairway To Heaven
CD2: Celebration Day/ Bron-Y-Aur Stomp/ That's The Way/ Going To California/ What Is And What Should Never Be/ Moby Dick
CD3: Whole Lotta Love Medley/ Communication Breakdown
Recording: Excellent audience.
Source: Tokyo September 23 1973.
Comments: Japanese CD. Deluxe gatefold cardboard sleeve.

CD - REFLECTIONS ON MY MIND
IMAGE QUALITY IQ-005/6
CD1: The Train Kept A Rollin' (3:08)/ I Can't Quit You (5:47)/ Dazed And Confused (10:58)/ Killing Floor (includes Lemon Song, Needle Blues) (6:07)/ Baby I'm Gonna Leave You (includes Reflections On My Mind) (6:45)/ How Many More Times (Incomplete) (11:14)
CD2: White Summer, Black Mountain Side (9:50)/ As Long As I Have You (includes Flesh Garbage, Shake And Hush) (13:22)/ You Shook Me (9:06)/ Pat's Delight (12:31)
Recording: Good to very good. Audience.
Source: The Image Club, Miami February 14 1969 not January 17 as listed on cover.
Comments: Japanese CD. B&w cover.

CD - ROCK 'N' ROLL CIRCUS
THE DIAGRAMS OF LED ZEPPELIN
TDOLZ 0012/13/14
CD1: The Song Remains The Same/ The Rover, Sick Again/ Nobody's Fault But Mine/ Over The Hills And Far Away/ Since I've Been Loving You/ No Quarter
CD2: Ten Years Gone/ The Battle Of Evermore/ Going To California/ Black Country Woman/ Bron-Y-Aur Stomp/ White Summer, Black Mountain Side/ Kashmir/ Out On The Tiles, Moby Dick
CD3: Heartbreaker/ Guitar Solo/ Achilles Last Stand/ Stairway To Heaven/ Whole Lotta Love/ Rock And Roll
Recording: Very good. Audience.
Source: Madison Square Garden, New York June 10 1977.
Comments: Japanese CD

CD - ROCK HOUR
ANTRABATA REFERENCE MASTER ARM 270669
D.J. Intro/ Communication Breakdown/ I Can't Quit You/ Interview/ Dazed And Confused/ Liverpool Scene Sketch/ White Summer, Black Mountain Side/ You Shook Me/ How Many More Times Medley
Recording: Excellent stereo. Soundboard. Allegedly from BBC master tapes.
Source: London June 27 1969.
Comments: Japanese CD. Deluxe color cover. Limited edition of 325 numbered copies.

CD - ROOM 2/3
IMAGE QUALITY IQ-019/20/21
CD1: Good Times Bad Times, Communication Breakdown (5:04)/ I Can't Quite You (6:41)/ Heartbreaker (5:45)/ Dazed And Confused (17:14)/ White Summer, Black Mountain Side (17:14)/ What Is And What Should Never Be (4:56)/ Moby Dick (11:47)
CD2: How Many More Times (21:25)/ C'Mon Everybody (3:15)/ Something Else (2:19)/ Good Times Bad Times, Communication Breakdown (4:33)/ I Can't Quite You (6:58)/ Heartbreaker (38:44)/ Dazed And Confused (18:45)
CD3: White Summer, Black Mountain Side (14:47)/ Babe I'm Gonna Leave You (6:34)/ What Is And What Should Never Be (5:04)/ Moby Dick (17:30)/ How Many More Times (12:09)
Recording: Very good. Audience.
Source: CD1 and CD2 tracks 1-3 Winterland Ballroom, San Francisco November 6 1969. CD2 tracks 4-7 and CD3 Winterland Ballroom, San Francisco November 7 1969.
Comments: Japanese CD. Deluxe color cover.

CD - RUNNING ON PURE HEART AND SOUL
DIAGRAMS OF LED ZEPPELIN TDOLZ 259701/2/3 VOL.025
CD1: The Song Remains The Same/ The Rover, Sick Again/ Nobody's Fault But Mine/ In My Time Of Dying/ Since I've Been Loving You/ No Quarter
CD2: Ten Years Gone/ The Battle Of Evermore/ Going To California/ Surrender/ Black Country Woman, Bron-Y-Aur Stomp/ White Summer, Black Mountain Side/

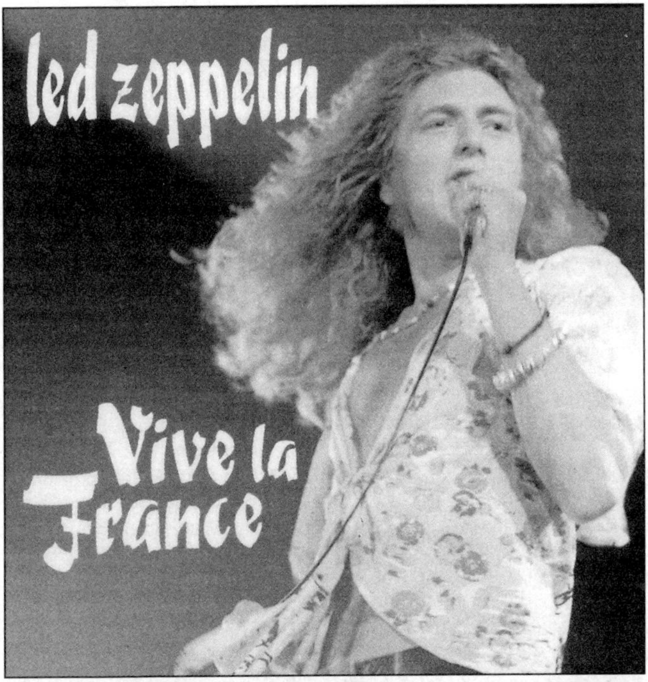
led zeppelin
Vive la France

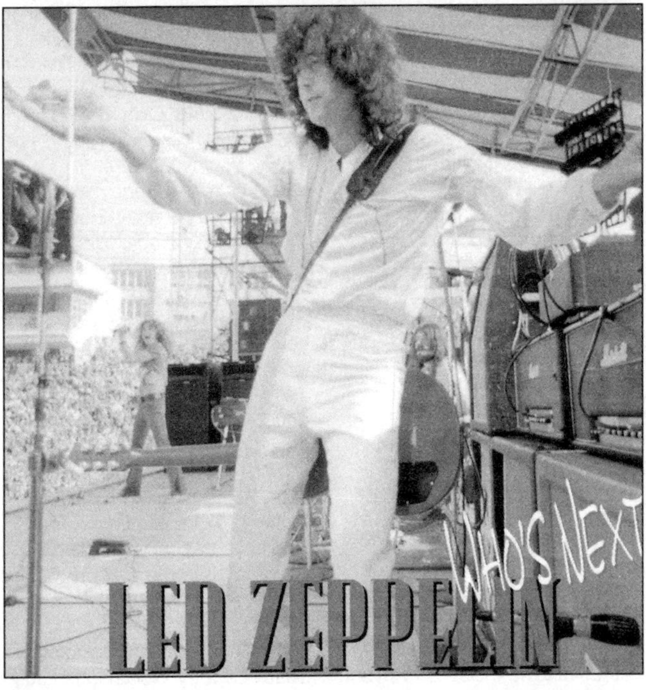
WHO'S NEXT
LED ZEPPELIN

LED ZEPPELIN

Kashmir/ Out On The Tiles, Moby Dick
CD3: Guitar Solo/ Achilles Last Stand/ Stairway To Heaven/ Whole Lotta Love/ Rock And Roll
Recording: Good. Audience.
Source: (Last Night) Capitol Center, Landover, Maryland May 30 1977.
Comments: Japanese CD. Part of the 'MARYLAND DE LUXE' 12-CD box set.

CD - THE SAFECRACKERS SHOW
MIDAS TOUCH 62211
Dazed And Confused (Outro Only)/ Stairway To Heaven/ Moby Dick/ Heartbreaker/ Whole Lotta Love/ The Ocean
Recording: Very good. Audience.
Source: Madison Square Garden July 27 1973.
Comments: Japanese CD.

CD - SEATTLE DAZE
IMAGE QUALITY IQ-007/8/9
CD1: Introduction (1:50)/ Rock And Roll (4:41)/ Celebration Day (3:22)/ Black Dog (5:55)/ Over The Hills And Far Away (6:40)/ Misty Mountain Hop (5:06)/ Since I've Been Loving You (8:22)/ No Quarter (12:57)/ The Song Remains The Same (5:38)/ The Rain Song (8:36)
CD2: Dazed And Confused (includes San Francisco) (33:51)/ Stairway To Heaven (12:29)
CD3: Moby Dick (31:44)/ Heartbreaker (8:00)/ Whole Lotta Love (includes Boogie Woogie) (14:55)/ The Ocean (6:01)
Recording: Excellent stereo. Audience.
Source: Seattle Center Coliseum, Seattle, Washington July 17 1973.
Comments: Japanese CD.

CD - SECOND CITY SHOWDOWN
MIDAS TOUCH 61831/2/3
CD1: Rock And Roll (4:32)/ Celebration Day (3:34)/ Bring It On Home Intro, Black Dog (6:32)/ Over The Hills And Far Away (6:51)/ Misty Mountain Hop (4:45)/ Since I've Been Loving You (9:18)/ No Quarter (11:44)/ The Song Remains The Same (6:23)/ The Rain Song (8:29)
CD2: Dazed And Confused Incl. San Francisco (29:48)/ Stairway To Heaven (11:16)
CD3: Moby Dick (24:54)/ Heartbreaker (6:07)/ Whole Lotta Love includes Let That Boy Boogie (16:59)/ Communication Breakdown (5:35)
Recording: Excellent. Soundboard.
Source: Chicago Auditorium, Chicago July 7 1973.
Comments: Japanese CD.

CD - '79
ANTRABATA REFERENCE MASTER ARM 23779
CD1: The Song Remains The Same/ Celebration Day/ Black Dog/ Nobody's Fault But Mine/ Over The Hills And Far Away/ Misty Mountain Hop/ Since I've Been Loving You/ No Quarter/ Hot Dog
CD2: The Rain Song/ White Summer-Black Mountain Side/ Kashmir/ Trampled Underfoot/ Achilles Last Stand/ Guitar-Bow Solo/ In The Evening/ Stairway To Heaven/ Rock And Roll
CD3: The Song Remains The Same/ Celebration Day/ Black Dog/ Nobody's Fault But Mine/ Over The Hills And Far Away/ Misty Mountain Hop/ Since I've Been Loving You/ No Quarter/ Ten Years Gone/ Hot Dog
CD4: The Rain Song/ White Summer-Black Mountain Side/ Kashmir/ Trampled Underfoot/ Sick Again/ Achilles Last Stand/ Guitar-Bow Solo/ In The Evening/ Stairway To Heaven/ Whole Lotta Love
CD5: The Song Remains The Same/ Celebration Day/ Black Dog/ Nobody's Fault But Mine/ Over The Hills And Far Away/ Misty Mountain Hop/ Since I've Been Loving You/ No Quarter
CD6: Ten Years Gone/ Hot Dog/ The Rain Song/ White Summer-Black Mountain Side/ Kashmir/ Trampled Underfoot/ Sick Again
CD7: Achilles Last Stand/ Guitar Solo-In the Evening/ Stairway To Heaven/ Rock And Roll/ You'll Never Walk Alone/ Whole Lotta Love/ Heartbreaker
CD8: The Song Remains The Same/ Celebration Day/ Black Dog/ Nobody's Fault But Mine/ Over The Hills And Far Away/ Misty Mountain Hop/ Since I've Been Loving You/ No Quarter
CD9: White Summer-Black Mountain Side/ Kashmir/ Trampled Underfoot/ Sick Again/ Achilles Last Stand/ Guitar Solo/ In The Evening/ Stairway to Heaven/ Rock And Roll/ Whole Lotta Love/ Communication Breakdown
Recording: Excellent. Audience.
Source: CD1-2 Copenhagen July 23 1979. CD3-4 Copenhagen July 24 1979. CD5-7

Knebworth Festival August 4 1979. CD8-9 Knebworth Festival August 11 1979.
Comments: 9-CD set made for the Japanese market. Limited edition of 325 numbered sets with certificate of authenticity. Each CD comes in a full color cardboard sleeve between two black bookboards. Time CD1 62:26. CD2 68:54. CD3 68:06. CD4 75:43. CD5 60:46. CD6 54:30. CD7 58:29. CD8 67:31. CD9 77:35.

CD - STUCK ON YOU
THE THE DIAGRAMS OF LED ZEPPELIN
TDOLZ VOL.030
CD1: Rock And Roll/ Over The Hill And Far Away/ Black Dog/ Misty Mountain Hop/ Since I've Been Loving You/ Dancing Days/ Bron-Y-Aur Stomp/ The Song Remains The Same/ The Rain Song
CD2: Dazed And Confused/ Stairway To Heaven/ Whole Lotta Love/ Heartbreaker
Recording: Fair audience.
Source: Glasgow Apollo, Glasgow, Scotland December 4 1972.
Comments: Japanese CD. Deluxe gatefold cardboard sleeve.

CD - STROLL ON!
THE DIAGRAM OF LED ZEPPELIN
TODLZ 179701 VOL. 017
Train Kept A Rollin'/ I Can't Quit You/ Dazed & Confused/ White Summer, Black Mountain Side/ How Many More Times/ Communication Breakdown
Recording: Excellent. Audience.
Source: Exhibition Hall, State Fair, West Allis, Wisconsin July 25 1969.
Comments: Japanese CD. Deluxe cardboard sleeve.

CD - TAKKA TAKKA
TARANTURA KAZAR-1/2
CD1: Rock And Roll (6:26)/ Celebration Day (3:28)/ Bring It On Home Intro, Black Dog (5:50)/ Over The Hills And Far Away (6:34)/ Misty Mountain Hop (5:36)/ Since I've Been Loving You (7:59)/ No Quarter (10:17)/ The Song Remains The Same (6:13)/ The Rain Song (8:29)
CD2: Dazed And Confused includes San Francisco (29:33)/ Stairway To Heaven (11:01)/ Moby Dick (4:28)/ Heartbreaker (8:01)/ Whole Lotta Love includes Let That Boy Boogie (12:34)/ Communication Breakdown (3:38)/ The Ocean (6:19)

Recording: Excellent. Audience.
Source: Kezar Stadium, San Francisco June 2 1973.
Comments: Japanese CD.

CD - THUNDEROUS BREAK
THE DIAGRAMS OF LED ZEPPELIN
TDOLZ 239701/2/3 VOL.023
CD1: The Song Remains The Same/ The Rover, Sick Again/ Nobody's Fault But Mine/ In My Time Of Dying/ Since I've Been Loving You/ No Quarter
CD2: Ten Years Gone/ The Battle Of Evermore/ Going To California/ Dancing Days, Black Country Woman, Bron-Y-Aur Stomp/ White Summer, Black Mountain Side/ Kashmir
CD3: Out On The Tiles, Moby Dick/ Guitar Solo/ Achilles Last Stand/ Stairway To Heaven/ Whole Lotta Love/ Rock And Roll
Recording: Good. Audience.
Source: (Second Night) Capitol Center, Landover, Maryland May 26 1977.
Comments: Japanese CD. Part of the 'MARYLAND DE LUXE' 12-CD box set.

CD - TIGHT BUT LOOSE
SAKA ZLCD 385
Train Kept A Rollin' (2:34)/ Nobody's Fault But Mine (5:40)/ Black Dog (5:58)/ Treat Her Right (6:13)/ Immigrant Song (4:01)/ Trying Too Hard (2:55)/ Judas Touch (5:46)/ Prison Blues (6:49)/ Train Kept A Rollin (3:16)/ Shake Your Money Maker (9:52)/ Going To California (8:57)/ Friends (6:07)
Source: Tracks 1-3 Nuremburg June 27 1980. Track 4 London December 13 1983. Track 5 in Bradford January 18 1973. Track 6 Page session 1966. Tracks 7-9 Outrider demos 1987. Track 10 Frankfurt July 1 1980. Tracks 11-12 Osaka, Japan September 29 1971.
Comments: European CD.

CD - TIGHTEST AND LOOSEST
THE DIAGRAMS OF LED ZEPPELIN
TDOLZ 249701/2/3 VOL.024
CD1: The Song Remains The Same/ The Rover, Sick Again/ Nobody's Fault But Mine/ In My Time Of Dying/ Since I've Been Loving You/ No Quarter/ Ten Years Gone
CD2: The Battle Of Evermore/ Going To California/ Black Country Woman, Bron-Y-Aur Stomp/ White Summer, Black Mountain Side/ Kashmir/ Out On The Tiles, Moby Dick

LED ZEPPELIN

CD3: Guitar Solo/ Achilles Last Stand/ Stairway To Heaven/ Whole Lotta Love/ Rock And Roll
Recording: Good. Audience.
Source: (Third Night) Capitol Center, Landover, Maryland May 28 1977.
Comments: Japanese CD. Part of the 'MARYLAND DE LUXE' 12-CD box set.

CD - THE TITANIC
IMAGE QUALITY IQ-016/17/18
CD1: Rock And Roll (4:22)/ Over The Hills And Far Away (6:35)/ Black Dog (6:17)/ Misty Mountain Hop (5:39)/ Since I've Been Loving You (8:14)/ Dancing Days (5:37)/ Bron-Yr-Aur Stomp (5:50)
CD2: The Song Remains The Same (6:30)/ The Rain Song (8:32)/ Dazed And Confused (includes San Francisco) (29:16)
CD3: Stairway To Heaven (12:11)/ Whole Lotta Love (Incls. The Crunge, Everybody Needs Somebody To Love, Boogie Woogie, Let's Have A Party, Heartbreak Hotel, I Can't Quite You, The Shap I'm In) (28:37)/ Heartbreaker (8:19)
Recording: Good. Audience.
Source: Alexandra Palace London UK Dec. 23 1972.
Comments: Japanese CD. Deluxe color cover.

CD - TRENTHAM GARDENS
MUSIC WITH LOVE MWL 009-010
CD1: Rock & Roll (3:45)/ Over The Hills And Far Away (5:45)/ Black Dog (6:18)/ Misty Mountain Hop (5:20)/ Since I've Been Loving You (8:02)/ Dancing Days (4:48)/ Dazed And Confused (29:23)/ Stairway To Heaven (11:20)
CD2: Bron-Y-Aur Stomp (5:44)/ The Song Remains The Same (5:31)/ The Rain Song (5:18)/ Whole Lotta Love Medley: Everybody Needs Someone To Love, Boogie Chillen, Baby I Don't Care, Let's Have A Party, Hang On Sloopy, Smokestack Lightning, You're A Better Man Than I, The Train Kept A Rollin', Shapes Of Things, Dust My Broom, Scratch My Back, Over Under Sideways Down, The Sun Is Shining, Shapes Of Things
Source: CD1 and CD2 tracks 1-4 at Stoke On Trent January 15 1973. Rest of tracks are Yardbirds' sessions recorded in London on various dates.
Comments: Japanese / German CD.

CD - TUNE UP
IMMIGRANT IM-052-53
CD1: Rock And Roll/ Sick Again/ Over The Hills And Far Away/ In My Time Of Dying/ The Song Remains The Same/ The Rain Song/ Kashmir/ No Quarter
CD2: Trampled Underfoot/ Moby Dick/ How Many More Times/ Stairway to Heaven/ Whole Lotta Love/ Black Dog
Recording: Good. Audience.
Source: Olympia, Detroit, Michigan January 31 1975.
Comments: Japanese CD.

CD - TYMPANI FOR THE BUTTER QUEEN
MIDAS TOUCH 62021/2
CD1: Rock And Roll (4:42)/ Celebration Day (3:53)/ Bring It On Home Intro, Black Dog (6:39)/ Over The Hills And Far Away (7:09)/ Misty Mountain Hop (4:48)/ Since I've Been Loving You (8:48)/ No Quarter (11:51)/ The Song Remains The Same (5:35)/ The Rain Song (8:47)
CD2: Dazed And Confused includes San Francisco (32:31)/ Stairway To Heaven (11:54)
Recording: Excellent. Soundboard.
Source: Convention Center, Fort Worth, Texas, May 19 1973.
Comments: Japanese CD.

CD - ULTRAVIOLENCE
SH OF5 A/B/C
CD1: Rock And Roll/ Sick Again/ Over The Hills And Far Away/ In My Time Of Dying/ The Song Remains The Same/ The Rain Song/ Kashmir
CD2: The Wanton Song/ No Quarter/ Trampled Underfoot/ Moby Dick
CD3: How Many More Times (includes The Hunter)/ Stairway To Heaven/ Whole Lotta Love, Black Dog/ Communication Breakdown (includes The Lemon Song)
Recording: Fair to good. Audience.
Source: Richfield Coliseum Cleveland Ohio January 24 1975.
Comments: Japanese CD.

CD - VIENNA 1970
OCEAN SOUND STUDIO
CD1: I Can't Quit You/ Dazed And Confused/ Heartbreaker
CD2: Moby Dick/ How Many More Times/ The Hunter/ Boogie Woogie/ Trucking Little Mama/ Lemon Song

Recording: Fair to good audience.
Source: Vienna 3/9/ 1970.
Comments: Japanese CD. Deluxe color cover. Time CD1 72:07. CD2 66:21.

CD - VIVA LA FRANCE
THE THE DIAGRAMS OF LED ZEPPELIN
TDOLZ VOL.028
CD1: Rock And Roll/ Over The Hills And Far Away/ Black Dog/ Misty Mountain Hop/ Since I've Been Loving You/ Dancing Days/ Bron-Y-Aur Stomp/ The Song Remains The Same/ The Rain Song/ Dazed And Confused
CD2: Moby Dick/ Stairway To Heaven/ Whole Lotta Love, Everybody Needs Somebody To Love, Boogie Woogie, Baby I Don't Care, Let's Have A Party, I Can't Quit You, Lemon Song
Recording: Poor audience.
Source: Palais Des Sports, Paris, France April 1 1973.
Comments: Japanese CD. Deluxe gatefold cardboard sleeve.

CD - THE WANDERER
LZRM010CD
CD1: Immigrant Song, Heartbreaker/ Black Dog/ Since I've Been Loving You (26:21)/] [Celebration Day/ Stairway To Heaven/ Going To California/ That's The Way (Start Only)/ That's The Way (Full Version) (33:29)/] [Tangerine/ Bron-Y-Aur Stomp (9:04)]
CD2: [Dazed & Confused/ What Is And What Should Never Be (29:14)/] [Moby Dick/ Whole Lotta Love, Boogie Woogie, Truckin' Little Mama, The Wanderer, Mary Lou, Let's Have A Party, Going Down Slow Blues (43:01)]
Recording: Poor to good mono. Audience.
Source: The Festival Hall, Brisbane, Australia February 29 1972.
Comments: CDR.

CD - WHERE THE ZEPPELIN ROAM
MIDAS TOUCH 62121/2
CD1: Rock And Roll (5:10)/ Celebration Day (3:35)/ Bring It On Home Intro, Black Dog (7:07)/ Over The Hills And Far Away (7:02)/ Misty Mountain Hop (4:58)/ Since I've Been Loving You (9:32)/ No Quarter (14:03)/ The Song Remains The Same (5:38)/ The Rain Song (9:08)
CD2: Dazed And Confused includes San Francisco (33:41)/ Stairway To Heaven (11:25)
Recording: Excellent. Soundboard.
Source: Buffalo Auditorium, Buffalo, NY July 15 1973.
Comments: Japanese CD.

CD - WHO'S NEXT
THE DIAGRAMS OF LED ZEPPELIN
TDOLZ 329701/2 VOL.032
CD1: Rock And Roll/ Celebration Day/ Black Dog/ Over The Hills And Far Away/ Misty Mountain Hop/ Since I've Been Loving You/ No Quarter/ The Song Remains The Same/ The Rain Song
CD2: Dazed & Confused/ Stairway To Heaven/ Moby Dick/ Heartbreaker/ Whole Lotta Love/ Communication Breakdown/ The Ocean
Recording: Excellent. Audience.
Source: Kezar Stadium San Francisco CA June 2 1973.
Comments: Japanese CD. Deluxe cardboard sleeve.

CD - YOUR TEENAGE DREAM
DIAGRAMS OF LED ZEPPELIN
TDOLZ229701/2/3 VOL.022
CD1: The Song Remains The Same/ The Rover, Sick Again/ Nobody's Fault But Mine/ In My Time Of Dying/ Since I've Been Loving You/ No Quarter
CD2: Ten Years Gone/ The Battle Of Evermore/ Going To California/ Black Country Woman, Bron-Y-Aur Stomp/ White Summer, Black Mountain Side/ Kashmir/ Out On The Tiles, Moby Dick
CD3: Guitar Solo/ Achilles Last Stand/ Stairway To Heaven/ Whole Lotta Love/ Rock and Roll
Recording: Good. Audience.
Source: (Opening Night) Capitol Center Landover Maryland May 25 1977.
Comments: Japanese CD. Part of the 'MARYLAND DE LUXE' 12-CD box set.

LENNON, JOHN

CD - CLOCK
SKY 101
Aisaimussen/ Honey Don't/ Glad All Over/ Lend Me Your Comb/ NYC/ Wake Up Little Susie/ Baby I Don't Care/ Vacation Has Just Begun/ Peggy Sue Got Married/ Peggy Sue 1&2
Recording: Good to very good.
Source: St. Regis Hotel, NYC, June 1971

LENNON, JOHN

Comments: European CD. B&w cover. CD numbered like a clockface. Time 28:31.

CD - THE DREAM IS OVER
PEGBOY PEGBOY 1006
Love/ Mother/ When A Boy Meets A Girl/ When A Boy Meets A Girl+/ God+/ God+/ God+/ God+/ Well Well Well/ I Found Out/ I Found Out/ My Mummy's Dead/ My Mummy's Dead/ Look At Me/ Mother/ I Found Out/ I Found Out/ Well Well Well/ Look At Me/ Look At Me (session outtake)/ Medley* That's All Right (Mama), Glad All Over, Honey Don't, Don't Be Cruel, Hound Dog, (unknown), Matchbox, Jam/ Love**
Source: +Previously unheard demos. Tracks 1-14 demos. Tracks 15-20 alternates. *Plastic Ono Band medley from a tape source. **Remix.
Comments: Cardboard slipcase. 28 page booklet.

CD - FREE AS A BIRD: THE DAKOTA DEMOS
PEGBOY 1001
Free As A Bird (take 1) (3:27)/ Real Love (take 1) (4:08)/ Now And Then (take 1) (5:03)/ Grow Old With Me (demo) (3:04)/ Free As A Bird (take 3) (3:40)/ Dear John (demo) (4:33)/ That's The Way The World Is (demo) (3:04)/ India (demo) (3:04)/ Mirror, Mirror (On The Wall) (take 1) (2:36)/ Gone From This Place (demo) (3:24)/ Across The River (unknown take) (2:42)/ Don't Be Crazy (demo) (3:12)/ Illusions (demo) (2:42)/ Baby Make Love To You (unknown take) (2:16)/ Life Begins At Forty (demo) (2:36)/ She's A Friend Of Dorothy's (take 7) (4:07)/ You Saved My Soul (demo) (1:34)/ Sally and Billy (demo) (3:28)/ Whatever Happened To... (demo) (4:39)/ One Of The Boys (take 2) (3:10)/ Help Me To Help Myself (demo) (2:08)/ Real Love (take 4) (4:00)
Source: Various.
Comments: Included are the original demos used by the 'Threetles' for the new ANTHOLOGY albums, Now And Then (which had been considered for ANTHOLOGY3 but was ultimately determined not up to the standards required) and three previously unreleased songs (India, Across The River, and Illusions).

CD - MISCELLANEOUS TRACKS
YELLOW DOG/ORANGE (YD-Orange 018)
Imagine*/ Now Or Never*/ Give Peace A Chance*/ Slippin' and Slidin'**/ Stand By Me, Imagine**/ I'm Losing You***/ Beautiful Boy***/ I'm Moving On***/Stand By Me+/ Slippin and Slidin'+/ Mucho Mungo (versions 1,2 & 3 - demos for Harry Nilsson 1974)++/ Goodnight Vienna (demo for Ringo 1974)++
Recording: Very good.
Source: *Jerry Lewis on Telethon, September 6, 72. **Salute To Sir Lew Grade, June 13, 75. ***Studio outtakes with Cheap Trick 1980. +Old Grey Whistle Test. ++Home demos.
Comments: European CD. Reissued by Cool Orangecicle. Time 53:53.

CD - TELECASTS
John Sinclair/ It's So Hard/ The Luck Of The Irish/ Sisters O Sisters/ We're All Water/ Woman Is The Nigger Of The World/ Attica state/ Midsummer New York/ Sakura Sakura/ Memphis*/ Johnny B. Goode*/ Imagine/ Imagine/ Now Or Never/ Give Peace A Chance
Recording: Very good to excellent. Soundboard.
Source: Tracks 1 and 7 David Frost Show January 13 1971. Tracks 5 and 6 Dick Cavett Show May 11 1972. Tracks 2-4, 8-12 Mike Douglas Show February 14-18 1972. Tracks 13-15 Jerry Lewis Telethon September 6 1972.
Comments: Japanese CD. Deluxe color cover. Picture CD. *With Chuck Berry. Time 57:03.

LOEB, LISA

CD - FALLING STARS
MOONRAKER 080
Alone/ Taffy/ Do You Sleep?/ Hurricane/ Stay/ It's Over/ Rose-Colored Times/ Alone/ Snow Day/ Do You Sleep?/ Dance With The Angels/ When All The Stars Were Falling/ All Day/ Hurricane/ Furious/ Stay/ Guessing Game/ Garden Of Delights/ Waiting For Wednesday/ Taffy
Recording: Excellent.
Source: Tracks 1-5 radio show, New York November 12 1995. Tracks 6-19 Pittsburgh, February 18 1996. Track 20 Conan O'Brien Show February 21 1996.
Comments: European CD.

LITTLE FEAT

CD - SNAKES ON EVERYTHING
GOLD STANDARD
CD1: Hamburger Midnight/ Got No Shadow/ On The Way Down/ Walkin' All Night/ Two Trains/ Willin'/ Cold Cold Cold, Dixie Chicken, Triple Face Boogie/ Fat Man In The Bathtub
CD2: Apolitical Blues/ Two Trains/ Got No Shadow, Wait Till The Shit Hits The Fans/ Texas Rose Cafe/ Snakes On Everything/ Cat Fever/ Walking All Night/ Smilin' Shoes/ Dixie Chicken
Recording: Excellent. Soundboard. Start of CD1 is a bit rough.
Source: Ebbet's Field, Denver, Colorado July 19 1973. CD1 early show. CD2 late show.
Comments: Japanese CD. Deluxe color cardboard gatefold cover. CDs in full color paper sleeves. Time CD1 54:26. CD2 61:35.

LIVE

CD - FOREVER ALONE
EMPIRE EMP 3
Operation Spirit/ Lightning Crashes/ I Alone/ All Over You/ The Beauty Of Grey/ T.B.D./ I Alone/ Supernatural/ Lightning Crashes/ White, Discussion/ Operation Spirit/ All Over You/ ?/ Lightning Crashes/ I Alone
Recording: Excellent. Soundboard. Tracks 11-15 very good to excellent audience.
Source: Tracks 1-3 Universal Amphitheater, Los Angeles, CA December 10 1994. Tracks 4-10 The Academy, New York February 15 1995. Tracks 11-15 Universal Amphitheater, Los Angeles, CA December 11 1994.
Comments: European CD. Time 69:22.

LYNYRD SKYNYRD & MOLLY HATCHET

CD - SOUTHERN CROSS
LSM 9637 A/B
CD1: LYNYRD SKYNYRD: Working For MCA/ I Ain't The One/ Down South Junkin'/ Double Trouble/ I Know A Little/ Saturday Night Special/ Swamp Music/ What's Your Name/ That Smell/ Simple Man/ Gimme Three steps/ Call Me The Breeze (includes guitar improvisations)/ Sweet Home Alabama
CD2: Free Bird/ MOLLY HAtCHET: Bounty Hunter/ It's All Over Now/ Gator Country/ Drum Solo/ Rolling Thunder/ Devil's Canyon/ Down From The Mountain/ Whiskey Man/ Dreams I'll Never See/ Guitar Solo/ Fall Of The Peacemakers/ Flirtin' With Disaster
Source: Loreley, June 23 1996.
Comments: European CD.

M

MALMSTEEN, YNGWIE

CD - FOREVER ONE
KOBRA RECORDS KRHM 09
Vengeance/ No Love Lost/ Never Die/ Instrumental/ Far Beyond The Sun/ Forever One/ I Am A Viking/ Instrumental, Red House/ Voodoo/ The Only One/ Fire In The Sky/ Heaven Tonight/ Burn/ I'll See The Light Tonight/ Burn/ I'll See The Light Tonight
Recording: Excellent. Soundboard.
Source: Sundsvall, Sweden November 17 1995. Tracks 12-14 Budokan, Tokyo, Japan March 16 1994.
Comments: European CD. Time 73:17.

CD - LIVE OPUS
BS-8/9
CD1: Vengeance/ No Love Lost/ Never Die/ Cross The Line/ Far Beyond The Sun/ I'd Die Without You/ Crush And Burn/ Keyboard Solo/ Time Will Tell, Pyramid Of Cheops/ Overture 1622, Trilogy Suite Op:5, Krakatau/ Red House
CD2: Guitar Solo/ Seventh Sign/ Band Introduction/ Voodoo, Bass Solo, Drum Solo, Jam/ The Only One/ Fire In The Sky/ Too Young To Die/ Forever One, Acoustic Solo, Black Star/ I'll See The Light Tonight
Recording: Poor. Audience.
Source: Sapporo Kouseinenkin Hall September 22 1995.
Comments: Japanese CD.

CD - SWEDISH MAGNUM IN JAPAN 1995
JAILBAIT RECORDS JBCD-009/010
CD1: Intro/ Vengeance/ No Love Lost/ Never Die/ Cross The Line/ Paganini, Adagio/ Far Beyond The Sun/ I'd Die Without You/ Crush And Burn

MANIC STREET PREACHERS

CD2: Seventh Sign/ Band Introduction/ Voodoo/ Bass, Drum Solo/ Voodoo/ Amberdawn, Brothers/ The Only One/ Fire In The Sky/ Too Young To Die, Too Drunk To Live/ Forever One/ Aria, Fugue/ Black Star/ I'll See The Light, Tonight/ Burn/ Spanish Castle Magic
Recording: Excellent. Audience.
Source: Kyoto, September 16 1995. CD2 track 14 Osaka September 15 1995. Track 15 Hyogo September 18 1995.
Comments: Japanese CD.

MANIC STREET PREACHERS

CD - BLACK ROSES
MOONRAKER 170
Enola, Alone/ La Tristessee Durera (A Scream To A Sigh)/ Everything Must Go/ Motorcycle Emptiness/ No Surface All Feeling/ I Need Your Love/ Motown Junk/ You Love Us/ A Design For Life/ Bonus Tracks: On So/ Everything Must Go/ Everything Must Go/ Kevin Carter/ Everything Must Go/ Interview
Recording: Excellent. Soundboard.
Source: Tracks 1-9 The Phoenix Festival July 19 1996. Tracks 10-11 The Later Show, British TV June 1 '96. Tracks 13-14 MTV Europe's Hanging Out May 17 1996. Track 15 The Phoenix Festival July 20 1996.
Comments: European CD.

CD - NO SUNSET, JUST SILENCE
KISS THE STONE KTS 572
From Despair To Where/ A Design For Life/ Faster/ Enola Alone/ La Tristessa/ Everything Must Go/ Yes/ Australia/ You Love Us/ Motorcycle Emptiness/ PCP/ Life Becoming A Landslide/ She Is Suffering/ Motorcycle Emptiness/ Roses In The Hospital/ Sleep Flower
Recording: Excellent stereo. Soundboard.
Source: Leeds, UK August 8 1996. Glastonbury June 24 1994. USA September 1993.
Comments: European CD.

CD - THE RETURN OF THE PREACHERS
TUBE TUCD 005
A Design For Life (instrumental)/ Australia/ From Despair To Where/ Everything Must Go/ Enola, Alone/ La Tristesse Durera (Scream To A Sigh)/ Faster/ No Surface, All Feeling/ Life Becoming A Landslide

Motown Junk/ A Design For Life/ Small Black Flowers That Grow In The Sky/ Raindrops Keep Falling On My Head/ Kevin Carter/ Motorcycle Emptiness/ Little Baby Nothing/ Yes/ You Love Us
Recording: Excellent stereo. Soundboard.
Source: Melkweg, Amsterdam June 11 1996.
Comments: European CD. Deluxe color cover. Time 69:14.

MARILLION

CD - GREAT AGAIN
THE WEB-RECORDS W 4570
Emanuelle/ Seasons End/ The King Of Sunset Town/ Beautiful/ Berlin/ King/ The Bell In The Sea/ The Party/ Afraid Of Sunrise/ Out Of This World/ Easter/ Cover My Eyes/ Slainte Mhath/ This Town/ The Rakes Progress/ 100 Nights/ The Last Of You/ Fallin' From The Moon/ Made Again/ Freaks/ Market Square Heroes/ Cover My Eyes/ The Bell In The Sea/ Beautiful/ Easter/ Sugar Mice/ Made Again
Recording: CD1 and CD 2 tracks I - 7 Excellent audience. CD 2 tracks 8 -12 Excellent soundboard.
Source: E-Werk, Koln April 23 1997 and KRO Radio Studio, Hilversum April 21 1996.
Comments: European 2 CD set.

MARILYN MANSON

CD - DEMONS IN MY LUNCHBOX VOL. 1
KISS THE STONE KTS 575
Cake And Sodomy/ Suicide Snowman/ Lunchbox/ Thrift/ Filth/ Wrapped In Plastic/ Intro, Misery Machine/ Booker T/ Cat In The Hat/ Justify My Love/ Dope Hat/ Strange Same Dogma/ Let Your Ego Die/ Thingmaker/ White Knuckles/ Luci In The Sky With Demons
Recording: Excellent stereo. Soundboard.
Source: Demos from 1993 and 1994.
Comments: European CD. Deluxe color cover. Picture CD. Time 72:55.

CD - FAMILY VALUES
SA 193743
Wrapped In Plastic/ Snake Eyes & Sissies/ Get Your Gun/ Dogma/ Cyclops/ Down In The Park/ Dop Hat/ My Monkey/ Inside My Head/ Organ Grinder/ Lunchbox/ Sweet Dreams/ Misery Machine

JOHN LENNON
MISCELLANEOUS TRACKS
Yellow Dog
RECORDS

Marilyn Manson
Selena's True Killers

MARILYN MANSON

Recording: Good to very good. Audience.
Source: Gothic Underground, Victoria, BC, Canada June 6 1996.
Comments: European CD. Deluxe color cover. Time 61:26.

CD - MONKEY MASSACRE
MK-701
Organ Grinder/ Cyclops/ Get Your Gun/ Dope Hat/ Wrapped In Plastic/ Sweet Dreams/ Snake Eyes And Sissies/ Dogma/ Down In The Park/ My Monkey/ Lunchbox/ Misery Machine/ Rock N Roll Nigger
Recording: Good to very good. Audience.
Source: Cambridge, Mass February 9 '95.
Comments: European CD. B&W cover. Time 68:58.

CD - RESIDENT EVIL
STK 645
Comments: European CD. Deluxe color cover. Copy of UNCUT (KISS THE STONE KTS 546). Picture CD. No doubt you've noticed STK 645 is KTS 546 backwards.

CD - SELENA'S TRUE KILLERS
HURRICANE HURR 50
Hands Of Small Children/ Wrapped In Plastic/ Snake Eyes And Sissies/ Get Your Gunn/ Dogma/ Cyclops/ Cake & Sodomy/ Down In The Park/ Dopehat/ My Monkey/ Smells Like Children/ Organ Grinder/ Lunch Box/ Rock 'N' Roll Nigger/ Sweet Dreams/ Misery Machine
Recording: Very good. Audience.
Source: Corpus Christi, Texas September 28 1995.
Comments: European CD. Deluxe color cover. Time 62:38.

CD - TRENT'S NASTY BABES
INSECT IST 100
Intro/ Organ Grinder/ Cyclops/ Get Your Gunn/ Dope Hat/ Wrapped In Plastic/ Sweet Dream/ Snake Eyes And Sissies/ Dogma/ Dawn In The Park/ My Monkey/ Lunchbox/ Misery Machine/ Rockn' Roll Nigger
Recording: Good to very good. Audience.
Source: Abyss, Houston, Texas January 11 1995.
Comments: European CD. Deluxe color cover. Time 61:53.

CD - UNCUT
KISS THE STONE KTS 546
Abuse Part 1/ Diary Of A Dope Fiend/ Shitty Chicken Gang Bang/ Kiddie Grinder/ Sympathy For The Parents/ Sweet Dreams (Are Made Of This)/ Everlasting Cocksucker/ Fuck Frankie/ I Put A Spell On You/ Abuse Part 2 (Confession)/ Scabs, Guns And Peanuts Butter/ Dance Of The Dope Hats/ White Trash/ Dancing With The One-Legged/ Rock And Roll Nigger/ Untitled/ Procardia/ My Monkey/ Choklit Factory
Recording: Excellent stereo. Soundboard.
Source: 'Smells Like Children' uncensored and uncut. Tracks 18-19 are unreleased demos.
Comments: European CD. Deluxe color cover. Picture CD. Time: 66:01.

MARION

CD - THE OLD SCHOOL GANG
OXYGEN OXY 082
I Stopped Dancing/ The Only Way/ Wait/ Time/ Vanessa/ Sparkle/ Your Body Lies/ The Collector/ Let's All Go Together/ Toys For Boys/ Sleep/ Fallen Through/ All For Love/ Time/ Sparkle/ Fallen Through/ Wait/ Your Body Lies/ The Collector
Recording: Excellent stereo. Soundboard.
Source: Tracks 1-12 Melkweg, Amsterdam, Holland March 1996. Tracks 13-16 Maida Vale Studios, London, UK, January 1996. Tracks 17-19 Maida Vale Studios, London, UK April 1996.
Comments: European CD. Deluxe color cover. Picture CD. Time 72:48.

MARLEY, BOB AND THE WAILERS

CD - CALIFORNIA SPECIAL
WEEPING GOAT WG-028-29
CD1: Trenchtown Rock/ Burnin' And Lottin'/ Them Belly Full (But We Hungry)/ Rebel Music/ I Shot The Sheriff/ Want More/ No Woman, No Cry
CD2: Lively Up Yourself/ Roots Rock Reggae/ Positive Vibration/ Get Up, Stand Up, No More Trouble, War
Recording: Good to very good. Audience.
Source: Paramount Theater, Oakland, CA May 30 '76.
Comments: Japanese CD. Deluxe color cover.

McCARTNEY, PAUL

CD - JAH IS NOT DEAD
WEEPING GOAT WG-027
Rastaman Chant/ Lion Of Judah/ Burnin' And Lootin'/ Them Belly Full (But We Hungry)/ Rebel Music/ I Shot The Sheriff/ No Woman, No Cry/ Roots Rock Reggae/ Kinky Reggae, Band Introduction/ Lively Up Yourself/ Positive Vibration
Recording: Good to very good. Audience.
Source: Boston, Massachusetts 1976.
Comments: Japanese CD. Deluxe color cover. Time 65:18.

CD - WITH A LITTLE HELP FROM MY FRIENDS
KISS THE STONE KTS 480/81
CD1: Seek Up/ Warehouse/ What Would You Say/ Say Goodbye/ Minarets/ Typical Situation/ Granny The Watchtower/ Recently/ Two Step/ Ants Marching/ Pay For What You Get/ Halloween
Recording: Excellent.
Source: The Roseland Ballroom, New York February 24 1995.
Comments: European CD.

MATTHEWS, DAVE BAND

CD - SOUTHERN COMFORT
KISS THE STONE KTS 583
Seek Up/ Dancing Nancies/ Ware House/ What Would You Say/ Lover Lay Down/ Too Much/ Ants Marching/ Crash, All Along The Watchtower (backstage acoustic session)
Recording: Excellent stereo. Soundboard.
Source: Tracks 1-6 Milan, Italy March 27 1995. Tracks 7-10 Pink Pop Fest, Holland 1996
Comments: European CD. Deluxe color cover. Picture CD. Time 60:19.

CD - WETLAND'S ACOUSTIC I
RUPERT 9582
Tripping Billies/ Typical Situation/ Pay For What You Get/ Satellite/ One Sweet World/ Stream/ I'll Back You Up/ Minaretes/ Warehouse/ Two Step
Recording: Excellent. Soundboard.
Source: Set 1, Wetlands Ballroom, New York January 29 1994.
Comments: European CD. Deluxe color cover. Time 52:10.

CD - WEDLAND'S ACOUSTIC II
RUPERT 9583
So Much To Say/ Dancing Nancies/ Lie On Our Graves/ You Are My Sanity/ Ants Marching/ Help Myself/ Christmas Song/ Recently/ Angel Of Montgomery/ All Along The Watchtower
Recording: Excellent. Soundboard.
Source: Set 2, Wetlands Ballroom, New York January 29 1994.
Comments: European CD. Deluxe color cover. Time 58:30.

MAYFIELD, CURTIS

CD - SMALL CLUB
MIDNIGHT BEAT MBCD063
Superfly/ It's Alright/ Gypsy Woman/ I'm So Proud/ Freddie's Dead/ Pusherman/ Billy Jack/ People Get Ready/ Do Be Down/ Give Me Your Love Song (Love Song)/ Move On Up/ (Don't Worry)/ If There's Hell Below, We're All Gonna Going To Go
Recording: Excellent stereo. Soundboard.
Source: The Troyan Horse, The Hague, Holland August 1990 during the 'Take It To The Streets' tour.

McCARTNEY, PAUL

OOBU JOOBU PART 10
YELLOW CAT RECORDS
Intro, Oobu Joobu/ Miss Ann (soundcheck)/ What's Going On (Marvin Gaye)/Blackbird & Blue Moon Of Kentucky (Mack version rehearsal)/ She's A Woman (rehearsal)/ Uh-Oh 7 (Desmond Dekker compact cassette)/ Live And Let Die (soundcheck)/ S M A (Heather & Paul)/ Mercury: The Planet Suite (London Philharmonic Orch.)/ Cut Across Shorty (rehearsal)/ Hi Heeled Sneakers (rehearsal)/ Oobu Joobu Intro (jingle)/ Riders On The Storm (Doors)/ Rough Ride (with Trevor Horn)/ Cook Of The House & Oobu Joobu Jingle (Linda's recipe)/ Bizarre Beatles Covers (5 pieces)/ Let Me Roll It (soundcheck)/ Oobu Joobu Jingle/Let It Be (Let It Lie) (Jingle)/ Bonus Tracks: Sea/ Cornish Wafer ('Rupert')/ Storm ('Rupert')/ Nutwood Scene ('Rupert')
Recording: Excellent. Soundboard.
Source: Broadcast the weekend of July 17, 1995.
Comments: European CD. Deluxe color cover. Time 57:43.

McCARTNEY, PAUL

OOBU JOOBU PART 11
YELLOW CAT RECORDS
Intro, Oobu Joobu/ Shake, Rattle & Roll (rehearsal)/ Rock It (Herbie Hancock)/ Oobu Joobu Intro (jingle)/ Honey Don't (Detroit soundtrack)/ If I Were Not Upon The Stage (partial)/ Intermezzo (sound effects)/ Like A Hurricane (Neil Young unplugged)/ Motor Of Love/ Oobu Joobu Outro Jingle (Rude Studios)/ Feel No Pain (unknown Jamaican artist)/ Your School (unreleased - partial)/ Get Back (rehearsal)/ Rodina: Song Of The Father Land (Woman's Choir - Bulgaria)/ Oobu Joobu (outtake)/ Oobu Joobu Intro/Cook Of The House (Linda's recipe)/ Tomorrow's Light (Detroit soundcheck)/ Three Pieces For Blues Band & Orchestra (William Rousseau)/ Oobu Joobu Outro (jingle)/ Vocal Jam (close harmony)/ Bonus Tracks: Walking In The Meadow ('Rupert')/ Sea Melody ('Rupert')/ Rupert Song #2 ('Rupert').
Recording: Excellent. Soundboard.
Source: Broadcast the weekend of July 24, 1995.
Comments: European CD. Deluxe color cover. Time 58:27.

OOBU JOOBU PART 12
YELLOW CAT RECORDS
Oobu Joobu Intro/Yesterday (Mack Version)/ Matchbox (rehearsal)/Blue Suede Shoes (rehearsal)/ Yesterday (rehearsal/Mack version)/Oobu Joobu Jingle/ Christmas Parade (unknown Jamaican Reggae artist)/ Yesterday (Boyz II Men - partial)/ Ballroom Dancing (film-take)/ Ready Teddy/About Yesterday (Little Richard)/ Rockestra Theme (with commentary)/ Yesterday (taped by Duane Eddy)/ Cook Of The House (Linda's recipe)/ Garlic (speech)/Little Daisy Root (unreleased)/ 3 Comments On Beatles And Yesterday (speech)/ Yesterday (parody)/ 3 Comments on Beatles and Yesterday/Human League (speech/Human League)/ True Love Baby (Carl and Paul)/ Get It (Carl and Paul)/Paul and George Martin about Yesterday (speech)/ Yesterday (live)/ Oobu Joobu Outro/ Yesterday (parody)/ Bonus Tracks: Lunchbox Odd Sox (from acetate)/ Tomorrow (from acetate).
Recording: Excellent. Soundboard.
Source: Broadcast the weekend of July 31, 1995.
Comments: European CD. Deluxe color cover. Time 55:25.

OOBU JOOBU PART 13
YELLOW CAT RECORDS
Oobu Joobu Intro/ Mean Woman Blues (Winnipeg soundcheck)/ When The Wind Blows She Blows Cool (Winnipeg jam)/ Comedy: Biff Stantial (Bonzo Dog Band)/ Outro/ Oobu Joobu Jingle/Introduction Coming Up (chat)/ Coming Up (outtake)/ I Want Love (Reggae from Jamaica)/ Another Day (rehearsal)? Praying Mantis/Mambo Baby (2 pieces from Rude Corner)/ Oobu Joobu Jingle/ Ann & Nancy Wilson About Wasting Water (chat)/ What About Love? (Heart)/ Cook Of The House (Linda's recipe)/ Sheep May Safely Graze/Paul About Meat (Go Veggie)/ Instrumental includes Oobu Joobu Jingles (different)/ Oobu Joobu Jingle/ Beautiful Boy (Lennon)/ Oobu Joobu Jingle/ Midnight Special (rehearsal)/ Oobu Joobu Outro/ Bonus Tracks: Rooster (aka The Great Cook And Seagull Race) (from acetate)/ Night Out (from acetate).
Recording: Excellent. Soundboard.
Source: Broadcast the weekend of August 7, 1995.
Comments: European CD. Deluxe color cover. Time 56:06.

OOBU JOOBU PART 14
YELLOW CAT RECORDS
Oobu Joobu Intro/ Sweetest Little Show In Town (Rude Studios)/ There's No Me Without You (The Manhattans)/ Gonna Set This Town On Fire Tonight (outtake)/ Suzy Q (Jamaica Reggae)/ Mr. Froggie Went A-Courtin (rehearsal)/ Sunny Goodge Street (Donovan)/ Soundcheck Song (improvisation)/ Every Night (Cincinnati soundcheck)/ Oobu Joobu Jingle/ Cook Of The House (Linda's recipe)/ Endless Days And Lonely Nights (Linda)/ Be A Vegetarian (demo)/ Ivory Madonna (UB 40)/ Outro/ Things We Said Today (rehearsal)/ Devoted To You (Everly Brothers)/ Don't Let The Sun Catch You Crying (Cincinnati rehearsal)/ Oobu Joobu Outro/ The Entertainer (film music)/ Bonus Tracks: Let Me Roll It (Scotland Ranachan Jams)/ With A Little Luck (Scotland Ranachan Jams)
Recording: Excellent. Soundboard.
Source: Broadcast the weekend of August 14, 1995.

Comments: European CD. Deluxe color cover. Time 59:4.

OOBU JOOBU PART 15
YELLOW CAT RECORDS
Oobu Joobu Intro/ Lady Madonna (soundcheck)/ Bring It On Home To Me (rehearsal)/ Sittin' On The Dock Of The Bay/Oobu Joobu Jingle (Otis Redding)/ Intro/ Tequila (rehearsal)/ Goldfinger (reggae)/ Intro to Song/Wanderlust (demo)/ Chinese Canon (World Music)/ Intro Jingle/Cook Of The House/Linda's Recipe/ Pull Away (soundcheck)/ Gymnopedes (Piano Music by Pascale Rogier)/ This One/Put It There (2 parodies)/ Oobu Joobu Jingle with Phil Collins/ Reason To Believe (Tim Hardin)/ I keep On Believing/Love Awake (Rude Studios)/ Hey Jude (rehearsal parody)/ Hey Jude (rehearsal)/ Oobu Joobu Outro/ Love Me Tender (parody)/ Bonus Tracks: I've Had Enough (Scotland Ranachan Jams)/ Band On The Run (Scotland Ranachan Jams)
Recording: Excellent. Soundboard.
Source: Broadcast the weekend of August 21, 1995.
Comments: European CD. Time 58:51.

OOBU JOOBU PART 16 & 17
YELLOW CAT RECORDS
CD1: PART 16 - Oobu Joobu Jingle/ Ain't That A Shame (outtake)/ I'm In Love Again (Fats Domino)/ Back In The USSR (rehearsal)/ We'll Be Right Back (vocals)/ New Moon Over Jamaica (Mix of Paul's demo and Johnny Cash)/ Intro to Baki Tribe (chants)/ Bring It To Jerome (Minneapolis soundcheck)/ Good Rockin' Tonight/Intro to Little Richard (acoustic jam)/ Lucille/Lucille (both versions mixed)/ Little Richard's Veg Story/Tutti Fruitti (Little Richard)/ Radio Play/Oobu Joobu Jingle (fun intermezzo)/ Cook Of The House/ Linda's Recipe/ New Orleans/Oobu Joobu Outro (unreleased Linda song)/ I Love This House (unfinished track with David Gilmour)/ Knock On Wood (Eddy Floyd)/ Blue Moon Of Kentucky/Oobu Joobu Jingle (mix: Monroe-Paul-Elvis)/ Bonus Track: Ode To A Koala Bear (alternate take).
CD2: PART 17 - Oobu Joobu Intro/Yesterday (jingle/parody)/ Love Mix (partial-unfinished song)/ Stop You Don't Know Where She Came From (demo from Rude Corner)/ Tintina (Professor Longhair)/ Oobu Joobu/I Wanna Be Your Man (Paul talks about the Stones first single)/ Oobu Joobu/I Wanna Be Your Man (NY soundcheck)/ Paul Talks About His Dad/ Flight Of The Bumble Bee (Marsalis)/ We Can Work It Out (soundcheck/rehearsal)/ Hey Jude (Mock Version) (rehearsal)/ Paul About Brian Wilson/God Only Knows (partial)/ God Only Knows (Elvis Costello & Brodsky Quartet)/ One After 909 (Paul & Costello & Brodsky Quartet)/ Lady Madonna (same as previous)/ Paul About Pet Sounds/You Still Believe In Me (Chat Paul/Beach Boys)/ Brian Wilson Interview/ Orange Crate Art (Brian Wilson)/ Brian Wilson at Piano: Hey Jude/She's Leaving Home (chatting and singing)/ San Francisco (Brian Wilson)/ Oobu Joobu's Thank You's/ C'mon People (soundcheck)/ Oobu Joobu Outro (last jingle)/ Bonus Track: Pre-Concert Warmup Tape World Tour '88-'93 (Daniel Lentz)
Recording: Excellent. Soundboard.
Source: Broadcast during the weekend of September 1-4 1995.
Comments: European CD. Time CD1 53:39. CD2 59:45.

MCKEE, MARIA

CD - GINO
MOONRAKER 154
Everybody (4:09)/ Smarter (3:35)/ Panic Beach (3:38)/ Panic Beach (3:02)/ I Know The Sound (5:30)/ Breathe (3:45)/ I'm Awake (4:33)/ Human (5:27)/ What Else You Wanna Know (6:29)/ Absolutely Barking Stars (4:18)/ Scarlover (5:28)/ Life Is Sweet, After Life (4:24)/ Life Is Sweet, After Life (6:22)*/ This Perfect Dress (4:31)*
Recording: Excellent stereo. Soundboard.
Source: Club Gino, Stockholm May 1 1996.
*MTV Europe April 24 1996.
Comments: European CD. Deluxe B&W cover. Picture CD.

MENSWE@R

CD - WIRED FOR SOUND
GOOD MIXER GMCD001
Day Dreamer/ Hollywood Girl/ Sleeping In/ Being Brave/ I'll Manage Somehow/ Stardust/ Day Dreamer/ 125 West 3rd Street/ I'll Manage Somehow/ Satellite/ Little Miss Pinpoint Eyes/ Sleeping In/ Day Dreamer/ Around You Again/ Star Dust
Recording: Excellent stereo. Soundboard.

METALLICA

Source: Tracks 1-6 Anson Rooms, Bristol April 17 '95. Tracks 7-9 MTV Studios, Camden, London August 8 '95. Tracks 10-17 The Underworld, Camden, London November 1 '95.
Comments: European CD. Deluxe color cover. Time 54:43.

METALLICA

CD - A CHANGE OF SEASONS
MASTER M 9601
Sad But True/ Ain't My Bitch/ King Nothing/ One/ Wasting My Hate/ Nothing Else Matters/ Until It Sleeps/ For Whom The Bell Tolls/ Wherever I May Roam/ Fade To Black/ 'Old Shit' - Medley: Ride The Lightning, No Remorse, Hit The Lights, Four Horsemen, Seek And Destroy, Fight Fire With Fire/ Master Of Puppets/ Enter Sandman
Recording: Excellent stereo. Radio broadcast.
Source: Prins van Oranjehal, Utrecht November 12 1996.
Comments: European CD.

CD - ALMOST THE LAST GIG... PART 1
SNAKE RECORDING METAL 1
Introduction/ Master Of Puppets/ For Whom The Bells Tole/ Welcome Home (Sanitarium)/ Ride The Lightning/ Cliff Burton Solo/ Whiplash/ Fade To Black
Recording: Very good to excellent. Audience.
Source: Olympen, Lund September 25 1986. The day before the death of Cliff Burton.
Comments: European CD. Deluxe color cover. Time 45:30.

CD - ALMOST THE LAST GIG... PART 2
SNAKE RECORDING METAL 2
Seek And Destroy/ Creeping Death/ The Four Horsemen/ Kirk Hammet Guitar Solo/ Am I Evil?/ Damage Inc./ Fight Fire With Fire
Recording: Very good to excellent. Audience.
Source: Olympen, Lund September 25 1986. The day before the death of Cliff Burton.
Comments: European CD. Deluxe color cover. Time 42:03.

CD - COURT IN THE ACT
MT-9601/2
CD1: Opening Jam/ So What?/ Creeping Death/ Sad But Blue/ Ain't My Bitch/ Jam Pt. 2/ Whiplash/ Bleeding Me/ King Nothing/ One/ Wasting My Hate/ Jason's Solo/ My Friends Of Misery/ Welcome Home (Sanitarium)/ Nothing Else Matters)
CD2: Until It Sleeps/ For Whom The Bell Tolls/ Wherever I May Roam/ Fade To Black/ Kill-Ride Medley: Ride The Lightning, No Remorse, Hit The Lights, The Four Horsemen, Seek And Destroy, Fight Fire With Fire/ London Dungeon/ Last Caress/ Master Of Puppets/ Enter Sandman/ Am I Evil?/ Breadfan/ Overkill
Recording: Good. Audience.
Source: Earls Court, London October 12 1996.
Comments: European CD. Deluxe color cover.

CD - CUT THE CRAP
KISS THE STONE KTS 632/33
CD1: Sad But True/ Ain't My Bitch/ King Of Nothing/ One/ Wasting My Hate/ Nothing Else Matters/ Until It Sleeps/ 2 x 4/ Wherever I May Roam
CD2: Fade To Black/ Ride The Lightning/ No Remorse/ Hit The Lights/ The Four Horsemen/ Seek & Destroy/ Fight Fire With Fire/ Master Of Puppets/ Enter Sandman/ Wasting My Hate/ Mama Said/ King Of Nothing
Recording: Excellent stereo. Soundboard.
Source: Jaarbeurs, Utrecht, Holland, November 12 1996. Tracks 10-12 studio November 16 1996.
Comments: European CD. Deluxe color cover. Picture CD. Total time 95:42.

CD - DONNINGTON
KISS THE STONE KTS 487
Master Of Puppets (4:06)/ Wherever I May Roam (7:08)/ Two By Four (6:00)/ Harvest Of Sorrow (8:32)/ Nothing Else Matters (6:05)/ Sad But True (5:47)/ One (10:52)/ Enter Sandman (6:56)
Recording: Excellent stereo. Soundboard.
Source: Donnington Festival August 26 '95.
Comments: European CD. Deluxe color cover. Picture CD.

CD - FADE TO BLACK
PARTY LINE PLCD-022/023
CD1: Enter Sandman/ Creeping Death/

Harvester Of Sorrow/ Welcome Home/ Sad But True/ Wherever I May Roam/ Guitar Solo/ The Unforgiven/ Justice Medley/ Bass Solo
CD2: Guitar Solo (includes Dazed And Confused)/ Through The Never/ For Whom The Bell Tolls/ Fade To Black/ Master Of Puppets/ Seek And Destroy/ Whiplash/ Nothing Else Matters/ Am I Evil?/ Last Caress/ One/ Battery/ Stone Cold Crazy
Recording: Fair to good audience.
Source: Olympiahalle, Munchen, Germany November 22 1992.
Comments: European CD. Deluxe color cover.

CD - FAILURE
KI 12.09.96 2/2
For Whom The Bell Tolls/ Wherever I May Roam/ Medley (Ride The Lightning, No Remorse, Hit The Lights, The Four Horsemen, Seek And Destroy, Fight Fire With Fire)/ The Shortest/ Straw/ Master Of Puppets/ Enter Sandman/ Last Caress/ Breadfan/ Motorbreath
Recording: Good to very good audience.
Source: Ostseehalle, Kiel September 12 1996 - Part 2.
Comments: European picture CD. See 'POWER' for part 1.

CD - FULL LOADED
KOBRA RECORDS KRHM 10-1/2
CD1: So What?/ Creeping Death/ Sad But True/ Ain't My Bitch/ Whiplash/ Bleeding Me/ King Nothing/ One/ Wasting My Hate/ Bass Solo, Welcome Home (Sanitarium) Nothing Else Matters/ Until It Sleeps
CD2: For Whom The Bell Tolls/ Wherever I May Roam/ Fade To Black/ Kill, Medley: Ride The Lightning, No Remorse, Hit The Light, The Four Horsemen, Seek And Destroy, Fight Fire With Fire/ Jam, The Shortest Straw/ Master Of Puppets/ Enter Sandman, Surprise/ Last Caress/ Breadfan/ Motorbreath
Recording: Poor to good. Audience.
Source: Milano, Italy, Forum September 28 1996.
Comments: European CD. Deluxe color cover.

CD - GARAGE DAYS FAR BEHIND
MEGA 001
2x2 (live)/ Medley: Kill A Melody, Ryde (Donnington August 26 1995)/ Devil'z Dance (Donnington August 26 1995)/ Until It Sleepz (Moby Mix '96)/ Jamming To The Oldies (live, February 13 1987)/ Hero Of The Day (Outta B-Sides Mix)/ Overkill (Motorhead song live)/ Damage Case (live)/ Stone Dead Forever (live)/ Too Late Too Late (live, December 13 1995)/ Until It Sleepz (demo December 8 1995)/ Such A Shame (by Trauma, Cliff Burton's first band 1982)/ Holier Than You (demo for 'Metallica')/ Disposable heroes (demo for 'Master Puppets')
Recording: Excellent stereo. Soundboard.
Comments: European CD. Deluxe color cover. Picture CD. Time 70:52.

CD - HIT THE FIRST SHIT
PORE THE SOUL PTS-010/11
CD1: Opening 'The Good, The Bad, The Ugly'/ Battery/ Master Of Puppets/ For Whom The Bell Tolls/ Welcome Home (Sanitarium)/ Ride The Lightning/ Jason Bass Solo/ Whiplash/ The Thing That Should Not Be/ Fade To Black/ Seek And Destroy/ Creeping Death
CD2: The Four Horsemen/ Kirk Guitar Solo/ Am I Evil/ Damage Inc./ Fight Fire With Fire/ The Four Horsemen/ For Whom The Bell Tolls/ Fade To Black
Recording: Excellent. Audience.
Source: Shibuya-Koukaido, Tokyo, Japan November 15 1986. CD2 tracks 6-13 Milton Keynes National Bowl June 5 1993.
Comments: Japanese CD.

CD - LIVE AT GREAT WESTERN FORUM
METUS1CD/2CD
CD1: Last Caress/ Creepin Death/ Sad But True/ Ain't My Bitch/ Whiplash/ Bleeding Me/ King Nothing/ One/ Devil's Dance/ Nothing Matters/ Until It Sleeps
CD2: For Whom The Bells Tolls/ Wherever I May Roam/ Fade To Black/ Ride The Lightning, No Remorse, Hit The Lights, Seek And Destroy, Fight Fire With Fire/ So What/ Master Of Puppets/ Enter Sandman/ Breadfan/ Overkill
Recording: Very good to excellent. Audience.
Source: Great Western Forum, Inglewood December 21 1996.
Comments: European CD. Deluxe color cover.

METALLICA

CD - LIVE METAL ATTACK
MA-01
Hit The Lights/ The Mechanics/ Phantom Lord/ Jump In The Fire/ Motorbreath/ No Remorse/ Seek And Destroy/ Whiplash/ Am I Evil/ Metal Militia
Recording: Good. Audience.
Source: Old Waldorf, San Francisco November 29 '82.
Comments: Japanese CD. Deluxe color cover. Time 55:00.

CD - LOAD AND ROLL LIVE
MOUNTAINS MTS 007/8
CD1: Intro/ So What!/ Creeping Death/ Sad But True/ Ain't My Bitch/ Disco Jam/ Whiplash/ Bleeding Me/ King Nothing/ One/ Wasting My Hate/ Medley: My Friends Of Misery, Welcome Home Sanitarium/ Nothing Else Matters/ Until It Sleeps
CD2: For Whom The Bell Tolls/ Wherever I May Roam/ Fade To Black/ Ride The Lightning/ No Remorse/ Hit The Lights/ The Four Horsemen/ Seek An Destroy/ Fight Fire With Fire/ The Shortest Straw/ Master Of Puppets/ Enter Sandman/ Last Caress/ Breadfan/ Motorbreath
Recording: Good to very good. Audience.
Source: Bercy, Paris September 15 1996.
Comments: European CD. Deluxe color cover.

CD - OSLO OVERLOAD
MTCD 376542-1/2
CD1: So What/ Creeping Death/ Sad But True/ Ain't My Bitch/ Whiplash/ Bleeding Me/ King Nothing/ One/ Wasting My Hate/ Nothing Else Matters
CD2: Until It Sleeps/ For Whom The Bell Tolls/ Wherever I May Roam/ Fade To Black/ Seek & Destroy/ Fight Fire With Fire/ Last Caress/ Master Of Puppets/ Enter Sandman/ Am I Evil/ Motorbreath/ Kirk Hammett Interview
Recording: Excellent stereo. Soundboard.
Source: Oslo Spextrum, Oslo November 23 1996.
Comments: European CD. Deluxe color cover. Time CD1 66:22. CD2 59:45.

CD - POWER
KI 12.09.96 1/2
So What?/ Creeping Death/ Sad But True/ Bitch/ Whiplash/ Bleeding Me/ King Nothing/ One Wasting My Hate/ Nothing Else Matters/ Until It Sleeps

Recording: Good to very good audience.
Source: Ostseehalle, Kiel September 12 1996 - Part 1.
Comments: European picture CD. See 'FAILURE' for part 2.

CD - PUPPIES IN EL PASO
BABYFACE BF019
Welcome Home (demo)/ Master Of Puppets (demo)/ Disposable Heroes (demo)/ Master Of Puppets/ For Whom The Bell Tolls/ Ride The Lightning/ Welcome Home/ Creeping Death/ Damage Inc.
Recording: Very good. Soundboard.
Source: El Paso, TX May 16 1986.
Comments: European CD. Time 60:30.

CD - THE REAL NO LIFE TILL LEATHER
DARK SIDE DS-003
Motorbreath/ Mechanix/ Jump In The Fire/ Seek And Destroy/ Phantom Lord/ Metal Militia/ Hit The Lights/ Hit The Lights/ Mechanix/ Motorbreath/ Jump In The Fire/ Whiplash/ No Remorse
Recording: Excellent. Soundboard.
Source: Tracks 1-7 Chateau East Studio, Trustin, CA June 7 '82. Tracks 8-11 Ron's Garage, CA April '82. Tracks 12-13 demos, San Francisco, CA March '83.
Comments: Japanese CD. Cover has 'Metallica - Power Metal' biz card inserted in it. Time 56:26.

CD - WAIT FOR THE FOUR HORSEMEN
MIDNIGHT BEAT MB CD 099/100
CD1: Intro/ Sad But True/ Ain't My Bitch/ King Nothing/ One/ Wasting My Hate/ Nothing Else Matters/ Until It Sleeps/ For Whom The Bell Tolls/ Where Ever I May Roam/ Fade To Black/ Kill Ride Medley: No Remorse, Hit The Lights, The Four Horsemen, Seek And Destroy, Fight Fire With Fire
CD2 (Shape): Interactive Multimedia Track (for Windows and Apple Macintosh)/ Master Of Puppets/ Enter Sandman
Recording: Excellent stereo. Soundboard.
Source: Prins Van Oranje Hal, Utrecht, Holland November 12 1996.
Comments: European CD. Deluxe color cover. CD2 shaped like a blade saw. Time CD1 72:07. CD2 10:20.

METALLICA

FADE TO BLACK

ALANIS MORISSETTE
PERFECT TIMING

MICHAEL, GEORGE

CD - FREE FOR LOVE
KISS THE STONE KTS 638
Everything She Wants (5:11)/ You Have Been Loved (5:35)/ Fast Love (5:01)/ Praying For Time (5:42)/ I Can't Make You Love Me (5:35)/ Freedom '90 (5:56)/ Father Figure (6:24)/ Strangest Thing (7:46)/ Star People (5:50)
Recording: Excellent stereo. Soundboard.
Source: Paris Theatre, London 1996.
Comments: European CD. Deluxe color cover. Picture CD.

CD - UNPLUGGED
MOONRAKER 212
Freedom/ Fastlove/ I Can't Make You Love Me/ Father Figure/ You Have Been Loved/ Everything She Wants/ Praying For Time/ Star People/ BONUS TRACKS Interview/ Star People
Recording: Excellent stereo. Soundboard.
Source: Three Miles Studios, London, England October 11 1996. Track 9 October 1996. Track 10 1996 MTV Europe Music Awards, London November 14 1996.
Comments: European CD. Deluxe color cover. Time 74:00.

MICHAEL SCHENKER GROUP, THE

CD - CRY OF THE AXEMAN
BONDAGE MUSIC DON056
Cry For The Nations/ Victim Of Illusion/ Natural Thing/ Feels Like A Good Thing/ Rock Bottom/ Lost Horizons/ Doctor Doctor/ Captain Nemo/ Rock My Nights Away/ Are You Ready To Rock/ Cry For The Nations/ On And On/ Attack Of The Mad Axeman
Recording: Poor.
Source: Tracks 1-7 Pink Pop Festival, Holland June 8 1981. Tracks 8-13 Portland, Oregon December 14 1983.
Comments: Japanese CD.

MIDNIGHT OIL

CD - ACOUSTIC NIGHTS
OXYGEN OXY 091
Feeding Frenzy (6:32)/ The Dead Heart (6:18)/ My Country (4:40)/ Blue Sky Mine (5:04)/ Sell My Soul (5:32)/ Truganini (5:00)/ Warakurna (5:13)/ Short Memory (5:04)/ Beds Are Burning (4:25)/ Earth And Sun And Moon (4:24)/ Sell 'n' Soul (4:16)/ Blue Sky Mine (4:18)/ In The Valley (3:24)/ Beds Are Burning (5:02)/ Truganini (4:41)
Recording: Excellent stereo. Soundboard.
Source: Tracks 1-10 acoustic set, Ronnie Scott's Club, London, UK June 22 1993. Tracks 11-15 'Unplugged Session', New York City April 16 1993.
Comments: European CD. Deluxe color cover.

MISFITS, THE

CD - SHOCKING RETURN
FLOOD RECORDINGS FLD005
Halloween/ Horror Business/ I Turned Into A Martian/ Death Comes Ripping/ All Hell Breaks Loose/ Hunger/ Static Age/ TV Casualty/ Hybrid Moments/ Last Caress/ Skulls/ Devil's Whorehouse/ She/ Teenagers From Mars/ Children In Heat/ Violent World/ Vampira/ Black Light/ The Haunting/ Night Of The Living Dead/ 20 Eyes/ Hollywood Babylon/ Horror Hotel/ Angelfuck/ Attitude/ London Dungeon/ Astro Zombies
Recording: Excellent. Soundboard.
Comments: European CD. Deluxe color cover. Tracks 6,18-19 are new songs. Time 51:21.

CD - VAMPIRA
BABYFACE BF010
Halloween/ 20 Eyes/ I Turned Into A Martian/ Horror Business/ Vampira/ Mommy, Can I Go Out And Kill Tonight/ London Dungeon/ Attitude/ Teenagers From Mars (Bobby Steele version)/ Night Of The Living Dead/ All Hell Breaks Loose/ Hate Breeders/ Bullet/ We Are 138/ Last Caress/ Horror Hotel/ Ghouls Night Out/ 20 Eyes/ I Turned Into A Martian/ Astro Zombie/ Vampira/ All Hell Breaks Loose/ Nike A Go Go/ Devil's Whorehouse/ Horror Business/ Teenagers From Mars/ Children In Heat/ Skulls/ Nike A Go Go/ Where Eagles Dare/ Demonomania/ Wolf's Blood
Recording: Good to very good.
Source: Tracks 1-17 Passaic, NJ February 25 '81. Tracks 18-24 Ambionic recording sessions '81. Tracks 25-27 New York '79. Tracks 28-32 Dearborn, MI January 7 '83.
Comments: European CD. Black and white cover with red type. Time 73:45.

MONTROSE

CD - HARD SHOOK DAYS
Good Rockin' Tonight (3:29)/ Bad Motor Scooter (4:24)/ Make It Last (5:41)/ I Don't Want It (3:22)/ Rock Candy (4:33)/ Roll Me Nice (4:41)/ One Thing On My Mind (3:33)/ Rock The Nation (5:06)/ You're Out Of Time (3:45)/ Roll Over Beethoven (4:47)/ I Got The Fire (3:20)/ Spaceage Sacrifice (7:44)/ This Beautiful Martin (4:38)/ Trouble (5:29)/ Space Station #5
Source: Tracks 1-10 Pacific Studios, San Francisco, CA 1973. Tracks 11-15 Sausalito (?) December 26 1974.
Comments: Japanese CD.

MOORE, GARY

CD - WISHING WELL
BONDAGE MUSIC BON 036
Wishing Well/ Murder In The Sky/ Shapes Of Things/ Don't Take Me For A Loser/ Guitar Solo/ End Of The World/ So Far Away, Empty Rooms/ Back On The Streets/ Nuclear Attack
Recording: Excellent stereo. Soundboard.
Source: Hammersmith Odeon, London February 11 '84.
Comments: Japanese CD. Picture CD. Time 48:31.

MORISSETTE, ALANIS

CD - FIND A SOULMATE
All I Really Want (7:08)/ Right Through You (3:39)/ Not The Doctor (7:39)/ Hand In My Pocket (4:49)/ Mary Jane (6:20)/ Ironic (4:25)/ You Learn (5:35)/ Forgiven (6:04)/ You Oughta Now (5:29)/ Wake Up (7:22)/ Head Over Feed (4:40)/ Perfect (3:35)/ King Of Intimidation (previously unreleased) (3:59)*/ Can Not (previously unreleased) (5:12)*/ Your House (previously unreleased) (3:05)*
Recording: Excellent stereo. Soundboard.
*Excellent. Audience.
Source: Amsterdam October 17 1995.
*Milan, April 2 1996.
Comments: European CD. Deluxe color cover. Picture CD. Time 78:41.

CD - FOR YOUR INFORMATION
MOONRAKER 169
You Oughta Know*/ You Learn*/ Mary Jane*/ Hand In My Pocket*/ All I Really Want*/ Ironic (Rock AM Ring, Germany 1996)/ Ironic, Hand In My Pocket**/ Forgiven**/ You Oughta Know**/ Wake Up**/ You Learn**/ Hand In My Pocket^/ Ironic^/ Forgiven^/ You Oughta Know^
Recording: Excellent stereo. Soundboard.
*Live & Loud MTV Studios, London April 1996. **Prince's Trust, Hyde Park, London June 29 1996. ^The Phoenix Festival, England July 19 1996.
Comment: European CD. Picture CD. Time 79:38.

CD - THE GIRL CAN'T HELP IT
KISS THE STONE KTS 550
Right Through You/ Not The Doctor/ Hand In My Pocket/ Mary Jane/ Ironic/ You Learn/ Forgiven/ You Oughta Know/ Wake Up/ Headover Feet/ Perfect/ You Oughta Know/ Mary Jane/ Hand In My Pocket/ You Learn
Recording: Excellent stereo. Soundboard.
Source: New Pop Festival, Baden Baden, Germany October 13 '95. Tracks 12-14 tour rehearsals '95. Track 15 Germany '96.
Comments: European CD. Picture CD. Time 73:37.

CD - THE GIRL WITH THE THORN IN HER SIDE
FORBIDDEN FRUIT FFCD 019
Intro (2:49)/ All I Really Want (5:18)/ Right Through You (3:29)/ Not The Doctor (7:26)/ Hand In My Pocket (4:51)/ Mary Jane (6:30)/ Ironic (4:29)/ You Learn (5:12)/ Forgiven (6:10)/ You Oughta Know (5:20)/ Wake Up (8:04)/ Head Over Feet (4:46)/ Perfect (3:24)/
Recording: Excellent. Audience.
Source: The Subterania, London September 28 1995.
Comments: European CD. Picture CD.

CD - HARD TO SWALLOW
KISS THE STONE KTS 515
Wake Me Up (acoustic)/ You Learn (acoustic)/ Not The Doctor (acoustic)/ Your House (acoustic)/ Headover Feete (acoustic)/ Forgiven (acoustic)/ All I Really Want (electric)/ Hand In My Pocket (acoustic)/ You Oughta To Know (electric)/ All I Really Want (electric)/ Right Through You (electric)
Recording: Excellent stereo. Soundboard.
Source: Tracks 1-6 LA, California. Tracks 12/11/95. Tracks 7-9 Germany 11/95. Tracks 10-11 Amsterdam 10/95

MORISSETTE, ALANIS

Comments: European CD. Deluxe color cover. Picture CD. Time 53:28.

CD - HEART & SOUL
KOBRA RECORDS KRCD 20
Intro/ All I Really Want/ Right Through You/ Not The Doctor/ Hand In My Pocket/ Mary Jane/ Head Over Feet/ King Of Intimidation/ Forgiven/ Perfect/ Can 't Not/ You Oughta Know/ Ironic/ You Learn/ You Oughta Know
Recording: Excellent stereo. Soundboard.
Source: Tracks 1-11 Hamburg April 9 1996. Tracks 12-14 Baden Baden October 13 1995.
Comments: European CD.

CD - HER FIRST TWO ALBUMS
OSA BONG NL767
Feel Your Love/ Too Hot/ Walk Away/ On My Own/ Superman/ Jealous/ Human Touch/ Oh Yeah!/ Party Boy/ Real World/ An Emotion Away/ Rain/ The Time Of Your Life/ No Apologies/ Can't Deny/ When We Meet Again/ Give What You Got
Recording: Excellent stereo. Soundboard.
Source: Studio.
Comments: European CD. Deluxe color cover. Time 71:56.

CD - HYDE 'N' CHIC
REV 26
Ironic (4:36)/ Hand In My Pocket (4:32)/ Forgiven (5:29)/ Wake Up (6:37)/ You Learn (6:41)/ All I Really Want (7:33)/ Right Through You (3:32)/ Not The Doctor (7:40)/ Hand In My Pocket (4:31)/ Ironic (6:10)/ Forgiven (5:40)/ You Oughta Know (4:40)/ Obvious Attraction (6:49)
Recording: Excellent stereo. Soundboard.
Source: Tracks 1-5 Hyde Park, London June 29 1996. Tracks 6-13 Roskilde Festival, Denmark June 30 1996.
Comments: European CD. Deluxe color cover. Picture CD. Time 74:39.

CD - I CAN'T NOT
STAR 037
Intro/ The Feeling Begins/ All I Really Want/ League/ Right Through You/ Introductions/ Not The Doctor/ League/ Hand In My Pocket/ League/ Mary Jane/ League/ Forgiven/ League/ Perfect (acoustic)/ League/ You Oughta Know/ Wake Up (acoustic)/ League/ Ironic/ You Learn/ Your House/ Outro
Recording: Excellent stereo. Soundboard.

Source: TV special from Lake Trout Stadium, New Orleans October 3 1996.
Comments: European CD. Deluxe color cover. Includes Alanis' interview segments from special. Time 71:57.

CD - LIGHT MY FIRE
KISS THE STONE KTS 570
The Feeling Begins/ All I Really Want/ Right Through You/ Not The Doctor/ Hand In My Pocket/ Head Over Feet/ I Don't Know/ Forgiven/ Perfect/ Can't Not/ You Oughta Know/ Wake Up/ No Pressure Over Capuccino/ Ironic/ You Learn/ Your House
Recording: Excellent stereo. Soundboard.
Source: New York February 8 1996.
Comments: European CD. Deluxe color cover.

CD - PERFECT TIMING
ELECTRIC 40023
Let's Talk About/ Right Through You/ 9 To 5/ Hand In My Pocket/ Mary Jane/ Ironic/ You Learn/ We Had Our Reasons/ You Outta Know/ Wake Up/ You Already Won Me Over/ Perfect/ Bonus Track: Hand In My Pocket (Best Album-Award, UK 1995)
Source: California September 1995.
Comments: Euro CD. Deluxe color cover.

CD - THE QUEEN OF INTIMIDATION
MOONRAKER 152
The Feeling Begins/ All I Really Want/ Right Through You/ You're Not The Doctor/ Hand In My Pocket/ Mary Jane/ Head Over Feet/ The King Of Intimidation/ Forgiven/ Perfect/ Can't Not/ You Oughta Know/ Wake Up/ You Oughta Know (1996 Grammy Awards)
Recording: Excellent stereo. Soundboard.
Source: The Grosse Frieheit, Hamburg April 9 '96
Comments: European CD. Deluxe color cover. Picture CD. Time 68:13.

CD - QUITE ALRIGHT
BLIZZARD BLZD140
Right Through You/ Not The Doctor/ Hand In My Pocket/ Mary Jane/ Ironic/ Forgiven/ You Outta Know/ Wake Up/ Hand Over Feet/ Perfect/ Hand In My Pocket
Recording: Excellent stereo. Soundboard.
Source: New Pop Festival, Baden Baden, Germany September 13 1995.
Comments: European CD. Deluxe color cover. Picture CD. Time 59:09.

CD - ROSELAND
MOONRAKER 076
The Feeling Begins/ All I Really Want/ Right Through You/ Not The Doctor/ Hand In My Pocket/ Head Over Feet/ I Don't Know/ Forgiven/ Perfect/ Can't Not/ You Oughta Know/ Wake Up/ No Pressure Over Capuccino/ Ironic/ You Learn/ Your House
Recording: Excellent stereo. Soundboard.
Source: Roseland Ballroom, New York City February 8 1996.
Comments: European CD. Deluxe color cover. Picture CD. Time 79:24.

CD - SOMETHING TO SHARE
KISS THE STONE KTS 625
Intro, All I Really Want (7:13)/ Band Intro, Not The Doctor (5:30)/ Hand In My Pocket (4:17)/ Mary Jane (5:24)/ You Oughta Know (4:49)/ Ironic (4:16)/ You Learn (4:56)/ Your House (3:06)/ Hand In My Pocket (4:39)/ Ironic (4:29)/ Forgiven (5:42)/ You Oughta Know (4:29)/ All I Really Want (5:07)/ You Learn (with Alanis on drums) (4:24)
Recording: Excellent stereo. Soundboard.
Source: Tracks 1-8 New Orleans 1996. Tracks 9-12 Phoenix Festival, England July 19 1996. Track 13 New York 1995. Track 14 Germany March 28 1996.
Comments: European CD. Deluxe color cover. Picture CD.

CD - WHAT COMES AROUND
MIDNIGHT BEAT MBCD070
All I Really Want/ Right Through You/ Not The Doctor/ Hand In My Pocket/ Mary Jane/ Ironic/ You Learn/ Forgiven/ You Oughta Know/ Wake Up/ Head Over Feet/ Perfect
Recording: Very good.
Source: De Melkweg, Amsterdam, The Netherlands, October 17 1995.

CD - YOU CAN KISS IT
KISS THE STONE KTS 591
The Feeling Begins/ All I Really Want/ Right Through You/ Band Intro, Not The Doctor/ Hand In My Pocket/ Mary Jane/ Ironic/ Forgiven/ You Oughta Know/ You Oughta Know/ Wake Up/ You Learn/ Ironic/ Forgiven
Recording: Excellent stereo. Soundboard.
Source: Track 1-9 Alabamahalle, Munich, Germany April 1 1996. Tracks 10-12 Pink Pop Festival, Landgraat, Holland May 27 1996. Tracks 13-14 The Rock Am Ring Festival, Germany May 26 1996.
Comments: European CD.

MORRISON, VAN

CD - EDINBURGH CASTLE
KISS THE STONE KTS 490
All Right, Okay, You Win (3:12)/ How Long Has This Been Going On? (4:29)/ Early In The Morning (3:01)/ Days Like This (3:23)/ Who Can I Turn To? (3:57)/ That's Life (3:34)/ I Will Be There (2:25)/ Vanlose Stairway (4:23)/ Blues In The Night (3:14)/ Haunts Of Ancient Peace (4:50)/ Your Mind Is On Vacation (4:19)/ Moondance (8:47)
Recording: Excellent stereo. Soundboard.
Source: The Edinburgh Jazz Festival August 1995.
Comments: European CD. Deluxe color cover. Picture CD.

CD - SUMMERTIME IN HOLLAND
VTM 936109-1/2
CD1: Sack O'Woe/ Satisfied/ Whenever God Shines His Light/ Summertime In England, Can You Feel The Silence/ Fire In The Belly/ This Weight/ Ain't That Lovin' You Baby?/ Wonderful Remark
CD2: Vanlose Stairway, Trans-Euro Train, Its Not The Twilight Zone/ The Burning Ground/ Tupelo Honey, Crazy Love/ Sometimes We Cry/ See Me Through, Soldier Of Fortune, When Heart Is Open, Thank You Fallentinme Be Mice Self Again/ Waiting Game/ The Healing Game/ Bright Side Of The Road/ Have I Told You Lately?
Recording: Very good. Audience.
Source: Utrecht, Vrendenburg, Holland, September 18 1996.
Comments: European CD. Deluxe color cover.

CD - VAN THE MAN
INSECT IST 47
Inarticulate Speech/ Baby, Please Don't Go/ Crawling King Snake/ Can't Feel It Anymore/ Always Explain/ Haunts Of Ancient Peace/ Sue Moves On Solid Ground/ All Saints Day/ Cleaning Windows/ Be-Bop-A-Lula/ Hey Hey/ Valouse Stairway/ Baby Blue/ Youth Of 1000 Summers/ Nightshirt/ Enlightenment/ No Guru
Recording: Very good to excellent. Audience.
Source: Glastonbury Festival June 28 1992.

MOTLEY CRUE

CD - CITY BOY BLUES
REEL MUSIC RMCD-95107
Hills Bros/ All Makers/ Freshness/ Exciting Night/ Pull It!/ Crazy Cats/ Sweet Sweet/ About Days/ Bench/ Deep Out/ Setting Love/ Apple Pie/ Try Try!
Recording: Good to very good. Audience.
Source: July 15 1995.
Comments: European CD. Deluxe color cover. Time 75:23.

CD - SHOOT TO KILL
DR. GIG DGCD 054
In The Beginning/ Shout At The Devil/ Knockin' Em Dead, Kid/ Too Young To Fall In Love/ Red Hot, Guitar Solo/ Piece Of Your Action/ Looks That Kill/ Helter Skelter/ Live Wire/ Take Me To The Top/ Looks That Kill/ Red Hot/ Starry Eyes/ Piece Of Your Action/ Merry-Go-Round/ Shout At The Devil/ Hotter Than Hell
Recording: Excellent stereo. Soundboard.
Source: Tracks 1-8 Tucson, Arizona '83. Tracks 9-16 Pasadena, California '82.
Comments: European CD. Deluxe color cover. Time 70:59.

MOTORHEAD

CD - DEAF FOREVER
THE SWINGIN' PIG TSP-CD-171
Doctor Rock/ Stay Clean/ Traitor/ Metropolis/ Dogs/ Ace Of Spades/ Eat The Rich/ Built For Speed/ Deaf Forever/ Just 'Cos You've Got The Power/ No Class/ Religion/ Stone Deaf In The U.S.A./ Killed By Death/ Overkill
Recording: Excellent stereo. Soundboard.
Source: The Hot Point Festival, Lausanne, Switzerland, September 1 1988.
Comments: European CD. Time 64:35.

MOTT THE HOOPLE

CD - HOOPING FURIOUSLY
HIWATT MTH 001
Thunderbuck Ram/ Whiskey Woman/ The Original Mixed-Up Kid/ Darkness Darkness/ The Moon Upstairs/ The Moon Upstairs/ Whiskey Woman/ Your Own Back Yard/ Darkness Darkness/ The Journey/ Death May Be Your Santa Claus/ One Of The Boys/ Midnight Lady/ All The Young Dudes/ It'll Be Me
Recording: Excellent. Soundboard.
Source: Track 1 BBC Radio, Top Gear February 1 1970. Tracks 2-3 BBC, Top Gear March 16 1971. Tracks 4-5 BBC Radio, Top Gear November 4 1971. Tracks 6-11 BBC Radio, In Concert December 31 1971. Tracks 12-14 The Tower Theatre, Philadelphia October 31 1972. Track 15 Rock 'N Roll Will Never Die recorded 1970.
Comments: Deluxe color cover. Time 75:26.

MOUNTAIN

CD - NANTUCKET HARD TIMES
ELEMENT OF CRIME ELEMENTS-016
Why Dontcha (4:34)/ Never In My Life (4:46)/ Theme For An Imaginary Western (8:10)/ Hard Times (3:02)/ Spark (7:27)/ Guitar Solo, Nantucket Sleighride, Drum Solo (13:50)/ Mississippi Queen (6:49)/ Rocky Mountain Way (10:02)
Source: L'Amours, New York December 4 1986.
Comments: Japanese CD.

CD - ROCKIN' AND ROLLIN' ALL OVER THE WORLD
DISCURIOUS 105
You Better Believe It**/ Get Off My Life Woman**/ By The River*/ House Of The Rising Sun*/ Theme For An Imaging Western**/ Nantucket Sleighride**/ Roll Over Beethoven/ Whole Lotta Shakin'**/ Intro Never In My Life***/ Silver Paper***/ Mississippi Queen***
Source: (*)New Jersey December 30 1973. (**)New York Dec 31 1973. (***)San Bernardino December 20 1971.
Comments: European CD.

N

NEW BARBARIANS, THE

CD - LIVE AT THE L.A. FORUM
THE SWINGIN' PIG TSP-CD-204
Mystifies Me/ Infekshun/ Rock Me Baby/ Sure The One You Need/ Lost And Lonely/ Band Introduction/ Breathe On Me/ Love In Vain/ Let's Go Steady/ Apartment No. 9/

Worried Life Blues/ I Can Feel The Fire
Recording: Excellent stereo. Soundboard.
Source: Inglewood Forum, Los Angeles
May 19 1979.
Comments: European CD. Time 61:10.

NINE INCH NAILS

CD - LOST ACTION HEROES
SLANG 43
Terrible Lie (4:50)/ March Of The Pigs (3:52)/ The Becoming (4:57)/ Sanctified (7:08)/ Piggy (4:25)/ Burn (4:54)/ Closer (6:26)/ Wish (3:40)/ Broken Machine (4:35)/ Down In It (4:42)/ Eraser (3:34)/ Scary Monsters (5:38)/ Reptile (6:01)/ Hurt (6:00)
Recording: Excellent stereo. Soundboard.
Source: Camden Entertainment Center, Philadelphia September 22 1995.
Comments: European CD. Deluxe color cover. Picture CD.

CD - MISSLETWISTER
TORNADO TOR020
Intro, Terrible Lie/ Sin/ Something I Can Never Have/ Justify/ That's What I Get/ Suck/ The Only Time/ Get Down Make Love/ Ringfinger/ Down In It/ Head Like A Hole
Recording: Good to very good. Audience.
Source: Melbourne, FL July 1 1990.
Comments: European CD. Deluxe color cover. Picture CD. Time 60:56.

CD - PUREST FEELING II
HAWK 066
Down In It I/ Suck I/ Supernaut/ Down In It II/ Twist/ Suck II Head Like A Hole/ Sanctified/ Down In It III/ Wish Kinda I Want To/ Head/ Down In It IV/ Sin
Recording: Excellent stereo. Soundboard.
Source: The Right Track, Cleveland November 1988.
Comments: European CD. Deluxe color cover. Time 42:56.

CD - SHALLOW GRAVE
INSECT 89
Terrible Lie (6:14)/ Sin (4:13)/ March Of The Pigs (3:54)/ Something I Can Never Have (6:36)/ Closer (6:41)/ Reptile (6:14)/ Wish (3:43)/ Suck (4:15)/ The Only Time (5:18)/ Get Down Make Love (3:36)/ Down In It (?)/ Big Man With A Gun (2:41)/ Head Like A Hole (6:48)/ Dead Souls (6:03)/ Help Me I Am In Hell (3:24)/ Happiness In Slavery (4:37)
Recording: Soundboard.
Source: Brixton Academy May 25 19/94
Comments: European CD.

CD - SHOW UP OR THROW UP...
HURRICANE HURR010
Sanctified/ Maybe Just Once/ The Only Time/ That's What I Get/ Ringfinger/ Down In It/ Intro/ Terrible Lie/ Sin/ Physical/ The Only Time/ Wish/ Get Down Make Love/ Down In It/ Head Like A Hole
Recording: Good. Audience.
Source: Tracks 1-6 Irving Plaza, NYC October 31 1988 (1st show ever). Tracks 7-15 Lollapalooza, Harriets Island, St. Paul, MN August 1 1991.
Comments: European CD. Deluxe color cover. Picture CD. Time 70:23.

CD - ULTRA RARE TRACKS
NINCD 100
Eraser (instrumental live version 1995)/ Scary Monsters (live with guest vocalist David Bowie 1995), Reptile, Hurt (live with guest vocalist David Bowie 1995)/ Dead Souls (outtake from the 'Downward Spiral' sessions 1994)/ Ruiner (rejected trance mix from the 'Downward Spiral' sessions 1994)/ Burn (outtake from the 'Downward Spiral' sessions 1994)/ Theme From The Right Track (unreleased studio instrumental 1988)/ Maybe Just Once, Purest Feeling, Twist (unreleased studio track 1988)/ Supernaut (unreleased studio track 1988 with Al Jorgenson 1990)/ Your Physical, Red Scab, Beat My Guest (live with guests Adam Ant and Marco Pirroni 1995)*/ Now I Am Nothing (unreleased live track 1991)
Recording: Excellent stereo. Soundboard. Excellent audience.
Comments: European CD. Deluxe color cover. Picture CD. Time 75:56.

NIRVANA

CD - A HIGHER STATE OF MIND
KISS THE STONE KTS 594
Breed/ Drain You/ Beeswax/ Spank Thru/ School/ Come As You Are/ Lithium/ Lounge Act/ Sliver/ About A Girl/ Polly/ Instrumental Improvisation/ In Bloom/ Territorial Pissing/ Been A Son/ On A Plain/ Negative Creep/ Blew/ Smells Like Teen Spirit/ Drain You/ Polly/ Territorial Pissing/ Lithium

NIRVANA

Recording: Excellent stereo. Soundboard.
Source: Buenos Aires, Argentina October 30 1992. Tracks 19-22 New York January 10 1992. Track 23 MTV Awards, Los Angeles September 8 1992.
Comments: European CD. CD looks like a record. Time 71:32.

CD - AMERICAN ACOUSTIC TOUR
P 910077
About A Girl (3:23)/ Come As You Are (4:18)/ Jesus Wants Me For A Sunbeam (4:15)/ Dumb (3:05)/ Man Who Sold The World (4:14)/ Pennyroyal Tea (3:45)/ Polly (3:16)/ On A Plain (4:17)/ Plateau (3:19)/ Lake Of Fire (2:53)/ All Apologies (4:06)/ Where Did You Sleep Last Night (4:53)
Recording: Excellent stereo. Soundboard.
Source: Various US locations 1993.
Comments: European CD. Deluxe color cover.

CD - COMPLETE COVER VERSIONS
SOL35
Here She Comes Now (from The Velvet's tribute LP)/ Do You Love Me (Kiss number recorded for Seattle radio June 1988)/ Jesus Wants Me For A Sunbeam (originally a Christian spiritual later recorded in his version by The Vaselines. This recording made in Washington October 31 1991)/ Dazed And Confused (Led Zep Song recorded in Europe November 1989)/ D-7 (live version of The Wipers song, Off Ramp Club, Seattle November 1990)/ Turnaround (Devo song recorded for Peel Session January 1991)/ Return Of The Rat (another Wipers song, this version appeared on the tribute 7" box set)/ The End (cover of The Doors classic live in Gent, Belgium 1991)/ The Man Who Sold The World (electric version of Bowie's song, Rome, February 22 1994)/ Molly's Lips (another Vaselines song, Peel Session January 1991)/ Love Buzz* (written by Robby Van Leewen, Nirvana's first single live in Vancouver March 1990)/ Plateau (acoustic version of The Meat Puppets song)/ Like Of Fire (as above)/ Baba O'Reilly (Who song live in France 1991)/ Son Of A Gun (another Vaselines song, Peel Session January 1991)/ Where Did You Sleep Last Night* (Kurt's solo version of the Leadbelly song)/ Here She Comes Now* (another version of The V.U. song, live in Seattle November 1990)

Recording: Excellent soundboard. *Very good to excellent audience.
Comments: European CD. Deluxe color cover. Picture CD. Time 57:26.

CD - HEART SHAPED ROME
KOBRA RECORDS KRCD 10
Radio Friendly Unit Shifter/ Drain You/ Breed/ Serve The Servants/ Come As You Are/ Smells Like Teen Spirit/ Sliver/ Dumb/ In Bloom/ About A Girl/ Scentless Apprentice/ Lithium/ Pennyroyal Tea/ School/ Polly/ Very Ape/ Lounge Act/ Rape Me/ Territorial Pissing/ All Apologies/ On A Plain/ Heart Shaped Box/ Improvisation (including Drum Solo)
Recording: Excellent stereo. Soundboard.
Source: The Palaghiaccio, Rome February 22 1994.
Comments: European CD. Deluxe color cover. Time 74:29.

CD - HORMOANING
MVCG-17002
Turnaround/ Aneurysm/ D-7/ Son Of A Gun/ Even In His Youth/ Molly's Lips
Recording: Excellent stereo. Soundboard.
Source: BBC Broadcast November 3 1990.
Comments: Japanese CD. Time 18:47.

CD - IN THE SHADOWS OF THE SUN
KISS THE STONE KTS 577
Radio Friendly Unit Shifter (4:36)/ Drain You (3:47)/ Breed (3:07)/ Serve The Servants (4:13)/ About A Girl (4:47)/ Heart-Shaped Box (2:38)/ Dumb (3:12)/ In Bloom (5:00)/ Come As You Are (3:46)/ Lithium (4:26)/ Pennyroyal Tea (3:35)/ Polly (3:02)/ Milk It (4:48)/ Rape Me (3:53)/ Territorial Pissing (2:50)/ Jesus Don't Want Me For A Sunbeam (2:13)/ Scentless Apprentice (6:00)/ Smells Like A Teen Spirit (4:12)
Recording: Excellent stereo. Soundboard.
Source: Bayfront Amphitheater, St. Petersburg, Florida November 27 1993.
Comments: European CD. CD looks like a record.

CD - KURT'S GRAND FINALE
INSECT IST 64
Radio Friendly Unit Shifter/ Drain You/ Breed/ Serve The Servants/ Come As You Are/ Smells Like Teen Spirit/ Silver/ Dumb/ In Bloom/ About A Girl/ Scentless Apprentice/ Lithium/ Pennyroyal Tea/ School/ (New Wave) Polly/ Very Ape/

NIRVANA
RARE TRAKS VOL. II

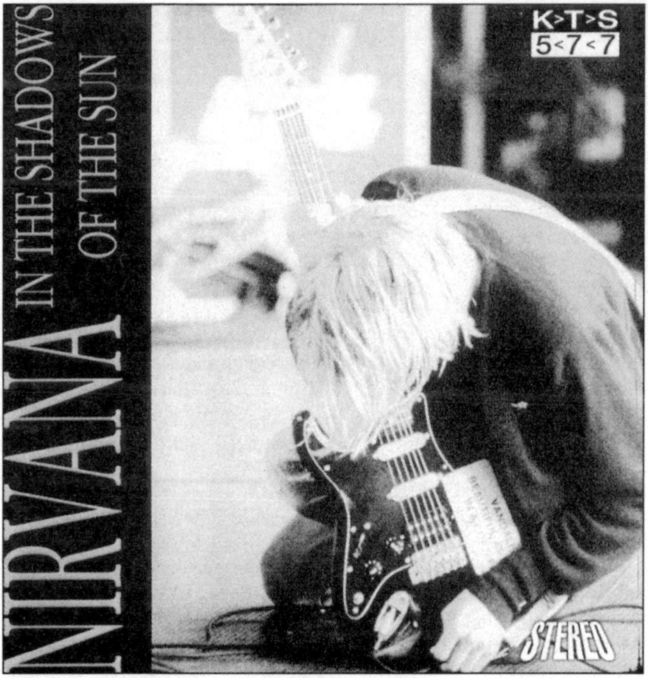
NIRVANA IN THE SHADOWS OF THE SUN
K>T>S
5<7<7
STEREO

NIRVANA

Lounge Act/ Rape Me/ Territorial Pissing/ All Apologies/ On A Plain/ Heard Shaped Box, Grand Finale
Recording: Excellent stereo. Soundboard.
Source: Ice Hockey Stadium, Rome February 22 1994. Kurt's final performance.
Comments: European CD. Deluxe B&w cover. Time 74:02.

CD - LAST CONCERT IN JAPAN
KISS THE STONE KTS 582
Negative Creep/ Been A Son/ On A Plain/ Blew/ Come As You Are/ Lithium/ Breed/ Sliver/ Drain You/ About A Girl/ School/ Aneurysm/ Love Buzz/ Polly/ Territorial Pissing/ Smells Like Teen Spirit/ Demolition/ Here She Comes Now/ Where Did You Sleep Last Night?
Recording: Excellent stereo. Soundboard.
Source: Nakano Sunplaza, Tokyo, Japan February 19 1992. Tracks 18-19 acoustic session, Holland November 24 1991.
Comments: European CD. CD looks like a record. Time 65:32.

CD - MR. KURDT KOBAIN
TUBE TUCD 006
School/ Scoff/ Love Buzz/ Floyd The Barber/ Dive/ Big Cheese/ Molly's Lips/ Spank Thru/ About A Girl/ Mr. Moustache/ Breed/ Negative Creep/ Blew
Recording: Excellent. Soundboard.
Source: Ku-Ba, Hanau, West Germany November 18 1989.
Comments: European CD. Deluxe color cover. Time 49:11.

CD - OUTCESTICIDE VOL. 6
KOBRA KRCD 007
Territorial Pissing (Jonathan Ross TV Show, London, UK December 1991)/ Opinion (unreleased acoustic song played by Kurt, includes short interview, Seattle radio session, September 1990)/ Smells Like Teen Spirit (Saturday Night Live TV show, New York City 1992)/ Love Buzz (Nozems A Gogo, Hilversum, Holland 1989)/ Rape Me, Lithium (Video Music Awards, Los Angeles, CA, September 10 1992)/ Serve The Servants (Arena, Seattle, December 31 1993)/ Jesus Doesn't Want Me For A Sunbeam (USA 1991)/ I Can Live (demo USA 1990)/ Dive/ About A Girl/ Disco Goddess/ Mexican Seafood/ Mr. Moustache/ Sifting/ Aero Zeppelin/ Scoff/ Love Buzz/ Floyd The Barber/ Dive/ Spank Through/ Big Cheese
Recording: Very good to excellent. Soundboard.
Source: Tracks 9-15 studio outtakes from Bleach recording session, Seattle 1989. Tracks 16-21 Austrian radio November 1989.
Comments: European CD. Time 74:00.

CD - RARE TRACKS VOL. I
INSECT IST 87
Mexican Seafood (early demo from volume one of the rare 7" compilations 'Teryaki Asthma')/ Her She Comes Now (demo from the '89 Velvet Underground tribute LP, 'Heaven & Hell')/ Beeswax (demo recorded late 1991, a contribution to the compilation LP on K Records, 'Kill Rock Stars')/ Been A Son & Stain (are rare B side demo tracks, from the first EP - 'Blew')/ Son Of A Gun, Molly's Lips, D-7, Turnaround (cover versions recorded for Radio One John Peel Sessions, Broadcast January 1991)/ Dumb, Untitled, Drain You (recorded for Radio One, John Peel Sessions, broadcast November 1990)/ Territorial Pissing (Jonathan Ross Tonight TV program recorded December 8 1991)/ Something In The Way, Been A Son (Radio One, The Mark Goodier Sessions, recorded August 1991)/ Spank Through, About Girl, Love Buzz, Polly. Everything & Nothing, Lithium, Breed (demos and practices with new drummer Dave Grohl Seattle late 1990)
Recording: Excellent. Soundboard.
Comments: European CD. Deluxe color cover. Picture CD. Time 71:40.

CD - RARE TRACKS VOL. II
INSECT IST 88
In Bloom (unissued Sub Pop 7" master tape May 1990)/ Omodium (early version of 'Breed' with different lyrics November 1989)/ Help Me (unreleased song from winter 1989)/ Oh, the Guilt (live version, November 1989)/ Smells Like Teen Spirit (with Flea from Red Hot Chili Peppers on trumpet January 1993)/ Pennyroyal Tea (early version with different lyrics October 1991)/ It's Closing Soon (Kurt & Courtney, The Rio Tape date unknown)/ Heart Shaped Box (early version with different lyrics January 1993)/ Scentless Apprentice (extended experimental feedback version January 1993)/ Been A Son (acoustic rehearsal October 1991)/ Something In The

Way (in store acoustic gig October 1991)/ Negative Creep (in store acoustic gig October 1991)/ Where Did You Sleep Last Night (Kurt solo at Castaic Lake September 1992)/ Baba O'Reilly (covering The Who in Rennes December 1991)/ The End (covering The Doors, Belgium November 1991)/ Lithium (mix six, unreleased studio version June 1991)/ Dumb (with Melora Craeger on cello February 1994)/ Molly's Lips (an early attempt at The Vaseline's song November 1989)/ In His Hands (unreleased song written circa summer 1990)/ The Man Who Sold The World (electric version December 1993)/ Smells Like Teen Spirit (live on The World TV Show November 1991)
Recording: Very good to excellent. Soundboard/audience.
Comments: European CD. Picture CD. Time 74:17.

CD - REVOLUTIONARY DEBRIS
BORED SOUND BS91
Jesus Doesn't Want Me For A Sunbeam/ Aneurysm/ School/ Floyd The Barber/ Drain You/ Smells Like Teen Spirit/ About A Girl/ Breed/ Polly/ Sliver/ Pennyroyal Tea/ Love Buzz/ Been A Son/ On A Plain/ Negative Creep/ Blew/ Noise Finale/ Lithium/ Rape Me/ Territorial Pissings/ Smells Like Teen Spirit/ Territorial Pissings
Recording: Excellent. Soundboard.
Source: Tracks 1-17 Cabaret Metro, Chicago October 12 1991. Tracks 18-20 The Palace, Hollywood October 25 1991. Tracks 21-22 Saturday Night Live January 11 1992.
Comments: European CD. Deluxe color cover. Time 74:36.

CD - SOMETHING IN MILWAUKEE
WKD-002/003
CD1: Radio Friendly Unit Shifter/ Drain You/ Breed/ Serve The Servants/ Heart Shaped Box/ Silver/ Dumb/ In Bloom/ Come As You Are/ Lithium/ Pennyroyal Tea/ School/ Polly (New Wave)/ Lounge Act/ Rape Me/ Territorial Pissings
CD2: Jesus Doesn't Want Me For A Sunbeam/ Something In The Way/ On A Plane/ Scentless Apprentice/ Blew/ Noise/ Heart Shaped Box/ Heart Shaped Box/ Rape Me
Recording: Good. Audience. CD2 tracks 7-9 very good soundboard.
Source: Meeca Auditorium, Milwaukee October 26 1993. CD2 tracks 7-9 Saturday Night Live Rehearsals 1993.

CD - STIFF DRINKS
BABYFACE BF005
School/ Shy/ Spank Thru/ In My Eyes/ Dive/ About A Girl/ Breed/ Big Chief/ Can You Feel/ Made Outta Wood/ Polly/ Pay To Play/ Been A Son/ The Same/ Daddy's Little Girl/ Disco Goddess/ Lithium/ Happy/ Polly/ Son Of A Gun/ Dive/ About A Girl
Recording: Excellent stereo. Soundboard. Tracks 16-22 Very good to excellent. Soundboard. Hiss.
Source: Duffy's Bar May 14 1990. Tracks 16-22 'Bleach' demos.
Comments: European CD. Deluxe color cover. Picture CD. Time 73:07.

CD - UP IN SMOKE
KISS THE STONE KTS 562/63
CD1: Radio Friendly Unit Shifter (4:36)/ Drain You (3:47)/ Breed (3:07)/ Serve The Servants (4:13)/ Heart-Shaped Box (4:47)/ Sliver (2:38)/ Dumb (3:12)/ In Bloom (5:00)/ Come As You Are (3:46)/ Lithium (4:26)/ Pennyroyal Tea (3:35)/ School (3:02)
CD2: Polly (4:48)/ Milk It (3:53)/ Rape Me (2:50)/ Territorial Pissing (2:13)/ Smells Like A Teen Spirit (6:00)/ All Apologies (4:12)/ Jesus Wants Me For A Sunbeam (4:30)/ Something In The Way (3:43)/ On A Plain (3:31)/ Scentless Apprentice (3:55)/ Blew (3:17)
Recording: Excellent. Audience.
Source: Milwaukee October 23 '93.
Comments: European CD. Picture CDs that look like records.

NO DOUBT

CD - HAPPY
MOONRAKER 230
Tragic Kingdom/ Excuse Me Mr./ Happy Now?/ Different People/ Just A Girl/ Sunday Morning/ Move On/ Don't Speak/ End On This/ Hey You/ Spiderwebs*
Recording: Excellent stereo. Soundboard.
Source: The City Hall Den Haag Holland Feb. 21 1997. *New York Sept. 6 1995.
Comments: European CD. Deluxe color cover. Time 52:43.

NOVA, HEATHER

CD - SUPERNOVA
MOONRAKER 167
Heal (4:23)/ Throwing Fire At The Sun (4:41)/ Island (6:24)/ Like A Hurricane (3:58)/ Walk This World (3:55)/ Heart And Shoulder (4:27)/ My Fidelity (4:15)/ Doubled Up (3:39)/ Maybe An Angel (4:42)/ Ear To The Ground (4:21)/ Truth And Bone (2:54)/ Island (4:48)/ Light Years (4:34)/ Walk This World (3:52)/ Island (5:38)/ Truth And Bone (4:49)/ I'm On Fire (2:41)
Recording: Excellent. Audience.
Source: Tracks 1-11 Club Knust, Hamburg March 2 1996. Track 12 MTV Europe's Hanging Out April 10 1996. Tracks 13-17 Loreley Festival, Germany June 22 1996.
Comments: European CD. Deluxe color cover. Picture CD.

O

OASIS

CD - ABEL & CAIN
KOBRA RECORDS KRCD 11
It's Good To Be Free/ Married With Children/ Sad Song*/ Talk Tonight*/ Whatever/ I'm The Walrus/ The Swamp Song/ Acquiesce/ Some Might Say/ Cigarettes & Alcohol/ Wonderwall*/ Live Forever/ Supersonic/ Hello/ Roll With it/ Whatever*/ Champagne Supernova/ Up In The Sky*
Recording: Excellent.
Source: Tracks 1-6 Fans Club Show, London December 1994. Tracks 7-17 Utrecht, Holland 10/01/96. Track 18 Maido Vale Studios London 1994. *Acoustic.
Comments: European CD. Time 79:37.

CD - ANOTHER STORY
KOBRA RECORDS KRCD 14
Cast No Shadow/ Wonderwall (radio session Rome Italy 1996)/ Married With Children (Fan Club, London May 1994)/ Take Me Away/ D'Yer Wanna Be A Spaceman (Manchester, UK December 18 1994)/ Whatever/ Live Forever/ Digsy Dinner (radio session 1994)/ You've Got To Hide Your Love Away (radio session 1995)/ Wonderwall (Seattle December 4 1995)/ Morning Glory/ Cast No Shadow (Stockholm November 20 1995)/ Fade Away Blackpool, UK October 2 1995)/ Life In Vain (live 1992)/ Don't Look Back In Anger (radio session UK 1995)/ Sad Song/ Supersonic (studio demo March 1994)/ Live Forever/ Shakermaker (demo 1994)
Recording: Excellent .
Comments: European CD. Time 68:49.

CD - BEHIND CLOSED DOORS
OXYGEN OXY 066
Supersonic/ Hello/ Shakermaker/ Roll With It/ Slide Away/ (It's Good) To Be Free/ Morning Glory/ Cigarettes & Alcohol/ Live Forever/ Cast No Shadow+/ Wonderwall+/ Don't Look Back In Anger+/ You've Got To Hide Your Love Away+/ Colour My Life*/ Take Me*/ See The Sun*/ Must Be The Music*
Recording: Excellent. Soundboard.
Source: Tracks 1-9 Roskilde Festival, Denmark June 30 1995. Tracks 10-11 acoustic radio session, Roma, Italy February 1996. Tracks 12-13 acoustic radio session, London, UK October 1995. Tracks 14-17 early demos, Manchester UK 1992. *Previously unreleased. +Acoustic.
Comment: Pic. Disc. Time 73:36.

CD - CITY V/S UNITED 1-0
DREAM ON RECORDS DOR 002
The Swamp Song/ The Masterplan/ I Am The Walrus/ Listen Up/ Bonehead's Bank Holiday (LP)/ Wonderwall (Top Of The Pops)/ Whatever (Later)/ I Am The Walrus (with strings)/ I Will Believe/ Step Out/ Underneath The Sky/ Cum On Feel The Noize/ Good To Be Free (White Room)
Recording: Excellent stereo. Soundboard.
Source: Rare live in studio songs, bonus tracks and B-Sides.
Comments: European CD. Deluxe color cover. Time 60:21.

CD - CLIMBING THE SKY
KOBRA RECORDS KRCD 17
Rock'N Roll Star/ Columbia/ Fade Away/ Digsy's Dinner/ Shakermaker/ Live Forever/ Bring It On Down/ Up In The Sky/ Slide Away/ Cigarettes & Alcohol/ Married With Children/ Supersonic/ I Am The Walrus
Recording: Excellent stereo. Soundboard.
Source: Cabaret Metro, Chicago October 15 1994.
Comments: European CD.

CD - CLOSET ENCOUNTERS
LIAM 96
Intro, Hello Hello, It's Good To Be Back (0:37)/ Don't Look Back In Anger (Top Of The Pops February 22 1996) (4:52)/ Cum On Feel The Noize (Top Of The Pops February 22 1996) (3:40)/ Step Out ('B' Side different mix) (3:40)/ Round Our Way (White Room January 26 1996) (4:42)/ Some Might Say (White Room January 26 1996) (4:54)/ Don't Look Back In Anger (White Room December 31 1995) (4:16)/ Wonderwall (White Room December 31 1995 - January 1 1996) (3:45)/ Roll With It (White Room January 1 1996) (3:55)/ Champagne Supernova (Brendan Lynch Beat Mob Mix, promo only) (4:46)/ Color My Life (unreleased demo 1992) (6:57)/ Take Me (unreleased demo 1992) (3:19)/ See The Sun (unreleased demo 1992) (5:52)/ Must Be The Music (unreleased demo 1992) (3:37)/ Better Let You Know (unreleased demo '92) (4:33)/ Snake Bite (unreleased demo 1992) (3:09)/ Untitled Jam #1 (5:30)/ Untitled Jam #2 (1:20)
Recording: Excellent stereo. Soundboard.

CD - DEFINITELY FLIP SIDES
OA 10905
Take Me Away/ Will Believe (live)/ Colombia (white label demo)/ D'Yer Wanna Be A Spaceman?/ Alive (8-track demo)/ Bring It On Down (live)/ Up In The Sky (acoustic)/ Cloudburst/ Supersonic (live)/ I Am The Walrus (live)/ Listen Up/ Fade Away/ Whatever/ (It's So Good) To Be Free/ Half The World Away
Recording: Excellent stereo. Soundboard.
Source: Pirate off following single sources. Tracks 1-3 Supersonic. Tracks 4-6 Shakermaker. Tracks 7-9 Live Forever. Tracks 1-12 Cigarettes & Alcohol. Tracks 13-15 Whatever.
Comments: Time 73:13.

CD - DEFINITIVE TOO
HISPANOLO RECORDS HISP 041
*Some Might Say (6:41)/ **Supersonic (3:05)/ **Married With Children (2:52)/ ^Rock 'N' Roll Stars (4:35)/ ^Shakermaker (4:48)/ ^Bring It On Down (4:09)/ ^Up In The Sky (4:17)/ ^Slide Away (5:57)/ ^Cigarettes And Alcohol (3:57)/ ^Sad Song (Acoustic) (4:36)/ *^What Ever (4:18)/ ^^Digsey's Diner (2:31)/ ^^Supersonic (3:10)/ #Acquiesce (3:50)/ #It's Good To Be Free (3:21)/ #Talk Tonight (With Paul Weller) (3:54)
Recording: Excellent stereo. Soundboard.
Source: *Unreleased long demo sung by Noel 1995 (FM Stereo). **Acoustic live on Mark Lamarr Show, May 3 1994 (FM Stereo). ^Live at Wolverhampton Civic Hall December 11 1994 (FM Stereo). ^^Acoustic live on GLR April 27 1994 (FM Stereo). #Live On The White Room April 17 1995 (Nicam Stereo). Mark Lamarr Show May 3 1994. Wolverhampton December 11 1994.
Comment: Picture CD.

CD - DUE NORTH
NOEL96
Cast No Shadow/ Don't Look Back In Anger/ Wonder Wall/ Don't Look Back In Anger/ You've Got To Hide Your Love Away/ Don't Look Back In Anger/ Boneheads Bank Holiday/ Fade Away/ Some Might Say/ Shakermaker/ Slide Away/ Morning Glory/ Cigarettes And Alcohol/ Don't Look Back In Anger/ I Am The Walrus
Recording: Excellent stereo. Soundboard.
Source: Tracks 1-2 Simon Mayo, Radio 1 November 3 '95. Tracks 3-5 Gary Crowley, GLR November 2 '95. Track 6 XFM session November 29 '95. Track 7 from vinyl. Track 8 Warchild album. Tracks 9-15 Glastonbury Festival June 23 '95.
Comments: European CD. Deluxe color cover. Time 65:54.

CD - THE GREAT ALTERNATIVE ALBUM
Hello (Denmark June 30 1995)/ Cigarettes & Alcohol (Denmark June 30 1995)/ It's Good To Be Free (Denmark June 30 1995)/ Morning Glory (Denmark June 30 1995)/ Acquiesce (The White Room April 17 1995)/ Married With Children (Maida Vale Studios, The Evening Session December 15 1994)/ Whatever (Maida Vale Studios orchestrated version)/ I Am The Walrus (orchestrated version, recorded with Jools Holland December 10 1994)/ Shakermaker (La Cigale, Paris November 3 1994)/ Fade Away (Paris, Top Live November 2 1994)/ Some Might Say (unissued long demo version sung by Noel, recorded 1996)/ Wonderwall (Noel on vocals and acoustic guitar Rome February 1996)/ Don't Look Back In Anger (acoustic radio session, Noel on vocals and acoustic guitar London October 1995)/ You've Got To Hide Your Love Away (acoustic radio session, Noel on

OASIS

vocals and acoustic guitar London October 1995)/ Talk Tonight (live duet with Paul Weller on The White Room)/ See The Sun (previously unreleased early demo 1992)/ Colour My Life (previously unreleased early demo 1992)/ Take Me (previously unreleased early demo 1992)/ Must Be The Music (previously unreleased early demo 1992)/ Conversation Piece
Comment: Picture disc. Time 79:44.

CD - FIRST FOOTING 96
NEDW96
You've Got To Hide Your Love Away/ Cum On Feel The Noize/ Wonderwall/ Up In The Sky/ Come Together/ Feel The Noize/ Don't Look Back In Anger/ Wonderwall/ Roll With It/ Good To Be Free/ Talk Tonight/ Boneheads Bankholiday/ Live Forever/ Bring It On Down/ Fade Away/ Wibbling Rivalry
Recording: Excellent stereo. Soundboard. Some very good mono.
Source: Track 1 Radio 1 November 30 1995. Tracks 2-4 Jools Holland December 1 1995. Track 5 different mix. Track 6 promo. Tracks 7-9 White Room, New Years Eve/Day 1995-1996. Tracks 10-11 White Room, April 14 1995. Track 12 different mix. Tracks 13-14 May 6 1995. Track 15 different mix. Track 16 NME Interview.
Comments: European CD. Deluxe color cover. Picture CD. Time 73:45.

CD - LISTEN UP
KISS THE STONE KTS 536
Rock And Roll Star/ Columbia/ Fade Away/ Digsy's Diner/ Listen Up/ Shaker Maker/ Live Forever/ Up In The Sky/ Bring It On Down/ Good To Be Free/ Married With Children/ Supersonic/ Slide Away
Recording: Excellent. Soundboard.
Source: The Commodore Ballroom, Vancouver, Canada February 25 1995.
Comments: European CD. Deluxe color cover. Picture CD. Time 56:54.

CD - LIVE AT EARLS COURT 1995
FORBIDDEN FRUIT FFCD 017
Acquiesce/ Supersonic/ Hello/ Some Might Say/ Shaker/ Roll With It/ Round Our Way, Up In The Sky/ Cigarettes And Alcohol/ Live Forever/ Champagne Supernova/ Wonderwall/ Cast No Shadow/ Morning Glory/ Don't Look Back In Anger/ Whatever/ I Am The Walrus (With The Bootleg Beatles)
Recording: Good stereo. Audience.
Source: Earls Court, London November 5 1995.
Comment: Picture CD. Time 74:01.

CD - LIVE AT THE WHISKEY
TOTONKA
Rock 'N' Roll Star/ Columbia/ Fade Away/ Digsy's Diner/ Shakermaker/ Live Forever/ Bring It On Down/ Up In The Sky/ Slide Away/ Cigarettes & Alcohol/ Married With Children/ Supersonic/ I Am The Walrus
Recording: Excellent stereo. Audience. Tape hiss.
Source: The Whiskey A Go Go September 29 1994.
Comment: Claims to be soundboard but it's audience. Time 64:21.

CD - LIVE FROM THE SKY
MOONRAKER 173
Intro/ Columbia/ Acquiesce/ Supersonic/ Roll With It/ Slide Away/ Morning Glory/ Round Are Way/ Up In The Sky/Cigarettes And Alcohol/ Whatever/ Cast No Shadow/ Wonderwall/ The Masterplan/ Don't Look Back In Anger/ Live Forever/ Champagne Supernova/ I Am The Walrus
Recording: Excellent. Soundboard.
Source: Knebworth, England August 11 1996.
Comments: European CD. Deluxe color cover. Picture CD. Time 79:59.

CD - THE LOST TAPES
KISS THE STONE KTS 561
See The Sun*/ Must Be The Music*/ Better Let You Know*/ Snakebite*/ Rock 'N' Roll Star/ Strange Thing*/ Bring It On Down/ Fade Away/ Columbia/ Cloudburst/ Take Me*/ Must Be The Music*/ Life In Vain*/ I Will Show You*/ Better Let You Know*/ Take Me*/ Color My Life*
Recording: Excellent stereo. Soundboard.
Source: Tracks 1-4 Manchester demos 1992. Tracks 5-10 Liverpool demos 1993. Tracks 11-15 live Manchester 1992. Tracks 16-17 Stockport demos 1992. *Previously unreleased.
Comments: European CD. Deluxe B&w cover. Picture CD. Time 73:25.

CD - MADE IN AMERICA
KISS THE STONE KTS 619
Swamp Song/ Acquiesce/ Hello/ Some

Might Say/ Roll With It/ Shakermaker/ Morning Glory/ Cigarettes And Alcohol/ Champagne Supernova/ Whatever, Octopus' Garden/ Wonderwall/ Slide Away/ Don't Look Back In Anger/ Live Forever/ I Am The Walrus
Recording: Excellent stereo. Soundboard.
Source: Patriot Centre, Fairfax, Virginia July 3 1996.
Comments: European CD.

CD - MAIN ROAD
MA 1N 2N
CD1: Swamp Song (4:32)/ Acquiesce (4:10)/ Supersonic (5:10)/ Hello (5:10)/ Some Might Say (5:36)/ Roll With It (4:32)/ Morning Glory (4:07)/ Round Our Way (4:52)/ Cigarettes And Alcohol (4:36)/ Champagne Supernova (10:28)/ Whatever (False Start) (1:14)/ Whatever, Octopus's Garden (5:27)/ Cast No Shadow (4:24)
CD2: Wonderwall (4:35)/ The Masterplan (5:52)/ Don't Look Back In Anger (4:480/ Live For Ever (4:45)/ I Am The Walrus (11:17)/ Cum On Feel The Noize (5:32)/ Whatever (4:09)/ Live Forever (4:02)/ Supersonic (4:21)
Recording: Excellent stereo. Soundboard.
Source: Manchester April 28 1996.
Comment: Picture CD. Time CD1 62:22. CD2 49:39.

CD - MAINE ROAD FIRST NIGHT
MASTER RECORDING MR 001
Acquiesce/ Supersonic/ Hello/ Some Might Say/ Roll With It/ Morning Glory/ Round Our Way/ Cigarettes And Alcohol/ Champagne Supernova/ Whatever/ Cast No Shadow/ Wonderwall/ Masterplan/ Don't Look Back In Anger/ Live Forever/ Cum On Feel The Noize
Recording: Excellent stereo. Soundboard.
Source: Manchester April 27 1996.
Comment: Picture CD. Time 78:55.

CD - MAINE ROAD SECOND NIGHT
MASTER RECORDING MR 002
Swamp Song/ Acquiesce/ Supersonic/ Hello/ Some Might Say/ Morning Glory/ Round Are Way/ Champagne Supernova/ Whatever/ Cast No Shadow/ Wonderwall/ Masterplan/ Don't Look Back In Anger/ I Am The Walrus
Recording: Excellent stereo. Soundboard.
Source: Manchester April 27 1996.
Comment: Picture CD. Time 75:30.

CD - NEW YORK CITY
VULGARTONE VU400
Rock 'N' Roll Star/ Columbia/ Fade Away/ Digsy's Dinner/ Shakermaker/ Live Forever/ Bring It On Down/ Up In The Sky/ Slide Away/ Cigarettes & Alcohol/ Married With Children/ Supersonic/ I Am The Walrus/ Rock 'N' Roll Star (Encore)
Recording: Excellent stereo. Soundboard.
Source: Wetlands, New York City October 24 1994.
Comments: European CD. Deluxe color cover. Picture CD. Time 75:01.

CD - THE NON-ALBUM TRACKS
OASIS OACD001
It's Good To Be Free (4:16)/ Half The World Away (4:22)/ Talk Tonite (4:22)/ Acquiesce (4:25)/ Headshrinker (4:38)/ It's Better People (4:00)/ Rockin' Chair (4:36)/ Live Forever (live) (4:40)/ Round Are Way (5:43)/ The Swamp Song (4:23)/ The Masterplan (5:17)/ Step Out (4:41)/ Underneath The Sky (3:22)/ Cum On Feel The Noize (5:08)/ Fade Away (re-recorded version) (4:11)/ Bonehead's Bank Holiday (3:56)
Recording: Excellent stereo. Soundboard.
Source: Tracks 1-2 from 'Whatever' CD single. Tracks 3-5 from 'Some Might Say' CD single. Tracks 6-8 from 'Roll With It' CD single. Tracks 9-11 from 'Wonderwall' CD single. Tracks 12-14 from 'Don't Look Back In Anger' CD single. Track 15 from 'Help' LP. Track 16 from The vinyl-only version of 'Morning Glory' LP.
Comments: European CD. Deluxe color cover.

CD - ODE TO THE WALRUS
FLASHBACK 03.96.0269
Rock 'N' Roll Star (5:16)/ Columbia (5:11)/ Fade Away (4:14)/ Digsy's Diner (2:21)/ Shakermaker (4:45)/ Live Forever (4:15)/ Bring It Down (4:56)/ Up In The Sky (4:55)/ Slide Away (6:30)/ Cigarettes + Alcohol (4:35)/ Married With Children (3:04)/ Supersonic (5:29)/ I'm A Walrus (9:22)
Recording: Excellent stereo. Soundboard.
Source: Cabaret Metro, Chicago October 15 1994.
Comments: European CD. Deluxe color cover.

OASIS

CD - ORPHEUM
MOONRAKER 052
The Swamp Song/ Acquiesce/ Supersonic/ Hello/ Roll With It/ Shakermaker/ Some Might Say/ Slide Away/ Cigarettes And Alcohol/ Champagne Supernova/ Wonderwall/ Cast No Shadow/ Morning Glory/ Don't Look Back In Anger/ Live Forever
Recording: Excellent stereo. Soundboard.
Source: The Orpheum, Boston October 14 1995.
Comments: European CD. Deluxe color cover. Time 77:08.

CD - POP UP IN BARCELONA
The Swamp Song/ Acquiesce/ Supersonic/ Hello/ Some Might Say/ Roll With It/ Shakermaker/ Morning Glory/ Cigarettes & Alcohol/ Champagne Supernova/ Take Me Away/ Whatever, Octopus' Garden/ Wonderwall/ Don't Look Back In Anger/ Live Forever/ I Am The Walrus
Recording: Very good stereo.
Source: Said Zeleste, Barcelona, Spain April 2 1996.
Comment: Picture CD. Time 74:04.

CD - RADIO SUPERNOVA
MOONRAKER 082
The Swamp Song/ Acquiesce/ Supersonic/ Hello/ Some Might Say/ Roll With It/ Slide Away/ (It's Good) To Be Free/ Morning Glory/ Cigarettes And Alcohol/ Don't Look Back In Anger/ Live Forever/ Rock 'N' Roll Star
Recording: Excellent. Soundboard.
Source: Glastonbury Festival, England, June 23 1995.

CD - RAGS TO RICHES
VULGARTONE VU 100
Rock 'N' Roll Star/ Strange Thing/ Bring It On Down/ Columbia/ Cloudburst/ D'Yer Wanna Be A Spaceman?/ Married With Children/ Whatever/ Live Forever/ Acquiesce/ It's Good To Be Free/ Morning Glory/ Roll With It/ Wonderwall/ Champagne Supernova
Recording: Excellent. Soundboard.
Source: Tracks 1-8 first demo tape recorded at The Real People Studio, Liverpool spring 1993. Tracks 9-10 recorded at Camden Studios, London August 18 1994 - Liam-vocals, Noel-acoustic guitar, Bonehead-keyboards. Tracks 11-12 recorded at White City Studios, London April 17 1995. Track 13 recorded at The Ed Sullivan Theatre, New York City October 19 1995 recorded as a four-piece with Bonehead on bass guitar. Tracks 15-16 The Arena, Seattle, WA December 4 1995.
Comments: European CD. Deluxe color cover. Time 59:57.

CD - ROCK 'N' ROLL
MOONRAKER 141
Rock 'N' Roll Star (5:06)/ Columbia (5:30)/ Fade Away (4:09)/ Digsy's Diner (2:46)/ Shakermaker (5:13)/ Live Forever (5:06)/ Bring It On Down (4:57)/ Up In The Sky (4:57)/ Slide Away (6:23)/ Cigarettes And Alcohol (4:39)/ Married With Children (3:00)/ Supersonic (5:18)/ I Am The Walrus (9:55)
Recording: Excellent stereo. Soundboard.
Source: Cabaret Metro, Chicago October 15 1994.
Comments: European CD. Picture CD.

CD - R & R WITH IT GLASTONBURY
3D REALITY 3D-0A-020
Opening Instrumental/ Some Might Say/ Shakermaker/ Slide Away/ It's Good To Be Free/ New Song/ Cigarettes & Alcohol/ New Song/ I Am The Walrus, Live In Tokyo '94/ Live Forever/ Cigarettes & Alcohol
Recording: Excellent. Soundboard.
Source: Glastonbury Festival June 23 1995.
Comment: Time 52:50.

CD - STEP INTO 1996
KISS THE STONE KTS 555
You've Got To Hide Your Love Away (Radio 1, November 30 1995) (2:10)/ Cum On Feel The Noize (3:46), Wonderwall (3:50), Up In The Sky (Jools Holland January 12 1995) (4:49)/ Come Together (different mix) (3:32)/ Cum On Fell The Noize (promo) (5:11)/ Don't Look Back In Anger (4:15), Wonderwall (3:46), Roll With It (White Room - New Years Eve/Day 1995/96) (3:54)/ Good To Be Free (3:25), Talk Tonight (White Room April 14 1995) (4:07)/ Boneheads Bankholiday (different mix) (3:49)/ Live Forever (4:18), Bring It On Down (live May 6 1995) (4:04)/ Fade Away (different mix) (4:09)/ Sad Song (4:16), Whatever (5:01), I Am The Walrus ('Later Show', London December 10 1994.
Recording: Excellent stereo. Soundboard.

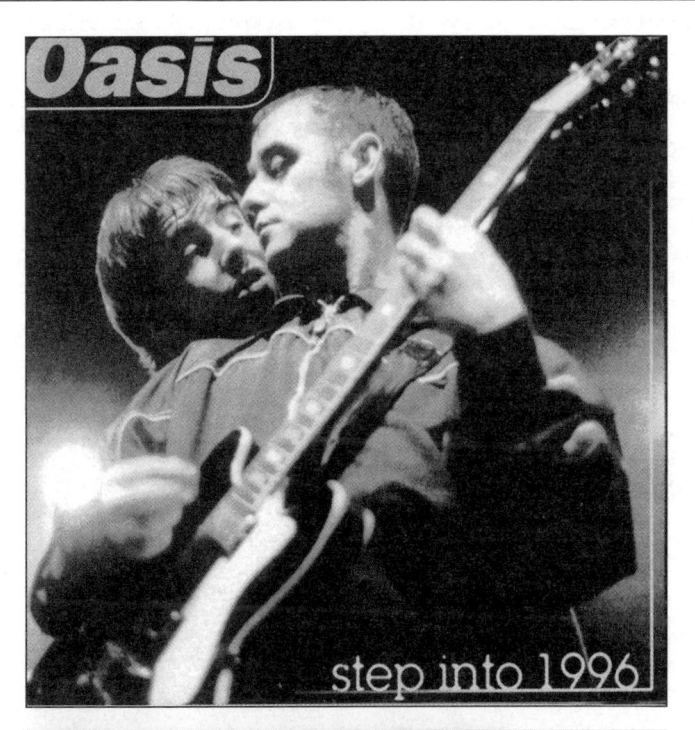

OASIS

OASIS

Comments: European CD. Picture CD. Time 72:23.

CD - TAKE THE HIGH ROAD
LOC 1
Champagne Supernova (7:44)/ I Am The Walrus (6:03)/ The Masterplan (5:04)/ Shakermaker (3:58)/ Whatever, Octopus's Garden (4:25)/ Morning Glory (3:42)/ Cigarettes And Alcohol (4:08)/ Live Forever (4:18)/ Slide Away (5:15)/ Some Might Say (4:53)/ Champagne Supernova (8:30)/ Don't Look Back In Anger (4:27)/ Day Tripper (Bonus: Ocean Colour Scene & Noel & Liam Gallagher, Electric Ballroom, Camden 9/5/96) (3:20)
Recording: Excellent stereo. Soundboard.
Source: Tracks 1-3 Knebworth 10/8/96. Tracks 4-12 Loch Lomond 3/8/96.
Comment: Picture CD.

CD - TAKE THE LOW ROAD
NEB 1
Columbia (5:04)/ Acquiesce (4:01)/ Supersonic (4:39)/ Hello (3:46)/ Some Might Say (5:47)/ Roll With It (4:19)/ Slide Away (6:40)/ Morning Glory (4:11)/ Round Our Way (4:37)/ Cigarettes And Alcohol (4:37)/ Whatever, Octopus's Garden (6:18)/ Cast No Shadow (4:22)/ Wonderwall (4:29)/ The Masterplan (4:35)/ Don't Look Back In Anger (4:50)/ Live Forever (4:44)
Recording: Excellent stereo. Soundboard.
Source: Knebworth 11/8/96.

CD - TARTAN DREAM
KISS THE STONE KTS 613
Champagne Supernova/ I Am The Walrus/ The Masterplan/ Shakermaker/ Whatever, Octopus's Garden/ Morning Glory/ Cigarettes And Alcohol/ Live Forever/ Slide Away/ Some Might Say/ Champagne Supernova/ Don't Look Back In Anger/ Day Tripper
Recording: Excellent stereo. Soundboard.
Source: Knebworth August 10 1996. Loch Lomond, Scotland August 3 1996. Camden, UK May 9 1996.
Comments: European CD.

CD - 250,000 FANS CAN'T BE WRONG
KISS THE STONE KTS 607/08
CD1: Intro/ Columbia/ Acquiesce/ Supersonic/ Hello/ Some Might Say/ Roll With It/ Slide Away/ Morning Glory/ Round Our Way, Up In The Sky/ Cigarettes & Alcohol/ Whatever, Octopus' Garden/ Wonderwall/ The Masterplan
CD2: Don't Look Back In Anger/ Live Forever/ Champagne Supernova/ I Am The Walrus/ Morning Glory/ Supersonic/ Live Forever/ Wonderwall (Acoustic)/ Don't Look Back In Anger/ Champagne Supernova/ My Big Mouth/ It's Getting Better Now
Recording: Excellent stereo. Soundboard. CD2 tracks 11-12 very good to excellent audience.
Source: Knebworth Park, England August 11 1996. CD2 tracks 5-10 Berkeley Community Theatre, Berkeley, CA December 12 1995. CD2 tracks 11-12 Knebworth Park, England August 10 1996. CD2 tracks 3-4 with John Squire from The Stone Roses.
Comments: European CD. Deluxe color cover. Picture CD. Time CD1 64:39. CD2 62:54.

CD - UNPLUGGED
FORBIDDEN FRUIT FFCD 016
Wonderwall (3:07)/ Cast No Shadow (4:22)/ Don't Look Back In Anger (3:58)/ You've Got To Hide Your Love Away (2:13)/ Talk Tonight (4:00)/ Morning Glory (3:19)/ Supersonic (3:05)/ Digsy's Diner (2:38)/ Fade Away (4:09)/ Married With Children (2:56)/ Live Forever (5:14)/ Shaker Maker (4:29)/ Sad Song (4:29)/ Slide Away (5:06)/ Do You Wanna Be A Spaceman (2:56)/ Talk Tonight (4:00)/ Live Forever (4:24)/ Take Me Away (4:25)/ Wonderwall (3:45)
Recording: Excellent stereo. Soundboard.
Source: Acoustic performances recorded for Radio 1's Aids Awareness Day. Tracks 2-3 Simon Mayo Show. Tracks 7, 10 Mark Lamarr. Tracks 11-13 Creation Records birthday party at Albert Hall. Track 19 Later With Jools Holland.
Comment: Picture CD.

CD - UNPLUGGED
MOONRAKER 194
Hello (3:38)/ Some Might Say (4:56)/ Live Forever (4:08)/ The Masterplan (5:04)/ Don't Look Back In Anger (5:03)/ Talk Tonight (4:37)/ Morning Glory (3:39)/ Round Are Way, Up In The Sky (5:12)/ Cast No Shadow (4:24)/ Wonderwall (4:36)
Recording: Excellent stereo. Soundboard.
Source: MTV Unplugged, Royal Festival Hall, London August 23 1996.
Comments: European CD. Purple cover.

White text. Picture CD.

CD - WONDERLIVE
MOONRAKER 051
The Swamp Song/ Acquiesce/ Some Might Say/ Cigarettes And Alcohol/ Wonderwall/ Live Forever/ Supersonic/ Hello/ Roll With It/ Whatever/ Champagne Supernova/ Interview (Dutch Radio, February '96)/ Some Might Say (The White Room, UK TV January 1996)
Recording: Excellent stereo. Soundboard.
Source: Utrecht, Holland, January 10 1996.
Comments: European CD. Deluxe color cover. Time 58:01.

OFFSPRING

CD - SMASH IT UP
HODDLE RECORDS HODD4
Bad Habit (4:00)/ We Are One (3:49)/ Killboy Powerhead (2:02)/ Burn It Up (3:27)/ Genocide (3:27)/ Gotta Get Away (4:05)/ Dirty Magic (3:30)/ Kick Him When He's Down (3:15)/ So Alone (1:28)/ It'll Be A Long Time (3:08)/ What Happened To You (4:03)/ Come Out And Play (3:31)/ Get It Right (2:54)/ Nitro (Youth Energy) (2:38)/ Undone (The Sweater Song) (Weezer Tribute) (0:40)/ Longview (Green Day Tribute) (1:16)/ Self Esteem (4:33)/ Smash (4:13)/ Session (2:57)/ Smash It Up (3:06)*
Recording: Good to very good. Audience.
Source: Brussels Luna April 23 '95.
*'Damned' cover, Glastonbury '95.
Comments: European CD. Green cover.

OLDFIELD, MIKE

CD - JUST ONE NIGHT
CANTEBURY DREAM CTD-001/002
CD1: Platinum, Part 1: Airborne, Part 2: Platinum (9:35)/ Conflict (3:27)/ Sheba (3:43)/ Mirage (5:54)/ Tubular Bells Part 2 (11:39)/ Taurus II (25:16)
CD2: Ommadawn Part 1 (21:47)/ Tubular Bells Part 1 (25:51)/ Mount Teide (4:26)/ Orabidoo (7:10)
Source: Shibuya Koukaidou, Tokyo, Japan May 26 1982.
Comments: Japanese CD.

CD - LOST IN SPACE
WISE RECORDS WISE 312
CD1: Tubular Bells (live '73)/ The Orchestral Hergest Ridge Part One (live, Royal Albert Hall, London December 9 1974. Featuring David Bedford as conductor and Steve Hillage on guitar. Taken from 'Space Movie' test pressing which was planned as an official release on a double-album but cancelled)/ Live Orabidoo (first live performance, New York April 8 1982)
CD2: Sentinel/ Dark Star/ Clear Light/ Blue Saloon/ Sun Jammer/ Red Dawn/ The Bell/ Weightless/ The Great Plane/ Sunset Door/ Tattoo/ Altered State/ Maja Gold/ Moonshine
Recording: Very good to excellent. Audience.
Source: CD2 USA 1992.
Comments: B&w cover. Time CD1 68:11. CD2 61:52.

CD - SYMPHONIES IN THE SHADOW
KOBRA RECORDS KRCR 13
Sentinel/ Dark Star/ Clear Light/ Blue Saloon/ Sun Jammer/ Red Dawn/ The Bell/ Finale/ Weightless/ The Great Plane/ Sunset Door/ Tattoo/ Altered State/ Maja Gold/ Moon Shine/ Tubular Bells II/ Dance Of The Daonhe Sidhe/ Passed You By
Recording: Excellent. Track 18 some surface noise.
Source: Tracks 1-15 USA 1992. Track 16 sampler for Nick Campbell Show 1989. Track 17, Mike with Tom Newman 1977 for 'The Faerie Symphony'. Track 18 with Phil Beer 1987.
Comments: European CD. Time 74:45.

CD - TUBULAR BELLS LIVE
MOTB-62573
Tubular Bells Pt. 1 (28:50)/ Tubular Bells Pt. 1 (28:33)
Source: Queen Elizabeth Hall June 25 1973.
Comments: Japanese CD.

OSBORNE, JOAN

CD - FALLING FROM GRACE
MOONRAKER 164
Pensacola (6:26)/ Right Hand Man (4:34)/ Help Me (6:39)/ St. Teresa (4:56)/ Century (4:52)/ Hammerhead (7:59)/ Mind Full Of Worries (3:38)/ Ladder (5:40)/ Let's Just Get Naked (5:55)/ One Of Us (4:51)
Recording: Excellent.
Source: The Phoenix Theatre, Toronto April 11 1996.
Comments: European CD.

OSBOURNE, OZZY

CD - LIVE IN LEICESTER
MIDAS TOUCH 95611
I Don't Know/ Mr. Crowley/ Rock & Roll Rebel/ Bark At The Moon/ Revelation/ Stealaway The Night/ So Tired/ Suicide Solution/ Journey To The Centre Of Eternity/ Flying High Again/ Iron Man/ Crazy Train/ Paranoid
Recording: Good. Soundboard.
Source: Leicester, UK November 10 1983.
Comments: Japanese CD. Deluxe color cover. Time 68:19.

CD - ONE UP THE B-SIDE
OZZY 1
I Don't Want To Change The World/ Mama, I'm Coming Home/ Desire/ Time After Time/ Won't Be Coming Home/ Mrs. J/ Voodoo Dancer/ Aimee/ Living With The Enemy/ Don't Blame Me/ The Whole World's Falling Down/ Party With The Animals/ One Up The B-Side/ Slow Down/ Don't Want To Be Your Hero/ The Liar
Recording: Excellent stereo. Soundboard.
Source: Tracks 1-6 'No More Tears' demo sessions. Tracks 7-9 B-Side from 'See You On The Other Side' 12". Track 10 B-Side from 'Mama, I'm Coming Home' 12". Track 11 B-Side from 'Perry Mason' 12". Track 12 Japanese bonus track from 'No More Tears' Album. Tracks 13-14 B-Side from 'Bark At The Moon' 12". Track 15 secret track from 'Bible Of Ozz'. Track 16 Japanese bonus track from 'No Rest For The Wicked' Album.
Comments: European CD. Deluxe color cover. Picture CD. Time 71:28.

CD - PHOENIX RISING
SBC 002/003
CD1: Flying High Again/ Goodbye To Romance/ Perry Mason/ No More Tears/ I Just Want You/ I Don't Want To Change The World/ Suicide Solution
CD2: Sabbath Bloody Sabbath/ Iron Man/ Sweet Leaf/ Children Of The Grave/ Mr. Crowley/ War Pigs/ Crazy Train/ Mama I'm Coming Home/ Bark At The Moon
Recording: Excellent stereo. Soundboard.
Source: Desert Skies Pavilion, Phoenix, Arizona April 13 1996.
Comments: European CD. Deluxe color cover.

CD - RETIREMENT SUCKS TOUR TOKYO 1996
PORE THE SOUL PRODUCTIONS PTS-032/3
CD1: Introduction/ Paranoid/ I Don't Know/ Flying High Again/ Goodbye To Romance/ Perry Mason/ No More Tears/ I Just Want You
CD2: I Don't Want To Change The World/ Suicide Solution/ Medley: Iron Man, Sweet Leaf, Children/ Mr. Crowley/ War Pigs/ Crazy Train/ Mama, I'm Coming Home/ Bark At The Moon
Source: Budokan, Tokyo March 8 1996.
Comments: Japanese CD.

P

PAGE, JIMMY AND ROY HARPER

CD - HAT OFF TO JIMMY PAGE
FIRE POWER FP-05
Short & Sweet/ Referendum/ Highway Blues/ True Story/ The Game/ Studio Jam
Recording: Good to very good soundboard. Track 6 excellent stereo soundboard.
Source: Tracks 1-5 Jimmy Page & Roy Harper, live in Battersea July 29 1984. Track 6 Jimmy Page, Nomis Studio, London January 21 1984.
Comments: Japanese CD.

PAGE, JIMMY AND ROBERT PLANT

CD - ANOTHER EVENING IN SYDNEY
TWO SYMBOLS TS 014-A/B
CD1: Babe I'm Gonna Leave You/ Celebration Day/ Ramble On/ Heartbreaker/ No Quarter/ The Song Remains The Same/ The Rain Song/ Since I've Been Loving You/ Whole Lotta Love Medley: In The Light, Season Of The Witch, Break On Through, Dazed And Confused
CD2: Nigel Eaton Hurdy Gurdy Solo/ Gallows Pole/ Four Sticks/ Yallah/ In The Evening, Carouselambra/ Dancing Days/ Kashmir/ Thank You/ Black Dog/ Rock And Roll
Recording: Very good to excellent. Audience.
Source: Entertainment Center, Sydney, Australia February 25 1996.
Comments: Japanese CD. Deluxe color

CD - ETERNAL BURNING
MAGNUM 005/6
CD1: Babe I'm Gonna Leave You, Stairway To Heaven/ Ramble On/ Custard Pie/ Heartbreaker/ Wonderful One/ The Song Remains The Same/ The Rain Song/ Celebration Day/ Hurdy Gurdy Solo/ Gallows Pole/ Since I've Been Loving You
CD2: Whole Lotta Love, Going Down, Break On Through, Dazed And Confused/ In The Evening/ Four Sticks/ Kashmir, Encore/ Black Dog/ Rock And Roll
Recording: Excellent. Audience.
Source: February 20 1995.

CD - EVENING CUSTARD
PORE THE SOLE PTS 024/25
CD1: Introduction, Immigrant Song Intro, The Wanton Song, Bring It On Home/ Heartbreaker/ Ramble On/ No Quarter/ Nigel Eaton's Hurdy Gurdy Solo/ Gallows Pole/ Tea For One/ The Song Remains The Same/ Going To California/ That's The Way/ Babe I'm Gonna Leave You (includes Stairway To Heaven Riff-Ending)
CD2: Whole Lotta Love Medley: Bring It On Home, Break On Through (To The Other Side), Dazed And Confused/ Yallah/ Four Sticks/ Kashmir (Encore)/ Custard Pie/ Rock And Roll
Recording: Excellent. Audience.
Source: Budokan, Tokyo February 12 1996.
Comments: Japanese CD.

CD - FIRST NIGHT IN JAPAN 1996
PORE THE SOLE PTS 016/7
CD1: Introduction, Immigrant Song Intro, The Wanton Song, Bring It On Home/ Heartbreaker/ Ramble On/ No Quarter/ Nigel Eaton's Hurdy Gurdy Solo/ Gallows Pole/ Since I've Been Loving You/ The Song Remains The Same/ Going To California/ Babe I'm Gonna Leave You (includes Stairway To Heaven-Riff ending)
CD2: Whole Lotta Love Medley: White Rabbit, Break On Through (To The Other Side), Dazed And Confused/ Yallah/ Four Sticks/ Kashmir (Encore)/ Black Dog/ Rock And Roll
Recording: Very good. Audience.
Source: Budokan, Tokyo, February 5 1996.
Comments: Japanese CD. Deluxe color cover. Time CD1 62:16. CD2 55:54.

cover. Time CD1 68:15. CD2 71:07.

CD - THE FIRST SHOW AT THE FAMOUS OLD BUILDING
REAL DRAGON RD-019/020
CD1: Eastern/ Immigrant Song (Intro), The Wanton Song/ Bring It On Home/ Heartbreaker/ Ramble On, What Is And What Should Never Be Tease/ No Quarter/ Nigel Eaton's Solo (Hurdy-Gurdy)/ Gallows Pole/ Since I've Been Loving You/ The Song Remains The Same/ Going To California/ Babe I'm Gonna Leave You, Stairway To Heaven Tease
CD2: Whole Lotta Love, Jimmy's Theremin Session, White Rabbit, Break On Through, Dazed & Confused, Whole Lotta Love/ Yallah/ Four Sticks/ Kashmir/ Encores: Out On The Tiles (Intro), Black Dog/ Rock And Roll
Source: Budokan Hall, Tokyo, Japan February 5 1996.

CD - THE FOURTH NIGHT LIVE
PORE THE SOUL PTS 022/3
CD1: The Rain Song/ No Quarter/ Babe I'm Gonna Leave You includes Stairway To Heaven/ Immigrant Song intro, The Wanton Song/ Heartbreaker, Ramble On/ Nigel Eaton's Hurdy Gurdy Solo/ Gallows Pole/ Whole Lotta Love Medley: Spoonful, Break On Through (To The Other Side), I Want To Take You Higher, Dazed And Confused/ Tea For One
CD2: Introduction Of Musicians, Dancing Days/ Yallah/ Four Sticks/ In The Evening includes Carouselambra/ Kashmir/ Out On The Tiles intro, Black Dog/ Rock And Roll
Recording: Very good. Audience.
Source: Budokan, Tokyo February 9 '96.
Comments: Japanese CD. B&w cover.
Time CD1 71:11. CD2 57:22.

THE FORTH SHOW AT THE FAMOUS OLD BUILDING
REAL DRAGON RD-021/022
CD1: The Rain Song/ No Quarter/ Babe I'm Gonna Leave You, Stairway To Heaven (Tease)/ Immigrant Song (Intro), The Wanton Song/ Heartbreaker/ Ramble On, What Is And What Should Never Be (Tease)/ Nigel Eaton's Hurdy-Gurdy Solo/ Gallows Pole/ Whole Lotta Love, Jimmy's Theremin Session, Spoonfull, Break On Through, Dazed And Confused, Whole Lotta Love/ Tea For One
CD2: Dancing Days/ Yallah/ Four Sticks/ Egyptian Pharaohs/ In The Evening (includ-

ing Carouselambla)/ Kashmir/ Encores: Out On The Tiles (Intro), Black Dog, In My Time Of Dying (Tease)/ Rock And Roll
Source: Budokan Hall, Tokyo, Japan February 9 1996.

CD - HAPPY SONGS FOR THE PEOPLE OF OSAKA
GENUINE FROG
CD1: Introduction/ Custard Pie/ Bring It On Home/ Heartbreaker/ What Is And What Should Never Be/ Hurdy Gurdy Solo/ Gallows Pole/ Wonderful One/ Going To California/ Ten Years Gone/ Babe, I'm Gonna Leave You/ Whole Lotta Love Medley
CD2: Tea For One/ Friends/ Yallah/ Four Sticks/ Kashmnir/ Black Dog/ Rock And Roll
Recording: Good to very good. Audience.
Source: Castle Hall, Osaka, Japan February 15 1996.
Comments: CDR. Deluxe color cover. Time CD1 70:01. CD2 62:26.

CD - IDAHO DAZE
TWO SYMBOLS TS 009-A/B
CD1: Immigrant Song, Wanton Song/ Bring It On Home/ Ramble On/ Thank You/ No Quarter/ Tangerine/ Hurdy Gurdy Solo/ Gallows Pole/ Since I've Been Loving you/ The Song Remains The Same/ Going To California
CD2: Babe, I'm Gonna Leave You, Stairway To Heaven/ Friends/ Four Sticks/ Whole Lotta Love, Light My Fire, For What It's Worth, Break On Through, Dazed And Confused/ In The Evening, Carouselambra/ Kashmir
Recording: Excellent. Audience.
Source: BSU Pavilion, Boise, Idaho, USA October 9 1995.
Comments: Japanese CD. Deluxe color cover. Time CD1 61:44. CD2 64:18.

CD - LIGHT MY FIRE
SONIC ZOOM SZ 2011/2012
CD1: Tales Of Bron/ Thank You/ Bring It On Home/ Ramble On/ Shake My Tree (includes theramin)/ Lullaby/ No Quarter/ Gallows Pole/ Hurdy-Gurdy solo/ When the Levee Breaks/ Hey Hey What Can I Do/ The Song Remains the Same
CD2: Since I've Been Loving You/ Friends/ Calling To You/ Light My Fire (includes Dazed & Confused)/ Four Sticks/ In the Evening (includes Carouselambra)/ Out On

The Tiles intro/ Black Dog/ Kashmir
Recording: Excellent. Audience.
Source: Market Square Arena, Indianapolis, Indiana April 26 1995
Comments: Time CD1 57:24. CD2 69:17.

CD - LITTLE JIMMY PLAY WITH BAD BOYS
PORE THE SOUL PTS-026/7
CD1: Introduction, Heartbreaker/ Bring It On Home/ Custard Pie/ Ramble On/ Tangerine/ Thank You/ Nigel Eaton's Hurdy Gurdy Solo/ Gallows Pole/ The Rain Song/ The Song Remains The Same/ Tea For One
CD2: Dancing Days/ In The Evening/ Four Sticks/ Kashmir (Encore)/ Celebration Day/ Black Dog/ Rock And Roll
Recording: Excellent. Audience.
Source: Century Hall, Nagoya February 17 1996.
Comments: Japanese CD.

CD - LIVE LEGEND
BLACK MOON PRODUCTS PP BOX-01
LIVE LEGEND CHAPTER ONE
BLACK MOON PRODUCTS PP-001-004
FIRST SHOW
CD1: Eastern Introduction, Immigrant Song Intro, The Wanton Song, Bring It On Home/ Heartbreaker/ Ramble On/ No Quarter/ Nigel Eaton's Hurdy Gurdy Solo/ Gallows Pole/ Since I've Been Loving You/ The Song Remains The Same/ Going To California
CD2: Babe I'm Gonna Leave You (includes Stairway To Heaven-riff ending)/ Whole Lotta Love Medley: White Rabbit, Break On Through (To The Other Side), Dazed And Confused/ Yallah/ Four Sticks/ Kashmir/ Out On The Tiles, Black Dog, In My Time Of Dying/ Rock And Roll
Source: Budokan Hall, Tokyo, February 5 1996.
SECOND SHOW
CD1: Babe I'm Gonna Leave You, Stairway To Heaven/ Bring It On Home/ Heartbreaker/ Thank You/ Gallows Pole/ Hurdy Gurdy Solo/ Nobody's Fault But Mine/ Going To California/ Since I've Been Loving You/ Dancing Days
CD2: Yallah/ Four Sticks/ Egyptian Pharaohs/ In The Evening includes Carouselambra/ Kashmir/ Tangerine/ Whole Lotta Love Medley: In The Light, Break On Through To The Other Side, Dazed And

Confused/ Rock And Roll
Source: Budokan Hall, Tokyo February 6 1996.
LIVE LEGEND CHAPTER TWO
BLACK MOON PRODUCTS PP-005-008
THIRD SHOW
CD1: Eastern Introduction, Celebration Day, Bring It On Home, Heartbreaker/ What Is And What Should Never Be/ The Rain Song (take 1 and 2)/ Hurdy Gurdy Solo/ When The Levee Breaks/ Gallows Pole/ Tea For One/ The Song Remains The Same/ Babe I'm Gonna Leave You, Stairway To Heaven
CD2: Whole Lotta Love Medley: Down By The Seaside, Break On Through (To The Other Side), Dazed And Confused/ Yallah (incomplete)/ Egyptian Pharaohs/ In The Evening includes Carouselambra Four Sticks/ Kashmir/ Black Dog, In My Time Of Dying/ Rock And Roll
Source: Budokan Hall, Tokyo February 8 1996.
FOURTH SHOW
CD1: The Rain Song/ No Quarter/ Babe I'm Gonna Leave You, Stairway To Heaven/ Immigrant Song, The Wanton Song/ Heartbreaker, Ramble On/ Hurdy Gurdy Solo/ Gallows Pole/ Whole Lotta Love Medley: Spoonful, Break On Through (To The Other Side), I Want To Take You Higher, Dazed And Confused
CD2: Tea For One/ Dancing Days/ Yallah/ Four Sticks/ Egyptian Pharaohs/ In The Evening includes Carouselambra/ Kashmir/ Out On The Tiles, In My Time Of Dying/ Rock And Roll
Source: Budokan Hall, Tokyo February 9 1996.
LIVE LEGEND CHAPTER THREE
BLACK MOON PRODUCTS PP-009-012
FIFTH SHOW
CD1: Eastern Introduction, Immigrant Song, The Wanton Song/ Bring It On Home/ Heartbreaker/ Ramble On/ No Quarter/ Hurdy Gurdy Solo/ Gallows Pole/ Tea For One/ The Song Remains The Same
CD2: Going To California/ That's The Way/ Babe I'm Gonna Leave You, Stairway To Heaven/ Whole Lotta Love Medley: Bring It On Home, Break On Through (To The Other Side), Dazed And Confused/ Yallah/ Four Sticks/ Kashmir// Rock And Roll
Source: Budokan Hall, Tokyo February12 1996.

SIXTH SHOW
CD1: Thank You/ Custard Pie/ Out On The Tiles, Black Dog, In My Time Of Dying/ Tangerine/ Hurdy Gurdy Solo/ Gallows Pole/ Tea For One/ The Song Remains The Same/ Going To California
CD2: Babe I'm Gonna Leave You, Stairway To Heaven/ Whole Lotta Love (includes I'm A King Bee, Break On Through, Dazed And Confused/ Friends)/ Yallar/ Four Sticks/ Kashmir
Source: Budokan Hall, Tokyo February13 1996.
LIVE LEGEND CHAPTER FOUR
BLACK MOON PRODUCTS PP-013-016
SEVENTH SHOW
CD1: Eastern Introduction/ Custard Pie/ Bring It On Home/ Heartbreaker/ What Is And What Should Never Be/ Hurdy Gurdy Solo/ Gallows Pole/ Wonderful One/ Going To California/ Ten Years Gone/ Babe I'm Gonna Leave You, Stairway To Heaven
CD2: Whole Lotta Love Medley: Whole Lotta Love Medley: You Shook Me, Break On Through (To The Other Side), Dazed And Confused/ Tea For One/ Friends/ Yallah/ Four Sticks/ Kashmnir/ Out On The Tiles, Black Dog, In My Time Of Dying/ Rock And Roll
Source: Castle Hall, Osaka February 15 1996.
EIGHTH SHOW
CD1: Eastern Introduction, Heartbreaker/ Bring It On Home/ Custard Pie/ Ramble On/ Tangerine/ Thank You/ Hurdy Gurdy Solo/ Gallows Pole/ The Rain Song/ The Song Remains The Same/ Tea For One
CD2: Dancing Days/ Egyptian Pharaohs/ In The Evening includes Carouselambra/ Four Sticks/ Kashmir// Celebration Day/ Black Dog, In My Time Of Dying/ Rock And Roll
Source: Century Hall, Nagoya February 17 1996.
LIVE LEGEND CHAPTER FIVE
BLACK MOON PRODUCTS PP-017-020
NINETH SHOW
CD1: Eastern Introduction/ Celebration Day/ Bring It On Home, Heartbreaker/ What Is And What Should Never Be/ Tangerine/ Thank You/ Hurdy Gurdy Solo/ Gallows Pole/ Nobody's Fault But Mine/ The Song Remains The Same/ Since I've Been Loving You
CD2: Whole Lotta Love Medley: It's All Over Now, Break On Through (To The Other Side), Dazed And Confused/

Egyptian Pharaohs/ In The Evening includes Carouselambra/ Four Sticks/ Kashmir/ Can You Feel It, Black Dog, In My Time Of Dying/ Rock And Roll
Source: Castle Hall, Osaka February 19 1996.
TENTH SHOW
CD1: Babe I Gonna Leave You, Stairway To Heaven/ Ramble On/ Custard Pie/ Heartbreaker/ Wonderful One/ The Song Remains The Same/ Rain Song/ Celebration Day/ Hurdy Gurdy Solo/ Gallows Pole/ Since I've Been Loving You
CD2: Whole Lotta Love (includes Baby Let Me Follow You Down, Going Down, Break On Through, Dazed And Confused)/ Egyptian Pharaohs/ In The Evening (includes Carouselambra)/ Four Sticks/ Kashmir/ Encore: Out On The Tiles, Black Dog, In My Time Of Dying/ Rock And Roll
Source: Marine Messe Hall, Fukuoka February 20 1996.
Recording: Good to very good. Audience.
Source: Milan, Italy June 10 1995.
Comments: Japanese limited edition numbered box set. Pictures from gigs on covers of CDs. Spines of cases form P/P logo.

CD - NO QUARTER-FANTASTIC NIGHT IN JUDO ARENA
OIRAN AMP2 5001
CD1: Babe I'm Gonna Leave You/ Bring It On Home/ Heartbreaker/ Thank You/ Gallows Pole/ Nigel Eaton's Hurdy Gurdy Solo/ Nobody's Fault But Mine/ Going To California/ Since I've Been Loving You/ Dancing Days/ Yallah/ Four Sticks
CD2: In The Evening includes Carouselambra/ Kashmir/ Tangerine/ Whole Lotta Love Medley: In The Night, Break On Through To The Other Side, Dazed And Confused/ Rock And Roll/ No Quarter/ Black Dog
Recording: Excellent. Audience.
Source: Nippon Budokan Hall, Tokyo February 6 1996. CD2 tracks 6-87 February 5 1996.
Comments: Japanese CD. Deluxe color cover. Picture CD.
Time CD1 65:21. CD2 62:40.

CD - THANK YOU
KIKO OVERUN CO. LTD
CD1: Yallah (only the last minute)/ Bring It On Home/ Celebration Day/ Dancing Days (only the first minute)/ Gallows Pole (only 2 minutes)/ Hurdy Gurdy solo/ Nobody's Fault But Mine (only the first 2 1/2 minutes) Plant dialogue/ Friends (contains a slight dropout),
Ramble On*/ Thank You*/ Hey Hey What Can I Do*/ Four Sticks*/ In the Evening (includes Carouselambra)*
CD2: Since I've Been Loving You (several takes including a great solo by Jimmy, chat, teaching orchestra, no vocals)/ Bring It On Home (no vocals)**/ Celebration Day (no vocals)**/ Dancing Days (no vocals)**/ Robert Plant interview (not broadcast)**
Recording: Excellent stereo. Soundboard.
Source: CD1 Civic Arena, Pensacola, Florida February 26 1995. *The Palace of Auburn Hills, Auburn Hills, Michigan April 1 1995. CD2 Pensacola, Florida February 26 1995 soundcheck. **Pensacola, Florida February 26, 1995 dress rehearsal.
Comments: Japanese CD.
Time CD1 50:03. CD2 46:21.

CD - TOUR OVER EUROPE
TWO SYMBOLS TS 008-A/B
CD1: Wanton Song/ Bring It On Home, Heartbreaker, Black Dog/ Thank You/ No Quarter/ Gallows Pole/ Yallah/ Since I've Been Loving You
CD2: The Song Remains The Same/ Calling To You, When The Levee Breaks, Break On Through, Dazed And Confused/ Dancing Days/ four Sticks/ In The Evening, Carouselambra
Recording: Good. Audience.
Source: Milan, Italy June 10 1995.
Comments: Japanese CD. Deluxe color cover. Time CD1 42:15. CD2 42:05.

CD - TWO SWANS ON A CENTURY LAKE
REAL DRAGON RD-031/32/33/34
CD1: Eastern/ Heartbreaker/ Bring It On Home/ Custard Pie/ Ramble On/ What Is And What Should Never Be (Tease)/ Tangerine/ Thank You/ Nigel Hurdy-Gurdy Solo/ Gallows Pole/ The Rain Song/ The Song Remains The Same/ Tea For One
CD2: Dancing Days/ Egyptian Pharaohs/ In The Evening (Including Caraselambra)/ Four Sticks/ Kashmir/ Encore Source: Celebration Day/ Black Dog, In My Time Of Dying (Tease)/ Rock And Roll
CD3: (Budokan, Tokyo February 5) Eastern/ Immigration Song (Intro)/ The Wanton Song/ Bring It On Home (Tease)/

PAGE, JIMMY AND ROBERT PLANT

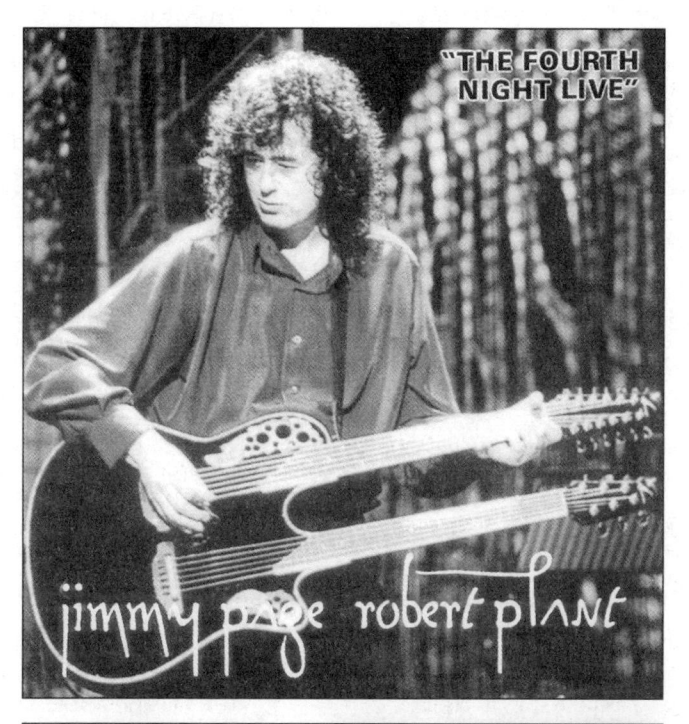

PAGE, JIMMY AND ROBERT PLANT

Heartbreaker/ Ramble On, What Is And What Should Never Be/ (Osaka-Jo Hall, Osaka Feb. 19) What Is And What Should Never Be/ (Budokan, Tokyo February 9) No Quarter/ (Budokan, Tokyo February 13) Going To California/ (Budokan, Tokyo February 12) That's The Way/ Babe I'm Gonna Leave You/ Stairway To Heaven (Tease)/ (Budokan, Tokyo February 6) Nigel Eaton's Hurdy-Gurdy Solo/ Nobody's Fault But Mine/ (Marine Messe Fukuoka, Fukuoka February 20) Wonderful One/ (Budokan, Tokyo February 13) Yallah
CD4: Friends/ Since I've Been Loving You/ (Osaka-Jo Hall, Osaka February 15) Ten Years Gone/ Whole Lotta Love/ Jimmy's Theremin Session/ In The Light/ Break On Through/ Dazed And Confused/ (Budokan, Tokyo February 6) Whole Lotta Love/ (Budokan, Tokyo February 8) Bonus: The Rain Song (intro), The Rain Song/ Nigel Eaton's Hurdy-Gurdy Solo/ When The Levee Breaks/ Tea For One (intro), Tea For One/ Yallah (incomplete version)
Recording: Excellent. Audience.
Source: CD1-2 Shirotori Century Hall, Nagoya, Japan February 17 1996.
Comments: Japanese CD. Deluxe color cover. Time CD1 64:57. CD2 60:09. CD3 66:12. CD4 71:19.

CD - WELCOME TO THE REHEARSALS
PORE THE SOUL PTS 020/1
CD1: Introduction, Celebration Day, Bring It On Home, Heartbreaker/ What Is And What Should Never Be/ The Rain Song (take 1 And 2)/ Nigel Eaton's Hurdy Gurdy Solo/ When The Levee Breaks/ Gallows Pole/ Tea For One/ The Song Remains The Same/ Babe I'm Gonna Leave You includes Stairway To Heaven
CD2: Whole Lotta Love Medley: Down By The Seaside, Break On Through (To The Other Side), Dazed And Confused/ Yallah (false version)/ Four Sticks/ Kashmir/ Black Dog/ Rock And Roll
Recording: Good to very good. Audience.
Source: Budokan, Tokyo February 8 1996.
Comments: Japanese CD. Deluxe color cover. Time CD1 67:30. CD2 66:06.

PANTERA

CD - NOIZE, BOOZE AND TATTOOS
KISS THE STONE KTS 485
A New Level/ Use My Third Arm/ Walk/ Strength Beyond Strength/ Slaughtered/ Domination, Hollow/ Becoming/ Five Minutes Alone/ This Love/ Mouth For War/ Primal Concrete Sledge/ Planet Caravan/ Cowboys From Hell
Recording: Excellent stereo. Soundboard.
Source: From 1995 World Tour.
Comments: European CD. Deluxe color cover. Picture CD. Time 68:05.

CD - UNSCARRED
SPIDER RECORDS 17
Suicide Note 1/ Suicide Note 2/ War Nerve/ New Level/ Walk/ Mouth For War/ Becoming/ Five Minutes Alone/ Sandblasted Skin/ Domination, Hollow Medley/ Phils Rant #1/ This Love/ Phils Rant #2 (Space Cowboy, Tales From The Hardside)/ Fucking Hostile/ Planet Caravan/ Cowboys From Hell (Cat Scratch Fever Mix)
Recording: Good to very good. Audience.
Source: Music Hall, Austin, TX Dec. 5 '96.
Comments: European CD. Deluxe color cover. Time 69:53.

PARSONS, GRAM AND THE FALLEN ANGELS

CD - YOURS TRULY, ANONYMOUS
COLOSSEUM 97-C-017
Buckaroo/ Still Feeling Blue/ That's All It Took/ California Cottenfields/ Cry One More Time/ A Song For You/ If You Don't Love Him/ Hang On Sloopy/ Baby What Do You Want Me To Do, Forty Days, Almost Grown/ If You Gotta Go, Go Now/ Do Right Woman/ You're Still On My Mind/ Lazy Days/ Close Up The Honky Tonk Woman/ Sing Me Back Home/ You Don't Miss Water/ You Don't Miss Water/ Hickory Wind/ The Christian Life/ Close Up the Honky Tonk Woman With The Sin City Crew
Recording: Good to very good. Audience. Track 16 very good soundboard. Tracks 17-19 Poor to fair.
Source: Tracks 1-9 Max's Kansas City, New York with The Fallen Angels March 9 '73. Tracks 10-15 Troubadour, Los Angeles '70. Track 16 studio demo with Fred Neil. Tracks 17-19 Piper Club, Roma with Byrds. Track 20 Armadillo World Headquarters, Austin, TX with Neil Young and Linda Ronstadt.

PEARL JAM

CD - ACT OF LOVE
KOBRA RECORDS KRCD 16/2
CD1: Long Road/ Last Exit/ Animal/ Hail Hail/ Don't Go/ Red Mosquito/ In My Tree/ Corduroy/ Betterman/ Lukin/ Mankind/ Hungry/ Even Flow/ Daughter/ Jeremy/ Sometimes/ Rearview Mirror/ Immortality/ Alive
CD2: Blood/ Who You Are/ State Of Love And Trust/ Not For You/ Present Tense/ Leaving Here/ Yellow Lead Better/ History Never Repeat/ Swallow My Pride/ Lukin/ I Got I.D./ Big Green Country/ Powder Finger/ Downtown/ Act Of Love
Source: CD1 and CD2 tracks 1-7 Berlin 1996. Tracks 8-10 tour 1995. Tracks 11-15 with Neil Young.
Comments: European CD.

CD - BLANK
KISS THE STONE KTS 639/40
CD1: Long Road/ Last Exit/ Animal/ Hail Hail/ Go/ Red Mosquito/ In My Tree/ Corduroy/ Better Man/ Lukin/ Mankind/ Goin' Hungry/ Even Flow/ Daughter/ Jeremy/ Sometimes/ Rearview Mirror
CD2: Immortality/ Alive/ Blood/ Who Are You/ State Of Love And Trust/ Not For You/ Present Tense/ Leaving Here/ Yellow Ledbetter/ Sonic Reducer/ History Never Repeats/ Swallow My Pride/ So You Wanna Be A Rock 'N Roll Star/ Needle And The Damage Done
Recording: Excellent stereo. Soundboard.
Source: CD1 and CD2 tracks 1-9 Deutchland Halle, Berlin, Germany November 3 1996. CD2 track 10 USA 1995. CD2 track 11 Auckland, New Zealand 1995. CD2 track 12 USA 1995. CD2 track 13 San Jose State University November 4 1995. CD2 track 14 Sydney Entertainment Center March 10 1995.
Comments: European CD. Deluxe color cover. Picture CD. Time 02:04:42.

CD - CHECKPOINT CHARLIE
MOONRAKER 203/4
CD1: Long Road/ Last Exit/ Animal/ Hail Hail/ Go/ Red Mosquito/ In My Tree/ Corduroy/ Better Man/ Hunger Strike/ Even Flow/ Daughter/ Jeremy/ Sometimes
CD2: Rearview Mirror/ Immortality/ Alive/ Blood, Fame, Suck You Dry/ Who Are You/ State Of Love And Trust/ Not For You/ Present Tense/ Leaving Here/ Yellow Ledbetter
Recording: Excellent stereo. Soundboard.
Source: The Deutschlandhalle, Berlin, Germany November 3 1996.
Comments: European CD.

CD - CIRCLES
TORNADO TOR070
Release/ Last Exit/ Spin The Black Circle/ Animal/ Tremor Christ/ Corduroy/ Whipping/ Not For You/ Small Town/ Why Go/ Jeremy/ Go/ Dissident/ Satan's Bed/ Daughter, Loser/ Even Flow
Recording: Excellent. Audience.
Source: Pan American Center, Las Cruces, NM, USA September 14 1995.
Comments: European CD. Deluxe color cover. Time 72:33.

CD - THE DELTA TAPES
KISS THE STONE KTS 604/05
CD1: Go/ Animal/ Last Exit/ Spin The Black Circle/ Tremor Christ/ Corduroy/ Not For You/ Luckin'/ It's Been Seven Years Tonight/ Elderly Woman Behind The Counter In A Small Town/ Deep/ Dissident/ Daughter, Pull Me Up/ Even Flow/ Rearviewmirror/ I Got I.D./ Whipping
CD2: Immortality/ Alive/ Black/ Blood/ Red Mosquito/ Betterman/ Leaving Here/ Footsteps/ Glorified G/ Jeremy/ Brain JFK/ State Of Love And Trust/ Porch/ Sonic Reducer
Recording: Excellent.
Source: Delta Center, Salt Lake City, Utah. CD1 tracks 1-17 and CD2 1-8 November 1 1995. CD2 tracks 9-14 November 2 1995.
Comments: European CD. Deluxe color cover. Time CD1 71:36. CD2 71:13.

CD - DOGS SAT PLAY
HURRICANE HURR019/20
CD1: Animal/ Satan's Bed/ Tremor Christ/ Even Flow/ Corduroy/ E.W.B.T.C.I.A.S.T./ Whipping/ Not For You/ Why Go/ Deep/ Jeremy/ Dissident/ Daughter, You Pull Me Up/ Rats/ Habit (soundcheck)
CD2: Chop It Down (M. McCready vocals)/ Immortal/ Rearviewmirror/ Alive/ Blood/ Better Man/ Sonic Reducer (with Joey Ramone)/ Rockin In The Free World/

PEARL JAM

Yellow Ledbetter/ Instrumental soundcheck/ Long Way Home (soundcheck)/ Soundcheck conclusion
Recording: Excellent. Audience.
Source: Tad Gormley Stadium, New Orleans September 17 1995.
Comments: European CD. Orange/white cover. Black type. Picture CD.

CD - DOWN THE ROAD
TORNADO TOR061/62
CD1: Go/ Animal/ Last Exit/ Spin The Black Circle/ Tremor Christ/ Corduroy/ Lukin'/ E.W.B.T.C.I.A.S.T./ Whipping/ Dissident/ Glorified G/ Daughter/ Habit/ Improv Jam/ Rearviewmirror/ Immortality
CD2: Alive/ Black/ Blood/ Not For You/ Hold The Line/ Better Man/ Open Road/ Porch/ Yellow Ledbetter
Recording: Very good. Audience.
Source: Phoenix, Arizona, September 13 1995.
Comments: European CD. Deluxe color cover. Picture CD.

CD - FREE LAND
KOBRA RECORDS KRCR 12
I've Got A Feeling (live '92)/ Black/ State/ Even Flow/ Rockin' In The Free World (USA Radio Show 11/05/92)/ Piece Of Crap (Eddie Vedder, Ministry demo)/ Lay Lady Lay (Pearl Jam and Neil Young demo)/ Alive (Europe '92)/ Jeremy (Europe '92)/ Daughter (including 'Another Brick On The Wall' Europe '92)/ Animal (USA '93)/ Mosquito (Salt Lake City '95)/ Little Wing (Salt Lake City '95)/ Sonic Reducer (Joey Ramone on vocals, '95)/ Leaving Here (Eddie Vedder solo live '95)
Recording: Excellent.
Comments: European CD. Deluxe color cover. Time 77:46.

CD - IN THE LAND OF THE RISING SUN
TORNADO RECORDS TORO068/69
CD1: Release/ Go/ Last Exit/ Tremor Christ/ Corduroy/ Lukin/ Even Flow/ Glorified G/ Daughter, Nonsense/ Alive/ I Got Shit/ Whippin'/ Jeremy/ Animal/ Blood
CD2: I'll Kick Your Ass/ Porch, Catholic Boys/ Satan's Bed/ Spin The Black Circle/ Sonic Reducer/ Footsteps/ Rearviewmirror/ Indifference/ Act Of Love/ W.M.A., Drum Solo/ Immortality/ Jam, My Presence/ Yellow Ledbetter
Recording: Very good. Audience.
Source: CD1 and CD2 tracks 1-8 Osaka, Japan February 21 1995. CD2 tracks 9-10 Sendai, Japan February 18 1995. CD2 tracks 11-13 Tokyo, Japan February 20 1995.

CD - LAST AMERICAN HEROES
METEOR FM 1101/2
CD1: Rearviewmirror/ Don't Need/ Go/ Animal/ Dissident/ Even Flow/ Glorified G/ Daughter/ Why Go Jeremy/ None
CD2: Garden/ Footsteps/ State Of Love And Trust/ Already In Love/ Blood/ This Notes For You/ Elderly Woman Behind The Counter In A Small Town/ Sonic Reducer
Recording: Excellent. Audience.
Source: Paramount, New York April 16 1994.
Comment: Time CD1 47:18. CD2 45:13.

CD - THE LIVE COVER E.P.
THE SWINGIN' PIG TSP-CD-006
Sonic Reducer/ Rocking In The Free World/ Fucking Up/ I've Got A Feeling
Recording: Excellent stereo. Soundboard.
Source: Track 1 Ahoy, Rotterdam July 16 1993. Track 2 Volkshaus, Zurich June 8 1992. Track 3 Ahoy, Rotterdam July 16 1993. Track 4 Melkweg, Amsterdam February 12 1992.
Comments: European CD. Time 21:50.

CD - LONG ROAD
HURRICANE HUR005/6
CD1: Long Road/ Corduroy/ Spin The Black Circle/ Last Exit/ Tremor Christ/ Animal/ Why Go/ Jeremy/ Better Man/ Lukin'/ Not For You/ Whipping/ Glorified G/ Daughter, W.M.A./ Go/ Alive/ Immortality
CD2: Blood/ Rearviewmirror/ Dissident/ Yellow Leadbetter/ Porch/ Release/ Jeremy/ Habit/ Sonic Reducer/ Improv, Porch/ Homeless/ Throw Your Arms Around Me
Recording: Good to very good. Audience.
Source: Casper Event Center, Casper, WY June 16 1995. CD2 tracks 6-9 California Expo Amphitheatre, Sacramento, CA June 22 1995. CD2 10-12 Eddie Vedder solo set, Palladium, Hollywood, CA January 23 1993.
Comments: European CD. Deluxe color cover.

CD - MAKE YOURSELF COMFORTABLE
LABOUR OF LOVE PRODUCTION
CD1: Intro Music/ The Long Road/ Hail

Hail/ Animal/ Last Exit/ In My Tree/ Corduroy/ Better Man/ Not For You/ Jeremy/ Red Mosquito/ Black/ Rearviewmirror/ Lukin/ Elderly Woman Behind The Counter In A Small Town CD2: State Of Love And Trust/ Alive Intro, Footsteps/ Alive/ Blood, Fame, Androgynous Mind/ Porch/ Encore Break/ Who You Are/ Even Flow/ Daughter, The Real Me, W.M.A./ Leaving Here/ Present Tense/ Encore Break/ Yellow Ledbetter/ Outro Music
Recording: Excellent stereo. Soundboard.
Source: Meadows Music Theatre, Hartford, CT October 2 1996.
Comments: CDR. Deluxe color cover. Picture CD. Gold disc. Time CD1 65:31. CD2 66:36.

CD - MALARIA
BLIZZARD BLZD106/7
Go/ Animal/ Last Exit/ Spin The Black Circle/ Tremor Christ/ Corduroy/ Not For You/ Lukin'/ It's Been 7 Years Tonight/ Small Town/ Deep/ Dissident/ Daughter, Pull Me Up/ Even Flow/ Rearview Mirror CD2: I Got I.D./ Whipping/ Immortality/ Alive/ Black/ Blood/ Mosquito/ Betterman/ Leaving Here/ Footsteps/ Porch
Recording: Excellent stereo. Soundboard.
Source: Delta Center, Salt Lake City, UT November 1 1995.
Comments: European CD. Deluxe color cover.

CD - ROAD RAGE
OXYGEN OXY 072/73
CD1: Go (4:48)/ Animal (2:32)/ Lost Exit (2:48)/ Spin The Black Circle (2:43)/ Tremor Christ (5:36)/ Corduroy (5:31)/ Not For You (5:51)/ Lukin (previously unreleased) (1:33)/ It's Been Seven Years Tonight (4:09)/ Elderly Woman Behind The Counter In A Small Town (3:47)/ Deep (5:05)/ Dissident (3:20)/ Daughter, Pull Me Up (8:00)/ Even Flow (5:59)/ Rearviewmirror (6:51)/ I Got I.D. (4:06)
CD2: Whipping (3:02)/ Immortality (6:49)/ Alive (5:28)/ Black (6:08)/ Blood (8:35)/ Mosquito (previously unreleased) (5:02)/ Betterman (5:15)/ Leaving Here (2:49)/ Footsteps (4:28)/ Jeremy (new version, previously unreleased) (6:40)/ Falling Down (previously unreleased) (5:55)/ Little Wing (Jimi Hendrix's tune, previously unreleased) (9:30)/ Be A Star, Boy (previously unreleased) (2:08)
Recording: Excellent stereo. Soundboard.
Source: The Delta Center, Salt Lake City November 1 '95. CD2 Tracks 10-13 throughout the '95 world tour.
Comments: European CD. Deluxe color cover. Picture CD. Time CD1 72:50. CD2 72:00.

CD - SELF POLLUTION 1
KTS OF AUSTRALIA 020 A/B
CD1: Intro - Intro (4:28)/ Don't You Ever (LP) + Eddie Talks (3:30)/ Away From Home (LP) (3:12)/ Spin The Black Circle (Live) (3:11)/ Satan's Bed (Live) (3:21)/ Corduroy (Live) (5:02)/ Not For You (Live) (5:19)/ Immortality (Live) (6:25)/ Don't Know Why I'm Here (LP) (3:27)/ West Seattle Acid Party (LP) (1:20)/ Eddie Talks (:29)/ Schmidt Rid (LP) (1:20)/ Eddie's Answering Machine Messages (4:19)/ City Girls (LP) (2:58)/ Take It Away (Live) (2:58)/ I Wonder (Live) (1:53)/ 10,000 Light Years (Live) (3:06)/ One Inch Masters (LP) (2:54)/ Little Restraint (LP) (2:00)/ Wishin' You Were (LP) (2:35)
CD2: Eddie Talks (5:07)/ Keep Your Mouth Off My Sisters (LP) (2:27)/ Primal Shit (LP) (3:17)/ Judgment Raid, Retribution & Time (Live) (3:14)/ Generation Spokesmodel (Live) (2:54)/ What Moves The Heart? (Live) (3:38)/ Eddie & Stone Talk (1:32)/ You Owe It To You (LP) (7:43)/ Chickenwing (LP) (6:47)/ Eddie & Jeff Talk (2:24)/ Jeff's Tape (2:45)/ Life Is Dead (Live) (4:49)/ I Don't Know Anything (Live) (5:40)/ Jeff's Tape & Talk (2:05)/ Solitude (LP) (3:40)
Source: Live digital recording from the airwaves to you. Recorded Sunday, 1-8-95. Over 2 hours of pirate radio from Eddie's House.
Comments: Made in Australia. Not related to KISS THE STONE label from Italy.

CD - SELF POLLUTION 2
KTS OF AUSTRALIA 020 C/D
CD1: Intro - How Do You Pass The President's Test? (LP) (4:11)/ Eddie Talks (1:27)/ No Action (Unreleased) (1:08)/ This Is The Call (Unreleased) (5:54)/ Why Fucking Why? (LP) (3:50)/ Eddie Talks (2:35)/ Make You Think (Live) (5:12)/ Fell On Black Days (Live) (4:51)/ Gonna Get To You (Live) (4:32)/ No Attention (Live) (4:45)/ Wanna Be A Star Boy (LP) (3:24)/ Eddie &

PEARL JAM

Chris Novasetic Talk (2:51)/ Johnny Get Out Of My ... (LP) (1:17)/ Eddie & Novasetic Talk + They Through Me Out Of The Church (LP) (15:38)
CD2: Kathleen Hanna's Song (5:50)/ Are You Fur (LP) (3:17)/ Chris Novaselic's Poem (5:16)/ My Brother (LP) (3:17)/ Eddie Talks (Live) (3:27)/ Last Exit (Live) (2:55)/ Blood (Live) (3:13)/ Tremor Christ (Live) (4:40)/ Porch (Live) (4:55)/ Indifference (Live) (5:06)/ Instrumental #1 (4:54)/ Instrumental #2 (5:00)/ Eddie Talks and Calls L7 and Neil Young (20:00)/ What A Wonderful World (LP)
Source: Live digital recording from the airwaves to you. Recorded Sunday, 1-8-95. Over 2 hours of pirate radio from Eddie's House.
Comments: Made in Australia. Not related to KISS THE STONE label from Italy.

CD - SELF POLLUTION 3
KTS OF AUSTRALIA 020 E
Intro + Eddie Talks (4:18)/ Spin The Black Circle (3:02)/ Satan's Bed (3:20)/ Corduroy (5:00)/ Not For You (5:20)/ Immortality (6:20)/ Eddie Talks To The Flashbacks (5:08)/ Eddie & Stone Talk (2:02)/ Eddie & Jeff Talk (6:23)/ Eddie & Chris Novaselic Talk (7:34)/ Eddie Talks & Pearl Jam Rocks (3:25)/ Last Exit (3:03)/ Blood (3:15)/ Tremor Christ (4:50)/ Porch (4:46)/ Indifference (5:09)/ Closing - Goodnight (5:35)
Source: Live digital recording from the airwaves to you. Recorded Sunday, 1-8-95. All the important Pearl Jam tunes and talk are here.
Comments: Made in Australia. Not related to KISS THE STONE label from Italy.

CD - SEVENTH HEAVEN
D R. GIG DGCD 050
Wash/ Once/ Even Flow/ State Of Love & Trust/ Alive/ Black/ Deep/ Jeremy/ Why Go/ Porch/ I've Got A Feeling/ Glorified G/ Daughter
Recording: Excellent stereo. Soundboard. Tracks 12-13 very good audience.
Source: Amsterdam, Holland, February 12 1992. Tracks 12-13 Holland 1993.
Comments: European CD. Deluxe color cover. Time 70:41.

CD - STEPPIN' STONES
TORNADO TOR040/41
CD1: Long Road/ Jeremy/ Ship Song/ Footsteps/ This Boy/ Better Man/ Last Exit/ Spin The Black Circle/ Animal/ Tremor Christ/ Corduroy/ Not For You/ Go/ State Of Love And Trust/ Daughter
CD2: Garden/ Calling Me Back/ Alive/ Whipping/ Lukin'/ Rearviewmirror/ E.W.B.T.C.I.A.S.T./ Blood/ Black/ Porch/ Immortality/ Indifference/ Habit/ I Got Shit/ Leaving Here/ Yellow Ledbetter
Recording: Excellent audience.
Source: Red Rocks Amphitheatre, Denver, Colorado June 20 1995.
Comments: European CD. Deluxe color cover. Picture CD.

CD - TIVOLI
MOONRAKER 118
Intro/ Release/ Evenflow/ Why Go?/ Jeremy/ Deep/ Alive/ Black/ State Of Love And Trust/ Once/ Improv/ Porch/ Eddie's Drum Solo/ Improv/ Alone/ Leash/ Hungerstrike/ Garden/ Improv
Recording: Excellent stereo. Soundboard.
Source: The Tivoli, Utrecht, Holland March 4 '92.
Comments: European CD. Deluxe color cover. Time 79:55.

PEARL JAM & NEIL YOUNG

CD - GOLDEN GATE
MOONRAKER 065/66
CD1: Last Exit/ Spin The Black Circle/ Go/ Animal/ Tremor Christ/ Corduroy/ Not For You/ Big Green Country/ Act Of Love/ Throw Your Hatred Down/ Powderfinger
CD2: Truth Be Known/ Rockin In The Free World/ Down By The River/ Downtown/ Cortez The Killer/ Peace And Love/ Rockin In The Free World
Recording: Excellent.
Source: Polo Field, Golden Gate Park, San Francisco June 24 1995.
Comments: European CD.

CD - IN DUBLIN
CRYSTAL CAT RECORDS CC 373/74
CD1: Intro/ Big Green Country/ Song X/ Act Of Love/ Downtown/ Mr. Soul/ Scenery/ Comes A Time/ The Needle & The Damage Done/ Don't Let It Bring You Down/ Mother Earth/ Throw Your Hatred Down
CD2: Cortez The Killer/ Powderfinger/

Rockin' In The Free World/ Intro/ Like A Hurricane/ My My, Hey Hey (Out Of The Blue)/ After The Goldrush/ I'm The Ocean/ Peace And Love
Recording: Excellent audience.
Source: Simmons Court Pavilion, RDS, Dublin, August 26 1995.
Comments: European CD.
Time CD1 70:23. CD2 71:22.

PENNYWISE

CD - TIME TO BURN
TORNADO TOR 014
Wouldn't It Be Nice/ Unknown Road/ Living For Today/ Rules/ Homesick/ Stand By Me/ The Secret/ Give Me Some More/ Pennywise/ No Reason Why/ Minor Threat Cover/ Time To Burn/ Kodiak/ Nothing/ Clean Your Head/ Bro Hymn
Recording: Poor. Audience.
Source: Trenton, NJ.
Comments: European CD. Time 50:33.

CD - UNDERDOGS
TORNADO TOR050
The Underdog/ Every Single Day/ Rules Made Up By You/ What You Give, Is What You Get/ Like We Did Before/ Stand By Me/ Today/ Gonna Do It My Way/ Touch Of Grey/ Living For Today/ Got A Lot To Learn/ Minor Threat/ Lowrider Improv/ Perfect People/ No Reason Why/ Killing Time/ Pennywise/ Slow Down/ Bro 'Em
Recording: Good to very good. Audience.
Source: Santa Monica, CA August 11 1995.
Comments: European CD. Pic CD.
Time 56:40.

PHISH

CD - ASTRAL INTERCOURSE
OXYGEN OXY 050
Loving Cup (6:17)/ Sparkle (3:36)/ Tweezer Medley: Tweezer, Gwa, Tweezer, Sparks, Makisupa, Policeman, Tweezer, Sweet Emotion, Walk Away, Tweezer, Cannonball, Purple Rain, Hyhu, Tweezer (67:50)
Recording: Excellent stereo. Soundboard.
Source: New York City May 7 '94.
Comments: European CD. Picture CD.

CD - I'D RATHER BE PHISHIN'
TORNADO TOR 019
Cd1: Buried Alive/ Poor Heart/ Sample In A Jar/ Foam/ The Mango Song/ Down With Disease/ Fee/ It's Ice/ Fast Enough For You/ I Didn't Know/ Split Open And Melt
CD2: Possum Blues Ending/ Cavern, Wilson, Cavern/ NJCV/ Tweezer/ Julius/ Tweezer/ BBFCFM/ Mound/ Slave To The Traffic Light/ Suzy Greenberg/ E: My Sweet One/ Tweezer (reprise)
Recording: Excellent. Audience.
Source: Big Birch, Patterson, NY July 13 '94.
Comments: European CD. Deluxe color cover.

CD - PHRESH PHISH
FLASHBACK FB 04.95.0260
CD1: Golgi Apparatus (4:37)/ High Time (5:15)/ Alumni Blues (5:20)/ Medley: You Enjoy Myself, Wilson, Peaches En Regalia (25:11)/ Low Rider (6:24)/ Divided Sky (13:06)/ Axis: Bold As Love (6:27)
CD2: Lizards (10:07)/ Walk Away (3:23)/ Possum (7:23)/ Fee (5:23)/ Sparks (3:30)/ Whipping Post (10:28)/ Good Times, Bad Times (4:25)/ Medley: Fluffhead, Fluff Travels (15:15)
CD3: Medley: No Regrets, AC/DC Bag (14:00)/ Suzy Greenberg (6:40)/ Dinner And A Movie (10:33)/ Bathtub Gin (5:56)/ I'm Hydrogen (13:31)/ Slit Open And Melt (7:16)/ Bouncing Around The Room (3:44)/ Foam (8:23)/ Highway To Hell (3:23)
Recording: Excellent.
Source: CD1, CD2 and CD3 track 1 'The Zoo' Amherst, MA September 24 1988.
CD3 tracks 2-9 'The Warfield' San Francisco, CA June 15 1988.
Comments: European CD. Box set with deluxe color cover.

PINK FLOYD

CD - ECHOES FROM OSAKA
BS 10/11
CD1: Speak To Me/ Breathe/ On The Run/ Time/ The Great Gig In The Sky/ Money/ Us And Them/ Any Colour You Like/ Brain Damage/ Eclipse/ One Of These Days
CD2: Careful With That Axe Eugene/ Echoes
Recording: Poor to good. Audience.
Source: Osaka, March 9 '72.
Comments: Japanese CD. Deluxe color cover. Time CD1 60:04. CD2 40:27.

PINK FLOYD

CD - LIVE IN TOKYO 1972
AMSTERDAM 9616-2-1/2
CD1: Dark Side Of The Moon/ Speak To Me/ Breathe/ On The Run/ Time/ The Great Gig In The Sky/ Money/ Us And Them/ Any Colour You Like/ Brain Damage/ Eclipse
CD2: One Of These Days/ Careful With That Axe, Eugine/ Echoes/ A Saucerful Of Secrets
Recording: Good. Audience.
Source: Tokyo Taiikukan Tokyo Japan March 6 1972.
Comments: Japanese CD. Deluxe color cover. Time CD1 50:45. CD2 61:05.

CD - NOT A CLOUD IN THE SKY
SILVER RARITIES SIRA185/186
CD1: Obscured By Clouds, When You're In/ Set The Controls For The Heart Of The Sun/ Careful With That Axe, Eugene/ Echoes
CD2: Speak To Me/ Breathe/ On The Run/ Time/ Breathe (Reprise)/ The Great Gig In The Sky/ Money/ Us And Them/ Any Colour You Like/ Brain Damage/ Eclipse/ One Of These Days
Recording: Very good. Audience
Source: Hollywood, Florida June 28 1973.
Comments: European CD.

CD - PROTOTYPE WISH YOU ARE ANIMALS
HIGHLAND HL 017/18#PF1
CD1: Shine On You Crazy Diamond (Part 1-9) (23:55)/ Raving And Drooling (Sheep) (16:10)/ You've Got To Be Crazy (Dogs) (18:35)/ The Dark Side Of The Moon, Speak To Me (3:16), Breathe (3:08), On The Run (5:13)
CD2: Time (6:53)/ The Great Gig In The Sky (7:43)/ Money (9:12)/ Us And Them (8:29)/ Any Colour You Like (8:38)/ Brain Damage (3:55)/ Eclipse (1:42)/ Echoes (24:40)
Recording: Good to very good. Audience.
Source: Wembley, London, UK November 16 1974.
Comments: Japanese CD. Deluxe color cover.

PLANT, ROBERT

CD - IN THE MOONLIGHT
MIDAS TOUCH MD95321/22
CD1: In The Mood/ Pledge Pin/ Messin' With The Mekon/ Worse Than Detroit/ Thru With The Two Step/ Other Arms
CD2: Horizontal Departure/ Moonlight In Samosa/ Wreckless Love/ Slow Dancer/ Like I've Never Been Gone
Recording: Excellent. Soundboard.
Source: Brighton, Centre December 17 1983.
Comments: Japanese CD.

CD - MIDNIGHT REHEARSALS
MIDAS TOUCH 61611
In The Mood (8:26)/ Pledge Pin (5:17)/ Pink And Black (5:13)/ Doo Doo A Do Do (8:31)/ Little By Little (8:46)/ Burning Down One Side (4:06)/ Rockin' At Midnight (4:36)/ Young Boy Blues (7:07)/ Once I Had A Girl (5:26)/ Mellow Saxophone (4:58)/ Sea Of Love (3:36)/ Honey Hush (7:05)
Recording: Excellent. Soundboard. Soundcheck.
Source: Vancouver, Canada June 9 1985.
Comments: Japanese CD.

PLANT, ROBERT AND JIMMY PAGE
See PAGE, JIMMY AND ROBERT PLANT

POLICE, THE

CD - FALL OUT
PARTY LINE PLCD-003
Don't Stand So Close To Me/ Walking On The Moon/ Deathwish/ Fall Out/ Man In A Suitcase/ Bring On the Night/ De Do Do, De Da Da Da/ Truth Hurts Everybody/ When The World Is Running Down, You Make The Best Of What's Still Around/ The Bed's Too Big Without You/ Driven To Tears/ Message In A Bottle/ Roxanne/ Can't Stand Losing You/ So Lonely
Recording: Good.
Source: February 2 1981.

POP, IGGY

CD - POP POWER
MOONRAKER 188
I Wanna Live (4:19)/ Down On The Street (3:24)/ Heart Is Saved (2:54)/ Raw Power (3:58)/ Search And Destroy (3:55)/ Five Foot One (4:11)/ Sixteen, Sister Midnight (7:02)/ I Wanna Be Your Dog (5:22)/ Look Away (5:09)/ The Passenger (4:37)/ Lust For Life (5:11)/ Home (4:16)/ Real Wild Child (2:26)/ Sick Of You (5:44)/ No Fun (3:38)/ 1969 (4:07)
Recording: Excellent stereo. Soundboard.

GRAM PARSONS
&
THE FALLEN ANGELS
YOURS TRULY, ANONYMOUS

PRINCE
TOKYO '90

PORTISHEAD

Source: Tracks 1-12 The Commodore, Vancouver, Canada April 29 1996. Tracks 13-16 The Lorely Festival, Germany June 22 1996.
Comments: European CD. Deluxe color cover.

PORTISHEAD

CD - WELCOME TO PORTISHEAD
GO!LIVE GLCD001
Numb/ Wandering Star/ Reaching Out/ Strangers/ Uncertainty/ It's A Fire/ Glory Box/ Pedestal/ Sour Times/ Intro/ Glory Box/ Uncertainty/ Wandering Star/ Reaching Out/ Sour Times
Recording: Excellent stereo. Soundboard.
Source: Tracks 1-9 Empress Ballroom, Blackpool May 25 1995. Tracks 10-15 La Cigale, Paris April 12 1995.
Comments: European CD. Deluxe color cover. Picture CD. Time 67:27.

POWELL, COZY

CD - OVER THE BBC
ELEMENT OF CRIME ELEMENTS-001
Theme 1/ Sweet Poison/ The Loner/ Take To The Water/ Killer/ Killer/ The Loner
Source: Tracks 1-5 BBC 'In Concert' January 20 1980. Tracks 6-7 BBC 'OGWT' Jan 8 1980.
Comments: Japanese CD.

PRAYING MANTIS

CD - LIVE + SINGLES
CD-010
Nightmare/ I Know It (Time Slipping Away)/ Tell Me The Nightmares Wrong/ Enough Is Enough/ Turn The Tables/ Flirting With Suicide/ Captured City/ The Reaper/ Johnny Cool/ Praying Mantis/ High Roller/ Thirty Pieces Of Silver/ Flirting With Suicide (live)/ Panic In The Street (live)/ Turn The Tables/ Tell Me The Nightmares Wrong/ A Question Of Time
Recording: Excellent. Soundboard.
Source: Tracks 1-6 Reading Festival Live. Tracks7-9 Sound House Tapes 12". Tracks10-11 Praying Mantis 7". Tracks12-14 Cheated Double 7". Tracks 15-17 Turn The Tables 7".
Comments: Japanese CD. Deluxe color cover. Time 71:45.

PRESIDENTS OF THE U.S.A.

CD - FUNK, PUNK AND TWANG
OXYGEN OXY 078
TV/ Kick Out The Jams/ Lunatic To Love/ Medley: Feather Pluckn, Baby You're A Rich Man/ Bug City/ Boll Weevil, Play That Funky Music/ Naked And Famous/ Lump/ Man/ Dune Buggy/ Video Killed The Radio Star/ Kitty/ Back Porch/ Twig In The Wind/ Medley: Feel Like Makin' Love, Peaches/ Candy/ Devil In The Sleeping Bag/ I Will Survive/ Body/ Stranger/ We Are Not Going To Make It
Recording: Excellent stereo. Soundboard.
Source: Tracks 1-15 Studion, Stockholm, Sweden March 29 '96. Tracks 16-21 Lee's Palace, Toronto, Canada November 9 '95.
Comments: European CD. Deluxe color cover. Picture CD. Time 72:47.

CD - PROVIDENZE
MOONRAKER 055
Kick Out The Jams/ Feather Pluckin', Baby You're A Rich Man/ Boll Weevil/ Back Porch/ Lump/ Stranger/ Candy Cigarettes/ Naked And Famous/ Dune Buggy/ Bug City/ Candy/ New Amplifier/ Supersonic (Supermodel)/ Feel Like Makin' Love/ Peaches/ Let's Rock/ Carolyn's Booty/ Kitty/ We Are Not Going To Make It
Recording: Excellent. Audience.
Source: Club Babyhead, Providence, Rhode Island November 13 1995.
Comments: European CD. Deluxe color cover. Time 58:10.

CD - ROCKIN' THE WHITE HOUSE
KISS THE STONE KTS 544
Kick Out The Jams/ Lunatic Love/ Feather Pluckin'/ Boll Weevil/ Dune Buggy/ Naked And Famous/ Lump/ Back Porch/ Kitty/ Video Killed The Radio Star/ Candy/ Peaches/ Lump/ Peaches/ Kick Out The Jams/ Feather Pluckin'/ Kitty/ Dune Buggy/ Lump/ Video Killed The Radio Star/ Peaches
Recording: Excellent.
Source: Tracks 1-5 Leeds, UK April 11 1996. Tracks 6-13 Camden, London November 11 1995. Tracks 14-19 Mount Rushmore spring '96
Comments: European CD. Deluxe color cover. Time 65:58

CD - VIDEO KILLED THE RADIO STAR
MOONRAKER 109
TV Eye/ Kick Out The Jams/ Lunatic To Love/ Feather Pluckn/ Baby You're A Rich Man/ Bug City/ Boll Weevil (Including Play That Funky Music)/ Naked And Famous/ Lump/ Man/ Dune Buggy/ Video Killed The Radio Star/ Kitty/ Back Porch/ Twig In The Wind/ Feel Like Makin Love/ Peaches
Recording: Excellent stereo. Soundboard.
Source: Studio, Stockholm, March 29 1996. First European gig.
Comments: European CD. Deluxe color cover. Time 53:49.

PRIMUS

CD - BEAVER TRAPPIN'
TORNADO TOR051
To Defy The Laws Of Tradition/ John The Fisherman/ Those Hamned Blue-Collar Tweekers/ Professor Nutbutdter's House Of Treats/ Mrs. Blaileen/ Nature Boy/ Southbound Pachyderm/ DeAnza Jig/ Seas Of Cheese, Pork Soda/ My Name Is Mud/ Jerry Was A Race Car Driver/ Over The Electric Grapevine/ Wynona's Big Brown Beaver/ Tommy The Cat
Recording: Excellent. Audience.
Source: Hollywood, CA, August 1995.
Recording: European CD. Deluxe color cover. Picture CD. Time 74:09.

CD - HOUSE OF TREATS
HURRICANE HURR014
Here Come The Bastards/ Pudding Time/ Those Damned Blue-Collar Tweekers/ Professor Nutbutter's House Of Treats/ Mrs. Blaileen/ Ground Hog's Day/ Southbound Pachyderm/ DeAnza Jig/ Seas Of Cheese, Pork Soda/ My Name Is Mud/ Over The Electric Grapevine/ Wynona's Big Brown Beaver/ Bob/ Jerry Was A Race Car Driver
Recording: Excellent. Audience.
Source: San Diego, CA August 1995.
Comments: European CD. Deluxe color cover. Picture CD. Time 69:24.

CD - RED ROCKS
PR-001
Here Come The Bastards/ Those Damned Blue-Collar Tweekers/ Professor Nuttbutter's House Of Treats/ Mrs. Baileen/ Spaghetti Western/ Too Many Puppies/ Southbound Pachyderm/ DeAnza Jig/ My Name Is Mud/ Over The Electric Grapevine/ Eleven/ Wynona's Big Brown Beaver/ Jerry Was A Race Car Driver
Recording: Very good. Audience.
Source: Red Rocks Amphitheater, Denver July 1995.
Comments: European CD. Deluxe color cover. Time 69:20.

PRINCE, THE ARTIST FORMERLY KNOWN AS

CD - THE AVENUE
MOONRAKER 089/90
CD1: Let's Go Crazy/ When You Were Mine/ A Case Of You/ Computer Blue/ Delirious/ Electric Intercourse/ Automatic/ I Would Die 4 U, Baby, I'm A Star/ Little Red Corvette/ Segue/ Purple Rain/ D.M.S.R.
CD2: Let's Go Crazy/ When You Were Mine/ A Case Of You/ Delirious/ Electric Intercourse/ Little Red Corvette/ D.M.S.R./ tracks 8-14 Jamming
Recording: Excellent.
Source: First Avenue, Minneapolis August 3 1983. CD1 the show, CD2 the afternoon rehearsal.
Comments: European CD.
Time CD1 70:36. CD2 45:54.

CD - BORN IN ST. PAUL
MOUNTAINS MTS001/002
CD1: Intro/ The Future/ 1999/ Housequake, Sexy Dancer/ Kiss, I'm In The Mood/ Purple Rain/ Take Me With U/ Alphabet Street/ The Question Of You, Electric Man/ Controversy/ Ain't No Way
CD2: Scandalous/ Baby I'm A Star, Respect/ Partyman/ Are You There?/ Brand New Boy/ Prison Of Love/ Bad Roses/ Good Man/ Kenny/ We Can Hang/ Curious Blue/ Boys Will Be Boys/ Good Bye
Recording: Poor audience recording. CD2 tracks 4-13 very good.
Source: Nude Tour preview gig, Civic Center, St. Paul May 6 1990. CD2 tracks 4-13 complete M.C. Flash sessions.

CD - BRAVE NEW WORLD
MOONRAKER 176
The Wedding: Friend, Lover, Sister, Mother, Wife/ Kamasutra/ Overture I/ Overture II/ Overture III/ Overture IV/ Overture V/ Overture VI/ Overture VII/ Overture VIII/ Overture IX/ Overture X/ Songs 4 A Brave New World: Starfish And Coffee '95/ Sarah/

PRINCE, THE ARTIST FORMERLY KNOWN AS

Five Women '95/ 18 & Over (extended version)/ 51 Hours/ The Ryde Dyvine/ Dark (alternate version)
Recording: Excellent stereo. Soundboard.
Comments: European CD. Time 78:37.

CD - FREEDOM
MOONRAKER 219
A Multimedia Tour Through The Moonraker Prince Catalogue/ Prince Interviews From Tokyo Radio & TV 1996 And The Following Quicktime Films: Gotta Stop Messin' About 1981/ A Case Of U 1983/ The Hard Life 1987/ Girls And Boys 1987/ Daddy Pop 1992/ Acknowledge Me 1994/ The Santana Medley 1994/ Talkin' Loud And Sayin' Nothing 1997/ Face Down 1997
Comments: European. Deluxe color cover. Simply said, a must for any Prince fan. An excellent presentation. The future of boots?

CD - HAPPY BIRTHDAY - PRINCE AND THE REVOLUTION
MOONRAKER 135
Around The World In A Day/ Christopher Tracy's Parade/ Raspberry Beret/ Controversy/ Mutiny/ Happy Birthday/ How Much Is That Doggy In The Window?/ Automatic/ D.M.S.R./ Anotherloverholenyohead/ I Wanna Be Your Lover/ Head/ Pop Life/ Life Can Be So Nice/ A Whole Lotta Shakin Goin' On/ Mountains/ Kiss
Recording: Excellent. Audience.
Source: Cobo Hall, Detroit June 7 '86.
Comments: European CD. Deluxe color cover. Picture CD. Time 55:12.

CD - THE HONEYMOON EXPERIENCE
MOONRAKER 057/58
CD1: 1999/ Endorphinmachine/ Shhh/ Days Of Wild/ Now/ Race, Girls And Boys/ The Most Beautiful Girl In The World/ P Control (Including Get Wild)/ Letitgo/ Starfish And Coffee/ Michael/ Drum Solo/ Sometimes It Snows In April/ The Ride
CD2: Sex Machine/ Johnny/ Sex Machine Jam/ Take Me With U/ Funky/ The Jam/ One Of Us/ Do Me, Baby/ Sexy MF/ If I Was Your Girlfriend/ Vicki Waiting/ The Purple Medley/ Purple Rain/ 7
Recording: Excellent. Audience.
Source: The Honey Moon Experience Honolulu, Hawaii February 19 '96.
Comments: European CD. Deluxe color cover. Time CD1 53:58. CD2 51:28.

CD - INTO THE VAULT
OXYGEN OXY 080
Mad/ Superhero/ Funky Design/ Strays Of The World/ Don't Talk To Strangers/ Be My Mirror/ I'll Do Anything/ Empty Room/ There Is Lonely/ Deuce & Aquator/ Black MF In The House/ This Groove/ Komastra/ Overture I/ Overture II/ Overture III
Recording: Excellent stereo. Soundboard.
Source: Track 1 recording session for the unreleased soundtrack for 'From Dusk 'Till Dawn' movie 1995. Track 2 original version of song given to Earth Wind And Fire. Track 3 unreleased 1995. Track 4 outtake from 'Come' album. Tracks 5-9 recording session for the unreleased soundtrack for 'I'll Do Anything' movie November 1993. Tracks 10-11 outtakes from the unreleased first NPG album. Track 12 unreleased track 1994. Tracks 13-16 Kamasutra opera written by Prince and The New Power Orchestra for his wedding on Feb. 14 1996.
Comments: European CD. Deluxe color cover. Picture CD. Time 70:09.

CD - JAPAN 96
MOONRAKER 047/48/49
CD1: 1999 Intro/ Endorphinmachine/ Shhh/ Days Of Wild (Including 777-9311)/ Now/ Sex Machine/ Funky Stuff/ Mary, Don't You Weep/ Johnny/ The Most Beautiful Girl In The World/ P Control (Including Get Wild)/ Letitgo/ Starfish And Coffee/ The Cross/ The Jam/ One Of Us/ Do Me, Baby/ Sexy MF
CD2: If I Was Your Girlfriend/ Vicki Waiting/ The Purple Medley/ 7/ Speech/ Billy Jack Bitch/ I Hate U Interlude/ 319/ Gold/ Bonus: Days Of Wild (January 11)/ Now (Including Babies Makin' Babies) (January 11)/ Sex Machine (January 11)/ Babies Makin' Babies (January 8)/ Funky Stuff (January 8)/ Oriental Intro (January 9)/ 7 (January 9)
CD3: Intro/ We March (January 8)/ Love...Thy Will Be Done (January 8)/ Funky (January 8)/ The Ride (January 8)/ One Of Us (January 16)/ Do Me, Baby (January 16)/ I Hate U (January 8)/ Johnny (January 16)/ The Glam Slam Boogie (January 16)/ Letitgo (January11)/ Starfish And Coffee (January 11)/ The Cross (January 9)/ If I Was Your Girlfriend (January 9)/ Vicki Waiting (January 9)/ The Purple Medley (January 11)/ I Hate U Interlude (January 13)/ 319 (January 13)/ Gold (January 8)
Recording: Excellent. Audience.

Source: The Budokan, Tokyo January 17 1995. Bonus Tracks: Tokyo January 8, 9, 16. Osaka January 11. Fukuoka Jan.13.
Comments: Euro CD. Deluxe color cover.

CD - LIVE SEXY
MOONRAKER 093/094
CD1: Escape/ Erotic City/ Housequake/ SLow Love/ Adore/ Delirious/ Jack U Off/ Sister/ Adore/ I Wanna Be Your Lover/ Head/ A Love Bizarre/ When You Were Mine/ If I Had A Harem/ When You Were Mine/ Little Red Corvette/ Controversy/ Dirty Mind/ Superfunkycalifragisexy/ Bob George/ Anna Stesia
CD2: Cross The Line Poem/ I No/ Lovesexy/ Glam Slam/ The Cross/ I Wish U Heaven/ Kiss/ Dance On/ Sheila E Drum Solo/ When 2 R In Love/ Venus De Milo/ Starfish And Coffee/ Raspberry Beret/ Condition Of The Heart/ Strange Relationship/ When 2 R In Love/ Lets Go Crazy/ When Doves Cry/ Purple Rain/ 1999/ Alphabet St.
Recording: Excellent.
Source: Dortmund, Germany Sept. 9 1988.
Comments: European CD.

CD - NPG-TV: CHANNEL THREE ['94-'96]
MOONRAKER 183
Prologue/ The Most Beautiful Girl In The World (Top Of The Pops Video '94)/ Speech (World Music Awards May 4 1994)/ Enporphinmachine (Canal May 5 1994)/ Speech (Soul Of America Music Awards May 7 1994)/ Interactive (VH-1 Honors June 26 1994)/ Love Sign (The Today Show July 12 1994)/ Peach (MTV Europe Music Awards November 24 1994)/ Dolphin (The Late Show With David Letterman December 13 1994)/ Speech (American Music Awards January 30 1995)/ Speech (The Brit Awards February 20 1995)/ Billy Jack Bitch (The Sunday Show March 5 1995)/ Get Wild (Top Of The Pops March 15 1995)/ Count The Days (The White Room April 6 1995)/ Get Wild (The White Room April 5 1995)/ Days Of Wild (VH-1 Love 4 One Another January 27 1996)/ The Ride (VH-1 Love 4 One Another January 27 1996)/ The Jam (VH-1 Love 4 One Another January 27 1996)/ Dinner With Delores (The Late Show With David Letterman July 8 1996)/ Dinner With Delores (The Today Show July 9 1996)/ Zannalee (The Today Show July 9 1996)/ Epilogue)

Recording: Excellent. Soundboard.
Comments: European CD. Deluxe color cover. Picture CD. Time 75:44.

CD - TOKYO '90
MOONRAKER 097
The Future/ 1999/ Housequake/ Sexy Dancer/ Kiss/ I'm In The Mood/ Purple Rain/ Take Me With You/ Bambi/ Alphabet St. (with It Takes Two)/ The Question Of U/ When Doves Cry/ Do Me Baby/ Ain't No Way/ Little Red Corvette/ Batdance/ Partyman (with What Have You Done For Me Lately?)/ Baby I'm A Star (with Respect)
Recording: Excellent stereo. Soundboard.
Source: Tokyo Dome August 31 1990.
Comments: European CD. Deluxe color cover. Picture CD. Time 73:59.

PRODIGY

CD - EVERLASTING FIRE
X-PERIENCE RECORDS X-P 7342
Charly (Alley Cat Mix)/ Everybody In The Place (Fairground Mix)/ G-Force (Part 1)/ Wind It Up (Rewound Edit)/ We Are The Ruffest/ Weather Experience/ (Top Buzz Remix)/ Out Of Space (Millenium Mix)/ Ruff In Jungle Bizness (Uplifting Vibes Mix)/ Jericho (Live Version)/ Rhythm Of Life (Original Mix)/ No Good (Start The Dance) (Bad For You-Mix)/ Rat Poison/ Firestarter (Instrumental)/ Molotov Bitch)
Recording: Excellent stereo. Soundboard.
Source: Studio.
Comments: European CD. Deluxe cover. Time 73:42.

PULP

CD - DISCORAMA
MOONRAKER 166
Prologue/ Disco 2000/ I Spy/ Do You Remember The First Time?/ Live Bed Show/ Sorted For E's And Wizz/ F.e.el.i.n.g.c.a.l.l.e.d.l.o.v.e.?/ Underwear/ Common People/ Monday Morning/ Underwear/ Mis-Shapes/ Sorted for E's And Wizz/ Acrylic Afternoons/ Do You Remember The First Time?
Recording: Excellent stereo. Soundboard.
Source: Tracks 1-9 The Alabama, Munich June 26 1996. Tracks 10-15 The Lollipop Festival, Stockholm July 29 1995.
Comments: European CD. Deluxe color cover. Time 73:53.

Q

QUEEN

CD - CHRISTMAS AT THE BEEB
YU 29
Now I'm Here/ Ogre Battle/ White Queen/ Bohemian Rhapsody, Killer Queen, The March Of Black Queen/ Keep Yourself Alive/ Brighton Rock, Son And Daughter/ Liar/ In The Lap Of The Gods/ Seven Seas Of Rhye/ See What I Fool I've Been/ God Save The Queen
Recording: Excellent. Soundboard.
Source: Hammersmith Odeon London England Dec. 24 1975.
Comments: Japanese CD. Deluxe color cover. Time 59:14.

CD - GREAT KING HANGMAN
BS-7
Now I'm Here/ White Queen/ Doing Allright/ In The Lap Of The Gods/ Killer Queen/ The March Of The Black Queen/ Bring Back That Leroy Brown/ Stone Cold Crazy/ In The Lap Of The Gods/ Modern Times Rock 'N' Roll/ Jailhouse Rock/ See What A Fool I've Been/ *Great King Rat/ *Seven Sea Of Rhye/ *Hang Man
Recording: Good to very good. Soundboard.
Source: Budokan, Tokyo April 19 1975.
*Budokan, Tokyo May 1 1975.
Comments: Japanese CD. Deluxe color cover. Time 65:20.

CD - JAZZ FINAL
CD1: We Will Rock You/ We Will Rock You (Hard Version)/ Let Me Entertain You/ Somebody To Love/ If You Can't Best Them/ Medley: Death On To Legs, Killer Queen, Bicycle Race, I'm In Love With My Car/ Get Down Make Love/ (You're) My Best Friend/ Now I'm Here/ Teo Torriatte/ Don't Stop Me Now/ Dreamers Ball/ Love Of My Life/ 39'
CD2: Fat Bottomed Girls/ Brighton Rock/ Keep Yourself Alive/ Bohemian Rhapsody/ Tie Your Mother Down/ Jail House Rock/ Sheer Heart Attack/ We Will Rock You/ We Are The Champions/ God Save The Queen/ *It's Late
Recording: Good to very good. Audience.
Source: Sapporo, Japan May 6 1979.
*Sapporo, Japan May 5 1979.
Comments: Japanese CD. Deluxe color cover. Time CD1 73:43. CD2 57:16.

CD - MAGIC VISION
KOBRA RECORDS KRCD 15
Thank God It's Christmas (from Queen V)/ Under Pressure (demo version with David Bowie)/ Misfire (demo written by J. Deacon)/ Mad The Swine (original version '73)/ April Lady (pre-Queen 'Smile' 1970)/ I Want It All (different text version)/ One Vision (alternate text version)/ I Go Crazy (B-Side of 'Radio Ga Ga')/ Man On The Prowl (extended version)/ One Vision (extended version)/ Breakthrough (extended version)/ Radio Ga-Ga (re-cut 1992)/ We Will Rock You (rock mix 1992)/ Stone Cold Crazy (trash version)/ Stealin' (B-Side)/ A Kind Of Magic (different version)/ I Want To Break Free (extended version)/ Too Much Love Will Kill You (Freddie on vocals)
Recording: Excellent. Soundboard.
Comments: European CD.

CD - MASTER OF "SHEETKEECKERS"
YU 49
Procession/ Father To Son/ Son & Daughter/ Ogre Battle/ Liar/ Procession/ Father To Son/ Ogre Battle/ Son & Daughter/ Keep Yourself Alive/ Seven Seas Of Rhye/ Modern Times Rock & Roll/ Liar
Recording: Excellent. Soundboard.
Source: Tracks 1-5 BBC Golders Green Hippodrome, London, England Sept. 13 1973. Tracks 6-13 Rainbow Theatre, London, England Mar. 31 1974.
Comments: Japanese CD. Deluxe B&w cover. Red type. Time 63:46.

R

RADIOHEAD

CD - THE BEST THING THAT YOU EVER HAD
KISS THE STONE KTS 590
My Iron Lung/ Bones/ High And Dry/ Bulletproof/ Planet Spirit/ Planet Telex/ Stop Whispering/ Nice Dream/ Lucky/ Creep/ Lurgee/ Anyone Can Play Guitar/ Just/

Blow Out/ Fake Plastic Trees/ The Bends
Recording: Excellent stereo. Soundboard.
Source: Boston April 13 1996. London July 30 1996.
Comments: European CD.

CD - BIG DAY OUT - GALWAY 96
WR005
Iron Lung/ Bones/ Bulletproof/ Planet Telex/ Black Star/ High & Dry/ Lucky/ Nice Dream/ Creep/ The Bends, Fake Plastic Trees/ Anyone Can Play Guitar/ Street Spirit/ Just/ Street Spirit/ Just/ Maquiladora
Source: Tracks 1-13 FM Broadcast, Galway July 28 1996. Tracks 14-15 acoustic demos. Track 16 radio session 1995.

CD - LIVE FROM PLANET EARTH
MOONRAKER 184
My Iron Long (5:13)/ Anyone Can Play Guitar (4:00)/ Bullet Proof...I Wish I Was (3:36)/ Planet Telex (4:20)/ High And Dry (4:26)/ Lucky (4:37)/ (Nice Dream) (3:59)/ Bones (3:23)/ Street Spirit (Fade Out) (4:40)/ The Bends (4:05)/ Just (4:12)/ Creep (4:44)/ Fake Plastic Trees (4:43)/ Thinking About You (2:57)/ Vegetable (3:49)/ Black Star (3:56)/ Creep (5:06)/ Stop Whispering (6:33)
Recording: Excellent.
Source: Tracks 1-14 Glasgow July 14 1996. Tracks 15-18 Stockholm December 1 1995.
Comments: European CD.

CD - PLANET ACOUSTIC
KISS THE STONE KTS 631
My Iron Lung (5:28)/ Anyone Can Play Guitar (3:55)/ Bullet Proof (3:38)/ Planet Telex (4:17)/ High & Dry (4:14)/ Lucky (4:34)/ Nice Dream (4:03)/ Bones (3:22)/ Street Spirit (4:43)/ The Bends (3:55)/ Just (3:46)/ Creep (4:36)/ Fake Plastic Trees (4:45)/ Thinking About You (2:58)/ Black Start (4:03)/ Street Spirit (4:18)/ Nobody Does It Better (3:31)
Recording: Excellent stereo. Soundboard.
Source: Tracks 1-14 In The Park Festival, Glasgow, Scotland July 31 1996. Tracks 15-16 acoustic session 1995. Track 17 studio session, Camden, London August 18 1995.
Comments: European CD. Deluxe color cover. Picture CD.

CD - POP IS DEAD
OXYGEN OXY 086
Bones/ High And Dry/ Lucky/ Creep/ Bishops Robes (New Song)/ You/ Fake Plastic Trees/ Just/ Street Spirit (Fade Out)/ Black Star/ (Nice Dream)/ Stop Whispering/ Street Spirit (Fade Out)/ Killer Cars/ Wonderwall/ Blow Out/ Subterranean Homesick Alien (New Song)/ My Iron Lung
Recording: Excellent stereo. Soundboard.
Source: Tracks 1-12 The Gino, Stockholm, Sweden December 1 1995. Tracks 13-16 acoustic radio session - Real Time Studio, Vancouver, BC March 22 1996. Track 17 acoustic radio session, Holland April 21 1995. Track 18 radio session - Vara Studios, Hilversum, Holland June 1995.
Comments: European CD.

CD - THE WAREHOUSE
MOONRAKER 079
The Bends/ Bones/ Bullet Proof .. I Wish I Was/ My Iron Lung/ Prove Yourself/ Street Spirit (Fade Out)/ Lucky/ Creep/ Nice Dream/ High And Dry/ Planet Telex/ Anyone Can Play Guitar/ Just/ Blow Out/ Fake Plastic Trees/ Thinking About You/ You/ Black Star/ Inside My Head
Recording: Excellent.
Source: The Warehouse, Toronto December 12 1995.
Comments: European CD. Deluxe color cover. Time 79:53.

RAGE AGAINST THE MACHINE

CD - BLOWN AWAY
KISS THE STONE KTS 626
Bulls On Parade (3:47)/ Viet Now (3:32)/ Bombtrack (2:23)/ Bullet In Your Head (7:41)/ Killing In The Name (5:17)/ Freedom (6:16)/ Bombtrack (4:17)/ War Without A Face (3:52)/ Bullet In Your Head (5:54)/ Zapata's Blood (3:48)/ Wind Below (5:42)/ Take The Power Back (6:18)/ Know Your Enemy (4:43)/ Producer (6:15)
Recording: Excellent stereo. Soundboard.
Source: Tracks 1-6 Tibet Freedom Festival, San Francisco June 16 1996. Tracks 7-9 Reading Festival, UK August 23 1996. Tracks 10-11 Red Rocks Amphitheater, Denver, Colorado September 13 1996. Tracks 12-14 Glastonbury Festival, UK 1994.
Comments: European CD. Deluxe color cover. Picture CD.

RAGE AGAINST THE MACHINE

CD - SNAPSHOT
KISS THE STONE KTS 596
Viet Now/ Bombtrack/ Fistful Of Steel/ Bullet In Your Head/ Tire Me/ Killing In The Name/ Zapara's Blood (with Chuck Dee Of Public Enemy)/ Bulls On Parade/ Year Of The Boomerang/ Darkness Of Greed/ Clear The Lane/ Mindsets A Threat/ Auto Logic/ The Narrows/ Hadda Be Playing On The Jukebox
Recording: Excellent. Soundboard.
Source: Tracks 1-7 Pink Pop Festival, Holland May 24 1996. Track 8 Rock AM Ring Festival, Germany May 26 1996. Track 9 Glastonbury Festival, UK June 1994. Tracks 10-14 Los Angeles, demos 1991. Track 15 Maida Vale Studios, London 1993.
Comments: European CD. Picture CD. Time 68:05.

RAINBOW

CD - ANOTHER ON LINE
NIGHTLIFE N-028/29
CD1: Over The Rainbow, Eyes Of The World/ Love's No Friend/ Since You've Been Gone, Over The Rainbow/ Stargazer/ Man On The Silver Mountain/ Catch The Rainbow
CD2: Keyboards Solo: Lost In Hollywood, Guitar Solo, Difficult To Cure, Keyboards Solo, Drums Solo, 1812 Overture, Lost In Hollywood/ Lazy, All Night Long/ Long Live Rock 'N' Roll/ Encore: Kill The King, Long Live Rock 'N' Roll, Over The Rainbow
Recording: Excellent. Audience. Cover says soundboard.
Source: Arhaus, Denmark August 8 1980.
Comments: Japanese CD. Deluxe color cover. Time CD1 44:04. CD2 43:23.

CD - PARISIAN MASQUERADE
CD1: Land Of Hope And Glory/ Over The Rainbow, Spot Light Kid, Too Late For Tears, Long Live Rock 'N' Roll Medley/ Black Night, Hunting Humans, Adlib, Wolf To The Moon, Difficult To Cure/ 'Key' Solo, Still I'm Sad/ 'Drs.' Solo, Man On The Silver Mountain, Adlib, Temple Of The King, Black Masquerade
CD2: Ariel, Since You Been Gone, Perfect Strangers, Woman From Tokyo, Adlib, Hall Of The Mountain King, (Encore) Blues, Burn, Smoke On The Water/ Over The Rainbow/ Hey Joe*, Rainbow Eyes*, Love Hurts*, Mistreated*, Black Night*/ Over The Rainbow*
Recording: Excellent. Audience.
Source: Paris, France October 31 1995.
*Ahoy, Rotterdam October 17 1995.
Comments: Japanese CD. Deluxe color cover. Picture CD.

CD - PERFECT ON LINE
NIGHTLIFE N-038/39
CD1: Over The Rainbow, Eyes Of The World/ Love's No Friend/ Since You've Been Gone, Over The Rainbow/ Stargazer/ Man On Silver Mountain/ Catch The Rainbow
CD2: Keyboard Solo, Lost In Hollywood, Guitar Solo, Difficult To Cure, Keyboard Solo, Drum Solo, Lost In Hollywood/ Lazy, All Night Long/ Blues, Long Live Rock 'N' Roll/ Kill The King, Long Live Rock 'N' Roll
Recording: Good. Audience. Cover says soundboard.
Source: Abork, Sweden August 10 '80.
Comments: Japanese CD. Deluxe color cover. Time CD1 47:58. CD2 44:38.

REM

CD - ACOUSTIC TOUR '91
REAL LIVE RL CD 04
World Leader Pretend (4:34)/ Half A World Away (3:30)/ Radio Song (4:31)/ Love Is All Around (3:20)/ Losing My Religion (4:40)/ Fall On Me (3:15)/ It's The End Of The World As We Know It (And I Feel Fine) (4:30)/ Belong (4:35)/ Low (4:58)/ Endgame (3:33)/// Swan Swan H. (2:47)/ Spookie (2:55)/ Disturbance At The Heron House (2:39)/ Fretless (5:30)/ Dallas (4:22)/ Losing My Religion (alternate version) (5:06)/ World Leader Pretend (alternate version) (4:41)
Recording: Excellent stereo. Soundboard.
Source: Acoustic tour 1991. Tracks 1-5 and 14 East Sound Studio, Toronto, Canada May 9. Tracks 6-8 and 15-17 Mountain Stage, West Virginia May 4. Tracks 9-13 SNAP FM studio, Los Angeles April 3.
Comments: European CD. Deluxe B&w cover.

CD - CLASSIC TRAXX
SHINOLA SH 69057
Wake Up B./ Bang And Blame/ What's The Frequency, Kenneth?/ Loosing My Religion/ Shiny Happy People/ I Don't Sleep, I

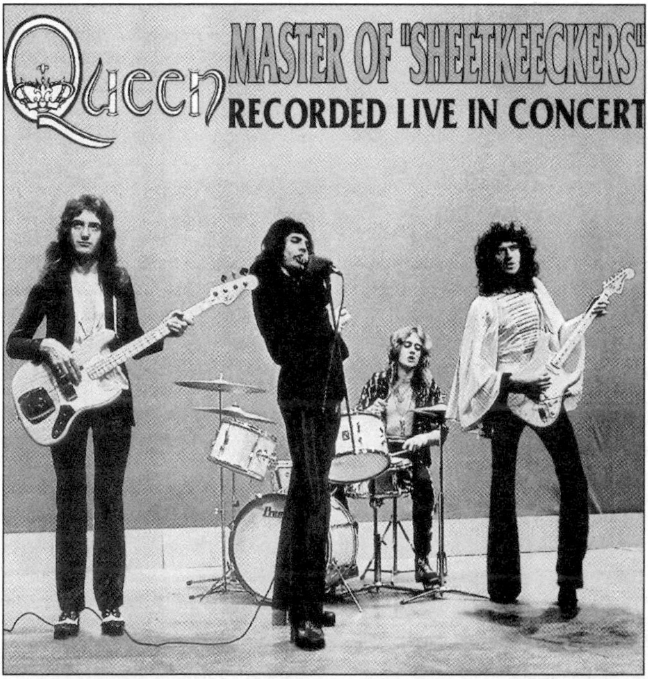
Queen
MASTER OF "SHEETKEECKERS"
RECORDED LIVE IN CONCERT

SNAPSHOT
RAGE
AGAINST
THE
MACHINE
commie

REM

Dream/ Drive/ Everybody Hurts/ Radio Song/ It's The End Of The World As We Know It (And I Feel Fine)/ Love Is All Around/ Man On The Moon/ Popsong/ Red Rain, South Central Rain/ The One I Love
Recording: Excellent.
Source: USA '93 - '95.
Comments: European CD. Time 63:45.

CD - FREAK MARMALADE
KOBRA RECORDS KRCD 12
Wake Up Bomb (MTV Music Awards September 7 '95)/ Undertown/ Revolution/ Baby Come (Milton Keynes, London July 29 '95)/ What's The Frequency Kenneth/ Bang And Blame/ I Don't Sleep, I Dream (Saturday Night Live November 12 '94)/ Everybody Hurts/ Losing My Religion/ Me In Honey/ Drive/ Funtime, Radio Free Europe (Green Peace Benefit November 19 '95)/ Half A World Away (acoustic) (Milton Keynes July 29 '95)/ So Central Rain (acoustic, Torino '95)/ Country Feedback (acoustic)/ Man On The Moon (acoustic, Milano '95)
Recording: Excellent.
Comments: European CD. Deluxe color cover. Time 78:10.

CD - MONSTER B-SIDES
QR7
What's The Frequency Kenneth?/ Bang And Blame/ I Don't Sleep, I Dream ('Saturday Night Live' November 12 '94)/ Monty Got A Raw Deal/ Everybody Hurts/ Man On The Moon/ Losing My Religion/ Country Feedback/ Begin The Begin/ Fall On Me/ Me In Honey/ Finest Worksong/ Drive/ Funtime/ Radio Free Europe (Greenpeace Benefit Concert, November 19 '92)/ Tighten Up (unreleased studio out-take from promo Flexi-disc)
Recording: Excellent stereo. Soundboard.
Comments: European CD. Deluxe color cover. Time 69:22.

CD - RARE TRAXX
SHINOLA SH 69041
Dallas/ It's A Free World Baby/ Hello There/ Red Rain/ See No Evil/ You Ain't Goin" Nowhere/ That Beat/ Jackson/ Ghost Rider/ All The Right Friends/ Tom's Diner/ Academy Flight Song/ Moon River/ Tainted Obligation/ Spooky/ The Back Beat Band (Mike Mills on bass)/ Money/ Long Tall Sally

Recording: Excellent.
Source: USA 1994.
Comments: European CD. Time 61:25.

CD - SOUND EMPORIUM
TORNADO TOR028
Moral Kiosk/ Pilgrimage/ Shaking Through/ Wolves Lover/ Laughing/ Easy Come, Easy Go/ Sitting Still/ Pretty Persuasion/ Catapult/ 1, 000, 000/ Gardening At Night/ 9-9/ Radio Free Europe/ White Tornado/ Ages Of You/ We Walk/ Neverland/ Gloria/ Carnival Of Sorts (Boxcars)/ Instrumental/ West Of The Fields
Recording: Excellent. Audience.
Source: Tupelo's Tavern, New Orleans, LA November 6 1982.
Comments: European CD. Deluxe color cover. Time 73:14.

CD - TO THE CLIMAX
DR. GIG DGCD 059
What's The Frequency, Kenneth?/ Crush With Eyeliner/ Drive/ Try Not To Breath/ Bang And Blame/ Undertow/ I Took Your Name/ Me In Honey/ Revolution/ Tongue/ Man On The Moon/ Departure/ Pop Song '89/ Finest Worksong/ Get Up/ Star 69/ Everybody Hurts
Recording: Good. Audience.
Source: The Torhout Festival, Belgium July 1 1995.
Comments: European CD. Deluxe color cover. Time 74:00.

RED HOT CHILI PEPPERS, THE

CD - FUNKAMENTAL
MOONRAKER 175
Give It Away (7:20)/ Suck My Kiss (4:00)/ Warped (7:20)/ Walkabout (4:12)/ Backwoods (4:21)/ My Friends (5:33)/ Higher Ground (3:22)/ Bloodsugarsexmagik (5:40)/ Pea (1:56)/ Coffee Shop (5:14)/ Aeroplane (5:26)/ One Big Mob (6:18)/ Under The Bridge (4:52)/ Me And My Friends (3:29)/ Sweet Home Alabama (1:27)/ Deep Kick (6:39)/ Nevermind (2:48)
Recording: Excellent stereo. Soundboard.
Source: The Sports Arena, San Diego April 16 1996.
Comments: European CD. Deluxe color cover. Picture CD. Time 79:51.

CD - THE GARDEN
MOONRAKER 078
Freaky Styley Jam/ Suck My Kiss/ Give It Away/ Warped/ Walkabout/ Come As You Are/ Backwoods/ My Friends/ Sound And Vision/ Higher Ground/ Pea/ Coffee Shop/ One Big Mob/ Under The Bridge/ Me And My Friends/ Deep Kick/ I Wanna Be Your Dog/ Nevermind
Recording: Excellent stereo. Audience.
Source: The Madison Square Garden, New York City February 9 '96. Special guest Iggy Pop.
Comments: European CD. Deluxe color cover. Time 79:22.

CD - GRAVITY
MOONRAKER 130
The Power Of Equality/ Warped/ Suck My Kiss/ Walkabout/ Blood Sugar Sex Magik/ My Friends/ Jesus!/ Higher Ground/ Pea/ Shallow Be Thy Name/ Aeroplane/ One Big Mob/ Under The Bridge/ Give It Away/ Deep Kick/ Coffee Shop
Recording: Excellent stereo. Audience.
Source: The Entertainment Centre, Sydney, Australia May 15 1996.
Comments: European CD.

REED, LOU WITH JOHN CALE AND NICO

CD - PARIS 29. 1. 72
VUCD-41
Waiting For The Man/ Berlin/ Black Angel's Death Song/ Wild Child/ Empty Bottle/ Heroin/ Ghost Story/ The Biggest, The Loudest, The Hairless/ Femme Fatale/ All Tomorrow's Parties/ Janitor Of Lunacy/ Black Angel's Death Song/ Heroin/ Pale Blue Eyes/ Candy Says
Recording: Good to very good. Audience

ROLLING STONES, THE

CD - A ROLLING STONE GATHERS NO MOSS
A VINYL GANG PRODUCT VGP-101
CD1: Everybody Needs Somebody To Love/ Around And Around/ Time Is On My Side/ It's All Over Now/ 19th Nervous Breakdown/ Get Off Of My Cloud/ The Last Time/ Paint It Black/ Under My Thumb/ Ruby Tuesday/ Let's Spend The Night Together/ (I Can't Get No) Satisfaction/ Introduction/ Everybody Needs Somebody To Love/ Tell Me (You're Coming Back)/ Around And Around/ Charlie's Intro, Little Red Rooster/ The Last Time
CD2: Everybody Needs Somebody To Love/ Around And Around/ Off The Hook/ Time Is On My Side/ Carol/ It's All Over Now/ Little Red Rooster/ Route 66/ Everybody Needs Somebody To Love/ The Last Time/ I'm Alright/ Craw-Dad/ Paint It Black/ 19th Nervous Breakdown/Lady Jane/ Medley: Get Off Of My Cloud/ Under My Thumb/ Ruby Tuesday/ Let's Spend The Night Together/ Goin' Home/ (I Can't Get No) Satisfaction
Source: CD1 Tracks 1-4 L'Olympia, Paris, France April 18 1995. Tracks 5-7 L'Olympia, Paris, France March 28 1966. Tracks 8-12 L'Olympia, Paris, France April 11 1967. Tracks 13-18 Swedish TV-Special, Stockholm April 2 1965. CD2 Tracks 1-12 L'Olympia, Paris, France April 18 1964. Tracks 13-22 L'Olympia, Paris, France April 11 1967.
Comments: Japanese CD.

CD - ACETATES
MIDNIGHT BEAT MBCD045
Silver Train/ Criss Cross Man/ Criss Cross Man/ Hide Your Love/ 100 Years Ago/ Ain't Too Proud To Beg/ If You Can't Rock Me/ Till The Next Goodbye/ Drift Away/ Dance Little Sister/ Fingerprint File/ Brown Sugar/ Bitch/ Let It Rock/ I Ain't To Proud To Beg
Recording: Good to very good. Surface noise.
Source: Various locations 1970 to 19074.

CD - ALL MEAT MUSIC
A VINYL GANG PRODUCT VGP-005
CD1: Brown Sugar/ Bitch/ Rocks Off/ Gimme Shelter/ Happy/ Tumbling Dice/ Love In Vain/ Sweet Virginia/ You Can't Always Get What You Want
CD2: Brown Sugar/ Bitch/ Rocks Off/ Gimme Shelter/ Happy/ Tumbling Dice/ Love In Vain/ Sweet Virginia/ You Can't Always Get What You Want/ Honky Tonk Women/ All Down The LIne/ Midnight Rambler/ Introductions/ Little Queenie/ Street Fighting Man
Recording: Very good.
Source: CD1 Auckland, New Zealand February 11 1973. CD2 Sydney, Australia February 27 1973.
Comments: Japanese CD.

ROLLING STONES, THE

CD - AN AMERICAN AFFAIR
VINYL GANG PRODUCTION VGP-080
Brown Sugar/ Bitch/ Rocks Off/ Gimme Shelter/ Happy Happy/ Love In Vain/ Sweet Virginia/ You Can't Always Get What You Want/ All Down Line/ Midnight Rambler/ Band Introduction/ Bye Bye Johnny/ Rip This Joint/ Jumping Jack Flash/ Street Fighting Man
Source: Civic Arena, Pittsburgh, Pennsylvania July 22 1972.
Comments: Japanese CD.

CD - BEAST OF BURDEN
VINYL GANG PRODUCT VGP-086
CD1: Under My Thumb/ When The Whip Comes Down/ Let's Spend The Night Together/ Shattered/ Neighbours/ Black Limousine/ Just My Imagination/ Twenty Flight Rock/ Going To A Go Go/ Chantilly Lace/ Let Me Go/ Time Is On My Side/ Beast Of Burden/ Let It Bleed
CD2: You Can't Always Get What You Want/ Band Introductions/ Little T & A/ Tumbling Dice/ She's So Cold/ Hang Fire/ Miss You/ Honky Tonk Women/ Brown Sugar/ Start Me Up/ Jumping Jack Flash/ (I Can't Get No) Satisfaction
Source: Berlin, West Germany June 8 1982.
Comments: Japanese CD.

CD - BEST OF KNEBWORTH FAIR, THE
MIDNIGHT MB CD 088
Around And Around (3:57)/ Little Red Rooster (5:29)/ Hot Stuff (5:33)/ Star Star (4:04)/ You Gotta Move (3:39)/ Route 66 (3:46)/ Wild Horses (7:02)/ Honky Tonk Woman (3:21)/ Country Honk Theme (0:29)/ Tumbling Dice (4:48)/ Midnight Rambler (13:34)/ Street Fighting Man (8:04)
Recording: Excellent stereo.
Source: Knebworth Fair, Knebworth Park, Stevenage, Hertfordshire, UK August 21 1976.

CD - BRING IT BACK ALIVE
A VINYL GANG PRODUCT VGP-054
Brown Sugar/ Bitch/ Rocks Off/ Gimme Shelter/ Happy/ Tumbling Dice/ Love In Vain/ Sweet Virginia/ You Can't Always Get What You Want/ All Down The Line/ Midnight Rambler/ Introductions/ Bye Bye Johnny/ Rip This Joint/ Jumping Jack Flash/ Street Fighting Man
Recording: Very good to excellent. Audience.
Source: Charlotte Coliseum, North Carolina July 6 1972. Track 1 second show, Madison Square Garden, New York July 25 1972.
Comments: Japanese CD.

CD - ELECTRIC MOTHERFUCKERS
KOBRA RECORDS KRCR 14
Fancy Man Blues (unreleased)/ Sympathy For The Devil ('69)/ Dirty Mac (instrumental, Great R'N'R Circus '68)/ Brown Sugar (K. Richards birthday December 18 '70 with Eric Clapton)/ Dead Flowers (Leeds '71)/ Just My Imagination (Passaic, New Jersey '78)/ Con Le Mie Lacrime (As Tears Go By - Italian version)/ Shake Rattle & Roll (Sevilla '92 Richards with Dylan)/ Connection (Sevilla '92)/ It's Only Rock' N' Roller (Tokyo March 23 '88 with Tina Turner)/ Checkin' Up On My Body (Take 3)/ Intro, Sweet Little Rock' N' Roller (New Barbarians, Canada)/ Like A Rolling Stone (Special TV '95)/ Love Is Strong (Richards on vocal)/ You Got Me Rockin' (early version with Richards on vocal)
Recording: Very good to excellent. Soundboard.
Comments: European CD. B&W cover. Red type. Time 76:17.

CD - EVERYTHING BUT THE COBRA
DR. GIG DG CD 037-2
CD1: Intro/ Note Fade Away/ Tumbling Dice/ You Got Me Rocking/ It's All Over Now/ Live With Me/ Sparks Will Fly/ (I Can't Get No) Satisfaction/ Out Of Tears/ Angie/ Midnight Rambler/ I Go Wild/ Miss You
CD2: Band Introduction/ Honky Tonk Women/ Happy/ Slipping Away/ Sympathy For The Devil/ Monkey Man/ Street Fighting Man/ Start Me Up/ It's Only /Rock 'N' Roll/ Brown Sugar/ Jumping Jack Flash/ Rock And A Hard Place*
Recording: Excellent stereo. Soundboard.
Source: Ellis Park Stadium, Johannesburg February 25 '95. *Johannesburg, February 24 '95.
Comments: European. Deluxe color cover.

CD - THE FOOTTAPPERS AND WHEEL SHUNTERS CLUB GIG
VINYL GANG PRODUCT VGP
CD1: Introductions/ Not Fade Away/ It's All Over/ Live With Me/ Let It Breed/ Beast Of Burden/ Angie/ Wild Horses/ Stand Up Charlie!/ Sweet Virginia/ Dead Flowers/ Still

A Fool/ Down In The Bottom/ Shine A Light
CD2: Like A Rolling Stone/ Jump On Top Of
Me/ Connection/ Band Introducing/ Before
They Make Me Run/ Slipping Away/
Monkey Man/ Can't Get Next To You/ All
Down The Line/ Street Fighting Man/ Rip
This Joint/ Respectable
Source: Paradiso Club, Amsterdam May 27
1995.
Comments: Japanese CD.

CD - GET YOUR LEEDS LUNGS OUT REVISITED
SWINGIN' PIG TSP-CD-215
Dead Flowers/ Stray Cat Blues/ Love In
Vain/ Midnight Rambler/ Bitch/ Band
Introduction/ Honky Tonk Women/ (I Can't
Get No) Satisfaction/ Little Queenie/ Brown
Sugar/ Street Fighting Man/ Let It Rock/ Let
It Rock (stereo version)
Recording: Excellent. Soundboard.
Source: Leeds University March 13 1971.
Comments: European CD. Remastered
from the original soundboard master tapes.

CD - GOING BACK TO THE ROOTS
WIZARDO REKORDS
CD1: Brown Sugar/ Bitch/ Rocks Off/
Gimme Shelter/ Happy/ Tumbling Dice/
Love In Vain/ Sweet Virginia/ You Can't
Always Get What You Want/ All Down The
Line/ Midnight Rambler/ Introductions/ Bye
Bye Johnny/ Rip This Joint/ Jumping Jack
Flash
CD2: Brown Sugar/ Bitch/ Rocks Off/
Gimme Shelter/ Happy/ Tumbling Dice/
Love In Vain/ Sweet Virginia/ You Can't
Always Get What You Want
Recording: CD1 very good audience. CD2
poor.
Source: CD1 The Scope, Norfolk, Virginia
July 5 1972. CD2 Convention Center,
Indianapolis July 12 1972.
Comments: Japanese CD.

CD - HANDSOME GIRLS
SWINGIN PIG TSP-CD-200-1/2/3/4
CD1: Let It Rock/ All Down The Line/ Honky
Tonk Women/ Starfucker/ When The Ship
Comes Down/ Beast Of Burden/ Miss You/
Just My Imagination/ Shattered/
Respectable/ Faraway Eyes/ Love In Vain/
Tumbling Dice/ Happy
CD2: Sweet Little Sixteen/ Brown Sugar/
Jumping Jack Flash (Alternate Mixes)/ All
Down The Line/ Honky Tonk Women/
Starfucker/ When The Ship Comes Down/
Beast Of Burden/ Shattered/ Faraway
Eyes/ Jumping Jack Flash
Source: CD1-CD2 Will Rogers Memorial
Center, Fort Worth July 18 1978.
CD3: Let It Rock*/ All Down The Line*/
Honky Tonk Women*/ Starfucker*/ When
The Whip Comes Down**/ Lies*/ Miss You*/
Beast Of Burden**/ Shattered**/
Respectable**/ Just My Imagination*/
Faraway Eyes***/ Love In Vain**/ Tumbling
Dice**/ Happy****
Source: *Masonic Hall, Detroit July 6 1978.
**Midsouth Coliseum, Memphis June 28
1978. ***Rupp Arena, Lexington, Kentucky
June 29 1978. ****Hofheinz Pavilion,
Houston July 19 1978.
CD4: Hound Dog*/ Sweet Little Sixteen**/
Brown Sugar**/ Jumping Jack Flash**/ Miss
You***/ Lies***/ Beast Of Burden***/
Shattered***/ Just My Imagination***
Respectable***/ Sweet Little Sixteen***
Source: *Midsouth Coliseum, Memphis
June 28 1978. **Hofheinz Pavilion, Houston
July 19 1978. ***Rupp Arena, Lexington,
Kentucky, June 29 1978.
Recording: Excellent stereo. Soundboard.
Comments: European CD. Remastered
from the original soundboard master tapes.

CD - L. A. CONNECTION
VINYL GANG PRODUCT VGP-085
CD1: Fanfare For The Common Man/
Honky Tonk Women/ All Down The Line/ If
You Can't Rock Me, Get Off My Cloud/ Star
Star/ Gimmie Shelter/ Ain't To Proud To
Beg/ You Gotta Move/ You Can't Always
Get What You Want/ Happy/ Tumbling Dice/
It's Only Rock 'N Roll/ Band Introductions/
Doo Doo Doo Doo (Heartbreaker)/
CD2: Fingerprint File/ Angie/ Wild Horses/
That's Life/ Outta Space/ Brown Sugar/
Midnight Rambler/ Rip This Joint/ Street
Fighting Man/ Jumping Jack Flash/
Sympathy For The Devil
Source: Inglewood Forum, Los Angeles
July 11 1975.
Comments: Japanese CD.

CD - LIVE AT WEST PALM BEACH 1969
IDOL MIND PRODUCTIONS IMP-CD-042
Introduction/ Jumpin' Jack Flash/ Carol/
Sympathy For The Devil/ Stray Cat Blues/
Love In Vain/ Under My Thumb/ Midnight
Rambler/ Gimme Shelter/ Live With Me/
Little Queenie/ Satisfaction/ Honky Tonk

ROLLING STONES, THE

Women/ Street Fighting Man
Recording: Very good. Audience.
Source: Palm Beach, Florida International Raceway, West Palm Beach, Florida November 30 1969.
Comments: Japanese CD.

CD - MORE STRIPPED
KISS THE STONE KTS 585
Wild Horses (5:03)/ Like A Rolling Stone (4:18)/ Angie (3:26)/ Dead Flowers (4:01)/ Live With Me (3:13)/ The Spider And The Fly (3:25)/ Shine A Light (4:10)/ Sweet Virginia (3:27)/ Rip This Joint (2:06)/ Gimme Shelter (5:14)/ Love In Vain (4:46)/ Street Fighting Man (3:39)/ Let It Bleed (0:55)/ Cook Cook Blues (4:08)/ Memphis (2:27)/ Da Do Ron Ron (2:20)/ Natural Magic (1:37)/ Fancy Man Blues (4:46)/ Highland Flying (4:09)/ We're Wasting Time (2:35)
Recording: Excellent. Soundboard.
Source: Tracks 1-13 Brixton Academy, London, UK; The Paradiso Club, Holland; The Olympia Theatre, Paris, France; and rehearsals at The Toshiba Studios, Tokyo, Japan and Estudios Valentim De Carvalho, Lisbon, Portugal. Tracks 14-20 are rare tracks; alternate versions; instrumentals and unreleased songs.
Comments: European CD. B&W cover. Orange type. CD looks like a record. 76:59.

CD - ONE DAY BEFORE FROM ALTEMONT
SHAVED DISC
Announce Of Delay Starting Concert For Airplane Trouble/ Jumping Jack Flash/ Carol/ Sympathy For The Devil/ Stray Cat Blues/ Love In Vain/ Under My Thumb/ Midnight Rambler/ Gimme Shelter/ Live With Me/ Little Queenie/ Satisfaction/ Honky Tonk Women/ Street Fighting Man
Recording: Good. Audience. Hiss.
Source: Palm Beach, Florida International Raceway, West Palm Beach, Florida November 30 1969.

CD - PARIS MATCH
GOLD STANDARD
Around And Around/ Off The Hook/ Time Is On My Side/ Carol/ It's All Over Now/ Little Red Rooster/ Route 66/ Everybody Needs Somebody To Love/ The Last Time/ I'm Alright/ Hey Crawdaddy/ Not Fade Away/ Mothers Little Helper/ Get Off My Cloud/ 19th Nervous Breakdown/ Satisfaction/ Connection/ It's All Over Now/ Going Home
Recording: Very good. Tracks 20-22 Poor to good.
Source: Tracks 1-11 recorded for French Radio at The Paris Olympia Theatre April 18 1965. Tracks 12-19 Honolulu, Hawaii, the final American concert with Brian Jones July 28 '66. Tracks 20-21 recorded for BBC Television's Sunday Night At The London Palladium January 20 '67. Track 22 The Paris Olympia Theatre April 11 '67.
Comments: Deluxe color cover. Time 74:52.

CD - SAN DIEGO '69
SWINGIN' PIG TSP-CD-214
Jumping Jack Flash/ Carol/ Sympathy For The Devil/ Stray Cat Blues/ Prodigal Son/ You Gotta Move/ Love In Vain/ I'm Free/ Under My Thumb/ Midnight Rambler/ Live With Me/ Little Queenie/ (I Can't Get No) Satisfaction/ Honky Tonk women/ Street Fighting Man
Source: The Sports Arena, San Diego November 10 1969.
Comments: European CD. Remastered from the original soundboard master tapes.

CD - SHATTERED EUROPE
THE SWINGIN' PIG TSP-CD-184
Under My Thumb/ When The Whip Comes Down/ Let's Spend The Night Together/ Shattered/ Neighbors/ Black Limousine/ Just My Imagination/ Band Introduction/ Little T & A/ Angie/ Tumbling Dice/ She's So Cold/ Hang Fire/ Miss You/ Honky Tonk Women/ Brown Sugar/ Start Me Up
Recording: Excellent stereo. Soundboard.
Source: Stadio San Paolo, Napoli, Italy July 17 1982.
Comments: European CD. Deluxe color cover. Gold disc. Time 76:25.

CD - SOMEWHERE IN GERMANY
CONTINENTAL DRIFT CDOO1/02
CD1: Start Me Up/ Sad Sad Sad/ Harlem Shuffle/Tumbling Dice/ Miss You/ Almost Hear You Sigh/ Ruby Tuesday/ Mixed Emotions/ Honky Tonk Women/ Midnight Rambler/ You Can't Always Get What You Want/ Can't Be Seen/ Happy
CD2: Paint It Black/ 2000 Lightyears From Home/ Sympathy For The Devil/ Street Fighting Man/ Gimme Shelter/ It's Only

Flash/ Satisfaction
Recording: Good. Audience.
Source: Parkstadion, Gelsenkirchen, Germany August 16 1990.
Comments: Japanese CD. Deluxe color cover.

CD - STATIC IN THE ATTIC
MIDNIGHT BEAT MB CD 084
Interview With Mick Jagger (1:32)/ Act Together (Instrumental) (5:32)/ Reggae Instrumental (4:25)/ Fool To Cry (Early Version) (6:02)/ Down In The Hole (3:56)/ Claudine #1 (3:37)/ We Had It All (2:52)/ Let's Go Steady (2:49)/ Indian Girl #1 (Long Version) (6:43)/ I Think I'm Going Mad (5:47)/ Let Me Go (Edit, No Sax) (3:52)/ Emotional Rescue (5:44)/ Claudine #2 (3:04)/ No Use Crying #1 (Long Version) (4:28)/ Summer Romance (Long Version) (3:52)/ Indian Girl #2 (Edit) (4:25)/ No Use Crying #2 (4:27)
Recording: Excellent stereo.
Source: Track 1 interview date unknown. All songs are alternate versions. Recorded at: Marconi EMI Studios, Paris January-March 1978. Musicland Studios, Munchen, December 7-15 1974. Compass Point Studios, Nassau, Bahamas January-February 8 1979.
Comments: European CD.

CD - STONED IN PERTH
WEEPING GOAT WG-045/6
CD1: Not Fade Away/ Tumbling Dice/ You Got Me Rocking/ Shattered/ Rocks Off/ Sparks Will Fly/ Satisfaction/ Beast Of Burden/ Angie/ Rock And A Hard Place/ I Go Wild/ Miss You
CD2: Band Introduction/ Honky Tonk Women/ Before They Make Me Run/ Slipping Away/ Sympathy For The Devil/ Gimme Shelter/ Street Fighting Man/ Start Me Up/ It's Only Rock'N Roll/ Brown Sugar/ Jumpin Jack Flash
Recording: Excellent. Audience.
Source: Perth, April 8 1995.
Comments: Japanese CD. Deluxe color cover.

CD - VERY ANCIENT, THANK YOU KINDLY
SCORPIO
Brown Sugar/ Bitch/ Rocks Off/ Gimme Shelter/ Dead Flowers/ Happy/ Tumbling Dice/ Love In Vain/ Sweet Virginia/ Ventilator Blues/ Torn And Frayed/ Loving Cup/ All Down The Line/ Bye Bye Johnny/ Rip This Joint/ Jumping Jack Flash/ Street Fighting Man/ Uptight, Satisfaction/ Don't Lie To Me/ It's All Over Now
Recording: Good to very good. Some excellent.
Source: Recorded at various North American venues during the 1972 summer tour, including Vancouver, Houston, Fort Worth, Pittsburgh, Philadelphia, New York City, Boston, Charlotte, NC and Honolulu.
Comments: Japanese CD. Deluxe color cover. Time 77:23.

CD - VOODOO, I LIKE IT
CRYSTAL CAT RECORDS CC 365/66
CD1: Intro/ The Show/ Intro Drums/ Not Fade Away/ Tumbling Dice/ You Got Me Rocking/ Respectable/ Rocks Off/ Live With Me/ Sparks Will Fly/ (I Can't Get No) Satisfaction/ Wild Horses/ Like A Rolling Stone/ Rock And A Hard Place/ I Go Wild/ Mis You/ Band Introduction
CD2: Honky Tonk Women/ Before They Make Me Run/ Slipping Away/ Paus Music/ Sympathy For The Devil/ Monkey Man/ Street Fighting Man/ Start Me Up/ It's Only Rock 'N Roll/ Brown Sugar/ Jumpin' Jack Flash/ Fireworks/ Beast Of Burden/ Gimmie Shelter/ Not Fade Away/ I Go Wild
Recording: Excellent. Audience.
Source: Stockholm June 3 '95. CD2 13, 14 Helsinki June 9 '95. CD2 15, 16 Stockholm June 3 '95.
Comments: European CD. Deluxe color cover. Time CD1 75:44. CD2 78:20.

CD - YOU'RE NOT SUGAR, I'M NOT SUGAR
A VINYL GANG PRODUCT VGP-072
CD1: Not Fade Away/ Tumbling Dice/ You Got Me Rocking/ Live With Me/ Just My Imagination/ Sparks Will Fly/ Satisfaction/ Beast Of Burden/ Far Away Eyes/ Rock And A Hard Place/ I Go Wild/ Miss You
CD2: Band Introduction/ Honky Tonk Women/ Before They Make Me Run/ Slipping Away/ Start Me Up/ It's Only Rock'N Roll/ Brown Sugar/ Keith Williams Interview With Mick And Keith/ Rachel Kerr Interview With Keith
Recording: Good.
Source: Football Park, Adelaide, Australia April 5 1995. CD2 Tracks 8 & 9 Sydney

Radio March & November 1995.
Comments: Japanese CD.

ROLLINS, HENRY BAND

CD - LIVE IN NEW YORK AND AT WOODSTOCK
Volume 4 (5:05)/ Divine Object Of Hatred (4:24)/ Disconnect (4:53)/ Civilized (4:40)/ Icon (3:47)/ Liar (8:03)/ Wrong Man (4:30)/ Right Here, Too Much (6:19)/ Alien Blueprint (3:53)/ Fool (3:57)
Recording: Excellent stereo. Soundboard.
Source: Tracks 1-6 New York. Tracks 7-10 Woodstock.
Comments: European CD. Time 51:19.

ROTH, DAVID LEE

CD - EAT'M AND SMILE WORLD TOUR 1986
JAILBAIT RECORDS JBCD-011
Shy Boy/ Tobacco Road/ Unchained/ Panama/ Drums Solo/ Pretty Woman/ Elephant Gun/ Everybody, Lighter Shade Of Green/ On Fire/ Bump And Grind/ Ice Cream Man/ Big Trouble/ Yankee Rose/ Steve Vai Vs Billy Sheehan: Strings Battle/ Ain't Talkin' 'Bout Love/ Goin' Crazy
Recording: Very good. Audience.
Source: California December 12 1986.

ROXY MUSIC

CD - MUSIKLADEN
COLOSSEUM RECORDS 96-C-007
Street Life/ Pyjamarama/ Mother Of Pearl/ Amazona/ Virginia Plain/ A Hard Rain's Gonna Fall/ Psalm/ Out Of The Blue/ If It Takes All Night/ Do The Strand/ Editions Of You/ In Every Dream Home A Nightmare/ Remake, Remodel/ Virginia Plain
Recording: Good to very good to excellent. Soundboard.
Source: Tracks 1-4, 7-9 German TV winter 1974. Track 5 Germany winter 1973. Track 6 German TV winter 1974. Tracks 10-14 Bremen Germany February 1973.
Comments: European CD. Deluxe color cover. Time 62:09.

CD - WILD WEEKEND
SCORPIO
Sentimental Fool/ The Thrill Of It All/ Love Is The Drug/ Mother Of Pearl/ Bittersweet/ Out Of The Blue/ Whirlwind/ Sea Breezes/ Both Ends Burning/ For Your Pleasure/ Diamond Head/ Wild Weekend
Recording: Excellent. Soundboard.
Source: The Calderone Theatre, Hempstead, New York March 8 1975.
Comments: Deluxe color cover. Time 63:51.

RUNDGREN, TODD

CD - LIVE IN MINK HOLLOW
BALBOA POP PRO. BPP-003
Real Men/ Sometimes I Don't Know How To Feel/ Love Of The Common Man/ Love In Action/ Abandoned City/ The Last Ride/ The Seven Rays/ Can We Still Be Friends?/ Death Of A Rock Star/ You Cried Wolf/ Gangrene/ Dream Goes On Forever/ Black And White/ Will the Real God Please Stand Up/ Couldn't I Just Tell You?/ Hello It's Me
Recording: Very good. Soundboard.
Source: Texas Opry House, Houston August 10 1978.

RUSH

CD - HEMISPHERES PERFORMANCE
ELEMENT OF CRIME ELEMENTS-042
Anthem/ By-Tor & Snow Dog, At The Tobes Of Hades, Across The Styx, Of The Battle/ Xanadu/ Cygnus X-1 Book II Hemispheres, Prelude, Apollo-Dionysus, Armageddon, Cygnus, The Sphere/ Closer To The Heart/ A Farewell To Kings/ La Villa Strangiato/ 2112 Overture, The Temples Of Syrinx, Discovery, Presentation, Oracle: The Dream, Soliloguy, Grand Finale
Recording: Good to very good.
Source: Oslo, Norway May 22 1979.
Comments: Japanese CD. Deluxe color cover. Time 78:21.

CD - 2112 DAYS
ELEMENT OF CRIME ELEMENTS-006
Bastille Day/ Anthem/ Lakeside Park/ 2112: Overture, The Temples Of Syrinx, Presentation/ Soliloquy, Grand Final/ Fly By Night, In The Mood/ Something For Nothing/ In The End/ By-Tor And The Snow Dog: At The Tobes Of Hades, Across The Styx, Of The Battle, Epilogue/ Working Man, Finding My Way/ What You're Doing
Recording: Very good. Soundboard.
Source: No source given.
Comments: Japanese CD. Deluxe color cover. Picture CD. Time 73:20.

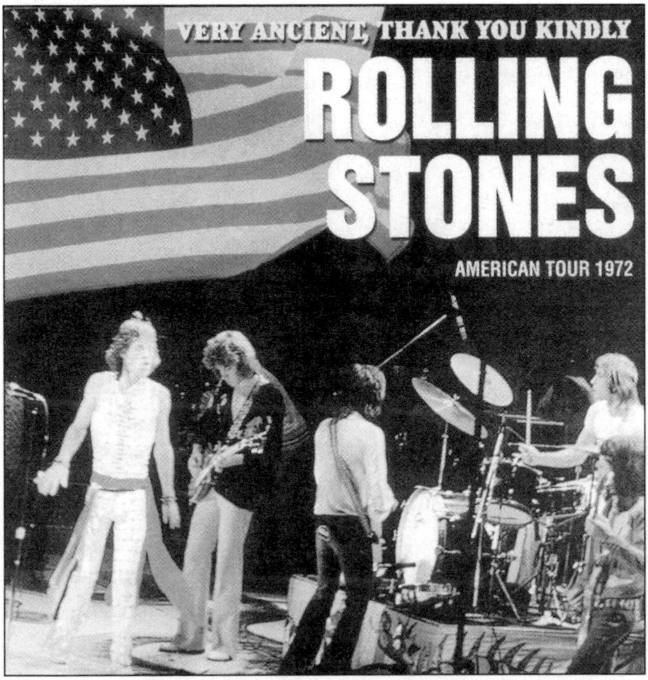
VERY ANCIENT, THANK YOU KINDLY
ROLLING
STONES
AMERICAN TOUR 1972

THE RUTLES
stereo
TRADE MARK
ELEMENT of CRIME
SWEET RUTLE TRACKS

RUTLES, THE

CD - SWEET RUTLE TRACKS
ELEMENT OF CRIME ELEMENTS-037
We'ved Armed/ Now She's Left You/ Number One/ Love Life/ Goose Step Mama/ It's Looking Good/ I Must Be In Love/ Baby Let Me Be/ Good Times Roll/ Let's Be Natural/ Get Up And Go/ Blue Suede Shubert/ Between Us/ Piggy In The Middle/ Livin' In Hope/ Double Back Alley/ Plenty Of Time
Source: Studio rehearsal. Unknown venue.
Comments: Japanese CD.

S

SEAL

CD - UNPLUGGED
MOONRAKER 148
Stone Free/ Prayer For The Dying/ Future Love Paradise/ Blues In E/ Crazy/ Quicksand/ Kiss From A Rose/ Violet/ Deep Water/ Don't Cry
Recording: Excellent stereo. Soundboard.
Source: The Brooklyn Academy Of Music, New York April 9 1996.
Comments: European CD. Deluxe color cover. Time 45:34.

SCHENKER, MICHAEL

CD - CRY OF THE AXEMAN
BONDAGE MUSIC BON056
Cry For The Nations/ Victim Of Illusion/ Natural Thing/ Feels Like A Good Thing/ Rock Bottom/ Lost Horizons/ Doctor Doctor/ Captain Nemo/ Rock My Nights Away/ Are You Ready To Rock/ Cry For The Nations/ On And On/ Attack Of The Mad Axeman
Recording: Excellent. Soundboard.
Source: Tracks 1-7 Pink Pop Festival, Holland June 8 1981. Tracks 8-13 Portland, Oregon December 14 1983.
Comments: Japanese CD. Deluxe color cover. Time 71:42.

SEPULTURA

CD - SET US FREE
MOONRAKER 155
Roots Bloody Roots/ Spit/ Territory/ Breed Apart/ Attitude/ Dusted/ Interlude/ Escape To The Void/ Ambush/ Straighthate/ Arise/ Slave New World/ Refuse, Resist/ Ratamahatta/ Bonus tracks From Canal+ French TV, May 29 1996: Roots Bloody Roots/ Ratamahatta
Recording: Excellent stereo. Soundboard.
Source: The Naval Museum, Stockholm, June 26 1996.
Comments: European CD. Picture CD. Time 62:57.

CD - PAIN & HATE
KOBRA RECORDS KRHM 11
Intro, Roots Bloody Roots/ Spit/ Territory/ Breed Apart/ Attitude/ Dusted/ Desperate Cry/ Escape To The Void/ We Who Are Not As Others/ Straight Hate/ Medley: Arise, Dead Embrionic Cells/ Slave New World/ Refuse - Resist/ Ratamahatta/ Territory/ Breed Apart/ Straight Hate/ Medley: Arise, Dead Embrionic Cells/ Ambush/ Biotech Is Godzilla
Recording: Excellent stereo. Soundboard.
Source: Tracks 1-14 Stockholm, Sweden June 26 1996. Tracks 15-20 Donnington Festival, England August 17 1996. (Andreas Kisser on vocals)
Comments: European CD.

SEVEN MARY THREE

CD - 41 MINUTES
MOONRAKER 146
Prologue/ Headstrong/ My My/ Roderico/ Devil Boy/ Margaret/ Anything/ Waters Edge/ Lame/ Cumbersome
Recording: Excellent.
Source: The Galaxy Theatre, Santa Ana February 3 1996.
Comments: European CD.

CD - WATER'S EDGE
KISS THE STONE KTS 547
Water's Edge (4:20)/ My My (3:39)/ Roderico (4:38)/ Devil Boy (5:16)/ Shelf Life (4:45)/ Margaret (3:54)/ Anything (4:38)/ Lame (5:20)/ Cumbersome (4:30)/ Honey Generation (5:23)/ Punch In Punch Out (2:58)/ Head Strong (4:56)/ Fortunate Son (3:08)
Recording: Excellent stereo. Soundboard.
Source: Lee's Palace, Toronto March 2 1996.
Comments: European CD. Deluxe color cover. Picture CD.

SEX PISTOLS, THE

CD - FAT, FORTY AND BACK (AND BOLLOCKS TO THE MAJORS)
KISS THE STONE KTS 593
Bodies/ Seventeen/ New York/ No Feelings/ Did You No Wrong/ God Save The Queen/ Liar/ Satellite/ I'm Not Your (Stepping Stone)/ Holidays In The Sun/ Submission/ Pretty Vacant/ EMI/ Anarchy In The U.K./ Problems/ No Fun/ New York/ Pretty Vacant
Recording: Excellent stereo. Soundboard.
Source: Finsbury Park, London June 26 1996.
Comments: European CD.

SIMON AND GARFUNKEL

CD - BEST LIVE COLLECTION 1966-1993
AQUARIUS 412-S-001
The Sounds Of Silence (3:42)/ Wednesday Morning 3 A.M. (2:33)/ I Am A Rock (2:52)/ For Emily, Whenever I May Find Her (2:27)/ Mrs. Robinson (2:56)/ Homeward Bound (2;31)/ Fakin' It (3:11)/ Old Friend (3:11)/ The Boxer (4:32)/ Bridge Over Troubled Water (5:05)/ Leaves That Are Green (2:51)/ So Long, Frank Lloyd Wright (3:06)/ Bye Bye Love (3:32)/ America (3:32)/ Scarborough Fair, Canticle (3:41)/ The 59th Street Bridge Song (Feeling Groovy) (2:21)/ Sound Of Silence (6:33)
Recording: Tracks 1-4 and 11-13 Good. Rest very good to excellent.
Source: Tracks 1-4 USA '66. Tracks 5-8 USA '68. Tracks 9-10 USA '69. Tracks 11-13 Europe '70. Tracks 14-17 USA '93.
Comments: European CD. Deluxe color cover.

CD - HEY, SCHOOL GIRL
MUSIC NATION MN 003
The Boxer/ America/ Homeward Bound/ We Belong Together/ Be Bop A Lula/ Black Slacks/ Hey, School Girl/ Mrs. Robinson/ El Condor Pasa (If I Could)/ April Come She Will/ The 59th Street Bridge Song/ Scarborough Fair/ Bridge Over Troubled Water/ Cecilia/ For Emily, Whenever I May Find Her/ The Sound Of Silence/ Old Friends
Recording: Excellent. Audience.
Source: Paramount, New York October 17 1993.
Comments: Japanese CD. Deluxe color cover. Time 57:26.

CD - FAR EAST REUNION
CD1: Mrs. Robinson/ Homeward Bound/ America/ Me And Julio Down By The Schoolyard/ Scarborough Fair, Cantile/ My Little Town/ Wake Up Little Suzie/ Still Crazy After All These Years/ Bright Eyes/ Late In The Evening/ Slip Slidin' Away/ El Condor Pasa/ Fifty Ways To Leave Your Lover/ American Tune/ The Later Great Johnny Ace/ Kodachrome, Mabellene/ Bridge Over Troubled Water/ The Boxer
CD2: Old Friends, Bookends/ 59th Street Bridge Song (Feelin' Groovy)/ Sound Of Silence/ Late In The Evening/ The Boxer/ Can't Help But Wonder Where I'm Bound/ Sparrow/ On The Side Of A Hill/ I Am A Rock/ A Church Is Burning/ Anji/ Ankji, So Long, Frank Lloyd Wright, Old Friends, Bookends/ Scarborough Fair, Cantile/ The House Carpenter Song/ Gospel Ship/ Pretty Boy Floyd/ A Church Is Burning/ Sounds Of Silence/ The Leaves That Are Green/ The Sun Is Burning/ Can't Help But Wonder Where I'm Bound/ Going To The Zoo/ He Was My Brother/ Homeward Bound/ Bye Bye Love
Source: CD1-CD2 tracks 1-5 Osaka Stadium May 7 1982. CD2 tracks 6-11 BBC Promo Show July '65. CD2 tracks 12-23 Queens College, London rehearsal 1964. CD2 Tracks 24-25 Saturday Night Live with George Harrison November 18 1976.
Comments: Japanese CD.

SIMPLY RED

CD - RED ALL OVER
KISS THE STONE KTS 597
So Beautiful/ Holding Back The Years/ You Make Me Believe/ Come To My Aid/ Open Up The Red Box/ Hillside Avenue/ If You Don't Know Me By Now/ Stars/ The Right Thing/ Money Too Tight To Mention/ Something Got Me Started/ Fairground
Recording: Excellent stereo. Soundboard.
Source: The Old Trafford, Manchester, England June 29 1996.
Comments: European CD.

SLADE

CD - LIVE IN LONDON
THE SWINGIN' PIG TSP-CD-218
Them Kinda Monkey's Can't Swing/ The Bangin' Man/ Gudbuy T'Jane/ Far Far Away/ Thanks For The Memory/ How Does

SMASHING PUMPKINS, THE

It Feel/ Just Want A Little Bit/ Everyday/ O.K. Yesterday Was Yesterday/ Raining In My Champagne/ Let The Good Times Roll/ Mama Weer All Crazee Now
Recording: Excellent stereo. Soundboard.
Source: London 1975.
Comments: European CD. Time 64:50.

SMASHING PUMPKINS, THE

CD - THE BERLIN BULLET
MOONRAKER 124/25
CD1: Mellon Collie And The Infinite Sadness/ Tonight, Tonight/ Zero/ Fuck You (An Ode To No One)/ Here Is No Why/ To Forgive/ Bullet With Butterfly Wings/ Thru The Eyes Of Ruby/ Porcelina Of The Vast Oceans/ Disarm/ By Starlight/ Geek U.S.A./ Cherub Rock/ Muzzle
CD2: 1979/ X.Y.U./ Interlude/ Today/ Mayonaise/ Bodies/ Silverfuck/ Farewell And Goodnight
Recording: Excellent. Audience.
Source: The Arena, Berlin, April 15, '96.
Comments: European CD. Deluxe color cover. Picture CD. Time CD1 69:68. CD2 60:42.

CD - BRIXTON
MOONRAKER 198
Tonight, Tonight/ Cupid De Locke/ Thirty Three/ 1979/ Zero/ Here Is No Why/ To Forgive/ Thru The Eyes Of Ruby/ Porcelina Of The Vast Oceans/ Jelleybelly/ Silverfuck/ Disarm/ Bullet With Butterfly Wings/ MTV Interview*/ Tonight Tonight*
Recording: Excellent.
Source: Brixton Academy, London May 15 1996. *MTV Video Awards, Radio City Music Hall, New York, September 5 1996.
Comments: European CD.

CD - DISCONNECT
OXYGEN OXY 046
Jellybelly (3:03)/ Zero (2:38)/ Disarm (3:04)/ Today (2:57)/ Fuck You (An Ode To No One) (4:39)/ Thru The Eyes Of Ruby (7:55)/ Where Boys Fear To Tread (4:03)/ Cherub Rock (4:18)/ X.Y.U. (7:20)/ Geek U.S.A. (5:02)/ Silverfuck (8:21)/ Siva (8:21)/ Mayonaise (6:05)/ Rudolph The Red Nose Raindeer (1:17)/ 1979 (4:25)/ Jackie Blue (4:41)
Recording: Excellent stereo. Soundboard.
Source: Tracks 1-11 Melkweg, Amsterdam, Holland December 12 '95. Tracks 12-13 Reading Festival, UK August 25 '95. Track 14 unreleased song Europe December '95. Track 15, American Music Awards, Shrine Auditorium, Los Angeles, CA January 29 '96. Track 16, Studio Outtake '95.
Comments: European CD. Deluxe color cover. Picture CD.

CD - DREAM
MOONRAKER 138
Geek U.S.A./ Rocket/ Today/ Disarm/ Drown/ Hummer/ Quiet/ Cherub Rock/ Mayonaise/ Bury Me
Recording: Excellent stereo. Soundboard.
Source: The Crosby Auditorium, San Diego, CA October 26 1993.
Comments: European CD. Deluxe color cover. Picture CD. Time 47:47.

CD - IN THE BELLY OF THE BEAST
SBC 005
Bullet With Butterfly Wings (Intro By David Bowie)/ Jellybelly/ Zero/ Today/ Disarm/ Bullet With Butterfly Wings/ Porcelina Of The Vast Oceans/ Rocket/ Thru The Eyes Of Ruby/ Siva/ Cherub Rock/ Mayonaisse/ X.Y.U./ Bullet With Butterfly Wings/ Siva
Recording: Excellent. Soundboard.
Source: Track 1 Taratata, French TV '95. Tracks 2-13 The Reading Festival, UK '95. Track 14 The White Room, UK TV '95. Track 15 BBC Session '95.
Comments: European CD. Deluxe color cover. Time 72:33.

CD - LIVE AT READING '95
FFCD022
Jellybelly/ Zero/ Today/ Disarm/ Bullet With Butterfly Wings/ Porcelina Of The Vast Oceans/ Rocket/ Thru The Eyes Of Ruby/ Siva/ Cherub Rock/ Mayonaise/ X.Y.U./ Dancing In The Moonlight/ Never Let Me Down/ Landslide/ Jackie Blue
Recording: Excellent stereo. Soundboard.
Source: Tracks 1-12 The Reading Festival, England August 25 1995. Tracks 13-16 live cover versions.
Comments: European CD. Deluxe color cover. Picture CD. Time 74:01.

CD - THE MELLON COLLIE DEMOS
MOONRAKER 123
Mellon Collie And The Infinite Sadness/ Lily (My One And Only)/ To Forgive/ Bullet With Butterfly Wings/ Here Is No Why/ Galapogos/ Instrumental/ Strolling (1979

demo)/ Ugly/ Wishing You Were/ Thirty-Three/ Beautiful/ Interview
Recording: Excellent stereo. Soundboard.
Source: Demos and outtakes from Mellon Collie And The Infinite Sadness.
Comments: European CD. Blue/green cover. Time 73:58.

CD - SECRET DESTROYERS
OXYGEN OXY 076
Landslide (3:09)/ Tonight, Tonight (4:29)/ 1979 (4:34)/ Cupid De Locke (3:00)/ Thirty-Three (4:00)/ Take Me Down (3:27)/ Bullet With Butterfly Wings (5:24)/ To Forgive (4:04)/ Tonight, Tonight (4:42)/ Zero (2:26)/ Fuck You (An Ode To No One) (4:28)/ To Forgive (3:46)/ By Starlight (3:53)/ Cherub Rock (5:02)/ Mayonaise (5:31)/ Bodies (4:11)
Recording: Excellent stereo. Soundboard.
Source: Tracks 1-8 acoustic session, Triple J Studio, Sidney, Australia March 13 1996. Tracks 9-17 The Palatrussardi, Milano, Italy April 24 1996.
Comments: European CD. Time 71:02.

CD - SECRETS OF YOUR DREAMS
KISS THE STONE KTS 545
Tonight Tonight/ Zero/ Fuck You (An Ode To No One)/ Today/ To Forgive/ Bullet With Butterfly Wings/ Thru The Eyes Of Ruby/ Porcelina Of The Vast Oceans/ Disarm/ Muzzle/ Cherub Rock/ 1979/ X.Y.U.
Recording: Excellent stereo. Soundboard.
Source: Dusseldorf Easter Festival, Germany April 7 1996.
Comments: European CD. Deluxe color cover. Picture CD.

CD - TURPENTINE KISSES
KISS THE STONE KTS 531
Tonight, Tonight (4:29)/ 1979 (4:28)/ Cupid De Locke (3:02)/ Thirty Three (4:07)/ Take Me Down (3:17)/ Bullet With Butterfly Wings (5:02)/ To Forgive (4:18)/ Muzzle (4:25)/ Today (3:19)/ Disarm (3:14)/ Bullet With Butterfly Wings (4:08)/ Siva (4:52)/ Mayonaise (5:32)/ Cherub Rock (4:29)
Recording: Excellent stereo. Soundboard.
Source: Tracks 1-8 acoustic, The Request Lounge, Sydney, Australia March 13 '96. Tracks 9-14 electric, The Reading Rock Festival August 25 1995.
Comments: European CD. Deluxe color cover. Picture CD.

CD - TWILIGHT
MOONRAKER 039
Porcelina Of The Vast Oceans/ Jellybelly/ Zero/ Disarm/ Today/ Fuck You (An Ode To No One)/ Thru The Eyes Of Ruby/ Where Boys Fear To Tread/ Cherub Rock/ X.Y.U./ Geek U.S.A./ Silver Fuck/ Bullet With Butterfly Wings/ Zero/ Bullet With Butterfly Wings
Recording: Excellent stereo. Soundboard.
Source: The Melkweg, Amsterdam December 12 '95. Tracks 13-14 'Saturday Night Live' November 11 '95. Track 15 Canal, French TV December 10 '95.
Comments: European CD. Deluxe color cover. Picture CD. Time 72:53.

CD - WRAPPED UP IN THE PLEASURES OF THE WORLD
KISS THE STONE KTS 542
Jelly Belly/ Zero/ Today/ Disarm/ Bullet With Butterfly Wings/ Porcelina Of The Vast Oceans/ Rocket/ Thru The Eyes Of Ruby/ Siva/ Cherub Rock/ Mayonaise/ X.Y.U.
Recording: Excellent stereo. Soundboard.
Source: The Reading Festival August 25 1995.
Comments: European CD. Time 60:12.

SMITH, PATTI

CD - FLASHES IN MY DREAMS (WATER FESTIVAL)
CRYSTAL CAT RECORDS CC 411/12
CD1: Wing (4:33)/ Beneath The Southern Cross (5:39)/ Redondo Beach (4:36)/ Wicked Messenger (4:09)/ Ghost Dance (4:35)/ Dancing Barefoot (5:04)/ Crystal Ship (2:58)/ When Doves Cry (2:25)/ Love Of The Common People (3:13)/ About A Boy (11:19)
CD2: Ain't It Strange (6:21)/ Not Fade Away (4:42)/ Poem: People (10:21)/ Gloria (2:39)/ Free Money (4:04)/ Gone Again (3:56)/ Wild Leaves (4:23)/ Because The Night (3:24)
Recording: Excellent. Audience.
Source: Riddarholmen, Stockholm, Sweden August 9 1996.
Comments: European CD. Deluxe B&W cover. Gold type. Picture CDs.

CD - LET'S DEODORIZE THE NIGHT
STRANGE IDOLS MUSIC VM-122875-A
My Mafia/ Nigger Book/ Sally/ Rape/ I Was Working Real Hard/ We're Gonna Have A Real Good Time Together/ Privilege (Set

SMITH, PATTI

Me Free)/ Ain't It Strange/ Space Monkey/ Redondo Beach/ Free Money/ Pale Blue Eyes, Louie Louie/ Pumping (My Heart)/ Land, Gloria/ Birdland/ Time Is On My Side/ My Generation/ Dedication
Recording: Excellent. Soundboard.
Source: The Bottom Line, New York City December 28 1975.
Comments: European CD. Deluxe color cover. Time 76:54.

CD - PATHS THAT CROSS
ARCHIVE RECORDS
CD1: Intro/ Piss Factory/ Somalia/ Dancing Barefoot/ Dylans Dog/ Dark Eyes/ Southern Cross/ Black Peter/ Not Fade Away/ Ghost Dance/ Because The Night/ Paths That Cross/ People Have The Power/ Farewell Reel/ Jacksons Song/ About A Boy
CD2: Piss Factory/ Horses/ Wicked Messenger/ About A Boy/ Poem, Dancing Barefoot/ Because The Night/ Ghost Dance/ Southern Cross/ Mortal Shoes/ Poem, Rock And Roll Nigger/ Not Fade Away/ Dark Eyes (with Bob Dylan)
Recording: Excellent. Audience.
Source: The 'Paradise Lost' Tour 1995. CD1 Theatre of Living Arts, Philadelphia Dec. 1995. CD2 Tracks 5-7, 9-12 Boston December 9. Tracks 1, 4 New York December 11. Track 8 Bethlehem December 13. Tracks 2-3, 13 Philadelphia December 17.
Comments: Japanese CD. Deluxe color gatefold cover. Each CD in a full color paper sleeve. Time CD1 64:35. CD2 74:44.

CD - TELL IT LIKE IT IS
KISS THE STONE KTS 628
Wing (5:07)/ People Have Power (3:55)/ Dancing Barefoot (5:21)/ Summer Cannibals (5:35)/ Wired Messenger (4:26)/ Ghost Dancer (4:37)/ Redondo Beach (4:37)/ Crystal Ship (3:17)/ When Doves Cry (10:45)/ Wild Leaves (4:35)/ People Have The Power (Poem) (2:13)/ Gone Again (3:50)/ Because The Night (3:32)
Recording: Excellent. Soundboard.
Source: Markethalle, Hamburg, Germany August 1 1996.
Comments: European CD. Deluxe color cover. Picture CD.

SONIC YOUTH

CD - EASTER
MOONRAKER 102
Teen Age Riot/ Bull In The Heather/ Starfield Road/ Washing Machine/ Junkie's Promise/ Saucer-Like/ Becuz/ Sugar Kane/ Skip Tracer/ Skink/ The Diamond Sea
Recording: Excellent stereo. Soundboard.
Source: The Philopshalle, Dortmund, Germany April 7 '96.
Comments: European CD. Deluxe color cover. Picture CD. Time 73:28.

CD - JUNKIE'S PROMISE
KISS THE STONE KTS 543
Teenage Riot (7:24)/ Bull In The Heather (2:47)/ Starfield Road (2:53)/ Washing Machine (9:02)/ Junkie's Promise (4:20)/ Saucer-Like (4:22)/ Becuz (6:07)/ Sugar Kane (7:56)/ Skip Tracer (3:48)/ Skink (4:43)/ The Diamond Sea (20:04)
Recording: Excellent stereo. Soundboard.
Source: Dusseldorf Easter Festival, Germany April 7 '96.
Comments: European CD. Deluxe color cover. Picture CD.

CD - SUGAR BABY
MOONRAKER 112
Schizophrenia/ Starfield Road/ Washing Machine/ Becuz/ Skip Tracer/ Skink/ The Diamond Sea/ BONUS TRACKS Interview*/ Junkie's Promise*/ Saucer-Like*/ Becuz*
Recording: Excellent.
Source: The Club Northern Light, Tilburg, Holland March 18 1996. *MTV'S Hanging Out April 15 1996.
Comments: European CD. Deluxe color cover. Time 58:54.

SOUL ASYLUM

CD - BROKEN GLASS
MOONRAKER 119
Hopes Up/ Shut Down/ Somebody To Shove/ Misery/ Black Gold/ Eyes Of A Child/ Promises Broke/ String Of Pearls/ Crawl/ Caged Rat/ Just Like Anyone/ Bonus: Soul Asylum-Iggy Pop 'Back Door Man'/ Soul Asylum-Lou Reed 'Sweet Jane'
Recording: Excellent.
Source: The Sudbahnhof, Frankfurt, Germany November 3 1995. Bonus tracks from The Rock And Roll Hall Of Fame, Cleveland September 2 1995.

Comments: European CD.

SOUNDGARDEN

CD - BLOW UP THE OUTSIDE
KISS THE STONE KTS 610/11
CD1: Spoon Man/ Searching With My Eyes Closed/ Let Me Drown/ Pretty Noose/ Burden In My Hand/ My Wave/ Ty Cobb/ Fell On Black Days/ Boot Camp/ An Unkind/ Rusty Cage
CD2: Black Hole Sun/ Out Shined/ Mail Man/ Drawing Flies/ Blow Up The Outside World/ Kick Stand/ Slaves And Bulldozers/ Never The Machine Forever/ Jesus Christ Pose
Recording: Excellent.
Source: Brixton Academy, London, UK September 19 1996.
Comments: European CD. Deluxe color cover. Picture CD. Total time 01:32:42.

CD - FRESH DEADLY RARITIES
TORNADO TOR022
Toy Box/ Heretic/ Come Together/ Fresh Deadly Roses/ Into The Void/ Girl You Want/ Stray Cat Blues/ She's A Politician/ Cold Bitch/ Show Me/ Touch Me/ I Don't Care About You/ Can You See Me/ I Can Give You Anything/ Homicidal Suicidal/ She Likes Surprises/ Like Suicide
Recording: Excellent stereo. Soundboard.
Comments: European CD. Deluxe color cover. Time 68:18.

SPOOKY TOOTH

CD - BERLIN WALL
COLOSSEUM 97-C-010
Something To Say/ I Am The Walrus/ The Wrong Time/ I Wanna Be Free/ Son Of Your Father/ Better By You, Better By Me/ A Long/ Soulful Lady/ Love Really Changed Me/ Pretty Woman/ Feelin' Bad/ I Can't Quite Her/ Evil Woman
Source: Tracks 1-8 Berlin, Germany December 1970. Tracks 9, 12 and 13 BBC June 23 1968. Tracks 10 and 11 BBC April 26 1969.
Comments: Japanese CD.

SPRINGSTEEN, BRUCE

CD - ACROSS THE BORDER
AMSTERDAM AMS 726A/B
CD1: The Ghost Of Tom Joad/ Atlantic City/ Adam Raised A Cain/ Highway 29/ Darkness On The Edge Of Town/ Johnny 99/ Nebraska/ Red Headed Woman/ Two Hearts/ The River/ Born In The U.S.A./ Dry Lightning
CD2: Spare Parts/ Sinaloa Cowboys/ The Line/ Balboa Park/ Across The Border/ Bobby Jean/ This Hard Land/ Streets Of Philadelphia/ No Surrender/ If I Should Fall Behind/ The Promised Land
Recording: Excellent. Audience.
Source: Tokyo International Forum, Hall 'A' January 30 1997.
Comments: Japanese CD.
Time CD1 59:49. CD2 63:11.

CD - ACROSS THE BORDER
MONSERRAT RECORDS BRCD 1902
Adam Raised A Cain (4:41)/ Straight Time (4:50)/ Highway 29 (4:18)/ Darkness (3:16)/ Murder Inc (4:19)/ Nebraska (5:06)/ It's The Little Things That Count (Unreleased) (3:52)/ Brothers Under The Bridge (Unreleased) (4:37)/ Born In The USA (4:14)/ Dry Lightning (6:03)/ Spare Parts (6:31)/ Youngstown (4:11)/ Shinola Cowboys (4:27)/ The Line (5:36)/ Balboa Park (3:52)/ Across The Border (6:00)
Recording: Excellent. Audience.
Source: January 7 '96
Comments: European CD. Deluxe color cover.

CD - AIN'T NOBODY HERE FROM BILLBOARD TONIGHT
MOONLIGHT ML 9619/20
CD1: Thunder Road/ Tenth Avenue Freeze-Out/ Spirit In The Night/ Pretty Flamingo/ She's The One/ Born To Run/ 4th Of July, Asbury Park (Sandy)/ Backstreets
CD2: Kitty's Back/ Jungleland/ Rosalita (Come Out Tonight)/ Goin' Back/ Devil With The Blue Dress Medley: Devil With The Blue Dress, Good Golly Miss Molly, C.C. Rider, Jenny, Take A Ride
Recording: Excellent. Audience.
Source: Roxy Theatre, Los Angeles October 17 1975.
Comments: European CD. Sepia-tone cover.

CD - ALONE IN COLTS NECK (THE COMPLETE NEBRASKA SESSION)
LABOUR OF LOVE 001
Nebraska/ Atlantic City/ Mansion On The Hill/ Born In The U.S.A./ Johnny 99/

SPRINGSTEEN, BRUCE

Downbound Train/ Losin' Kind/ State Trooper/ Used Cars/ Open All Night/ Pink Cadillac/ Deputy (Later Retitled 'Highway Patrolman')/ Reason To Believe/ Child Bride (Later Retitled 'Working On The Highway')/ Bonus Tracks Dream Baby/ Precious Memories/ Nebraska #1/ Nebraska #2
Recording: Excellent stereo.
Source: Springsteen acoustic home demos - four track mixes. Colts Neck, New Jersey late December 1981 through January 1982. Compiled and edited by Bruce possibly on January 3 1982.

CD - ASBURY PARK NIGHT
CRYSTAL CAT RECORDS CC 421-23
CD1: Intro/ For You/ It's Hard To Be A Saint In The City/ Atlantic City/ Straight Time/ Tougher Than The Rest/ Darkness On The Edge Of Town/ Johnny 99/ All That Heaven Will Allow/ Wild Billy's Circus Story/ Red Headed Woman/ Two Hearts/ When Your Alone/ Shut Out The Light/ Born In The U.S.A./ The Ghost Of Tom Joad
CD2: Intro/ Sinaloa Cowboys/ The Line/ Racing In The Street/ Across The Border/ I Don't Wanna Go Home/ Spirit In The Night/ Rosalita/ This Hard Land/ 4th Of July, Ashbury Park (Sandy)
CD3: Intro/ Long Time Coming/ The River/ The Hitter/ Two Hearts/ Independence Day/ Working On The Highway/ I Wanna Marry You/ Spirit In The Night/ Rosalita/ 4th Of July, Asbury Park (Sandy)/ If I Should Fall Behind/ Stop Prop 209
Recording: Excellent. Audience.
Source: Paramount Theatre, Asbury Park, NJ November 26 1996.
Comments: European CD. Deluxe color cover. Time CD1 76:2. CD2 75:30. CD3 68:41

CD - BORN AGAIN
OXYGEN OXY 087
The Ghost Of Tom Joad (6:01)/ Straight Time (5:50)/ Darkness On The Edge Of Town (3:42)/ Born In The U.S.A. (5:06)/ Dry Lightning (4:27)/ Youngstown (6:37)/ The Line (9:53)/ Across The Border (5:27)/ Streets Of Philadelphia (3:25)/ The Promised Land (6:41)/ The Ghost Of Tom Joad (5:05)/ Angel Eyes (with Bruce's Introduction) (5:15)/ Streets Of Philadelphia (3:22)
Recording: Excellent.

Source: Tracks 1-10 ICC Concert Hall, Berlin, Germany April 19 1996. Track 11 Sanremo Music Festival, Sanremo, Italy February 20 1996. Track 12 Frank Sinatra Tribute, USA December 14 1995. Track 13 Shrine Auditorium, Los Angeles, CA March 1 1995 (37th Annual Grammy Awards).
Comments: European CD.

CD - BORN IN THE U.S.A. RARE MASTERS
LABOUR OF LOVE 019
Down, Down, Down (Working Title For The Original Take Of 'I'm Goin' Down')/ Murder Incorporated/ TV Movie/ County Fair #2 (Full Band Version With Female Vocals)/ Born In The U.S.A (Complete Take)/ Sugarland #4 (Slow Acoustic Version)/ My Love Will Not Let You Down/ My Hometown (With Female Background Vocals)/ Glory Days (With Extra Verse)/ Frankie/ Darlington County/ Working On The Highway/ Downbound Train
Recording: Excellent stereo.
Source: Springsteen and The E Street Band, Power Station Studio, New York City. Tracks 1-4 November 9 1983. Tracks 5-9 January through May 1983. Original rough mix of 'Born In The USA' album compiled May 10 1983. Tracks 10-13 possibly May 1982.

CD - BRIXTON NIGHT
CRYSTAL CAT RECORDS CC 395/96
CD1: Intro (1:16)/ The Ghost Of Tom Joad (5:07)/ Atlantic City (4:16)/ Straight Time (4:53)/ Highway 29 (3:59)/ Darkness On The Edge Of Town (3:10)/ State Trooper (2:54)/ Mansion On The Hill (3:56)/ The Pilgrim Of Temple Of Love (4:38)/ Red Headed Woman (3:20)/ Brothers Under The Bridges (4:22)/ Born In The U.S.A. (4:24)/ Dry Lightning (4:16)
CD2: Seeds(3:19)/ Youngstown (3:42)/ Sinaloa Cowboys (4:01)/ The Line (5:14)/ Balboa Park (3:25)/ Across The Border (5:04)/ Bobby Jean (3:27)/ This Hard Land (4:47)/ Streets Of Philadelphia (3:02)/ Galveston Bay (5:16)/ The Promised Land (6:29)
CD3: Johnny 99 (4:07)/ Highway Patrolman (4:56)/ The Wish (4:07)/ If I Should Fall Behind (3:38)/ Spare Parts (3:33)/ Point Blank (4:02)/ Does This Bus Stop At 82nd Street? (2:22)/ No Surrender (3:12)/ Blowin' Down The Road (I Ain't Going To Be

THE SMASHING PUMPKINS
Dream
And run away with me

bruce
springsteen

SPRINGSTEEN, BRUCE

Treated This Way) (3:23)/ The Angel (2:40)/ Blinded By The Light (5:03)/ Pony Boy (1:02)/ Dead Man Walkin' (2:33)
Recording: Excellent.
Source: Solo acoustic tour, Brixton Academy, London, England April 24 1996.
Comments: European CD. Deluxe color cover.

CD - BROTHERS UNDER THE BRIDGES
AMSTERDAM AMS 725A/B
CD1: The Ghost Of Tom Joad/ Atlantic City/ Adam Raised A Cain/ Highway 29/ Darkness On The Edge Of Town/ Johnny 99/ Nebraska/ Red Headed Woman/ Two Hearts/ Brothers Under The Bridges/ Born In The U.S.A./ Dry Lightning
CD2: Spare Parts/ Sinaloa Cowboys/ The Line/ Balboa Park/ Across The Border/ Bobby Jean/ This Hard Land/ Streets Of Philadelphia/ No Surrender/ If I Should Fall Behind/ The Promised Land
Recording: Excellent. Audience.
Source: Tokyo International Forum, Hall 'A' January 29 1997.
Comments: Japanese CD. Time CD1 58:49. CD2 64:15.

CD - CIRKUS NIGHT
CRYSTAL CAT RECORDS CC 392/93
CD1: The Ghost Of Tom Joad (4:46)/ Adam Raised Cain (3:46)/ Straight Time (4:55)/ Highway 29 (4:01)/ Darkness On The Edge Of Town (3:07)/ Johnny 99 (3:58)/ Nebraska (4:07)/ Dead Man Walkin' (2:37)/ It's The Little Things That Count (2:29)/ Sell It And They Will Come (3:41)/ Brothers Under The Bridges (4:19)/ Born In The U.S.A. (3:36)/ Dry Lightning (3:57)/ Reason To Believe (4:14)
CD2: Intro, Storyteller (1:30)/ Youngstown (3:28)/ Sinaloa Cowboys (3:59)/ The Line (5:13)/ Bobby Jean (3:34)/ This Hard Land (4:33)/ Streets Of Philadelphia (2:48)/ Galveston Bay (5:09)/ Promised Land (5:46)/ Bonus Track: The Wish (3:51)*
Recording: Excellent. Audience.
Source: Cirkus, Stockholm, Sweden March 13 1996. *Spectrum, Oslo, Norway March 14 1996.
Comments: European CD.

CD - DRY LIGHTNING
AMSTERDAM 727A/B
CD1: The Ghost Of Tom Joad/ Atlantic City/ Adam Raised A Cain/ Highway 29/ Darkness On The Edge Of Town/ Murder Incorporated/ Highway Patrolman/ Red Headed Woman/ Two Hearts/ The River/ Born In The U.S.A./ Dry Lightning/ Youngstown
CD2: Spare Parts/ Sinaloa Cowboys/ The Line/ Balboa Park/ Across The Border/ Bobby Jean/ This Hard Land/ No Surrender/ Galveston Bay/ If I Should Fall Behind/ The Promised Land
Recording: Excellent. Audience.
Source: Tokyo International Forum, Hall 'A' January 31 1997.
Comments: Japanese CD.
Time CD1 64:39. CD2 66:23.

CD - FREEHOLD NIGHT
CRYSTAL CAT CC 419/20
CD1: The River (4:53)/ Adam Raised A Cain (3:43)/ Straight Time (4:38)/ Highway 29 (4:01)/ Darkness On The Edge Of Town (3:10)/ Johnny 99 (4:08)/ Mansion On The Hill (4:12)/ The Wish (3:51)/ Red Headed Woman (3:08)/ Two Hearts (3:11)/ When You're Alone (3:02)/ Open All Night (3:28)/ Used Cars (2:19)/ Born In The U.S.A.
CD2: Intro (1:35)/ The Ghost Of Tom Joad (4:43)/ Sinaloa Cowboys (3:35)/ The Line (4:54)/ Balboa Park (3:09)/ Across The Border (4:21)/ Grown' Up (2:52)/ This Hard Land (4:23)/ My Hometown (5:07)/ Racing In The Street (5:08)/ Promised Land (5:48)/ Freehold
Recording: Excellent. Audience.
Source: St. Rose Of Lima School, Freehold, NJ November 8 1996.
Comments: European CD. Deluxe color cover. Time CD1 76:34. CD2 74:50.

CD - HAMBURG NIGHT
CRYSTAL CAT RECORDS CC 385/86
CD1: The Ghost Of Tom Joad (5:10)/ Adam Raised Cain (3:57)/ Straight Time (4:53)/ Highway 29 (3:59)/ Darkness On The Edge Of Town (3:11)/ Murder Incorporated (3:31)/ Mansion On The Hill (3:54)/ Dead Man Walkin' (3:04)/ Sell It And They Will Come (4:09)/ Brothers Under The Bridges (4:18)/ Born In The U.S.A. (3:55)/ Dry Lightning (3:58)/ Reason To Believe (3:49)/ Youngstown (3:52)
CD2: Intro, Storyteller (4:15)/ Sinaloa Cowboys (4:02)/ The Line (5:18)/ Balboa Park (3:25)/ Across The Border (5:11)/ Does This Bus Stop At 82nd Street? (2:21)/ This Hard Land (4:32)/ Streets Of

Philadelphia (2:55)/ Galveston Bay (5:23)/ My Best Was Never Good Enough (2:12)/ Promised Land (3:46)/ No Surrender (2:49)/ Nebraska (4:13)
Recording: Excellent. Audience.
Source: Congress Centrum, Saal 1, Hamburg, Germany. Track 12 Philipshalle, Dusseldorf, Germany February 18 1996. Track 13 Rudi-Sedelmayer-Halle, Munchen, Germany February 15 1996.
Comments: European CD. Deluxe B&w cover.

CD - I'M SO GLAD TO BE HERE TONIGHT
GAMBLE RECORDS BSGR 06/07/08
CD1: Darkness On The Edge Of Town/ Mansion On The Hill/ This Hard Land/ Better Days/ Lucky Town/ Atlantic City/ 57 Channels (And Nothing On)/ Badlands/ Living Proof/ Many Rivers To Cross/ Leap Of Faith/ Man's Job/ Roll Of The Dice
CD2: Prove It All Night/ Because The Night/ Brilliant Disguise/ Human Touch/ The River/ Who'll Stop The Rain/ Souls Of The Departed/ Born In The USA/ Light Of Day
CD3: Hungry Heart/ Glory Days/ Thunder Road/ Born To Run/ My Beautiful Reward/ Rockin' All Over The World/ Working On The Highway/ Seeds/ Adam Raised A Cain/ Trapped/ Darkness On The Edge Of Town/ My Hometown/ I'm On Fire
Recording: Good to very good. Audience.
Source: The Ahoy, April 20 1993. CD3 tracks 8-13 April 19 1993.
Comments: European CD. Deluxe color cover.

CD - IN FREEHOLD
MIDNIGHT BEAT MB CD 097/98
CD1: The River/ Adam Raised A Cain/ Straight Time/ Highway 29/ Darkness On The Edge Of Town/ Johnny 99/ Mansion On The Hill/ The Wish/ Red Headed Woman/ Two Hearts/ When You're Alone/ Open All Night/ Used Cars/ Born In The U.S.A.
CD2: The Ghost Of Tom Joad/ Sinaloa Cowboys/ The Line/ Balboa Park/ Across The Border/ Growin' Up/ This Hard Land/ My Hometown/ Racing In The Streets/ The Promised Land/ In Freehold
Recording: Excellent. Audience.
Source: St. Rose Of Lima Gymnasium, St. Rose Of Lima School, Freehold, NJ November 8 1996.
Comments: European CD.

CD - JACKSONVILLE (AND MY FATHER'S PLACE)
MIDNIGHT BEAT MBCD064/65
CD1: Night/ Rendezvous/ Spirit In The Night/ It's My Life/ Thunder Road/ Mona, She's The One/ Tenth Avenue Freeze-Out/ Action In The Street/ Backstreets
CD2: Jungleland/ Rosalita (Come Out Tonight)/ Spirit In The Night/ Does This Bus stop At 82nd Street?/ It's Hard to Be A Saint In The City/ You Mean So Much To Me/ Thundercrack
Recording: Very good. Audience
Source: The Auditorium, Jacksonville, Florida March 4 1977. CD2 tracks 3-7 Roslyn, New York July 31 1973.
Comments: European CD.

CD - JESSE JAMES & THE WAGES OF SIN (SOLO MASTERS VOLUME IV)
LABOUR OF LOVE 010
Long Way Home/ Ruled By The Gun #1/ Ruled By The Gun #2 (harmonies & guitar solos)/ Downbound Train/ Wages Of Sin #1/ I Need You #1/ I Need You #2 (background vocals)/ Ruled By The Gun #3/ Ruled By The Gun #4 (harmonies)/ Baby I'm So Cold (Turn The Lights Down Low) (early version of 'Follow That Dream' with lyrics from 'Loose Ends')/ Untitled Riff/ Wages Of Sin #2/ Wages Of Sin #3 (harmonies)/ Wheels Make The World Go Round/ Glory Days (original demo)/ Wages Of Sin #4/ Fade To Black/ Your Love (Is All Around Me Now) #1/ Your Love (Is All Around Me Now) #2/ Jesse James #1 (harmonies similar to 'None But The Brave')/ Jesse James #2 (harmonies)/ They Killed Him In The Street By #1/ They Killed Him In The Street By #2 (harmonies)/ True Love Is Hard To Come By #1/ True Love Is Hard To Come By #2/ True Love Is Hard To Come By #3 (early version of 'Janey Don't Lose Heart')
Recording: Excellent. Soundboard.
Source: Acoustic home demos, Hollywood Hills, Los Angeles early 1983.

CD - LIVE AT THE AGORA
E. ST. RECORDS ES-46/47/48
CD1: Summertime Blues/ Badlands/ Spirit In The Night/ Darkness On The Edge Of Town/ Factory/ The Promised Land/ Prove It All Night/ Racing In The Street/ Thunder

SPRINGSTEEN, BRUCE

Road/ Jungleland
CD2: Paradise By The C/ Fire/ Sherry Darling/ Not Fade Away/ Gloria/, She's One Up/ Growin' Up/ Backstreets/ Rosalita (Come Out Tonight)
CD3: 4th Of July, Asbury Park (Sandy)/ Born To Run/ Because The Night/ Raise Your Hand/ Twist & Shout/ Kitty's Back*/ Point Blank*
Recording: Excellent stereo. Soundboard.
Source: From the original reels. Agora Ballroom, Cleveland, OH August 9 1978. *Palladium, New York September 17 1978.
Comments: European CD. Deluxe B&w cover. Time CD1 71:36. CD2 68:18. CD3 58:41.

CD - NASSAU NIGHT
CRYSTAL CAT RECORDS CC 387/89
CD1: Intro (0:31)/ Night (3:07)/ Prove It All Night (5:57)/ Spirit In The Night (6:38)/ Darkness On The Edge Of Town (4:05)/ Independence Day (5:27)/ Who'll Stop The Rain (3:23)/ This Land Is Your Land (3:05)/ The Promised Land (5:57)/ Out In The Street (4:34)/ Racing In The Street (8:15)/ Piano ();46)/ The River (6:58)/ Badlands (4:57)/ Thunder Road (5:32)
CD2: Intro (0:27)/ Cadillac Ranch (4:55)/ Sherry Darling (5:15)/ Hungry Heart (4:13)/ Merry Christmas Baby (4:36)/ Fire (4:18)/ Candy's Room (3:10)/ Because The Night (6:23)/ 4th Of July, Asbury Park (Sandy) (6:21)/ Rendez Vous (2:43)/ Fade Away (9:16)/ The Price You Pay (5:22)/ Wreck On The Highway (4:42)/ Two Hearts (2:41)/ Ramrod (4:23)
CD3: You Can Look (But You Better Not Touch) (3:32)/ Held Up Without A Gun (1:09)/ Midnight Hour (1:39)/ Auld Lang Syne (2:03)/ Rosalita (Come Out Tonight) (12:48)/ Santa Claus Is Coming To Town (4:14)/ Jungleland (10:00)/ Born To Run (4:38)/ Devil With A Blue Dress On (12:20)/ Good Golly Miss Molly (0:42)/ C.C. Rider (1:17)/ Jenny Take A Ride, Boogie (2:55)/ I Hear A Train, Devil With ... (6:09)/ Twist And Shout (4:41)/ Raise Your Hand (2:47)
Recording: Excellent. Audience.
Source: Nassau Coliseum, Uniondale, N.Y., December 31 1980.
Comments: European CD.

CD - NEWCASTLE NIGHT
CRYSTAL CAT RECORDS CC 390-91
CD1: The Ghost Of Tom Joad/ Adam Raised A Cain/ Straight Time/ Highway 29/ Darkness On The Edge Of Town/ Murder Incorporated/ Mansion On The Hill/ Dead Man Walkin'/ Sell It And They Will Come/ Little Things That Count/ Brothers Under The Bridges/ Born In The U.S.A./ Dry Lightning/ Reason To Believe/ Youngstown
CD2: Intro/ Sinaloa Cowboys/ The Line/ Balboa Park/ Across The Border/ Bobby Jean/ This Hard Land/ Streets Of Philadelphia/ Galveston Bay/ The Promised Land/ Interview* (by Pelle Gustafson City Hall, New Castle March 2 1996 after the show)
Recording: Excellent. Audience. *Excellent. Soundboard.
Source: City Hall, Newcastle, England March 2 1996.
Comments: European CD. Deluxe color cover. Time CD1 75:60. CD2 75:02.

CD - NICK'S FAT CITY
STAR 003/4
CD1: No Strings Attached/ Only Lovers Left Alive/ What Did You Do In The War/ Talkin' To The King/ Chain Smokin'/ Labor Of Love/ Never Be Enough Time/ Murder Inc.
CD2: Dark And Bloody Ground/ Pumpin' Iron/ American Babylon/ Homestead/ Down The Road Of Peace/ Just Around The Corner/ The Ghost Of Tom Joad
Recording: Excellent.
Source: Nick's Fat City, Pittsburgh October 20 1995. CD2 track 7 NBC, November 11 1995.
Comments: European CD. Deluxe color cover. Picture CDs.

CD - OLD HABITS
KISS THE STONE KTS 566
The Ghost Of Tom Joad/ Straight Time/ Darkness On The Edge Of Town/ Born In The USA/ Dry Lightning/ Youngstown/ The Line/ Across The Border/ Streets Of Philadelphia/ The Promised Land/ Sinaloa Cowboys*/ Balboa Park*/ Does This Bus Stop At 82nd Street?*/ This Hard Land*
Recording: Excellent.
Source: I.C.C. Concert Halle, Berlin March 31 '96. *The Tower Theatre, Philadelphia December 9 '95.
Comments: European CD.

CD - ONE WAY STREET (DARKNESS MASTERS VOLUME I)
LABOUR OF LOVE 002
One Way Street/ Don't Look Back (instrumental)/ Frankie/ Drive All Night #1 (original version)/ Drive All Night #2 (alternate version)/ Something In The Night/ Candy's Boy #1/ Fire/ The Fast Song #1 (instrumental)/ Streets Of Fire #1 / Badlands #1 (instrumental)/ The Promise/ Talk To Me (instrumental)/ Get That Feeling/ Racing In The Street #1 (alternate version with harp)
Recording: Excellent stereo. Soundboard.
Source: Bruce Springsteen And The E Street Band, Atlantic Studios, New York City. Tracks 1-8 June 1977. Tracks 9-15 August 1977.
Comments: European CD. Best ever quality Darkness outtakes.

CD - ORPHEUM
MOONRAKER 067/68
CD1: The Ghost Of Tom Joad/ Adam Raised A Cain/ Straight Time/ Highway 29/ Darkness On The Edge Of Town/ Murder Incorporated/ Mansion On The Hill/ Little Things That Count/ Brothers Under The Bridges/ Born In The USA/ Dry Lightning/ Spare Parts
CD2: Youngstown/ Sinaloa Cowboys/ The Line/ Balboa Park/ Across The Border/ Does This Bus Stop At 82nd Street?/ This Hard Land/ Streets Of Philadelphia/ Galveston Bay/ The Promised Land/ My Best Was Never Good Enough
Recording: Excellent. Audience.
Source: The Orpheum, Boston December 16 '95.
Comments: European CD. Deluxe color cover. Picture CD. Time CD1 59:53. CD2 61:11.

CD - PARIS 96
MOONRAKER 069/70
CD1: The Ghost Of Tom Joad/ Adam Raised A Cain/ Straight Time/ Highway 29/ Darkness On The Edge Of Town/ Murder Incorporated/ Nebraska/ Little Things That Count/ Brothers Under The Bridges/ Born In The USA/ Dry Lightning/ Reason To Believe
CD2: Youngstown/ Sinola Cowboys/ The Line/ Balboa Park/ Across The Border/ Does This Bus Stop At 82nd Street?/ This Hard Land/ Streets Of Philadelphia/ Galveston Bay/ My Best Was Never Good Enough/ The Promised Land
Recording: Excellent. Audience.
Source: Le Zenith, Paris February 21 '96.
Comments: European CD.

CD - PHILADELPHIA NIGHT
CRYSTAL CAT RECORDS CC 382
Intro/ the Ghost Of Tom Joad/ Straight Time/ Darkness On The Edge Of Town/ Born In The U.S.A./ Youngstown/ Sinaloa Cowboys/ Balboa Park/ Does This Bus Stop At 82nd Street?/ This Is Hard Land/ Streets Of Philadelphia/ (Springsteen interviewed by Bob Costas, Count Basie Theatre, Red Bank, NJ November 21 1995) Talking About Ghost.../ John Ford Film Grapes Of Wraith/ Stories And Characters/ Short History Of Music Scene In Late Sixties/ Is Love Real?? Book, Journey To Nowhere/ Photograph Of Your Own Landscape/ Inspiration To Youngstown/ Made Records He Wanted To Make/ Straight Time Laying Around/ About The Acoustic Show/ Best Days? You Can't Generalize People
Recording: Excellent stereo. Soundboard.
Source: Solo acoustic tour, Tower Theatre, Philadelphia December 8-9 1995.
Comments: European CD. Deluxe color cover. Picture CD. Time 78:36.

CD - RATTLING THE CHAINS (DARKNESS MASTERS VOLUME II)
LABOUR OF LOVE 003
Badlands #2 (with different lyrics)/ Adam Raised A Cain (alternate take with different lyrics)/ Factory (alternative Lyrics)/ Racing In The Street #2 (with different lyrics)/ Prove It All Night (with lyrics from 'Something In The Night')/ Because The Night (early version)/ Racing In The Street #3 (slow version with different lyrics)/ Streets Of Fire #2 (different lyrics)/ The Fast Song #2/ Sherry Darling/ Candy's Boy #2/ Badlands #3 (different lyrics)/ Spanish Eyes/ Independence Day (original version)/ Break Out (early version)/ Someday, Tonight (instrumental)
Recording: Excellent stereo. Soundboard.
Source: Tracks 1-5, Bruce Springsteen And The E Street Band, Atlantic Studios or The Record Plant, New York City, August 1977. Tracks 6-13 Bruce Springsteen And The E Street Band, Atlantic Studios, New York City June through August '77. Tracks 14-16 Bruce Springsteen And The E Street Band

SPRINGSTEEN, BRUCE

The Record Plant, New York City September 1977.

CD - SHIT HOT AND ROCKIN'
HAMM 01/02
CD1: Thunder Road/ Tenth Avenue Freeze Out/ Sprit In The Night/ Lost In The Flood/ She's The One/ Born To Run/ Pretty Flamingo/ Growin' Up/ It's Hard To Be Saint In The City/ Backstreets/ Sha La La/ Jungleland
CD2: Rosalita/ 4th July, Asbury Park (Sandy)/ Wear My Ring (Around Your Neck)/ Medley: Devil With Blue Dress, Good Golly Miss Molly, C.C. Rider, Jenny Takes A Ride/ For You/ Every Time That You Walk In The Room/ Quarter To Three/ Twist & Shout/ Carol/ Little Queenie
Source: Hammersmith Odeon, London November 24 1975.

CD - THE SKY OVER BERLIN
MOONRAKER 127
The Ghost Of Tom Joad/ Straight Time/ Darkness On The Edge Of Town/ Born In The USA/ Dry Lightning/ Youngstown/ The Line/ Across The Border/ Streets Of Philadelphia/ Promised Land/ Bonus: Mansion On The Hill (Boston December 16 '95)/ Nebraska (Paris February 21 '96)/ Sell It And They Will Come (Stockholm March 13 '96)
Recording: Excellent.
Source: The ICC Berlin, Germany April 19 1996.
Comments: European CD. Deluxe color cover. Time 67:59.

CD - STRAIGHT TIME
AMSTERDAM 724A/B
CD1: The Ghost Of Tom Joad/ Atlantic City/ Straight Time/ Highway 29/ Darkness On The Edge Of Town/ Johnny 99/ Mansion On The Hill/ Red Headed Woman/ Two Hearts/ Brothers Under The Bridges/ Born In The U.S.A./ Dry Lightning
CD2: Spare Parts/ Sinaloa Cowboys/ The Line/ Balboa Park/ Across The Border/ Bobby Jean/ This Hard Land/ No Surrender/ Streets Of Philadelphia/ If I Should Fall Behind/ The Promised Land
Recording: Excellent. Audience.
Source: Tokyo International Forum, Hall 'A' January 27 1997.
Comments: Japanese CD.
Time CD1 59:16, CD2 62:34

CD - RUNNING DRY
PARTY LINE PLCD-020
Jungleland/ Rosalita (Come Out Tonight)/ Detroit Medley/ Quarter To Three
Recording: Good. Audience.
Source: Jay Alley Palladium, Tampa. Florida November 9 1975.
Comments: B&w cover. Yellow/red type. Time 37:15.

CD - USA BLUES II
CRYSTAL CAT CC 415
Intro (0:51)/ Tom Joad - Part 1 (6:42)/ Blowin' Down The Road (I Ain't Going To Be Treated This Way) 4:04/ Oklahoma Hills (2:38)/ Car Car (1:06)/ Deportee (Plane Wreck At Los Gatos) (3:01)/ Across The Border (4:46)/ Hard Travelling (3:08)/ I Got To Know (6:07)/ Homestead (3:54)/ My Fathers House (6:03)/ In Michigan (1:31)/ Shut Out The Light (3:40)/ Born In The U.S.A. (5:14)/ There'll Never Be Any Other For Me But You (2:54)
Recording: Excellent stereo.
Source: Tracks 1-9 a tribute concert for Woody Guthrie, Severance Hall, Cleveland, Ohio September 29 1996. Track 10 Benedum Center, Pittsburgh, PA September 16 1996. Track 11 Oakdale Theatre, Wallingford, Connecticut September 18 1996. Track 12 James W. Miller Auditorium, Western Michigan University Kalamazoo, MI September 24 1996. Tracks 13-15 Northrop Auditorium, Minneapolis, MN October 3 1996.

CD - WHERE THE RIVERS MEET
DOBERMAN 047/048/049
CD1: Born In The USA/ Out In The Streets/ Spirit In The Night/ Atlantic City/ State Trooper/ Highway Patrolman/ Prove It All Night/ Who'll Stop The Rain/ Glory Days/ Promised Land/ The River
CD2: Trapped/ Badlands/ Thunder Road/ Hungry Heart/ Dancing In The Dark/ Cadillac Ranch/ Candy's Room/ Downbound Train/ I'm On Fire/ Cover Me Up/ Growin' Up/ Bobby Jean
CD3: Jersey Girl/ Rosalita (Come Out Tonight)/ Jungleland/ Born To Run/ Detroit Medley (including Travellin' Band)/ Twist And Shout (including Do You Love Me)/ Santa Claus Is Coming To Town
Recording: Excellent stereo. Audience.
Source: The Civic Arena, Pittsburgh, PA September 22 1984.

STATUS QUO

Comments: UK CDR.

CD - WORKING CLASS HERO
SUMO 03/04
CD1: Adam Raised A Cain/ Straight Time/ Highway 29/ Darkness On The Edge Of Town/ Murder Inc./ Nebraska/ The Wish/ Brothers Under The Bridge/ Born In The U.S.A./ Dry Lightning/ Reason To Believe
CD2: Youngstown/ Sinaloa Cowboys/ The Line/ Balboa Park/ Across The Border/ Bobbie Jean/ This Hard Land/ Streets Of Philadelphia/ Galveston Bay
Recording: Excellent. Audience.
Source: Oslo Spektrum, Oslo, Norway March 14 1996.
Comments: European CD. Deluxe color cover.

CD - YOU BETTER NOT TOUCH VOL. 2
CRYSTAL CAT RECORDS CC 378
Back In Your Arms Again #1 (band) (0:36)/ Back In Your Arms Again #2 (band) (3:16)/ Blood Brothers (vocals, guitar, saxophone) (1:15)/ Blood Brothers (band) (1:53)/ Blood Brothers (vocals, guitar) (1:21)/ Blood Brothers (band, vocals, guitar) (1:26)/ Blood Brothers (band) (5:01)/ Without You (band) (4:34)/ High Hopes (band) (1:50)/ This Hard Land (2 different takes) (1:57)/ Secret Garden (piano) (0:21)/ Secret Garden (band alternate raw take) (4:09)/ Clarence Improvisation, Happy Birthday (1:16)/ You Can't Look (But You Better Not Touch) (0:45)/ Intro (0:27)/ Seeds (2:48)/ Adam Raised A Cain (2:47)/ Sinaloa Cowboys (4:17)/ Point Blank (3:46)/ I Don't Want Any More Of This Army Life (0:42)/ This Hard Land (3:54)/ The Ghost Of Tom Joad (4:28)/ Down By The River (with Neil Young (5:22)
Recording: Excellent. Soundboard. Tracks 16-24 Excellent. Audience.
Source: Tracks 1-15 studio '95. Tracks 16-24 Shoreline Amphitheatre, Mountain View, California October 28 1995.
Comments: European CD. Deluxe color cover. Picture CD.

STATUS QUO

CD - AUSTRALIEN ASSAULT
THE NL ARMY RWFC 97-2
Caroline/ Roll Over Lay Down/ Backwater/ Rockers Rollin'/ Is There A Better Way/ You Don't Own Me/ Hold You Back/ Rockin' All Over The World/ Down Down/ Dirty Water/ Big Fat Mama/ Don't Waste My Time/ Roadhouse Blues
Recording: Very good audience.
Source: Civic Centre, Newcastle July 18 1978.
Comments: European CD.

CD - BRITISH FUN INVASION
QUO VADIS RECORDS BTG 3316
Paper Plane/ Softer Ride/ The Wanderer/ Backwater/ Medley (Mystery Song, Railroad, Most Of The Time, Wild Side Of Life, Rollin' Home, Again And Again, Slow Train)/ Gerdundula/ Get Back/ Get Out Of Denver/ Whatever You Want/ In The Army Now/ Something 'Bout You Baby I Like/ Don't Waste My Time/ Come Rock With Me/ Rockin' On/ Roadhouse Blues/ Caroline
Recording: Excellent stereo. Radio broadcast.
Source: Philipshalle, Dusseldorf May 16 1996.
Comments: European picture CD.

CD - GREAT BALLS OF FIRE
THE NL ARMY RWFC 97
Paper Plane/ Softer Ride/ The Wanderer/ Proud Mary/ Fun Fun Fun/ Backwater/ Medley (Mystery Song, Railroad, Most Of The Time, Wild Side Of Life, Rollin' Home, Again And Again, Slow Train)/ Gerdundula/ Get Back/ Get Out Of Denver/ Whatever You Want/ In The Army Now/ Something 'Bout You Baby I Like/ Don't Waste My Time/ Rockin' All Over The World/ Roadhouse Blues/ Caroline/ All Around My Hat/ The Anniversary Waltz/ Medley (Let's Dance, Red River, Rock, No Particular Place To Go, The Wanderer, I Hear You Knocking, Lucille, Great Balls Of Fire)/ Rock'n'Roll Music/ Dizzy Miss Lizzy/ Long Tall Sally/ Sweet Soul Music/ Bye Bye Johnny
Recording: Very good audience.
Source: Wembley Arena, London December 16 1996.
Comments: European 2 CD set.

CD - IS IT REALLY QUO?
STONE DEAF RECORDS SDR 9701
Roadhouse Blues/ Down The Dustpipe/ Spinning Wheel Blues/ Is It Really Me?/ Gotta Go Home

STATUS QUO

Radio broadcast.
Source: BBC Studios, London February 26 1970.
Comments: European CD.

CD - LIVE IN BRIGHTON
STONE DEAF RECORDS SDR 9702
Paper Plane/ The Wanderer/ Proud Mary/ Fun Fun Fun/ Get Back/ Whatever You Want/ In The Army Now/ Something 'Bout You Baby I Like/ Don't Waste My Time/ Rockin' All Over The World/ Roadhouse Blues/ Caroline/ All Around My Hat
Recording: Excellent stereo. Radio broadcast.
Source: The Centre, Brighton December 11 1996.
Comments: European CD.

STING

CD - GOOD TIMES FADE AWAY
OSA BONG
Let Your Soul Be A Pilot (5:37)/ Ob-La-Di Ob-La-Da (3:22)/ If You Love Somebody, Set Them Free (4:52)/ I Was Brought To My Senses (6:36)/ You Still Touch Me (4:22)/ Synchronicity (5:02)/ If I Ever Lose My Faith In You (5:13)/ Fields Of Gold (3:44)/ Shape Of My Heart (2:54)/ Roxanne (6:44)/ Englishman In New York (5:04)/ Bring On The Night, When The World Is Running Down (8:08)/ When We Dance (5:49)/ Every Breath You Take (5:11)
Recording: Excellent stereo. Soundboard.
Comments: European CD. Deluxe color cover. Pic CD.

STONE ROSES, THE

CD - HIGH TIMES IN DOPE LAND
SKINUP 002
Intro/ I Wanna Be Adored/ She Bangs The Drums/ Waterfall/ Ten Story Love Song/ Daybreak, Breaking, In To Heaven/ Your Star Will Shine/ Tightrope/ Elizabeth My Dear/ Love Spreads/ Good Times/ I Am The Resurrection/ Begging You/ Made Of Stone
Recording: Very good audience recording.
Source: The Paradiso, Amsterdam April 14 1995.

CD - STONE ROSES
3D REALITY 3D-SR-050
I Wanna Be Adored/ She Bangs The Drum/ Waterfall/ Ten Story Love Song, Day Break, Breaking Into Heaven/ Love Spreads/ Good Times/ Made Of Stone/Driving South/ Elizabeth My Dear/ I Am The Resurrection
Recording: Excellent audience recording.
Source: Mielpargue, Hall, Hiroshima September 20 1995.

STONE THE CROWS

CD - DON'T THINK TWICE
HF 9543
158 (6:48)/ Keep On Rollin' (5:14)/ Big Jim Salter (15:41)/ Mr. Wizard (7:58)/ Don't Think Twice (5:41)/ Goin' Down (5:06)/ Think (9:06)
Recording: Excellent. Soundboard.
Source: Recorded Live, London '71.
Comments: European CD. Deluxe color cover. Picture CD.

CD - ODE TO JOHN LAW
HF 9541
Sad Mary (6:50)/ Friend (6:25)/ Love 74 (6:35)/ Mad Dogs & Englishmen (3:32)/ Things Are Getting Better (6:08)/ Ode To John Law (5:45)/ Danger Zone (6:20)
Recording: Excellent. Soundboard.
Comments: European CD. Deluxe color cover. Picture CD.

CD - ON THE HIGHWAY
HF 9544
On The Highway (6:36)/ Palace Of The King (4:59)/ Penicillin Blues (5:43)/ Sunset Cowboy (6:48)/ Niagara (9:06)/ Mr. Wizard (9:06)/ I'm Not A Good Time Girl (3:43)/ Goin' Down (5:38)
Recording: Excellent. Soundboard.
Source: Recorded Live, London '72.
Comments: European CD. Deluxe color cover. Picture CD.

CD - STONE THE CROWS
HF 9540
The Touch Of Your Loving Hand (6:01)/ Raining In Your Heart (5:10)/ Blind Man (5:09)/ Fool On The Hill (4:13)/ I Saw America (17:28)
Recording: Excellent. Soundboard.
Source: Studio.
Comments: European CD. Deluxe color cover. Picture CD.

STONE THE CROWS

STONE THE CROWS

CD - TEENAGE LICKS
HF 9542
Big Jim Salter/ Faces/ Mr. Wizard/ Don't Think Twice/ Keep On Rollin'/ Alien Mochre/ One Five Eight/ I May Be Right I May Be Wrong/ Seven Lakes
Recording: Excellent. Soundboard.
Source: Studio.
Comments: European CD. Deluxe color cover. Picture CD. Time 39:06.

STYLE COUNCIL

CD - ANOTHER COUNTRY
3D REALTY 3D-SC-026
You Are The Best Thing/ (When You) Call Me/ The Lodgers/ Our Favorite Shop/ Have You Ever Had It Blue/ Mr. Cool's Dream/ Party Chambers/ Le Depart/ Spin' Drifting/ The Cost Of Loving, The Cost/ All Year Round/ Soul Deep/ Everybody's On The Run/ Promised Land/ Can You Still Love Me?

SUPERGRASS

CD - CAUGHT BY THE FUZZ
MOONRAKER 160
Sitting Up Straight (2:43)/ I'd Like To Know (4:08)/ Odd? (4:18)/ Lose It (2:45)/ Richard The Third (3:34)/ Time (3:30)/ Alright (3:05)/ We're Not Supposed To (3:28)/ She's So Loose (3:28)/ Melaine Davis (3:21)/ Going Out (5:01)/ Interviews (3:17)/ Going Out (4:16)*/ We're Not Supposed To (3:03)*/ Strange Ones (3:44)*
Recording: Excellent stereo. Soundboard.
Source: The RDS, Dublin June 22 '96.
*British TV March 1 1996.
Comments: European CD. Deluxe color cover. Picture CD.

SUEDE

CD - EUROPE IS OUR PLAYGROUND
MOONRAKER 199
Filmstar/ Trash/ Heroine/ She/ Lazy/ By The Sea/ Starcrazy/ Animal Nitrate/ The Wild Ones/ Saturday Night/ So Young/ New Generation/ Beautiful Ones/ Picnic By The Motorway
Lazy/ Europe Is Our Playground/ Starcrazy/ Saturday Night
Recording: Excellent stereo. Soundboard.
Source: Tracks 1-14 The Kilburn National, London October 11 1996. Tracks 15-18 BBC radio session, Manchester September 23 1996.
Comments: European CD.

CD - TRASHY
KISS THE STONE KTS 644
Filmstar (4:02)/ Trash (4:34)/ Heroine (3:03)/ She (4:44)/ Lazy (3:13)/ By The Sea (4:41)/ Starcrazy (3:23)/ Animal Nitrate (3:28)/ The Wild Ones (4:54)/ Saturday Night (5:01)/ So Young (3:43)/ New Generation (4:37)/ Beautiful Ones (5:16)/ Picnic By The Motorway (4:17)
Recording: Excellent stereo. Soundboard.
Source: Kilburn National Ballroom, London October 11 1996.
Comments: European CD. Deluxe color cover. Picture CD.

SWEET SAVAGE

CD - SWEET SAVAGE
CD-008
Take No Prisoners/ Killing Time/ Eye Of The Storm/ Straight Thru The Heart/ Teaser/ Into The Night/ Queen's Vengeance/ Eye Of The Storm/ Killing Time/ Finders Keepers/ Sweet Surrender/ Prospector Of Greed/ The Raid/ Lady Marion/ Queen's Vengeance/ Take No Prisoners/ Bottle Of Wine/ Eye Of The Storm/ Lady Of The Night
Recording: Tracks 1-5 excellent stereo. Soundboard. Tracks 6-19 poor to good.
Source: Tracks 1-2 from the 'Killing Time' single. Track 3 from the 'Friday Rock Show' LP. Tracks 4-5 from the 'Straight Thru The Heart' single. Tracks 6-19 live.
Comments: Japanese CD. B&W. Red type. Time 72:07.

SYKES, JOHN

CD - BY REQUEST
NIGHTLIFE N-045
JOHN SYKES: Don't Say Goodbye (Studio Outtake '90)/ TYGERS OF PAN TANG: Love Potion #9 (Old Grey Whistle Test '81)/ WHITESNAKE: Crying In The Rain (Canada '84)/ BLUE MURDER: Riot (New York November 18, '89)/ Blue Murder (New York November 28, '89)/ Thunder & Lightning (Dallas, April 8, '94)/ Still Of The Night (Dallas, April 8, '94)/ THIN LIZZY: The Sun Goes Down (Leicester, February 13, '83)/ Are You Ready (Leicester '83)/ JOHN

SYKES: She Knows (Tokyo September 5 '93)/ Please Don't Leave Me, Kings Call (Tokyo September 5 '93)
Recording: Good-very good. Some excellent. Audience/Soundboard.
Comments: Japanese CD. Deluxe color cover. Time 70:90.

T

TAYLOR, JAMES

CD - CARNEGIE HALL
KISS THE STONE KTS 537
You Can Close Your Eyes (3:00)/ Riding On A Railroad (2:50)/ Blossom, Band Intro (3:06)/ Long Ago And Far Away (2:53)/ Country Roads (4:05)/ You've Got A Friend (5:05)/ Promised Land (3:35)/ Let It Fall Down (4:24)/ Brighten Your Night With Day (2:56)/ Walking Man (3:32)/ Don't Be Lonely Tonight (2:41)/ Fire And Rain (3:59)/ Mockingbird (4:20)/ Ain't No Song (3:56)/ Sweet Baby James (3:10)
Recording: Excellent stereo. Soundboard.
Source: Carnegie Hall, New York, May 1974. Track 13 duet with Carly Simon.
Comments: European CD. Deluxe color cover. Picture CD.

TEENAGE FANCLUB

CD - GLAND SLAM
3D REALITY 3D-TF-023
The Cabbage/ Don't Look Back/ Radio/ Mellow Dought/ Star Sign/ About You/ Sparky's Dream/ The Concept, Stain/ The Concept, Stain/ God Knows It's True/ Metal Baby/ So Far Gone/ What You Do To Fe/ December/ Star Sign/ Mr. Tambourine Man/ Goody Goody Gum Drops/ It's Hard To Fall In Love/ Alcoholiday/ Long Hair/ Gene Clarke
Source: Tracks 1-8 Bristol, England 1995. Tracks 9-15 Amsterdam, Holland 1993. Tracks 19-21 outtakes 1995.
Comments: Japanese CD.

TELEVISION

CD - THIS IS CLOSED
COLOSSEUM 97-C-016
Fire Engine/ Glory/ Grip Of Love/ Foxhole/ Dreams Dream/ Ain't That Nothing/ Friction/ Prove It/ Marquee Moon/ Kingdom Come/ Satisfaction
Source: The First Farewell Show, The Bottom Line, NYC July 29 1978.
Comments: Japanese CD.

THERAPY?

CD - INFERNAL GUM
TROUBLE 959493
Nowhere (Sabres Of Paradise Mix)/ Nowhere (Therapeutic Distortion Mix)/ Nice 'N' Sleazy/ Reuters/ Tatty Seaside Town/ Evil Elvis (The Lost Demo)/ Isolation/ Lunacy Booth (String Version)/ Isolation (Consolidated Mix)/ Stories (Cello Version)/ Isolation (Consolidated Synth Mix)/ Our Love Must Die/ Nice Guys/ Loose (Photek Remix)/ Misery (Acoustic Version)/ Die Laughing (Acoustic Version)/ Screamager (Acoustic Version)/ Die Laughing (Live)/ Nowhere (Live)/ Unbeliever (Live)
Recording: Excellent stereo. Soundboard.
Comments: European CD. Deluxe color cover. Time 76:16

THIN LIZZY

CD - FINAL LIGHTNING
NIGHTLIFE N-046
Jailbreak/ Cold Sweat/ The Sun Goes Down/ Holy War/ The Boys Are Back/ Rosalie/ Baby Please Don't Go/ Still In Love/ With You/ Dancing In The Moonlight
Recording: Excellent stereo. Soundboard.
Source: Hitchin January 26 1983.
Comments: Japanese CD. Dbw. Red type. Time 54:53.

CD - OSAKA SUNDOWN
NIGHTLIFE N-011
Thunder And Lightning/ Waiting On An Alibi/ Jailbreak/ Baby Please Don't Go/ Angel Of Death/ Are You Ready/ Holy War/ The Sun Goes Down/ Cold Sweat/ Sha La La/ Baby Drives Me Crazy/ Still In Love With You/ Rosalie
Recording: Excellent. Audience.
Source: Banpaku Hall, Osaka May 21 1983.
Comments: Japanese CD. Deluxe color cover. Time 73:24.

THIN LIZZY

CD - SOLDIER OF FORTUNE
L602
Soldier Of Fortune/ Jailbreak/ Warriors/ Dancing In The Moonlight/ Massacre/ Still In Love With You/ Cowboy Song/ The Boys Are Back In Town/ Don't Believe A Word/ Emerald/ Bad Reputation
Recording: Good. Audience. Hiss.
Source: Reading Festival, England, August 27 1977.
Comments: Japanese CD. Deluxe color cover. Time 55:15.

311

CD - DOWN IN L.A.
SNOW 021
Independence Day/ Lucky/ Freakout/ Misdirected Hostility/ Feels So Good/ All Mixed Up/ Nick Hex/ Hysteria/ Down/ Do You Right/ From The Earth/ Hive/ Unity/ Do You Right
Recording: Excellent. Audience.
Source: Tracks 1-13 live at 'Choose Or Lose' benefit concert, Hospitality Point, San Diego, CA August 13 1996. Track 14 live from Irvine, CA June 15 1996.
Comments: European CD. Deluxe color cover.

THUNDERS, JOHNNY

CD - JOHNNY ON THE ROCKS
NIGHTLIFE N-048
Intro, The Man With The Golden Arm/ Pipeline/ Personality Crisis/ A Little Bit Of Whore/ Mia/ Steppin' Stone/ Alone In A Crowd/ Endless Party/ Green Onions/ Talkin' 'Bout You/ Copy Cat/ Don't Mess With Cupid/ Born Too Loose/ Too Much Junkie Business/ Pills/ Gloria/ Lightning Bar Blues/ Looking At You/ Blitzkreig
Recording: Very good-excellent. Audience.
Source: Mr Keisa's, Leicester, England, October 21 1984.
Comments: Japanese CD. Deluxe color cover. Time 61:26

TRAFFIC

CD - A GROUP, A DOG, A GHOST
COLOSSEUM RECORDS 97-C-012
Who Knows What Tomorrow Might Bring?/ Every Mothers Son/ Medicated Goo/ Pearly Queen/ Dear Mr. Fantasy/ John Barleycorn Must Die/ Empty Pages/ 40,000 Headmen/ Glad/ Freedom Rider/ Can't Find My Way Home/ No Time To Live
Recording: Good to very good. Audience. Hiss.
Source: Fillmore West, San Francisco, CA June 30 1970.
Comments: Japanese CD. Deluxe color cover. Time 74:37.

CD - GLAD
VINTAGE RARE MASTERS VRM-016
Medicated Goo/ John Barleycorn Must Die/ Pearly Queen/ Stranger To Himself/ Dear Mr. Fantasy/ Empty Pages/ 40, 000 Headmen/ Glad/ Freedom Rider/ Can't Find My Way Home
Recording: Excellent. Audience.
Source: Fillmore West, San Francisco July 1 1970.
Comments: Japanese CD. Deluxe color cover. Time 63:27.

TRAGICALLY HIP, THE

CD - ANOTHER ROADSIDE
35525
Locked In The Trunk Of A Car/ Three Pistols/ At The Hundredth Meridian/ The Last Of The Unplucked Gems/ Lionized/ Courage/ Eldorado/ Wheat Kings/ New Orleans Is Sinking (includes National Disaster)/ Fully Completely/ The Wherewhithal/ Pigeon Camera/ We'll Go Too/ 50 Mission Cap/ Little Bones
Recording: Excellent stereo. Soundboard.
Source: Landsdowne Park, Ottawa July 26 1993.
Comments: CDR. Deluxe color cardboard sleeve. Picture CD. Gold Kodak disc. Time 70:11.

CD - BON APPETITE
GOLDEN BOY GBCD004
Fifty Mission Cap/ At The Hundredth Meridian/ Locked In the Trunk Of A Car/ The Wherewithal/ Untitled Jam/ Eldorado/ So Hard Done By/ Fully Completely/ We'll Go Too/ Pigeon Camera/ Lionized/ Looking For A Place To Happen/ Blonde Solid/ You See The Details/ Radio Show/ Last Of The Unplucked Gems/ Fully Completely/ New Orleans
Recording: Excellent stereo. Soundboard.
Source: Tracks 1-15 recorded 1992 for 'Fully Completely'. Tracks 16-17 Northwestern University, IL 1993. Track 18

The Roxy Theatre, Hollywood, CA May 3 1991.
Comments: CDR. Deluxe color cover. Time 69:44.

CD - FISHERMAN'S PARADISE
GOLDEN BOY GBCD003
Little Bones/ She Didn't Know/ Highway Girl/ Everytime You Go/ Cordelia/ Trickle Down/ 38 Years Old/ Three Pistols/ Fight/ I Believe In You/ New Orleans/ On The Verge/ Blow At High Dough/ Locked In The Trunk Of A Car/ At The Hundredth Meridian
Recording: Excellent stereo. Soundboard.
Source: Tracks 1-13 The Cabaret Metro, Chicago, IL April 20 1991. Tracks 14-15 Northwestern University 1993.
Comments: CDR. Deluxe color cover. Time 72:44.

CD - 'FREAKED' IN SWEDEN
35526
Fully Completely/ Inevitability Of Death/ Greasy Jungle/ The Last Of The Unplucked Gems/ New Orleans Is Sinking/ Grace, Too/ Daredevil/ Titanic Terrarium/ At The Hundredth Meridian/ Nautical Disaster/ Fire In The Hole/ Thugs/ Little Bones
Recording: Excellent stereo. Soundboard.
Source: Gino, Sweden, December 7 1994.
Comments: CDR. Deluxe color cardboard sleeve. Picture CD. Gold Kodak disc. Time 62:56.

TURNER, TINA

CD - WILDEST DREAMS 1996
ELECTRIC 666045/46
CD1: Whatever You Want (5:38)/ Do What You Do (3:57)/ River Deep, Mountain High (3:42)/ Missing You (3:53)/ In Your Wildest Dream (6:09)/ Golden Eye (5:03)/ Private Dancer (8:38)/ We Don't Need Another Hero (5:39)/ Unplugged: Let's Stay Together (4:02)/ I Can't Stand The Rain (3:10)/ Undercover Agent For The Blues (3:35)/ Steamy Windows (3:23)
CD2: Give It Up For Your (2:57)/ Better Be Good To Me (5:36)/ Addicted To Love (5:05)/ The Best (6:57)/ What's Love Got To Do With It (5:44)/ Group Announcement (3:09)/ Proud Mary (9:49)/ Nutbush City Limits (5:03)/ Something Beautiful Remains (4:13)/ On Silent Wings (5:06)
Source: New Ajax Arena, Amsterdam September 7 1996.

Comments: European CD.

TYRANNOSAURUS REX

CD - FOR THE LION AND THE UNICORN
LITTLE HOBBIT RECORDS LHCD 1111
Unicorn, Hot Rod Mama/ Afghan Woman/ Debora/ Mustang Ford/ Stacey Grove/ Salamanda Palaganda/ Wind Quartets/ One Inch Rock/ Chariots Of Silk/ Seal Of Season/ Conesuala/ Nijinski Hind/ Once Upon The Seas Of Abyssina/ Interstellar Overdrive/ Do You Remember/ The Wizard/ Eastern Spell/ Strange Orchestras/ Misty Coast Of Albany/ Evenings Of Damask/ Pewter Suitor/ Travelling Tradition
Recording: Fair to good. Audience.
Source: The Lyceum, London April 11 1969. Tracks 17 and 18 Broendby Club, Copenhagen 1969. Tracks 19 Cafe Au Gogo, New York August 16 1969. Tracks 20-22 Queen Elizabeth Hall, London January 13 1969.
Comments: European CD. Picture CD. Time 56:00.

CD - T.K.Y. BLUES
H-BOMB MUSIC HBM 9507
20th Century Boy/ Chariot Choogle/ Telegram Sam/ Buick Mackane/ Jeepster/ Tokyo Blues/ Get It On
Recording: Poor. Audience.
Source: Budokan, Tokyo October 25 1973.
Comments: Japanese CD. Deluxe color cover. Time 72:15.

TURNER, JOE LYNN

CD - SPOTLIGHT KID
NIGHTLIFE N-013
Intro/ Death Alley Driver/ I Surrender/ Day Of The Eagle/ Wishing Well/ Jealous Lover/ Stone Cold/ Street Of Dreams/ Never In My Life/ Can't Happen Here/ Highway Star/ Smoke On The Water
Recording: Excellent stereo. Soundboard.
Source: Milwaukee Summer Fest July 7 1994.
Comments: Japanese CD. Deluxe color cover. Time 66:07.

TYGERS OF PAN TANG

CD - FIRST TYGER
NIGHTLIFE N-047
Euthanasia/ Bad Times/ Rock N Roll Man/

Badger Badger/ Slave To Freedom/ John Sykes Solo/ Wild Cats/ Fireclown/ Suzie Smiled/ Straight As A Die/ Money/ Don't Touch Me There/ Tush
Recording: Good to very good. Audience.
Source: Reading Festival, August 24 1980.
Comments: Japanese CD. Deluxe color cover. Time 42:39.

U

U2

CD - THE COMPLETE BOSTON '83 TAPES
SWINGING PIG TSP-CD-222-2
CD1: Out Of Control/ Twilight/ An Cat Dubh, Into The Heart/ Surrender/ Two Hearts Beat As One/ Seconds/ Sunday Bloody Sunday/ Cry, The Electric Co./ I Fall Down/ October/ New Year's Day
CD2: Gloria/ I Threw A Brick/ A Day Without Me/ Party Girl/ 11 O'Clock Tick Tock/ I Will Follow/ 40/ I Will Follow/ An Cat Dubh, Into The Heart/ A Day Without Me/ 11 O'Clock Tick Tock
Recording: Excellent stereo. Soundboard.
Source: Orpheum Theatre, Boston May 29 1983. Four tracks from Hilversum October 14 1980.
Comments: European CD.

CD - FIRST NIGHT ON EARTH
LZCD 034/035
CD1: Intro/ Mofo/ I Will Follow/ Even Better The The Real Thing/ Do You Feel Loved/ Pride (In The Name Of Love)/ I Still Haven't Found What I'm Looking For/ Last Night On Earth/ Gone/ Until The End Of The World/ If God Sends His Angels/ String At The Sun (Take 1)/ String At The Sun (Take 2)/ Daydream Believer
CD2: Miami, Bullet The Blue Sky/ Please, Sunday Bloody Sunday/ Where The Streets Have No Name/ Intro/ Discotheque/ If You Wear That Velvet Dress/ With Or Without/ Hold Me, Thrill Me, Kiss Me, Kill Me/ Mysterious Way/ One/ Mofo/ I Will Follow
Source: Sam Boyd Stadium Las Vegas NV Apr. 25 1997.
Comments: European CD. Deluxe color cover.

CD - FOUR WILD IRISH ROSES PART 2
OXYGEN OXY 084
Two Hearts Beat (As One) (5:48) ('83 different version)/ October (2:26) ('81 different version with Wally Badarou)/ The Ocean (1:26) (Old Grey Whistle Test, UK February 28 '81)/ 11 O'Clock Tick Tock (4:57) (Old Grey Whistle Test, UK February 28 '81)/ The Dream Is Over (2:52) ('78 previously unreleased song)/ Lost On A Silent Planet (3:45) ('78 previously unreleased song)/ Another Time, Another Place (4:38) (different version)/ City At Night (2:28) ('78 Previously Unreleased Song)/ Street Mission (4:15) ('78 previously unreleased song)/ Scarlet (2:23) (Kid Jensen Session, UK October 14 '81)/ Stories For Boys (2:44) (Dublin, Ireland, RTE Studios '79)/ Lost Highway (1:19) (US Radio Sessions December '87)/ People Get Ready (3:06) (Belfast, McCordie Hall March 13 '87)/ Southern Man (3:42) (Belfast, McCordie Hall March 13 '87)/ Trip Through Your Wires (3:43) (Belfast, McCordie Hall March 13 '87)/ Exit (3:33) (Belfast, McCordie Hall March 13 '87)/ In God's Country (2:52) (Belfast, McCordie Hall March 13 '87)/ Pride (In The Name Of Love) (4:05) (Belfast, McCordie Hall March 13 '87)/ Twist And Shout (1:47) (L. Mullen solo, Aussie Radio November 14 '89)/ All Over Now (2:14) (L. Mullen, Aussie Radio November 14 '89)/ Trip Through Your Wires, She's A Mystery To Me (2:52) (Sun Studios, Memphis, TN November '87)/ Can't Help Falling In Love (2:10) (Sun Studios,Memphis, TN November '87)
Recording: Excellent. Soundboard.
Comments: European CD.

CD - HEART BEAT
KOBRA RECORDS KRCD 13
Bullet The Blue Sky/ Love Rescue Me/ People Get Ready/ When Love Comes To Town (with B.B. King, Rotterdam, December 31 '89)/ I Will Follow (R. Skinner Session September 18 '80)/ Sunday Bloody Sunday (alternate version February '83)/ Surrender (alternate version February '83)/ Be There (outtake '82)/ The Ocean (Old Grey Whistle Test, UK February 28 '81)/ 11 O'Clock Tick Tock (Old Grey Whistle Test, UK February 28 '81)/ The Dream Is Over Lost On A Silent Planet (previously unreleased '78)/ Street Mission (previously unreleased '78)/ In

God's Country (Belfast McCorde Hall March 13 '87)/ Pride (In The Name Of Love) (Belfast McCorde Hall March 13 '87) Twist And Shout / Mullen Solo (Aussie Radio November 14 '89)/ All Over You/ Mullen Solo (Aussie Radio November 14 '89)/ My Wild Irish Rose (from the film documentary 'The Roost Of Irish Rock, '95)
Recording: Very good to excellent.
Comments: European CD. B&W cover. Red type. Time 75:40.

CD - LIVE IN TOKYO 1983
AMSTERDAM AMS 9613-1-1
Out Of Control (4:28)/ Twilight (4:38)/ An Cat Dubh, Into The Heart (7:23)/ Surrender (5:09)/ Two Hearts Beat As One (4:46)/ Seconds (3:08)/ Sunday Bloody Sunday (includes The Midnight Hour) (5:32)/ Cry, The Electric Co. (5:34)/ I Fall Down (3:41)/ October, New Year's Day (6:46)/ Gloria (5:05)/ Trash, Trampoline And The Party Girl (3:26)/ 11 O'Clock Tick Tock (6:15)/ I Will Follow (4:47)/ '40' (4:55)
Source: Shibuya Public Hall, Tokyo, Japan November 26 1983.
Comments: Japanese CD.

UFO

CD - BY REQUEST
NIGHTLIFE N-050
Give Her The Gun/ Time On My Hands/ Space Child/ Rock Bottom/ Cold Turkey/ Prince Kajuku/ Boogie For George/ Back To The USA/ C'Mon Everybody/ Try Me, Just Another Suicide
Recording: Tracks 1-2 Excellent. Soundboard. Tracks 3-10 Poor-Good. Audience.
Source: Tracks 1-2 BBC Studio '74. Tracks 3-9 Zurich March 5 '74. Track 10 Blackpool soundcheck November 6 '77.
Comments: Japanese CD.

ULMER, JAMES BLOOD

CD - BLOODY GUITAR
IMPROVISATION LABEL IL-3366815
Love Dance/ Would You Like To Go To America?/ Show Time/ Please Tell Her/ Swing And Dance
Source: Pithecanthoropus, Tokyo April 13 1983.
Comments: Japanese CD.

URIAH HEEP

CD - BEAST PARTY
DIRTY13 D13-006
Roll, Overture/ Sell Your Son I/ Stealin/ The Other Side Of Midnight/ Too Scared To Run/ Rockarama/ Angel/ The Wizard/ July Morning/ Bad Blood/ Party Line/ Mick Box Solo/ Gypsy/ Easy Living
Source: Cardiff New Ocean Club March 19 1985.
Comments: Japanese CD.

CD - RETURN TO WETTON
GYPSY EYE 004
Gypsy (5:24)/ Impro Guitar Number (5:25)/ Sweet Lorrain (includes Wetton solo) (6:24)/ July Morning (4:38)/ Midnight (6:12)/ Easy Livin' (2:23)/ Bird Of Prey (2:08)/ Love Machine (4:30)/ Look At Yourself (5:10)/ Intro (1:06)/ Devil's Daughter (4:39)/ Sterlin' (5:51)/ Suicide Man (4:56)/ Shady Lady (6:04)/ Prima Donna (7:24)
CD2: The Wizzard (4:35)/ July Morning (11:37)/ Return to Fantasy (5:45)/ Easy Livin'/ Gypsy (5:05)/ Mick Box Solo (6:41)/ Sweet Lorrain (includes Wetton solo) (10:15)/ Bird Of Prey (3:14)/ Love Machine (4:23)/ Look At Yourself (5:24)/ Rainbow Demon (6:09)
Recording: CD1 tracks 1-9 good soundboard. Tracks 10-15 fair to good audience. CD2 tracks 1-10 poor to good audience - shoot the guy singing along. Track 11 poor to fair audience.
Source: CD1 tracks 1-9 Pink Pop Final, Yeelen 1976. Tracks 10-15 ??? CD2 tracks 1-10 Jaap Eden Hall, Amsterdam February 17 1976. Track 11 Central Park, NY September 3 1975.

V

VAN HALEN

CD - A.F.U.
REAL THING RTCD-008/9
CD1: One Way To Rock/ Summer Night/ Panama/ A.F.U./ Bass Solo/ Running With The Devil/ Why Can't This Be Love/ Mine All Mine, Drums Solo/ Cabowabo/ Finish What Ya Started/ '5150'
CD2: When It's Love/ Eagles Fly/ I Can't

VAN HALEN

Drive 55/ Best Of Both Worlds/ Guitar Solo/ Black And Blue/ Ain't Talkin' About Love/ You Really Got Me, It's Only Rock 'N' Roll, You Really Got Me/ Rock And Roll
Recording: Good. Audience.
Source: January 25 1989.
Comments: Japanese CD. Deluxe color cover. Time CD1 59:05. CD2 59:27.

CD - ASSAULTS QUEBEC
CD1: Unchained/ Hot For The Teacher/ Drums Solo/ Little Guitars/ Cathedral, House Of Pain/ I'll Wait/ Everybody Wants Some!!/ Girl Gone Bad/ Ice Cream Man/ Summertime Blues/ 1984, Jump/ Guitar Solo/ Panama
CD2: You Really Got Me/ Ain't talkin' Bout Love/ Hot For The Teacher/ Drums Solo/ On Fire/ Runnin' With The Devil/ Little Guitars/ I'll Wait/ 1984, Jump/ Guitar Solo/ Panama
Recording: Very good. Audience. CD2 Tracks 3-11 good to very good. Audience.
Source: Quebec City Coliseum, Quebec, Canada April 21 1984. CD2 Tracks 3-11 Nuremburg, Germany September 2 1984.
Comments: European CD. Deluxe color cover. Time CD1 69:48. CD2 61:32.

CD - CRACK THE SECRET
BONDAGE MUSIC BON058
The Seventh Seal/ Judgement Day/ Don't Tell Me (What Love Can Do)/ Amsterdam/ Panama/ Top Of The World/ Feelin' Best Of Both Worlds/ Ain't Talkin' 'Bout Love/ *Your Really Got Me/ *Jump/ *There's Only One Way To Rock/ *5150
Recording: Excellent. Soundboard. *Very good.
Source: Secret Gig, Arnheim, Holland January 27 1995. *Budokan, Tokyo, Japan November 1 1995.
Comments: Japanese CD. Deluxe color cover. Time 70:07.

CD - ON FIRE IN FRESNO
BABYFACE BF016
Interview (KROQ December 14 1976)/ House Of Pain (demo)/ Running With The Devil (demo)/ Light Up The Sky/ Running With The Devil/ Beautiful Girls/ On Fire/ Feel Your Love Tonight/ Out Of Love Again/ Ice Cream Man/ Ain't Talkin' 'Bout Love/ Dead Or Alive/ You Really Got Me/ Bottoms Up
Recording: Tracks 2-3 excellent. Soundboard. Tracks 4-15 good. Audience.
Source: Tracks 2-3 1976. Tracks 4-15 Fresno, CA March 25 1979.
Comments: European CD. Deluxe color cover. Time 73:00.

'77 + LIVE
BABY FACE BF2302
Show Your Love/ Voodoo Queen/ Little Dreamer/ Last Night/ Get The Show On The Road/ Babe Don't Leave Me Alone/ Big Trouble/ She's The Woman/ Put Out The Lights/ Happy Trails/ If You Can't Rock Me/ Jean Genie/ Dave Raps, Intro of band/ Women In Love/ Rock Steady/ Rock N' Roll Hoochie Koo
Recording: Very good to excellent.
Source: Outtakes. Tracks 11-16 Pasadena Hilton 1976.
Comments: European CD. Deluxe color cover. Time 59:04.

CD - '77 + LIVES ON
BABYFACE BF027
Show Your Love/ Running With The Devil/ Somebody Get Me A Doctor/ In A Simple Rhyme/ I Wanna Be Your Lover/ Last Night (Hang 'Em High)/ Peace Of Mind/ Eruption/ House Of Pain/ D.O.A./ You Really Got Me/ Jamie's Crying/ Feel Your Love Tonight/ Ain't Dalkin Bout Love
Recording: Poor to good. Audience.
Source: January 18 1977. Tracks 12-14 Fresno 1978.
Comments: European CD. Deluxe color cover. Time 61:51.

VAUGHAN, STEVIE RAY

CD - FORCE OF NATURE II
BALBOA PRODUCTIONS BP-95012/13
CD1: Opening Jam/ Come On/ Mary Had A Little Lamb/ Rude Mood/ Dirty Pool/ Voodoo Child/ Heartfixer/ Drivin' South/ Texas Flood/ Testify/ Jam 292
CD2: Instrumental/ Instrumental/ Voodoo Child/ Tell Me/ Texas Flood/ I'm Leaving You/ Piece And Joy/ Little Wing/ Third Stone From The Sun/ Lenny
Recording: Poor audience.
Source: Fitzgeralds Club, Houston, Texas June 20 1983.

CD - GOOD VIBES AT THE SPECTRUM!
MIDNIGHT BEAT MB CD 082
Shuffle (4:54)/ Voodoo Chile (Slight Return)

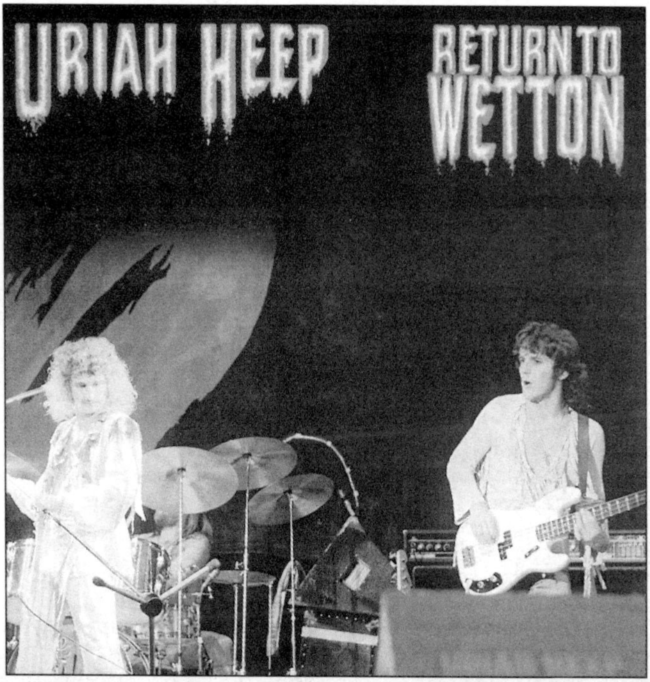
URIAH HEEP
RETURN TO WETTON

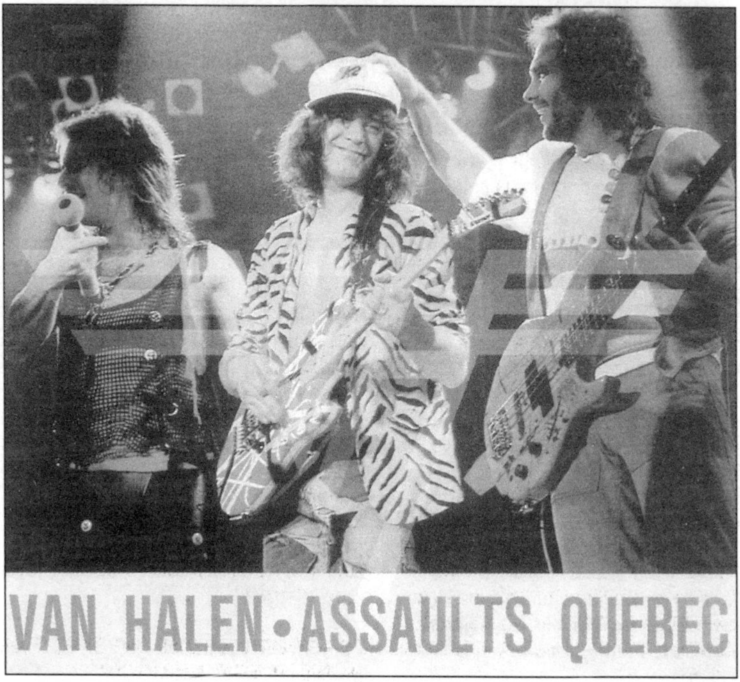
VAN HALEN • ASSAULTS QUEBEC

VAUGHAN, STEVIE RAY

(11:38)/ Honey Bee (2:19)/ Mary Had A Little Lamb (3:28)/ Couldn't Stand The Weather (4:58)/ Cold Shot (4:11)/ Pride And Joy (4:38)/ Riviera Paradise (9:02)/ Testify (4:14)/ So Excited (4:59)/ Voodoo Chile (Slight Return) (7:02)/ Pride And Joy (4:07)/ Mary Had A Little Lamb (3:13)/ Love Struck Baby (2:46)/ Texas Flood (7:30)
Recording: Excellent. Soundboard.
Source: Tracks 1-8 The Spectrum, Montreal. Tracks 9-15 The Reading Festival, England 1983.
Comments: Deluxe color cover.

CD - THANKS FOR THE MEMORIES
MIDNIGHT BEAT MB CD 083
So Excited (3:28)/ Voodoo Chile (Slight Return) (10:36)/ The Things I Used To Do (6:59)/ Pride And Joy (4:14)/ Tin Pan Alley (12:11)/ Little Sister (4:09)/ Change It (4:19)/ Come On (4:29)/ Cold Shot (5:33)/ Love House (4:21)/ Texas Flood (8:02)/ Pride And Joy (4:27)/ Willy The Wimp (6:38)
Recording: Excellent. Soundboard.
Source: Tracks 1-5 Antones, Austin, Texas 1983. Tracks 6-13 Dallas, Texas 1986.
Comments: Deluxe color cover.

CD - THE WILD MAN FROM TEXAS PLAYS HOUSTON
MIDNIGHT BEAT MB CD 081
House Is A Rockin' (2:37)/ Tightrope (5:20)/ Let Me Love You (3:43)/ Crossfire (4:04)/ Riviera Paradise (10:21)/ Wall Of Denial (5:52)/ Superstition (4:49)/ Cold Shot (6:37)/ Texas Flood (7:09)/ Voodoo Chile (Slight Return) (11:32)/ Leave My Little Girl Alone (5:48)
Recording: Excellent. Soundboard.
Source: Houston, Texas 1990.
Comments: Deluxe color cover.

VELVET UNDERGROUND, THE

CD - THE LEGENDARY GUITAR TAPES
VUCD-37/38
CD1: I Can't Stand It/ Candy Says/ I'm Waiting For The Man/ Ferry Boat Bill/ I'm Set Free/ What Goes On/ White Light, White Heat/ Beginning To See The Light/ Jesus
CD2: Heroin, Sister Ray/ Move Right In/ Run Run Run/ Foggy Notion
Recording: Good.
Source: March 15 1969. CD2 track 2 December 12 1968. Track 3 July 11 1969. Track 4 December 12 1968.

CD - ULTRA RARE TRAX VOL. 2
3D-REALITY CRASSICS 3DC-VU-003
I Love You/ Wild Child/ Ride Into The Sun/ Lisa Says/ She Is My Best Friend/ Hanging' Round/ Walk On A Wild Side/ Kid/ What Goes On/ Sheltered Life/ Sheltered Life/ Here She Comes Now/ Here She Comes Now/ Inside Your Heart/ Move Right In/ Rock And Roll/ Andy's Chest/ Index
Source: Tracks 1-9 Lou Reed's first home demo recording 1970 for the first solo album 'Lou Reed'. Tracks 11-13 very early recordings winter 1966, New York City without Moe. Tracks 14-17 studio outtakes from legendary 'VU' session New York City 1969 - different mix from the 'Vu' album. Track 18 flexidisc from Andy Warhol's Index Book. At Factory looking through and talking about the book.
Comments: Japanese CD.

CD - ULTRA RARE TRAX VOL. 3
3D-REALITY CRASSICS 3DC-VU-004
Venus In Furs/ Heroin/ Guess I'm Falling In Love/ Loop/ Heroin/ Venus In Furs/ White Light, White Heat/ Jesus/ Sister Ray, Murder Mystery/ Noise
Source: Tracks 1 & 2 WNET TV, NYC February 1966. Speaker is Andy Warhol. Track 3 The Gymnasium, NYC April 1967. Track 4 flexidisc from Aspen Magazine, #Issue 3 December 1966. Written by John Cale And Credit To The V. U.
Tracks 5, 6 from Exploding Plastic Inevitable Film Soundtrack. Live at Poor Richard, Chicago summer 1966. Reed in hospital, Cale singing, Moe on bass and Angus Maclise on drums. Tracks 7-9 live at Boston Tea Party, Boston March 13 1969. Track 10 from East Village Other/Electric Newspaper L, August 1966.
Comments: Japanese CD.

W

WEEZER

CD - AMERICAN HOLIDAY
TORNADO TOR038
I Want A Girl/ Do You Believe/ Buddy Holly/ No-One Hears Me/ Say It Ain't So/ Get'ch You/ Holiday/ Sweater Song/ What America Needs/ Bet On You/ I Want A Girl/ Do You Believe/ Buddy Holly/ I Love You So/ Say It Ain't So/ Sweater Song/ What America Needs
Recording: Very good to excellent. Audience.
Source: Tracks 1-9 St. Louis, MO 1994. Tracks 10-17 Madison Square Garden, New York May 12 1994.
Comments: European CD. Deluxe color cover. Time 63:03.

WELLER, PAUL

CD - A MAN OF GREAT PROMISE
KISS THE STONE KTS 521
Sun Flower (4:23)/ Changing Man (3:53)/ Out Of The Sinking (3:56)/ Broken Stones (3:29)/ Porcelain Gods (5:44)/ Butterflies (2:48)/ Wildwood (3:48)/ A Man Of Great Promise (2:45)/ Tales From The Riverbank (3:16)/ Want You More (4:34)/ Foot Of The Mountain (4:05)/ Into Tomorrow (3:22)/ Stanley Road (4:10)/ Wood Cutters Son (4:36)/ You Do Something To Me(Acoustic Version) (3:40)/ Whirlpool's End (6:17)/ She Comes To Me (Piano & Voice Version) (3:13)/ Walk On Guilded Splinters (3:54)
Recording: Excellent. Soundboard.
Source: London, England February 23 1996. Tracks 7-11. Acoustic session.
Comments: European CD. Time 60:12.

CD - BUTTERFLY
MOONRAKER 113
Out Of The Sinking/ Didn't Mean To Hurt You/ The Changing Man/ Time Passes/ Sunflower/ Introductions/ The Changing Man/ Out Of The Sinking/ Broken Stones/ Porcelain Gods/ Amongst Butterflies/ Wild Wood/ A Man Of Great Promise/ Tales From The Riverbank/ Make Me Want You More/ Woodcutter's Son/ Something To Me/ Whirlpool's End
Recording: Excellent.
Source: Tracks 1-5 The Roskilde Festival, Denmark July 2 1995. Tracks 6-18 London February 23 1996.
Comments: European CD.

CD - TELL ME MORE (THE OTHER SIDE OF STANLEY ROAD)
SR2
Stanley Road (demo) (5:14)/ Porcelain Gods (demo) (4:57)/ Time Passes (demo) (3:33)/ Broken Stones (demo) (4:26)/ You Do Something To Me (demo) (3:32)/ Broken Stones (Maida Vale April 26 1995) (3:07)/ Woodcutters Son (Maida Vale April 26 1995) (4:14)/ I Walk On Guilded Splinters (Maida Vale April 26 1995) (2:58)/ Time Passes (Maida Vale April 26 1995) (4:09)/ Out Of The Sinking (Oxford Street May 17 1995) (3:27)/ You Do Something To Me (Maida Vale May 22 1995) (3:35)/ Out Of The Sinking (US Radio May 10 1994) (3:23)/ Out Of The Sinking (Emma Freud June 15 1994) (3:21)/ Steam (different mix) (6:15)/ I'd Rather Go Blind (different mix) (3:52)/ The Changingman (White Room May 17 1994) (3:41)/ Porcelain Gods (White Room May 17 1994) (2:14)/ Wildwood (Portishead remix) (3:26)
Recording: Excellent stereo. Soundboard.
Comments: European CD. Color cover.

WESTERBERG, PAUL

CD - GRAVEL PIT
KISS THE STONE KTS 331
Waiting For Somebody (3:27)/ Mannequin Shop (2:59)/ Achin' To Be (3:48)/ Waitress In The Sky (2:35)/ Dice Behind Your Shades (4:10)/ Merry Go Round (4:05)/ Seein' Her (3:36)/ I Will Dare (2:27)/ Whole Wide World (2:44)/ Knockin' On Mine (4:31)/ Skyway (2:06)/ Dyslexic Heart (3:35)/ Daydream Believer (2:32)/ Smokey (2:16)/ I'll Be You (3:21)/ Can't Hardly Wait (4:02)/ Here Comes A Regular (5:22)/ World Class Fad (3:12)/ Alex Chilton (3:08)/ Left Of The Dial (4:18)/ The Ledge (5:04)/ Silver Naked Ladies (4:40)
Recording: Excellent.
Source: The Stone Pony, Asbury Park, NJ 7/08/93.
Comments: European CD. Deluxe color cover. Picture CD.

WIDESPREAD PANIC

CD - PANIC ON
HURRICANE HURR 016/17
CD1: Let's Get Down To Business/ Lights/ Charlie/ Junior/ My Town's Hero/ Back At The House/ She's Got Wings/ Feelin' Alright
CD2: Good Times Today/ Won't Be The Same/ Mama's Pride/ In The Shade/ Time Again/ Mother Nature's Taking Over/ Bertha/ Makes Sense To Me/ Turn On Your Love Light
Recording: Excellent. Audience.
Source: Bogart's, Cincinnati, OH October 3 1995.
Comments: European CD. Deluxe color cover.

WHITESNAKE

CD - BLACK AND BLUE
NIGHTLIFE N-020
Come On/ You And Me/ Walking In The Shadows Of The Blues/ Black And Blue/ Ready An' Willing/ Ain't No Love In The Heart Of The City/ Love Hunter/ Mistreated
Recording: Poor-good. Audience.
Source: Marquee Club, London, February 4 1980.
Comments: Japanese CD. Deluxe color cover. Time 56:43.

WHITE ZOMBIE

CD - DEMONIC POSSESSIONS
TORNADO TOR 042
Super-Charger Heaven/ Real Solution #9/ Black Sunshine/ Welcome To Planet Motherfucker/ Psychoholic Slag/ Electric Head Part 2 (The Ecstasy)/ I Zombie/ More Human Than Human/ Creature Of The Wheel/ Soul Crusher/ Thunder Kiss '95/ Grease Paint And Monkey Brains/ Children Of The Grave/ Blood Milk And Sky
Source: Hara Arena, Dayton, OH June 24 1995
Comments: European CD.

CD - KICKING IN HEAVENS DOOR
KISS THE STONE KTS 516
Intro/ Electric Head Pt. 1 (The Agony)/ Super-Charger Heaven/ Red Solution #9/ More Human Than Human/ Thunder Kiss '65/ Super-Charger Heaven/ Real Solution #9/ Welcome To Planet Motherfucker, Psychoholic Slag/ Electric Head Pt. 2 (The Ecstacy)/ More Human Than Human/ Thunder Kiss '65/ More Human Than Human
Recording: Excellent.
Source: Tracks: 1-5 Donnington, August 26 1995. Tracks 6-11 Cologne, Germany August 19 1995. Track 12 The Ed Sullivan Theatre, New York July 14 1995.
Comments: European CD.

CD - SYNTHETIC DELUSIONS
WZ-01
Electric Head Part 1/ Super-Charger Heaven/ Real Solution #9/ Black Sunshine/ I Am Legend (Intro)/ Electric Head Part 2/ I, Zombie/ More Human Than Human/ Soul Crusher/ Thunder Kiss '65/ Grease Paint And Monkey Brains/ Children Of The Grave
Recording: Very good. Audience.
Source: San Jose, June 28 1995.
Comments: Japanese CD. Deluxe color cover. Time 60:04.

WHO, THE

CD - ALTERNATE TOMMY
ELEMENT OF CRIME ELEMENTS-027
Overture (4:44)/ It's A Boy (0:42)/ 1921 (3:14)/ Amazing Journey (3:38)/ Sparks (5:57)/ Christmas (4:42)/ Cousin Kevin (4:04)/ The Acid Queen (3:34)/ Underture (1:48)/ Do You Think It's Alright? (0:26)/ Fiddle About (1:22)/ Pinball Wizard (3:43)/ There's A Doctor (0:24)/ Go To The Mirror, Success (4:44)/ Tommy Can You Hear Me? (1:15)/ Smash The Mirror (1:43)/ Sensation (2:46)/ Miracle Cure (0:12)/ Sally Simpson (4:51)/ I'm Free (2:29)/ Welcome (3:25)/ Tommy's Holiday Camp (0:57)/ We're Not Gonna Take It (5:07)
Recording: Excellent stereo. Soundboard.
Source: Original recording at IBC Studio, London.
Comments: Japanese CD. Deluxe color cover.

CD - THE CAPITOL TAKING
PLANET RECORDS
I Can't Explain/ Summertime Blues/ My Generation/ I Am The Sea/ The Real Me/ I'm The One/ Sea And Sand/ Drowned/ Bell Boy/ Doctor Jimmy/ Won't Get Fooled Again/ Pinball Wizard*/ See Me Feel Me*
Recording: Excellent stereo. Soundboard.
Source: Capitol Center, Landover, Maryland

December 6 1973. *Spectrum, Philadelphia December 4 1973.
Comments: European CD. Deluxe color cover. Time 72:34. A copy of Great Dane's 'Tales From The Who' (GDR CD 8910).

CD - DANGEROUS 1982
MIDNIGHT BLUE MB 001
I Can't Explain/ Young Man Blues/ Quiet One/ Dangerous/ Eminence Front/ Dr. Jimmy/ Drowned/ Sister Disco/ Baba O'Reily/ Pinball Wizard/ See Me, Feel Me
Recording: Excellent. Soundboard.
Source: Live 1982.
Comments: European CD. Deluxe color cover. Time 51:32.

CD - DREAM OF '69
MUM MUCD 007
Heaven And Hell/ I Can't Explain/ Fortune Teller/ Tattoo/ Young Man Blues/ Substitute/ Happy Jack/ I'm A Boy/ Tommy Medley: Overture, If It's A Boy, 1921, Amazing Journey, Sparks, Undurture, Tommy's Holiday Camp, We're Not Gonna Fake It, See Me Feel Me, Listening To You/ Summertime Blues/ Shaking All Over/ Little Billy/ Relax*
Recording: Excellent. Soundboard.
Source: USA '69. *Fillmore East, New York April 5 1968.
Comments: European CD. Time 73:12.

CD - EARL'S COURT 1996
AMSTERDAM AMS 723
CD1: I Am The Sea/ The Real Me/ Quadrophenia/ Cut My Hair/ The Punk And The Godfather/ I'm One/ The Dirty Jobs/ Helpless Dancer/ Is It My Head/ I've Had Enough/ 5:15/ Sea And Sand/ Drowned
CD2: Bell Boy/ Dr. Jimmy/ The Rock/ Love Reign Over Me/ Won't Got Fooled Again/ Behind Blue Eyes/ Who Are You
Source: Earl's Court Arena, London December 6 1996.
Comments: Japanese CD.

CD - GREATEST HITS LIVE
CHARTBUSTERS CHER-022-A
Summertime Blues (3:39)/ My Generation (6:11)/ Pinball Wizard (2:54)/ See Me Feel Me (We're Not Gonna Take It) (5:06)/ Won't Get Fooled Again (8:30)/ I Can't Explain (2:19)/ Happy Jack (2:15)/ I'm A Boy (2:50)/ 5:15 (5:31)/ Don't Let Go The Coat (4:04)/ Sister Disco (4:12)/ You Better Bet (5:22)/ Behind Blue Eyes (3:35)/ Substitute (3:49)/ Baba O'Reily (2:33)/ Boris The Spider (2:33)/ Who Are You (6:30
Recording: Excellent stereo. Soundboard.
Source: Tracks 1-2, 5-6 Landover, MD December 6 1973. Tracks 3-4 Philadelphia December 4 1973. Tracks 7-8 'Live At Leeds' February 14 1970. Tracks 9-13 Essen, West Germany March 28 1981. Tracks 14-16 New York June 27 1989. Track 17 Toronto December 17 1982.
Comments: Deluxe color cover. Time 73:52.

CD - IT'S A BOY
ALEGRA CD 9040 AAD
Tommy: Overture (3:18)/ It's A Boy (1:40)/ 1921 (2:20)/ Eyesight To The Blind (1:51)/ Christmas (3:08)/ The Acid Queen (3:20)/ Pinball Wizard (2:21)/ Pictures Of Lily (2:30)/ Easy Going Guy (2:15)/ See Me, Feel Me (4:42)/ Amazing Journey (4:26)/ Sparks (2:41)/ Do You Think It's Alright - Fiddle About, Tommy Can You Hear Me? - There's A Doctor I've You Found (3:03)/ Go To The Mirror (4:15)/ I'm Free (2:19)/ My Generation (6:31)/ Happy Jack (2:08)/ Can't Explain (2:20)
Recording: Excellent stereo. Soundboard.
Source: Amsterdam September 27 1969. Track 8 Monterey Pop Festival June 18 1967. Tracks 9, 16-18 Fillmore East April 5 1968
Comments: Deluxe color cover. Time 55:45.

CD - LAST STAND WITH KEITH MOON
MONTSERRAT RECORDS BRCD 1903/1904
CD1: Can't Explain (2:43)/ Substitute (3:38)/ My Wife (7:37)/ Baba O'Riley (5:48)/ Squeeze Box (3:04)/ Behind Blue Eyes (5:02)/ Dreaming From The Waist (5:41)/ Magic Bus (11:36)
CD2: Amazing Journey (includes Sparks, Undurture) (11:09)/ The Acid Queen (3:41)/ Fiddle About (2:10)/ Pinball Wizard (2:56)/ I'm Free (2:53)/ Tommy's Holiday Camp (0:55)/ We're Not Gonna Take It (10:05)/ Summertime Blues (4:13)/ My Generation, Join Together, My Generation Reprise (17:50)/ Won't Get Fooled Again (10:00
Recording: Excellent stereo. Soundboard.
Source: Maple Leaf Garden, October 21 1976. Complete show.

WHO, THE

CD - MY GENERATION
ON STAGE CD 12012 AAD
Can't Explain (2:16)/ Fortune Teller (2:30)/ Tattoo (2:56)/ Young Man Blues (5:25)/ Pinball Wizard (2:39)/ Substitute (2:01)/ Happy Jack (2:10)/ I'm Free (2:20)/ 1921 (2:22)/ Summertime Blues (3:34)/ See Me, Feel Me (4:40)/ I'm A Boy (2:34)/ Christmas (0:48)/ The Acid Queen (3:21)/ Shakin' All Over (8:18)/ My Generation (13:17)
Recording: Excellent. Soundboard.
Source: Amsterdam Opera House, September 29 1969.
Comments: European CD. Deluxe color cover. Time 61:28.

CD - NEW YEARS EVE
FIRE POWER FP-015
I Don't Even Know Myself/ Naked Eyes/ I'm Free/ Tommy's Holiday Camp/ Welcome/ Were Not Gonna Take It/ Go To The Mirror/ Smashing The Mirror/ Miracle Cure/ Sally Simpson/ I'm Free/ Tommy's Holiday Camp/ We're Not Gonna Take It
Source: Tracks 1, 2 Lulu Show December 31 1970. Tracks 3-13 Tommy Rehearsals.

WILSON, DENNIS

CD - DENNY REMEMBERED VOL.ONE
SURF002
News Report/ Holy Evening/ Companion/ It's Not Too Late/ Carry Me Home/ 10, 000 Light Years/ River Song/ Wild Situation (take one)/ New Orleans/ Love Surrounds Me (take one)/ Organ Duets/ Barbara/ Quad Instrumentals/ Nixon Joke 1973/ You Are So Beautiful/ Good Timin'/ Lady/ Moon Light/ News Report
Recording: Very good to excellent.
Source: The cover says 'Classic lost tracks from Bamboo to Malibu from a sadly missed Beach Boy'.
Comments: European CD. Deluxe color cover. 'Brothers Records' logos on disc and cover.

WOOD, RON

CD - LIVE IN AUSTIN
SWINGIN' PIG TSP-CD-203
Testify/ Show Me/ Flying/ Breathe On Me/ (I Know) I'm Losing You/ Josephine/ Black Limousine/ Pretty Beat Up/ Band Introduction/ Silicon Grown/ Little Red Rooster/ It's Only Rock 'N' Roll/ Stay With Me
Recording: Excellent stereo. Soundboard.
Source: Terrace, Austin, Texas November 13 1992.
Comments: European CD.

Y

YARDBIRDS, THE

CD - LAST RAVE-UP IN L.A.
GLIMPSES RECORDS GR001CD-1/2
CD1: The Train Kept A Rollin'/ You'er A Better Man Than I, Heart Full Of Soul/ Dazed And Confused/ Shapes Of Things/ I'm A Man/ White Summer/ Smokestack Lightning, Beck's Bolero, I'm Waiting For The Man
CD2: Bye Bye Bird/ Drinking Muddy Waters/ Happenings Ten Years Time Ago/ New York Blues (Become My Friend)/ I Wish You Would, Hey Gyp/ I Ain't Done Wrong/ Over Under Sideways Down
Recording: Poor. Audience. Surface noise.
Source: The Shrine Auditorium, Los Angeles May 31 1968 and June 1 1986.

YES

CD - ALTERNATE YESSONGS
HIGHLAND HL 003/4#Y2
CD1: Opening (Excerpt From 'Firebird Suite') (1:23)/ Siberian Khatru (8:49)/ I've Seen Good People, Your Move, All Good People (7:23)/ Heart Of The Sunrise (11:26)/ The Clap, Mood For A Day (7:15)/ And You And I, Cord Of Love, Eclipse, The Preacher The Teacher, The Apocalypse (10:37)/ Close To The Edge, The Solid Time Of Change, Total Mass Retain, I Get Up I Get Down, Seasons Of Man (18:18)/ Excerpt From 'Six Wives Of Henry VII' (7:31)
CD2: Roundabout/ Yours Is No Disgrace (4:34)/ Yours Is No Disgrace (11:10)/ I've Seen Good People, Your Move, All Good People (7:25)/ The Clap (5:00)/ Perpetual Change (14:51)
Source: CD1 and CD2 tracks 1 and 2 Duke University, Durham, NC November 11 1972. CD2 tracks 3 to 6 Yale Bowl, New Haven,

CT July 24 1971.
Comments: Japanese CD.

CD - BIG GENERATOR SHOW & RARE TRACKS
HIGHLAND HL005/6#Y3
CD1: Rhythm Of Love (6:45)/ Drum Solo, Hold On (7:17)/ Heart Of The Sunrise (10:54)/ Big Generator (6:01)/ Changes (7:33)/ Shoot High Aim Low (8:27)/ Owner Of A Lonely heart (5:17)/ And You And I (10:51)/ Your Is No Disgrace (11:28)
CD2: Love Will Find Away (5:08)/ Big Generator (4:48)/ Rhythm Of Love (5:35)/ Final Eyes (7:36)/ I'm Running (8:31)/ Shoot High Aim Low (7:51)/ Shoot High Aim Low (7:14)/ Rhythm Of Love ('Dance To The Rhythm' mix) (6:53)/ Love Will Find A Way (extended version) (7:19)/ Owner Of A Lonely Heart (special 'Red & Blue' remix dance version) (7:51)/ Leave It ('Hello, Goodbye' mix) (6:38)
Source: CD1 Summit, Houston February 21 1988. CD2 Tracks 1-7 studio outtakes. CD2 tracks 8-11 12" remixes.
Comments: Japanese CD.

CD - DRAMASHOW
HIGHLAND HL 014#Y4
The Clap (4:30)/ And You And I, Cord Of Life, Eclipse, The Preacher The Teacher, Apocalypse (10:46)/ Go To This (4:02)/ Keyboard Solo (includes 'Video Killed The Radio Star' and 'Man In The Car') (6:43)/ We Can Fly From Here (6:36)/ Tempus Fugit (5:30)/ Into The Lens (I Am A Camera) (8:24)/ Machine Messiah (12:13)/ Starship Trooper, Life Seeker, Disillusion, Wurm (11:41)/ Roundabout (8:46)
Recording: Poor to good audience.
Source: Madison Square Garden, New York June 9 1980.
Comments: Japanese CD. Deluxe color cover.

CD - LONG BEACH ARENA '74
PIG'S EYE BS6
Close To The Edge/ The Revealing/ The Ancient/ Round-About/ Starship Trooper
Recording: Good to very good. Soundboard.
Source: The Long Beach Arena, March 19 1974.
Comments: Japanese CD. Copy of original slick cover. Time 75:53.

YOUNG, NEIL

CD - A HOT NIGHT IN GLASGOW
DOBERMAN 041/042
CD1: Hey, Hey, My, My/ Bite The Bullet/ Barstool Blues/ Big Time/ Pocahontas/ Roll Another Number For The Road/ Slip Away/ The Needle And The Damage Done/ Long May You Run/ Four Strong Winds/ Cinnamon Girl
CD2: Fuckin' Up/ Cortez The Killer/ Music Arcade/ Like A Hurricane/ Welfare Mothers/ Danger Bird/ Sedan Delivery
Recording: Excellent stereo. Audience.
Source: The SECC, Glasgow July 20 1996.
Comments: UK CDR. With Crazy Horse.

CD - AUSTIN '84
REALIVE RL CD 08
Are You Ready For The Country? (3:27)/ Hawks & Doves (3:43)/ Comes A Time (3:00)/ Bound For Glory (6:10)/ Are There Anymore Real Cowboys? (3:04)/ Heart Of Gold (3:05)/ Roll Another Number (For The Road) (2:49)/ Southern Pacific (8:00)/ Helpless (5:00)/ Field Of Opportunity (3:32)/ Old Man (3:36)/ Powderfinger (5:11)/ Down By The River (9:46)/ Forever Young (with The Grateful Dead) (6:46)
Recording: Excellent stereo. Soundboard.
Source: Austin 1984.
Comments: European CD. Deluxe color cover. With The International Harvesters.

CD - BIG TIME WITH CRAZY HORSE
CRYSTAL CAT RECORDS CC 405/06
CD1: Country Girl/ Pocahontas/ Stupid Girl/ Big Time/ Drive Back/ I Am A Child/ Heart Of Gold/ The Loner/ Fuckin' Up/ Cortez The Killer/ Scattered
CD2: Music Arcade/ Welfare Mothers/ Like A Hurricane/ Hey Hey, My My/ Powderfinger/ Sedan Delivery/ The Losing End/ Roll Another Number For The Road/ Rockin' In The Free World/ Cinnamon Girl
Recording: Very good. Audience.
Source: Sjohistoriska Museet, Stockholm, Sweden June 25 1996.
Comments: European CD. Deluxe color cover. Picture CD.

CD - BIGTIME IN FRANKFURT
NY-14796-A/B
CD1: Hey, Hey, My, My (Out Of The Blue) (6:00)/ Down By The River (12:00)/ Drive

Back (7:28)/ Big Time (7:32)/ Slip Away (13:45)/ The Needle & The Damage Done (2:33)/ I Am A Child (3:47)/ Sugar Mountain (7:10)
CD2: Cinnamon Girl (3:54)/ Fuckin' Up (8:53)/ Cortez The Killer (9:55)/ Music Arcade (4:16)/ Roll Another Number (3:47)/ Like A Hurricane (14:42)/ Loosing End (7:36)/ Sedan Delivery (6:07)/ Tonight's The Night (12:15)
Recording: Good-Very good. Audience.
Source: The Complete Show, Festhalle, Frankfurt, Germany July 14 1996.
Comments: European CD. Deluxe color cover. With Crazy Horse.

CD - BLUE NOTES
CRYSTAL CAT RECORDS CC 413/14
CD1: Intro (0:35)/ Ten Men Working (6:31)/ Hello Lonely Woman (4:32)/ I'm Goin' (5:33)/ Married Man (2:44)/ Coupe De Ville (4:52)/ Ordinary People (12:20)/ The Days That Used To Be (4:41)/ After The Gold Rush (4:08)/ Crime In The City (7:17)/ Bad News (7:39)/ Life In The City (3:37)
CD2: Intro (0:36)/ Twilight (6:36)/ Ain't It The Truth (5:03)/ Hey Hey (4:13)/ This Notes For You (6:27)/ Welcome To The Big Room (6:20)/ Tonight's The Night (14:27)/ Sixty To Zero (17:47)/ Soul Of A Woman (5:43)/ On The Way Home (2:48)
Recording: Very good. Audience.
Source: Jones Beach Music Center, Wantaugh, NY August 27 1988.
Comments: European CD. Deluxe color cover. Picture CD.

CD - BRIDGE BENEFIT 1995
CRYSTAL CAT RECORDS CC 379
Intro/ Comes A Time/ The Needle And The Damage Done/ Heart Of Gold/ Pocahontas/ Look Out For My Love/ Cortez The Killer/ Powderfinger/ Tonight's The Night/ Rockin' In The Free World/ My Heart/ Prime Of Life/ Change Your Mind/ Piece Of Crap
Recording: Very good to excellent. Audience. Tracks 11-14 excellent stereo. Soundboard.
Source: Shoreline Amphitheatre, Mountain View, CA October 28 1995. Tracks 11-14 The Complex Recording Studios, Los Angeles October 3 1994.
Comments: European CD. Time 75:15.

CD - THE CATALYST CLUB ONE
BROKEN ARROW RECORDS BA2684 A
Rock, Rock, Rock/ So Tired/ I Got A Problem/ Stand By Me/ Your Love/ Powderfinger/ Barstool Blues/ Welfare Mothers/ Touch The Night/ Tonight's The Night/ Hey Hey, My My (Into The Black)
Source: Catalyst Club, Santa Cruz, first set February 8 1984.
Comments: Japanese CD.

CD - THE CATALYST CLUB THREE
BROKEN ARROW RECORDS BA2784 A
Rock, Rock, Rock/ So Tired/ Violent Side/ Stand By Me/ I Got A Problem/ Your Love/ Powderfinger/ Homegrown/ Welfare Mothers/ Touch The Night/ Hey Hey, My My (Into The Black)/ Cinnamon Girl
Source: Catalyst Club, Santa Cruz, first set February 7 1984.
Comments: Japanese CD.

CD - THE CATAYLST CLUB FOUR
BROKEN ARROW RECORDS BA2784 B
Rock, Rock, Rock/ So Tired/ Violent Side/ Stand By Me/ I Got A Problem/ Your Love/ Powderfinger/ Barstool Blues/ Welfare Mothers/ Touch The Night/ Tonight's The Night/ Cortez The Killer/ Cinnamon Girl
Source: Catalyst Club, Santa Cruz, second set February 7 1984.
Comments: Japanese CD.

CD - DREAM MACHINE
CRYSTAL CAT RECORDS CC 331/32
CD1: Mr. Soulman/ The Loner/ Southern Man/ Helpless/ This Notes For You/ Motorcycle Mama/ Like A Hurricane/ I Believe In You/ Love To Burn/ Separate Ways
CD2: Powder Finger/ Only Love Can Break Your Heart/ Harvest Moon/ The Needle And The Damage Done/ Ride My Dream Machine/ Down By The River/ (Sitting On) The Dock Of The Bay/ All Along The Watchtower/ Keep On Rockin' In The Free World (with Pearl Jam)
Recording: Very good to excellent. Audience.
Source: Rotterdam July 5 1993. *Stockholm June 28 1993.
Comments: European CD. Deluxe color cover. Time CD1 65:06. CD2 64:31.

CD - FARM AID AT THE SUPERDOME
TORNADO TOR065
Country Home/ Home Grown/ Down By The River/ All Along The Watchtower (with Willie Nelson)/ Piece Of Crap/ Farmer John/ Change Your Mind
Recording: Good to very good. Audience.
Source: September 18 '94.
Comments: European CD. Deluxe color cover. Picture CD. Time 65:04.

CD - THE FARM AID SESSIONS
OTA-006
Harvest Moon/ Unknown Legend/ Old King/ Old Man/ Heart Of Gold/ Mother Earth/ Helpless/ For Strong Winds/ From Hank To Hendrix/ Are There Anymore Real Cowboys..?/ Rockin' In The Free World/ Mother Earth/ Piece Of Crap/ Rockin' In The Free World W/ Willie Neilson
Recording: Excellent.
Source: Tracks 1-5 Farm Aid Festival 1992. Tracks 6-12 Farm Aid Festival 1993. Track 13 Bridge Benefit, Mountain View, California October 2 1994. Track 14 Stockholm June 28 '93. Tracks 11-12 1990.

CD - HORSE POWER
RO 03.06.96 1/2
CD1: Pocahontas/ Powderfinger/ Big Time/ Slip Away/ Welfare Mothers (first try)/ Welfare Mothers/ The Needle And The Damage Done/ Heart Of Gold/ I Am A Child/ Cinnamon Girl/ Fuckin' Up
CD2: Cortez The Killer/ Music Arcade/ Like A Hurricane/ Hey Hey My My/ Sedan Delivery/ Rockin' In A Free World/ Act Of Love (Washington July 14 1995)/ Down By The River (Mountain View October 28 1995)
Recording: Very good. Audience.
Source: The Ahoy, Rotterdam June 3 1996.
Comments: European CD. Deluxe color cover.

CD - HURRICANE OVER BOSTON
REALIVE RL CD 40-1/2
CD1: Tell Me Why (3:55)/ Roll Another Number (For The Road) (2:50)/ Journey Through The Past (3:37)/ The Needle And The Damage Done (2:21)/ Harvest (2:59)/ Campaigner (3:46)/ Pocahontas (3:36)/ A Man Needs A Maid (4:32)/ Sugar Mountain (6:15)/ Country Home (5:02)/ Don't Cry No Tears (3:01)/ Drive Back (4:03)/ Cowgirl In The Sand (9:38)/ Bite The Bullet (includes band introduction) (4:34)/ Lotta Love (3:27)/ Like A Hurricane (9:43)
CD2: After The Goldrush (4:28)/ Are You Ready For The Country (4:08)/ Cortez The Killer (6:34)/ Cinnamon Girl (4:20)/ Homegrown (2:45)/ Down By The River (7:03)/ Razor Love (6:54)/ Give Me Strength (3:23)/ Good Phone (a.k.a. 'Let Your Fingers Do The Walking') (3:49)/ Amber Jean (5:25)/ California Sunset (5:22)/ It Might Have Been (Traditional) (4:02)/ Soul Of A Woman (4:13)/ Everybody's Alone (2:40)/ Wonderin' (1:48)
Recording: Very good. Audience.
Source: Boston, MA Music Hall November 22 1976.
Comments: European CD. Deluxe color cover. With Crazy Horse.

CD - LEIPZIG 10. JULI 1996
GAE 333 A/B
CD1: Hey, Hey, My, My (Out Of The Blue) (5:05)/ Powderfinger (5:20)/ Pocahontas (4:18)/ Big Time (7:30)/ Slip Away (13:43)/ The Needle And The Damage Done (3:57)/ Heart Of Gold (3:56)/ I'm A Child (4:11)/ Sugar Mountain (7:17)/ Fuckin' Up (8:14)/ Cortez The Killer (13:41)
CD2: Cinnamon Girl (2:29)/ Music Arcade (4:14)/ Like A Hurricane (15:34)/ This Time (3:01)/ Sedan Delivery (5:31)/ Rocking The Free World (9:48)/ Down By The River (14:13)*/ Drive Back (7:12)/ Tonight's The Night (14:19)
Recording: Very good to excellent. Audience.
Source: Leipzig, July 10 1996. *Frankfurt, July 14 1996.
Comments: European CD. Picture CD. Disney won't like this cover.

CD - LIVE AT THE GOLDEN GATE PARK
BABYFACE BF017/18
CD1: On The Wall/ America/ Throw Your Weapons Down/ Mama/ Truth Be Known/ Rockin' In The Free World/ Damage Done/ Hey Hey, My My/ The Ocean/ Down By The River
CD2: Jam/ Dancing Across The Water/ Peace And Love/ Rockin' In The Free World
Recording: Excellent. Audience.
Source: San Francisco June 24 '95.
Comments: European CD. B&w cover.

YOUNG, NEIL

Purple/yellow type.

CD - MOTHER EARTH
KISS THE STONE KTS 584
Country Home/ Down By The River/ All Along The Watchtower/ Farm John/ Change Your Mind/ Harvest Moon/ Old Man/ Heart Of Gold/ Rockin' In The Free World/ Mother Earth
Recording: Excellent stereo. Soundboard.
Source: The Superdrome, New Orleans, Louisiana September 18 1994.
Comments: European. Deluxe color cover. Picture CD. With Crazy Horse. 72:04.

CD - THE PHOENIX ARCADE
MOONRAKER 174
Big Time (7:36)/ Sedan Delivery (5:54)/ Music Arcade (4:18)/ Like A Hurricane (18:10)/ Hey Hey, My My (5:49)/ Rockin' In The Free World (8:33)/ Cinnamon Girl (10:56)
Recording: Tracks 1-4 Excellent. Soundboard. Tracks 5-7 good audience.
Source: Tracks 1-4 The Phoenix Festival, England, July 19 '96. Tracks 5-7 The Royal Naval Museum, Stockholm June 25 '96.
Comments: European CD. Deluxe color cover. Picture CD.

CD - SOMETIME IN NEW YORK CITY
GOLD STANDARD
CD1: Mr. Soul/ Old Laughing Lady/ Journey Through The Past/ Pocahontus/ Mellow My Mind/ Needle And The Damage Done/ Roll Another Number/ A Man Needs A Maid/ Sugar Mountain/ Country Home/ Don't Cry No Tears/ Down By The River/ Bite The Bullet/ Lotta Love/ Like A Hurricane
CD2: Peace Of Mind/ After The Gold Rush/ Cortez The Killer/ Cinnamon Girl/ Helpless/ Old Man/ Too Far Gone/ Don't Say You Win, Don't Say You Lose/ Heart Of Gold/ The Losing End/ Drive Back/ Southern Man/ Last Trip To Tulsa
Recording: Very good-excellent. Audience.
Source: CD1 and CD2 tracks 1-5 early show, Palladium, NYC Nov. 20 '76. Tracks 6-12 Koln Germany March 20 '76. Track 13 Hamburg Germany March 21 '76.
Comments: Japanese CD. Deluxe color gatefold cover. Each CD in a full color paper sleeve. With Crazy Horse.

YOUNG, NEIL AND PEARL JAM
See listings under
PEARL JAM & NEIL YOUNG

Z

ZAPPA, FRANK

CD - IN NEW YORK & SAN FRANCISCO
P 910106
Prelude To Bobby Brown (2:53)/ Bobby Brown (3:01)/ Conehead (6:03)/ Moe's Vacation (1:18)/ I Have Been In You (7:53)/ The Little House I Used To Live In (8:49)/ Tell Me You Love Me (2:40)/ Yo Mama (8:59)/ Heavy Duty Judy (4:09)/ Presentation (1:33)/ City Of Tiny Lights (8:25)/ You Are What You Is (3:55)/ Mud Club (2:53)
Recording: Very good. Some good to very good.
Source: San Francisco and New York '78.
Comments: European. B&w cover. Orange type.

ZZ TOP

CD - HI-FI MAMA
STENTOR STEN 91.086
I Thank You/ Waiting For The Blues/ Jesus Just Left Chicago/ I'm Bad, I'm Nationwide/ Low Down In The Streets/ A Fool For Your Stockings/ Cheap Sunglasses/ Arrested For Driving While Blind/ She Love My Automobile/ Hi-Fi Mama/ Dust My Broom/ Jailhouse Rock/ Tush
Source: Passaic, NJ 1980.
Comments: European CD. Time 47:53.

CD - WAITING FOR THE SHOW
DEAD DOG RECORDS SE 453
Intro/ World Of Swirl/ Pincushion/ Breakaway/ Waiting On The Bus/ Jesus Just Left Chicago/ I'm Bad, I'm Nationwide/ Cheep Sunglasses/ Tell It To Me, Baby/ Fool For Your Stockings/ Sleeping Bag/ She Loves My Automobile/ Antenna Head/ Legs/ Gimme All Your Lovin'
Source: Hartford, USA May 24 1994.
Comments: European CD.

STEREO
SOUNDBOARD
DANGERROUS 1982
The Who

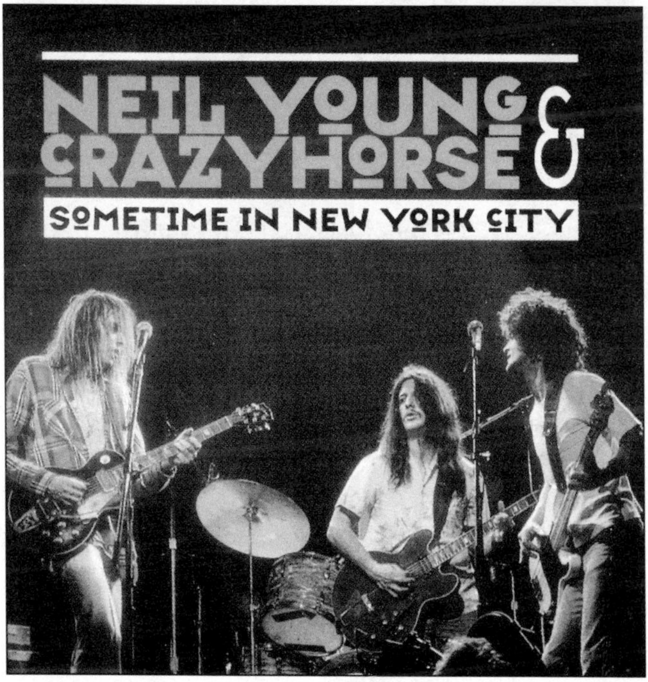
NEIL YOUNG & CRAZYHORSE
SOMETIME IN NEW YORK CITY

OTHER BOOKS

These books are bootleg rating guides and discographies that can $ave you money! They give you the information you need to help you make the right boot purchase choices because for over 20 years HOT WACKS BOOKS have been indispensible tools for bootleg collectors.

You'll find bootleg listings with song titles, matrix numbers, recording sources, sound quality and specific comments in each of the info-packed books for artists ranging from AC/DC to Frank Zappa. All entries are arranged alphabetically by the artist's name making these complete & easy-to-use guides. The books also include pictures of rare cover art and special articles. HOT WACKS is a must for you to keep up to date with the ever-expanding world of bootlegs. No other single publication gives so much bootleg information in such a concentrated form.

FROM HOT WACKS

Belmo's Beatleg News says: "...the bootleg Bible."

ICE says: "...an invaluable resource."

Record Collector says: "... a vital tool."

HOT WACKS BOOK 15
The master guide - over 800 pages of comprehensive listings for thousands of boots.
In the USA $22.95 US FUNDS (surface mail) or $24.95 US FUNDS (airmail)
In Europe/Asia $24.95 US FUNDS (surface mail) or $32.95 US FUNDS (airmail)
In Canada $24.95 Canadian Funds

HOT WACKS BOOK Supplement 1
This '93 publication has almost 200 pages of comprehensive info not in 15.
In the USA $12.95 US FUNDS (surface mail) or $14.95 US FUNDS (air mail)
In Europe/Asia $14.95 US FUNDS (surface mail) or $17.95 US FUNDS (air mail)
In Canada $14.95 Canadian Funds

HOT WACKS BOOK Supplement 2
This '94 publication contains new info and articles about special packaging and legality.
In the USA $14.95 US FUNDS (surface mail) or $16.95 US FUNDS (air mail)
In Europe/Asia $16.95 US FUNDS (surface mail) or $17.95 US FUNDS (air mail)
In Canada $16.95 Canadian Funds

HOT WACKS BOOK Supplement 3
This '95 publication has over 225 pages of new boot info and articles about The Beatles, Led Zeppelin, Pink Floyd, Nirvana, EQing for bootlegs and legality.
In the USA $15.95 US FUNDS (surface mail) or $17.95 US FUNDS (air mail).
In Europe / Asia $17.95 US FUNDS (surface mail) or $20.95 US FUNDS (air mail)
In Canada $16.95 Canadian Funds

HOT WACKS BOOK Supplement 4
This NEW 1996 publication has over 200 pages of new bootleg information and over 30 pages of articles about The Beatles, PInk Floyd, Nirvana, THE STONES and legal issues
In the USA $17.95 US FUNDS (surface mail) or $19.95 US FUNDS (air mail)
In Europe / Asia $19.95 US FUNDS (surface mail) or $21.95 US FUNDS (air mail)
In Canada $17.95 Canadian Funds

ORDER MORE THAN ONE BOOK AND SAVE!
Deduct $2.00 from the total amount of your order for each additional book.

Order your books today! Please send payment by cheque or international money order in US FUNDS (except for the U.K.) to:
THE HOT WACKS PRESS
POB 544, Dept. 5, Owen Sound, ON, N4K 5R1, CANADA OR
Use your **VISA** and order by Fax (Dial 519 376 9449) OR E-mail (hotwacks@log.on.ca)
Visit HOT WACKS on the Web @ http://www.bootlegs.com OR http://log.on.ca/hotwacks

JOHN, PAUL & ME
BEFORE THE BEATLES
THE TRUE STORY OF THE EARLY DAYS

If ever there was a seminal moment in modern music it must surely have been a sunny afternoon in 1957. As so often happens important moments in history take place away from the light of public scrutiny and often are left to the speculations of latter day scholars.

Fortunately for music fans and historians alike Len Garry was there. Not seeing it through the eyes of a jaded critic but with the perspective of optimistic youth. More than a casual observer, Len Garry was a significant participant at the birth of a phenomenon.

At the age of fourteen he was to witness the first stirrings of this centuries greatest song-writing team. As "Tea-chest bass" player in the "Quarrymen" Len was an enthusiastic accomplice in events which so many others have speculated about. He was there sharing the same stage with John Lennon And Paul McCartney when they Gave their first concert together. He was in the same small backstage dressing room when Lennon and McCartney were first introduced and Paul showed John how to play guitar chords.

Through a boisterous couple of years Len shared everything with the young John Lennon, from cigarettes to musical ideas, from teenage school pranks to girlfriends.

Relating the years before the legends were born, John Paul and Me is a highly personal documentary, a crystal-clear trip back through time to when John Lennon, Paul McCartney, Len Garry and their friends were nothing more than a group of optimistic teenagers with ambition in their eyes and music in their hearts.

LEN GARRY: In 1955 John Lennon, Pete Shotton, & Len Gary were best friends. In 1957 Len Garry was actually in the same room when John Lennon first met Paul McCartney. For a few halcyon years Len Garry was the "tea-chest" bass player in the John Lennon's band The Quarrymen. The story of those first early days has never been told: until now.

With the benefit of anecdotes supplied by the other surviving Quarrymen including Pete Shotton (ex-Apple General Manager). Len Gary relates a touching and informative look at the birth of this centuries most influential musical phenomenon.

JOHN, PAUL & ME includes an exclusive interview CD with Len Gary and Pete Shotton recorded in 1997 at JOHN LENNON's childhood home 'Mendips' in Liverpool!

Order your copy of JOHN, PAUL & ME today!

In the USA $17.95 US FUNDS plus postage ($3.00 surface mail) or ($5.00 for airmail)
In the U.K. £12 plus postage (£2 for surface mail) or (£4 for airmail)
In Europe/Asia/Australia $17.95 US FUNDS plus postage ($4.00 surface) or ($8.00 air)
In Canada $22.95 Canadian Funds (includes surface mail)

Please send payment by cheque or international money order in US FUNDS (except the U.K.) to:
THE HOT WACKS PRESS - POB 544, Dept. 5, Owen Sound, ON, N4K 5R1, CANADA
OR
Use your **VISA** and order by Fax (Dial 519 376 9449) OR E-mail (hotwacks@log.on.ca)
Visit HOT WACKS on the Web @ http://www.bootlegs.com OR http://log.on.ca/hotwacks

THE BEATLES BOOTLEG DISCOGRAPHY YOU'VE ALL BEEN WAITING FOR!

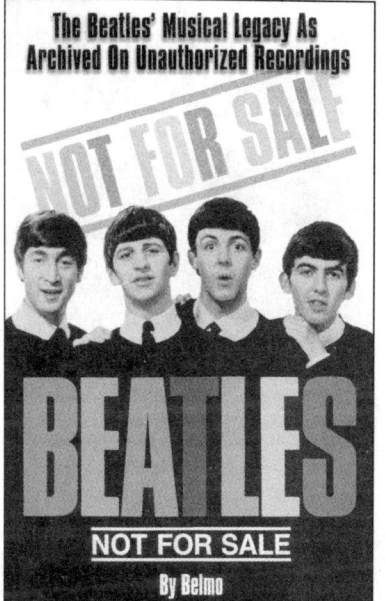

The Beatles' Musical Legacy As Archived On Unauthorized Recordings

NOT FOR SALE

By Belmo

Destined to be THE BIBLE of Beatles bootles, NOT FOR SALE examines nearly 1000 titles (group and solo Beatlegs) in this 440 page book.

Forty years of unreleased music are reviewed in this easy-to-use reference. All the notable and important bootlegs here are - from the earliest vinyl of the 1970s to the latest compact discs from Midnight Beat, Vigotone and Yellow Dog Records.

The topically arranged discography includes album titles, years of release, song titles, catalog numbers, record companies, historical background, stereo/mono content and album ratings (1 to 5 stars).

NOT FOR SALE includes the largest listing EVER compiled of known unreleased and unbootlegged Beatles songs and performances from 1957 to 1997, pages of rare cover art, alphabetized index for easy reference, an analysis of The Beatles Anthology series, Beatleg trivia, secrets from the underground, and a listing of the essential Beatlegs.

Belmo, the author of NOT FOR SALE, is the editor and publisher of the international newsletter, Belmo's Beatleg News, and co-author of Black Market Beatles (the definitive history of Beatles bootlegs).

"NOT FOR SALE is the reference guide most long-time Beatles collectors have wished for and is indispensible to newcomers lured into those forbidden record bins. It is certain to become one of the most dogeared, frequently-thumbed volumes on Beatles bookshelves everywhere."

Allen J. Wiener (author of The Beatles: The Ultimate Recording Guide)

Order your copy of NOT FOR SALE today!

In the USA $19.95 US FUNDS plus postage ($5.00 surface mail) or ($8.00 for airmail)
In the U.K. £14 plus postage (£4 for surface mail) or (£8 for airmail)
In Europe/Asia/Australia $19.95 US FUNDS plus postage ($8.00 surface) or ($14.00 air)
In Canada $24.95 Canadian Funds (includes surface mail)

Please send payment by cheque or international money order in US FUNDS (except the U.K.) to:
THE HOT WACKS PRESS - POB 544, Dept. 5, Owen Sound, ON, N4K 5R1, CANADA
OR
Use your **VISA** and order by Fax (Dial 519 376 9449) OR E-mail (hotwacks@log.on.ca)
Visit HOT WACKS on the Web @ http://www.bootlegs.com OR http://log.on.ca/hotwacks

ANOTHER BOOK FROM BELMO
BLACK MARKET BEATLES

BY BELMO AND BERKENSTADT
FOREWORD BY ADRIAN BELEW

Nationally-recognized Beatles recording experts Belmo (editor and publisher of BELMO'S BEATLEG NEWS) and Jim Berkenstadt (archivist and writer) have joined forces to conceive BLACK MARKET BEATLES, the most comprehensive guide ever written about the bootleg recordings of the Fab Four.

Besides containing the world's largest Beatles underground discography (which stands at a staggering 1,600 entries) the book also features interviews with several Beatle bootleggers, a photo survey of bootleg trademarks and logos, a bootleg label 'family tree' and much more, including over 225 photos and illustrations.

BLACK MARKET BEATLES also has a history of bootlegging.

All in all, this is one of the most significant and unique books about The Beatles ever published.

"...intriguing and well-written..."
"...excellent research..."
"...a genuine feel for Beatles music and bootleg history..."

(Allen J. Wiener - GOLDMINE)

Order your copy of BLACK MARKET BEATLES today!

In the USA $14.95 US FUNDS plus postage ($3.00 surface mail) or ($5.00 for airmail)
In the U.K. £7 plus postage (£2 for surface mail) or (£4 for airmail)
In Europe/Asia/Australia $14.95 US FUNDS plus postage ($4.00 surface) or ($8.00 air)
In Canada $16.95 Canadian Funds (includes surface mail)

Please send payment by cheque or international money order in US FUNDS (except the U.K.) to:
THE HOT WACKS PRESS - POB 544, Dept. 5, Owen Sound, ON, N4K 5R1, CANADA
OR
Use your **VISA** and order by Fax (Dial 519 376 9449) OR E-mail (hotwacks@log.on.ca)
Visit HOT WACKS on the Web @ http://www.bootlegs.com OR http://log.on.ca/hotwacks

RECORD COLLECTOR'S BEST BOOK OF THE YEAR

In the summer of 1969, in a small cluster of LA record stores, there appeared a white-labelled two-record set housed in a plain cardboard sleeve. This was Great White Wonder, a motley collection of unreleased Bob Dylan recordings. It was the first rock bootleg and it spawned an entire industry dedicated to making unofficial recordings available to the fans.

In the 442 page book, THE GREAT WHITE WONDERS (released in the U.S. as *Bootleg*), author Clinton Heylin examines bootlegs, their complex legal status as well as their production and distribution.

Though the record industry claims that it has lost millions of dollars to the bootlegger, Heylin seeks to debunk this notion. THE GREAT WHITE WONDERS tells a story as much about individual enthusiasm and creativity as about big business: of a fan acquiring an illicit tape which he wants to circulate to other enthusiasts, of small pressing plants, nondescript retail outlets ... and wonderfully inventive packaging. Clinton Heylin has tracked down and interviewed some of the important individuals involved in the business since 1969 and the result is the first indepth account of the bootleg business.

EXCLUSIVE OFFER! The first 300 copies of THE GREAT WHITE WONDERS softback edition purchased from THE HOT WACKS PRESS will be numbered and come with the author's autograph as well as a limited edition sticker.

David Fricke of ROLLING STONE says:

"...highly entertaining...."

RECORD COLLECTOR says:

"...a damn good read."

Order your copy of GREAT WHITE WONDERS today!

In the USA $19..95 US FUNDS plus postage ($5.00 surface mail) or ($8.00 for airmail)
In the U.K. £10 plus postage (£4 for surface mail) or (£8 for airmail)
In Europe/Asia/Australia $19.95 US FUNDS plus postage ($8.00 surface) or ($14.00 air)
In Canada $24.95 Canadian Funds (includes surface mail)

Please send payment by cheque or international money order in US FUNDS (except the U.K.) to:
THE HOT WACKS PRESS - POB 544, Dept. 5, Owen Sound, ON, N4K 5R1, CANADA
OR
Use your **VISA** and order by Fax (Dial 519 376 9449) OR E-mail (hotwacks@log.on.ca)
Visit HOT WACKS on the Web @ http://www.bootlegs.com OR http://log.on.ca/hotwacks

FROM ROBERT GODWIN, AUTHOR OF *THE ILLUSTRATED COLLECTOR'S GUIDE TO LED ZEPPELIN*

LED ZEPPELIN THE PRESS REPORTS

By July of 1968, the British blues band The Yardbirds had played their last concert, leaving newcomer guitarist, Jimmy Page, with a manager, some contracts and a name. Page and manager Peter Grant determined to create a new band - a phoenix of gargantuan proportions - Led Zeppelin. From their first concerts in Scandinavia to their final sad separation, Jimmy Page, Robert Plant, John Paul Jones, John Bonham and manager Peter Grant proved themselves to be consummate professionals, especially in the way they presented themselves to the media.

For twelve years the music tabloids and mainstream press followed the band's every move, extracting interviews at any opportunity. Thousands of fans around the world kept abreast of their movements through the press, especially in the United Kingdom where radio was still a government monopoly.

In his new **496 page** book, **LED ZEPPELIN - THE PRESS REPORTS**, noted Led Zeppelin expert Robert Godwin has collected and reviewed over a thousand articles from around the globe. Reports of the band's activities from Tokyo to New York and from Sydney to London are compiled and collated in chronological order.

Robert Godwin has been writing music reference books for 15 years. He has written for Goldmine, Guitar World and the American Forces Network.

Praise for Robert's last book about Led Zeppelin:
New Musical Express reports.... **a massive fix of facts**....
Record Collector reports.... **The way that rock publishing should be**....
Metal Hammer reports.... **A mass of vital information**....
Kerrang reports.... **A fascinating tome**....

LED ZEPPELIN - THE PRESS REPORTS includes an exclusive interview compact disc with JIMMY PAGE from 1977 in which he discusses his amazing career as one of the world's top rock musicians.

Order your copy of LED ZEPPELIN - THE PRESS REPORTS today!
In the USA $23.95 US FUNDS plus postage ($5.00 for surface mail) or ($8.00 for airmail)
In the U.K. £15 plus postage (£4 for surface mail) or (£8 for airmail)
In Europe/Asia/Australia $23.95 US FUNDS ($8.00 surface mail) or ($14.00 airmail)
In Canada $29.95 Canadian Funds (includes surface mail)

Please send payment by cheque or international money order in US FUNDS (except the U.K.) to:
THE HOT WACKS PRESS - POB 544, Dept. 5, Owen Sound, ON, N4K 5R1, CANADA
OR
Use your **VISA** and order by Fax (Dial 519 376 9449) OR E-mail (hotwacks@log.on.ca)
Visit HOT WACKS on the Web @ http://www.bootlegs.com OR http://log.on.ca/hotwacks

No Gossip, No Rumor Just Rock And Roll
Led Zeppelin Live
The Final Edition

is an updated, information-packed, 552-page finalized edition based on more than 20 years of detailed analysis of underground concert tapes by author Luis Rey. It closely examines over 250 concerts, from the early days of the band in 1968, through to the group's final performance in 1980. The book also studies and reviews more than 25 rehearsal, television, radio and/or studio sessions.

Dates, places, times, track listings and sound quality are all documented chronologically. Detailed comments about each show and information regarding corresponding bootleg records and CDs are included. An extensive 16-page list of concert dates follows. The book also includes a 37-page list of songs played in concerts and sessions, as well as a section clearing up some of the common mistakes made in dating underground tapes and bootlegs.

The book also contains: 48 pages of black and white pictures; 24 pages of color pictures; 32 pages of concert posters and programs in full color and old newspaper concert ads. Some of this material is published here for the first time.

MOJO says:
"...entertaining and insightful."

GUITAR says:
"...the definative study..."

Zep fanzine THE ONLY ONE says:
"...an excellent source of reference."

Zep fanzine PROXIMITY says:
"Here's a guy that knows his stuff."

Never before has there been a book with so much information about Zeppelin live. If you want scandal, look somewhere else. If you want to know about **LED ZEPPELIN** in concert, **LIVE** is the book for you.

Order your copy of LED ZEPPELIN LIVE - THE FINAL EDITION today!
In the USA $22.95 US FUNDS plus postage ($5.00 for surface mail) or ($8.00 for airmail)
In the U.K. £15 plus postage (£4 for surface mail) or (£8 for airmail)
In Europe/Asia $22.95 US FUNDS ($8.00 for surface mail) or ($14.00 for airmail)
In Canada $28.95 Canadian Funds (includes surface mail)

Please send payment by cheque or international money order in US FUNDS (except the U.K.) to:
THE HOT WACKS PRESS - POB 544, Dept. 5, Owen Sound, ON, N4K 5R1, CANADA
OR
Use your **VISA** and order by Fax (Dial 519 376 9449) OR E-mail (hotwacks@log.on.ca)
Visit HOT WACKS on the Web @ http://www.bootlegs.com OR http://log.on.ca/hotwacks

THE ILLUSTRATED COLLECTOR'S GUIDE TO LED ZEPPELIN NOW ON CD-ROM

THE ILLUSTRATED COLLECTOR'S GUIDE TO LED ZEPPELIN CD-ROM is the 5th edition of the world's most comprehensive guide to collecting Led Zeppelin recordings. The previous four editions have reached Led Zeppelin collectors in over 50 countries. This digital book contains all of the information from previous editions plus many new entries and updates. It also has more rare concert adverts some of which reveal dates long since forgotten.

The CD-ROM also features over 500 bootleg CDs and nearly 400 boot LPs. Each is cross-referenced to the extensive concert dates itinerary which documents over 500 Led Zeppelin concerts. It also contains over 2150 pictures of records, CDs, posters and news clippings. In addition, this CD book also documents over 1,000 non-boot Led Zeppelin and solo records from Jimmy Page's first sessions up to the 'Unledded' reunion album.

NME says: "...exhaustive research."
KERRANG says: "...a mass of information."

Order your copy of THE ILLUSTRATED COLLECTOR'S GUIDE TO LED ZEPPELIN ON CD-ROM today!

In the USA $19.95 US FUNDS plus postage ($3.00 surface mail) or ($5.00 for airmail)
In the U.K. £10 plus postage (£2 for surface mail) or (£4 for airmail)
In Europe/Asia/Australia $19.95 US FUNDS plus postage ($4.00 surface) or ($8.00 for airmail)
In Canada $24.95 Canadian Funds (includes surface mail)

Please send payment by cheque or international money order in US FUNDS (except for the U.K.) to: THE HOT WACKS PRESS POB 544, Dept. 5, Owen Sound, ON, N4K 5R1, CANADA
OR
Use your **VISA** and order by Fax (Dial 519 376 9449) OR E-mail (hotwacks@log.on.ca)
Visit HOT WACKS on the Web @ http://www.bootlegs.com OR http://log.on.ca/hotwacks

PLEASE NOTE: This CD-ROM is a digital book. It contains no audio or video clips and is in no way associated with the artists, their management or their representatives. SYSTEM REQUIREMENTS: Computer - IBM Compatible PC / Operating System - Windows 3.1 or higher / CD-ROM drive required / Memory - 4MB RAM, 8MB RAM recommended / Imput Device - Keyboard and mouse/ Graphics - 256 colour Super VGA (small fonts).

BLACK DIAMOND

THE UNAUTHORISED BIOGRAPHY OF KISS
by Dale Sherman

Meet the band whose mythology precedes them.....KISS has been around for nearly a quarter of a century in one form or another. From street-gang rock n' roll sadists, to swashbuckling super-heroes; from kiddie show monsters to serious musicians; from glam rock to heavy metal and back again.

Love them or hate them, everyone remembers KISS. But what about the truths behind the legends that have grown up around the band over the years.

BLACK DIAMOND peels back the myths and stories for fans, non-fans and the curious alike. Eight years in the making, here is the real and complete history of the band from before it was even called KISS to the triumphant return of the original line-up to the concert stage in 1996. More so, it is a look at the changing world of rock music from the early 1970's to the present day and what it takes for a band to stay on top.

Dale Sherman, an Ohio-native, has been writing about KISS since early 1984 when he helped co-create the short lived, but much sought after, KISS fan-magazine Strange Ways (once listed by Gene Simmons as his favourite fanzine about the band.) Dale has written articles about KISS for other fanzines and his own KISS Forum as well, besides writing articles on other topics in and outside of the music industry.

Black Diamond includes an exclusive interview compact disc with ex-KISS drummer Eric Carr.

Order your copy of BLACK DIAMOND today!

In the USA $17.95 US FUNDS plus postage ($3.00 surface mail) or ($5.00 for airmail)
In the U.K. £12 plus postage (£2 for surface mail) or (£4 for airmail)
In Europe/Asia/Australia $17.95 US FUNDS plus postage ($4.00 surface) or ($8.00 air)
In Canada $22.95 Canadian Funds (includes surface mail)

Please send payment by cheque or international money order in US FUNDS (except the U.K.) to:
THE HOT WACKS PRESS - POB 544, Dept. 5, Owen Sound, ON, N4K 5R1, CANADA
OR
Use your **VISA** and order by Fax (Dial 519 376 9449) OR E-mail (hotwacks@log.on.ca)
Visit HOT WACKS on the Web @ http://www.bootlegs.com OR http://log.on.ca/hotwacks

THE ALTERNATIVE MUSIC ALMANAC

Over 400 fact-filled pages. Loaded with Photos and Hundreds of trivia items, lists, and other tidbits. Plenty of info to please alternative aficionados, while not too complicated for novice fans. Includes fanclub and internet addresses for every major artist and label.

No music fan can deny that alternative music is the most popular and important genre of music to emerge in the last two decades. Ironically, the bands which originally defied the mainstream are now defining it.

Acclaimed Toronto DJ Alan Cross (102.1 The Edge, CFNY-FM) tracks the progress of this exciting style of music from its origins in this incredibly-detailed, fact-filled guide of everything you wanted to know about alternative music.

*the complete history of alternative music
*a 365-day guide to alternative music milestones and artist's birthdays
*stories behind over 200 band names
*internet and fanclub addresses for every major artist, label and related web sites
*hundreds of trivia items, lists and other tidbits, including a list of the 20 Essential Alternative Albums

The Alternative Music Almanac is an indispensable tool for both music fans and music industry professionals.

Order your copy of The Alternative Music Almanac today!

In the USA $19.95 US FUNDS plus postage ($5.00 surface mail) or ($8.00 for airmail)
In the U.K. £14 plus postage (£4 for surface mail) or (£8 for airmail)
In Europe/Asia/Australia $19.95 US FUNDS plus postage ($8.00 surface) or ($14.00 air)
In Canada $24.95 Canadian Funds (includes surface mail)

Please send payment by cheque or international money order in US FUNDS (except for the U.K.) to:
THE HOT WACKS PRESS
POB 544, Dept. 5, Owen Sound, ON, N4K 5R1, CANADA
OR
Use your VISA and order by Fax (Dial 519 376 9449) OR E-mail (hotwacks@log.on.ca)
Visit HOT WACKS on the Web @ http://www.bootlegs.com OR http://log.on.ca/hotwacks

the collector's guide to
heavy metal

Riff Kills Man.... Again!
by Martin Popoff

....for who can resist the unswerving majesty of the power chord? Read about it, as we batter, praise, and otherwise penetrate the essence of over 3,300 bruising records comprising a large wedge of the world's Most Powerful Music. Designed to guide the discerning fan through the jungle of releases competing for your CD dollar. Hard Rock, Heavy Metal, Grunge, Thrash, Funk Metal, Black Metal, Death Metal, Euro Metal, Prog Metal, Punk, etc etc. **576 pages**.

***The Collector's Guide To Heavy Metal* also includes an exclusive nineteen track Heavy Metal sampler compact disc.**

Lollipop Magazine says: "....**Martin Popoff is to heavy metal what Hunter S. Thompson was to politics...this is a completists guide to Heavy Metal. By any definition....**"

Terminal City says: "**What a necessary brain stuffer this humungous belch of hard rock fan spoo is!**"

Order your copy of The Collector's Guide To Heavy Metal today!
In the USA $19.95 US FUNDS plus postage ($5.00 surface mail) or ($8.00 for airmail)
In the U.K. £14 plus postage (£4 for surface mail) or (£8 for airmail)
In Europe/Asia/Australia $19.95 US FUNDS plus postage ($8.00 surface) or ($14.00 air)
In Canada $24.95 Canadian Funds (includes surface mail)

Please send payment by cheque or international money order in US FUNDS (except the U.K.) to:
THE HOT WACKS PRESS - POB 544, Dept. 5, Owen Sound, ON, N4K 5R1, CANADA
OR
Use your **VISA** and order by Fax (Dial 519 376 9449) OR E-mail (hotwacks@log.on.ca)
Visit HOT WACKS on the Web @ http://www.bootlegs.com OR http://log.on.ca/hotwacks

GRACELAND

#601 MIKASA-BLDG. 7-8-1, NISHISHINJUKU, SHINJUKUKU, TOKYO 160 JAPAN
FAX: 81-3-3366-3906

JAPANESE RAREST LIVE CDS!
MAIL ORDER
WHOLESALERS WELCOME!

VARIOUS LABELS AVAILABLE

IQ LABEL, MIDAS TOUCH, HIGHLAND, AMSTERDAM, BONDAGE MUSIC, SCARECROW, ELEMENT OF CRIME, 8-BALL, H-BOMB, THE DIAGRAMS OF LED ZEPPELIN, AND MORE!

VARIOUS ARTISTS AVAILABLE

LED ZEPPELIN, JEFF BECK, THE WHO, ROLLING STONES, DEEP PURPLE, ERIC CLAPTON, KISS, AEROSMITH, BLACK SABBATH, KING CRIMSON, RUSH, QUEEN, PINK FLOYD, VAN HALEN, GENESIS, YES, AND MORE!

NEW RELEASE INFORMATION

★ IQ LABEL
LED ZEPPELIN/ROOM 2/3(3CD)
LED ZEPPELIN/SEATTLE DAZE(3CD)
LED ZEPPELIN/NEWCASTLE SYMPHONY(2CD)
LED ZEPPELIN/FLAWLESS PORFORMANCE(3CD)
LED ZEPPELIN/THE TITANIC(3CD)
LED ZEPPELIN/KNEES UP MOTHER BROWN(2CD)
JIMMY PAGE/CHICAGO PRELUDE(2CD)

★ THE DIAGRAMS OF LED ZEPPELIN
LED ZEPPELIN/HOT AUGUST NIGHT(2CD)
LED ZEPPELIN/LIGHT & SHADE(3CD)
LED ZEPPELIN/REFLECTION FROM A DREAM(3CD)

★ MIDAS TOUCH
THE WHO/LIVE AT CHARLTON 1974(2CD)
HUMBLE PIE/ON STAGE(1CD)

★ SCARECROW
JEFF BECK GROUP/LAID OF GIG(1CD)
JEFF BECK GROUP/COME BACK GIG(2CD)
JEFF BECK/JEFF'S GEAR(1CD)
JEFF BECK/JELLYWAY JAM(1CD)
JEFF BECK/PLAY WITH FRIENDS (1CD)
JEFF BECK/OPENING SHOP(1CD)

★ 8-BALL
YES/BBC SESSIONS 69-70(1CD)

★ BONDAGE MUSIC
AEROSMITH/KING'S CHRONICLE(6CD BOX)
OZZY OSBOURNE/LOUDER THAN EVERYTHING(2CD)
DEEP PURPLE/WITH PURPLE FROM RUSSIA(2CD)
KISS+AEROSMITH/TWO KINGS IN GERMANY(1CD)
BLACK SABBATH/PARISIAN BITCH(1CD)

★ HIGHLAND
YES/THE STORY OF RELAYER(2CD)
E.L.&P./PROMENADE GATES(2CD)
YES/READING 8.22.75(2CD)
STEVE HACKETT/STAR OF SIRIUS(2CD)
GENESIS/REAL IMPERIAL(2CD)
YES/IN THE BEGINNING(1CD)
GENESIS/SECOND NATURE(2CD)
AND MORE!

PLEASE SEND $3 FOR OUR COMPLETE CATALOGUE

WORLD WIDE

INSECT RECORDS
- IST 6/7 METALLICA DAMAGED JUSTICE
- IST 8/9 PRINCE SMALL CLUB
- IST 11 R.E.M. ROCK PERUGIA
- IST 19 ROBERT PLANT PROMISED LAND
- IST 20 LED ZEPPELIN MANY MORE EARLY TIMES
- IST 21/22 RUSH GANSTER OF BOATS
- IST 23 NIRVANA SEATTLE SOUND, SOUNDS GREAT
- IST 24 MOTLEY CRUE THE RED HOT SPOT
- IST 25 JAPAN ORIENTAL PERFORMANCE
- IST 26/27 KISS PETER, PAUL, GENE & ACE
- IST 28 U 2 LOOKING BACK IN THE MIRROR
- IST 29 SIMPLES MINDS DUTCH DAZE
- IST 30 JANE'S ADDICTION CARNIVAL OF SOULS
- IST 31/32 QUEEN THE JEWELS
- IST 33 BOB MARLEY THE LAST CLUB TOUR' 75
- IST 34/35 U 2 BONO IS A DINKY
- IST 38 SUEDE WHAT'S YOUR NAME LONDON...
- IST 39/40 PINK FLOYD 1994 WEST COAST TRIP
- IST 41 FRANKIE GOES TO HOLLYWOOD FRANKIE SAYS...
- IST 42 NINE INCH NAILS MUDSTOCK
- IST 43 SIGUE SIGUE SPUTNIK ORANGE DEVIL
- IST 44 ELVIS COSTELLO BUDDY HOLLY ON ACID
- IST 46 COLLECTIVE SOUL SWEET HOME CHICAGO
- IST 47 VAN MORRISON VAN THE MAN
- IST 48 JIMI HENDRIX MOONS AND RAINBOWS
- IST 49/50 METALLICA CANDY FOR THE KIDS
- IST 51 SUEDE OLD MAN'S CAR
- IST 53 THERAPHY? I WANT MY MONEY BACK
- IST 54 PARADISE LOST NORTHERN DARKNESS
- IST 55 SIOUXSIE & THE BANSHEES SKREECHING
- IST 56/57 THE STRANGLERS ..AND THEN THERE WERE 3
- IST 58 PORNO FOR PYROS ECCENTRIC
- IST 59/60 STING ..LIKE A BEE
- IST 61 LIVE ALDOUS HUXLEY
- IST 62/63 TORI AMOS CHILDHOOD MEMORIES
- IST 64 NIRVANA KURT'S GRAND FINALE
- IST 65/66 ROLLING STONES OFF WITH OUR HEADS
- IST 67 BAD RELIGION POWER POP
- IST 68 LUSH SHOW US YOUR TITS
- IST 69/70 PAUL RODGERS IN BAD COMPANY
- IST 71 ROLLINS BAND HARD AS NAILS
- IST 72/73 PHISH HOLIDAY RECORDING SNAP
- IST 77/78 MARILLION ONE-OFF SHOWS
- IST 87 NIRVANA RARE TRACKS VOL. I
- IST 88 NIRVANA RARE TRACKS VOL. II
- IST 89 NINE INCH NAILS SHALLOW GRAVE
- IST 90 JOHN CALE UNIQUE
- IST 93 NIRVANA RARE TRACKS VOL. III
- IST 94 NIRVANA RARE TRACKS VOL. IV
- IST 100 MARILYN MANSON TRENT's NASTY BABES

HAWK
- HAWK001 STONE TEMPLE PILOTS MIGHTY JOE YOUNG
- HAWK002 PAVEMENT SUMMER BABE
- HAWK003 NINE INCH NAILS SLAVES
- HAWK004 HELMET EARTH TONES
- HAWK005 SUGAR WHATEVER MAKES YOU HAPPY
- HAWK006 HOLE PRETTY PLEASE
- HAWK007/8 THE CURE FROM THE EDGE...
- HAWK009 U2 WELCOME TO THE VIBE
- HAWK010/11 PETER GABRIEL SECRET WORLD TOUR
- HAWK012 SCREAMING TREES WINTER SONGS
- HAWK013 SMASHING PUMPKINS DAYDREAM KISSES
- HAWK014 SOUL ASYLUM WE'RE THE OPENING BAND
- HAWK015 PORNO FOR PYROS PORN AGAIN
- HAWK016 BABES IN TOYLAND MOCKING BIRD'S
- HAWK017 LEMONHEADS SECRET LIFE OF EVAN DANDO
- HAWK018 NEIL YOUNG RIVERS EDGE
- HAWK019 FRANK BLACK THE RETURN OF FU MANCHU
- HAWK021 IZZY STRADLIN SOMEBODY KNOCKIN'
- HAWK022 STING AIN'T NO SUNSHINE
- HAWK023 DURAN DURAN WORLD BROADCAST
- HAWK024 BLIND MELON HIGH TIMES
- HAWK026 NINE INCH NAILS PUREST FEELING
- HAWK028 RAGE AGAINST THE MACHINE WHO'S ON FIRST?
- HAWK029 STONE TEMPLE PILOTS TROUBLE NO MORE
- HAWK030 PAUL WESTERBERG LUCKY'S REVENGE
- HAWK031 BELLY SOFT WHITE UNDER
- HAWK032/33 PEARL JAM MANIFESTING MORRISON
- HAWK034/35 STEELY DAN BOOK OF LIARS
- HAWK036 TORI AMOS AFTER BURN
- HAWK038 RAGE AGAINST THE MACHINE PEOPLE OF THE SUN
- HAWK039/40 THE GREATFUL DEAD SCARLET FIRE
- HAWK043 SMASHING PUMPKINS OUT OF FOCUS
- HAWK044 /45 PEARL JAM LEAVING BABYLON
- HAWK046 DEAD CAN DANCE EXIT TO EDEN
- HAWK047 BJORK THE GIRL FROM OUTER SPACE
- HAWK048 THE CREAM LONG TIME COMMIN'
- HAWK049/50 ERIC CLAPTON BIG BLUE
- HAWK051 COUNTING CROWS CHILDREN IN BLOOM
- HAWK053 BELLY SWEET RIDE
- HAWK054 REPLACEMENTS HANGING IT UP
- HAWK055 PORNO FOR PYROS 100 WAYS
- HAWK057 SEPULTURA ENTER CHOAS
- HAWK059 THE GRATEFUL DEAD SPRING BREAK '94
- HAWK060 TOOL SHED
- HAWK061 STEVIE RAY VAUGHAN CITY OF LIGHTS
- HAWK062 K.D. LANG LOVE SO SWEET
- HAWK063 ELVIS COSTELLO GOING STATESIDE
- HAWK065 BLACK FLAG LAST SHOW
- HAWK066 NINE INCH NAILS PUREST FEELING II
- HAWK068/69 PAGE & PLANT 15 YEARS ON
- HAWK073 BOB DYLAN YOU FIGURE IT OUT
- HAWK074 LIVE PLAYIN' BACK 'OME
- HAWK076/77 PEARL JAM N.W.
- HAWK086 NO FX LONDON'S BURNING
- HAWK087 BEASTIE BOYS WHITE TRASH
- HAWK088 STONE ROSES BLOW THE DAM
- HAWK089 PENNYWISE LAST NIGHT IN TOWN
- HAWK090 RANCID WILD THING
- HAWK091 CRANBERRIES SUPPORT SLOTTED
- HAWK092 NIRVANA IT'S ALL GOING WRONG
- HAWK093 OPERATION IVY RANCID
- HAWK094 OASIS MORE MANCUNIANS
- HAWK095 NINE INCH NAILS THE ODDBALL COUPLE
- HAWK096 DAVE MATTHEWS MADE THE GRAIN

hawk — Most Trusted Name in Music

MAIL ORDER

PUMPKIN BROTHERS
__ PUMP 01/02 U2 FIRST NIGHT OF THE 1992 TOUR

OCTOPUSS
__ OCT 001 THE BEATLES HAIL, HAIL, ROCK & ROLL
__ OCT 005 THE BEATLES PRIME CUTS VOL. 4 (1967-1968)

X RECORDS
__ X 001/002 DEPECHE MODE SWISS DEVOTIONX RECORDS

RUPERT

__ RUP 9673 NIRVANA LIVE AT DUFFY'S
__ RUP 9674 SILVERCHAIR SURFIN' IN THE RAIN
__ RUP 9676 MARILYN MANSON GOD DAMN LITTLE CHILDREN
__ RUP 9677 TRACY BOHNAM KILL THE BULLDOG
__ RUP 9678 BEASTIE BOYS CHECK YOUR THRAEDS
__ RUP 9679 RAGE AGAINST THE MACHINE AFFIRMATIVE ACTION
__ RUP 9680 ALANIS MORISSETTE A MOMENT OF CLARITY
__ RUP 9681 PATTI SMITH DIVINE INTERVENTION
__ RUP 9682 HOOTIE & THE BLOWFISH GREEN DESERTS
__ RUP 9683 MINISTRY OVERFLOW
__ RUP 9684 NO FX WHO SAID WE'RE SHITE.??
__ RUP 9685 OFFSPRING UNDERWORLD
__ RUP 9686 KORN THRASHIN' BAGPIPES
__ RUP 9687 STEVIE RAY VAUGHAN THREEE BAR BLUES
__ RUP 9688 SMASHING PUMPKINS SQUASHED ZUCCHINI
__ RUP 9689 GARBAGE TRASH
__ RUP 9690 FOO FIGHTERS AN EVENING WITH ......
__ RUP 9691 PRESIDENTS OF THE USA AWESTRUCK
__ RUP 9692/3 TORI AMOS SWEET OL' ENGLAND
__ RUP 9694 BUSH CEASE IN POINT
__ RUP 9695 THE BLUETONES COMIN' UP
__ RUP 9696 MANIC STREET PREACHERS MSP IN LEEDS
__ RUP 9697 BRUCE SPRINGSTEEN CHECKPOINT BRUCE
__ RUP 9698 FILTER INDUSTRIAL DOSE
__ RUP 9699 BLUR IMPULSE

DINASAUR

__ DNS 95002 QUICKSILVER MESSANGER SERVICE SMOKIN' SOUND
__ DNS 95005 GRATEFUL DEAD PHIL & FRIENDS
__ DNS 95006 GRATEFUL DEAD GARDEN ROCK
__ DNS 95007 GRATEFUL DEAD NEW YEAR '78 Set I
__ DNS 95008 GRATEFUL DEAD NEW YEAR '78 Set II
__ DNS 95009 GRATEFUL DEAD NEW YEAR '78 Set III
__ DNS 95010 GRATEFUL DEAD APRIL FOOLS Set I
__ DNS 95011 GRATEFUL DEAD APRIL FOOLS Set II
__ DNS 95012 GRATEFUL DEAD UNIVERSAL RYTHMIC SOUND Set I
__ DNS 95013 GRATEFUL DEAD UNIVERSAL RYTHMIC SOUND Set II

KALEIDO (Original 1989 Pressing)
__ KMCD 3 LED ZEPPELIN SAN FRANCISCO I
__ KMCD 3 LED ZEPPELIN SAN FRANCISCO II

CAPITAL
__ CAP 72348 FRANK SINATRA SINGS TO THE NEW YORKERS
Order

Mail Order Service

Cd Prices (Euro clients only)
Disc cost
1Cd = Lit. 25,000
2Cd = Lit. 50,000
Postage & Packaging   First Cd = Lit. 5,500
Each Additional Lit. 2,500

Cd Prices (Clients from the US & Rest of the world)
Disc cost
1Cd = Us$ 22
2Cd = Us$ 44
Postage & Packaging   First Cd = Us$ 4,50
Each Additional Us$ 2,00
Payment with orders please.
Send complete Credit card details
(all cards will be charged in Italian Lira)
or Advanced payment : Cash (by registered letter),
International Money Order (I.M.O.) in
Italian Lira payable to : Octopuss Srl

With every 10 Cd's ordered 1 FREE.!!!!!!

Mailing Address
Octopuss Mail Order
00052 Cerveteri
Italy

PROXIMITY LED-ZEPPELIN Collector's Journal

All the Zep you need!

You've read every word of Led Zeppelin Live and you still want more? PROXIMITY is the place to get it!

Proximity is America's finest Zeppelin fanzine and the single most authoratative, literate and consistent source of collector-oriented info on Led Zeppelin, Page & Plant, and all related topics.

Four times a year, Proximity gives you in-depth articles such as "Zeppelin Tour Programs," "U.S. Promotional Items," "Equalizing Unauthorized Audio," "Fairport Convention, Zeppelin, & the Birth of British Folk/rock" and "Peter Grant in His Own Words."

Also included in every issue are rare photos & artifacts, regular columns on new bootlegs & current Zeppelin-related goings-on, vintage illustrated concert reviews, "Clippings From The Archives" and much more.

"Proximity is the best, most informative source ever published about Led Zeppelin."
- Luis Rey, author of Led Zeppelin Live

SUBSCRIPTIONS:
USA & Canada: $16.00 per year
(4 issues)
Overseas: $24.00 per year
Single issues: $4.00 ($6.00 overseas)

Send check or MO payable to: HUGH JONES
P.O. BOX 45541, SEATTLE, WA 98145-0541   USA
email: mr.prox@halcyon.com
Proximity on the web: www.dnaco.net:80/~buckeye/prox
•Wholesale inquiries welcome•
•Display & classified ad rates available upon request•

Also available at: Tower Records/Books (everywhere), Revolver Records (NYC),
Cellophane Square Records (Seattle), Rockin' Rudy's Records (Missoula)
and other fine music periodical dealers everywhere.